AMERICAN NOVEL

❗

American Novel
Crane to Faulkner

Edited by
FRANK N. MAGILL

Derived from Library Editions
Published by Salem Press, Inc.

SALEM SOFTBACKS
Pasadena, California

LIBRARY OF CONGRESS CATALOG CARD NUMBER: 81-51768

ISBN 0-89356-308-0

Some of this material has appeared previously in
works published under the titles *Masterplots*: Revised Edition, *Cyclopedia of World Authors*, *Cyclopedia of Literary Characters*, and *Magill's Bibliography of Literary Criticism*.

First Printing

PUBLISHER'S NOTE

MAGILL SURVEYS form a series of integrated study guides designed to provide sources for augmenting classroom work in the Humanities. These guides offer ready-reference information about authors and their works and are structured with classroom requirements strictly in mind. Articles include biographical information about authors and their total canon, and, where appropriate, they provide plot summaries, character studies, critical evaluations, and extensive bibliographical references.

Magill Surveys are intended to take the student far beyond the immediate assignment. For example, if the program calls for the study of "a Dickens novel," the appropriate Survey will present to the student half a dozen or more pages on each of several Dickens novels, including a critical biography of Dickens, plot summaries and critical evaluations of the novels, individual character analyses of scores of the characters appearing in these novels, and finally an average of about twenty bibliographical references for *each* of the novels—the latter element a highly valuable resource whether for class work or term papers. Thus, the student may gain extensive background information about the author and his canon while concentrating on in-depth study of a particular work.

The text for this Survey derives from a series of extensive library references in world literature edited by Frank N. Magill, including the following sources: *Masterplots*, *Cyclopedia of World Authors*, *Cyclopedia of Literary Characters*, and *Magill's Bibliography of Literary Criticism*.

All the material drawn from the above sources has been revised and supplemented where necessary to reflect current critical opinion. The text has been arranged to provide convenient access to a great amount of basic information condensed in one handy volume. Elaborate indexing techniques have been employed to assure information retrieval with a minimum of time and effort.

The original material reproduced in *Magill Surveys* has been developed through consultations with and contributions by hundreds of professors and scholars throughout the United States and abroad over a period of years. Its authoritativeness is attested by the thousands of academic and public libraries where the basic works from which this material is drawn will be found. The student who wishes to go beyond his assignment will find here ample means to satisfy his desire.

This collection on the American novel deals with forty authors and seventy-five representative late-nineteenth and twentieth century novels. It provides an overview of important American long fiction from Stephen Crane to William Faulkner. Many lesser-known authors and their works are included to provide a full picture of the development of the genre in this century. An examination of the influence of these writers on American fiction will enhance the students' appreciation of American literature.

v

CONTENTS

CONTENTS

CONTENTS

Special Consultant

Mary Rohrberger

List of Contributors

Kenneth John Atchity
Nancy G. Ballard
Judith Bolch
Peter A. Brier
Sally Buckner
Eric H. Christianson
Constance A. Cutler
Jan Kennedy Foster
Bonnie Fraser
William Freitas
Leslie E. Gerber
William E. Grant
Frederick W. Gwynn
Howard Lee Hertz
Glenda Lindsey Hicks
Clarence O. Johnson

Jennifer Kidney
Henderson Kincheloe
Dayton Kohler
Margaret McFadden-Gerber
Elaine Mathiasen
Frank Joseph Mazzi
Leslie B. Mittleman
Keith Neilson
Margaret F. Nelson
Vina Nickels Oldach
Dorothy Petty
Michael S. Reynolds
Mary Rohrberger
John Saunders
William Shute
Charles Johnson Taggart

AMERICAN NOVEL

SHERWOOD ANDERSON

Born: Camden, Ohio (September 13, 1876)
Died: Colón, Panama (March 8, 1941)

Principal Works

NOVELS: *Windy McPherson's Son*, 1916; *Marching Men*, 1917; *Poor White*, 1920; *Many Marriages*, 1923; *Dark Laughter*, 1925; *Beyond Desire*, 1932; *Kit Brandon*, 1936.

SHORT STORIES: *Winesburg, Ohio*, 1919; *The Triumph of the Egg*, 1921; *Horses and Men*, 1923; *Death in the Woods and Other Stories*, 1933.

ESSAYS AND STUDIES: *Sherwood Anderson's Notebook*, 1926; *Hello Towns!*, 1929; *Perhaps Women*, 1931; *No Swank*, 1934; *Puzzled America*, 1935; *Home Town*, 1940.

POEMS: *Mid-American Chants*, 1918; *A New Testament*, 1927.

AUTOBIOGRAPHY: *A Story Teller's Story*, 1924; *Tar: A Midwest Childhood*, 1926; *Sherwood Anderson's Memoirs*, 1942.

PLAYS: *Plays: Winesburg and Others*, 1937.

LETTERS: *Letters of Sherwood Anderson*, edited by Howard Mumford Jones, 1953.

Sherwood Anderson was born in Camden, Ohio, September 13, 1876. His wanderings began in boyhood as his family moved from town to town in Ohio. The father ran a harness shop, worked in harness shops, and painted signs in a succession of jobs, each bringing in less money for his large family. Sherwood, an active young boy, sold newspapers, picked up odd jobs, and wandered around the Ohio towns that were to become the setting for his later stories and novels. Although he read avidly, he had finished only one year of high school when he went to Chicago, in 1896, to work as a day laborer. After serving in the Spanish-American War and attending a prep school for a short time, he returned to Chicago and worked for an advertising agency. He did well in business and soon moved to Elyria, Ohio, where he managed a factory and sold a roof paint called "Roof Fix." Outwardly, during those years, he led a conventional young businessman's life, but at the same time he was trying in poems, short stories, and novels to record his puzzled impressions of American life.

Legend has it that Anderson simply walked out of his factory one afternoon in 1912, after deciding to leave industry for writing. Actually, the decision was neither that conscious nor that simple, for the conflicts between life and his literary ambition had been growing for years, and he seemed to suffer a kind of breakdown. After leaving the factory, he wandered aimlessly for four days until he was discovered in Cleveland. Later, leaving his family, he went to Chicago and began to write more seriously and intensely. In Chicago, as a member of a literary group which included Dreiser, Sandburg, Hecht, and others, and stimulated by Harriet Monroe's *Poetry* (founded 1912) and Margaret Anderson's *Little Review* (begun in 1914), Sherwood Anderson found an artistic climate in which he could write.

His first novel, *Windy McPherson's Son*, the story of a Midwestern boy's revolt against his father and against his small home town, appeared in 1916 but received little attention. Three years and several publications later, however, Anderson became well known and widely acclaimed following the publication of *Winesburg, Ohio*. The book is a loosely-structured series of episodes dealing with life and character in a small Midwestern town. Anderson attempted to show, with enormous sympathy, the grim and quietly desperate lives in the small half-industrial town. The collection is centered around young George Willard as he learns to see and understand the town around him. Anderson concentrated on the weak and the maimed, the characters beaten by life in a competitive and mechanical society. He attempted to give life to the groping, half-inarticulate protests of these people.

Winesburg, Ohio was hailed as the authentic voice of the Midwest. Distinguished eastern literary figures such as Waldo Frank, Van Wyck Brooks, and Paul Rosenfeld admired and befriended Anderson. Other writers, such as Theodore Dreiser and Hart Crane, valued his power and insight. *Poor White*, Anderson's next work, dealt with American society more comprehensively in presenting the wanderings of a lonely, inarticulate young man. Again the novel was well received, and this success, in combination with the short stories in *The Triumph of the Egg* and *Horses and Men*, made Anderson one of the most frequently honored figures on the American literary scene in the early twenties. He received the first annual award given by *The Dial* in December, 1921. His fame spread to Europe, and, a few years later, Virginia Woolf wrote that "Of all American novelists the most discussed and read in England at the present moment are probably Mr. Sherwood Anderson and Mr. Sinclair Lewis."

About this time Anderson began to feel the influence of D. H. Lawrence strongly. He read Lawrence over and over again and attempted to incorporate some of Lawrence's search for the meaning of life through sexual experience into his own novels. *Many Marriages* expresses the point of view that Americans are crippled by the attitude that sexual discussion and experience should be repressed. *Dark Laughter*, in many ways his best novel, uses sex as one of several means for the hero to scrape away the superficialities of modern cosmopolitan life and to get back to the primitive and basic meanings of human experience. In this novel, as well as in most of his other work, Anderson seemed probing, groping, to get at the really meaningful and essential experience of modern society.

After becoming successful, Anderson wandered around both America and Europe, finally settling in Marion, Virginia, where he edited two newspapers, one Republican, one Democrat. He continued to write, although after 1925 his work never reached the depth or the public of his earlier work. He died at Colón,

Panama, while on a State Department mission, March 8, 1941.

Critics during the 1920's talked of the depth of his insight, of his warmth and concern for humanity, of his clumsy efforts toward conveying his simple people through a rugged and effective style, of his genuine quality as a spokesman for the frustrations of the man from the small Midwestern town. In recent years critics have been less inclined to acclaim Anderson as a homespun American genius or to speak of his depth of insight. He is still regarded as a writer of warmth and sympathy who managed to create a rugged, half-articulate style through which to present his characters doomed by society. Much of the literary world today is inclined to agree with an early estimate made by F. Scott Fitzgerald: "He is the possessor of a brilliant and almost inimitable prose style, and of scarcely any ideas at all." For this reason his short stories and his autobiographical writings seem more likely to survive because they are less thesis-ridden than his novels.

Bibliography

There is no collected edition. Convenient one-volume editions are *The Sherwood Anderson Reader*, edited by Paul Rosenfeld, 1947, and *The Portable Sherwood Anderson*, edited by Horace Gregory, 1949. The two leading biographical studies are Irving Howe, *Sherwood Anderson*, 1951, and James Schevill, *Sherwood Anderson: His Life and Work*, 1951. A selection of the letters was edited by Howard Mumford Jones and Walter B. Rideout in 1953. An early critical study was C. B. Chase, *Sherwood Anderson*, 1927. See also T. K. Whipple, *Spokesmen*, 1928; Harlan Hatcher, *Creating the Modern American Novel*, 1935; Alfred Kazin, *On Native Grounds*, 1942; Rex Burbank, *Sherwood Anderson*, 1964; Ray L. White, editor, *The Achievement of Sherwood Anderson: Essays in Criticism*, 1966; and David D. Anderson, *Sherwood Anderson: An Introduction and Interpretation*, 1967.

Among the outstanding articles on Anderson are Lionel Trilling, "Sherwood Anderson," *Kenyon Review*, III (1941), 293–302; Robert Morss Lovett, "Sherwood Anderson, American," *Virginia Quarterly Review*, XVII (1941), 379–388; Norman Holmes Pearson, "Anderson and the New Puritanism," *Newberry Library Bulletin*, Series 2, No. 2 (1948), 52–70; Bernard Raymund, "The Grammar of Not-Reason: Sherwood Anderson," *Arizona Quarterly*, XII (1956), 48–60, 137–148; John J. Mahoney, "An Analysis of *Winesburg, Ohio*," *Journal of Aesthetics and Art Criticism*, XV (1956), 245–252; and Jarvis Thurston, "Anderson and *Winesburg*," *Accent*, XVI (1956), 107–128.

DARK LAUGHTER

Type of work: Novel
Author: Sherwood Anderson (1876–1941)
Time of plot: 1920's
Locale: Old Harbor, Indiana
First published: 1925

Sherwood Anderson's most popular novel, Dark Laughter *deals with the escape of a Chicago newspaperman from a life he regards as oppressive and ruled by machines, and the similar escape of an employer's wife, with whom he ultimately falls in love and elopes. The "dark laughter" of this book of moods rather than plot comes from the American black who, uncorrupted by white society and morals, is the only one still capable of pure, uninhibited joy.*

Principal Characters

Bruce Dudley, born John Stockton, who revolts against the sort of rational sterility that characterizes modern technological society. Dudley wanders around the country taking various jobs. He travels from Chicago to New Orleans, and from there to Old Harbor, Indiana, the town where he grew up. He is a reporter, an auto worker, a gardener. His love affair with Aline Grey, his employer's wife, which results in her pregnancy, as well as his flight with Aline towards an unknown destination, are for Anderson facets of the conduct to be expected of two people who love each other but who are unable to reconcile their values with a society dedicated only to material manipulation and acquisition.

Aline Grey, the unhappy wife of an automobile wheel factory owner. She is attracted to Dudley and encourages his love, though she knows her behavior is likely to cause comment in the small Indiana town where she lives. Her affair with Dudley ruins her husband's life.

Fred Grey, practically an Anderson symbol for blind devotion to technology. Grey is incapable of dealing with any situation that depends for its resolution on a knowledge of human nature. When Dudley and Aline leave, Grey becomes completely confused. Not knowing whether to use a revolver on himself, on Dudley and Aline, or simply on Dudley, he fires a wild shot into the river. Confused, desperate, ineffectual in the knowledge of his wife's desertion, Grey is scorned by the easy laughter of some uneducated Negro domestics for whom his problem is childishly simple.

Sponge Martin, a worker in the Grey factory. He loves the simple things: fishing, sipping moonshine whiskey, making love to his carefree wife. Martin is used in the novel to lend authority to Dudley and Aline's love affair.

Rose Frank, an acquaintance of Aline. It was at Rose's apartment in Paris, just after World War I, that Aline met a man she wanted in much the same way she was to want Dudley years later in Old Harbor.

The Story

Bruce Dudley's name was not Bruce Dudley at all. It was John Stockton. But he had grown tired of being John Stockton, reporter on a Chicago paper, married to Bernice who worked on the same paper and who wrote magazine stories on the side. She thought him flighty and he admitted it. He wanted adventure. He wanted to go down the Mississippi as Huckleberry Finn had done. He wanted to go back to Old Harbor, the river town in Indiana where he had spent his childhood. And so, with less than three hundred dollars, he left Chicago, Bernice, and his job on the paper. He picked up the name Bruce Dudley from two store signs in an Illinois town. After his trip to New Orleans he went to Old Harbor and got a job varnishing automobile wheels in the Grey Wheel Company.

Sponge Martin worked in the same room with Bruce. Sponge, a wiry old fellow with a black mustache, lived a simple, elemental life. That was the reason, perhaps, why Bruce liked him so much. Sometimes when the nights were fair and the fish were biting, Sponge and his wife took sandwiches and some moonshine whiskey and went down to the river. They fished for a while and got drunk, and then Sponge's wife made him feel like a young man again. Bruce wished he could be as happy and carefree as Sponge.

When Bruce was making his way down the Mississippi and when he stayed for five months in an old house in New Orlean—that was before he came to Old Harbor—he watched the Negroes and listened to their songs and laughter. It seemed to him that they lived as simply as children and were happy, laughing their dark laughter.

Aline, the wife of Fred Grey, who owned the Grey Wheel Company, saw Bruce Dudley walking out the factory door one evening as she sat in her car waiting for Fred. Who he was she did not know, but she remembered another man to whom she had felt attracted in the same way. It happened in Paris after the war. She had seen the man at Rose Frank's apartment and she had wanted him. Then she had married Fred, who was recovering from the shock of the war. He was not what she wished for, but, somehow, she had married him.

One evening Bruce Dudley passed by the Grey home as Aline stood in the yard. He stopped and looked first at the house and then at Aline. Neither spoke but something passed between them. They had found each other.

Aline, who had advertised for a gardener, hired Bruce after turning down several applicants. Bruce had quit his job at the factory shortly before he saw her advertisement. When Bruce began to work for her, the two maintained some reserve, but each was determined to have the other. Bruce and Aline carried on many imaginary conversations. Fred apparently resented Bruce's presence about the grounds, but he said nothing to the man. When he questioned his wife, he learned that she knew nothing of Bruce except that he was a good worker.

As Aline watched her husband leave for the factory each morning she wondered how much he knew. She thought a great deal about her own life and about life in general. Her husband was no lover. Few women nowadays had true lovers.

Modern civilization told one what he could not have. One belittled what he could
not possess. Because one did not have love, one made fun of it, was skeptical of it,
and besmirched it. The little play of the two men and the woman went on silently.
Two Negro women who worked in Aline's house watched the proceedings. From
time to time they laughed, and their dark laughter seemed mocking. White folks
were queer. They made life so involved. Negroes took what they wanted—simply,
openly, happily.

One day in June, after Fred had gone to march in a veterans' parade and the
Negro servants had gone to watch the parade, Aline and Bruce were left alone.
She sat and watched him working in the garden. Finally he looked at her, and he
followed her into the house through a door she purposely left open. Before Fred
returned, Bruce had left the house. He disappeared from Old Harbor. Two
months later Aline told Fred she was going to have a child.

As Fred came home one evening in the early fall, he saw his wife and Bruce
together in the garden. Aline calmly called to him and announced that the child
she was expecting was not his. She and Bruce had waited, she went on, so that
she might let him know they were leaving. Fred pleaded with her to stay, knowing
she was hurting herself, but they walked away, Bruce carrying two heavy bags.

Fred told himself, as he stood with his revolver in his hand a few minutes later,
that he could not dispassionately let another man walk away with his wife. His
mind was filled with confused anger. For a moment he thought of killing himself.
Then he followed the pair along the river road. He was determined to kill Bruce.
But he lost them in the darkness. In a blind fury he shot at the river. On the way
back to his house he stopped to sit on a log. The revolver fell to the ground and he
sat crying like a child for a long time.

After Fred had returned to his home and gone to bed, he tried to laugh at what
had happened. He could not. But outside in the road he heard a sudden burst of
laughter. It was the younger of the two Negresses who worked in the Grey home.
She cried out loudly that she had known it all the time, and again there came a
burst of laughter—dark laughter.

Critical Evaluation

Dark Laughter is an interesting, serious novel that emerged from the aftermath of World War I. Anderson's novel reflects the literary and stylistic
devices pioneered in the era following that war.

World War I meant, for writers, artists, and thinkers, the end of intellectual,
scientific, political, moral, and psychological certainties. Before the outbreak
of war, intellectuals considered Western culture the finest flowering, the highest expression of human civilization. But the outbreak of the war, and its bar-
barism, and the duration and intensity of its savagery, unprecedented in human
history, shattered that belief. Scientific discoveries shook hitherto unquestioned
assumptions about the Newtonian universe. Marx's theories and the Russian

Revolution undermined confidence in social classes and political systems. Freud, by elaborating a theory of an active unconscious, and an unconscious life, destroyed the idea that man was a given, known quantity.

All these developments form the context for "literary modernism," a movement in literature in which accepted patterns of characterization, sequence, and symbols were altered radically. It is in this context that Anderson's *Dark Laughter* can be understood best. *Dark Laughter* is a novel that tries both to formulate a criticism of the old values (made disreputable by the war), and at the same time to set forth new values by which men can live.

Given this disillusionment *and* hope, it is appropriate that Anderson establishes two dramatic poles in the novel: one embodies a natural, honest, sincere relationship to life; the other (embodying the old, prewar values) represents an artificial, mechanical, and dishonest approach.

Fred Grey and Bernice Stockton are characters leading superficial and distant lives. Grey, who imagines himself sensitive, cultured, and generous is actually a morally coarse, suspicious, and tight-fisted factory owner. He is, above all, separated from the realities of life by his economic position and his inner sterility.

Bernice Stockton, the wife that Bruce Dudley fled, is a variation of the same type. Her "specialty" is literature, but from hints of the story she is writing—a precious, unreal thing—her characters and plot only reflect her own superficial romanticism, not the actual conditions of life. She is a member of an "in group" of writers and intellectuals, and Anderson indicates that this membership is more important to her than infusing her art with truth.

Standing in opposition to these characters are Bruce Dudley, Sponge Martin and, to an extent, Aline Grey. For Anderson, these people represent the new, hopeful values which have come to life after the trauma of war. Sponge Martin (and his wife), for example, have a genuine connection to real life. Their sexual life is natural and unaffected; they have few pretensions; they are generous and simple. Dudley himself, the central character in the novel, is a writer more interested in the truth than in "word slinging." Leaving Bernice was a rejection of her literary pretensions. Falling in love with Aline, and fathering her child, meant answering the deeper, underlying currents in life.

For Aline, who vacillated between these poles, the marriage to Grey represented a confused surrender to the conventional life. Running away with Dudley meant coming to terms with life as it is—not as it exists in the decadent literary circles of postwar France, in the romantic fantasies of her adolescence, or in the expected routines of upper-middle-class-life in the United States.

It is also clear that, just as Anderson is criticizing an outworn and mechanical value system, he is also criticizing an earlier literary tradition. Does literature come to terms with the natural, primitive side of life? Does it seek out

the unconscious and explore it? Does it portray the uncertainties and difficulties of life? If the answer to these questions is yes, then Anderson approves;
but if literary tradition only discusses the superficial and agreeable aspects
of life, then Anderson heartily disapproves. Thus, as literature, Anderson
hopes *Dark Laughter* both supports and represents a new literary tradition
that corresponds to the new postwar values.

Anderson himself said the literary quality of *Dark Laughter* was influenced
by James Joyce, and it is true that Anderson uses a number of modernist
techniques: sections of narrative broken into fragments; parts of poems
scattered through the text; subjective, semi-stream-of-consciousness narration;
switches in point of view. But Anderson does not have Joyce's verbal facility,
depth of allusion, grammatical mastery, or density of detail.

The techniques of *Dark Laughter* probably reflect the more general literary climate of the 1920's rather than Joyce's specific influence. In a period
of intellectual uncertainty, when old beliefs were brought into question, prose
style itself assumed a fragmented, subjective, and somewhat disjointed
character.

At the same time, *Dark Laughter* also displays certain negative features
of the American literary climate of the 1920's. One of these negative qualities,
perhaps the most visible, is the racist aspect of many of Anderson's passages.
For example, the title of the novel, *Dark Laughter,* refers to the natural, honest
pole that Anderson supports. But associated with this naturalness is the
"primitive," "uncivilized," and "amoral" qualities that Anderson links to
black people. In fact, *Dark Laughter* refers to the laughter of black maids in
the Grey household when they learn of Aline's adultery.

Such prejudices, commonplace in the era in which *Dark Laughter* was
written, need not overshadow the major intent of the book. *Dark Laughter*
expresses an important opposition of ideas in modernist literary terms; the
reader is asked to choose between real life and superficial life; and, in that
sense, Anderson has presented the reader with a profound moral choice.

Bibliography

Anderson, David D. *Sherwood Anderson: An Introduction and Interpretation.* New York: Barnes & Noble, 1967, pp. 122–129.

Cargill, Oscar. *Intellectual America: Ideas on the March.* New York: Macmillan, 1941, pp. 322–331, 676–685.

Chase, Cleveland B. *Sherwood Anderson.* New York: Robert M. McBride,
1927, pp. 16–27.

Howe, Irving. "Sherwood Anderson and D.H. Lawrence," in *Furioso.* V (Fall,
1950), pp. 21–33.

Krutch, Joseph Wood. *American Criticism.* New York: Harcourt, 1926, pp. 108–111.

Lovett, Robert Morss. "Sherwood Anderson, American," in *Virginia Quarterly Review.* XVII (Summer, 1941), pp. 379–388.

McHaney, Thomas L. "Anderson, Hemingway, and Faulkner's *The Wild Palms*," in *PMLA.* LXXXVII (May, 1972), pp. 465–474.

Rahv, Philip. *Image and Idea: Fourteen Essays on Literary Themes.* Norfolk, Conn.: New Directions, 1949, pp. 3–5.

Sherman, Stuart P. *Critical Woodcuts.* New York: Scribner's, 1926, pp. 3–17

Tugwell, Rexford Guy. "An Economist Reads *Dark Laughter*," in *New Republic.* XLV (December 9, 1925), pp. 87–88.

White, Ray Lewis. "Hemingway's Private Explanation of *The Torrents of Spring*," in *Modern Fiction Studies.* XIII (Summer, 1967), pp. 261–263.

Wickham, Harvey. *The Impuritans.* New York: L. MacVeagh, 1929, pp. 268–282.

POOR WHITE

Type of work: Novel
Author: Sherwood Anderson (1876–1941)
Time of plot: 1880–1900
Locale: Missouri and Ohio
First published: 1920

Poor White *is the story of one man's rise from origins of poverty and laziness to a career of creativity and self-realization. The novel is also significant as a study of the invasion of pioneer, rural America by industrialism. Anderson graphically describes not only the growth of America, but also the frustrations of individual men in conflict with an encroaching machine age.*

Principal Characters

Hugh McVey, a Midwestern American whose genius for inventing and manufacturing machinery accounts for his rise from drab poverty to material success. He is, according to many critics, Anderson's example of the force that produced the problems attendant on the impact of technology upon rural America at the turn of the century.

Steve Hunter, McVey's partner in business. He is a capable publicist who convinces the town fathers of Bidwell to invest in a plant to manufacture McVey's invention. The plant makes the town prosperous.

Clara Butterworth, a rather shy, plain, melancholy girl who in a week's time abandons her studies at the state university, returns to Bidwell, falls in love with McVey, and elopes with him. She is not suited by temperament to a man like McVey and their marriage becomes a strained relationship. Adversity and the prospect of a child finally bring them together.

Joe Wainsworth, a harness maker who invests his savings in McVey's invention

and is almost financially ruined when the money is lost. The reversal disturbs his disposition, and he becomes sullen and irritable. A trivial incident sets him off and, seriously deranged, he kills his employee, shoots Steve Hunter, and tries to strangle McVey.

Sarah Shepard, McVey's foster mother, who instills in him respect for knowledge, hard work, social success, and industrial progress.

Henry Shepard, Sarah's husband and McVey's first employer. He befriends McVey and provides a home for him.

Jim Gibson, a braggart and Wainsworth's employee. His unfortunate boast precipitates Wainsworth's derangement and its concomitant violence. Gibson becomes Wainsworth's first victim.

Tom Butterworth, Clara's father, who is the richest man in town.

Allie Mulberry, a simple-minded workman who makes a model of McVey's invention.

The Story

As a young boy in Missouri, Hugh McVey was incredibly lazy. Hour after hour he would lie on the grass by the river doing absolutely nothing. Not having gone to school, he was ignorant and his manners were rude.

When the railroad came to town, Hugh got work sweeping the platform and doing odd jobs. His boss, Henry Shepard, took an interest in him, and bought him clothes. Soon Hugh went to live with Henry and his wife Sarah. Sarah, who was from New England, always preserved her memory of quiet Eastern villages and large industrial cities. Determined to educate Hugh, she lavished on him the discipline and affection she would have given her own child.

The situation was difficult, at first, for both of them. But Sarah Shepard was a determined woman. She taught Hugh to read, to write, to wonder about the world beyond the little town. She instilled within him the belief that his family had been of no account, so that he grew to have a repulsion toward the poor white farmers and workers. Always she held out before him the promise of the East, the progress and growth of that region. Gradually, Hugh began to win his fight against natural indolence and to adjust himself to his new way of life. When the Shepards left town, Hugh was appointed station agent for the railroad.

He kept the job for a year. During that time the dream of Eastern cities grew more and more vivid for Hugh. He gave up his job and traveled east, working wherever he could. Always lonely, always apart from people, he felt an impenetrable wall between him and the rest of the world. He kept on, through Illinois, Indiana, Ohio.

Hugh was twenty-three when he settled down in Ohio. By accident, he got the job of a telegraph operator, just a mile from the town of Bidwell. There he lived alone, a familiar and puzzling figure to the people of the town. The rumor began to spread that he was an inventor working on a new device. Others suggested that he was looking over the town for a possible factory site. But Hugh was doing neither as yet. Then during his walks around the farmlands, he became fascinated by the motions of the farmers planting their seeds and their crops. Slowly there grew in his mind an idea for a crop-setting machine that would save the labor of the farmers and their families.

Steve Hunter, who had just come back from school in Buffalo, was another dreamer. He dreamed of being a manufacturer, the wealthiest in Bidwell. He succeeded in convincing the town's important people that Hugh was his man, and that he was working on an invention that would make them both rich. He persuaded them to invest in a new company which would build a factory and promote Hugh's invention. Steve went to see Hugh, who had progressed so that the blueprint for a plant-setting machine was complete. The two young men came to an agreement.

The town idiot, who had skill in woodworking, made models of the machine, and the machine itself was finally constructed in an old building carefully guarded from the curious. When the machine was not successful, Hugh invented another, his mind more and more preoccupied with the planning of devices and machines. A factory was then built and many workers were hired. With the factory, Bidwell's industralization began.

What was happening in Bidwell was the same growth of industralism that was changing the entire structure of the nation. It was a period of transition. Bidwell, being a small town, felt the effects of the new development keenly. Workers be came part of the community, in which there had been only farmers and merchants.

Joe Wainsworth, the harness-maker, had invested his life-savings in Hugh's invention, and he had lost them. An independent man, a craftsman, he came to resent the factory, the very idea of the machine. People came into his shop less often. They were buying machine-made harness. Joe became a broken man. His employee, Jim Gibson, a spiritual bully, really ran the business, and Joe submitted meekly.

Meanwhile, Clara Butterworth came back to Bidwell after three years at the university in Columbus. She too was lonely, unhappy. When she returned, she saw that the old Bidwell was gone, that her father, Tom Butterworth, was wealthier than before, that the growth of the town was due primarily to one person, Hugh McVey. A week after she met Hugh, he walked up to the farm and asked her to marry him. They eloped and were married that night.

For four years they lived together in a strange, strained relationship. During those four years Joe Wainsworth's fury against Steve Hunter, against the new age of industry which had taken his savings, increased. One day he heard Jim Gibson brag about his hold over his employer. That night Joe Wainsworth killed Jim Gibson. As he fled from the scene, he met Steve Hunter and shot him.

Clara, Hugh, and Tom Butterworth were returning from a drive in the family's first automobile when they learned what had happened. Two men had captured Joe, and when they tried to put him into the automobile to take him back to town, Joe jumped toward Hugh and sank his fingers into his neck. It was Clara who broke his grip upon her husband. Somehow the incident brought Hugh and Clara closer together.

Hugh's career as an inventor no longer satisfied him. Joe Wainsworth's attack had unnerved him, made him doubt the worth of his work. It did not matter so much if someone in Iowa had invented a machine exactly like his, and he did not intend to dispute the rights of the Iowan. Clara was bearing his child, an individual who would struggle just as he had. Clara told him of the child one night as they stood listening to the noises of the farm and the snoring of the hired hand. As they walked into the house side by side, the factory whistles blew in the night. Hugh hardly heard them. The dark Midwestern nights, men and women, the land itself—the full, deep life current would go on in spite of factories and machines.

Critical Evaluation

The intent of *Poor White* is, first of all, to describe the opening stages of industrialization in the great Ohio Valley; but this description, rather than being merely social or statistical, is set in profoundly human terms. That is, the birth and development of American industry are made specific and concrete through the individual lives of the people who invent the machines, who finance the enterprises, and who run the factories. Thus, *Poor White* is as much a historical novel as a novel dealing with the dramas of love and hate and individual psychology. Anderson catches a particular historical moment, and, almost in the manner of Tolstoy, explores individual reactions and contributions.

The two most significant human dramas are Hugh McVey's development on the one hand, and Clara Butterworth's relationship to him on the other. McVey, an inventor, and prototype of a creative personality—a genius of sorts—is shown by Anderson to have been influenced by the various regions of the United States. McVey is a product of "poor whites" dreaming near the banks of the Mississippi River and of discipline imposed on that dreaminess by a tough New England lady. If Anderson's attribution of innate characteristics to various regions of the country seems thin and stereotyped, Anderson does succeed in capturing the strengths and weaknesses of this individual and in exploring why this man in particular could play the historical role assigned to him in the novel.

The character of Clara Butterworth is mainly explored in terms of her sexual relationship with men, and this characterizaton lacks the force and focus of Hugh McVey's. Part of her vagueness may have resulted from Anderson's trying to describe her subjective confusion. Another reason may be that Anderson has made certain naturalist assumptions about her. Sexual urges that move her, and that drive the men around her, are heavily stressed by Anderson; and these urges, biologically irresistible, external and abstract, tend to rob her of her personality.

A final note should be added on the appearance of a socialist agitator near the end of the novel. The period Anderson describes is one in which the ideas of socialism, first introduced into this country, assumed vast popularity, especially in the farming regions of the midwest. Anderson suggests at the end of the novel that this agitator, and the ideas he supports, embody the next historical stage, the new society brought about by industrialization.

Bibliography

Anderson, David D. "The Uncritical Critics: American Realists and the Lincoln Myth," in *Midamerica II*. Edited by David D. Anderson. East Lansing, Mich.: Midwestern Press, 1975, pp. 17–23.

Burbank, Rex. *Sherwood Anderson.* New York: Twayne, 1964, pp. 48–60.

Gelfant, Blanche Housman. *The American City Novel.* Norman: University of Oklahoma Press, 1954, pp. 95–132.

Hoffman, Frederick John. *The Twenties.* New York: Viking, 1955, pp. 302–306.

Howe, Irving. "Sherwood Anderson and the American Myth of Power," in *Tomorrow.* VII (August, 1949), pp. 52–54.

Rideout, Walter B. "Introduction," in *Poor White.* By Sherwood Anderson. New York: Viking, 1966, pp. ix–xx.

Ward, A.C. *American Literature, 1880–1930.* New York: Dial Press, 1932, pp. 111–113, 120–133.

ARNA BONTEMPS

Born: Alexandria, Louisiana (October 13, 1902)
Died: Nashville, Tennessee (June 4, 1973)

Principal Works

NOVELS: *God Sends Sundays*, 1931; *Black Thunder*, 1936; *Drums at Dusk*, 1939.

JUVENILE LITERATURE: *Popo and Fifina: Children of Haiti* (with Langston Hughes), 1932; *Sad-Faced Boy*, 1937; *The Fast Sooner Hound* (with Jack Conroy), 1942; *Chariot in the Sky*, 1951.

POETRY: *Personals*, 1963.

PLAY: *St. Louis Woman* (with Countee Cullen), 1946.

BIOGRAPHY: *We Have Tomorrow*, 1945; *The Story of George Washington Carver*, 1954; *Frederick Douglass: Slave, Fighter, Freeman*, 1959; *Famous Negro Athletes*, 1964.

MISCELLANEOUS: *The Harlem Renaissance*, 1972.

Arna Bontemps, although not as well known as Richard Wright, James Baldwin, or other of his contemporaries, has nevertheless made a remarkable contribution to American literature. As chroniclers of black experience, few writers can match his prolific output. As editor, co-author, and author, he produced some thirty books, a volume of poetry, a Broadway play, and over thirty articles. Most of this material was written while he held full-time positions either as teacher or librarian.

Arna Bontemps was born in Alexandria, Louisiana, on October 13, 1902. "Mine has not been a varmint-infested childhood so often the hallmark of Negro American autobiography," Bontemps once wrote. Yet his handsome construction worker father moved the family to California after an encounter with two drunk white men. The Bontemps were to be the only black family in the Los Angeles neighborhood where they settled, and the young Arna was largely divorced from black culture. He attended a white boarding school and carried out his father's wish: "Now don't go up there acting colored." However, after he graduated from Pacific Union College in 1923, young Bontemps, finding it "impossible" and "unthinkable" to shed his blackness, went to Harlem. There he met the young intellectuals and writers, such as Claude McKay, James Weldon Johnson, and Countee Cullen. To support himself, Bontemps taught at the Harlem Academy.

During the seven years that Bontemps lived in New York, he produced a significant amount of work. In addition to his first novel, *God Sends Sundays*, he produced poetry that won the Alexander Pushkin Award in 1926 and 1927. He won first prize in *The Crisis* poetry contest with "Nocturne at Bethesda."

The Depression claimed as its victims the Harlem Renaissance in general and

Bontemps in particular. When publishing became as economically depressed as other industries, the young talented people in Harlem began to move elsewhere. Bontemps moved to Alabama. For three years Bontemps, his wife, and two children lived in Huntsville, Alabama, while he taught at Oakwood Junior College. During this turbulent period Bontemps published his first piece of juvenile literature, *Popo and Fifina*, in collaboration with Langston Hughes. His interest in literature for children continued throughout his life, as evidenced by his anthologies of poetry, his fiction, and biographies.

Sensing a lack of opportunity in Alabama, the Bontemps family, after a short sojourn in California, went to Chicago in 1935. Once again he taught, but he eventually entered the Graduate Library School of the University of Chicago. During this period he also supervised the Illinois Writers Project, published his second and most highly praised novel, *Black Thunder*, and won the Julius Rosenwald Fund fellowship for creative writing. This award allowed him to travel in the Caribbean and publish his third novel, *Drums at Dusk*, in 1939.

In 1943, having completed his M.A. in library science, Bontemps took a position as head librarian at Fisk University in Nashville, Tennessee. He held this post until 1965. Fisk was not new to Bontemps. He had visited the school in the early 1930's to meet men such as James Weldon Johnson, refugees from the Harlem Renaissance. They lived there "surrounded by bleak hostilities" in the hope that they could keep alive the short-lived beginning of a black awakening which they observed in the Harlem Renaissance. It was also at Fisk that Bontemps first read of Gabriel Prosser's unsuccessful Virginia rebellion. The "yeasty" atmosphere of Fisk proved to be a welcome relief to Bontemps after the social unrest in Alabama and the ghetto crime of Chicago.

After he retired as head librarian in 1965, Bontemps continued to be active in a variety of situations. Among them were a visiting professorship in literature at the University of Chicago and the curatorship of the James Weldon Johnson Collection at Yale University. At his death in 1973, Bontemps was writer-in-residence at Fisk. He was survived by his wife and six children.

Although critics have noted a number of themes in Bontemps' work, his considerable output makes generalizing difficult. One is startled by the range of his literary interests: athletes, musicals, poetry, biography, literary history, black history, juvenile literature, and more. Writing in 1965, Bontemps stated, "For my own part, I am staying on in the South to write something about the changes I have seen in my lifetime, and about the Negro's awakening and regeneration. That is my theme. . . ." What he saw is partly denied us; he died while writing his autobiography.

Bibliography

There are no authorized editions of Bontemps' work, nor is there a biography. Although histories of black literature make mention of Bontemps, particularly in his relationship to the Harlem Renaissance, there is no full-length study of his work. Secondary sources are generally scarce. The most valuable single source is Bontemps' article, "Why I Returned," *Harper's*, CCXXX (April, 1965), 176–182.

BLACK THUNDER

Type of work: Novel
Author: Arna Bontemps (1902–1973)
Locale: Henrico County, Virginia
Time of plot: 1800
First published: 1936

    Arna Bontemps spent three years meticulously researching court records in Virginia to reconstruct in Black Thunder *the slave rebellion of 1800. In the character of Gabriel, leader of the revolt, Bontemps created a mythic figure of tragic dignity and courage.*

Principal Characters

Gabriel Prosser, the mythic "gen'l" who leads the abortive rebellion against Richmond. The most powerful of three strong brothers, he had defeated his chief rival, Ditcher, to assume leadership among the slaves. Although not a complex figure psychologically, he proves to be a man of considerable dignity and courage. Once the rebellion is thwarted by an unprecedented rain storm, he must avoid arrest since his fellow conspirators, Pharoah and old Ben, have informed the white authorities of his role in the revolt. Rather than hide shamefully, Gabriel keeps the citizens and soldiers in Richmond nervous by his repeated appearances. His arrest aboard a ship, where he has hidden in order to reach Norfolk, comes only when he is enervated by fatigue and thirst. Even though he does not find the success of his idol, Toussaint, he faces death without fear. Because of his refusal to accept the role of slave, he dies a free man.

Juba, Gabriel's woman who rides the black colt Araby as a signal of the revolt's beginning. Her courage and daring is a match for any of the black males she urges on to rebellion. After the slaves' defeat, she continues to defy her master, Prosser, who beats her savagely in return. On the day of Gabriel's execution, Prosser sells her at the block.

Ben Woodfolk, an aged retainer of the Sheppard household. Referred to by his owner as "a good boy," Ben prefers his soft security in slavery to bloody freedom. His confession to his master of his minor role in the rebellion and his subsequent testimony to the court are the first steps in Gabriel's demise.

Ditcher, a gigantic powerful black whom Gabriel physically defeats to emerge as leader of the blacks. Ditcher joins the rebellion as Gabriel's second-in-command. When he surrenders, he does so with dignity and awaits his sure death serenely.

Criddle, a hog-butchering slave who uses his skills to kill a white-trash farmer. His action triggers the full exposure of the insurrection by Pharoah and old Ben. White soldiers later kill him.

Mingo, a free black whose knowledge of Toussaint and his reading of biblical passages about freedom inspire Gabriel and his companions. One of the leaders of the rebellion, he is arrested, and the white authorities unsuccessfully attempt to make him confess to being the link between the so-called Jacobins and the slaves.

Pharoah, a pumpkin-colored mulatto salve whose pettiness and cowardice cause him to tell the citizens of Richmond of the rebellion. His guilt afterwards leads him to paranoia and insanity.

Bundy, a worn-out, rum-drinking slave killed by his master, Thomas Prosser. His death serves as the catalyst for the rebellion.

Melody, a beautiful, apricot-colored, free mulatto whose name is first linked with the young white heir, Robin Sheppard. Yet she proves to be sympathetic with the rebellion and helps Gabriel find his way onto the ship bound for Norfolk. Fearing for her own safety, she goes to Philadelphia to join Biddenhurst.

Thomas Prosser, Gabriel and Juba's cruel owner whose murder of Bundy ignites the rebellion.

Mosley Sheppard, owner of old Ben. Although free of Prosser's cruelty, he still takes old Ben into Richmond to testify against the other rebels.

Alexander Biddenhurst, a white liberal who espouses freedom for blacks. However, once rumors of a black revolt are in the air, he conveniently leaves Richmond for Philadelphia. In spite of his dubious honor, he does help other refugees from Richmond, such as the Creuzot family and Melody.

M. Creuzot, a French immigrant whose printing shop is destroyed by Richmond mobs that suspect he is the Jacobin source of the revolt. With his family, he escapes to Philadelphia.

Essay-Review

Richard Wright has praised *Black Thunder* as the first Negro proletarian novel. Indeed, before *Black Thunder* no full-length black novel had developed the subject of black violence against white society. For these reasons, if no other, Arna Bontemps has made a reremarkable contribution to American literary history. Yet interest in *Black Thunder* remains largely extrinsic. While Bontemps makes scrupulous use of historical materials, manipulates point-of-view in a sophisticated manner, and creates some convincing characters, the novel does not succeed where it must—as felt drama.

When Thomas Prosser, one of the cruelest slave owners, runs down and kills Old Bundy, Gabriel decides it is time for black men to be free. He plans an attack on the city of Richmond. However, the plan meets with failure. The night of the revolt, an unexpected storm swells the creeks and slows the men in their march from the surrounding countryside to the city. Gabriel sends the men home to await further word. Before they can act, a slave murders a white-trash farmer, whose daughter escapes and tells of the crime. Then some of the slaves who fear the rebellion betray their fellows. Word spreads quickly of the slave revolt, and the state of Virginia arms itself. Finally, the rebellion is subdued and Gabriel is captured. He goes to his death with pride and courage.

Bontemps chose the history of Gabriel Prosser's rebellion rather than Denmark Vesey's or Nat Turner's because "Freedom was a less complicated affair in his case. It was, it seemed to me, a more unmistakable equivalent of the yearning I felt and which I imagined to be general." Bontemps subsequently combed the court records of the state of Virginia for three years to gather the material for his novel. Bontemps, however, goes beyond judicial transcripts to create a full historical context for *Black Thunder*. The rebellion takes place against the background of the volatile election of 1800 between the Federalist John Adams and the Democrat Thomas Jefferson. The issues are philosophical, and in the state of Virginia any friend of the egalitarian principles of the French Revolution or Voltaire is seen as a Jacobin. Even so, such men are to be found in Richmond, and as Gabriel overhears Alexander Biddenhurst of Philadelphia and M. Creuzot, the French immigrant, speak of universal freedom, gooseflesh covers his body.

Gabriel hears other tales of freedom. Mingo, the free black saddle-maker, reads him the letters of Toussaint L'Ouverture and the Biblical exhortations about release from bondage. In the process of tracing the possible historical currents feeding into the rebellion, Bontemps becomes unfortunately cerebral and academic. Such figures as Biddenhurst and Creuzot appear wooden and contrived. The more affecting source of the rebellion, the grevious misery that is slavery, receives relatively little attention. Other than Prosser's vicious assault on Old Bundy, the worn-out slave, the inhuman conditions of plantation life are slighted. The one slave life seen in much detail, that of old Ben, the major-domo at the Sheppard mansion, is one of relative ease and comfort. The reader learns little of the life of field hands, such as the hog-butcher Criddle, who supply the manpower for the rebellion.

Although there are questions about the priorities of the exposition, the major flaw in the novel is the handling of the rebellion itself. Dramatically it is difficult to have as the focal point of a novel an event postponed because of rain. Working within the limitations of historical fact, Bontemps attempts to create some sense of suspense before the revolt fails by shifting the point-of-view from one conspirator to another. Such a technique, however, does not compensate for the inherent lack of drama in an event which does not take place. Furthermore, a rebellion had apparently been in the wind for some time, yet the novel is vague about this matter. Much less attention is given to it than to the less compelling affairs of Creuzot and Biddenhurst.

The aftermath of the rebellion is also unsatisfying as drama. While the shifting point-of-view has some validity prior to the rebellion, it undercuts the reader's concern for Gabriel once he is forced into hiding. One simply cannot feel much anxiety or concern for him when the focus regularly shifts from Juba to Melody to Biddenhurst in Philadelphia. One senses that Bontemps must adopt such a strategy to disguise the fact that Gabriel is one-dimensional. The reader must believe in his courage, although it is never revealed in a direct dramatic manner; but beyond that virtue, and his somewhat abstract desire for freedom, Gabriel is not a complex character. Much more compelling is old Ben, divided between his sense of loyalty and fear toward Bundy and the revolt and his life of ease as "a good boy" with the Sheppards. Even Juba, Gabriel's rebellious and indomitable woman, is a more engaging character.

Clearly Bontemps' novel has as its chief aim the creation of a heroic symbol, an emblem of defiance and courage. Gabriel's profound realization that freedom and death are inextricably connected is a gut feeling that the effete, intellectual Biddenhurst could never know. Gabriel's success as a symbol is seen most clearly in his statement to his white jury. With simple dignity and clear vision he says, "I been studying about freedom a heap, me. I heard a plenty folks talk and I listened a heap. And everything I heard made me feel like I wanted to be free....On'erstand? That's all. Something keep telling me that anything what's equal to a gray squirrel wants to be free. That's how it all come about." Although the novelist does not always succeed, the poet and the polemicist in Bontemps can soar.

Bibliography

"Arna Bontemps: Dedication and Bibliography," in *Black World*, XXI (September, 1971).

Bone, Robert A. *The Negro Novel in America*. Rev. ed. New Haven, Conn.: Yale University Press, 1965.

Davis, Arthur P. *From the Dark Tower*. Washington, D.C.: Howard University, 1974.

Gloster, Hugh M. *Negro Voices in American Fiction*. Chapel Hill, N.C.: University of North Carolina Press, 1948.

Inge, M. Thomas, Maurice Duke, and Jackson R. Bryer. *Black American Writers*. New York: St. Martin's Press, 1978.

Littlejohn, David. *Black on White: A Critical Survey of Writings by American Negroes*. New York: Grossman, 1966.

"Sad-Faced Author," in *Horn Book*, XV (January, 1939), 7–12.

Weil, Dorothy. "Folklore Motifs in Arna Bontemps' *Black Thunder*," in *Southern Folklore Quarterly*, March, 1971.

Young, James O. *Black Writers of the Thirties*. Baton Rouge: Louisiana State University Press, 1973.

PEARL S. BUCK

Born: Hillsboro, West Virginia (June 26, 1892)
Died: Danby, Vermont (March 6, 1973)

Principal Works

NOVELS: *The Good Earth*, 1931; *Sons*, 1932; *A House Divided*, 1935; *This Proud Heart*, 1938; *Dragon Seed*, 1942; *The Promise*, 1943; *Pavilion of Women*, 1946; *Peony*, 1948; *Kinfolk*, 1949; *The Hidden Flower*, 1952; *Imperial Woman*, 1956; *Letter from Peking*, 1957; *The Living Reed*, 1963; *Death in the Castle*, 1965; *The Time Is Noon*, 1966; *The Three Daughters of Madame Liang*, 1969; *Mandala*, 1970.

BIOGRAPHY AND AUTOBIOGRAPHY: *The Exile*, 1936; *Fighting Angel: Portrait of a Soul*, 1936; *My Several Worlds*, 1954; *A Bridge for Passing*, 1962; *China As I See It*, 1970.

TRANSLATIONS: *All Men Are Brothers*, 1933 (*Shui hu chuan*, 2 vols.)

Pearl S(ydenstricker) Buck was born in West Virginia on June 26, 1892, into a missionary family. Her parents, Absalom and Caroline Sydenstricker, took her to China when she was still an infant, and China was her home, except during her college undergraduate days, until 1932. When she was ready to go to college, Pearl Buck's parents sent her back to the United States, where she attended Randolph-Macon Woman's College, in Lynchburg, Virginia, graduating in 1914. While she was an undergraduate Pearl Buck distinguished herself by becoming president of her class and by some amateur literary accomplishments. In 1917 she married John Lossing Buck, also an American missionary to China. Their first five years of marriage were spent in the highly unsettled regions of North China. When her husband became head of the farm-management departments at Nanking University, Pearl Buck began to teach English at the same institution, serving until 1924. She later taught at National Southeastern University, from 1925 to 1927, and at Chung-Yang University, from 1928 to 1930. She lived in Nanking until publication of *The Good Earth* in 1931 made her world-famous as a popular novelist. With that book she achieved fame, not only as a novelist, but as the foremost interpreter of China to Westerners. She and her first husband had two daughters, who returned to America with her. Following her return to the United States she divorced her first husband, later marrying Richard J. Walsh, president of the John Day Company, her publishers. They settled on a farm in Pennsylvania and later adopted nine children. Her second husband died in 1960.

In addition to her undergraduate degree, Pearl Buck earned a master's degree from Cornell University. Honorary degrees were awarded her by several institutions, including Harvard and Yale. She was also one of the first women to be elected to the American Academy of Arts and Letters. *The Good Earth*, which was highly successful in many ways, won many awards for its author, including the Pulitzer Prize in 1932 and the Howells Medal of the American Academy of Arts and Letters in 1936. Her crowning award was the Nobel Prize for Literature, which she received in 1938.

The Good Earth was the first novel of a trilogy The House of Earth, which includes Sons and A House Divided. The trilogy presents the history of a Chinese family through several generations, and it has been compared to the Rougon-Macquart series of novels by Zola. Similarities are especially strong between Pearl Buck's The Good Earth and Zola's La Terre, the similarities running much deeper than the titles. The Good Earth was an exceptionally popular novel. With its American sales alone approximating a million copies, and translations made into twenty or more other languages, the novel stood at the top of the best-seller lists in the United States for more than two years. Despite its vast popularity, or perhaps partly because of it, critics and scholars have been slow to grant Pearl Buck's work a place in literary history, and not only because her books have been concerned with a culture alien to America. Critical appraisals of The Good Earth and the later novels have said that the books have their greatest merit in the truthfulness with which China and its people are portrayed, a statement which can scarcely be interpreted as aesthetic acclaim.

Following The Good Earth, which is a point of departure in any discussion of Pearl Buck, came other novels which had a more modest success, such books as The Young Revolutionist (1932), portraying the Chinese Communist movement, and The Mother (1934), which relates the tribulations of a Chinese peasant woman. During the 1930's Pearl Buck also turned to writing books other than novels. The First Wife and Other Stories (1932) was her first volume of published short fiction. Like a later volume, Today and Forever (1941), it had relatively little appeal to the public, which seemed to have quickly categorized Pearl Buck as a novelist. In addition to her other work, there appeared two volumes of biography, The Exile in 1936 and Fighting Angel in 1936, portraits of the author's missionary parents. These two books offer a suggestion as to why Pearl Buck broke away from missionary work, inasmuch as they show that she believed that the Christianity of the missions failed to arouse Chinese sympathy for Christianity or the people who represented it. Perhaps that belief also played a large part in Pearl Buck's continued efforts to help improve understanding between the Chinese and Western peoples. In 1941 she founded the East and West Association, serving as its president for many years. Her work to improve understanding continued through such volumes as Dragon Seed, The Promise, Hidden Flower, and Imperial Woman. An autobiographical volume, My Several Worlds, relates the author's experiences as a person, a writer, and a humanitarian. Also worthy of mention in Pearl Buck's amazing volume of writings is All Men Are Brothers, a translation of a Chinese classic, Shui hu chuan. She also wrote and published a number of books for children.

Pearl Buck considered herself a writer in the Chinese tradition of fiction, a tradition which stresses as its primary purpose the entertainment of the people. Such was her declaration in her Nobel lecture, *The Chinese Novel* (1939). She also said that she had to write, especially novels, and that she could not be truly happy unless she was writing, either to entertain or to further her humanitarian and liberal beliefs in religion and politics. In 1964 she started the Pearl Buck Foundation with a one million dollar contribution. The foundation has helped more than two thousand Asian children fathered and abandoned by American servicemen.

In failing health, Miss Buck continued to write until her death. Her last book, *All Under Heaven*, was published less than a week before her death on March 6, 1973.

Bibliography

The only full length critical-biographical studies are Paul A. Doyle, *Pearl Buck*, 1965; and Theodore F. Harris, *Pearl Buck: A Biography*, 1969. See Robert Van Gelder, *Writers and Writing*, 1946; Harry R. Warfel, *American Novelists of Today*, 1951; and Phyllis Bentley, "The Art of Pearl S. Buck," *English Journal*, XXIV (1935), 791–800.

THE GOOD EARTH

Type of work: Novel
Author: Pearl S. Buck (1892–1973)
Time of plot: Early twentieth century
Locale: Northern China
First published: 1931

With a detached, pastoral style, this novel follows the cycles of birth, marriage, and death in the Chinese peasant family of Wang Lung. The good years of plentiful harvest, marriage, and healthy children are balanced by the times of near starvation and stillborn progeny. Wang Lung finally finds himself a wealthy man, but his grown sons for whom he has worked so hard have no respect for their father's love of the good earth; they plan to sell his hardearned property as soon as he dies.

Principal Characters

Wang Lung, an ambitious farmer who sees in the land the only sure source of livelihood. But at the end of his life his third son has left the land to be a soldier and his first and second sons callously plan to sell the land and go to the city as soon as Wang dies.

O-Lan, a slave bought by Wang's father to marry Wang. She works hard in their small field with Wang, and during civil war violence she loots in order to get money to buy more land. She dies in middle age of a stomach illness.

Nung En, their oldest son, who, when he covets his father's concubine, Lotus Blossom, is married to the grain merchant Liu's daughter.

Nung Wen, their second son, appren-ticed to Liu.

The Fool, their feeble-minded daughter.

Liu, a grain merchant in the town.

The Uncle, who brings his wife and shiftless son to live on Wang's farm. Secretly a lieutenant of a robber band, he also brings protection.

Lotus Blossom, Wang Lung's concubine, who is refused entrance into the house by O-Lan.

Ching, a neighbor hired by Wang Lung as overseer, as the farm is extended.

Pear Blossom, a pretty slave taken by Wang after the death of his wife.

The Story

His father had chosen a slave girl to be the bride of Wang Lung, a slave from the house of Hwang, a girl who would keep the house clean, prepare the food, and not waste her time thinking about clothes. On the morning he led her out through the gate of the big house, they stopped at a temple and burned incense. That was their marriage.

O-lan was a good wife. She thriftily gathered twigs and wood, so that they would not have to buy fuel. She mended Wang Lung's and his father's winter clothes and scoured the house. She worked in the fields beside her husband, even on the day she bore their first son.

The harvest was a good one that year. Wang Lung had a handful of silver dollars from the sale of his wheat and rice. He and O-lan bought new coats for themselves and new clothes for the baby. Together they went to pay their respects, with their child, at the home in which O-lan had once been a slave. With some of the silver dollars Wang Lung bought a small field of rich land from the Hwangs. The second child was born a year later. It was again a year of good harvest.

Wang Lung's third baby was a girl. On the day of her birth crows flew about the house, mocking Wang Lung with their cries. The farmer did not rejoice when his little daughter was born, for poor farmers raised their daughters only to serve the rich. The crows had been an evil omen. The child was born feeble-minded.

That summer was dry, and for months no rain fell. The harvest was poor. After the little rice and wheat had been eaten and the ox killed for food, there was nothing for the poor peasants to do but die or go south to find work and food in a province of plenty. Wang Lung sold their furniture for a few pieces of silver, and after O-lan had borne their fourth child, dead with bruises on its neck when he saw it for the first time, the family began their journey. Falling in with a crowd of refugees, they were lucky. The refugees led them to a railroad, and with the money Wang Lung had received for his furniture they traveled on a train to their new home.

In the city they constructed a hut of mats against a wall, and, while O-lan and the two older children begged, Wang Lung pulled a ricksha. In that way they spent the winter, each day earning enough to buy rice for the next.

One day an exciting thing happened. There was to be a battle between soldiers in the town and an approaching enemy. When the wealthy people in the town fled, the poor who lived so miserably broke into the houses of the rich. By threatening one fat fellow who had been left behind, Wang Lung obtained enough money to take his family home.

O-lan soon repaired the damage which the weather had done to their house during their absence; then, with jewels which his wife had managed to plunder during the looting in the city, Wang Lung bought more land from the house of Hwang. He allowed O-lan to keep two small pearls which she fancied. Now Wang Lung had more land than one man could handle, and he hired one of his neighbors, Ching, as overseer. Several years later he had six men working for him. O-lan, who had borne him twins, a boy and a girl, after their return from the south, no longer went out into the fields to work, but kept the new house he had built. Wang Lung's two oldest sons were sent to school in the town.

When his land was flooded and work impossible until the water receded, Wang Lung began to go regularly to a tea shop in the town. There he fell in love with Lotus and brought her home to his farm to be his concubine. O-lan would have nothing to do with the girl, and Wang Lung was forced to set up a separate establishment for Lotus in order to keep the peace.

When he found that his oldest son visited Lotus often while he was away, Wang Lung arranged to have the boy marry the daughter of a grain merchant in the town. The wedding took place shortly before O-lan, still in the prime of life, died of a chronic stomach illness. To cement the bond between the farmer and the grain merchant, Wang Lung's second son was apprenticed to Liu, the merchant, and his youngest daughter was betrothed to Liu's young son. Soon after O-lan's death Wang Lung's father followed her. They were buried near one another on a hill on his land.

When he grew weathly, an uncle, his wife, and his shiftless son came to live with Wang Lung. One year there was a great flood, and although his neighbors' houses were pillaged by robbers during the confusion, Wang Lung was not bothered. Then he learned that his uncle was second to the chief of the robbers. From that time on he had to give way to his uncle's family for they were his insurance against robbery and perhaps murder.

At last Wang Lung coaxed his uncle and aunt to smoke opium, and so they became too involved in their dreams to bother him. But there was no way he could curb their son. When the boy began to annoy the wife of Wang Lung's oldest son, the farmer rented the deserted house of Hwang and he, with his own family, moved into town. The cousin left to join the soldiers. The uncle and aunt were left in the country with their pipes to console them.

After Wang Lung's overseeer died, he did no more farming himself. From that time on he rented his land, hoping that his youngest son would work it after his death. But he was disappointed. When Wang Lung took a slave young enough to be his granddaughter, the boy, who was in love with her, ran away from home and became a soldier.

When he felt that his death was near, Wang Lung went back to live on his land, taking with him only his slave, young Pear Blossom, his foolish-witted first daughter, and some servants. One day as he accompanied his sons across the fields, he overheard them planning what they would do with their inheritance, with the money they would get from selling their father's property. Wang Lung cried out, protesting that they must never sell the land because only from it could they be sure of earning a living. He did not know that they looked at each other over his head and smiled.

Critical Evaluation

Pearl Sydenstricker Buck referred to herself as "mentally bifocal" with respect to her American and Chinese ways of looking at things. The daughter of American missionaries in China, Pearl Buck came to know that land better than any other. She spent her early formative years in China and that time was extremely significant in developing her ideas, viewpoints, and philosophy. She attended schools both in China and the United States and made several trips back and forth, some unwillingly as when she and her parents were expelled from China during the Boxer Rebellion of 1900.

Pearl Buck began her writing as a girl in China with articles and short stories. There is no doubt that she had a gift for making the strange, unknown, and distant appear familiar. Until the time of her first published success, *East Wind, West Wind,* very little had been written about simple Chinese life although China was becoming of increasing interest to businessmen, diplomats, and missionaries. Nevertheless, the general public thought of the Chinese in rather strange terms, not as people with whom they could easily identify. Buck's feeling for the fundamental truths of life transcended any preconceived notions that the reading public may have had about China, and portrayed her people as understandable human beings who struggled for happiness and success like anyone else.

The Good Earth was published in 1931 and is probably Buck's most popular and widely read novel. It depicts a simple picture, the cycle of life from early years until death. Some Americans who first read the book thought the simple detailed descriptions of everyday Chinese life were "too Chinese" and, therefore, unappealing. Then, too, some Chinese felt that the author's portrayal of their people was inaccurate and incomplete. Most Chinese intellectuals objected to her choice of the peasant farmer as a worthy subject of a novel. They preferred to have the Western world see the intellectual and philosophical Chinese, even though that group was (and is) definitely in the minority. Buck's only answer to such criticism was that she wrote about what she knew best and these were the people whom she saw and came to know and love during her years in the interior of China.

The theme of *The Good Earth* is an uncomplicated one with universal appeal. The author tries to show how man can rise from poverty and relative insignificance to a position of importance and wealth. In some ways, the story is the proverbial Horatio Alger tale that so many Americans know and admire. The difference with this novel and the feature which makes it unique is its setting. Wang Lung, the main character around whom the action in the novel resolves, is a poor man who knows very little apart from the fact that land is valuable and solid and worth owning. Therefore, he spends his entire life trying to acquire as much land as he can in order to insure his own security as well as that of his family and descendants for generations to come. Ironically, he becomes like the rich he at first holds in awe. He has allowed himself to follow in their path and separate himself from the land and live above toil and dirt. The earth theme appears repeatedly throughout the book. Wang Lung's greatest joy is to look out over his land, to hold it in his fingers and to work it for his survival. Even at the end of the novel he returns to the old quarters he occupied on his first plot of land so that he can find the peace he knows his kinship with the land can bring him.

Buck's style is that of a simple direct narrative. There are no complicated literary techniques such as foreshadowing, flashbacks, or stream of consciousness. Neither are there any involved subplots to detract from the main story line. Wang Lung is, as has been noted, the central character and all the other characters and their actions relate in one way or another to him. *The Good Earth* is structured upon characterization, and it is a book of dramatic episodes which are projected through the sensitivities and experiences of those characters. It may be said that a strength of the author's characterization is her consistency, that is to say, all of her characters act and react in keeping with their personalities. None are stereotypes, as their motives are too complex. O-lan is typically good, but there are aspects of her personality which give her depth, dimension, and originality. When she does some seemingly dishonest thing such as steal the jewels she found at the home of the plundered rich, or kill the small baby girl born to her in ill health, she is consistent with her character in the context of these situations. She is realistic and sees both acts as producing more good than evil. O-lan is courageous and faithful and throughout the novel she maintains a beautiful dignity which gives her a special identity of her own, even if she is an unpretty common slave.

One of the most obvious and significant Chinese customs which appears repeatedly in the novel is the submission of the wife in all things to the will of the man. Girl children were born only to be reared for someone else's house as slaves, while men were born to carry on family names, traditions, and property. This situation is based on the Chinese position that women are inferior to men. The reader cannot help but be struck by this attitude as it manifests itself in the lives of the men and women in *The Good Earth*.

The novel may be criticized as having no high point or climax. True enough, there is no point of great and significant decision. There is no one who causes Wang Lung any serious struggle. His only antagonists are the adversity of the elements and the occasional arguments he has with his lazy uncle and his worthless nephew. Dramatic interest is sustained in the novel by well placed turning points which give the story new direction. The first is Wang Lung's marriage to O-lan and their first satisfying years together. Then, in the face of poverty, destitution, and little hope of recovery, Wang Lung demands and receives the handful of gold from the rich man and is thus able to get back to his land. At this point we see how very much Wang Lung's land means to him and what he is willing to do to have it back. In the closing pages of the novel, the quiet servitude and devotion of Pear Blossom, his slave, brings him the only peace and contentment he is to know in his late years. While there is no moralizing as such, Pear Blossom and her relationship to her master leads one to reflect on the fruits of such hard labor and sacrifice. A simple slave girl in a house full of discord—this is all Wang Lung has.

The success of *The Good Earth* is apparent. Pearl Buck won the Pulitzer Prize for it and it has been dramatized as well as made into a motion picture. It is widely read in many languages, undoubtedly because of its universal appeal as a clear and to the point portrayal of one man's struggle for survival, success, and ultimate happiness.

Bibliography

Canby, Henry S. "*The Good Earth*: Pearl Buck and the Nobel Prize," in *Saturday Review of Literature*. XIX (November 19, 1938), p. 8.

Cevasco, G.A. "Pearl Buck and the Chinese Novel," in *Asian Studies*. V (December, 1967), pp. 437–450.

Doyle, Paul A. *Pearl Buck*. New York: Twayne, 1965, pp. 36–54.

Gray, J. *On Second Thought*. Minneapolis: University of Minnesota Press, 1969, pp. 30–32.

Henchoz, Ami. "A Permanent Element in Pearl Buck's Novels," in *English Studies*. XXV (1943), pp. 97–103.

Langlois, Walter G. "*The Dream of the Red Chamber, The Good Earth*, and *Man's Fate*: Chronicles of Social Change in China," in *Literature East and West*. XI (March, 1967), pp. 1–10.

Shimizu, Mamoru. "On Some Stylistic Features, Chiefly Biblical, of *The Good Earth*," in *Studies in English Literature*. IV (1964), pp. 117–134.

Stuckey, W.J. *Pulitzer Prize Novels: A Critical Backward Look*. Norman: University of Oklahoma Press, 1966, pp. 90–93.

Thompson, Dody W. "Pearl Buck," in *American Winners of the Nobel Literary Prize*. Edited by Warren G. French and Walter E. Kidd. Norman: University of Oklahoma Press, 1968, pp. 85–110.

JAMES M. CAIN

Born: Annapolis, Maryland (July 1, 1892)
Died: University Park, Maryland (October 27, 1977)

Principal Works

NOVELS: *The Postman Always Rings Twice,* 1934; *Double Indemnity,* 1936; *Serenade,* 1937; *Career in C Major,* 1938; *The Embezzler,* 1940: *Mildred Pierce,* 1941: *Love's Lovely Counterfeit,* 1942; *Past All Dishonor,* 1946; *The Butterfly,* 1947; *The Moth,* 1948: *Galatea,* 1953; *Mignon,* 1963; *The Magician's Wife,* 1965.

NONFICTION: *Our Government,* 1930.

James M. Cain is a master of the hard-boiled or tough guy novel that flourished during the 1930's. The raw materials of his novels are simple, basic universals: sexual desire, money, murder, and other forms of violence. His typical hero is an educated roughneck, his typical heroine a ruthless woman. As lovers, they embark upon some high adventure and end up on what Cain calls "the loverack." For them, the wish that comes true proves a terrifying thing; when they get away with murder—the victim being, usually, the woman's husband—and collect the insurance money, they turn on each other. The sex usually has a fake religious aura and often borders on the abnormal; for instance, the action in *Serenade* derives from the hero's homosexual inclinations. Cain depicts the criminal behavior of men and women who are not too remote from the average American. He also creates a sense of place, as in his Glendale, California, novels. And in *Mildred Pierce,* he portrays a certain type of American female.

Cain has been admired for his technique, which is most evident in his extraordinary sense of pace. His best novels are brief and are narrated by men who are disinclined to embellish the telling. With no interest in past action, only in the immediacy of the present careening into the future, Cain lets a story "secrete its own adrenalin" and "needles it at the least hint of a letdown." In his best works, he comes close to creating examples of what has been called the pure novel—the novel that, like nonobjective painting, is its own subject.

Cain's parents, both Irish, were born in New Haven, Connecticut. His father taught at St. John's College, Annapolis, and was president of Washington College in Chestertown, Maryland. His mother, Rose Mallahan, was a professional singer. James Mallahan Cain was born in Annapolis in 1892. Although baptized a Catholic, he left the church when he was thirteen. In 1910, he graduated "without distinction" from Washington College, where he was nonactive, to his father's dismay, in extracurricular activities; he received an M.A. in 1917 from Johns Hopkins. He once studied singing with great concentration, but was finally told that his voice was not good enough for a successful career.

Having lost a number of jobs for reason, he said, of incompetence, Cain became a reporter in 1917 for the Baltimore *American*, where he met Mencken. While working on the Baltimore *Sun* in 1918, he enlisted in the army and served in France, where he edited *The Lorraine Cross*, one of the most successful weeklies of the American Expeditionary Forces. From 1919 to 1923 he worked for the Baltimore *Sun*; in 1923, he was also Professor of Journalism at St. John's College. He wrote editorials under Walter Lippman for the New York *World* from 1924 until he went to Hollywood; his weekly political dialogues were compiled in his controversial book, *Our Government*.

While Mencken was editor, Cain wrote a number of plays, stories, and articles, mostly political, for *The American Mercury*. He contributed rather tough-styled articles on labor strife and other aspects of the American scene during the 1920's and 1930's to the leading periodicals. After the enormous success of his first novel, *The Postman Always Rings Twice*, which was banned in Canada and made into a play (1937) and a movie (1946), Cain gave up journalism permanently. As a Hollywood scriptwriter in the 1930's and 1940's, he learned a great deal about cinematic technique; though he proved unsuccessful as a screenwriter, his own novels became famous movies: *Mildred Pierce* and *Double Indemnity* (adapted by Raymond Chandler). A planner, like many of the heroes he created, he organized the American Authors Authority in 1946 to get justice for writers.

Cain was married four times, his last wife, being the former Chicago opera singer, Florence McBeth. He last lived in Hyattsville, Maryland, just outside Baltimore. He died in 1977 in University Park, Maryland.

Bibliography

The only full-length study is David Madden, *James M. Cain*, 1970. Sources of biographical information on Cain are *Twentieth Century Authors* and *Current Biography*, 1947. For briefer critical commentary see Edmund Wilson, "The Boys in the Back Room," *Classics and Commercials*, 1950, 19–22; Max Lerner, "Cain in the Movies," *Public Journal*, 1945, 46–48; James T. Farrell, "Cain's Movietone Realism," *Literature and Morality*, 1947, 78–89; W. M. Frohock, "Tabloid Tragedy," *The Novel of Violence in America*, 1950; David Madden, "James M. Cain and the Pure Novel," *The University Review-Kansas City*, December, 1963 and March, 1964, 143–148, 235–239; and Joyce Carol Oates, "Man under Sentence of Death: The Novels of James M. Cain," in *Tough Guy Writers of the Thirties*, David Madden, editor, 1968.

THE POSTMAN ALWAYS RINGS TWICE

Type of work: Novel
Author: James M. Cain (1892–1977)
Time of plot: 1933
Locale: Southern California
First published: 1934

Essay-Review

Three related genres that developed in the novel form during the 1930's were the hard-boiled private detective (which departed from the genteel English novel of detection), the proletarian (which derived from European naturalism and American selective realism), and the tough guy (which derived from the former two). But perhaps for the best and most influential work of all three genres "the tough-guy novel" is a good term: Dashiell Hammett's *The Maltese Falcon*, published in 1929, and Raymond Chandler's *The Big Sleep*, published in 1939, in the private detective realm; B. Traven's *The Death Ship*, which appeared in an American edition in 1934, among proletarian novels; and Horace McCoy's *They Shoot Horses, Don't They?* published in 1935, among the pure tough-guy books are all minor classics in American literature. These and similar novels expressed the mood of American society during the depression, influenced action in motion pictures, affected the tone and attitude of more serious writers, and inspired certain European novelists during the 1940's. The quintessence of all these is James M. Cain's *The Postman Always Rings Twice*.

Although Frank Chambers, the twenty-four-year-old narrator of Cain's novel, belongs to that legion of unemployed who became tramps of the road, hoboes of the rails, and migrant workers, Cain is not deliberately interested in depicting the social ills of his time; if there is an attack on conditions that produced a man like Frank, it is only implicit. Frank is an easy-going fellow, remarkably free of bitterness, even when given cause; although he commits murder and pistol whips a blackmailer, he is not willfully vicious. A spontaneous creature of action whose psychological nature readily accomodates ambivalent attitudes, he can be fond of Nick Papadakis and weep at his funeral, yet seduce his young wife Cora, and attempt to kill him twice.

And although this novel is concerned, as many of Cain's are, with murder and other forms of violence, and although it satisfies momentarily the average American's inexhaustible craving for details of crime and punishment, it cannot be classified as a detective tale. Cain, like the readers he has in mind, is fascinated by the intricacies of the law and of insurance claims, but his primary interest is in presenting an inside view of the criminal act. However, Frank is no gangster and Cora is no moll; they are not far removed in status or aspiration from the average anticipated reader of Cain.

For Frank and Cora lie down in the great American dreambed of the 1920's, only to wake up in a living nightmare in the 1930's. A lurid decade produced such a lurid relationship and such a lurid tale. When they meet at Nick's Twin Oaks Tavern on a highway outside Los Angeles, Frank has just been thrown off a truck, having sneaked into the back for a ride up from Tiajuana, and Cora is washing dishes in the restaurant. To demonstrate the animal impact of their encounter, Cain has them meet on page 5, make love on page 15, and decide to murder the obese, middle-aged Greek on page 23. Sharing the dream of getting drunk and making love without hiding, they go on what Cain calls "the Love-Rack." He regards the concept of "the wish that comes true" as a terrifying thing. This terror becomes palpable as soon as Frank and Cora believe that they have gotten away with murder and have acquired money, property, and freedom.

But in the background each has another dream which mocks the shared realization of the immediate wish. Cora came to Hollywood from a small town in Iowa bemused by the dream most girls of the Thirties cherished: to become a movie star. She failed, and Nick rescued her from a hash house. But basically her values are middle-class, and above all she wants respectability, even if murder is the prerequisite. An anachronism in the age of technology, though he has a certain skill as a garage mechanic, Frank desires to be always on the move, compelled by something of the spirit of the open road that Whitman cleebrated. For a moment, but only for a moment, he shares this romantic, idyllic vision with Cora. After the failure of their first attempt to murder Nick, they set out together for a life of wandering. Thus, in the criminal affair of these lovers, these deliberate outsiders, two central dreams of the American experience—unrestrained mobility and respectable sedentariness—and two views of the American landscape—the open road and the mortgaged house—collide. As the dreams finally betray them, they begin, ironically, to turn on each other, for basically what Frank wants is Cora, the sexual dynamo, and what Cora wants is an instrument to be used to gain her ends—money and respectability. Though she may convince herself that the right man, instead of a fat foreigner, is a necessary part of her aspirations, this man would soon wake up in the wrong dream.

While the novel's larger thematic dimensions exist in the background, as a kind of fable of the American experience, giving it a lasting value in our literature, Cain is more immediately concerned with the lovers and with the action that results from their wish. This action keeps in motion certain elements that almost guarantee the reader's interest: illicit love; murder; the smell of tainted money; sexual violence that verges on the abnormal; and the strong characterizations of such men as Sackett (the district attorney), Katz (the eccentric lawyer), and Madge (the pick-up who takes Frank to South America to capture jaguars). Cain plays upon the universal wishes of the average American male.

What fascinates serious readers of literature is Cain's technique for manipulating reader response. Not only does he almost automatically achieve certain thematic ironies inherent in his raw material, but the ironies of action are stunningly executed. For instance, Frank cons Nick out of a free meal, but the con backfires in a way when Nick cons Frank into staying on to operate the service station; thus Frank becomes involved in a situation that will leave three people dead. After recovering from what he took to be an accident in the bathtub, Nick searches for Frank and persuades him to return to the roadside restaurant, thus helping to bring about his own death. Cleared of killing the Greek, Frank and Cora collect the insurance. Later, when she is waiting for a taxi to leave Frank, Cora sticks a note for him in the cash register; it refers to their having killed the Greek for his money. But Frank catches her and insists that he loves her. To test his love, Cora, who is now pregnant, swims so far out to sea that Frank will have to help her back. He does help her, but driving back from the beach, they have a wreck and she is killed. The police find the note in the cash register and conclude that Frank has engineered the wreck so that he can have all the money. Because he cannot be tried twice for killing the Greek, they execute him for murdering Cora. A careful pattern of minor ironies contributes to the impact of the major ones.

Cain's structural techniques are impressive. The swift execution of the basic situation in the first twenty-three pages has been noted, and each development, each scene, is controlled with the same narrative skill; inherent in each episode is the inevitability of the next. Everything is kept strictly to the essentials. The characters, for instance, exist only for the immediate action; there is almost no exposition as such. Cain is the acknowledged master of pace. Violence and sexual passion are thrust forward at a rate that is itself part of the reader's vicarious experience. Contributing to this sense of pace is the swift rhythm of the dialogue, which also manages to keep certain undercurrents flowing. Frank's character justifies the economy of style, the nerve-end adherence to the spine of the action. Albert Camus modeled the style of *The Stranger* on Cain's novel, and Meursault is cut to the pattern of Frank Chambers. But Cain has written what has been called a pure novel, for his deliberate intentions go no further than the immediate experience, brief as a movie is, as unified in its impression as a poem usually is. Though Frank writes his story on the eve of his execution, Cain does not even suggest the simplest moral: crime does not pay. An intense experience, which a man tells in such a way as to make it, briefly, our experience, it is its own reason for being. Camus' novel, however, operates on this premise only in the first half; in the second, he begins to develop a philosophical point of view that affects man in every phase of life.

For Cain, the postman, whose custom is always to ring twice, rang thrice. This first novel is one of America's all-time best sellers and has gone through a great many editions; Cain adapted it to the stage; and it was made into a famous motion picture. After many years it is still being read widely, both as popular entertainment and as a work of art of a very peculiar sort, respected, with severe qualifications, by students of literature.

ERSKINE CALDWELL

Born: White Oak, Georgia (December 17, 1903)

Principal Works

NOVELS: *The Bastard*, 1930; *Tobacco Road*, 1932; *God's Little Acre*, 1933; *Journeyman*, 1935; *Georgia Boy*, 1943; *Tragic Ground*, 1944; *A House in the Uplands*, 1946; *The Sure Hand of God*, 1947; *The Courting of Susie Brown*, 1952; *Love and Money*, 1954; *Grette*, 1955; *Claudelle Inglish*, 1958; *Jenny by Nature*, 1961; *Close to Home*, 1962; *Miss Mamma Aimee*, 1967; *Summertime Island*, 1968; *The Weather Shelter*, 1969; *The Earnshaw Neighborhood*, 1972.

SHORT STORIES: *American Earth*, 1931; *We Are the Living*, 1933; *Kneel to the Rising Sun*, 1935; *Southways*, 1938; *Jackpot*, 1940; *The Complete Stories of Erskine Caldwell*, 1953; *Gulf Coast Stories*, 1956; *Certain Women*, 1957; *When You Think of Me*, 1959.

AUTOBIOGRAPHY: *Moscow Under Fire: A Wartime Diary*, 1941; *Call It Experience*, 1951.

MISCELLANEOUS: *You Have Seen Their Faces*, 1937 (with Margaret Bourke-White); *Say, Is This the U. S. A.*, 1941; *Around About America*, 1964; *In Search of Bisco*, 1965.

His novels having sold millions of copies, particularly in paperback reprints, Erskine (Preston) Caldwell has become one of the most popular novelists in America. Born into a ministerial household in White Oak, Georgia, on December 17, 1903, he moved widely about the United States in his early years. Although he has ranged as far away as Maine and Russia, his representative fiction has always been associated with the South. His topic is usually the life of the dispossessed, the down-trodden, the sharecropper, the underdog, white or black. Before he became successful as a writer, he held a wide variety of jobs—football player, pool hall worker, real estate salesman—and attended briefly Erskine College, the University of Pennsylvania, and the University of Virginia.

Although he has published an astounding quantity of fiction, Caldwell also found time to be foreign correspondent for *Life, P.M.*, and the Columbia Broadcasting System. During the 1930's he collaborated with his second wife, the photographer Margaret Bourke-White, in the production of pictorial, sociological books. His *Tobacco Road* was not only a best-seller as a book (and a successful movie), but as dramatized by Joseph Kirkland it broke all records for the New York stage, including that of the amazing *Abie's Irish Rose*.

A tall, good-humored man, Caldwell has not let either success or the charge of sensationalism turn his head. Consciously leftist in his attitude, he looks upon his books as more than mere entertainment; they are social documents of protest.

Bibliography

There is no authorized biographical study of Caldwell and, in recent years, very little criticism, the most recent being James Korges, *Erskine Caldwell*, 1969. See also Joseph Warren Beach, *American Fiction, 1920–1940*, 1941; W. M. Frohock, *The Novel of Violence in America, 1920–1950*, 1950; Kenneth Burke, "Caldwell: Maker of Grotesques," *New Republic*, LXXXII (1935), 232–235; John Donald Wade, "Sweet Are the Uses of Degeneracy," *Southern Review*, I (1936), 449–466; Peter A. Carmichael, "Jeeter Lester, Agrarian Par Excellence," *Sewanee Review*, XLVIII (1940), 21–29; and John M. Maclachlan, "Folk and Culture in the Novels of Erskine Caldwell," *Southern Folklore Quarterly*, IX (1945), 93–101.

GOD'S LITTLE ACRE

Type of work: Novel
Author: Erskine Caldwell (1903–)
Time of plot: Early twentieth century
Locale: Georgia
First published: 1936

Erskine Caldwell, like many of his literary peers, frequently concerned himself with the society of a changing South and in so doing participated in the Southern literary Renaissance. Despite the uneveness of his work and charges of obscenity, God's Little Acre *remains (along with* Tobacco Road*) an artistic work worthy of notice.*

Principal Characters

Ty Ty Walden, patriarch of a burgeoning family and master of "God's little acre." Ty Ty is a comic and tragic "man of the land" who lets his fields lie fallow while he searches for the buried lode of gold that will make him rich and his family content. Ty Ty not only prides himself on his apparently futile search for gold but also on the "scientific" methods he employs. (His scientific approach includes the kidnapping of an albino to divine the gold's location.) Ty Ty also prides himself on his acceptance of man's animal instincts, his bevy of attractive daughters and daughter-in-law, and his unorthodox relationship with God. His goals in life are simple: he wants to discover gold and to keep his family from fighting.

Will Thompson, a "mill man" ostensibly opposite Ty Ty walden in profession and life style. Will and Ty Ty are, according to Griselda, "real men." Both men appear to know a "secret of living" that ties prurient matters to strength, committment, and even religion.

Rosamond Thompson, Will's faithful wife who endures Will's infidelities and erratic behavior, living in her yellow mill town house until the death of her husband in the workers' rebellion.

Griselda Walden, Buck Walden's wife. Griselda is a "perfect little female," "the prettiest of them all," who in spite of her husband's jealousy and the sexual looseness of her in-laws, remains faithful to her husband until just prior to Will Thompson's death. It is Griselda who sees Ty Ty in Will Thompson and succumbs to the sexual intensity that marks a "real man" to her.

Darling Jill Walden, Ty Ty's only remaining single child who bluntly proclaims that she will not marry until she is "a few months gone." Jill is incorrigible in social as well as sexual matters. She browbeats and abuses Pluto, her suitor, and has no compunction about even her incestual relationship with men.

Pluto Swint, the browbeat suitor of Darling Jill. Pluto, because of his involvement with Jill's family, has no time to campaign for the coveted sherrif's position. His lack of time is rivaled only by the lack of energy that the hot Southern sun and Pluto's obesity bring on.

Buck Walden, Griselda's violent and jealous husband who, with Ty Ty, spends his life in the various caverns digging for gold. When he is not digging, Buck is quarreling with his family or threatening Will Thompson's life.

Jim Leslie Walden, Ty Ty's rich son who abandoned the Waldens and their wild gold fever. Though seemingly respectable, he is married to a "diseased" wife and in wild pursuit of Griselda.

Essay-Review

Expatriated from Georgia to Maine, Erskine Caldwell, widely read and much debated Southern novelist, functions, particularly in his early works, as both realist and humorist in defining a new poor white proletariat of the South. In this context *God's Little Acre* can be seen as a social novel by a regional novelist.

In a symmetrical seven-part structure, the action of the novel moves from farm to mill town, farm to Augusta, farm to mill town, and back to farm. Though the vocabulary may change, in each of the settings the same themes dominate. Caldwell consistently concerns himself with family, gold, sex, and God and the points at which these elements merge and diverge.

Darling Jill, Ty Ty's daughter, adds Will, whom she and Pluto have gone to the mill town to recruit as a worker, to the list of men she has conquered. As usual, she causes a fracas, but all parties are somehow reconciled by the time they return to the farm. Upon their return they find the others digging frantically, having obtained an albino to divine the location of gold. While the usual arguments ensue over women, they all decide to go to Augusta to obtain a loan from Ty Ty's wealthy son, Jim Leslie. Sexual favors are the encouragement Jim Leslie needs to agree to the loan. After returning to the farm, they are off again to return Will to the mill town. There, Will leads the workers in protest against the company. He is killed by a guard. Back on the farm, Jim Leslie has arrived to claim the sexual favors promised him by Griselda. Buck, her husband, kills him, causing Ty Ty to question his search for gold for the first time. However, he resolves the problem by willing the one acre of land he has made mobile and bequeathed to God to "follow Buck, stopping when he did so that he would always be upon it."

The Walden family is in many ways quite traditional: it is an extended family radiating from a patriarchal center. Ty Ty is always concerned with the fate of his children and freely shares whatever he possesses with his family.

Much of his strength he derives from his fiercely independent relationship with God.

"... When you get God in your heart," Ty Ty claims, "you have a feeling that living is worth striving for night and day. I ain't talking about the God you hear about in churches, I'm talking about the God inside of a body. I've got the greatest feeling for Him, because he helps me to live. That's why I set aside God's little acre out there on the farm when I was just a young man starting in. I like to have something around me that I can go to and stand on and feel God in."

His faith gives Ty Ty the strength and will to pursue gold on his land, but his insistent digging also marks a variance from faith that ultimately brings guilt to Ty Ty. His guilt comes from mobilizing God's acre so that he can dig for gold at any spot on his land: "He felt guilty of something—maybe it was sacrilege or desecration—whatever it was, he knew he had not played fair with God."

Ty Ty's gold fever also jeopardizes his faith with his family. Ty Ty's bad faith is symbolically marked by the digging next to his house. The family finds itself "balanced on the rim of a lantern-lit crater at the side of the house." This crater grows with digging until by the end of the novel the stability of the house is seriously threatened. As the hole grows bigger, it becomes apparent, even to Ty Ty, that the house will need some support if it is to continue to stand. Besides literally undermining the house, Ty Ty's gold fever distracts him so that he cannot farm even the small space of land allotted to farming. He had planted his crop late that year; he had no time since he had been busy digging.

Metaphorically Ty Ty's gold fever extends to another problem with the Walden family: their salacious attitudes and activities. This problem proceeds from Ty Ty's religious attitude and the extent to which he carries his views. To Ty Ty, people think God wants them to be different than the way they know they are. He is certain that most people believe the preacher, who tries to convince them that they have gone astray from their true nature. Ty Ty's creed is, "When you sit down by yourself and feel what's in you, that's the real way to live."

But Ty Ty's gold fever, his constant digging, and his religious feelings all run together and manifest themselves in his unconventional sexual attitudes that, like his digging, undermine his family. Mirrored in his children Ty Ty witnesses his own sexual freedom with pride. Of Darling Jill's "teasing and fooling with a lot of men" Ty Ty is "tickled to death" since Darling Jill is the "baby of the family . . . coming along at last." But it is Jim Leslie's lascivious attitudes, like Will's, that ultimately bring dissension, death, and destruction on the family, and leave Ty Ty hopelessly digging for a lode that by definition docs not and cannot exist in dry soil.

Bibliography

Allen, Walter. *The Modern Novel in Britain and the United States.* New York: Dutton, 1964, pp. 119–120.

Beach, Joseph Warren. *American Fiction, 1920–1940.* New York: Russell and Russell, 1960, pp. 240–245.

Bradbury, John M. *Renaissance in the South: Critical History of the Literature 1920–1960.* Chapel Hill: University of North Carolina Press, 1963, pp. 100–101.

Burke, Kenneth. "Caldwell: Maker of Grotesques," in *Psychoanalysis and American Fiction.* Edited by Irving Malin. New York: Dutton, 1965, pp. 248–253.

Holman, Hugh. "Southern Social Issues and the Outer World," in *Southern Fiction Today*. Edited by George Gore. Athens: University of Georgia Press, 1969, pp. 21–28.

Itofuji, Horomi. "An Aspect of Erskine Caldwell in *God's Little Acre*," in *Kyusha American Literature*. II (May, 1959), pp. 17–22.

Korges, James. *Erskine Caldwell*. Minneapolis: University of Minnesota Press, 1968, pp. 25–32.

Kukie, Lawrence S. "*God's Little Acre*: An Analysis," in *Saturday Review of Literature*. XI (November 24, 1934), pp. 305–306, 312.

Wagenknecht, Edward. "Novelists of the Thirties: Erskine Caldwell," in *Cavalcade of the American Novel*. New York: Holt, 1952, pp. 415–417.

TOBACCO ROAD

Type of work: Novel
Author: Erskine Caldwell (1903–   )
Time of plot: 1920's
Locale: Georgia
First published: 1932

Although certain exaggerated, Rabelaisian episodes of Tobacco Road *make the novel appear to be merely a burlesque on backwoods Georgia life, Caldwell's serious purpose is to show with realism the social problems of his region.*

Principal Characters

Jeeter Lester, a Georgia poor white, the father of seventeen, of whom twelve are surviving and two are still at home. Shiftless but always vaguely hopeful, he makes several half-hearted and futile attempts to feed himself first and afterward his starving family. He burns to death in his shack as a result of a fire he set to burn broomsedge.

Ada Lester, his wife, who shares his fate.

Dude Lester, his sixteen-year-old son, who is persuaded into marriage with a middle-aged widow by her purchase of a Ford, which subsequently runs over and kills a Negro and, later, the Lesters' grandmother, both to no one's particular regret.

Bessie Lester, the wife of Dude. She uses her authority as a backwoods evangelist to perform her own marriage ceremony.

Pearl Bensey, Jeeter's fifteen-year-old married daughter. Tied to their bed by her husband, she manages to free herself and run away.

Lov Bensey, Pearl's husband. After Pearl's flight, he is advised by Jeeter to take Ellie May instead.

Ellie May Lester, Jeeter's harelipped daughter, who uses her charms to distract Lov's attention, first from his bag of turnips, later from his marital loss.

The Story

Lov Bensey, husband of Pearl, fifteen-year-old daughter of Jeeter Lester, felt low in his mind when he stopped by the Lester house on his way home with a bag of turnips. Pearl, he complained, refused to have anything to do with him; she would neither sleep with him nor talk to him.

The Lesters lived in a one-room shack which was falling apart. They had nothing to eat but pork-rind soup. Jeeter was trying to patch an inner tube so that the Lester car, a nondescript wreck which had been refused even by the junk dealer, could be used to carry firewood to Augusta. Jeeter's harelipped daughter Ellie

TOBACCO ROAD by Erskine Caldwell. By permission of the author and the publishers, Duell, Sloan & Pearce, Inc. Copyright, 1932, by Erskine Caldwell.

May charmed Lov away from his bag of turnips. While she and Lov were dallying in the yard in front of the shack, the other Lesters pounced upon the bag of turnips. Jeeter grabbed it and ran into the scrub woods, followed by his worthless son Dude. Jeeter ate his fill of turnips. He gave Dude several and even saved a handful for the rest of the family. They returned from the woods to find Lov gone. Sister Bessie, a woman preacher, had come for a visit. Bessie, middle-aged, and Dude, sixteen, were attracted to each other. Bessie, upon leaving, promised to return to take Dude away to be her husband.

The Lesters were starving. Jeeter had long since been unable to get credit at the local stores in order to buy seed, fertilizer, and food. His land was exhausted and there was no chance of reclaiming it because of Jeeter's utter laziness. Jeeter and his wife Ada had had seventeen children. Twelve of them survived, but all except Ellie May and Dude had left home.

Bessie returned and announced that God had given her permission to marry Dude, but Dude refused to listen until Bessie said that she was planning to buy a new car with some money that her late husband had left her. She and Dude went to town and bought a new Ford, the loud horn of which Dude highly approved. At the county courthouse, over the mild protestations of the clerk because of Dude's youth, Bessie got a marriage license. Back at the Lester shack, Bessie, using her authority as preacher, married herself to Dude.

The newlyweds went for a ride in their new car; they returned to the tobacco road at sundown with one fender of the car completely ruined. They had run into a farm wagon on the highway and had killed a Negro whom they left lying by the roadside.

Jeeter, anxious to get food and snuff, persuaded Bessie and Dude to take him to Augusta with a load of firewood. Their arrival in Augusta was delayed, however, by the breakdown of the car. A gallon and a half of oil poured into the crank case enabled them to get to the city, where Jeeter failed to sell one stick of wood. The trio sold the car's spare tire, for which they could see no use, and bought food. They mistook a house of ill-repute for a hotel; Bessie was absent from Jeeter and her young husband for most of the night.

During the return trip to the tobacco road, Jeeter unloaded the wood beside the highway and set fire to it. He was about to suggest another trip in the car, but Bessie and Dude rode away before he could stop them.

As the car rapidly fell apart, the warmth between Bessie and her young husband cooled. In a fight between Bessie and the Lesters over Jeeter's right to ride in the car again, Dude sided with his wife. After all, the car still ran a little.

Meanwhile Pearl ran away from Lov; she had managed to escape after he had tied her to their bed. Jeeter advised Lov not to look for Pearl, but to take Ellie May in her place. He asked Ellie May to bring back victuals and clothes from Lov's house. The grandmother, who had been run over by Bessie's Ford, died in the yard.

Jeeter anticipated seeding time by burning the broomsedge off his land. A wind blew the fire to the house while Jeeter and Ada were asleep. The destitute sharecroppers were burned to death on the land that Jeeter's family had once owned as prosperous farmers.

Critical Evaluation

Tobacco Road, published in the midst of the Great Depression, reflects the social and economic concerns of the 1930's, as well as principles of literary naturalism. During the 1930's, a time of extreme economic hardship, novels such as *Tobacco Road* helped make Americans (and others) aware of the destructive poverty and alienation at the bottom of society.

Naturalism, a significant movement in American literature from before the beginning of the twentieth century through World War II, stresses the impersonal and powerful forces that shape human destinies. The characters of *Tobacco Road* are caught in the backwaters of industrialization, in the grip of irresistible forces. Unable to farm effectively, yet bound to the land, and so unable to migrate to the factories, they are trapped from one generation to the next. Jeeter, for instance, cannot farm his land, and yet instinct binds him (and, finally, his son) to it.

These characters are also prisoners of other forces, most notably the past and their sexuality. They find modern technology beyond their understanding, and they ruin a new car Bessie has managed to buy. Unable to use modern farming methods, Jeeter and Ada die trying to burn the fields to clear them for an imaginary cotton crop. Sexuality also operates powerfully on these characters. Bessie's marriage to Dude and Lov's attraction for Ellie May are based entirely on sex; and, in fact, the reader is left with the impression that the characters of *Tobacco Road* are as little able to cope with sexual forces as with economic forces.

The style of the novel, marked by simple, declarative sentences and catching the rhythms of the dialect used by poor white Southerners, is appropriate for the tragically self-destructive life Caldwell describes. This plain style, typical of naturalism, corresponds to the basic drives for food, sex, and survival, drives which are not hidden or disguised by the demands of civilization, but which Caldwell lays bare for all to see in the changeless lives of his characters.

Bibliography

Beach, Joseph Warren. "Erskine Caldwell: The Comic Catharsis," in *American Fiction 1920–1940.* New York: Macmillan, 1941, pp. 225–231.

Bradbury, John M. *Renaissance in the South: Critical History of the Literature 1920–1960.* Chapel Hill: University of North Carolina Press, 1963, pp. 100–101.

Burke, Kenneth. "Caldwell: Maker of Grotesques," in *Psychoanalysis and American Fiction.* Edited by Irving Malin. New York: Dutton, 1965, pp. 248–253.

Couch, W.T. *"Tobacco Road,"* in Virginia Quarterly Review. XIII (Spring 1938), p. 309.

Frohock, W.M. *The Novel of Violence in America.* Boston: Beacon Press, 1957, pp. 106–123.

Gossett, Louise Y. *Violence in Recent Southern Fiction.* Durham, N.C.: Duke University Press, 1965, pp. 16–29.

Holman, Hugh. "Southern Social Issues and the Outer World," in *Southern Fiction Today.* Edited by George Gore. Athens: University of Georgia Press, 1969, pp. 21–28.

Korges, James. *Erskine Caldwell.* Minneapolis: University of Minnesota Press, 1969, pp. 22–24.

Krutch, Joseph Wood. "Tragedy: Eugene O'Neill," in *American Drama Since 1918.* New York: Random House, 1939, pp. 122–126.

Marion, H.H. "Star Dust Above *Tobacco Road,"* in *Christian Century.* LX (February 16, 1938), pp. 204–206.

Sievers, W. David. *Freud on Broadway.* New York: Hermitage House, 1955, pp. 237–238.

Snelling, Paula. "Ground Itch, Art and Erskine Caldwell," in *From the Mountain.* Edited by Helen White. Memphis, Tenn.: Memphis State University Press, 1972, pp. 148–195.

Wagenknecht, Edward. "Novelists of the Thirties: Erskine Caldwell," in *Cavalcade of the American Novel.* New York: Holt, 1952, pp. 415–417.

WILLA CATHER

Born: Gore, Virginia (December 7, 1873)
Died: New York, N.Y. (April 24, 1947)

Principal Works

NOVELS: *Alexander's Bridge*, 1912; *O Pioneers!* 1913; *The Songs of the Lark*, 1915; *My Ántonia*, 1918; *One of Ours*, 1922; *A Lost Lady*, 1923; *The Professor's House*, 1925; *My Mortal Enemy*, 1926; *Death Comes for the Archbishop*, 1927; *Shadows on the Rock*, 1931; *Lucy Gayheart*, 1935; *Sapphira and the Slave Girl*, 1940.

SHORT STORIES: *The Troll Garden*, 1905; *Youth and the Bright Medusa*, 1920; *Obscure Destinies*, 1932; *The Old Beauty and Others*, 1948.

POEMS: *April Twilights*, 1903 (enlarged edition, 1923).

ESSAYS: *Not Under Forty*, 1936; *Willa Cather on Writing*, 1949.

Willa Cather was the last of a generation of writers who lived through the passing of the old frontier, who saw at first hand the region of the homesteader transformed into a countryside of tidy farms and small towns; and she found in the primitive virtues of the pioneer experience her own values as an artist. When the prairie roads "no longer ran about like wild things, but followed the surveyed section lines," they led inevitably to Main Street. This fact colored all her perceptions of a place and its people, gave her writing its center and its roots. The West, the past—one was the physical background of her best work, the other its spiritual climate. The very nature of her materials determined her course as a writer: to record the decline of the prairie frontier and later to find in more traditional societies of the Spanish Southwest and French-Colonial Quebec those resources of the human spirit which have been almost overwhelmed in the complexities and confusion of the present.

For a talent as special as hers, Willa Cather was fortunate in her time and place. She was born on December 7, 1873, in the Back Creek Valley of northern Virginia, not far from Winchester, where her ancestors had settled late in the eighteenth century. In 1883 her father moved his family to a ranch near Red Cloud, Nebraska, and there she grew up in a region still marked by trails of the Indian and the buffalo. This change from the stability and ordered pattern of life in rural Virginia made a lasting impression on the nine-year-old girl, so that for the rest of her life she was to be concerned with the effects of continuance and change on human character.

During the year the Cathers lived on the Nebraska Divide they had few American neighbors, but Bohemian, Scandinavian, French, and German farmers lived nearby. Free to come and go as she pleased, Willa Cather found a new set of experiences among these people struggling to master a new language and a stubborn soil and to hold their lands through periods of drought and failing credit. Friendships with immigrant neighbors and the classics she read aloud to her grandmothers at night—there was at the time no school she could attend—gave her a deeper knowledge of old cultures than the prairie towns of that day could provide. The lasting impressions of those early years are reflected in that passage in *My Ántonia* in which Jim Burden ponders the lines of the classic poet, *Primus ego in patriam mecum* . . . *deducam Musas*, and realizes that Vergil had in mind not the Roman state or even a province, but a rural neighborhood, a landscape of fields "sloping down to the river and to the old beech trees with broken tops." Here is the narrow gap that Miss Cather eventually crossed between the frontier of the prairie and the frontier of art.

In 1885 the Cathers moved into Red Cloud, where Willa attended the high school for two years. A great influence on her life at that time was an English storekeeper who taught her to read Latin and Greek; after she matriculated at the University of Nebraska in 1891 she continued her unofficial studies under his guidance during vacations. Graduated in 1895, she went to Pittsburgh a year later to do editorial work for a small magazine before joining the staff of the Pittsburgh *Daily Leader* in 1897. About the same time her poems and short stories began to appear in *McClure's Magazine* and *Cosmopolitan.* Finding newspaper work too exacting for creative writing, she taught in the Pittsburgh high schools from 1901 to 1906. *April Twilights*, a book of poems, was published in 1903, followed two years later by a collection of short stories, *The Troll Garden.* In 1906 she joined the staff of *McClure's Magazine*, where she remained until she published her first novel in 1912.

The first novel is likely to be an unguarded one, and *Alexander's Bridge* was no exception. Brining together a young Westerner's impressions of charming Boston teas and London drawing rooms, a moral problem out of Edith Wharton, and moral symbolism out of Henry James, the book failed because it did not come out of Cather's own experience but out of her respect for literary tradition. In the meantime, however, she had met Sarah Orne Jewett, who advised her to write of her own region in her own way. Cather profited by this advice; her next three novels enclose vast spaces of prairie, hills, and sky in a world rich and sustaining with homely realism. In *O Pioneers!* the immigrant heroine, Alexandra Bergson, develops the brooding wisdom and deep strength we find in the women of racial myths as she struggles to tame the wild land and bring it to fruition. *The Song of the Lark* tells the story of Thea Kronborg, rising from the crudeness and vulgarity of a Colorado mountain town to have a great career as a singer. In *My Ántonia* the simplicity and generous good nature of Ántonia Shimerda leave her untouched by years of farm drudgery and village spite; her serenity and happiness have their source in her passion for order and motherhood.

But the land which ennobled some natures could also corrupt the weak and breed the mean. As the pioneering impulses dwindled to a second generation's desire for soft jobs and easy money, Cather's disillusionment deepened and found expression in the books of her middle period. The short stories in *Youth and the Bright Medusa* contain pictures of the barrenness and waste imposed by the frontier effort and a career in art. *One of Ours* is a novel of defeat which fails to convince because Claude Wheeler is little more than an abstraction in a conventional novel of art, a fable of the creative spirit blighted by a crass, stupid world. *A Lost Lady* is another story of frustration, but in it Cather had her vision of a dying age and her own disillusionment in its passing under firm control. This was the first example of what she called the novel *démeublé,* fiction stripped of all furnishings to leave the scene bare for the play of emotions. From this time on she was to abandon the full-bodied realistic method in her novels; in her later works her plots take shape naturally from the development of character or the interplay and clash of personalities, and her deeper meanings are conveyed indirectly by images and symbols. In *The Professor's House,* for example, the Blue Mesa looms behind the story of Godfrey St. Peter, an enduring symbol overshadowing the four stories of corruption and betrayal which give the novel its underlying strength and critical force. Beneath its quiet and autumnal mood *The Professor's House* is Cather's most intimate and bitter work, touching American life at so many weak points in our national self-esteem.

This novel also marks a crisis in Cather's career and in her personal reaction against modern materialism. Either she could ease her disillusionment with satire, as many of her contemporaries were doing, or she could preserve in another time and place the mood of serenity and acceptance with which her book ends. The artist who had written "The Sculptor's Funeral" and "A Wagner Matinee" more than twenty years before could not turn back to repeat herself. Her Godfrey St. Peter was a spiritual brother who had written of the conquistadores and the Franciscan friars; she chose to follow him into his region of imagination and history. In her earlier novels she had celebrated, as all America has done, the industry and courage of the pioneer, but she had also showed what no one before her had seen, the essential humanism of his legend. Now she was to trace the fundamental likenesses, presented in the same images of heroism and endurance, between the frontier in its best phase and the influence of historical civilizations. The result was *Death Comes for the Archbishop,* an American masterpiece recreating a region, a society, and a culture in its account of two dedicated missionary priests and their experiences in the Southwest shortly after the Mexican War. *Shadows on the Rock,* a somewhat similar chronicle of Quebec in the days of Frontenac, is less effective, possibly because the novel lacks, in the French tradition for order and reason, the grander passions of place and human nature that light up *Death Comes for the Archbishop* like desert sunlight.

Willa Cather was to publish three more books before her death in New York City on April 24, 1947. Of the stories in *Obscure Destinies,* "Neighbor Rosicky" is among her best. *Lucy Gayheart* is a minor work bringing together two of Cather's favorite themes, the West and music. In *Sapphira and the Slave Girl* she drew for the first time on memories of her Virginia childhood in a novel of pre-

Civil War days, a work suggesting allegorical intentions and filled with disturbing subtleties that criticism has not yet attempted to resolve. *The Old Beauty and Others*, containing her last three stories, was published posthumously in 1948.

Willa Cather thought of the novel as an instrument of culture, not a vehicle for social reportage or character-mongering, and art worth a lifetime's effort and devotion. Her literary masters were the European craftsmen whom she so greatly admired, but her own writing was American in subject and mood. Coming at the end of an era, she tried to recapture a past that existed largely in memory, a past which was once innocent and romantic and heroic. That was her aim and her achievement, and what she had to say she said with honesty and simplicity, with moral subtlety and stylistic evocation. Her fidelity to this vision of experience testifies to her integrity as a person and an artist.

Bibliography

Willa Cather's books have been collected in the Library Edition, 13 vols., 1937–1941. In addition to *The Old Beauty and Others*, 1948, and *Willa Cather on Writing*, 1941, posthumous publications have included *Willa Cather in Europe*, a collection of travel sketches and impressions edited by George N. Kates, who also appended to *Five Stories by Willa Cather*, 1956, a discussion of her unfinished Avignon story which was destroyed at her request after her death. James R. Shively in *Writings from Willa Cather's Campus Years*, 1950, reprints six stories written as an undergraduate at the University of Nebraska. Mildred R. Bennett has also edited *Willa Cather's Collected Short Fiction, 1892–1912*, 1965; and Bernice Slote has edited *The Kingdom of Art: Willa Cather's First Principles and Critical Statements*, 1966.

The authorized biography is E. K. Brown, *Willa Cather: A Critical Biography*, 1953, completed by Leon Edel. Much of the material in the official biography derives from Edith Lewis, *Willa Cather Living: A Personal Record*, 1953. Mildred R. Bennett, *The World of Willa Cather*, is useful for the Red Cloud background of Miss Cather's writing. Elizabeth Shepley Sergeant, *Willa Cather: A Memoir*, 1953, is both an informal biography and the record of a friendship. James R. Shively's *Writings from Willa Cather's Campus Years* brings together interesting material from her university days, including reminiscences of classmates.

The most extensive critical study is David Daiches, *Willa Cather: A Critical Introduction*, 1950. For briefer studies in books and periodicals see Stuart P. Sherman, *Critical Woodcuts*, 1926; Elizabeth Shepley Sergeant, *Fire Under the Andes*, 1927; Rebecca West, *The Strange Necessity*, 1931; Arthur H. Quinn, *American Fiction*, 1936; Alfred Kazin, *On Native Grounds*, 1942; Maxwell Geismar, *The Last of the Provincials*, 1947; Francis X. Connolly, "Willa Cather: Memory as Muse," in *Fifty Years of the American Novel*, edited by Harold C. Gardiner, S.J., 1951; Frederick J. Hoffman, *The Modern Novel in America, 1900–1950*, 1951; Edward Wagenknecht, *Cavalcade of the American Novel*,

1952; John H. Randall, *The Landscape and the Looking Glass: Willa Cather's Search for Values*, 1960; Robert McNamara, "Phases of American Religion in Thornton Wilder and Willa Cather," *Catholic World*, CXXXV (1932), 641–649; E. K. Brown, "Willa Cather and the West," *University of Toronto Quarterly*, V (1936), 544–566, and "Homage to Willa Cather," *Yale Review*, XXXVI (1946), 77–92; Robert H. Footman, "The Genius of Willa Cather," *American Literature*, X (1938), 123–141; Dayton Kohler, "Willa Cather," *College English*, IX (1947), 8–18; Edward A. and Lillian D. Bloom, "Willa Cather's Novels of the Frontier: A Study in Thematic Symbolism," *American Literature*, XXI (1949), 71–93, and *"Shadows on the Rock*: Notes on the Composition of a Novel," *Twentieth Century Literature*, II (1956), 70–85; Bernard Baum, "Willa Cather's Waste Land," *South Atlantic Quarterly*, XLVIII (1949), 589–601; and John P. Hinz, "Willa Cather: Prairie Spring," *Prairie Schooner*, XXIII (1949), 82–89, and "A Lost Lady and *The Professor's House*," *Virginia Quarterly Review*, XXIX (1953), 70–85. For a complete bibliographical listing see Phyllis Martin Hutchinson, "The Writings of Willa Cather: A List of Works by and about Her," *Bulletin of the New York Public Library*, LX (1956), 267–288, 338–356, 378–400.

DEATH COMES FOR THE ARCHBISHOP

Type of work: Novel
Author: Willa Cather (1873–1947)
Time of plot: Last half of the nineteenth century
Locale: New Mexico and Arizona
First published: 1927

Based on the lives of two eminent nineteenth century French clerics, this novel tells of the missionary efforts of the French bishop, Jean Latour, and his vicar, Father Joseph Vaillant, to establish a diocese in the territory of New Mexico. Besides a skillful reconstruction of these dedicated lives, the novel also provides a vivid picture of a particular region and culture. Tales and legends from Spanish colonial history and from the primitive tribal traditions of the Hopi and Navajo enter the chronicle at many points, creating an effect of density and variety.

Principal Characters

Father Jean Marie Latour, a devout French priest consecrated Vicar Apostolic of New Mexico and Bishop of Agathonica in partibus in 1850. With Father Vaillant, his friend and fellow seminarian, he journeys from his old parish on the shores of Lake Ontario to Santa Fé, seat of the new diocese in territory recently acquired from Mexico. In those troubled times he finds many of the old missions in ruins or abandoned, the Mexican clergy lax and unlearned, the sacraments corrupted by native superstitions. The travels of these two dedicated missionary priests over a desert region of sand, arroyos, towering mesas, and bleak red hills, the accounts of the labors they perform and the hardships they endure to establish the order and authority of the Church in a wild land, make up the story of this beautifully told chronicle. Father Latour is an aristocrat by nature and tradition. Intellectual, fastidious, reserved, he finds the loneliness of his mission redeemed by the cheerfulness and simple-hearted warmth of his old friend and by the simple piety he often encoun-

ters among the humblest of his people; from them, as in the case of old Sada, he learns lessons of humility and grace. For years he dreams of building a cathedral in Santa Fé, and in time his ambition is realized. By then he is an Archbishop and an old man. In the end he decides not to return to his native Auvergne, the wet, green country of his youth that he had often remembered with yearning during his years in the hot desert country. He retires to a small farm outside Santa Fé, and when he dies his body rests in state before the altar in the cathedral he had built. Father Latour's story is based on the life of a historical figure, Jean Baptiste Lamy, the first Archbishop of Santa Fé.

Father Joseph Vaillant, Father Latour's friend and vicar. The son of hardy peasant stock, he is tireless in his missionary labors. If Father Latour is an intellectual aristocrat, Father Vaillant is his opposite, the hearty man of feeling, able to mix with all kinds of people and to move them as much by his good humor and physical vitality as by his eloquence. Doctrine, he holds, is good enough in its place, but he prefers to put his trust in miracles and the working of faith. When the gold rush begins in Colorado, he is sent to Camp Denver to work among the miners. There he continues his missionary labors, traveling from camp to camp in a covered carriage that is both his sleeping quarters and an improvised chapel. Borrowing and begging wherever he can, he builds for the Church and for the future. When he dies, the first Bishop of Denver, there is not a building in the city large enough to hold the thousands who come to his funeral. Like Father Latour, Father Vaillant is modeled after a real person, Father Joseph P. Machebeuf.

Padre Antonio José Martinez, the vigorous but arrogant priest at Taos credited with having instigated the revolt of the Taos Indians. A man of violence and sensual passions, he has lived like a dictator too long to accept the authority of Father Latour with meekness or reason. When Father Latour visits him in Taos, he challenges his Bishop on the subject of celibacy. After the Bishop announces his intention to reform lax practices throughout his diocese, Padre Martinez tells him blandly that he will found his own church if interfered with. As good as his promise, he and Padre Lucero defy Father Latour and Rome and try to establish a schism called the Old Holy Catholic Church of Mexico. Until his death a short time later Padre Martinez carries on his personal and ecclesiastical feud with Father Taladrid, appointed by Father Latour to succeed the old tyrant of Taos.

Padre Marino Lucero, the priest of Arroyo Hondo, who joins Padre Martinez in defying Father Latour's authority. Padre Lucero is said to have a fortune hidden away. After he repents of his heresy and dies reconciled to Rome, buckskin bags containing gold and silver coins valued at almost twenty thousand dollars are found buried under the floor of his house.

Padre Gallegos, the genial, worldly priest at Albuquerque, a lover of whiskey, fandangos, and poker. Although Father Latour likes him as a man, he finds him scandalous and impossible as a priest. As soon as possible he suspends Padre Gallegos and puts Father Vaillant in charge of the Albuquerque parish.

Manuel Lujon, a wealthy Mexican. During a visit at his rancho Father Vaillant sees and admires a matched pair of white mules, Contento and Angelica. The priest praises the animals so highly that Lujon, a generous, pious man, decides to give him one of them. But Father Vaillant refuses to accept the gift, saying that it would not be fitting for him to ride on a fine white mule while his Bishop rides a common hack. Resigned, Lujon sends the second mule to Father Latour.

Buck Scales, a gaunt, surly American at whose house Father Latour and his vicar stop on one of their missionary journeys. Warned away by the gestures of his frightened wife, they continue on to the next town. The woman follows them to tell that in the past six years her husband has murdered four travelers as well as the three children she has borne. Scales is arrested and hanged.

Magdalena, the Mexican wife of Buck Scales, a devout woman who reveals her husband's crimes. After her husband's hanging she lives for a time in the home of Kit Carson. Later Father Latour makes her the housekeeper in the establishment of the Sisters of Loretto in Santa Fé. She attends the old Archbishop in his last days.

Kit Carson, the American trapper and scout. He and Father Latour become friends when they meet after the arrest of Buck Scales.

Jacinto, an intelligent young Indian from

the Pecos pueblo, often employed as Father Latour's guide on the priest's missionary journeys. On one of these trips the travelers are overtaken by a sudden snowstorm. Jacinto leads Father Latour into a cave which has obviously been used for ceremonial purposes. Before he builds a fire Jacinto walls up an opening in the cave. Waking later in the night, Father Latour sees his guide standing guard over the sealed opening. He realizes that he has been close to some secret ceremonial mystery of the Pecos, possibly connected with snake worship, but he respects Jacinto's confidence and never mentions the matter.

Don Antonio Olivares, a wealthy ranchero who has promised to make a large contribution to Father Latour's cathedral fund. He dies suddenly before he can make good his promise, leaving his estate to his wife and daughter for life, after which his property is to go to the Church. Two of his brothers contest the will.

Doña Isabella Olivares, the American wife of Father Latour's friend and benefactor. After her husband's death two of his brothers contest the will on the grounds that Doña Isabella is not old enough to have a daughter of the age of Señorita Inez and that the girl is the child of one of Don Antonio's indiscreet youthful romances, adopted by Doña Isabella for the purpose of defrauding the brothers. Father Vaillant convinces the vain woman that it is her duty to tell the truth about her age in order for her and her daughter to win the case. Much against her will Doña Isabella confesses in court that she is fifty-two years old and not forty-two, as she has claimed. Later she tells Father Vaillant and Father Latour that she will never forgive them for having made her tell a lie about a matter as serious as a woman's age.

Señorita Inez, the daughter of Doña Isa-

bella and Don Antonio Olivares. Her age and her mother's are questioned when the Olivares brothers try to break Don Antonio's will.

Boyd O'Reilly, a young American lawyer, the manager of Don Antonio Olivares' affairs.

Sada, the wretched slave of a Protestant American family. One December night she escapes from the stable where she sleeps and takes refuge in the church. Father Latour finds her there, hears her confession, blesses her, and gives her a holy relic and his own warm cloak.

Eusabio, a man of influence among the Navajos. Though he is younger than Father Latour, the priest respects him greatly for his intelligence and sense of honor. Father Latour grieves when the Navajos are forced to leave their country and rejoices that he has been able to live long enough to see them restored to their lands. When the old Archbishop dies, Eusabio carries word of his death to the Indians.

Bernard Ducrot, the young priest who looks after Father Latour in his last years. He becomes like a son to the gentle old man.

Padre Jesus de Baca, the white-haired, almost blind priest at Isleta. An old man of great innocence and piety, he lives surrounded by his tame parrots.

Trinidad Lucero, a slovenly young monk in training for the priesthood whom Father Latour meets in the house of Padre Martinez. He passes as Padre Lucero's nephew, but some say he is the son of Padre Martinez. When Padre Martinez and Padre Lucero proclaim their schism, Trinidad acts as a curate for both.

Padre Taladrid, the young Spanish priest whom Father Latour appoints to succeed Padre Martinez at Taos.

The Story

In 1851 Father Jean Marie Latour reached Santa Fé, where he was to become Vicar Apostolic of New Mexico. His journey from the shores of Lake Ontario had been long and arduous. He had lost his belongings in a shipwreck at Galveston and had suffered painful injury in a wagon accident at San Antonio.

Upon Father Latour's arrival, in company with his good friend, Father Joseph Vaillant, the Mexican priests refused to recognize his authority. He had no choice but to ride three thousand miles into Mexico to secure the necessary papers from the Bishop of Durango.

On the road he lost his way in an arid landscape of red hills and gaunt junipers. His thirst became a vertigo of mind and senses, and he could blot out his own agony only by repeating the cry of the Saviour on the Cross. As he was about to give up all hope, he saw a tree growing in the shape of a cross. A short time later he arrived in the Mexican settlement called *Agua Secreta*, Hidden Water. Stopping at the home of Benito, Bishop Latour first performed the marriage ceremonies and then baptized all the children.

At Durango he received the necessary documents and started the long trip back to Santa Fé. Meanwhile Father Vaillant had won over the inhabitants from enmity to amity and had set up the Episcopal residence in an old adobe house. On the first morning after his return to Santa Fé the bishop heard the unexpected sound of a bell ringing the Angelus. Father Vaillant told him that he had found the bell, bearing the date 1356, in the basement of old San Miguel Church.

On a missionary journey to Albuquerque in March, Father Vaillant acquired as a gift a handsome cream-colored mule and another just like it for his bishop. These mules, Contento and Angelica, served the men in good stead for many years.

On another such trip the two priests were riding together on their mules. Caught in a sleet storm, they stopped at the rude shack of an American, Buck Scales. His Mexican wife warned the travelers by gestures that their lives were in danger, and they rode on to Mora without spending the night. The next morning the Mexican woman appeared in town. She told them that her husband had already murdered and robbed four travelers, and that he had killed her three babies. The result was that Scales was brought to justice, and his wife, Magdalena, was sent to the home of Kit Carson, the famous frontier scout. From that time on Kit Carson was a valuable friend of the bishop and his vicar. Magdalena later became the housekeeper and manager for the kitchens of the Sisters of Loretto.

During his first year at Santa Fé, the bishop was called to a meeting of the Plenary Council at Baltimore. On the return journey he brought back with him five nuns sent to establish the school of Our Lady of Light. Next, Bishop Latour, attended by the Indian Jacinto as his guide, spent some time visiting his own vicarate. Padre Gallegos, whom he visited at Albuquerque, acted more like a professional gambler than a priest, but because he was very popular with the natives Bishop Latour did not remove him at that time. At last he arrived at his destination, the top of the mesa at Acoma, the end of his long journey. On that trip he heard the legend of Fray Baltazar, killed during an uprising of the Acoma Indians.

A month after the bishop's visit, he suspended Padre Gallegos and put Father Vaillant in charge of the parish at Albuquerque. On a trip to the Pecos Mountains the vicar fell ill with an attack of the black measles. The bishop, hearing of his illness, set out to nurse his friend. Jacinto again served as guide on the cold, snowy trip. When Bishop Latour reached his friend's bedside, he found that Kit Carson had arrived before him. As soon as the sick man could sit in the saddle, Carson and the bishop took him back to Santa Fé.

Bishop Latour decided to investigate the parish of Taos, where the powerful old priest, Antonio José Martinez, was the ruler of both spiritual and temporal matters. The following year the bishop was called to Rome. When he returned, he brought with him four young priests from the Seminary of Montferrand and a Spanish priest to replace Padre Martinez at Taos.

Bishop Latour had one great ambition; he wanted to build a cathedral in Santa Fé. In that project he was assisted by the rich Mexican *rancheros,* but to the greatest extent by his good friend, Don Antonio Olivares. When Don Antonio died, his will stated that his estate was left to his wife and daughter during their lives, and after their decease to the Church. Don Antonio's brothers contested the will on the grounds that the daughter, Señorita Inez, was too old to be Doña Isabella's daughter, and the bishop and his vicar had to persuade the vain, coquettish widow to swear to her true age of fifty-three, rather than the forty-two years she claimed. Thus the money was saved for Don Antonio's family and, eventually, the Church.

Father Vaillant was sent to Tucson, but after several years Bishop Latour decided to recall him to Santa Fé. When he arrived, the bishop showed him the stone for building the cathedral. About that time Bishop Latour received a letter from the Bishop of Leavenworth. Because of the discovery of gold near Pike's Peak, he asked to have a priest sent there from Father Latour's diocese. Father Vaillant was the obvious choice.

Father Vaillant spent the rest of his life doing good works in Colorado, though he did return to Santa Fé with the Papal Emissary when Bishop Latour was made an archbishop. Father Vaillant became the first Bishop of Colorado. He died there after years of service, and Archbishop Latour attended his impressive funeral services.

After the death of his friend, Father Latour retired to a modest country estate near Santa Fé. He had dreamed during all his missionary years of the time when he could retire to his own fertile green Auvergne in France, but in the end he decided that he could not leave the land of his labors for his faith. Memories of the journeys he and Father Vaillant had made over thousands of miles of desert country became the meaning of his later years. Bernard Ducrot, a young Seminarian from France, became like a son to him.

When Father Latour knew that his time had come to die, he asked to be taken into town to spend his last days near the cathedral. On the last day of his life the church was filled with people who came to pray for him, as word that he was dying spread through the town. He died in the still twilight, and the cathedral bell, tolling in the early darkness, carried to the waiting countryside the news that at last death had come for Father Latour.

Critical Evaluation

When writing of her great predecessor and teacher, Sarah Orne Jewett, Willa Cather expressed her own belief that the quality that gives a work of literature greatness is the "voice" of the author, the sincere, unadorned, and unique vision of a writer coming to grips with his material. If any one characteristic can be said to dominate the writings of Willa Cather, it is a true and moving sincerity. She never tried to twist her subject matter to suit a preconceived purpose, and she resisted the temptation to dress up her homely material. She gave herself absolutely to her chosen material, and the result was a series of books both truthful and rich with intimations of the destiny of the American continent. By digging into the roots of her material, she found the greater meanings and expressed them with a deceptive simplicity. Her vision and craftsmanship were seldom more successful than in *Death Comes for the Archbishop*. So completely did Willa Cather merge her "voice" with her material, that some critics have felt that the book is almost too polished, without the sense of struggle necessary in a truly great novel. But this, in fact, indicates the magnitude of the author's achievement and the brilliance of her technical skill. *Death Comes for the Archbishop* resonates with the unspoken beliefs of the author and the resolved conflicts that went into its construction. On the surface, it is cleanly wrought and simple, but it is a more complicated and profound book than it appears at first reading. Cather learned well from her early inspiration, Sarah Orne Jewett, the secret of artless art, of craftsmanship that disarms by its very simplicity, but which is based in a highly sophisticated intelligence.

It is true that this novel is an epic and a regional history, but, much more than either, it is a tale of personal isolation, of one man's life reduced to the painful weariness of his own sensitivities. Father Latour is a hero in the most profound sense of the word, at times almost a romantic hero, with his virtues of courage and determination, but he is also a very modern protagonist, with his doubts and inner conflicts and his philosophical nature. His personality is held up in startling contrast to that of his friend and vicar, Father Vaillant, a more simple, although no less good, individual. Cather's austere style perfectly captures the scholarly asperity and urbane religious devotion that compose Father Latour's character. And always in this book, the reader is aware of a sense of the dignity of human life, as exemplified in the person of this individual. Cather was not afraid to draw a good man, a man who could stand above others because of his deeds and because of his innate quality. The novel must stand or fall on this character, and it stands superbly.

Although this book is based on a true sequence of events, it is not a novel of plot. It is a chronicle and a character study, and perhaps, more specifically, an interplay of environment and character. Throughout the book, the reader is aware of the reaction of men to the land, and of one man to the land he has chosen. Subtly and deeply, the author suggests that the soul of man is profoundly altered by the soul of the land, and Cather never doubts for a moment that the land does possess a soul or that this soul can transform a human being in complex and important ways. Willa Cather was fascinated by the way the rough landscape of the Southwest, when reduced to its essences, seemed to take human beings and reduce them to their essences. She abandoned traditional realism in this book, turning toward the directness of symbolism. With stark pictures and vivid styles, she created an imaginary world rooted in realism, but transcending realism. The rigid economy with which the book is written forces it to stand with a unique power in the reader's mind long after his reading. And the personality of Bishop Latour stands as the greatest symbol, like a wind-swept crag or precipice in the vast New Mexico landscape, suggesting the nobility of the human spirit, despite the inner conflicts against which it must struggle.

The descriptions of place set the emotional tone of the novel. The quality of life is intimately related to the landscape, and the accounts of the journeys and the efforts to survive despite the unfriendliness of the barren land, all help to create an odd warmth and almost surreal passion in the narrative. The personalities of Bishop Latour and Father Vaillant establish a definite emotional relationship with the country, and if the other characters in the book are less vividly realized as individuals, perhaps it is because they do not seem to have this relationship with the land. Some of them have become part of the land, worn down by the elements like the rocks and riverbeds, and others have no relationship to it at all; but none of them is involved in the intense love-hate relationship with the land with which the two main characters struggle for so many years.

Although the chronology of the book encompasses many years, the novel is essentially static, a series of rich images and thoughtful moments highlighted and captured as by a camera. This quality of the narrative is not a fault; it is a fact of Cather's style. The frozen moments of contemplation, the glimpses into Father Latour's inner world and spiritual loneliness, are the moments that give the book its greatness. Despite the presence of Kit Carson, the novel is not an adventure story any more than it is merely the account of a pair of churchmen attempting to establish their church in a difficult new terrain. The cathedral becomes the most important symbol in the final part of the book, representing the earthly successes of a man dedicated to nonworldly ambitions. This conflict between the earthly and the spiritual is at the heart of Bishop Latour's personality and at the heart of the book. But the reader understands, at the end, when the bell tolls for Father Latour, that the temptations were never very deep and the good man's victory was greater than he ever knew. The author does not spell out her meaning, but the emotional impact of her narrative brings it home to the reader.

Bibliography

Bloom, Edward A. and Lillian D. Bloom. "The Genesis of *Death Comes for the Archbishop*," in *American Literature*. XXVI (January, 1955), pp. 479–506.

————. "On the Composition of a Novel," in *Willa Cather and Her Critics*. Edited by James Schroeter. Ithaca, N.Y.: Cornell University Press, 1967, pp. 323–355. Reprinted in *Willa Cather's Gift of Sympathy*. Carbondale: Southern Illinois University Press, 1962, pp. 19–21, 197–236.

Brown, Edward Killoran and Leon Edel. *Willa Cather: A Critical Biography*. New York: Knopf, 1953, pp. 251–265.

Charles, Sister Peter Damian, O.P. "*Death Comes for the Archbishop*: A Novel of Love and Death," in *New Mexico Quarterly*. XXXVI (Winter, 1966–1967), pp. 389–403.

Connolly, Francis X. "Willa Cather: Memory as Muse," in *Fifty Years of the American Novel: A Christian Appraisal*. Edited by Harold C. Gardiner. New York: Gordian Press, 1968, pp. 82–87.

Daiches, David. *Willa Cather: A Critical Introduction*. Ithaca, N.Y.: Cornell University Press, 1951, pp. 104–118.

Dinn, James M. "A Novelist's Miracle: Structure and Myth in *Death Comes for the Archbishop*," in *Western American Literature*. VII (Spring, 1972), pp. 39–46.

Fox, Maynard. "Proponents of Order: Tom Outland and Bishop Latour," in *Western American Literature*. IV (Summer, 1969), pp. 107–115.

Gale, Robert L. "Cather's *Death Comes for the Archbishop*," in *Explicator*. XXI (May, 1963), item 75.

Gerber, Philip L. *Willa Cather*. Boston: Twayne, 1975, pp. 120–127.

Giannone, Richard. "*Death Comes for the Archbishop*," in *Music in Willa Cather's Fiction*. Lincoln: University of Nebraska Press, 1968, pp. 185–200.

————. "The Southwest's Eternal Echo: Music in *Death Comes for the Archbishop*," in *Arizona Quarterly*. XXII (Spring, 1966), pp. 6–18.

Greene, George. *"Death Comes for the Archbishop,"* in *New Mexico Quarterly.* XXVII (Spring–Summer, 1957), pp. 69–82.

McFarland, Dorothy Tuck. *Willa Cather.* New York: Frederick Ungar, 1972, pp. 95–110.

Powell, Lawrence Clark. *"Death Comes for the Archbishop:* Willa Cather," in *Southwest Classics: The Creative Literature of the Arid Lands. Essays on the Books and Their Writers.* Los Angeles: Ward Ritchie Press, 1974, pp. 121–135.

Randall, John H., III. *The Landscape and the Looking Glass: Willa Cather's Search for Value.* Boston: Houghton Mifflin, 1960, pp. 257–310.

Rapin, René. *Willa Cather.* New York: McBride, 1930, pp. 69–71.

Robinson, Cecil, *With the Ears of Strangers: The Mexican in American Literature.* Tucson: University of Arizona Press, 1963, pp. 237–238, 265–267.

Stewart, D.H. "Cather's Mortal Comedy," in *Queen's Quarterly.* LXXIII (Summer, 1966), pp. 244–259.

Stouck, David. *Willa Cather's Imagination.* Lincoln: University of Nebraska Press, 1975, pp. 117–119, 129–149.

Stouck, Mary-Ann and David Stouck. "Art and Religion in *Death Comes for the Archbishop,"* in *Arizona Quarterly.* XXIX (1973), pp. 293–302.

Van Ghent, Dorothy. *Willa Cather.* Minneapolis: University of Minnesota Press, 1964, pp. 35–38.

West, Rebecca. "The Classic Artist," in *The Strange Necessity.* New York: Viking, 1928, pp. 233–248. Reprinted in *Willa Cather and Her Critics.* Edited by James Schroeter. Ithaca, N.Y.: Cornell University Press, 1967, pp. 62–71.

Whittington, Curtis, Jr. "The Stream and the Broken Pottery: The Form of Willa Cather's *Death Comes for the Archbishop,"* in *McNeese Review.* XVI (1965), pp. 16–24.

MY ÁNTONIA

Type of work: Novel
Author: Willa Cather (1873–1947)
Time of plot: Late nineteenth and early twentieth centuries
Locale: Nebraska prairie land
First published: 1918

My Ántonia *is the story of a Bohemian girl whose family came from the Old Country to settle on the open prairies of Nebraska. While she lives on her farm and tills the soil, she is a child of the prairie, but when Ántonia goes to the city, she meets heartbreak, disillusionment, and social ostracism. Only after her return to the land which is her heritage does she find peace and meaning in life.*

Principal Characters

Ántonia Shimerda, a young immigrant girl of appealing innocence, simple passions, and moral integrity, the daughter of a Bohemian homesteading family in Nebraska. Even as a child she is the mainstay of her gentle, daydreaming father. She and Jim Burden, the grandson of a neighboring farmer, become friends, and he teaches her English. After her father's death her crass mother and sly, sullen older brother force her to do a man's work in the fields. Pitying the girl, Jim's grandmother finds work for her as a hired girl in the town of Black Hawk. There her quiet, deep zest for life and the Saturday night dances lead to her ruin. She falls in love with Larry Donovan, a dashing railroad conductor, and goes to Denver to marry him, but he soon deserts her and she comes back to Black Hawk, unwed, to have her child. Twenty years later Jim Burden, visiting in Nebraska, meets her again. She is now married to Cuzak, a dependable, hardworking farmer, and the mother of a large brood of children. Jim finds her untouched by farm drudgery or village spite. Because of her serenity, strength of spirit, and passion for order and motherhood, she reminds him of stories told about the mothers of ancient races.

James Quayle Burden, called **Jim,** the narrator. Orphaned at the age of ten, he leaves his home in Virginia and goes to live with his grandparents in Nebraska. In that lonely prairie country his only playmates are the children of immigrant families living nearby, among them Ántonia Shimerda, with whom he shares his first meaningful experiences in his new home. When his grandparents move into Black Hawk he misses the freedom of life on the prairie. Hating the town, he leaves it to attend the University of Nebraska. There he meets Gaston Cleric, a teacher of Latin who introduces the boy to literature and the greater world of art and culture. From the university he goes on to study law at Harvard. Aided by a brilliant but incompatible marriage, he becomes the legal counsel for a Western railroad. Successful, rich, but unhappy in his middle years and in the failure of his marriage, he recalls his prairie boyhood and realizes that he and Ántonia Shimerda have in common a past that is all the more precious because it is lost and almost incommunicable, existing only in memories of the bright occasions of their youth.

Mr. Shimerda, a Bohemian farmer unsuited to pioneer life on the prairie. Homesick for the Old World and never happy in his Nebraska surroundings, he finds his loneliness and misery unendurable, lives more and more in the past, and ends by blowing out his brains.

Mrs. Shimerda, a shrewd, grasping woman whose chief concern is to get ahead in the world. She bullies her family, accepts the assistance of her neighbors without grace, and eventually sees her dream of prosperity fulfilled.

Ambrož Shimerda, called **Ambrosch,** the Shimerdas' older son. Like his mother, he is insensitive and mean. Burdened by drought, poor crops, and debt, he clings to the land with peasant tenacity. Even though he repels his neighbors with his surly manner, sly trickery, and petty dishonesties, everyone admits that he is a hard worker and a good farmer.

Yulka Shimerda, Ántonia's younger sister, a mild, obedient girl.

Marek Shimerda, the Shimerdas' youngest child. Tongue-tied and feeble-minded, he is eventually committed to an institution.

Mr. Burden, Jim Burden's grandfather, a Virginian who has bought a farm in Nebraska. Deliberate in speech and action, he is a just, generous man, bearded like an ancient prophet and sometimes speaking like one.

Mrs. Burden, his wife, a brisk, practical woman who gives unstinted love to her orphan grandson. Kind-hearted, she gives assistance to the immigrant families of the region, and without her aid the needy Shimerdas would not have survived their first Nebraska winter.

Lena Lingard, the daughter of poor Norwegian parents, from childhood a girl attractive to men. Interested in clothes and possessing a sense of style, she is successful as a designer and later becomes the owner of a dress shop in San Francisco. She and Jim Burden become good friends while he is a student at the University of Nebraska. Her sensuous beauty appeals greatly to his youthful imagination, and he is partly in love with her before he goes to study at Harvard.

Tiny Soderball, a girl of all work at the hotel in Black Hawk. She moves to Seattle, runs a sailors' boarding house for a time, and then goes to Alaska to open a hotel for miners. After a dying Swede wills her his claim, she makes a fortune from mining. With a comfortable fortune put aside, she goes to live in San Francisco. When Jim Burden meets her there, she tells him the thing that interests her most is making money. Lena Lingard is her only friend.

Wycliffe Cutter, called **Wick,** a miserly moneylender who has grown rich by fleecing his foreign-born neighbors in the vicinity of Black Hawk. Ántonia Shimerda goes to work for him and his suspicious, vulgar wife. Making elaborate plans to seduce Ántonia, he puts some of his valuables in his bedroom and tells her that she is to sleep there, to guard them, while he and his wife are away on a trip. Mrs. Burden sends her grandson to sleep in the Cutter house, and Wick, returning ahead of his wife, is surprised and enraged to find Jim Burden in his bed. Years later, afraid that his wife's family will inherit his money if he should die first, he kills her and then himself.

Mrs. Cutter, a woman as mean and miserly as her husband, whom she nags constantly. He murders her before committing suicide.

Larry Donovan, a railroad conductor and gay ladies' man. He courts Ántonia Shimerda, promises to marry her if she will join him in Denver, seduces her, and then goes off to Mexico, leaving her pregnant.

Mrs. Steavens, a widow, the tenant on the Burden farm. She tells Jim Burden, home from Harvard, the story of Ántonia Shimerda's betrayal by Larry Donovan.

Otto Fuchs, the Burdens' hired man during their farming years. Born in Austria, he came to America when a boy and lived an adventurous life as a cowboy, a stage driver, a miner, and a bartender in the West. After the Burdens rent their farm and move into Black Hawk he resumes his drifting life.

Jake Marpole, the hired man who travels with young Jim Burden from Virginia to Nebraska. Though a kind-hearted man, he has a sharp temper and is violent when angry. He is always deeply ashamed if he swears in front of Mrs. Burden.

Christian Harling, a prosperous, strait-laced grain merchant and cattle buyer, a neighbor of the Burden family in Black Hawk.

Mrs. Harling, his wife, devoted to her family and to music. She takes a motherly interest in Ántonia Shimerda, who works for her as a hired girl for a time, but feels compelled to send her away when the girl begins to go to the Saturday night dances attended by drummers and town boys.

Peter and
Pavel, Russian neighbors of the Burden family and Mr. Shimerda's friends. Just before he dies Pavel tells a terrible story of the time in Russia when, to save his own life, he threw a bride and groom from a sledge to a pack of wolves.

Anton Jelinek, the young Bohemian who makes the coffin for Mr. Shimerda's funeral. He becomes a friend of the Burdens and later a saloon proprietor.

Cuzak, Anton Jelinek's cousin, the sturdy farmer who marries Ántonia Shimerda. Though he has had many reverses in his life, he remains good-natured. Hard-working, dependable, considerate, he is a good husband to Ántonia.

Rudolph,
Anton,
Leo,
Jan,
Anna,
Yulka,
Nina, and
Lucie, Ántonia's children by Cuzak.

Martha, Ántonia's daughter by Larry Donovan. She marries a prosperous young farmer.

Gaston Cleric, the young Latin teacher who introduces Jim Burden to the classics and the world of ideas. When he accepts an instructorship at Harvard, he persuades Jim to transfer to that university.

Genevieve Whitney Burden, Jim Burden's wife. Though she does not figure in the novel, her presence in the background helps to explain her husband's present mood and his nostalgia for his early years in Nebraska. Spoiled, restless, temperamental, independently wealthy, she leads her own life, interests herself in social causes, and plays patroness to young poets and artists.

The Story

Jim Burden's father and mother died when he was ten years old, and the boy made the long trip from Virginia to his grandparents' farm in Nebraska in the company of Jake Marpole, a hired hand who was to work for Jim's grandfather. Arriving by train late at night in the prairie town of Black Hawk, the boy noticed an immigrant family huddled on the station platform. He and Jake were met by a lanky, scar-faced cowboy named Otto Fuchs, who drove them in a jolting wagon across the empty prairie to the Burden farm.

Jim grew to love the vast expanse of land and sky. One day Jim's grandmother suggested that the family pay a visit to the Shimerdas, an immigrant family just arrived in the territory. At first the newcomers impressed Jim unfavorably. The Shimerdas were poor and lived in a dugout cut into the earth. The place was dirty. The children were ragged. Although he could not understand her speech, Jim made friends with the oldest girl, Ántonia.

Jim found himself often at the Shimerda home. He did not like Ántonia's surly brother, Ambrosch, or her grasping mother, but Ántonia, with her eager smile and great, warm eyes won an immediate place in Jim's heart. One day her father, his English dictionary tucked under his arm, cornered Jim and asked him to teach the girl English. She learned rapidly. Jim respected Ántonia's father. He was a tall, thin, sensitive man, a musician in the old country. Now he was saddened by poverty and burdened with overwork. He seldom laughed any more.

Jim and Ántonia passed many happy hours on the prairie. Then tragedy struck the Shimerdas. During a severe winter, Mr. Shimerda, broken and beaten by the prairie, shot himself. Ántonia had loved her father more than any other member of the family, and after his death she shouldered his share of the farm work. When spring came, she went with Ambrosch into the fields and plowed like a man. The harvest brought money. The Shimerdas soon had a house, and with the money left over they bought plowshares and cattle.

Because Jim's grandparents were growing too old to keep up their farm, they dismissed Jake and Otto and moved to the town of Black Hawk. There Jim longed for the open prairie land, the gruff, friendly companionship of Jake and Otto, and the warmth of Ántonia's friendship. He suffered at school and spent his idle hours roaming the barren gray streets of Black Hawk.

At Jim's suggestion, his grandmother arranged with a neighbor, Mrs. Harling, to bring Ántonia into town as her hired girl, Ántonia entered into her tasks with enthusiasm. Jim saw a change in her. She was more feminine; she laughed oftener; and though she never shirked her duties at the Harling house, she was eager for recreation and gaiety.

Almost every night she went to a dance pavilion with a group of hired girls. There, in new, handmade dresses, the immigrant girls gathered to dance with the village boys. Jim Burden went, too, and the more he saw of the hired girls, the better he liked them. Once or twice he worried about Ántonia, who was popular and trusting. When she earned a reputation for being a little too gay, she lost her position with the Harlings and went to work for a cruel money-lender, Wick Cutter, who had a licentious eye on her.

One night, Ántonia appeared at the Burdens and begged Jim to stay in her bed for the night and let her remain at the Burdens. Wick Cutter was supposed to be out of town, but Ántonia suspected that, with Mrs. Cutter also gone, he might return and harm her. Her fears proved correct, for as Jim lay awake in Ántonia's bed Wick returned and went to the bedroom where he thought Ántonia was sleeping.

Ántonia returned to work for the Harlings. Jim, eager to go off to college, studied hard during the summer and passed his entrance examinations. In the fall he left for the state university and although he found there a whole new world of literature and art, he could not forget his early years under the blazing prairie sun and his friendship with Ántonia. He heard little of Ántonia during those years. One of her friends, Lena Lingard, who had also worked as a hired girl in Black Hawk, visited him one day. He learned from her that Ántonia was engaged to be married to a man named Larry Donovan.

Jim went on to Harvard to study law, and for years heard nothing of his Nebraska friends. He assumed that Ántonia was married. When he made a trip back to Black Hawk to see his grandparents, he learned that Ántonia, deceived by Larry Donovan, had left Black Hawk in shame and returned to her family. There she worked again in the fields until her baby was born. When Jim went to see her, he found her still the same lovely girl, though her eyes were somber and she had lost her old gaiety. She welcomed him and proudly showed him her baby.

Jim thought that his visit was probably the last time he would see Ántonia. He told her how much a part of him she had become and how sorry he was to leave her again. Ántonia knew that Jim would always be with her, no matter where he went. He reminded her of her beloved father, who, though he had been dead many years, still lived nobly in her heart. She told Jim goodbye and watched him walk back toward town along the familiar road.

It was twenty years before Jim Burden saw Ántonia again. On a Western trip he found himself not far from Black Hawk, and on impulse he drove out in an open buggy to the farm where she lived. He found the place swarming with children of all ages. Small boys rushed forward to greet him, and then fell back shyly. Ántonia had married well, at last. The grain was high, and the neat farmhouse seemed to be charged with an atmosphere of activity and happiness. Ántonia seemed as unchanged as she was when she and Jim used to whirl over the dance floor together in Black Hawk. Cuzak, her husband, seemed to know Jim before they were introduced, for Ántonia had told all her family about Jim Burden. After a long visit with the Cuzaks, Jim left, promising that he would return the next summer and take two of the Cuzak boys hunting with him.

Waiting in Black Hawk for the train that would take him East, Jim found it hard to realize the long time that had passed since the dark night, years before, when he had seen an immigrant family standing wrapped in their shawls on the same platform. All his memories of the prairie came back to him. Whatever happened now, whatever they had missed, he and Ántonia had shared precious years between them, years that would never be forgotten.

Critical Evaluation

The figure of the pioneer woman Ántonia Shimerda concentrates in itself a complex of values, an axis about which *My Ántonia* revolves. The novel in its turn illustrates two classical themes of American literature. Written in 1918, it reaches backward into the nineteenth century and beyond for its artistic and moral direction.

Willa Cather, the product of a genteel Virginia upbringing, found herself early in life transplanted to the frontier and forced to confront those vast blank spaces over which men had not yet succeeded in establishing the dominion of custom and convention. She saw a few brave settlers bearding the wilderness, meeting the physical challenge as well as the moral one of having to act straight out of their instincts without benefit of civilized constraints; for her these people, particularly the women, were a race apart. Ántonia, with her noble simplicity, is among other things a monument to that vigorous race.

She is also an embodiment of a long tradition of fictional heroes of British and American romance. At the time the novel was written, literature and criticism in America were undergoing a change of direction. The thrust of literature in the new century owed much to the developing sciences; Lewis and Dreiser appeared on the scene with their sociological novels, signaling the rise of naturalism. Fictional characters would henceforth be viewed as interpreting in their acts the flaws and beauties of laws, institutions, and social structures. *My Ántonia* fits an older mold, a form in which the effects of colonial Puritanism can be detected. Specifically, the mode demands that the hero overcome or fail to overcome the strictures and hazards of his situation by his own wit, strength, or courage. This convention draws from the very wellspring of American life, the democratic belief in the wholeness and self-sufficiency of the individual, that is, in personal culpability, and in the absolute value of the personal conscience. Cather makes no real indictment of the society that scorns and undervalues Ántonia and the other hired girls; the social conventions are, with the land, simply the medium through which she fulfills her destiny. It is the peculiarly American sense of starting out brand-new in a new land, that sense of moral isolation, that adds poignance to the struggles of the individual against the vagaries of fortune. This theme of American newness and innocence, which R. B. Lewis calls "The Theme of the American Adam," has as a natural concomitant elements of temptation and fortunate fall. The serpent in Ántonia's story is the town of Black Hawk, where she quarrels with her benefactors and runs afoul of Larry Donovan. Seduced and abandoned, she returns to the land; but her experience has made her better able, as she tells Jim Burden, to prepare her children to face the world.

But if the town is Ántonia's downfall in terms of one theme, it is the grey backdrop against which she shines in terms of another; in the same way the prairie is her antagonist in one sense, and the natural force of which she is the flower in another. Jim Burden first finds her, significantly, actually living in the earth. Early on she begins to take on characteristics of the land: "Her neck came up strongly out of her shoulders, like the bole of a tree out of the turf"; " 'But she has such splendid color in her cheeks—like those big dark red plums.' " She works the land; she makes gardens; she nourishes the Harling children with food and stories. Her connection with the fertile earth is insisted upon. And the earth, the virgin land, is in this novel the source of physical vigor and the best resource of the soul. Jim Burden describes his first experience of the land as a feeling of cosmic unity: "Perhaps we feel like that when we die and become part of something entire, whether it is sun and air, or goodness and knowledge. At any rate, that is happiness; to be dissolved into something complete and great." The people who live on the prairie seem to him open and giving like the land; for instance, he says of Ántonia that "everything she said seemed to come right out of her heart." By contrast, the life of the town is pinched and ungenerous: "People's speech, their voices, their very glances, became furtive and repressed. Every individual taste, every natural appetite, was bridled by caution." Ántonia, in all her acts, shows the naturalness and boundless generosity of the plains; gives unstintingly of her strength and loyalty to her surly brother, to Jim and the Harling children, to Larry Donovan, and to her husband Cuzak; and pours out a flood of love and nurture upon her children. She alludes several times to her dislike of towns and cities and to her feeling of familiar friendship with the country. Toward the end of the book the figure of Ántonia and the infinite fertility of the land come together symbolically in an extremely vivid and moving image. Ántonia and her children have been showing Jim Burden the contents of their fruit cellar, and as they step outside, "[the children] all came running up the steps together, big and little, tow heads and gold heads and brown, and flashing little naked legs; a veritable explosion of life out of the dark cave into the sunlight." The cave might be the apotheosis of Ántonia's first home on the prairie, the latter redeeming the former by its fruitfulness.

Above all, the novel celebrates the early life on the plains of which Jim Burden and Ántonia were a part. The long digressions about Peter and Pavel, Blind D'Arnault, the Cutters and others, the profoundly elegiac descriptions of Jake Marpole and Otto Fuchs, the sharply caught details of farm life, town life, landscape—these things are bent to the recreation of a simpler and better time, a hard life now gone beyond recall, but lovingly remembered.

Bibliography

A., G.W. "Cather's *My Ántonia*," in *Explicator*. V (March, 1947), item 35.

Bowden, Edwin T. *The Dungeon of the Heart: Human Isolation and the American Novel.* New York: Macmillan, 1961, pp. 43–54.

Bridges, Jean B. "The Actress in Cather's Novel *My Ántonia*," in *Society for the Study of Midwestern Literature Newsletter.* VI (1976), pp. 10–11.

Brown, Edward Killoran and Leon Edel. *Willa Cather: A Critical Biography.* New York: Knopf, 1953, pp. 199–209.

Charles, Sister Peter Damian, O.P. "*My Ántonia*: A Dark Dimension," in *Western American Literature.* II (Summer, 1967), pp. 91–108.

Connolly, Francis X. "Willa Cather: Memory as Muse," in *Fifty Years of the American Novel: A Christian Appraisal.* Edited by Harold C. Gardiner. New York: Gordian Press, 1968, pp. 75–77.

Dahl, Curtis. "An American Georgic: Willa Cather's *My Ántonia*," in *Comparative Literature.* VII (Winter, 1955), pp. 43–51.

Daiches, David. *Willa Cather: A Critical Introduction.* Ithaca, N.Y.: Cornell University Press, 1951, pp. 43–61.

Gerber, Philip L. *Willa Cather.* Boston: Twayne, 1975, pp. 87–92.

Giannone, Richard. "*My Ántonia*," in *Music in Willa Cather's Fiction.* Lincoln: University of Nebraska Press, 1968, pp. 107–123.

Havighurst, Walter. "Introduction," in *My Ántonia.* Boston: Houghton Mifflin, 1949.

Helmick, Evelyn Thomas. "The Mysteries of Ántonia," in *Midwest Quarterly.* XVII (Winter, 1976), pp. 173–185.

McFarland, Dorothy Tuck. *Willa Cather.* New York: Frederick Ungar, 1972, pp. 39–50.

Mencken, H.L. "*My Ántonia*," in *Willa Cather and Her Critics.* Edited by James Schroeter. Ithaca, N.Y.: Cornell University Press, 1967, pp. 8–9.

Miller, James E., Jr. "*My Ántonia*: A Frontier Drama of Time," in *American Quarterly.* X (Winter, 1958), pp. 476–484. Reprinted in *Quests Surd and Absurd: Essays in American Literature.* Chicago: University of Chicago Press, 1967, pp. 66–75.

———. "*My Ántonia* and the American Dream," in *Prairie Schooner.* XLVIII (Summer, 1974), pp. 112–123.

Randall, John H., III. *The Landscape and the Looking Glass: Willa Cather's Search for Value.* Boston: Houghton Mifflin, 1960, pp. 105–149. Reprinted in *Willa Cather and Her Critics.* Edited by James Schroeter. Ithaca, N.Y.: Cornell University Press, 1967, pp. 272–322.

Rapin, René. *Willa Cather.* New York: McBride, 1930, pp. 47–51.

Rucker, Mary E. "Prospective Focus in *My Ántonia,*" in *Arizona Quarterly.* XXIX (1973), pp. 303–316.

Scholes, Robert E. "Hope and Memory in *My Ántonia,*" in *Shenandoah.* XIV (Autumn, 1962), pp. 24–29.

Stegner, Wallace. "Willa Cather: *My Ántonia,*" in *The American Novel from James Fenimore Cooper to William Faulkner.* New York: Basic Books, 1965, pp. 144–153.

Stouck, David. *Willa Cather's Imagination.* Lincoln: University of Nebraska Press, 1975, pp. 45–58.

Van Ghent, Dorothy. *Willa Cather.* Minneapolis: University of Minnesota Press, 1964, pp. 21–25.

O PIONEERS!

Type of work: Novel
Author: Willa Cather (1873–1947)
Time of plot: 1880–1910
Locale: Nebraska
First published: 1913

Willa Cather began her illustrious career as a novelist with two powerful narratives of pioneer life on the Nebraska prairie, O Pioneers! *and* My Antonia *(1918). The heroine of* O Pioneers!, *Alexandra Bergson, is the first of the sturdy young immigrant women who tame the harsh prairie land through strength of character, tenacity, and an ability to become one with it.*

Principal Characters

Alexandra Bergson, the daughter of a Swedish immigrant homesteader on the Divide in Nebraska. A strong-willed girl of great courage and resourcefulness, she takes charge of the farm after her father's death and through good years or bad uses the land wisely. When times are hard and neighbors become discouraged and move away, she scrimps and saves to add their acres to her own. She is the first on the Divide to try new agricultural methods, to plant alfalfa, to build a silo. She keeps Oscar and Lou, her younger brothers, from leaving the farm for easier work and softer living in town. At the end she can look out over her cultivated fields and know that she has won prosperity for herself and her brothers. But her success as a farmer is bought at the price of her experience as a woman. Twice she sees Carl Linstrum, whom she loves, leave the Divide with no words of love spoken. She is over forty when the death of Emil, her youngest brother, killed by a jealous husband, teaches her the need of love and the grace of compassion; and she and Carl are reunited. Alexandra Bergson is a character almost epic in stature, a fertility goddess of the plains subduing the wild and stubborn land and making it fruitful.

John Bergson, an immigrant farmer who dreams of regaining on his Nebraska homestead a family fortune lost in Sweden. He dies after eleven years of failure, his faith in the land still unshaken. On his deathbed he asks his two older sons to be guided by their sister, for he sees in her qualities of imagination, energy, desire, and wisdom that her brothers lack.

Mrs. Bergson, a devoted wife and mother who tries to maintain household order by clinging to old, familiar European ways. Her twin passions are gardening and preserving.

Carl Linstrum, a grave, introspective young man unsuited to farm life on the Nebraska frontier. His predicament is that of many transplanted Europeans, divided as he is between his Old World heritage and his prairie environment. When his father sells the Linstrum farm and moves back to St. Louis, Carl goes to the city to learn the engraver's trade. Sixteen years later, dissatisfied with commercial life, he returns to the Divide, but

Oscar and Lou Bergson, Alexandra's brothers, insult him and drive him away with accusations that he has come back to marry their sister for her money. Carl goes off to Alaska but returns when he reads the news of Emil Bergson's murder. This time he and Alexandra plan to marry.

Oscar and
Lou Bergson, Alexandra's younger brothers. Dull, insensitive, greedy, they respect their sister but have no real affection for her. Their great hope is that they or their children will inherit her land.

Emil Bergson, Alexandra's youngest brother, whose relationship to his sister seems more like that of a son than of a brother. He grows into a moody, restless young man. Less stolid than the Scandinavian Bergsons, he finds his friends among the more volatile, merrier Bohemians and French settlers in nearby communities. In love with Marie Shabata, a young married woman, he goes to Mexico for a time. After his return he plans to study law in Omaha. One night Frank Shabata finds Emil and Marie together and in his jealous rage kills them.

Marie Shabata, a pretty Bohemian housewife, innocently flirtatious from childhood, always merry and teasing. Having eloped with Frank Shabata, she tries to make the best of a bad situation and endures as cheerfully and patiently as possible his jealous suspicions and wild outbreaks of rage. At first she refuses to acknowledge her true feelings for handsome young Emil Bergson, but circumstances bring them together until, one disastrous night, Frank Shabata finds the two in the orchard and shoots them.

Frank Shabata, a wildly jealous, bad-tempered man distrustful of his pretty young wife. After shooting Marie and Emil Bergson when he finds them together, he makes a futile effort to escape before surrendering to the authorities. Alexandra Bergson shows the true bigness and generosity of her nature after

Frank has been sentenced to prison. Convinced that he had acted only as his rash and violent nature compelled him and that his punishment can serve no purpose for the dead, she visits him in the penitentiary at Lincoln and promises to do everything she can to get him pardoned.

Crazy Ivar, a Swedish hermit and horse doctor whom the uncharitable call crazy; others believe him touched by the hand of God. He is wise in homely folklore concerning animals, birds, and crops, and Alexandra Bergson asks his advice on many farm matters. After he loses his land during a period of depression, she gives him a home. Behind his clouded mind he is a man of deep faith and shrewd wisdom.

Amédée Chevalier, a jolly, high-spirited young French farmer, Emil Bergson's best friend. He dies suddenly after an emergency operation for appendicitis.

Angélique Chevalier, his young wife, widowed after a year of marriage.

Annie Lee, the neighbor girl whom Lou Bergson marries. Like her husband, she is ashamed of old-fashioned European ways and apes American dress and customs.

Milly,
Stella, and
Sadie, the daughters of Lou and Annie Bergson.

Mrs. Lee, Annie Bergson's mother, a spry, wholesome old woman who holds nostalgically to the Old World ways her daughter and son-in-law dislike. Every winter she visits Alexandra Bergson, who allows the old woman to do as she pleases during her stay.

Signa, Alexandra Bergson's hired girl and friend.

Nelse Jensen, Signa's husband.

Barney Flinn, the foreman on Alexandra Bergson's farm.

The Story

Hanover was a frontier town huddled on the windblown Nebraska prairie. One winter day young Alexandra Bergson and her small brother Emil went into town from their new homestead. The Bergsons were Swedes. Their life in the new country was one of hardship because the father was sick and the children were too young to do all the work on their prairie acres. Alexandra went to the village doctor's office to get some medicine for her father. The doctor told her there was no hope for Bergson's recovery.

Emil had brought his kitten to town with him. He was crying on the street because it had climbed to the top of the telegraph pole and would not come down. When Alexandra returned, she met their neighbor, Carl Lindstrum, who rescued the cat. The three rode toward home together and Carl talked of his drawing. When Alexandra and Emil arrived home, their supper was waiting and their mother and father were anxious for their return. Shortly afterward Bergson called his family about him and told them to listen to Alexandra, even though she was a girl, for she had proved her abilities to run the farm capably. Above all, they were to keep the land.

Alexandra was still a girl when her father died, but she assumed at once the family's domestic and financial troubles; she guided everything the family did, and through her resourcefulness she gained security and even a measure of wealth for her brothers and herself.

Emil, the youngest brother, remained the dreamer of the family, in his mooning over Marie Tovesky, whom he had first loved as a little child. Marie had married Frank Shabata. Frank was wildly possessive and mistrusted everyone who showed the slightest kindness to Marie.

Alexandra was in love with Carl Lindstrum, whose father gave up his farm because the new, stubborn land seemed too hard to subdue. He returned to more settled country and took Carl with him to learn the engraver's trade.

Alexandra depended upon Crazy Ivar for many things. He was a hermit, living in a hole dug into the side of a river bed. The kinder Swedes claimed he had been touched by God. Those who were unsympathetic were sure he was dangerous. Actually, he was a kindhearted mystic who loved animals and birds and who let his beard grow according to the custom of ancient prophets. Through his lack of concern for worldly matters he lost his claim, and Alexandra gave him shelter on her own farm, much to the dismay of her brothers and their wives. They demanded that she send Crazy Ivar to an institution, but she refused. She respected Crazy Ivar as she did few other people.

In the same way, Alexandra defended Carl Lindstrum. After an absence of sixteen years he came back to their settlement. He had studied much, but in the eyes of the thrifty Swedes his life was a failure because he had not married, because he had no property, because he seemed willing to marry Alexandra, who was by now quite wealthy. Her brothers, Oscar and Lou, told Alexandra that she must not marry Carl, and she ordered them from her house. Carl, hearing of the disagreement, set out for the West at once.

Alexandra applied herself to new problems. She paid passage for other Swedes to come to America; she experimented with new farming methods. She became friendlier with Marie Shabata, whose husband was growing more jealous. She saw to it that Emil received an education, let him go off to the university despite the criticism of the other brothers. By now Emil knew he loved Marie Shabata, and he went away to study because he felt that if he stayed in the community something terrible would happen. Even attending the university did not help him. Other girls he met seemed less attractive. His secret thoughts were always about Marie.

Frank Shabata discharged hired hands because he suspected them. He followed Marie about everywhere. Even at the Catholic Church he was at her heels scowling at every one to whom she talked. His jealousy was like a disease. At the same time he treated her coldly and insulted her publicly in front of their friends. She, on her part, was headstrong and defiant.

At last Emil returned from college. His friend Amédée became ill while working in his wheat fields and died shortly afterward. Following the funeral, Emil resolved to see Marie, to say goodbye to her before leaving the neighborhood permanently. He found her in her orchard under the mulberry tree. There for the first time they became lovers.

Frank returned from town slightly drunk. Finding a Bergson horse in his stable, he took a weapon and went in search of Emil. When he saw the two he fired, killing both. Then Frank, mad with horror, started to run away.

Crazy Ivar discovered the dead bodies and ran with the news to Alexandra. For the next few months Alexandra seemed in a daze and spent much of her time in the cemetery. She was caught there during a terrible storm, and Crazy Ivar had to go after her. During the storm she regained her old self-possession. Frank Shabata, who had been captured soon after the shooting, had been tried and sentenced to prison. Alexandra determined to do what she could to secure his freedom. If she could no longer help her brother, she would help Frank.

While trying to help Frank, she heard that Carl Lindstrum had returned. He had never received her letter telling of the tragedy, but on his return from Alaska he had read of the trial and had hurried to Alexandra. His mine was a promising venture. The two decided that they could now marry and bring their long separation to an end.

Critical Evaluation

Born in Virginia, Willa Cather grew up on Hamlin Garland's Middle Border. In 1884, her parents moved to Nebraska. Later, in 1895, she was graduated from the University of Nebraska. The gift of writing flowed through her veins, and before she wrote *O Pioneers!* and her other more memorable novels, she was the editor of *McClure's Magazine.* Even with fame and a comfortable life style, Willa never wanted to lose her past; she did not condemn it.

In her hands, the vivid recollections of youth on the limitless prairie became one of her most effective techniques. Firsthand experiences lent an authenticity to her work that was surpassed by few others at the time. Through her eyes and her sense of feeling, just as Alexandra Bergson sensed the potential of her homestead, the reader is presented with the personal meaning of an America of vast, open lands, and will more fully appreciate the "why" behind the winning of a very fertile section of the country.

The Bergsons were not the only Scandinavian immigrants attempting to carve out a new life in the Midwest. Over one million Norwegians and Swedes emigrated to the United States between 1820 and 1900. Many others, like Marie Tovesky's family, came from Eastern Europe. Still others, with roots deep in American soil, gave up their farms and businesses east of the Mississippi for a chance at the opportunities out West. The Swedish Bergson family was the author's primary subject in *O Pioneers!*, and yet, the flavor of cultural pluralism enhances the theme of the interface between settler and hostile land.

With skill and sympathy, the author re-creates the realities of prairie life that were undeveloped in most other sagas of the West. The reader experiences the uncertainties of the planting seasons, the frenzied activity at harvest time, and the numerous droughts and blizzards. The climate, with all of its unpredictable changes, is not over played. Only one who had lived there could so persuasively describe the potent forces of weather. Cather wrote of a region that was just beginning to enter the scientific age. Long before the arrival of the Bergsons, the Morrill Act of 1862 established state agricultural schools, and the land-grant college system, of which Nebraska was a part, started to grow. Created in the same year, the U.S. Department of Agriculture would disseminate scientific knowledge to farmers through the colleges, animal husbandry journals, and the like. Unlike her brothers Lou and Oscar, and many other settlers, Alexandra was receptive to these new ideas; they offered assistance in the taming of the land. Imaginative integration of real developments into the story became a necessity, if not a desire for the author. Perhaps the most impressive element in the author's testimony on prairie living is the epic struggle of immigrant pioneer women. Here lies the greatness of Cather's creativity.

Emotions and personal responses to circumstances are often left unrecorded for future generations, but the author's poignant memory of her own pioneer experiences and of inhabitants of towns similar to Hanover preserves their bleak lot. Environment and character development are carefully blended. Monotonous rolling hills, severe winters, the routine tilling of the resisting soil, the piercing wind, and the frustration over meager results created a restlessness in many settlers. Alexandra's brothers Lou and Oscar were bored with farming. The cultural shock of Americanization had been too much for them. Yet, her youngest brother, Emil, represented the brighter side of American opportunities. Frank Shabata's possessiveness, especially his concern over Marie's fidelity, became a fatal disease. Marie, the free spirit, was not to be possessed by any one man. Alexandra's independence was born of her inner spirit and sense of purpose. The West was subdued by people with her strength of character and perseverance.

Alexandra's self-control and determination were traits developed early in her life in a small seaport in Sweden. The primitive environment of Nebraska and the additional family responsibilities following her father's premature death forced her youthful personality into a demanding maturity. As a woman, she did not have the idle moments to display her feminine attributes as did others of more secure status. Life to Alexandra meant more than spending time to make herself attractive to possible suitors. Women, as would-be wives with handsome dowries or as extramarital lovers, were in demand throughout the West. She possessed a motherly instinct for her brood, often referring to her youngest brother, Emil, as her boy. There was a more important purpose to her life, making her land bountiful.

Alexandra regarded the potentiality of her land with a spiritual reverence and as an obligation to the future. The mysticism of Crazy Ivar, and his appreciation of nature's creatures and of the seasonal procession, were understood by Alexandra, but she was no ordinary settler. She could have sold the farm and moved to the city as thousands of others had done when faced with severe hardship. The farm, the open lands, and the challenge, however, represented to her the essence of life. Alexandra believed in the supremacy of moral and spiritual values over material possessions. Owning her own piece of the earth and making it productive, with a modest income, were possessions enough.

Novels concerning the inner conflicts of women, or about the attitudes of social disapproval toward single women of the frontier, would not have appealed to the reading public of rustic Hanover. They would have viewed her standing in the community in a variety of ways, and men were her most harsh critics. To frontier men, women were to be married and to have children. They considered the gentle sex subservient creatures to the wills of men. Women did not possess the same faculties of reason the men allegedly held. They were not supposed to own land. A woman's ownership of property was considered the freak result of a hardworking husband's untimely death, a mere temporary state of affairs until she married and the new mate gained title to the land. These were some of the reasons why Alexandra's brothers were concerned about her plans to marry Carl. They feared that Alexandra lacked enough sense to prevent Carl from assuming ownership of

78   *O Pioneers!* / CATHER

some of the land that also belonged to them. Other men might have been jealous.

Near forty, Alexandra was not a young, irresponsible girl. Carl was five years her junior, but earlier they had gone their separate ways and then finally decided to marry. Even with the tragedies of Emil's murder and of his murderer, Frank Shabata, Carl and Alexandra would endow the prairie with life and hope.

Bibliography

Bohlke, L. Brent. "The Ecstasy of Alexandra Bergson," in *Colby Library Quarterly*. XI (1975), pp. 139–149.

Brown, Edward Killoran and Leon Edel. *Willa Cather: A Critical Biography*. New York: Knopf, 1953, pp. 173–179.

Charles, Sister Peter Damian, O.P. "Love and Death in Willa Cather's *O Pioneers!*" in *College Language Association Journal*. IX (December, 1965), pp. 140–150.

Daiches, David. *Willa Cather: A Critical Introduction*. Ithaca, N.Y.: Cornell University Press, 1951, pp. 15–29.

Fox, Maynard. "Symbolic Representation in Willa Cather's *O Pioneers!*" in *Western American Literature*. IX (Fall, 1974), pp. 187–196.

Gerber, Philip L. *Willa Cather*. Boston: Twayne, 1975, pp. 75–80.

Giannone, Richard. "*O Pioneers!*" in *Music in Willa Cather's Fiction*. Lincoln: University of Nebraska Press, 1968, pp. 69–81.

————. "*O Pioneers!*: Song of the Earth and Youth," in *South Dakota Review*. II (Spring, 1965), pp. 52–68.

McFarland, Dorothy Tuck. *Willa Cather*. New York: Frederick Ungar, 1972, pp. 19–28.

Rapin, René. *Willa Cather*. New York: McBride, 1930, pp. 21–26.

Randall, John H., III. *The Landscape and the Looking Glass: Willa Cather's Search for Value*. Boston: Houghton Mifflin, 1960, pp. 64–105.

Reaves, J. Russell. "Mythic Motivation in Willa Cather's *O Pioneers!*," in *Western Folklore*. XXVII (January, 1968), pp. 19–25.

Schneider, Sister Lucy, C.S.J. "*O Pioneers!* in the Light of Willa Cather's 'Land Philosophy,'" in *Colby Library Quarterly*. VIII (June, 1968), pp. 55–70.

Stouck, David. *Willa Cather's Imagination*. Lincoln: University of Nebraska Press, 1975, pp. 23–32.

Van Ghent, Dorothy. *Willa Cather*. Minneapolis: University of Minnesota Press, 1964, pp. 15–18.

WALTER VAN TILBURG CLARK

Born: East Orland, Maine (August 3, 1909)
Died: Reno, Nevada (November 10, 1971)

Principal Works

NOVELS: *The Ox-Bow Incident*, 1940; *The City of Trembling Leaves*, 1945; *The Track of the Cat*, 1949.
SHORT STORIES: *The Watchful Gods and Other Stories*, 1950.

Walter Van Tilburg Clark was born in East Orland, Maine, August 3, 1909, but spent his early childhood in West Nyack, New York. In 1917 the family moved to Reno, Nevada, where the elder Clark assumed the presidency of the University of Nevada. Educated in the Reno public schools, he took his B.A. degree at the University of Nevada in 1931 and an M.A. the following year. He then returned to New England to attend the University of Vermont for two years, taking a second M.A. there in 1934. By this time he had married. For the next ten years he taught English and dramatics and coached athletics in the public schools in Cazenovia, New York.

During this period of school teaching he wrote and published his first two novels and several short stories. *The Ox-Bow Incident* reveals Clark at once as a Western novelist. The novel, laid in the Nevada of 1885, deals with a lynching. But Clark's story of cowboys and cattle rustling is not the ordinary local color tale. It is, in the first place, a carefully and tightly constructed narrative. In the second place, it is a perceptive and imaginative examination of the nature and meaning of justice and man's moral responsibility in administering it; it is an investigation into the implications of mob violence. Clark skillfully explores varying reactions to the lynching, from the lawless expression of man's hunting instincts to the delicate subtleties in moral cowardice.

The City of the Trembling Leaves is by comparison a sprawling book. What it has in common with *The Ox-Bow Incident*, however, is its Western setting—Reno—and its sensitivity to the landscape of the West, which Clark sees always with a clear and knowledgeable eye. It is a story of maturation, of how a young artist grows to adulthood, finally finding a satisfactory relationship with the girl he loves and composing the symphony he had to write. The book has a certain value as a portrait of the artist as a young man in an indifferent society. The novel is too long because Clark masses detail indiscriminately in the description of places and persons and gives serious attention to almost every adolescent itch felt by his protagonist.

With these two novels behind him, Clark decided in 1945 to give up teaching and devote all his time to writing. He moved with his wife and two children first to Taos, New Mexico, and later to Nevada and California, and Montana.

The Track of the Cat, published in 1949, is the story of how the three sons of a ranching family hunt down and kill a marauding panther, but only after it has caused the death of two of them. This novel represents Clark's most ambitious effort to explore the myth of the West and the place of the white man there. The panther is a symbol of many meanings: of the pristine West before the white man despoiled it, of the Indians' revenge because the white man took the land from them, simply of the power of myth. Through these levels of interpretation the book presents a searching and provocative view of man and nature in the American West.

The Watchful Gods and Other Stories is a selection of Clark's short stories, ten in number, including "The Wind and the Snow of Winter," which won the O. Henry prize in 1945.

Bibliography

There is no full study of Clark. John R. Kuehl, "Walter Van Tilburg Clark: A Bibliography," *Bulletin of Bibliography*, XXII, 1 (1956), 18–20, includes a list of articles about Clark. See Otis W. Coan, *America in Fiction*, 1949. Useful articles are Vernon Young, "Gods Without Heroes: The Tentative Myth of Walter Van Tilburg Clark," *Arizona Quarterly*, VII, 2 (1951), 110; Frederic I. Carpenter, "The West of Walter Van Tilburg Clark," *College English*, XIII (1952), 243–248; L. L. Leo, "Walter Van Tilburg Clark's Ambiguous American Dream," *College English*, XXVI (1965), 382–387; Max Westbrook, "The Archetypal Ethic of *The Ox-Bow Incident*," *Western American Literature*, I (1966), 105–118; and Barclay Bates, "Clark's Man for All Seasons: The Achievement of Wholeness in *The Ox-Bow Incident*," *Western American Literature*, III (1968), 37–49.

THE OX-BOW INCIDENT

Type of work: Novel
Author: Walter Van Tilburg Clark (1909–1971)
Time of plot: 1885
Locale: Nevada
First published: 1940

What seems in its beginning pages to be a typical Western with all the stage settings and characters of a cowboy thriller is actually a tense story of the cruel laws of survival. As the plot moves slowly but inexorably to its climax, the mob assumes the nature of a Greek chorus, now arguing on one side, now on the other, as Clark unfolds his saga of human misery.

Principal Characters

Gil Carter, a wandering ranch hand who drifts into Bridger's Wells looking for a girl. When she returns to the town, after having reportedly gone to San Francisco, with a husband, Gil is furious. He joins a posse, but thinks more of his disappointment in love than of the hanging of three innocent men.

Art Croft, Gil's friend and companion. Though wounded by mistake by a stage driver, he goes on with the posse in search of rustlers.

Rose Mapen, the girl Gil loves and who disappoints him by marrying another man while gone from Bridger's Wells.

Canby, the saloonkeeper at Bridger's Wells.

Farnley, a cowboy who assists in hanging the three innocent men. When one of them, Donald Martin, dies too slowly in the hangman's noose, Farnley shoots him.

Kinkaid, Farnley's friend, supposedly killed by rustlers. He turns up alive after three innocent men have been hanged for his murder.

Davies, a storekeeper in the town. He tries to prevent the hanging of innocent men and fails. He takes a ring and a farewell letter to Martin's wife and two children. After the lynching he comes to believe, erroneously, that the fault was his.

Osgood, a Baptist minister. He tries to help Davies prevent mob action.

Joyce, a young cowboy who goes with Croft to ask Judge Tyler to swear in the posse.

Judge Tyler, the local magistrate. He tries to prevent mob action but ironically stimulates it.

Sheriff Risley, whose absence from town allows the mob to act. He returns just too late. He refuses to arrest the members of the posse, claiming lack of evidence.

Mapes, the sheriff's swaggering deputy who leads the posse he illegally deputizes.

Jenny Grier, called Ma, keeper of a boarding house. She helps hang the supposed rustlers and murderers.

Tetley, a rancher. He forces his son to participate in the mob's precipitate action. After his son commits suicide, he does, too.

Gerald Tetley, an emotional young man. Horrified by having to participate in the mob killings, he commits suicide.

Donald Martin, a rancher. Wrongly ac-cused of being a rustler, he is hanged unlawfully by the mob.

A Mexican, Martin's rider, also hanged by the mob.

An Old Man, Martin's simple-minded worker, the mob's third victim.

Drew, a rancher. He failed to hand Martin a bill of sale for cattle purchased, thus contributing to the man's death.

The Story

Gil Carter, a cow puncher, and his friend Croft rode into the little frontier town of Bridger's Wells. At Canby's saloon they reined in their horses. Canby was alone at the bar, and he served Gil and Croft with silent glumness.

Canby told them that Rose Mapen, the girl Gil sought, had gone to Frisco. He also told the two cowboys that all the local cowhands and their employers were on the lookout for rustlers who were raiding the ranches in the valley. More than six hundred head of cattle had been stolen and the ranchers were even regarding one another with suspicion. Gil and Croft felt suspicion leveled at them when a group of riders and town men came into the bar.

Gil began to play poker and won hand after hand. The stakes and the bad feeling grew higher until finally Gil and a man named Farnley closed in a rough row. Gil downed his opponent but was himself knocked unconscious when Canby hit him over the head with a bottle.

A rider rode up to the saloon with the word that rustlers had killed Kinkaid, Farnley's friend. Farnley did not want to wait for a posse to be formed, but cooler heads prevailed, among them old Davies, a storekeeper, and Osgood, the Baptist minister. Everyone there joined in the argument, some for, some opposed to, immediate action.

Davies sent Croft and a young cowboy named Joyce to ask Judge Tyler to swear in a posse before a lawless man hunt began. The judge was not eager to swear in a posse in the absence of Risley, the sheriff, but Mapes, a loud, swaggering, newly appointed deputy, demanded that he be allowed to lead the posse.

Meanwhile the tempers of the crowd began to grow sullen. Ma Grier, who kept a boarding-house, joined the mob. Then Judge Tyler arrived and his long-winded oration against a posse stirred the men up more than anything else could have done. Davies took over again and almost convinced the men they should disband. But at that moment Tetley, a former Confederate officer and an important rancher, rode up with word that his Mexican herder had seen the rustlers.

Mob spirit flared up once more. Mapes deputized the men in spite of Judge Tyler's assertion that a deputy could not deputize others. The mob rode off in the direction of Drew's ranch, where Kinkaid had been killed.

There the riders found the first trace of their quarry. Tracks showed that three riders were driving forty head of cattle toward a pass through the range.

Along the way Croft talked to Tetley's sullen son, Gerald. Gerald was not cut out to be a rancher, a fact ignored by his stern, domineering father. Croft thought the boy appeared emotional and unmanly.

The stagecoach suddenly appeared over a rise. In the darkness and confusion, the driver thought that the riders were attempting a holdup. He fired, hitting Croft high in the chest. When he learned his mistake, he pulled up his horses and stopped. One of the passengers was Rose Mapen, the girl Gil had hoped to find in Bridger's Wells. She introduced the man with her as her husband. Gil was furious.

Croft had his wound doctored and continued on with the posse. On a tip from the passengers, the posse headed for the Ox-Bow, a small valley high up in the range.

Snow was falling by the time the riders came to the Ox-Bow. Through the darkness they saw the flicker of a campfire and heard the sound of cattle. Surrounding the campfire, they surprised the three men sleeping there, an old man, a young, dark-looking man, and a Mexican. The prisoners were seized and tied.

The dark-looking young man insisted there was some mistake. He said that he was Donald Martin and that he had moved into Pike's Hole three days before. But one of the members of the posse, a man from Pike's Hole, claimed he did not know Martin or anything about him. Martin began to grow desperate. He demanded to be taken to Pike's Hole, where his wife and two children were. The members of the posse were contemptuous.

Only Davies tried to defend Martin, but Mapes soon silenced the old storekeeper. The cattle were proof enough. Besides, Martin had no bill of sale. He claimed that Drew, who had sold him the cattle, had promised to mail a bill of sale later.

The posse was for an immediate hanging. Tetley wanted to force a confession, but most of the riders said it was no kindness to make the three wait to die. Martin told them that the Mexican was only his rider, that he did not know much about him because the man spoke no English. The old man was a simple-minded fellow who had agreed to work for Martin for very little pay.

Martin was permitted to write a letter to his wife. Shortly afterward it was discovered that the Mexican possessed Kinkaid's gun. He began to speak English. He claimed that he had found Kinkaid's gun.

Tetley appointed three of the posse to lead the horses out away from the men, whose necks would then be caught in the nooses of the ropes tied to the overhanging limb of a tree. He insisted that his milksop son was to be one of the three. Farnley was another. Ma Grier was the third.

Martin became bitter and unforgiving. He made Davies promise to look after his wife and he gave Davies the letter and a ring. A fine snow continued to fall.

The three were executed. The Mexican and the old man died cleanly. Martin, whose horse had been slowly started by Gerald, had to be shot by Farnley. Tetley felled his son with the butt of his pistol for bungling the hanging. Then the posse rode away.

As they rode out of the Ox-Bow they met Sheriff Risley, Judge Tyler, Drew, and Kinkaid, who was not dead after all. The judge shouted that every member of the posse would be tried for murder. The sheriff, however, said that he could not arrest a single man present for the murders because identity was uncertain in the swirling snow. He asked for ten volunteers to continue the search for the real rustlers.

Only old Davies seemed moved by the affair, more so after he learned that Martin's story was true and that the cattle had been bought from Drew without a bill of sale. Nearly maddened, he gave the ring and letter to Drew, who promised to look after Martin's widow.

After Croft and Gil had returned to Canby's saloon, Davies began to moan to Croft. Davies now had the idea that he himself had caused the hanging of the three men. Gil got drunk. That day Gerald Tetley hanged himself. A few hours later Gerald's father also committed suicide. The cowhands took up a collection for Martin's widow. In their room at Canby's, Gil and Croft could hear Rose laughing and talking in the bar. They decided to leave town.

Critical Evaluation

Clark's *The Ox-Bow Incident* is set against a Nevada landscape in 1885, but its portrayal of mob justice is timeless. The tragedy in the novel involves not only the obvious one of innocent people who are wrongly punished. Clark illustrates how unjust and cruel acts can be carried out by intelligent and moral men who allow their sense of social duty to corrupt their greater, if less dominant, sense of human justice.

Bridger's Wells, Nevada, the initial setting for the novel's development, offered its citizens a limited variety of recreational diversions—eating, sleeping, drinking, cards, and fighting. Into that frontier setting stepped Gil Carter and Art Croft to learn that rustlers, who were at once murderers, had provided the place with an exciting alternative. Osgood, the Baptist minister from the only "working church" in town, realized early how tempers could sublimate one's reason and sense of justice. For the minister, however, the timing, if not also the place, was wrong. In times of despair, reason and justice become less attractive when immediate action seems convenient. Bartlett, a rancher who found rustling a particularly vile threat, argued that "justice" often proved ineffective and worked too slowly to guarantee that guilty men would pay the penalties for their crimes. "I say, stretch the bastards." Bartlett proved effective enough to persuade two score townspeople into forming an illegal posse even though none of the men he exhorted owned any cattle, and only two or three even knew the allegedly murdered man.

Bartlett, the one rancher, physically weak and unsound though he appeared, had stigmatized any among his listeners who opposed his argument. Davies, the storekeeper, proved unsuccessful in his efforts to delay the manhunt by his words: "True law, the code of justice, the essence of our sensations of right and wrong, is the conscience of society. It has taken thousands of years to develop, and it is the greatest, the most distinguishing quality which has evolved with mankind." Notwithstanding the thoughtfulness of his argument, a new leader, Tetley, had by then emerged who, capitalizing on his own frustrations as well as on the gullibility of others, effected a peculiar reversal of the "conscience of society" so as to produce, in effect, a new concept of "justice."

Major Tetley's son Gerald, who was forced by his father to take part in the posse, painfully realized the weakness of individual men too afraid to challenge the mob, who convince themselves that to resist would be to admit weakness, to be the only hunter in a pack to quit. "How many of us do you think are really here because there have been cattle stolen, or because Kinkaid was shot?" he asks. In the absence of Sheriff Risley, who as the legally constituted police authority might have impeded the development toward lynch law, the formation of an illegal posse, the manhunt, and the lynchings all went ahead with the inevitability of a Shakespearean tragedy.

In the eleventh hour, no gesture which suggested innocence could spare the doomed men. Martin's emotional letter to his wife was to be shared among the posse by Davies in an effort to save the life of a man Davies believed was innocent. The effort was challenged by Martin himself, however, who used the incident to make another point, that even an initial promise to preserve the integrity of his letter would have proved futile among men in whom conscience had long since failed as a measure of just conduct. In a moment where bravery might understandably have failed among men about to be hanged, the Mexican removed a bullet from his own leg, washed the wound and dressed it with a fire-heated knife. He tossed the knife into the ground within an inch of where its owner's foot would have been had he not, in fear, drawn quickly away. The Mexican, who smiled often at the proceedings, did so again, seeing in the posse the absence of the very bravery they thought they all possessed. All sympathy that Martin's letter and the Mexican's courage might otherwise have created for the three doomed men never materialized, however, because most of the posse had simply made up their minds about the prisoners' fate already, or because they believed the rest had, and since they believed fledgling signs of sympathy were wrong and something which had to be concealed, Tetley had his day.

Davies, the one man who had had least to do with the hangings, and perhaps did most to prevent them, was himself riddled with guilt for the occasion of the crime. "Tetley couldn't help what he did," Davies believed. "Tetley's a beast. . . . But a beast is not to blame." The leader of the posse was successful only to the extent that he was allowed to achieve his goal. Davies, a peaceful man, even thought that he should have resorted to the gun, to violence if necessary, to prevent the illegal executions from taking place. He admitted too, however, that in not having a weapon he was glad his convictions did not have to be tested. Davies' sense of guilt and his sense of justice made him realize, as no one else could, how little he actually did to prevent the hangings from taking place. "I had everything, justice, pity, . . . and I let those three men hang because I was afraid. The . . . only thing Tetley had, guts, plain guts, and I didn't have it." The sensitive man, lacking the brute convictions of his opposite, is rendered impotent. His final confession is accompanied by laughter in the background.

The Ox-Bow Incident has no hero; yet it cries out for one in a world where the lessons of the Ox-Bow may not be remembered, much less learned. Inasmuch as the novel was written in 1937 and 1938, while Nazism bullied a world into submission, it is not a theme which was then out of step with world developments. Neither, according to Clark, does the story lack American application. "What I wanted to say was 'It can happen here. It has happened here, in minor but sufficiently indicative ways, a great many times.' "

Bibliography

Andersen, Kenneth. "Character Portrayal in *The Ox-Bow Incident*," in *Western American Literature*. IV (Winter, 1970), pp. 287–298.

————. "Form in Walter Van Tilburg Clark's *The Ox-Bow Incident*," in *Western Review*. VI (Spring, 1969), pp. 19–25.

Banks, Loy Otis. "The Credible Literary West," in *Colorado Quarterly*. VIII (Summer, 1959), pp. 45–49.

Bates, Barclay W. "Clark's Man for All Seasons: The Achievement of Wholeness in *The Ox-Bow Incident*," in *Western American Literature*. III (Spring, 1968), pp. 37–49.

Carpenter, Frederic I. "The West of Walter Van Tilburg Clark," in *College English*. XIII (February, 1952), pp. 243–248. Reprinted in *English Journal*. XLI (February, 1952), pp. 64–69.

Cochran, Robert W. "Nature and the Nature of Man in *The Ox-Bow Incident*," in *Western American Literature*. V (Winter, 1971), pp. 253–264.

Eisinger, Chester E. "The Fiction of Walter Van Tilburg Clark: Man and Nature in the West," in *Southwest Review*. XLIV (Summer, 1959), pp. 215–218. Reprinted in *Fiction of the Forties*. Chicago: University of Chicago Press, 1963, pp. 311–314.

Gurian, Jay. "The Unwritten West," in *The American West*. II (Winter, 1965), pp. 61–62.

Houghton, Donald E. "The Failure of Speech in *The Ox-Bow Incident*," in *English Journal.* LIX (December, 1970), pp. 1245–1251.

Lee, L.L. *Walter Van Tilburg Clark.* Boise, Id.: Boise State University, 1973.

————. "Walter Van Tilburg Clark's Ambiguous American Dream," in *College English.* XXVI (February, 1965), pp. 382–387.

Milton, John R. "The Western Attitude: Walter Van Tilburg Clark," in *Critique.* II (Winter, 1959), pp. 59–62.

Peterson, Levi S. "Tragedy and Western American Literature," in *Western American Literature.* VI (1972), pp. 243–249.

Portz, John. "Idea and Symbol in Walter Van Tilburg Clark," in *Accent.* XVII (Spring, 1957), pp. 112–128.

Redman, Ben Ray. "Magnificent Incident," in *Saturday Review of Literature.* XXIII (October 26, 1940), p. 6.

Stein, Paul. "Cowboys and Unicorns: The Novels of Walter Van Tilburg Clark," in *Western American Literature.* V (Winter, 1971), pp. 265–275.

Webb, Walter Prescott. "Afterword," in *The Ox-Bow Incident.* New York: Signet, 1960, pp. 219–224.

Westbrook, Max. "The Archetypal Ethic of *The Ox-Bow Incident*," in *Walter Van Tilburg Clark.* New York: Twayne, 1969, pp. 54–67.

Wilner, Herbert. "Walter Van Tilburg Clark," in *Western Review.* XX (Winter, 1956), pp. 103–122.

STEPHEN CRANE

Born: Newark, New Jersey (November 1, 1871)
Died: Badenweiler, Germany (June 5, 1900)

Principal Works

NOVELS: *Maggie: A Girl of the Streets*, 1893; *The Red Badge of Courage: An Episode of the American Civil War*, 1895; *George's Mother*, 1896; *The Third Violet*, 1897; *Active Service*, 1899; *The O'Ruddy*, 1903 (completed by Robert Barr).

SHORT STORIES: *The Little Regiment and Other Episodes of the American Civil War*, 1896; *The Open Boat and Other Tales of Adventure*, 1898; *The Monster and Other Stories*, 1899; *Whilomville Stories*, 1900; *Wounds in the Rain: War Stories*, 1900.

POEMS: *The Black Riders*, 1895; *War Is Kind*, 1899.

HISTORY: *Great Battles of the World*, 1901.

Stephen Crane was the fourteenth child born into the ministerial household of the Reverend Jonathan Crane and his wife Mary, at Newark, New Jersey, on November 1, 1871. The father's frequent moves to pastorates in New Jersey and New York gave the youngest Crane an opportunity to grow up under changing environments and stimuli. As a boy he shocked his family by announcing his disbelief in hell, a protest against the apparent futility of his father's devoted service to Methodism. Ideals with which the Reverend Jonathan Crane sternly allied himself did not correspond to life as his son came to know it. Stephen later wrote, "He was so simple and good that I often think he didn't know much of anything about humanity." Although physically frail, Stephen was essentially an outdoorsman. At Lafayette College (1889–1890) and at Syracuse University (1890–1891) he distinguished himself at boxing and as a shortstop on the varsity team. Years later, Joseph Conrad paid tribute to him as a good shot and a fine horseman. Mary Crane's death ended her son's college career, and he was never to be formally well educated. His real education sprang from a keen ability to observe and learn from the life around him.

Crane moved to New York City where he lived a precarious five years as a free-lance writer for the newspapers. While working for *The Herald*, the fledgling reporter studied the intimate nature of the Bowery. He slept in Bowery shelters, for he wanted the truth of the life he witnessed. None escaped his keen observation: the beggar, the vagrant, the harlot—the life of the East Side world. During the two days before Christmas of 1891, the twenty-year-old reporter wrote his first novel. The characters were nameless and the book untitled. A brother, William Crane, suggested a title, *Maggie: A Girl of the Streets*. Meanwhile *The Herald* had either fired Crane or he had dismissed himself. Actually, Crane was not a successful reporter. Copy which he submitted was rich in impressions but often lacked the basic facts of the event.

Maggie was not a respectable book. Its author, having borrowed a thousand dollars from his brother William, published it early in 1893 under a pseudonym, Johnston Smith. Impressed by *Maggie*, Hamlin Garland became the first established writer to show faith in Crane's talent, but the book did not sell; only a hundred copies of the seven hundred printed were sold. It was not until 1896 that the book was reissued under its author's name. In it Crane had discovered the slum as literary material; thus naturalism entered American letters, and from that obscure beginning his feeling for dialect and his knowledge of American life fastened his fiction in reality. In contrast to the light romances of its period, *Maggie* proclaimed a world without virtue. Since Crane's outlook was cynical, he was not disposed to cry the cause of his heroine, Maggie Johnson, nor to expect a reform of the environment which spawned her. Then, too, Maggie is never lifelike enough to evoke pity. She resembles a figure in a Greek drama whose fate is sealed before the play begins.

Through his reading and endless conversations with Civil War veterans, young Stephen had grown up intrigued by war. In ten days and nights of intense labor he wrote the first American novel to describe not only what a soldier did but how he felt. Written in Edmund Crane's home at Lakeview, New Jersey, *The Red Badge of Courage* first appeared in installment form in *The Philadelphia Press*, the manuscript having been sold to Irving Bacheller's newspaper syndicate in February, 1894, for less than a hundred dollars. Publication in book form was delayed until October 3, 1895, for the author, commissioned by the Bacheller syndicate, was away traveling in the West, the Southwest, and Mexico. With his second novel Crane was established as a major novelist, but success and fame were never to bring him much money.

The Red Badge of Courage depicted a youth confused and battered about by war as Crane had been by life. Written about the little man, the book appealed to the American mind. Henry Fleming, the farmer's boy, seemed real enough. Even the officers were human. Crane, always eager for new sensations and with a seeming personal delight in danger, wrote of war as he imagined it. In the tense and telegraphic manner peculiar to him, he flashed a series of individual pictures of war, each heightened by color images reflecting the psychological horror of the event. Henry Fleming's fear was one which Crane himself felt, and Henry's victory over fear was not a true victory. It stands for that effort which man manages somehow to make. Man sees; despite his seeing, he goes onward.

Crane's characters do not fashion their worlds. Things happen to them, and under stress they react as the event dictates. The author feels no sentimental concern for Maggie or Henry; they mirror the brutal forces of their environments and are not distinct personalities. Maggie's mind is not entered by the novelist, but it seems certain that she will be battered to death by an environment which she is powerless to escape. Henry's mind is entered, and in entering it the author unlocks the thoughts and emotions of mankind at war.

Shipwrecked off the coast of Florida while serving with a Cuban filibustering expedition in 1896, Crane experienced hardships which may have contributed to his early death. In Jacksonville he met Cora Taylor, a woman older than himself, who was to follow him as he covered the Greco-Turkish War for *The New York Journal*. Stephen and Cora were married in Greece.

Notoriety arising from false reports that he was addicted to liquor and morphine may have influenced Crane's decision to establish residence in England. Having developed strong friendships with Joseph Conrad and Henry James, he remained in England except for a brief return to cover the Spanish-American War for *The World*. Crane was brave if not foolhardy under fire, and the fatigue of battle further broke his health. Conrad, perhaps Crane's most intimate friend, was displeased to witness at Brede Place, Sussex, shortly before Crane's death, an unhappy talent lost in a maze of hack work.

On assignment as a special writer for the *London Morning Post*, he collapsed, ill from the tuberculosis which caused his death in Badenweiler, Germany, on June 5, 1900, after a futile trip to the Black Forest in search of a cure. His body was returned to the family plot in Elizabeth, New Jersey.

A trail-blazer of unquestioned sincerity, Crane felt and knew that what he wrote was of the essence of truth. Portraying a universe without meaning or order, he sensed only that his task was to point out the cutting irony of circumstances and to probe the fate of his experimental men and women as they reacted to the intensely cruel pressures of a meaningless yet always victorious circumstance. Within these limits he perfected an art; beyond them, during the short time allotted him, he did not care to explore. It may be that he saw no reason to explore, for it may be that he saw nothing there.

Bibliography

The definitive edition is that edited by Fredson Bowers. An older edition is *The Works of Stephen Crane*, edited by Wilson Follett, 12 vols., 1925–1927; and by the same editor, *The Collected Poems of Stephen Crane*, 1930. The definitive biography is R. W. Stallman, *Stephen Crane*, 1968. See also Thomas Beer, *Stephen Crane: A Study in American Letters*, with an Introduction by Joseph Conrad, 1923; John Berryman, *Stephen Crane*, in the American Men of Letters Series, 1950; Edward Garnett, "Stephen Crane and His Work," in *Friday Nights*, 1922; Matthew Josephson, *Portrait of the Artist as American*, 1930; Alfred Kazin, *On Native Grounds*, 1942; V. S. Pritchett, *The Living Novel*, 1946; Alexander Cowie, *The Rise of the American Novel*, 1948; R. W. Stallman, Introduction to *The Red Badge of Courage*, Modern Library edition, 1951; Daniel G. Hoffman, Introduction to *The Red Badge of Courage*, Harper's Modern Classics edition, 1957; Maurice Bassan, *Stephen Crane: A Collection of Critical Essays*, 1967; Donald B. Gibson, *The Fiction of Stephen Crane*, 1968; and Jean Cazemajou, *Stephen Crane*, 1969; also H. T. Webster, "Wilbur F. Hinman's *Corporal Si Klegg* and Stephen Crane's *Red Badge of Courage*," *American Literature*, II (1939),

285–293; John Schroeder, "Stephen Crane Embattled," in *University of Kansas City Review*, XVII (1950), 119–129; and Scott C. Osborn, "Stephen Crane's Imagery: 'Pasted Like a Wafer,'" *American Literature, XXIII* (1951), 362.

MAGGIE: A GIRL OF THE STREETS

Type of work: Novel
Author: Stephen Crane (1871–1900)
Time of plot: Late nineteenth century
Locale: New York
First published: 1893

Maggie: A Girl of the Streets *was the first novel to deal realistically and straightforwardly with the sordid life of the slums. It gave rise to the school of naturalistic fiction of Norris, Dreiser, and others. Despite its faults of style and structure, it remains of historical and literary importance.*

Principal Characters

Maggie, a girl who has grown up in the slums of New York. Although surrounded by corruption of all sorts throughout her youth, she has remained uncontaminated by it. When she falls in love with Pete, a friend of her brother, her moral deterioration begins. After she has lived with him, her family, who are anything but models of decorum, will have nothing to do with her. She turns to prostitution but finds it hard to support herself, and eventually she commits suicide.

Jimmy, Maggie's brother. After his father's death, he goes to work to support Maggie and their mother. He quickly falls into the normal patterns of life for men of his class, has a succession of affairs, and fathers several illegitimate children. When Maggie tries to return home after her affair with Pete, he is highly indignant and will do nothing to help her.

Pete, Jimmy's friend and Maggie's lover. After seducing Maggie he quickly tires of her and turns her out. Thereafter he denies any responsibility toward her.

The Mother, a woman given to drink and constant haranguing with her husband and children. When Maggie and Jimmy were small she left them to shift for themselves most of the time, but it is she who assumes an attitude of outraged virtue when Maggie tries to return home. After her daughter's death she is inconsolable.

The Story

In the slum section of New York City, Maggie and her two brothers grew up in the squalor and corruption, both moral and physical, of that poverty-stricken area. Her father usually came home from work drunk, and her mother, too, was fond of the bottle. The children were neglected. When the drunken parents ranted at each other, the children hid in terror under the table or the bed.

Somehow Maggie managed to remain untouched by that sordidness. Her

MAGGIE: A GIRL OF THE STREETS, by Stephen Crane. By permission of the publishers, Alfred A. Knopf, Inc.

younger brother died; Jimmy, her older brother, went to work after the father died. He fought, drank, and had many affairs with women. From time to time he was hounded by some of the women, who demanded support for themselves and the illegitimate children he had fathered. Jimmy brushed them aside.

When Jimmy brought his best friend home with him, Maggie fell in love. Pete, a bartender, was handsome, flashy, and exciting. One night he took her out to show her the night life of the city. Maggie's wonder knew no bounds, for to her the experience was the height of luxury. On the doorstep she allowed Pete to kiss her goodnight. Pete was disappointed, but not discouraged. He took Maggie out again. The next time she surrendered and went to live with him.

But Pete soon grew tired of Maggie, and she was compelled to return home. In furious indignation, her mother ordered her out of the house. She had done everything, the mother insisted, to bring Maggie up to be a fine, decent girl. She had been an excellent mother and had spared no pains to keep her daughter on the path of virtue. Now her daughter would be dead to her. The neighbors joined in, denouncing Maggie. Jimmy, the seducer of other men's sisters, became indignant. He and a companion went to the bar where Pete worked, intent upon beating him up. When they failed, Jimmy contented himself by shrugging his shoulders and condemning his sister.

Maggie was now homeless and penniless. She went to see Pete, but he sent her away, irritated and fearful lest he should lose his job. She turned to prostitution, plying her trade by night, accosting poor and wealthy alike. But she did not have much luck. One night she walked forlornly and unsuccessfully in the waterfront district. Resignedly she trudged on, toward the pier and the black, murky depths of the river.

A short time later, Jimmy came home from one of his prolonged absences. Maggie, the mother wailed, was dead. With the neighbors around her, she sobbed and moaned. What the Lord had given the Lord had taken away, the neighbors told her. Uncomforted, Maggie's mother shrieked that she forgave her daughter; oh yes, she forgave Maggie her sins.

Critical Evaluation

Published in 1893 when Crane was only twenty-two years old, *Maggie: A Girl of the Streets* heralded a major new talent in American literature. Little in Crane's early background would seem to have anticipated a work such as *Maggie: A Girl of the Streets,* or the deeply pessimistic attitude toward life reflected there. Son of a small-town Methodist minister, Crane had never really experienced the sort of life and community environment indigenous to the novel except for his observations during some months in New York. But, as he was to prove so brilliantly in *The Red Badge of Courage,* Crane's imagination and genius could extrapolate with uncanny accuracy the patterns of lives he had seen remotely if at all. This may be accounted for at least in part by the fact that Crane, even at the youthful age of twenty-two, already was developing the style and technique of a literary naturalism which essentially saw the novel as a kind of theoretical scientifically-controlled experiment into which characters were placed for observation. As Émile Zola, the acknowledged father of naturalism, had written, "a novelist must be only a scientist, an analyst, an anatomist, and his work must have the certainty, the solidity, and the practical application of a work of science."

Many of Crane's contemporaries, here and abroad, arrived at their naturalistic philosophy through reading in the biological sciences, particularly in the works of Charles Darwin and Herbert Spencer, both of whom contributed immeasurably to the development of the movement. Crane, however, does not appear to have reached his position so much through reading science as from his study of the French and Russian authors who were the earliest pioneers of naturalism in literature. The literary sources of his philosophy of the novel, though, in no way weaken Crane's theoretical framework, and he stands among Hamlin Garland, Frank Norris, Jack London, and Theodore Dreiser as a major figure of American Naturalism. As an artist, Crane is, in his best work, superior to any of these writers. Since *Maggie: A Girl of the Streets* is not of that caliber artistically, however, it is best treated as representational of the naturalistic novel.

An extreme form of the realism which had characterized the previous generation of writers—especially Henry James and Mark Twain in the United States—naturalism resulted from the adaption of the principles of pessimistic scientific determinism to literature. According to these principles, man is a helpless and weak animal caught up in internal or external forces over which he can assert no control, and which ultimately threaten to destroy him. The universe, as perceived from this point of view, operates entirely on Newtonian mechanical principles and has neither intelligent guidance nor moral purpose. From Darwin the naturalists adopted the concept of biological determinism which characterizes his *On the Origin of Species,* while Herbert Spencer gave them a theory of society reflecting the law of tooth and claw and the survival of the fittest. In general, these writers fall into one of two camps: those who emphasize the biological nature of man and show him attempting to utilize his animal instincts to survive in a hostile world, and those who are more concerned with man in the social environment and present him as a product of socio-economic forces against which he can hardly hope to prevail. Crane, who wrote in Hamlin Garland's copy of *Maggie: A Girl of the Streets* that the novel illustrated the way in which environment was a shaping force in man's life, was at this stage of his career clearly in the latter camp.

In one sense, *Maggie: A Girl of the Streets* is as much about environment as about Maggie and the other characters in any specific sense. Crane, after all, did not even name his characters in his early drafts, preferring to treat them as generalized and representative types rather than as individualized characters. Also, he shows no interest in getting into the mental or psychic lives of his characters to discover for us their private selves. All this suggests the extent to which environment, rather than character, is at the heart of the work. Later Crane would develop more interest in the psychological dimension than he shows here, though he would never entirely abandon the view of man caught up in external forces beyond his control. On these grounds, most readers are likely to quarrel with William Dean Howells, who professed to see an approximation of the Fate characteristic of Greek tragedy in Crane's determinism. Stephen Crane's sense of the environment both as shaping force and destructive power is so strong that Maggie can only dramatize man's pathetic weakness in the face of cosmic power—lacking even the illusion of freedom, she cannot illustrate the powerful sense of human potential even in adversity found in true tragedy.

But the faults—and they are many—of this novel should not be allowed to detract from its important place in the development of the American novel. It has been variously called the first truly modern American novel, and the novel which first clearly differentiated the American from the English novel tradition, and persuasive arguments can be made for both insights. Crane was able in this early novel to open up for consideration by his successors an entire level of social life not heretofore seriously treated by American authors, though many writers had sentimentalized the slums. Even more revolutionary was his challenge, well before Dreiser's *Sister Carrie,* to the Victorian taboos against any real treatment of sex in the novel by writing honestly and frankly and sympathetically about a "fallen woman." Further, Crane's treatment of the hypocritical religious values his characters frequently mouth to justify their most inhumane acts anticipates that loss of traditional values which looms so large in the writing of this century. Though he published his greatest work, *The Red Badge of Courage,* in 1895, Crane was essentially a twentieth century writer, and his *Maggie: A Girl of the Streets* was America's first novel which could truly be called modern. Without Crane's short and brilliant career, modern literature might not have developed as it did in this country.

Bibliography

Brennan, Joseph. "Irony and Symbolic Structure in Crane's *Maggie,*" in *Nineteenth-Century Fiction.* XVI (March, 1962), pp. 303–315.

Brooks, Van Wyck. *Maggie: A Girl of the Streets and George's Mother.* Greenwich, Conn.: Fawcett, 1960, pp. 5–8.

Bruccoli, Matthew J. "Maggie's Last Night," in *Stephen Crane Newsletter.* II (Fall, 1967), pp. 10–11.

Cady, Edwin Harrison. "Stephen Crane's *Maggie: A Girl of the Streets,*" in

Landmarks of American Writing. Edited by Hennig Cohen. New York: Basic Books, 1969, pp. 172–181.

Colvert, James B.   "Structure and Theme in Stephen Crane's Fiction," in *Modern Fiction Studies.* V (Autumn, 1959), pp. 199–208.

Cunliffe, Marcus.   *The Literature of the United States.* Baltimore: Penguin, 1954, pp. 204–207.

————.   "Stephen Crane and the American Background of *Maggie*," in *American Quarterly.* VII (Spring, 1955), pp. 31–44.

Fitelson, David.   "Stephen Crane's *Maggie* and Darwinism," in *American Quarterly.* XVI (Summer, 1964), pp. 182–194.

Fox, Austin M.   *Maggie and Other Stories.* New York: Washington Square Press, 1960, pp. v-xviii.

Gullason, Thomas A.   "The Sources of Stephen Crane's *Maggie*," in *Philological Quarterly.* XXXVIII (Oct., 1959), pp. 497–502.

————.   "Thematic Patterns in Stephen Crane's Early Novels," in *Nineteenth-Century Fiction.* XVI (June, 1961), pp. 59–67.

Kahn, Sholom J.   "Stephen Crane and Whitman: A Possible Source for *Maggie*," in *Walt Whitman Review.* VII (Dec., 1961), pp. 71–77.

Katz, Joseph.   "The *Maggie* Nobody Knows," in *Modern Fiction Studies.* XII (Summer, 1966), pp. 200–212.

La France, M.   "George's Mother and the Other Half of Maggie," in *Stephen Crane in Transition.* Edited by Joseph Katz. De Kalb: Northern Illinois University Press, 1972, pp. 35–53.

Martin, John.   "Childhood in Stephen Crane's *Maggie*, 'The Monster' and *Whilomville Stories*," in *Midwestern University Quarterly.* II (1967), pp. 40–46.

Overmyer, Janet.   "The Structure of Crane's *Maggie*," in *University of Kansas City Review.* XXIX (October, 1962), pp. 71–72.

Pizer, Donald.   "Stephen Crane's *Maggie* and American Naturalism," in *Criticism.* VII (Spring, 1965), pp. 168–175.

Seymour-Smith, Martin.   *Fallen Women.* London: Nelson, 1969, pp. 182–185.

Simoneaux, Katherine G.   "Color Imagery in Crane's *Maggie: A Girl of the Streets*," in *College Language Association Journal.* XVIII (1974), pp. 91–100.

Stallman, Robert Wooster.   "Crane's *Maggie*: A Reassessment," in *Modern Fiction Studies.* V (Autumn, 1959), pp. 251–259.

————.   *The Houses That James Built and Other Literary Studies.* East Lansing: Michigan State University Press, 1961, pp. 63–72.

————. "Stephen Crane's Revision of *Maggie: A Girl of the Streets*," in *American Literature*. XXVI (January, 1955), pp. 528–536.

Stein, William Bysshe. "New Testament Inversions in Crane's *Maggie*," in *Modern Language Notes*. LXXIII (April, 1958), pp. 268–272.

Wertheim, Stanley. "The Saga of March 23rd: Garland, Gilder, and Crane," in *Stephen Crane Newsletter*. III (Winter, 1968), pp. 1–3.

THE RED BADGE OF COURAGE

Type of work: Novel
Author: Stephen Crane (1871–1900)
Time of plot: Civil War
Locale: A Civil War battlefield
First published: 1895

Marking a dramatic departure from the traditional treatment of war in fiction, this novel ignores powerful generals and historic victories and defeats in favor of probing the personal reactions of unknown foot soldiers fighting unknown enemies in skirmishes of indeterminate outcome. Henry Fleming is motivated not by courage or patriotism, but by cowardice, fear, and finally egoism, and events in the novel are all filtered subjectively through his consciousness.

Principal Characters

Henry Fleming, a young recruit under fire for the first time in an unnamed battle of the Civil War, possibly Chancellorsville. A farm boy whose struggle with his emotions might be that of the eternal recruit in any battle of any war, Henry has dreamed of fighting heroically in "Greeklike" battles. Irritated and unnerved by his regiment's inactivity, he tortures himself with the fear that he may run away when the actual firing begins. He does so. Sheepishly rejoining his regiment, he learns that his cowardice is not known to his fellow soldiers. In the next attack he keeps firing after the others have stopped. When a color-bearer falls, he picks up the flag and carries it forward. Later he hears that the colonel has complimented his fierceness. Henry's psychological battle with himself is now ended; it has gone from fear to cowardice to bravery and, finally, to egotism.

Jim Conklin, "the tall soldier," a veteran who comforts Henry and squabbles with the braggart Wilson. He predicts that the regiment is about to move into battle. When it does so, he is mortally wounded.

Henry and "the tattered man" find him stumbling to the rear, still on his feet, fearful of falling under the wheels of an artillery wagon. He wanders into a field, as if it were a place of rendezvous with death. Henry and the tattered man follow him, trying to bring him back. He brushes them off and, with a great convulsion, drops dead.

Wilson, "the loud one." At first he seems confident, absolutely sure of his courage. But as the battle begins he suddenly thinks he may be killed, and he turns a packet of letters over to Henry Fleming. After the first attack he asks for the return of the letters. Some of his loudness and swagger is now gone. He and Henry struggle to get the flag from the fallen color-bearer. Henry seizes it, but Wilson aids him in going forward and setting an example to the wavering troops.

"The Tattered Man," a soldier encountered by Henry Fleming just after he has run away. The man embarrasses the recruit by asking where he is wounded. Later he and Henry follow Jim Conklin into the field. The soldier is so impressed by the manner of Jim's death that he calls the dead man a "jim-dandy." Then he cautions Henry to "watch out fer ol' number one."

Lieutenant Hasbrouck, a young officer of Henry Fleming's company. He is shot in the hand in the early part of the battle but is able to drive a fleeing soldier back into the ranks and tries vainly to stop the disorganized retreat. He later compliments Henry and Wilson by calling them "wild cats."

Colonel MacChesnay, the officer who also compliments Henry Fleming and Wilson. He is berated by the general, shortly after Henry's advance with the flag, for not forcing the partial success of the charge to a complete one.

The Story

The tall soldier, Jim Conklin, and the loud soldier, Wilson, argued bitterly over the rumor that the troops were about to move. Henry Fleming was impatient to experience his first battle, and as he listened to the quarreling of the seasoned soldiers he wondered if he would become frightened and run away under gunfire. He questioned Wilson and Conklin, and each man stated that he would stand and fight no matter what happened.

Henry had come from a farm, where he had dreamed of battles and longed for army life. His mother had held him back at first. When she saw that her son was bored with the farm, she packed his woolen clothing and with a warning that he must not associate with the wicked kind of men who were in the military camps sent him off to join the Yankee troops.

One gray morning Henry awoke to find that the regiment was about to move. With a hazy feeling that death would be a relief from dull and meaningless marching, Henry was again disappointed. The troops made only another march. He began to suspect that the generals were stupid fools, but the other men in his raw regiment scoffed at his idea and told him to shut up.

When the fighting suddenly began, there was very little action in it for Henry. He lay on the ground with the other men and watched for signs of the enemy. Some of the men around him were wounded. He could not see what was going on or what the battle was about. Then an attack came. Immediately Henry forgot all his former confused thoughts, and he could only fire his rifle over and over; around him men behaved in their strange individual manner as they were wounded. Henry felt a close comradeship with the men at his side who were firing at the enemy with him.

Suddenly the attack ended. To Henry, it seemed strange that the sky above should still be blue after the guns had stopped firing. While the men were recovering from the attack, binding wounds, and gathering equipment, another surprise attack was launched from the enemy line. Unprepared and tired from the first fighting, the men retreated in panic. Henry, sharing their sudden terror, ran, too.

When the fearful retreat had ended, the fleeing men learned that the enemy had lost the battle. Now Henry felt a surge of guilt. Dreading to rejoin his companions, he fled into the forest. There he saw a squirrel run away from him in fright. The fleeing animal seemed to vindicate in Henry's mind his own cowardly flight; he had acted according to nature whose own creatures ran from danger. Then, seeing a dead man lying in a clearing, Henry hurried back into the retreating column of wounded men. Most were staggering along in helpless bewilderment and some were being carried on stretchers. Henry realized that he had no wound and that he did not belong in that group of staggering men. There was one pitiful-looking man, covered with dirt and blood, wandering about dazed and alone. Everyone was staring at him and avoiding him. When Henry approached him, the young boy saw that the soldier was Jim Conklin. He was horrified at the sight of the tall soldier. He tried to help Jim, but with a wild motion of despair Jim fell to the ground dead. Once more Henry fled.

His conscience was paining him. He wanted to return to his regiment to finish the fight, but he thought that his fellow soldiers would point to him as a deserter. He envied the dead men who were lying all about him. They were already heroes; he was a coward. Ahead he could hear the rumbling of artillery. As he neared the lines of his regiment, a retreating line of men broke from the trees ahead of him. The men ran fiercely, ignoring him or waving frantically at him as they shouted something he could not comprehend. He stood among the flying men, not knowing what to do. One man hit him on the head with the butt of a rifle.

Henry went on carefully, the wound in his head paining him a great deal. He walked for a long while until he met another soldier, who led Henry back to his regiment. The first familiar man Henry met was Wilson. Wilson, who had been a terrible braggart before the first battle, had given Henry a packet of letters to keep for him in case he were killed. Now Henry felt superior to Wilson. If the man asked him where he had been, Henry would remind him of the letters. Lost was Henry's feeling of guilt; he felt superior now, his deeds of cowardice almost forgotten. No one knew that he had run off in terror. Wilson had changed. He no longer was the swaggering, boastful man who had annoyed Henry in the beginning. The men in the regiment washed Henry'· head wound and told him to get some sleep.

The next morning Wilson casually asked Henry for the letters. Half sorry that he had to yield them with no taunting remark, Henry returned the letters to his comrade. He felt sorry for Wilson's embarrassment. He felt himself a virtuous and heroic man.

Another battle started. This time Henry held his position doggedly and kept firing his rifle without thinking. Once he fell down, and for a panicky moment he thought that he had been shot, but he continued to fire his rifle blindly, loading and firing without even seeing the enemy. Finally someone shouted to him that he must stop shooting, that the battle was over. Then Henry looked up for the first time and saw that there were no enemy troops before him. Now he was a hero. Everyone stared at him when the lieutenant of the regiment complimented his fierce fighting. Henry realized that he had behaved like a demon.

Wilson and Henry, off in the woods looking for water, overheard two officers discussing the coming battle. They said that Henry's regiment fought like mule drivers, but that they would have to be used anyway. Then one officer said that probably not many of the regiment would live through the day's fighting. Soon after the attack started, the color bearer was killed and Henry took up the flag, with Wilson at his side. Although the regiment fought bravely, one of the commanding officers of the army said that the men had not gained the ground that they were expected to take. The same officer had complimented Henry for his courageous fighting. He began to feel that he knew the measure of his own courage and endurance.

His outfit fought one more engagement with the enemy. Henry was by that time a veteran, and the fighting held less meaning for him than had the earlier battles. When it was over, he and Wilson marched away with their victorious regiment.

Critical Evaluation

The Red Badge of Courage, Stephen Crane's second novel (*Maggie: A Girl of the Streets* had appeared under a pseudonym in 1893) and his most famous work, has often been considered the first truly modern war novel. The war is the American Civil War and the battle is presumed to be the one fought at Chancellorsville, though neither the war nor the battle is named in the novel. Nor is there mention of Abraham Lincoln or the principal battle generals, Joseph Hooker (Union) and Robert E. Lee and "Stonewall" Jackson (Confederate). This is by design, since Crane was writing a different kind of war novel. He was not concerned with the causes of the war, the political and social implications of the prolonged and bloody conflict, the strategy and tactics of the commanding officers, or even the real outcome of the battle in which historically the combined losses were nearly thirty thousand men (including "Stonewall" Jackson, mistakenly shot in darkness by one of his own men).

From beginning to end the short novel focuses upon one Union Army volunteer. Though other characters enter the story and reappear intermittently, they are distinctly minor, and they are present primarily to show the relationship of Henry Fleming (usually called only "the youth") to one person, to a small group of soldiers, or to the complex war of which he is such an insignificant part.

Much of the story takes the reader into Henry's consciousness. We share his boyish dreams of glory, his excitement in anticipating battle action, his fear of showing fear, his cowardice and flight, his inner justification of what he has done, his wish for a wound to symbolize a courage he has not shown, the ironic gaining of his false "red badge," his secret knowledge of the badge's origin, his "earning" the badge as he later fights fiercely and instinctively, his joy in musing on his own bravery and valiant actions, his anger at an officer who fails to appreciate his soldiery, and his final feeling that "the great death" is, after all, not a thing to be feared so much. Now, he tells himself, he is a man. In centering the story within the consciousness of an inexperienced youth caught in a war situation whose meaning and complexities he cannot understand, Crane anticipates Ford Madox Ford, Ernest Hemingway, and other later novelists.

Crane has been called a realist, a naturalist, an impressionist, and a symbolist. He is all of these in *The Red Badge of Courage*. Though young Stephen Crane had never seen a battle when he wrote the novel, he had read about them; he had talked with veterans and had studied history under a Civil War general; and he had imagined what it would be like to be a frightened young man facing violent death amid the confusion, noise, and turmoil of a conflict which had no clear meaning to him. Intuitively he wrote so realistically that several early reviewers concluded that only an experienced soldier could have written the book. After Crane had later seen the Greeks and Turks fighting in 1897 (he was a journalist reporting the war), he told Joseph Conrad, "My picture of war was all right! I have found it as I imagined it."

Although naturalistic passages appear in the novel, Crane portrays in Henry Fleming not a helpless chip floating on the indifferent ocean of life but a youth sometimes impelled into action by society or by instinct yet also capable of consciously willed acts. Before the first skirmish Henry wishes he could escape from his regiment and considers his plight: " . . . there were iron laws of tradition and law on four sides. He was in a moving box." In the second skirmish he runs "like a rabbit." When a squirrel in the forest flees after Henry throws a pine cone at him, Henry justifies his own flight: "There was the law, he said. Nature had given him a sign." But he is not content to look upon himself as on the squirrel's level. He feels guilt over his cowardice. When he carries the flag in the later skirmishes, he is not a terrified chicken or rabbit or squirrel but a young man motivated by pride, by a sense of belonging to a group, and by a determination to show his courage to an officer who had scornfully called the soldiers in his group a lot of "mule drivers."

From the beginning, critics have both admired and complained about Crane's impressionistic writing and his use of imagery and symbols in *The Red Badge of Courage*. Edward Garnett in 1898 called Crane "the chief impressionist of our day" and praised his "wonderful fervour and freshness of style." Joseph Conrad (himself an impressionist) was struck by Crane's "genuine verbal felicity, welding analysis and description in a continuous fascination of individual style," and Conrad saw Henry as "the symbol of all untried men." By contrast, one American critic in 1898 described the novel as "a mere riot of words" and condemned "the violent straining after effect" and the "absurd similes." Though H. G. Wells liked the book as a whole, he commented on "those chromatic splashes that at times deafen and confuse in the *Red Badge,* those images that astonish rather than enlighten."

Yet judging by the continuing popularity of *The Red Badge of Courage,* most readers are not repelled by Crane's repeated use of color—"blue demonstration," "red eyes," "red animal—war," "red sun"—or by his use of images—"dark shadows that moved like monsters," "The dragons were coming," guns that "belched and howled like brass devils guarding a gate." Only in a few passages does Crane indulge in "arty" writing—"The guns squatted in a row like savage chiefs. They argued with abrupt violence"—or drop into the pathetic fallacy—"The flag suddenly sank down as if dying. Its motion as it fell was a gesture of despair." Usually the impressionistic phrasing is appropriate to the scene or to the emotional state of Henry Fleming at a particular moment, as when, after he has fought he feels heroically, the sun shines "now bright and gay in the blue, enameled sky."

A brilliant work of the imagination, *The Red Badge of Courage* will endure as what Crane afterward wrote a friend he had intended it to be, "a psychological portrayal of fear."

Bibliography

Albrecht, Robert C. "Content and Style in *The Red Badge of Courage,*" in *College English.* XXVII (March, 1966), pp. 487–492.

Berryman, John. *The Freedom of the Poet.* New York: Farrar, Straus and Giroux, 1976, pp. 176–184.

Breslin, Paul. "Courage and Convention: *The Red Badge of Courage,*" in *Yale Review.* LXVI (1976), pp. 209–222.

Burhans, Clinton S., Jr. "Judging Henry Judging: Point of View in *The Red Badge of Courage,*" in *Ball State University Forum.* XV (1974), pp. 38–48.

————. "Twin Lights on Henry Fleming: Structural Parallels in *The Red Badge of Courage,*" in *Arizona Quarterly.* XXX (1974), pp. 149–159.

Cazemajou, J. "*The Red Badge of Courage*: The 'Religion of Peace' and the War Archetype," in *Stephen Crane in Transition.* Edited by Joseph Katz. De Kalb: Northern Illinois University Press, 1972, pp. 54–65.

Cox, James T. "The Imagery of *The Red Badge of Courage,*" in *Modern Fiction Studies.* V (Autumn, 1959), pp. 209–219.

Gollin, Rita K. " 'Little Souls Who Thirst for Fight' in *The Red Badge of Courage,*" in *Arizona Quarterly.* XXX (1974), pp. 111–118.

Greenfield, Stanley B. "The Unmistakable Stephen Crane," in *PMLA.* LXXIII (December, 1958), pp. 562–572.

Hart, John E. "*The Red Badge of Courage* as Myth and Symbol," in *University of Kansas City Review.* XIX (Summer, 1953), pp. 249–256.

Hoffman, Michael J. *The Subversive Vision; American Romanticism in Literature.* Port Washington, N.Y.: Kennikat, 1973, pp. 129–139.

Hungerford, Harold R. "That Was at Chancellorsville: The Factual Framework of *The Red Badge of Courage*," in *American Literature.* XXXIV (January, 1963), pp. 520–531.

Klotz, Marvin. "Romance or Realism?: Plot, Theme, and Character in *The Red Badge of Courage*," in *College Language Association Journal.* VI (December, 1962), pp. 98–106.

Lorch, Thomas M. "The Cyclical Structure of *The Red Badge of Courage*," in *College Language Association Journal.* X (March, 1967), pp. 229–238.

Mangum, Bryant. "Crane's Red Badge and Zola's," in *American Literary Realism, 1870–1910.* IX (1976), pp. 279–280.

Marcus, Mordecai. "The Unity of *The Red Badge of Courage*," in The Red Badge of Courage: *Text and Criticism.* Edited by Richard Lettis. New York: Harcourt, Brace, 1960, pp. 189–195.

Maynard, Reid. "Red as Leitmotiv in *The Red Badge of Courage*," in *Arizona Quarterly.* XXX (1974), pp. 135–141.

Morace, Robert A. "A 'New' Review of *The Red Badge of Courage*," in *American Literary Realism, 1870–1910.* VIII (1975), pp. 163–165.

Rathbun, John W. "Structure and Meaning in *The Red Badge of Courage*," in *Ball State University Forum.* X (Winter, 1969), pp. 8–16.

Rechnitz, Robert M. "Depersonalization and the Dream in *The Red Badge of Courage*," in *Studies in the Novel* (North Texas State University). VI (1974), pp. 76–87.

Solomon, Eric. "The Structure of *The Red Badge of Courage*," in *Modern Fiction Studies.* V (Autumn, 1959), pp. 220–234.

Van Meter, Jan. "Sex and War in *The Red Badge of Courage*: Cultural Themes and Literary Criticism," in *Genre.* VII (1974), pp. 71–90.

Vanderbilt, Kermit and Daniel Weiss. "From Rifleman to Flagbearer: Henry Fleming's Separate Peace in *The Red Badge of Courage*," in *Modern Fiction Studies.* XI (Winter, 1965/66), pp. 371–380.

Weiss, Daniel. "*The Red Badge of Courage*," in *Psychoanalytic Review.* LII (Summer, 1965), pp. 35–52 and LII (Fall, 1965), pp. 130–154.

Zambrano, Ana Laura. "The Role of Nature in *The Red Badge of Courage*," in *Arizona Quarterly.* XXX (1974), pp. 164–166.

COUNTEE CULLEN

Born: New York, N.Y. (May 30, 1903)
Died: Tuckahoe, New York (January 10, 1946)

Principal Works

POETRY: *Color*, 1925; *Copper Sun*, 1927; *Ballad of the Brown Girl*, 1927; *The Black Christ and Other Poems*, 1929; *The Medea and Some Poems*, 1935; *On These I Stand*, 1947.
ANTHOLOGY: *Caroling Dusk*, 1927.
CHILDREN'S BOOKS: *The Lost Zoo*, 1940; *My Lives and How I Lost Them*, 1942.
NOVEL: *One Way to Heaven*, 1932.

Countee Cullen wrote and published his work during a period which was known as the Harlem Renaissance. In the late 1920's and early 1930's Americans were, for the first time, beginning to take a serious interest in Negro art; Negro nightclubs were sought out by white patrons, Negro poetry and novels were published by major companies, and Harlem was a cultural center. Yet life in Harlem during this period was not typical of life for Negroes throughout the United States, and Countee Cullen grew up in isolation from many of the problems facing black Americans. As a result, his work is not written in great protest or in excessive self-consciousness of his racial condition; perhaps for this reason, his work always found a publisher. At the same time, Cullen's one novel and his poems which depict the conditions of Negro life strike the contemporary reader as presenting a very unbiased, clear picture of a world in which good and evil are balanced and in which man finally must be judged as an individual rather than as a representative of his race.

Countee (pronounced Coun-tay) Cullen was born Countee Porter in New York City on May 30, 1903. Little is known of his early childhood except that he attended Sunday school regularly and was a bright student at public school. In 1918, his grandmother, with whom he lived, died, and Countee was adopted by the Reverend Frederick Asbury Cullen, pastor of the Salem Methodist Episcopal Church in Harlem which Countee attended. Reverend Cullen and his wife Carolyn were childless and were attracted by young Countee's devoutness and intellectual precocity.

On February 4, 1918, Countee Cullen enrolled in DeWitt Clinton High School, a predominantly white college preparatory school. At DeWitt Clinton, Cullen was editor-in-chief of the *Clinton News* and associate editor of *The Magpie*, the student literary magazine where he first published his poetry. In January 1921 his poem "I Have a Rendezvous with Life" won first prize in a poetry contest and was published in several local newspapers. Cullen was vice president of his graduating class at DeWitt Clinton, a member of Arista (the honor society), chairman of the Senior Publications Committee, and treasurer of the Inter-High School Poetry Association.

In 1922 Cullen began studies at New York University, majoring in literature. In 1923, his sophomore year at New York University, Cullen's poem "Ballad of the Brown Girl" won second prize in the Witter Bynner undergraduate poetry contest sponsored by the Poetry Society of America. By the spring of 1924 Cullen had published poetry in *Harper's*, *Poetry*, and *The Nation*. In 1925, his senior year, Cullen was elected to Phi Beta Kappa and had his first book of poetry, *Color*, published by Harper and Brothers.

In the summer of 1925 the NAACP magazine, *The Crisis*, sponsored a literature and art competition. The judges for the literature contest included Sinclair Lewis and Eugene O'Neill. Countee Cullen received the first place award for poetry while his friends, Frank Horne and Langston Hughes, received the second and third place awards.

Cullen's poetics were conservative; he distrusted "free verse" and admired the English Romanticists, especially Keats. Yet the subject matter of his poetry frequently focused on the problems facing American Negroes or on the Negro heritage. Still Cullen was able to admire the very different work of his contemporary and friend, Langston Hughes, although he satirizes a Hughes-like poet in his novel, *One Way to Heaven*. Cullen's politics, as well, were somewhat conservative at this time, despite his father's active role in obtaining rights for Negroes.

Cullen's success as a poet began to bring invitations to read his poems and to address various audiences on the subject of poetry. In the spring of 1926, the Civic Club of Baltimore invited Cullen to read his poetry at the Emerson Hotel in that city. When Cullen arrived by train in Baltimore, he was met by representatives of the Civic Club who informed him that the management of the Emerson Hotel refused to allow the reading to take place as they only allowed white guests. The Civic Club had sent Cullen a letter informing him that the reading had been cancelled, but it had not arrived in Cambridge (where Cullen was attending graduate school) by the time Cullen left for Baltimore. For the first time in his life Cullen had come face to face with racial discrimination.

In June of 1926 Cullen received the degree of Master of Arts from Harvard University. That summer he and his father toured Europe and the Holy Land; the congregation of Reverend Cullen's church paid for the trip in recognition of his twenty-five years of service in the church.

After returning from Europe, Cullen began working on the editorial staff of *Opportunity: A Journal of Negro Life*, the magazine published by the Urban League. He developed a column of his own, "The Dark Tower," in which he reviewed Negro achievements in art, literature, and theater. In December of 1926 Cullen won a poetry award from the Harmon Foundation for *Color*, and early in 1927 his second book of poetry, *Copper Sun*, was published. *Copper Sun* did not achieve the acclaim of his first book, but an interesting review of the book in *The Nation* stated that Cullen "can forget that he is of the colored race and be just 'poet' most of the time."

Because of his work on *Opportunity*, Cullen was made aware of the work of other Negro artists, and this allowed him to prepare an anthology of verse by black poets, *Caroling Dusk*, which was published in 1927. Included in the anthology were poems by Paul Laurence Dunbar (who Cullen considered the first Negro to achieve recognition as an American poet), Claude McKay, Langston Hughes, and Arna Bontemps. Cullen felt that black writers should not be restricted to subject matter dealing with their race and tried to include poems in the anthology which were universal in their topics—among these were poems written by an eight-year-old Negro girl named Lula Lowe Weeden. The anthology and Cullen's philosophy in preparing it were important because they revealed the desire on the part of the Negro artist to be considered as an artist first. Cullen stated in his introduction to the anthology that "this country's Negro writers may here and there turn some singular facet toward the literary sun, but in the main, since theirs is also the heritage of the English language, their work will not present any serious aberration from the poetic tendencies of their times."

On April 9, 1928, Cullen married Yolande Du Bois, the daughter of W. E. B. Du Bois. Cullen had known Yolande for several years—while he was at New York University and Yolande was attending Fisk University, they frequently met during school vacations. The wedding itself was an elaborate affair, with sixteen bridesmaids and decorations consisting of live canaries in gilded cages. After their honeymoon, Cullen returned to his job on the *Opportunity* in New York, and Yolande returned to her teaching job in Baltimore. The marriage ended in divorce in 1929.

In June of 1928 Cullen moved to Paris to work under a Guggenheim Fellowship. In Paris he completed a long narrative poem, "The Black Christ," which tells the story of a Negro boy who is lynched yet miraculously resurrected. It is the story of how Christian faith is tried by prejudice and cruelty. Early in 1929 Cullen's third volume of poetry, *The Black Christ and Other Poems*, was published.

Cullen returned to New York in the fall of 1930 and began working on a novel in which he planned to contrast the two sides of life in Harlem. The novel was published under the title *One Way to Heaven* in February 1932. In the novel Cullen incorporates the life of Harlem with which he was familiar, including portraits of persons he might have known, prefacing the novel with the intriguing note: "Some of the characters in this book are fictitious."

During this period Cullen collaborated with Arna Bontemps to rewrite Bontemps' novel, *God Sends Sunday*, as a play, thus beginning a venture which was not to be completed until after Cullen's death. (Cullen and Bontemps later rewrote the play as a musical with Harold Arlen and Johnny Mercer, and it was finally performed on Broadway as "St. Louis Woman," with Pearl Bailey in the cast, in April of 1946.)

In December of 1934 Cullen began a career as a public school teacher at Frederick Douglass Junior High School 139, teaching French and English. As a teacher, Cullen taught poetry-writing, established literary awards for his students, and gave them an annual Christmas party at his home.

In September 1940 Cullen married Ida Mae Roberson whom he had met through her brother Harry in 1931. Also in 1940 he published a book for children, *The Lost Zoo*, which was originally written for his godchildren and supposedly co-authored by his cat Christopher. The success of *The Lost Zoo* led Cullen to tell more of Christopher's story in *My Lives and How I Lost Them* (1942).

In the last years of his life Cullen suffered from ulcers and hypertension but continued teaching and writing. In 1945 he wrote to Harper and Brothers with regard to a volume of selected poems, including what he considered to be his best work. The volume was published posthumously in 1947 (*On These I Stand*). Cullen died of uremic poisoning on January 10, 1946.

Bibliography

The only complete biographical study of Countee Cullen is Blanche E. Ferguson's *Countee Cullen and the Negro Renaissance*, 1966. *A Bio-Bibliography of Countee P. Cullen 1903–1946* by Margaret Perry, 1971, contains a useful biographical sketch as well as an assessment of Cullen's poetry and complete bibliographical information. Houston A. Baker, Jr., has written a study of Cullen's poetry, *A Many-Colored Coat of Dreams: The Poetry of Countee Cullen*, 1974.

ONE WAY TO HEAVEN

Type of work: Novel
Author: Countee Cullen (1903–1946)
Time of plot: 1929
Locale: Harlem, New York City
First published: 1932

In his only novel, Countee Cullen presents, against the background of Harlem in the period of the Negro Renaissance, the unregenerate Sam Lucas, a con man who uses the church as the setting for his game, a womanizer who falls in love, a liar whose final lie finds him "one way to heaven."

Principal Characters

Sam Lucas, a one-armed drifter from Texas who makes his living by faking dramatic conversions at church revivals. By throwing a deck of cards and razor on the altar, he earns a living from the donations of other church members who are impressed by the drama and feel pity for the one-armed man. He is a womanizer who has never really been in love, but who falls in love with Mattie Johnson because she is different, a non-believer who nonetheless sees the opulent Mount Hebron African Methodist Episcopal Church as a sign that his "people sure are rising." More crafty than intelligent, his striking appearance belies this fact.

Mattie Johnson, first seen as a Mary Magdelene figure, an attractive girl dressed flashily in red and black. After her conversion, effected by Sam Lucas's dramatic gesture, she is revealed to have been innocent both of sin and of any particular feeling for religion. Employed as Constancia Brandon's maid, she is proud to be working for one of her own people. She is sensible except in matters of love and religion where she reveals herself to be both too impressionable and too rigid. After her conversion, she becomes even more devout than Aunt Mandy and ultimately drives Sam away from her.

Aunt Mandy, a thin yellow woman, Mattie's aunt, who represents one set of dualities in the Negro world—the church vs. popular superstition, the sacred versus the secular. At church she is seen soberly dressed, without jewelry; while at home she wears golden hoops in her ears and rings "of dubious value." She represents a balance of which Mattie is incapable and realizes that "loving" is more important than religion.

Constancia Brandon, a sophisticated Harlem socialite. A doctor's wife, a Radcliffe graduate, and daughter of a well-to-do well-educated Negro family, she changes her name from Constance to Constancia in order to fit her more flamboyant and secular self-image. Constancia enjoys "pranks"—manipulating the guests at her soirées to see how they will respond, baiting them with her comments. She is intelligent, warm, and generous.

Reverend Drummond, the minister of the Mount Hebron African Methodist Episcopal Church. He is portrayed as understanding, realistic, and tolerant.

Reverend Clarence Johnson, the Texas evangelist who preaches the sermon at the Mount Hebron Church the night Sam Lucas arrives in Harlem. He is capable of sarcasm, which he turns on Sam after recognizing him at the revival, and of discretion—he does not give Sam away out of sympathy for Mattie.

Emma May, the attractive usher at the theater where Sam works as ticket chopper. She becomes Sam's mistress after he leaves Mattie.

Bradley Norris, the free verse poet. He attempts a sonnet at one of Constancia's soirées and fails utterly.

Lady Hyacinth and the **Duchess of Uganda,** Negro women who are participants in the Back to Africa movement and frequent guests of Constancia Brandon's.

Mrs. Harold De Peyster Johnson, a public school teacher who is said to have "midwifed at the New Negro's birth." She is often present at Constancia Brandon's soirées.

Professor Seth Calhoun, a white Southerner, tall, thin-lipped, and pale. He has written a book on his theory of the racial inferiority of the Negro, which he discusses at one of Constancia Brandon's gatherings.

Lottie Smith, a blues singer, "slight, brown, and indescribably chic," she frequently attends Constancia's soirées.

Essay-Review

Countee Cullen is best known for his poetry, yet his one novel, *One Way to Heaven,* is probably more accessible than his poetry to the contemporary student of literature. The qualities of irony and sarcasm which are apparent in many of his epitaphs are more effectively used in the novel, enhanced by the technique of understatement. Cullen's poetry generally tends to be conservative in statement and traditional in form and does not tend to dwell on the special position of the Negro. His novel, however, presents a realistic portrayal of Negro life during the period of the Negro Renaissance in Harlem; because of its realism, the novel inevitably deals with the dilemmas confronting black Americans in that era.

When Sam Lucas arrives in Harlem, his first stop is the Mount Hebron Methodist Episcopal Church. It is here, following his con-game conversion, that he meets Mattie Johnson, who herself is converted as a result of Sam's act. A short time later, Sam and Mattie are married, and Sam moves in with Mattie and her Aunt Mandy. While Mattie goes to work as maid for Constancia Brandon, a well-educated Harlem socialite, Sam stays at home and plays cards with Aunt Mandy. As Mattie becomes more devoted to religion, Sam becomes disenchanted with the woman he married. When he finds work in a theater with the help of Constancia Brandon, he also finds a companion more to his liking in the usher, Emma May. He finally leaves Mandy to live with Emma May. However, when he becomes seriously ill, Mattie takes him in. Sam's final con-game comes when he overhears Mattie tell Aunt Mandy that she would like to know if Sam will be saved. Overhearing Aunt Mandy's stories of deathbed visions, Sam fakes such a vision to satisfy Mattie's wish.

One Way to Heaven, in its subject matter and selection of characters, would seem to be a forerunner of more recent black fiction, such as James Baldwin's *Go*

Tell It on the Mountain or Ralph Ellison's *Invisible Man*; but its broader scope of presentation and its style indicate more conservative antecedents, such as Theodore Dreiser or Sinclair Lewis. Like Dreiser or Lewis, Cullen presents with reportorial accuracy an all-inclusive picture of the society in which he actually lived. His prefatory remark that "some of the characters in this book are fictitious" tempts the reader to search for those characters which are not. Cullen's father was the minister of a large African Methodist Episcopal church in Harlem—is Reverend Drummond a portrait of Frederick Cullen? Cullen attended literary soirées at the homes of A'Leilia Walker and Lillian Alexander (like Constancia Brandon in the novel, a doctor's wife)—is the character of Constancia Brondon modeled after these ladies? Could the "free verse" poet, Bradley Norris, who badly bungles his attempt at a sonnet at one of Constancia's parties, be traditionalist Cullen's gentle sarcasm at the expense of his friend Langston Hughes? It might also be noted that canaries in golded cages appeared when Cullen and Yolande Du Bois married as well as at the fictional wedding of Sam Lucas and Mattie Johnson.

One Way to Heaven portrays life in Harlem in terms of various dualisms. Some critics, in fact, see *One Way to Heaven* as two novels: the satirical novel dealing with the world of Constancia Brandon and the realistic novel dealing with Mattie Johnson and Sam Lucas. These critics see the satirical portions of Cullen's novel as a flaw, but in light of the central dualisms persented in the story of Sam and Mattie, they can be seen to play an important part.

The successful characters in the novel—Aunt Mandy and Constancia Brandon—are those who can carry these dualisms in balance within themselves. The unsuccessful characters—Mattie Johnson and Sam Lucas—feel that their lives have room for only one world view.

The worlds of black and white, poor and rich, exist in harmony in the character of Constancia Brandon, who is Cullen's vehicle for social comment in the novel. Constancia "had never experienced any racial disturbances or misgivings, attributing her equanimity on this score to one English grandfather, one grandfather black as soot, one grandmother the color of coffee and cream in the most felicitous combination, one creole grandmother, and two sane parents." When she arranges Mattie's wedding, Constancia responds to Mattie's request that no white people be invited with dismay at Mattie's prejudice and with practicality—Constancia's white friends would have provided substantial wedding gifts. Her own literary gatherings are fully integrated, reflecting her belief that everyone is as enlightened as she is. Two of these evenings are fully described in Chapters 9 and 10 of the novel. The day that "Professor Seth Calhoun of Alabama lectured at the home of Mrs. Constancia Brandon" is reported as a landmark in Harlem social history. Constancia has invited the professor to lecture to her guests on the subject of his book, *The Menace of the Negro to Our American Civilization*; the occasion provides Constancia and the reader with an opportunity to observe the reactions of certain "stock-figures" of the era. Among the guests are Mrs. De

Peyster Johnson, the Harlem school teacher who insists on black racial purity to the extent of rejecting a light-colored suitor in favor of a darker man for whom she feels no real love; Miss McGoffin, the missionary who naïvely assumes that all Negroes long to be Christianized; Donald Hewitt, the wealthy young Englishman who finds real "Yankee freedom of speech" only among American Negroes; Lottie Smith, the blues singer who shocks Miss McGoffin with her pagan appearance; and the Duchess of Uganda and Lady Hyacinth Brown—the former an elocutionist, the latter a housewife—who are ardent participants in the Back to Africa movement. Each of these characters is subjected to Constancia's straight-faced sarcasm; of all the assembled guests, only Miss McGoffin, Mrs. De Peyster Johnson, and Donald Hewitt are offended by Professor Calhoun's lecture. The Duchess and Lady Hyacinth arrive just as Professor Calhoun is concluding his remarks with the suggestion that all American Negroes should be returned to Africa; having missed his statement of reasons for this suggestion, the ladies applaud him vehemently. Constancia herself views the evening's events as a kind of test of the sense of perspective and the sense of humor among her people—qualities of which she has an abundance.

Aunt Mandy represents the balance between the secular and the religious. She has respect for both worlds but sees neither as absolute. She attends church regularly but also observes the traditions of popular superstition, such as serving black-eyed peas and rice on New Year's Day to ensure good luck and telling fortunes with her cards. She recognizes that love is more important than religion and tries to warn Mattie of the dangers of depending wholly on the church to solve her problems with Sam.

The story of *One Way to Heaven*, however, is not the story of Constancia Brandon or of Aunt Mandy, but the story of Sam Lucas and Mattie Johnson, their divergent views on love and religion, and their diverging paths. Sam and Mattie meet at the Mount Hebron African Methodist Episcopal Church on Watch Day, New Year's Eve; they have gone there for the wrong reasons—Sam to fulfill the next episode in his career con-game, Mattie to assuage her aunt. Both are skeptical of the reality in religion—Sam because of his own success with his mock-conversions, Mattie because she simply has never been convinced. Throughout their relationship the church functions as a catalyst while the deck of cards and the razor—the tools of Sam's game and Mattie's conversion—are the major symbols of their differing attitudes.

The church itself is never presented as hypocritical or disruptive of the lives of its members. Both Reverend Johnson and Reverend Drummond are portrayed as wise and reasonable men: the former does not give Sam's treachery away, the latter saves the relationship of Sam and Mattie for a while. It is only the reactions of individuals to the church, Sam's extreme contempt and fear and Mattie's total devotion, that are potentially destructive.

The cards and razor symbolize the greatly different characters of Sam and Mattie. To Sam they are tools to be used in the secular world (he is a gambler and a scrapper) at first she prays over them and finally she uses them in an occult ritual to bring Sam back to her). Aunt Mandy, who is able to separate the worldly from the religious and to exist comfortably on both levels, sees Sam's cards as cleansed by his gesture in church and therefore no longer special and adds that "it all depends on the kind of cards you have and what you do with them." She has her own deck of cards for fortune-telling and readily learns to gamble with Sam. Mattie is horrified when she discovers them playing with "her" cards after Aunt Mandy's cards have been accidentally burned.

One Way to Heaven is a successful novel because of its overriding ambiguity. After her husband nearly murders her, after she loses her baby, Mattie nears Aunt Mandy's view of the great importance of loving, of an acceptance of the "sweet trouble" which men bring; but when Sam is dying, she cares more to have some concrete evidence of his being saved. Sam plays one more trick on the faithful of the world by faking a deathbed vision, thus saving himself in her eyes and allowing Mattie to return to the complacency of her dependence on religion. Does Sam's ultimate selfless gesture constitute his "way to heaven" or is he eternally damned for never giving up the game?

Bibliography

Bone, Robert. *The Negro Novel in America.* New Haven: Yale University Press, 1958; rev. 1965, pp. 78–80.

Bronz, Stephen H. *Roots of Negro Racial Consciousness.* New York: Libra, 1964, pp. 63–64.

Ferguson, Blanche E. *Countee Cullen and the Negro Renaissance.* New York: Dodd, Mead, & Co., 1966.

Turner, Darwin T. "Countee Cullen: The Lost Ariel," in *In a Minor Chord.* Carbondale: Southern Illinois Univ. Press, 1971, pp. 77–82.

JOHN DOS PASSOS

Born: Chicago, Illinois (January 14, 1896)
Died: Baltimore, Maryland (September 23, 1970)

Principal Works

NOVELS: *One Man's Initiation: 1917*, 1920; *Three Soldiers*, 1921; *Streets of Night*, 1923; *Manhattan Transfer*, 1925; *The 42nd Parallel*, 1930; *1919*, 1932; *The Big Money*, 1936; *U. S. A.*, 1937 (The 42nd Parallel, *1919*, and *The Big Money*); *Adventures of a Young Man*, 1939; *Number One*, 1943; *The Grand Design*, 1948; *District of Columbia*, 1953 (*Adventures of a Young Man, Number One*, and *The Grand Design*); *Chosen Country*, 1951; *Most Likely to Succeed*, 1954; *Midcentury, 1961*, 1961.

POEMS: *A Pushcart at the Curb*, 1922.

MEMOIR: *The Best Times*, 1966.

PLAYS: *The Garbage Man*, 1926; *Airways, Inc.*, 1928; *Three Plays*, 1934.

TRAVEL AND REPORTING: *Rosinante to the Road Again*, 1922; *Orient Express*, 1927; *In All Countries*, 1934; *Journeys Between Wars*, 1938; *State of the Nation*, 1944; *Tour of Duty*, 1946; *Brazil on the Move*, 1961; *The Portugal Story*, 1969; *Easter Island: Island of Enigma*, 1971.

HISTORICAL ESSAYS AND STUDIES: *The Ground We Stand On*, 1941; *The Head and Heart of Thomas Jefferson*, 1953; *The Men Who Made Our Nation*, 1956; *Mr. Wilson's War*, 1962; *The Shackles of Power: Three Jeffersonian Decades*, 1966.

Of Portuguese-American ancestry, John (Roderigo) Dos Passos was born in Chicago on January 14, 1896, and educated at Harvard, from which he was graduated in 1916. During the First World War he served in the ambulance corps, and from his experiences grew his first novel to attract attention, *Three Soldiers*, a contribution to a large body of fiction, both European and American, which aimed to strip war of any shreds of glamour or romance that might still cling to it. Disillusioned like so many of the now famous "lost generation," Dos Passos next turned his attention to an exhaustive study of the American scene, trying to pack into *Manhattan Transfer* and the trilogies that followed it a picture, as nearly complete as possible, of American society during a significant and crucial period of our national history.

During his early career as a novelist Dos Passos displayed distinctly leftist and unorthodox sympathies that he carried into practice to the extent of being jailed for joining a picket line during the furor that attended the Sacco-Vanzetti case. This was the period of the so-called "proletarian" novel, a type that he did much to form, not only by his technical devices but especially by his sympathies with the underdog, those whom he considered to be exploited and abused by the American system. During the depression years, when so much in our national life was under sharp criticism, the point of view maintained by Dos Passos and his imitators had great popularity and influence.

In massive novels crowded with characters, like *U. S. A.* and *District of Columbia*, the real protagonist is, as has often been remarked, society itself. That is to say, the author exerts as much effort to describe and make real the social scene of a given period as a traditional novelist would expend upon the development of a human hero. The "characters," in the conventional sense of the word, are subordinate to society; the important point is the effect that the social and particularly the economic milieu has upon the individual. Thus it is vital for the success of the book that the reader be given as vivid a picture of the era as is possible. To accomplish this purpose, Dos Passos employed a variety of technical devices: the "Camera Eye," which focused on atmospheric details subjectively and impressionistically rendered; the "Newsreel," made up of snatches of popular songs, quotations from speeches, reproductions of newspaper headlines and related reportage of the time, and interpolated biographical sketches of real personages whose activities coincided with those of his fictional creations. It was a kind of literary *découpage* which at times was very successful. The accuracy of detail, adding up to a portrait of modern America, won the highest praise of Sinclair Lewis, himself a master of realistic reporting.

The Spanish Civil War was a disillusioning experience to Dos Passos, as it was to many writers; it was to turn his sympathies toward the political Right and to deepen his interest in American history and the democratic tradition. It was a shift, however, which lost him the support of some of his earlier admirers. Further, critics were not so kind to his more recent novels; the documentary style, they felt, had been overworked. Nevertheless, Dos Passos' novels are important in that they reveal varied aspects of American life from a sociological viewpoint hitherto largely ignored.

Bibliography

There is a recent biographical study, *John Dos Passos: A Twentieth Century Odyssey* by Townsend Ludingtion, 1980. For evaluations of Dos Passos' work see Granville Hicks, *The Great Tradition*, 1933; Joseph Warren Beach, *American Fiction, 1920–1940*, 1941; Maxwell Geismar, *Writers in Crisis*, 1942; Alfred Kazin, *On Native Grounds*, 1942; George Snell, *The Shapers of American Fiction*, 1947; W. M. Frohock, *The Novel of Violence in America*, 1950; J. W. Aldridge, *After the Lost Generation*, 1951; John H. Wrenn, *John Dos Passos*, 1961; Robert G. Davis, *John Dos Passos*, 1962; John D. Brantley, *The Fiction of John Dos Passos*, 1968; and Allen Belkind, ed., *John Dos Passos: The Critics and the Writer's Intention* (essays by various hands), 1971.

See also Alan Calmer, "John Dos Passos," *Sewanee Review*, XL (1932), 341–349; Michael Gold, "The Education of John Dos Passos: Anatomist of Our

Time," *Saturday Review of Literature*, XIV (1936), 3–4, 12–13, Delmore Schwartz, "John Dos Passos and the Whole Truth,"*Southern Review* IV (1938), 351–367; Lionel Trilling, "The America of John Dos Passos," *Partisan Review*, IV (1938), 26–32; Granville Hicks, "Politics and John Dos Passos," *Antioch Review*, X (1950), 85–98; and Milton Rugoff, "Dos Passos, Novelist of Our Time," *Sewanee Review*, XLIX (1941), 453–494.

U.S.A.

Type of work: Novel
Author: John Dos Passos (1896–1970)
Time of plot: 1900–1935
Locale: The United States
First published: 1930, 1932, 1936

The separate titles of Dos Passos' major trilogy are The 42nd Parallel. Nineteen Nineteen. *and* The Big Money. *A sprawling, powerful collective novel written from the point of view of Marxist determinism,* U. S. A. *attempts to offer a complete cross-section of American life covering the political, social, and economic history of the people from the beginning of the century to the depression-ridden 1930's.*

Principal Characters

Fenian O'Hara McCreary, called **Fainy Mac,** a young Irishman who learns the printing trade from an uncle, whose bankruptcy puts McCreary out of a job and makes a tramp of him. Because of his skill as a printer McCreary is able to find work here and there, one with a shoddy outfit called the Truthseeker Literary Distributing Co., Inc., and he travels from place to place, usually riding on freight trains. In his travels he falls in with members of the I.W.W. and becomes an earnest worker in that labor movement. He marries Maisie Spencer, but eventually they quarrel and he leaves his family in California when he goes to become a labor organizer in Mexico. There he lives a free and easy life.

Maisie Spencer, a shopgirl who marries Fainy McCreary. She is unable to share his radical views and they part.

Janey Williams, a girl who wants a career in business. She becomes a stenographer and through her luck and skill is hired as secretary to J. Ward Moorehouse, a prominent man in public relations. She becomes an efficient, if sour, woman who makes a place for herself in

business. Her great embarrassment is her brother Joe, a sailor who shows up periodically in her life with presents for her.

Joe Williams, Janey Williams' brother, a young man who cannot accept discipline. He loves life at sea and becomes a merchant seaman after deserting from the Navy. Although he is in and out of scrapes all the time he manages to qualify as a second officer during World War I. His life ends when a Senegalese hits him over the head with a bottle in a brawl over a woman in the port of St. Nazaire.

Della Williams, Joe Williams' wife. Although she is cold to her husband and claims that she is modest, she comes to believe during World War I that it is her patriotic duty to entertain men in uniform all she can, much to her husband's chagrin.

J. Ward Moorehouse, an opportunist who becomes a leading public relations and advertising executive. He is anxious to succeed in life and to have a hand in many activities. His first wife is Annabelle Strang, a wealthy, promiscuous woman, his second, Gertrude Staple, who helps him in his career. Though he succeeds as a businessman, he is unhappy in his domestic life, to which he gives all too little time because he prefers a whole series of women to his wife. A heart attack finally persuades him that the life he leads is not a fruitful one.

Annabelle Strang, the wealthy, amoral woman who becomes J. Ward Moorehouse's first wife.

Gertrude Staple, J. Ward Moorehouse's second wife, a wealthy young woman whose family and fortune help her husband become established as a public relations counselor. She becomes mentally ill and spends many years in a sanitarium.

Eleanor Stoddard, a poor girl from Chicago. Gifted with artistic talent, she sets herself up an interior decorator and succeeds professionally. She becomes a hard, shallow, but attractive woman. While serving as a Red Cross worker in Europe, she becomes J. Ward Moorehouse's mistress for a time. Always climbing socially, she becomes engaged to an exiled Russian nobleman in New York after World War I.

Eveline Hutchins, the daughter of a liberal clergyman. She becomes Eleanor Stoddard's erstwhile business partner. A young woman who spends her life seeking pleasure and escape from boredom, her life is a series of rather sordid love affairs, both before and after marriage. She finally commits suicide.

Paul Johnson, Eveline Hutchins' shy and colorless soldier husband, whom she meets in France while doing Red Cross work.

Charley Anderson, a not very promising youth who becomes famous as an aviator during World War I. He cashes in on his wartime reputation and makes a great deal of money, both as an inventor and as a trader on the stock market. His loose sexual morality and his heavy drinking lose him his wife, his jobs, his fortune, and finally his life. He dies as the result of an auto accident which happens while he is drunk. He has a brief love affair with Eveline Hutchins.

Margo Dowling, the daughter of a ne'er-do-well drunkard. Through her beauty and talent she makes her own way in the world and becomes a movie star after many amatory adventures. For a time she is Charley Anderson's mistress.

Agnes Mandeville, Margo Dowling's stepmother, friend, and financial adviser. She is a shrewd woman with money.

Frank Mandeville, a broken-down vaudeville actor and Agnes' husband. A lost man after the advent of motion pictures, he spends much of his time trying to seduce Margo Dowling and eventually rapes her.

Tony de Carrida, Margo Dowling's first husband, an effeminate Cuban musician who is finally reduced to being Margo's uniformed chauffeur.

Sam Margolies, a peculiar but successful movie producer who "discovers" Margo Dowling and makes her a movie star. He becomes her second husband.

Richard Ellsworth Savage, called **Dick,** a bright young man and a Harvard graduate who wishes to become a poet. He meets J. Ward Moorehouse and ends up as a junior partner in Moorehouse's firm.

The Story

The Spanish-American War was over. Politicians with mustaches said that America was now ready to lead the world.

Mac McCreary was a printer for a fly-by-night publisher in Chicago. Later he worked his way to the West Coast. There he got work as a printer in Sacramento and married Maisie Spencer, who could never understand his radical views. They quarreled and he went to Mexico to work in the revolutionary movement there.

Janey Williams, growing up in Washington, D.C., became a stenographer. She was always ashamed when her sailor brother, Joe, showed up, and even more ashamed of him after she became secretary to J. Ward Moorehouse. Of all Moorehouse's female acquaintances, she was the only one who never became his mistress.

J. Ward Moorehouse's boyish manner and blue eyes were the secret of his success. They attracted Annabelle Strang, the wealthy nymphomaniac he later divorced. Gertrude Staple, his second wife, helped to make him a prominent public relations expert. His shrewdness made him an ideal man for government service in France during World War I. After the war he became one of the nation's leading advertising executives.

Because Eleanor Stoddard hated the sordid environment of her childhood her delicate, arty tastes led her naturally into partnership with Eveline Hutchins in the decorating business, and eventually to New York and acquaintanceship with J. Ward Moorehouse. In Europe with the Red Cross during the war, she lived with Moorehouse. Back in New York in the twenties she used her connections in shrewd fashion and became engaged to a member of the Russian nobility.

Charley Anderson had been an aviator in the war. A successful invention and astute opportunism made him a wealthy airplane manufacturer. He married a wife who had little sympathy for his interest in mechanics. In Florida, after a plane crash, he met Margo Dowling, an actress. Charley Anderson's series of drunks ended in a grade crossing accident.

Joe Williams was a sailor who had been on the beach in Buenos Aires. In Norfolk he met Della, who urged him to give up seafaring and settle down. Unable to hold a job, he shipped out again and almost lost his life when the ship he was on was sunk by a German submarine. When Joe got his third mate's license, he and Della were married. He was ill in the East Indies, arrested in New York for not carrying a draft card, and torpedoed once more off Spain. Della was unfaithful to him. Treated coldly the few times he looked up his sister Janey, he shipped for Europe once more. One night in St. Nazaire he attacked a huge Senegalese who was dancing with a girl he knew. His skull was crushed when he was hit over the head with a bottle.

Teachers encouraged Dick Savage in his literary talents. During his teens he worked at a summer hotel and there he slept with a minister's wife who shared his taste in poetry. A government official paid his way through Harvard, where Dick cultivated his estheticism and mild snobbery before he joined the Norton-Harjes ambulance service and went to Europe. There some of his letters about the war came to the attention of censorship officials and he was shipped back to the United States. His former sponsor got him an officer's commission and he returned to France. In Italy he met a relief worker named Anne Elizabeth Trent, who was his mistress for a time. When he returned to the United States, he became an idea man for Moorehouse's advertising agency.

Eveline Hutchins, who had a small artistic talent, became Eleanor Stoddard's partner in a decorating establishment in New York. All her life she tried to escape from boredom through sensation. Beginning with the Mexican artist who was her first lover, she had a succession of affairs. In France, where she was Eleanor's assistant in the Red Cross, she married a shy young soldier named Paul Johnson. Later she had a brief affair with Charley Anderson. Dissatisfied, she decided at last that life was too dull for endurance and died from an overdose of sleeping pills.

Anne Elizabeth Trent, known as Daughter, was the child of moderately wealthy Texans. In New York she met Webb Cruthers, a young anarchist. One day, seeing a policeman kick a woman picketer in the face, Daughter attacked him with her fists. Her night in jail disturbed her father so much that she returned to Texas and worked in Red Cross canteens. Later she went overseas. There she met Dick Savage. Pregnant, she learned he had no intention of marrying her. In Paris she went on a drunken spree with a French aviator and died with him in a plane crash.

Benny Compton was the son of Jewish immigrants. After six months in jail for making radical speeches, he worked his way West through Canada. In Seattle he and other agitators were beaten by deputies. Benny returned East. One day police broke up a meeting where he was speaking. On his twenty-third birthday Benny went to Atlanta to serve a ten-year sentence. Released after the war, he lived for a time with Mary French, a fellow traveler in the party.

Mary French spent her childhood in Trinidad, where her father, a physician, did charity work among the native miners. Mary, planning to become a social worker, spent her summers at Jane Addams' Hull House. She went to Washington as secretary to a union official, and later worked as a union organizer in New York City. There she took care of Ben Compton after his release from Atlanta. While working with the Sacco-Vanzetti Committee she fell in love with Don Stevens, a fellow party member. Summoned to Moscow with a group of party leaders, Stevens returned to New York with a wife assigned to him by the party. Mary went back to her committee work for laboring men's relief.

Margo Dowling grew up in a rundown house in Rockaway, Long Island, with her drunken father and Agnes, her father's mistress. At last Agnes left her lover and took Margo with her. In New York Agnes became the common-law wife of an actor named Frank Mandeville. One day, while drunk, Mandeville raped the girl. Margo ran off to Cuba with Tony, an effeminate Cuban guitar player, whom she later deserted. She was a cheerful companion for Charley Anderson, who gave her a check for five thousand dollars on his deathbed. In Hollywood she met Sam Margolies, a successful producer, who made a star of her.

Jobless and hungry, a young hitchhiker stood by the roadside. Overhead droned a plane in which people of the big money rode the skyways. Below the hitchhiker with empty belly thumbed cars speeding by. The haves and the have-nots—that was America in the depression thirties.

Critical Evaluation

John Dos Passos' statement at the beginning of *U.S.A.* that America is, more than anything else, the sounds of its many voices, offers several insights into the style and content of the trilogy. The style, for example, reflects the author's attempt to capture some sense of characteristically American "voices," not just in the idiomatic narration of the chronicles (or novel sections), but in "Newsreels," "Biographies," and "The Camera Eye" as well. While these sections reflect, respectively, the public voice of the media and popular culture, the oratorical and eulogistic voice of the biographies, and the personal and private voice of the artist, the most important voices in the trilogy are those of the chronicles in which Dos Passos introduces a cross-section of American voices ranging from the blue collar worker to the professional and managerial classes, and representing a variety of regional and ethnic backgrounds. Like Walt Whitman, who profoundly influenced him, Dos Passos takes all America as his subject matter as he tries to capture through the sounds of the many voices which characterize its people and institutions the meaning of *U.S.A.*

Many people have associated the social, political, and economic views expressed in *U.S.A.* with Marxism—as leftists in the 1930's liked to believe this important author made common cause with them—but it is really the American economist Thornstein Veblen, rather than Marx, who seems to have shaped Dos Passos' thinking about the economic and political situation in the United States during the first quarter of this century. Dos Passos had read Veblen's *The Theory of the Leisure Class, The Theory of Business Enterprise,* and other writings, and it was from these sources that his attack on the American business economy stems. In *The Big Money,* Dos Passos offers a "Biography" of Veblen in which he summarizes this economist's theories of the domination of society by monopoly capitalism and the sabotage of the workers' human rights by business interests dominated by the profit motive. According to Dos Passos, the alternatives Veblen saw were either a society strangled and its workers destroyed by the capitalists' insatiable greed for profit or a society in which the needs of those who do the work would be the prime consideration. Veblen, writing just at the turn of the century, still held out hope that the workers might yet take control of the means of production before monopoly capitalism could plunge the world into a new dark age. Dos Passos goes on to develop the idea that any such hope died with World War I, and that the American dream of democracy was dead from that time forward.

Against the background of Veblen's ideas, *U.S.A.* can be seen as a documentary chronicling the growing exploitation of the American worker by the capitalist system, and a lamentation for the lost hope of Veblen's dream of a society which would make the producer the prime beneficiary of his own labor. The best characterization of the blue collar worker is Mac McCreary— a rootless laborer constantly searching for some outlet for his idealistic hope of restoring power to the worker. Certainly one of the most sympathetic characters in *U.S.A.*, Mac dramatizes the isolation and frustration of the modern worker, who is only a human cog in the industrial machine, unable either to take pride in his work or finally to profit significantly by it. Other characters as well fit within the pattern of the capitalist system as Veblen described it, or else, like Mac, revolt against the injustice of the system. There are the exploiters and the exploited, and there are some few, like Mary French and Ben Compton, who make opposition to the system a way of life. Equally prevalent are those characters who dramatize Veblen's theory of conspicuous consumption by serving as playthings (Margo Dowling), lackeys (Dick Savage), or promoters (J. Ward Moorehouse) for those who control the wealth and power.

Throughout the trilogy, the essential conflict is that between the business interests who control the wealth, and the workers who produce it. But Dos Passos is almost equally concerned with the way in which the system of monopoly capitalism exploits and destroys even those of the managerial class who seem to profit most immediately from it. Dick Savage, for example, starts out as a talented young writer only to be corrupted by the system. And Charlie Anderson, who early could be seen as typifying the American dream of success through ingenuity and imagination, dies as much a victim of the system as any of its workers. J. Ward Moorehouse, on the other hand, makes nothing and produces nothing, but his is the talent that can parlay nothing into a fortune, and the mentality that can survive in the world of *U.S.A.*

The two national historical events to which Dos Passos gives most attention are World War I, and the execution of the anarchists Sacco and Vanzetti. The war, as Dos Passos saw it, under the pretense of making the world safe for democracy, gave the capitalists the opportunity they needed to solidify their power by actually crushing the democratic spirit. For Dos Passos, democracy was dead in America from World War I, and the Sacco and Vanzetti case proved it. The death of these two immigrant Italian radicals on a trumped-up charge of murder was, in Dos Passos' eyes, the ultimate demonstration of the fact that our traditional freedoms were lost and that monopoly capitalism had usurped power in America. When, in his later and more conservative years, John Dos Passos was accused of having deserted the liberal positions of his youth, he maintained that his views had not shifted from those he argued in *U.S.A.* The evidence of the novel would seem to bear him out. The *U.S.A.* trilogy is a more nostalgic than revolutionary work, and it looks back to that point in American history before the options were lost rather than forward to a socialist revolution. His finest work shows Dos Passos as a democratic idealist rather than as a socialist revolutionary.

Bibliography

Aldridge, John W. *After the Lost Generation.* New York: McGraw-Hill, 1951, pp. 71–77.

Allen, Walter. *The Modern Novel in Britain and the United States.* New York: Dutton, 1964, pp. 144–148.

Beach, Joseph Warren. *American Fiction, 1920–1940.* New York: Russell and Russell, 1960, pp. 52–66.

Blake, Nelson Manfred. *Novelist's America: Fiction as History, 1910–1940.* Syracuse, N.Y.: Syracuse University Press, 1969, pp. 168–183.

Brantley, John D. *The Fiction of John Dos Passos.* The Hague: Mouton, 1968, pp. 55–78.

Cowley, Malcolm. "The Poet Against the World," in *After the Genteel Tradition: American Writers, 1910–1930.* Carbondale: Southern Illinois University Press, 1964, pp. 134–146.

Davis, Robert G. *John Dos Passos.* Minneapolis: University of Minnesota Press, 1962, pp. 21–31.

Feied, Frederick. *No Pie in the Sky: The Hobo as American Cultural Hero in the Works of Jack London, John Dos Passos and Jack Kerouac.* New York: Citadel, 1964, pp. 41–56.

Geismar, Maxwell. *Writers in Crisis: The American Novel, 1925–1940.* Revised Edition. Boston: Houghton Mifflin, 1961, pp. 109–120, 123–130.

Gelfant, Blanche Housman. *The American City Novel.* Norman: University of Oklahoma Press, 1954, pp. 166–174.

Goldman, Arnold. "Dos Passos and His U.S.A.," in *New Literary History.* I (1970), pp. 471–483.

Gurko, Leo. "John Dos Passos' *U.S.A.*: A 1930's Spectacular," in *Proletarian Writers of the Thirties.* Edited by David Madden. Carbondale: Southern Illinois University Press, 1968, pp. 46–63.

Hoffman, Arnold R. "An Element of Structure in *U.S.A.*," in *CEA Critic.* XXXI (October, 1968), pp. 12–13.

Knox, George. "Voice in the *U.S.A.* Biographies," in *Texas Studies in Literature and Language.* IV (1962), pp. 109–116.

Lydenberg, John. "Dos Passos' *U.S.A.*: The Words of Hollow Men," in *Essays on Determinism in American Literature.* Edited by Sydney J. Frause. Kent, Oh.: Kent State University Press, 1964, pp. 97–107.

Magney, Claude-Edmonde. "Dos Passos' *U.S.A.*, or the Impersonal Novel," in *The Age of the American Novel: The Film Aesthetic of Fiction Between the Two Wars.* Translated by Eleanor Hochman. New York: Frederick Ungar, 1972, pp. 105–123.

Maynard, Reid. "John Dos Passos' One-Sided Panorama," in *Discourse.* XI (Autumn, 1968), pp. 468–474.

Millgate, Michael. *American Social Fiction: James to Cozzens.* New York: Barnes & Noble, 1965, pp. 130–135.

Sanders, David, Editor. *Studies in* U.S.A. Columbus, Oh.: Charles E. Merrill, 1971.

Schwartz, Delmore. "John Dos Passos and the Whole Truth," in *Southern Review.* IV (Autumn, 1938), pp. 351–365.

Smith, James S. "The Novelist of Discomfort: A Reconsideration of John Dos Passos," in *College English.* XIX (May, 1958), pp. 332–338.

Walcutt, Charles Child. *American Literary Naturalism, A Divided Stream.* Minneapolis: University of Minnesota Press, 1956, pp. 283–289.

THEODORE DREISER

Born: Terre Haute, Indiana (August 27, 1871)
Died: Hollywood, California (December 28, 1945)

Principal Works

NOVELS: *Sister Carrie*, 1900; *Jennie Gerhardt*, 1911; *The Financier*, 1912; *The Titan*, 1914; *The "Genius,"* 1915; *An American Tragedy*, 1925; *The Bulwark*, 1946; *The Stoic*, 1947.

SHORT STORIES: *Free and Other Stories*, 1918; *Twelve Men*, 1919; *Chains: Lesser Novels and Stories*, 1927; *A Gallery of Women*, 1929.

PLAYS: *Plays of the Natural and Supernatural*, 1916 *(The Girl in the Coffin, The Blue Sphere, Laughing Gas, In the Dark, The Spring Recital, The Light in the Window, "Old Ragpicker"); The Hand of the Potter: A Tragedy in Four Acts*, 1918.

AUTOBIOGRAPHY: *A Book About Myself*, 1922 (republished as *Newspaper Days*, 1931); *Dawn*, 1931.

ESSAYS: *Hey Rub-a-Dub-Dub*, 1920.

TRAVEL SKETCHES: *A Traveler at Forty*, 1913: *A Hoosier Holiday*, 1916; *The Color of a Great City*, 1923.

POLITICAL AND SOCIAL STUDIES: *Dreiser Looks at Russia*, 1928; *Tragic America*, 1931.

POEMS: *Moods, Cadenced and Declaimed*, 1926, 1928.

Theodore Dreiser, born in Terre Haute, Indiana, on August 27, 1871, is probably the most puzzling figure in twentieth century American literature. No other major author has survived so much hostile criticism. Nor has any other author of his stature displayed so much paradoxical thinking. Yet despite his inconsistencies and blunders, Dreiser's position is unshakable. His influence on the naturalistic American novel has been enormous; moreover, there is in his writing a peculiar power and honesty that is not to be found anywhere else.

The son of a desperately poor and narrowly religious family, Dreiser developed intense feelings about poverty and social restraint that are manifest in all his work. After a spotty schooling in various Indiana towns, he became a journalist and worked for newspapers and magazines in several cities. This work and his searching reading formed the education for his literary career. The greatest influence on Dreiser's thinking was his study of the evolutionary writers—especially Spencer, Huxley, and Darwin—who taught him to view life as a massive struggle for survival. Starting from these ideas he worked out his own theories about human behavior in terms of compulsions or "chemisms."

Sister Carrie, his first novel, was suppressed by its publisher, thus initiating

Dreiser's long series of battles with censorship. This novel tells the story of a beautiful, materialistic girl who accepts a liaison in preference to the conditions of sweatshop labor. Especially impressive is the documentation of George Hurstwood's gradual collapse and suicide. What the Grundy clan found objectionable in *Sister Carrie* was not the use of a "fallen woman," but rather Dreiser's unconventional view of her; instead of punishing Carrie, he seems to say that she was justified in seeking her welfare as best she could. *Sister Carrie* exhibits all of Dreiser's merits and defects: the clumsy writing, the overpowering earnestness, the loose construction, the massing of realistic detail.

Dreiser's next novel, *Jennie Gerhardt*, is another study of a kept woman; but Jennie is a nobler character, a lower-class girl who leaves her wealthy lover when she realizes that she stands in the way of his career. After this work came the first volume of the Frank Cowperwood "trilogy of desire": *The Financier* (published 1912, revised 1927), followed by *The Titan* in 1914, and *The Stoic* in 1947. These novels comprise a wide examination of American finance from the time of Lincoln and deal with the life of a ruthless tycoon. As a boy Cowperwood sees a lobster devour a squid and realizes, "Things lived on each other—that was it." *The "Genius"* again brought Dreiser into conflict with the censors, but this time he was championed by H. L. Mencken. Eugene Witla, the hero of the novel, is a gifted realistic painter whose sexuality conflicts with his artistic career.

An American Tragedy, Dreiser's highest achievement, was also the victim of censorship. The protagonist, Clyde Griffiths, attempts to drown his pregnant mistress because marriage to her would ruin his hopes of a rich marriage. He proves too indecisive; but the boat overturns, and he is convicted of murder. While awaiting execution, Clyde comes to understand the extent of his guilt. In contrast to this angry book, *The Bulwark*, Dreiser's mellowest novel, tells the story of a Quaker banker whose faith is deepened by the failure of his family life.

Dreiser's stories have been collected in *Free*, *Twelve Men*, *Chains*, and *A Gallery of Women*. *Plays of the Natural and Supernatural*, published in 1916, was followed by a tragedy, *The Hand of the Potter*. *Hey Rub-a-Dub-Dub* is a collection of essays. His other writings include political studies and poems, as well as books of travel sketches and reminiscence. Dreiser's autobiography, written with characteristic frankness, is contained in *A Book About Myself*—republished in 1931 as *Newspaper Days* and *Dawn*.

Theodore Dreiser was neither a clear nor original thinker. Though he assimilated many of the ideas of the evolutionists, he remained enough of a skeptic to show marked ambiguities in his work. He is both a determinist and a sentimentalist, evoking considerable pity for his defeated characters. Although he appears to believe that it is proper for a man to grab as much as possible from an indifferent or malevolent society, he came to accept many of the ideas of communism. The main theme in Dreiser's work is that of the conflict between the individual and society. In keeping with this theme, his characters are, typically, either weaklings or strong figures who seize what they want.

Dreiser died in Hollywood, California, on December 28, 1945. Although it now seems certain that his reputation will endure, it is difficult to forecast what final judgment the critics and literary historians will pass on him. It is hard to measure a giant.

Bibliography

The best biography is W. A. Swanberg, *Dreiser*, 1965. Other biographical and critical studies include Burton Rascoe, *Theodore Dreiser*, 1925; Dorothy Dudley, *Dreiser and the Land of the Free*, 1946; Robert H. Elias, *Theodore Dreiser: Apostle of Nature*, 1949; Helen Dreiser, *My Life with Dreiser*, 1951; F. O. Matthiessen, *Theodore Dreiser*, 1951; Richard Lehan, *Theodore Dreiser: His World and His Novels*, 1970; and Ellen Moers, *Two Dreisers: The Man and the Novelist*, 1970.

See also H. L. Mencken, "Theodore Dreiser," in *A Book of Prefaces*, 1917; Vernon L. Parrington, *Main Currents of American Thought*, III, 1930; Joseph Warren Beach, *The Twentieth Century Novel*, 1932; Granville Hicks, *The Great Tradition*, 1933; E. B. Burgum, *The Novel and the World's Dilemma*, 1947; George Snell, "Theodore Dreiser: Philosopher," in *Shapers of American Fiction*, 1947; F. J. Hoffman, *The Modern Novel in America, 1900–1950*, 1951; Edward Wagenknecht, *Cavalcade of the American Novel*, 1952; and Maxwell Geismar, *Rebels and Ancestors*, 1953.

AN AMERICAN TRAGEDY

Type of work: Novel
Author: Theodore Dreiser (1871–1945)
Time of plot: Early twentieth century
Locale: Kansas City, Chicago, and Lycurgus, New York
First published: 1925

Considered by most to be Dreiser's best novel, An American Tragedy *is a naturalist's indictment of the American economic system, which instills the craving and expectation for material prosperity in all its citizens, while allowing only a few to attain the dream of luxury and privilege with which it bedazzles the masses. The novel follows the career of Clyde Griffiths, a weak-willed man whose greed and false values lead him to attempt murder, and end finally in his own destruction.*

Principal Characters

Clyde Griffiths, the tragic hero. The son of itinerant evangelists and raised in poverty and in an atmosphere of narrow-minded religiosity, he has always longed for the things that money can buy. At sixteen, he gets a job as a bellboy in a Kansas City hotel and uses his unexpectedly large earnings for his own pleasure rather than to help his family. When his sister is left penniless and pregnant, he contributes only a small sum; he is buying a coat for Hortense Briggs, a shopgirl whom he is trying to seduce. Because of a wreck in a stolen car, he has to leave Kansas City. In Chicago he meets his rich uncle, Samuel Griffiths, who gives him a job in his factory at Lycurgus, New York. The job is an unimportant one, and Clyde is resented by his cousins, particularly by Gilbert. Clyde is forbidden to associate with the factory girls, but out of loneliness he becomes friendly with one of them, Roberta Alden, whom he persuades to become his mistress. Meanwhile he is taken up by Sondra Finchley, the daughter of a wealthy family, who wishes to spite Gilbert. They fall in love, and Clyde dreams of a rich marriage. But Roberta becomes pregnant and demands that he marry her, thus shattering his hopes of having all that his life has lacked. When their attempts at abortion fail, Clyde, inspired by a newspaper account of a murder, plans to murder Roberta. Though he intends to kill her, her death is actually the result of an accident. A long trial ensues; but in spite of all efforts, Clyde is convicted, and the story ends with his electrocution.

Roberta Alden, Clyde's mistress. A factory girl and the daughter of poor parents, she falls in love with Clyde, whom she meets at the factory. In spite of her moral scruples, she becomes his mistress. When she finds herself pregnant, she tries to force him to marry her, though she knows that he no longer loves her. This situation leads to her accidental death at Clyde's hands.

Titus Alden, Roberta's shiftless father.

Sondra Finchley, a wealthy girl who takes up Clyde to spite his cousin Gilbert. She falls in love with him and is planning to marry him when he is arrested for murder.

Asa Griffiths, Clyde's father, a poverty-stricken itinerant evangelist.

Elvira Griffiths, Clyde's mother, the strongest member of the family.

Hester (Esta) Griffiths, Clyde's sister, who is seduced and abandoned by an actor.

Samuel Griffiths, Clyde's uncle, a rich manufacturer who gives Clyde a job in his factory.

Elizabeth Griffiths, Samuel's wife.

Gilbert Griffiths, their son, a pompous young man who resents Clyde.

Myra Griffiths and
Bella Griffiths, daughters of Samuel and Elizabeth.

Hortense Briggs, a crude, mercenary shopgirl whom Clyde tries to seduce. She is interested only in what she can per-

suade him to spend on her.

Thomas Ratterer, a bellboy who works with Clyde and introduces him to fast life.

Willard Sparser, the boy who steals the car and causes the accident that drives Clyde from Kansas City.

Orville Mason, a ruthless and politically ambitious district attorney who prosecutes Clyde.

Burton Burleigh, Mason's assistant. In the morgue he threads some of Roberta's hair into Clyde's camera to provide the evidence necessary for conviction.

Alvin Belknap and
Reuben Jephson, defense attorneys.

Governor Waltham, of New York, who rejects Clyde's plea for commutation of sentence.

The Rev. Duncan McMillan, an evangelist. He brings Clyde spiritual comfort just before the execution.

The Story

When Clyde Griffiths was still a child, his religious-minded parents took him and his brothers and sisters around the streets of various cities, where they prayed and sang in public. The family was always very poor, but the fundamentalist faith of the Griffiths was their hope and mainstay throughout the storms and troubles of life.

Young Clyde was never religious, however, and he always felt ashamed of the existence his parents were living. As soon as he was old enough to make decisions for himself, he decided to go his own way. At sixteen he got a job as a bellboy in a Kansas City hotel. There the salary and the tips he received astonished him. For the first time in his life he had money in his pocket, and he could dress well and enjoy himself. Then a tragedy overwhelmed the family. Clyde's sister ran away, supposedly to be married. Her elopement was a great blow to the parents, but Clyde himself did not brood over the matter. Life was too pleasant for him; more and more he enjoyed the luxuries which his job provided. He made friends with the other bellhops and joined them in parties that centered around liquor and women. Clyde soon became familiar with drink and brothels.

One day he discovered that his sister was back in town. The man with whom she had run away had deserted her, and she was penniless and pregnant. Knowing his sister needed money, Clyde gave his mother a few dollars for her. He promised to give her more; instead he bought an expensive coat for a girl in the hope that she would yield herself to him. One night he and his friends went on a party in a car that did not belong to them. Coming back from their outing, they ran over a little girl. In their attempt to escape, they wrecked the car. Clyde fled to Chicago.

In Chicago he got work at the Union League Club, where he eventually met his wealthy uncle, Samuel Griffiths. The uncle, who owned a factory in Lycurgus, New York, took a fancy to Clyde and offered him work in the factory. Clyde went to Lycurgus. There his cousin, Gilbert, resented this cousin from the Middle West. The whole family, with the exception of his uncle, considered Clyde beneath them socially and would not accept him into their circle. Clyde was given a job at the very bottom of the business, but his uncle soon made him a supervisor.

In the meantime Sondra Finchley, who disliked Gilbert, began to invite Clyde to parties she and her friends often gave. Her main purpose was to annoy Gilbert. Clyde's growing popularity forced the Griffiths to receive him socially, much to Gilbert's disgust.

In the course of his work at the factory Clyde met Roberta Alden, with whom he soon fell in love. Since it was forbidden for a supervisor to mix socially with an employee, they had to meet secretly. Clyde attempted to persuade Roberta to give herself to him, but the girl refused. At last, rather than lose him, she consented and became his mistress.

At the same time Clyde was becoming fascinated by Sondra. He came to love her and hoped to marry her, and thus acquire the wealth and social position for which he yearned. Gradually he began breaking dates with Roberta in order to be with Sondra every moment that she could spare him. Roberta began to be suspicious and eventually found out the truth.

By that time she was pregnant. Clyde went to drug stores for medicine that did not work. He attempted to find a doctor of questionable reputation. Roberta went to see one physician who refused to perform an operation. Clyde and Roberta were both becoming desperate, and Clyde saw his possible marriage to the girl as a dismal ending to all his hopes for a bright future. He told himself that he did not love Roberta, that it was Sondra whom he wished to marry. Roberta asked him to marry her for the sake of her child, saying she would go away afterward, if he wished, so that he could be free of her. Clyde would not agree to her proposal and grew more irritable and worried.

One day he read in the newspaper an item about the accidental drowning of a couple who had gone boating. Slowly a plan began to form in his mind. He told Roberta he would marry her and persuaded her to accompany him to an isolated lake resort. There, as though accidentally, he lunged toward her. She was hit by his camera and fell into the water. Clyde escaped, confident that her drowning would look like an accident, even though he had planned it all carefully.

But he had been clumsy. Letters that he and Roberta had written were found, and when her condition became known he was arrested. His uncle obtained an attorney for him. At his trial, the defense built up an elaborate case in his favor. But in spite of his lawyer's efforts, he was found guilty and sentenced to be electrocuted. His mother came to see him and urged him to save his soul. A clergyman finally succeeded in getting Clyde to write a statement—a declaration that he repented of his sins. It is doubtful whether he did. He died in the electric chair, a young man tempted by his desire for luxury and wealth.

Critical Evaluation

Few readers claim to "like" the works of Theodore Dreiser, for his novels are not ones which charm or delight. Nor are they clever stories which we explore for their plot. Even his characters are mostly obnoxious beings who fail to appeal in any usual sense. Why then is Dreiser considered by some a genius? Why do we read his books at all? The answer lies in a strange paradox: Dreiser's very faults are what attract us again and again. His stumbling, awkward style, his convoluted philosophies, and his pitiable personages combine to present us with a world view which, perhaps more successfully than that of any other American writer, conveys the naturalistic atmosphere. Dreiser's books, like the universe he seeks to describe, impress and repel us by their very disorder, their mystery, their powerful demands on our comfortable assumptions.

All of Dreiser's characteristics are most clearly reflected in *An American Tragedy,* the masterpiece of an author who had earlier published three important novels, *Sister Carrie, Jennie Gerhardt* and *The Financier.* In this book Dreiser the naturalist asserts the doctrine that man is struggling endlessly to survive in an uncaring world where he is a victim of heredity, environment, and chance which leave him small room for free choice or action. Dreiser's theory of life is basically mechanistic, and for *An American Tragedy* he invented the term "chemism" to explain the chemical forces which he believed propelled man to act in a certain way. Man, Dreiser said, is a "mechanism, undevised and uncreated and a badly and carelessly driven one at that." Such a poor creature is Clyde Griffiths, the central character of *An American Tragedy.* The book, which is full of scientific imagery, shows us how Clyde is driven to his final destruction.

Dreiser chooses to concentrate on man's struggle against one particular force: society and its institutions. Clyde in each of the novel's three sections strives not against a malign God nor a malevolent fate but against the unyielding structure of his culture. In other times men have defined themselves by other touchstones (religion, honor, war), but Clyde can answer his craving for meaning in only one way. For to matter in America means, in the book's terms, to be masterful, to have material goods and status. His America tempts him with its powerful businesses, its glittering social affairs, and its promises that anyone who is deserving can share in these riches. That is, of course, a false promise, for the American tragedy is the gap between the country's ideals and its reality.

Doomed to failure in his quest, Clyde, whose story has been called a "parable of our national experience," cannot be blamed for desiring what he sees all about him. Nor can he be criticized for the weaknesses and handicaps which assure his end. Immature and shallow, offering a "Gee" on all occasions, uneducated and poor, Clyde is willing to compromise in any necessary fashion in order to become materially successful. Yet his very lack of moral or intellectual distinction, when coupled with the intensity of his desires, makes him the ideal and innocent representative of a culture where achievement is gauged by such measurements. In the novel, inspired by a 1906 murder case involving a Chester Gillette who killed an inconveniently pregnant girl friend for reasons much like those in the book, Clyde's attorney calls him a "mental as well as a moral coward—no more and no less," but later adds that Clyde cannot help this state. "('After all, you didn't make yourself, did you?')"

What did "make" Clyde includes poor parents just as inept as he. Impractical and ineffectual, the Griffiths offer him only their God who, as he can plainly see, has brought them none of the things he (or they) want. Religion is one obstacle Clyde can and does remove when he ignores their protests and responds instead to his environment and inner urgings. His adaptability is exploited in the Arabian Nights atmosphere of the hotels in which he works, places where luxury alone is vital and kindness and honesty mere trifles. When in the second part of the novel Clyde finds himself in Lycurgus, he once again gravitates helplessly toward the surrounding values. Named after the Spartan who initiated that society's rigid rules, Lycurgus is just as tantalizing as the hotels. It is a "walled city" which, as one of the novel's major symbols, allows outsiders to peek at its glories but rarely permits them to enter its gates. Clyde, fascinated and overwhelmed, abandons the simple pleasures he has found with Roberta and attempts to climb its walls.

Whenever Clyde struggles free of his environmental influences, he is frustrated by the accidents and coincidences which haunt him. He unwillingly leaves Kansas City because of the car accident, and he leaves Chicago because of a seemingly happy encounter with his uncle. His chance meeting with Sondra and the mistaken identity developed their relationship, just as Roberta's unplanned pregnancy so rudely obstructs his dreams. Even his murder scheme is derived from a chance newspaper article, and the murder itself is in a sense self-initiated, for Clyde *allows* rather than *forces* Roberta's drowning.

Other characters in the novel are equally victims of the roles in which they find themselves. While many of them are compellingly presented, their main importance is to provide background and stimuli for Clyde. Since he rarely sees them as people but rather as impediments (his family, Roberta) or as exciting objects (Sondra), we too are interested in them mostly in this respect, and the book belongs almost entirely to Clyde.

In *An American Tragedy,* Dreiser, a former newspaperman and editor of women's publications, watches his world and its foibles and is moved by men's shared helplessness. He shows us how useless moral judgment is in solving such dilemmas and insists, as he does in all his works, that all we may expect of one another is compassion for our common plights. Although he offers us little encouragement, Dreiser does hint that perhaps the human condition may improve. The final scene—"Dusk, of a summer night"—closely resembles the opening. A small boy once again troops reluctantly with a group of street missionaries. Yet Mrs. Griffiths responds to the frustrations of Esta's child as she had never done to Clyde's and gives him money for an ice-cream cone. This child, she promises herself, will be different.

Bibliography

Campbell, Charles L. *"An American Tragedy*; or Death in the Woods," in *Modern Fiction Studies.* XV (Summer, 1969), pp. 251–259.

Coursen, Herbert R. "Clyde Griffiths and the American Dream," in *New Republic.* CXLV (September 4, 1961), pp. 21–22.

Davidson, Donald. "Theodore Dreiser," in his *The Spyglass.* Nashville, Tenn: Vanderbilt University Press, 1963, pp. 67–70.

Farrell, James T. "Dreiser's *Tragedy*: The Distortion of American Values," in *Prospects: Annual of American Cultural Studies.* I (1975), pp. 19–27.

Frohock, W.M. "Theodore Dreiser," in *Seven Novelists in the American Naturalist Tradition.* Edited by Charles Walcutt. Minneapolis: University of Minnesota, 1974, pp. 92–130.

Gerber, Philip L. *Theodore Dreiser.* New York: Twayne, 1964, pp. 127–153.

Grebstein, Sheldon N. *"An American Tragedy*: Theme and Structure," in *The Twenties.* Edited by R.E. Langford and W.E. Taylor. Deland, Fla.: Edwards, 1966, pp. 62–66.

Harter, Carol C. "Strange Bedfellows: *The Wasteland* and *An American Tragedy,"* in *The Twenties.* Edited by W.G. French. Deland, Fla.: Everett/ Edwards, 1975, pp. 51–64.

Hoffman, Frederick J. "The Scene of Violence: Dostoevsky and Dreiser," in *Modern Fiction Studies.* VI (Summer, 1960), pp. 91–105.

Howe, Irving. "Dreiser: The Springs of Desire," in his *Decline of the New.* New York: Harcourt, Brace and World, 1970, pp. 137–150.

————. "Dreiser and Tragedy," in *Dreiser: A Collection of Critical Essays.*

Edited by John Lydenberg. Englewood Cliffs, N.J.: Prentice-Hall, 1971, pp. 141–152.

Lane, Lauriat, Jr. "The Double in *An American Tragedy*," in *Modern Fiction Studies*. XII (Summer, 1966), pp. 213–220.

Lehan, Richard. "Dreiser's *An American Tragedy*: A Critical Study," in *College English*. XXV (December, 1963), pp. 187–193. Also in *The Modern American Novel*. Edited by Max R. Westbrook. New York: Random House, 1967, pp. 21–32.

McAleer, John J. *Theodore Dreiser*. New York: Holt, Rinehart and Winston, 1968, pp. 127–146.

Matthiessen, F.O. "Of Crime and Punishment," in *The Stature of Theodore Dreiser*. Edited by Alfred Kazin. Bloomington: Indiana University Press, 1955, pp. 204–218.

Mencken, H.L. "Dreiser," in *Mencken Christomathy*. New York: A.A. Knopf, 1949, pp. 501–505.

Moers, Ellen. *Two Dreisers*. New York: Viking, 1969, pp. 209–306.

Morgan, W. Wayne. "Theodore Dreiser: The Naturalist as Humanist," in his *American Writers in Rebellion*. New York: Hill and Wang, 1965, pp. 175–180.

Pizer, Donald. *The Novels of Theodore Dreiser*. Minneapolis: University of Minnesota, 1976, pp. 203–289.

Salzman, Jack, Editor. *Theodore Dreiser: The Critical Reception*. New York: David Lewis, 1972, pp. 439–502.

Samuels, Charles Thomas. "Mr. Trilling, Mr. Warren, and *An American Tragedy*," in *Yale Review*. LIII (June, 1964), pp. 629–640. Also in *Dreiser: A Collection of Critical Essays*. Edited by John Lydenberg. Englewood Cliffs, N.J.: Prentice-Hall, 1971, pp. 163–173.

Shafer, Robert. "*An American Tragedy*: A Humanistic Demurer," in *The Stature of Theodore Dreiser*. Edited by Alfred Kazin. Bloomington: Indiana University, 1955, pp. 113–126.

Shapiro, Charles. "*An American Tragedy*: The Dream, the Failure, and the Hope," in his *Theodore Dreiser*. Carbondale: Southern Illinois University Press, 1962, pp. 81–113.

Walcutt, Charles Child. "The Divided Stream," in *Dreiser: A Collection of Critical Essays*. Edited by John Lydenberg. Englewood Cliffs, N.J.: Prentice-Hall, 1971, pp. 120–122.

Warren, Robert Penn. "*An American Tragedy*," in *Yale Review*. LII (Autumn, 1962), pp. 1–15. Also in *Dreiser: A Collection of Critical Essays*. Edited by John Lydenberg. Englewood Cliffs, N.J.: Prentice-Hall, 1971, pp. 129–140.

JENNIE GERHARDT

Type of work: Novel
Author: Theodore Dreiser (1871–1945)
Time of plot: The last two decades of the nineteenth century
Locale: Chicago and various other Midwestern cities
First published: 1911

This naturalistic novel tells the story of a beautiful and vital young girl who is beaten by the forces of life. These forces are accidental and inevitable, and stronger than any man's will or purpose. The social and economic details in the book provide an interesting picture of urban life in the American Middle West at the end of the nineteenth century.

Principal Characters

Genevieve Gerhardt (Jennie), the oldest of six children of a poor, hard-working glass blower in Columbus, Ohio. Both beautiful and innocent, Jennie is forced to work at a local hotel when her father becomes ill; there she attracts Senator Brander, who stays at the hotel. When Brander helps her family and keeps her brother out of jail for stealing coal from the railroad, Jennie, in gratitude, sleeps with him. At his sudden death she is left pregnant. She later moves to Cleveland, where she meets Lester Kane. With her family in need again, she goes on a trip to New York with him in return for his help: In Chicago Lester finds out about Jennie's daughter and agrees to allow the child to live with them. Jennie realizes that his family's disapproval of their relationship is harming Lester both financially and socially, and she influences him to leave her. He later marries an old childhood sweetheart. Jennie's daughter dies and she adopts two orphan children. Some years later, while his wife is in Europe, Lester has a heart attack and sends for Jennie, who nurses him until his death.

Lester Kane, the son of a wealthy carriage manufacturer. A weak man, Lester is torn between his desire for social and financial affluence and his feeling for Jennie. He neither marries her nor leaves her, until his father's will demands that he act within three years. Pursued by Mrs. Gerald, a widow, he finally follows his family's wishes and leaves Jennie with a generous settlement.

William Gerhardt, Jennie's father, a poor glass blower. After his wife dies and his family grows up he lives with Jennie, the daughter he disapproved of but who is ultimately kindest to him. He dies in Chicago.

George Sylvester Brander, a Senator from Ohio. A bachelor, he intends to marry Jennie but dies of a heart attack.

Wilhelmina Vesta, Jennie's daughter by Senator Brander; she dies of typhoid fever at the age of fourteen.

Mrs. Letty Pace Gerald, a wealthy widow and childhood sweetheart of Lester Kane. Lester finally marries her but is not happy.

Mrs. Gerhardt, Jennie's mother, hard-working and sympathetic. She dies in Cleveland before Jennie moves to Chicago.

Robert Kane, Lester's older brother, vice president of the carriage company. A ruthless financier, interested only in power, he influences his father to make the will that cripples Lester.

Archibald Kane, Lester's father. According to his will, Lester must abandon Jennie to get his share in the business. If he marries Jennie, he is to receive ten thousand dollars a year for life; if he continues to live with her without marriage, he gets nothing after three years.

Sebastian Gerhardt (Bass), Jennie's oldest brother and the closest to her.

George Gerhardt, another brother.

Martha Gerhardt, a sister; she becomes a teacher.

William Gerhardt, Jr., a brother who becomes an electrical engineer.

Veronica Gerhardt, a sister who marries a wholesale druggist in Cleveland.

Louise Kane, Lester's youngest sister, a cold, social woman who discovers that Lester is living with Jennie in a Chicago hotel.

Amy and
Imogene Kane, other sisters.

Mrs. Kane, Lester's mother.

Mrs. Henry Bracebridge, Jennie's Cleveland employer at whose home she meets Lester Kane.

Mr. O'Brien, a lawyer, the executor of Archibald Kane's estate; he suggests that Jennie influence Lester to leave her.

Rose Perpetua and
Henry Stover, orphans adopted by Jennie.

Samuel E. Ross, a real estate promoter through whom Lester loses money in Chicago.

The Story

Jennie Gerhardt, the beautiful and virtuous eighteen-year-old, was the eldest of six children of a poor, hard-working German family in Columbus, Ohio, in 1880. Her father, a glass blower, was ill, and Jennie and her mother were forced to work at a local hotel in order to provide for the younger children in the family. Jennie did the laundry for the kind and handsome Senator Brander (he was fifty-two at the time), and attracted his eye. Senator Brander was kind to Jennie and her family. When he was able to keep Jennie's brother Sebastian out of jail for stealing some needed coal from the railroad, Jennie, full of gratitude, allowed him to sleep with her. Senator Brander, struck by Jennie's beauty, charm, and goodness, promised to marry her. He died suddenly, however, while on a trip to Washington.

Left alone, Jennie discovered that she was pregnant. Her father, a stern Lutheran, insisted that she leave the house, but her more understanding mother allowed her to return when her father, now in better health, left to find work in Youngstown. Jennie's child was a daughter whom she named Vesta. At Sebastian's suggestion, the family moved to Cleveland to find work. While her mother looked after Vesta, Jennie found a job as a maid in the home of Mrs. Bracebridge. One of Mrs. Bracebridge's guests, Lester Kane, the son of a rich carriage manufacturer, found Jennie temptingly attractive. When he tried to seduce Jennie, the girl, though greatly attracted to him, managed to put off his advances.

Mrs. Gerhardt was injured in a glass-blowing accident and lost the use of both of his hands. Again, the family needed money badly, and Jennie decided to accept Lester's offer of aid for her family. The price was that she become his mistress, go on a trip to New York with him, and then allow him to establish her in an apartment in Chicago. Although Jennie loved Lester, she knew that he did not intend to marry her because his family would be horrified at such an alliance, but once again she sacrificed her virtue because she felt that her family needed the offered aid. After Jennie had become Lester's mistress, he gave her family money for a house. Jennie was afraid, however, to tell Lester about the existence of her daughter Vesta.

Jennie and Lester moved to Chicago and lived there. Her family began to suspect that, contrary to what Jennie had told them, she and Lester were not married. When Mrs. Gerhardt died, several years later, Jennie moved Vesta to Chicago and boarded the child in another woman's house. One night Jennie was called because Vesta was seriously ill, and Lester discovered Vesta's existence. Although upset at first, when Jennie told him the story, Lester understood and agreed to allow Vesta to live with them. They soon moved to a house in Hyde Park, a middle-class residential district in Chicago. Mr. Gerhardt, now old and ill and willing to accept the situation between Jennie and Lester, also came to live with them and to tend the furnace and the lawn.

Although they were constantly aware of the increasing disapproval of Lester's family, Jennie and Lester lived happily for a time. Lester's father, violently opposed to the relationship with Jennie, whom he had never met, threatened to disinherit Lester if he did not leave her. Lester's brother Robert urged his father on and attempted to persuade Lester to abandon Jennie. Nevertheless, Lester felt that he owed his allegiance, as well as his love, to her, and he remained with her in spite of the fact that they were snubbed by most of Lester's society connections.

When Lester's father died, still believing that his son's relationship with Jennie demonstrated irresponsibility, he left Lester's share of the estate in trust with Robert. Lester was given three alternatives: he could leave Jennie and receive all his money; he could marry Jennie and receive only $10,000 a year for life, or he could continue his present arrangement with the knowledge that if he did not either abandon or marry Jennie within three years, he would lose his share of the money. Characteristically, Lester hesitated. He took Jennie to Europe, where they met Mrs. Letty Pace Gerald, a beautiful and accomplished widow who had been Lester's childhood sweetheart and who was still fond of him. In the meantime Robert had expanded the carriage business into a monopoly and eased Lester into a subordinate position. When Lester returned to Chicago, he decided to attempt to make an independent future for himself and Jennie. He put a good deal of money into a real estate deal and lost it. Mrs. Gerald also moved to Chicago in pursuit of Lester.

After old Mr. Gerhardt died, Jennie found herself in a difficult situation. Lester, out of the family business because of her, was finding it difficult to earn a living. Mrs. Gerald and Robert's lawyers kept pressing her to release him, claiming this suggestion was for his own economic and social good. Jennie, always altruistic, began to influence Lester to leave her. Before long both were convinced that separation was the only solution so that Lester could return to the family business. Finally Lester left Jennie. Later he set up a house and an income for her and Vesta in a cottage an hour or so from the center of Chicago.

Once more established in the family business, Lester married Mrs. Gerald. Six months after Lester had left Jennie, Vesta, a fourteen-year-old girl already showing a good deal of sensitivity and talent, died of typhoid fever.

Jennie, calling herself Mrs. Stover, moved to the city and adopted two orphan children. Five years passed. Jennie, although still in love with Lester, accepted her quiet life. At last she was able to cope with experience in whatever terms it presented itself to her, even though she had never been able to impose her will on experience in any meaningful way.

One night, Lester, having suffered a heart attack while in Chicago on some business matters, sent for Jennie; his wife was in Europe and could not reach Chicago for three weeks. Jennie tended Lester throughout his last illness. One day he confessed that he had always loved her, that he had made a mistake ever to permit the forces of business and family pressure to make him leave her. Jennie felt that his final confession, his statement that he should never have left her, indicated a kind of spiritual union and left her with something that she could value for the rest of her life. Lester died. Jennie realized that she would now be forced to live through many years that could promise no salvation, no new excitement—that would simply impose themselves upon her as had the years in the past. She was resolved to accept her loneliness because she knew there was nothing else for her to do.

Jennie went to see Lester's coffin loaded on the train. She realized then, even more clearly, that man was simply a stiff figure, moved about by circumstance. Virtue, beauty, moral worth could not save man; nor could evil or degeneracy. Man simply yielded and managed the best he could under the circumstances of his nature, the society, and the economic force that surrounded him.

Critical Evaluation

In his second novel, *Jennie Gerhardt,* Theodore Dreiser continues his exploration of themes first introduced in *Sister Carrie.* Central to the novel's vision is Dreiser's belief that the misery in people's lives arises from the conflict between natural human instincts and artificial social and moral standards. Man denies his basic animal appetites, condemning them because they violate the codes of society; yet, ironically, he himself has not only created, but come to believe in, those very social mores which thwart his true desires and bring him great unhappiness. Thus, Jennie is condemned by society for acting on motives of selfless love and generosity. She violates moral codes in becoming Lester Kane's mistress, although she does so in order to save her family from poverty; and when that relationship proves to be a loving and happy one, it is nevertheless considered sinful because it lacks the legal sanction of a marriage license. Likewise, Lester's natural desires are blocked on both sides: if he marries Jennie he will be disinherited and ostracized for marrying beneath his social class, while if he does not, he will be condemned for "living in sin."

In terms of the novel, the people most guilty of perpetuating a social framework so destructive of human happiness are the fathers, who represent the rigid old morality. Mr. Gerhardt, who stands for the blindness and bigotry of religious conviction, turns his own daughter out of her home for trying to help him in a time of financial distress. For similar reasons, Mr. Kane condemns his son's alliance with Jennie, although for his moral arbiter he has replaced the Christian God with the gods of money and respectability.

Within the naturalistic vision embodied in *Jennie Gerhardt,* man is seen as a powerless victim, a creature without free will who therefore lacks the means to control his own destiny. It would be a mistake, however, to assume that, in the absence of free will, chance rules men's lives. It is true that the story of Jennie's career is filled with chance incidents which seemingly bring about important changes in her life; but actually, these chance occurrences are mere catalysts. What really dictates the course which each character's life takes is his or her temperament and personality. Dreiser creates in each character a particular set of limitations which predetermine how he or she will respond to any new circumstances. Thus, when it appears that Jennie or Lester have a free choice to make between two alternatives, what is actually the case is that their respective temperaments cause them to choose as they do. Given Jennie's generous and caring nature, she has no choice but to become Lester's mistress; given Lester's lack of ambition, and his love of an easy life, it is inevitable that he leave Jennie in order to secure his inheritance. By the same token, such seemingly crucial chance events as Senator Brander's untimely death or Letty Pace Gerald's sudden appearance do not materially affect the characters' lives in the long run; if it were not for these *particular* two incidents, some other incidents would eventually occur through which Jennie and Lester would play out the inevitable roles determined for them by the essential qualities of their personalities.

Bibliography

Elias, Robert H.   *Theodore Dreiser: Apostle of Nature.* Ithaca, N.Y.: Cornell University Press, 1970, pp. 152–176.

Fiedler, Leslie. "Dreiser and the Sentimental Novel," in *Dreiser: A Collection of Critical Essays*. Edited by John Lydenberg. Englewood Cliffs, N.J.: Prentice-Hall, 1971, pp. 45–51.

Howe, Irving. "Dreiser: The Springs of Desire," in his *Decline of the New*. New York: Harcourt, Brace and World, 1970, pp. 139–142.

McAleer, John J. *Theodore Dreiser*. New York: Holt, Rinehart and Winston, 1968, pp. 93–102.

Mookerjee, R.N. *Theodore Dreiser: His Thought and Social Criticism*. Delhi, India: National Publishing House, 1974, pp. 45–49.

Morgan, W. Wayne. "Theodore Dreiser: The Naturalist as Humanist," in his *American Writers in Rebellion*. New York: Hill and Wang, 1965, pp. 171–174.

Pizer, Donald. *The Novels of Theodore Dreiser*. Minneapolis: University of Minnesota, 1976, pp. 96–130.

Salzman, Jack, Editor. *Theodore Dreiser: The Critical Reception*. New York: David Lewis, 1972, pp. 56–96.

Shapiro, Charles. "*Jennie Gerhardt*: The American Family and the American Dream," in his *Twelve Original Essays on Great American Novels*. Détroit: Wayne State University Press, 1960, pp. 177–195. Also in his *Theodore Dreiser*. Carbondale: Southern Illinois University Press, 1962, pp. 14–24.

Sherman, Stuart. "The Barbaric Naturalism of Mr. Dreiser," in *Dreiser: A Collection of Critical Essays*. Edited by John Lydenberg. Englewood Cliffs, N.J.: Prentice-Hall, 1971, pp. 63–72.

Walcutt, Charles Child. "The Divided Stream," in *Dreiser: A Collection of Critical Essays*. Edited by John Lydenberg. Englewood Cliffs, N.J.: Prentice-Hall, 1971, pp. 109–115.

SISTER CARRIE

Type of work: Novel
Author: Theodore Dreiser (1871–1945)
Time of plot: 1889
Locale: Chicago and New York
First published: 1900

Critically controversial and commercially unnoticed when first published, Sister Carrie *is now recognized as one of America's finest naturalistic novels. The book demonstrates a survival of the fittest ethic, with the survival qualities being largely accidental. Carrie Meeber not only survives, but even flourishes, despite any exceptional physical, intellectual, or moral qualities, merely because she has the right instincts and her luck is good. George Hurstwood is destroyed because his instincts betray him and his luck turns bad.*

Principal Characters

Caroline Meeber, called **Sister Carrie, a** young Middle Western girl who rises from her small-town origins to success as an actress. Her story illustrates one part of Dreiser's division of mankind between the Intellectual and the Emotional. Members of the latter division he calls "harps in the wind," hopelessly seeking to satisfy an inexplicable yearning for beauty, accomplishment, the good life. Caroline Meeber belongs to this second group, which performs its sad, forsaken quest in the manner of dancers after a flame. Although Carrie is not capable of much rationalization, she is capable of sensing an ideal, and she has a tenacious energy to bend toward its realization. The key to Carrie's apparently simple character is that she is a rather complex person. Moved by desires which at first she sees as ends in themselves—to have money, to own fine clothes, to be socially accepted—she enters into an affair with Hurstwood and contributes to his degeneration while remaining virtually untouched herself. Her restlessness and seeming disregard for others are really manifestations of her inability to recognize anything outside of concrete representation. Throughout the book she is never given to reflection. Although she uses Drouet and Hurstwood to her advantage, she is no gross country girl grasping at opportunity. There is something monolithic in her nature, and certain gifts or curses of sensitivity and pluck combine to give her an appeal that her fellows recognize as representative of themselves. As Carrie Madena, she scores a success on the stage by acting in flimsy, superficial parts. What is sad about Carrie is that each time she steps up to the much prized rung that has been just above, her ideal eludes her and she becomes vaguely disillusioned with still another symbol of happiness and success. Thus she becomes Dreiser's commentary on man's pathetic reach for the ideal on the distant peak; reality is the intractable stuff he has to work with to achieve it.

George Hurstwood, the manager of a Chicago saloon, a man who has worked his way into a carefully balanced niche of the social order. In that class just below the luxurious rich, he has created for himself an air of success made substantial by good food, good company, comfortable living. When he encounters Carrie, Hurstwood has fallen into the practice of maintaining only the semblance of marital order; he denies himself little in the way of pleasures that he genuinely covets, but he has the saving grace of discretion on his side. He begins to fancy himself as quite clever, something of a commander on the field of life, and this self-deception brings about his eventual collapse. With Carrie, he imagines nothing can stay his success, and in a weak moment he discards the last shreds of caution. Because he never fully understands Carrie, a pall of reality weights their relationship. Hurstwood has betrayed his place of trust by stealing money from his employers, has hoodwinked Carrie into running off with him, and these conditions prove insufferable. Faced with a much lower status in society, Hurstwood, now using the alias of Wheeler, is unable to reconcile himself to fact and begins to indulge in the attrition of living in the past. One by one his carefully structured conceptions of himself and his flamboyance crumple, and he learns that he is no match for grubbiness. The painstaking chronicle of Hurstwood's decline into apathy becomes the signal merit of this novel. Hurstwood is incapable of checking his downhill slide because, even to his end, a desolate, grimy suicide in a flop house, the granules of former pride remain with him, actually sapping his powers of adaptation.

Charles Drouet, a traveling salesman and a superficial egotist, Carrie Meeber's first lover. Drouet has no real depth to his nature. Uncomplex, he has no wish to inflict harm on others and tries, while pleasing himself, to bring them happiness. He serves as Carrie's first introduction to a form of the good life, but she quickly outgrows him as she passes on to George Hurstwood. At the end of the novel Drouet is shown essentially as he was at the beginning: handsome, flashy, gay, boylike, effervescent, and entirely without scope or perspective.

Bod Ames, a young man intellectually inclined. Of the people in the novel he is the only one who really understands or genuinely moves Carrie. Ironically, he causes the most painful reawakening of the quest for the "ideal" in Carrie's nature.

Minnie and
Sven Hanson, Carrie's sister and brother-in-law with whom she lives when she comes to Chicago. They live a sterile, plodding life that Carrie earnestly wishes to avoid.

Mrs. Hurstwood, the deceived, deserted wife who has watched her marriage deteriorate steadily, even before her husband's affair with Carrie Meeber. Cold and social-minded by nature, she ends up in possession of all property accumulated by Hurstwood over the years.

Jessica and
George Hurstwood, Jr., the Hurstwood children, rather selfish offspring, without depth, who conform to their mother's way.

Mr. and Mrs. Vance, a couple who live next to Carrie and Hurstwood in New York. They impress Carrie with their sophistication and put her life with Hurstwood under a shabbier light.

The Story

When Carrie Meeber left her home town in Wisconsin, she had nothing but a few dollars and a certain unspoiled beauty and charm. Young, inexperienced, she was going to Chicago to live with her sister and to find work. While on the train, she met Charles Drouet, a genial, flashy traveling salesman. Before the train pulled into the station, they had exchanged addresses, and Drouet promised to call on Carrie at her sister's house.

When she arrived at her sister's home, Carrie discovered that her life there would be far from the happy, carefree existence of which she had dreamed. The Hansons were hard-working people, grim and penny-pinching, allowing themselves no pleasures, and living a dull, conventional life. It was clear to Carrie that Drouet could not possibly call there, not only because of the unattractive atmosphere, but also because the Hansons were sure to object to him. She wrote and told him that he was not to call, that she would get in touch with him later.

Meanwhile Carrie went job-hunting and finally found work in a small shoe factory. Of her first wages, all but fifty cents went to her sister and brother-in-law. Then she fell ill and lost her job. Once again she had to look for work. Day after day she trudged the streets, without success. It seemed as if she would have to go back to Wisconsin, and the Hansons encouraged her to do so. If she could not bring in money, they did not want her.

One day, while Carrie was looking for work, she met Drouet and told him her troubles. He offered her money which, with reluctance, she finally accepted. The money was for clothes she needed, but she did not know how to explain the source of the money to her sister. Drouet solved the problem by suggesting that he rent a room for her, where she could keep her clothing. A few days later Carrie went to live with Drouet, who had promised to marry her as soon as he had completed a business deal.

In the meantime Drouet introduced her to a friend, G. W. Hurstwood. Hurstwood had a good job as the manager of a saloon, a comfortable home, a wife, and two grown children. More than twice Carrie's age, he nevertheless accepted Drouet's suggestion that he look in on her while the salesman was out of town on one of his trips. Before long Hurstwood was passionately in love with her. When Drouet came back, he discovered from a chambermaid that Carrie and Hurstwood had been going out together frequently. A scene followed. Carrie was furious when Drouet told her that Hurstwood was already married. She blamed Drouet for her folly, saying that he should have told her that Hurstwood was a married man.

Meanwhile, Mrs. Hurstwood had become suspicious of her husband. Drouet had secured for Carrie a part in a theatrical entertainment which a local lodge was presenting. Hurstwood, hearing that Carrie was to appear, persuaded many of his friends to go with him to the show. Mrs. Hurstwood learned of the affair and heard, too, that her husband had been seen riding with an unknown woman. She confronted Hurstwood and told him that she intended to sue for divorce. Faced with social and financial ruin, Hurstwood was in despair. One night he discovered that his employer's safe was open. He robbed it of several thousand dollars and went to Carrie's apartment. Drouet had just deserted her. Pretending that Drouet had been hurt, Hurstwood succeeded in getting Carrie on a train bound for Montreal. In Montreal Hurstwood was approached by an agent of his former employer, who urged him to return the money and to settle the issue quietly. Hurstwood returned all but a relatively small sum.

Under the name of Wheeler, he and Carrie were married, Carrie being all the while under the impression that the ceremony was legal. Then they left for New York. There Hurstwood looked for work, but with no success. Finally he bought a partnership in a small tavern. After a time the partnership was dissolved and he lost all his money. Every day he went looking for work. Gradually he grew less eager for a job, and began staying at home all day. When bills piled up, he and Carrie moved to a new apartment to escape their creditors.

Carrie set out to find work and was lucky enough to get a job as a chorus girl. With a friend, she took an apartment and left Hurstwood to himself. Soon Carrie became a well-known actress, and a local hotel invited her to become a guest there, at a nominal expense. Carrie had many friends and admirers. She had money and all the comforts and luxuries which appealed to a small-town girl.

Hurstwood had not fared so well. He could find no work. Once he worked as a scab, during some labor troubles, but he left that job because it was too hazardous. He became a bum, living in Bowery flophouses and begging on the streets. One day he went to see Carrie. She gave him some money, largely because she had seen Drouet and had learned for the first time of Hurstwood's theft in Chicago. She believed that Hurstwood had kept his disgrace a secret in order to spare her feelings.

Although Carrie was a toast of the town, she was not happy in spite of her success. She was invited to give performances abroad. In the meantime Hurstwood died and, unknown to Carrie, was buried in the potter's field. As Carrie was sailing for London, Hurstwood's ex-wife, daughter, and son-in-law were in the city, eager for pleasure and social success, a success made possible by the daughter's marriage and by Hurstwood's divorce settlement, which had given the family all of his property.

Critical Evaluation

Sister Carrie, like most of Theodore Dreiser's novels, embodies his naturalistic belief that while men are controlled and conditioned by heredity, instinct, and chance, a few extraordinary and usually unsophisticated human beings refuse to accept their fate wordlessly and instead strive, unsuccessfully, to find meaning and purpose for their existence. Carrie, the title character, senses that she is merely a cipher in an uncaring world yet seeks to grasp the mysteries of life and thereby satisfy her need to matter. In pointing out "how curious are the vagaries of fortune," Dreiser suggests that even though life may be cruel, its enigmatic quality makes it all the more fascinating.

Despite its title, the novel is not a study of a family but of Carrie's strangely unemotional relationships with three men and of the resulting and unexpected changes which occur in her outlook and status. A "half-equipped little knight" with small talent, Carrie's instincts nevertheless raise her from a poor maiden to a successful actress. Basically the novel traces the rise, through Carrie's increasing reliance on instinct, in a three-stage development. Initially Carrie is at least partially ruled by reason, but by the end of the first phase of her rise—marked by her accidental second meeting with Drouet and her submission to his promises—Carrie begins to abandon the reason which has not served her well. During this second portion, her blossoming instinct pulls her to the material advantages offered by Drouet, and her life with him is evidence of her growing commitment to these instincts. Yet it is her almost unconscious and unplanned switch to Hurstwood which reveals how totally she is now following her instincts. Hurstwood offers finer material possessions and more emotional rapport, and Carrie drifts easily into his orbit. Now fully and irrevocably tied to her instincts, Carrie throughout the rest of the novel considers it an obligation to self to let these impulses lead her where they will. When a stage career and her association with Ames replace Hurstwood, she is merely proceeding further toward the end to which she is bound once she leaves Drouet and all trace of reason. As a plant must turn toward the sun, Carrie must feed her unsatisfied urge for happiness.

Closely related to Dreiser's belief that instinct must prevail is his thesis that man lacks responsibility for his fate, a thesis suggested by all three main characters. Drouet leads Carrie to what some consider her moral downfall, but, Dreiser tells us, "There was nothing evil in the fellow." His glands, not he, are to blame. Neither is there any question of guilt in Hurstwood's case. Since he rarely makes a choice, he cannot be expected to answer for what happens to him. Chance, not conviction, makes him a thief. His wife, not Hurstwood, ends their marriage. And even his attraction to Carrie is a thing of chance, for "He was merely floating those gossamer threads of thought which, like the spider's, he hoped would lay hold somewhere." Although merely a sham without true power or greatness (a fact Dreiser, dazzled by his own creation, seems to forget), Hurstwood in his decline from semi-prominence to degradation reminds the reader that the forces which send Carrie to stardom can with equal ease reduce a man to nothing. Similarly, we must neither praise Carrie nor be shocked because she is not punished for her sins.

Dreiser presents his ideas through many symbolic images, but most important are the city, the sea, and the rocking chair. The city, in the book represented by both New York and Chicago, is a microcosm of Dreiser's universe. Nature is grim and unfeeling; so is the city. Unless a man is strong and productive and fortunate, he faces the world's indifference, a state magnified in the city where man is perhaps more isolated than elsewhere. When Hurstwood, for example, is dying, he does so alone despite Carrie's presence in a nearby apartment, Drouet's relative closeness in a hotel, and his wife's pending arrival on the train, for none know, nor care, about his tragedy. Dreiser's concept of an uncaring and ever-changing universe is equally conveyed by his use of the sea and the rocking chair. Again and again Carrie is described as a "lone figure in a tossing, thoughtless sea." Like its counterpart, the city, the sea symbol suggests that only the strong or the lucky survive. And the rocking chair hints at the futility of this constant flux, for a rocking chair is in continual motion but goes nowhere. Although Carrie's life would seem to improve, she is sitting miserably in the rocking chair not only at the novel's beginning but also at its end. While this circular development suggests that Carrie has small chance to become truly happy, the fact that she continues to rock provides evidence of her never-ceasing aspiration.

Part of the book reflects events from Dreiser's own turbulent life. In 1886, L. A. Hopkins, a clerk in a Chicago saloon, took $3,500 from his employers, and with Emma Dreiser, one of the author's many troubled siblings, fled to New York. Using this incident as the genesis for his novel, Dreiser modeled Carrie on his sister and used Hopkins for aspects of Hurstwood's personality. By the time Dreiser finished the novel in 1900, however, he had gone far beyond the cheap story of adultery and theft and had created a work which presented complex questions of innocence and guilt.

Surrounding the publication of Dreiser's first novel were the controversy and confusion which were to mark the career of this man from a poor and disturbed Indiana family in whose plight he saw reflected much of the irony of the world. Apparently the novel was accepted by Doubleday, Page during the absence of Frank Doubleday, the senior partner, who upon his return expressed doubt about its content and style. Refusing to release the firm from its unwritten commitment, however, Dreiser demanded that the book be published, and it appeared in 1900. Although it sold poorly (earning for Dreiser only $68.40) and was not aggressively promoted by the publishers, stories relating Mrs. Doubleday's violent objections to its moral view and the resulting suppression of the novel are unverified legend. In his own typical confusion of fact and half-fact, Dreiser added to the myths by telling conflicting accounts of what had happened.

Reaction to the book was surprisingly widespread, and many critics attacked its philosophical premises as immoral. Such charges and those that the novel was poorly written, wordy, and melodramatic would later greet each of Dreiser's productions. Yet as Dreiser wrote book after book exploring the yearning of the young for riches, position, and understanding, a yearning he personally experienced in an overwhelming form, readers were struck by the sincerity, powerful detail, and massive impact of his work. Especially known for *Jennie Gerhardt* (1911), and *An American Tragedy* (1925), Dreiser has a secure niche among top-ranking American naturalists.

Bibliography

Auchincloss, Louis. *Louis Auchincloss on* Sister Carrie. New York: Merrill, 1968.

Cowley, Malcolm. "Sister Carrie's Brother," in *The Stature of Theodore Dreiser.* Edited by Alfred Kazin. Bloomington: Indiana University Press, 1955, pp. 171–181. Also in his *A Many Windowed House.* Carbondale: Southern Illinois University Press, 1970, pp. 153–165.

Elias, Robert H. *Theodore Dreiser: Apostle of Nature.* Ithaca, N.Y.: Cornell University Press, 1970, pp. 103–117.

Farrell, James T. "Dreiser's *Sister Carrie,*" in his *The League of Frightened Philistines.* New York: Vanguard, 1945, pp. 12–19.

Gerber, Philip L. *Theodore Dreiser.* New York: Twayne, 1964, pp. 51–70.

Griffin, R.J. "Carrie and Music: A Note on Dreiser's Technique," in *From Irving to Steinbeck.* Edited by Motley Deakin and Peter Lisca. Gainesville: University Presses of Florida, 1972, pp. 73–81.

Griffith, Clark. *"Sister Carrie:* Dreiser's Wasteland," in *American Studies.* XVI, pp. 41–47.

Hakutani, Yoshinobu. *"Sister Carrie* and the Problem of Literary Naturalism," in *Twentieth Century Literature.* XIII (April, 1967), pp. 3–17.

Hoffman, Michael J. "From Realism to Naturalism: *Sister Carrie* and the Sentimentality of Nihilism," in his *The Subversive Vision: American Romanticism in Literature.* Port Washington, N.Y.: Kennikat, 1972, pp. 139–153.

Hussman, Lawrence E., Jr. "Thomas Edison and *Sister Carrie*: A Source for Character and Theme," in *American Literary Realism.* VIII (Spring, 1975), pp. 155–158.

Kazin, Alfred. "The Stature of Theodore Dreiser," in *Dreiser: A Collection of Critical Essays.* Edited by John Lydenberg. Englewood Cliffs, N.J.: Prentice-Hall, 1971, pp. 11–15. Also in his *The Stature of Theodore Dreiser.* Bloomington: Indiana University Press, 1955, pp. 3–12.

Lynn, Kenneth S. *"Sister Carrie,"* in *Visions of America.* Compiled by David Kherdian. New York: Macmillan, 1973, pp. 137–148.

McAleer, John J. *Theodore Dreiser.* New York: Holt, Rinehart and Winston, 1968, pp. 76–92.

Martin, Jay. *Harvests of Change, American Literature 1865–1914.* Englewood Cliffs, N.J.: Prentice-Hall, 1964, pp. 252–253, 256–258.

Matthiessen, F.O. *Theodore Dreiser.* New York: William Sloane, 1951, pp. 55–108.

Moers, Ellen. "The Finesse of Dreiser," in *American Scholar.* XXXIII (Winter, 1963–1964), pp. 109–114. Also in *Dreiser: A Collection of Critical Essays.* Edited by John Lydenberg. Englewood Cliffs, N.J.: Prentice-Hall, 1971, pp. 153–162.

————. *Two Dreisers.* New York: Viking, 1969, pp. 73–154.

Mookerjee, R.N. *Theodore Dreiser: His Thought and Social Criticism.* Delhi, India: National Publishing House, 1974, pp. 38–41.

Noble, D.W. "Progress vs. Tragedy: Veblin and Dreiser," in *Intellectual History in America,* Volume II. Edited by Cushing Strout. New York: Harper & Row, 1968, pp. 70–72.

Pizer, Donald. "Nineteenth-Century American Naturalism: An Essay in Definition," in *Bucknell Review.* XIII (December, 1965), pp. 1–18. Also in his *Realism and Naturalism in Nineteenth Century American Literature.* Carbondale: Southern Illinois University Press, 1966, pp. 11–32.

————. *The Novels of Theodore Dreiser.* New York: Holt, Rinehart and Winston, 1976, pp. 31–95.

Salzman, Jack, Editor. *Theodore Dreiser: The Critical Reception.* New York: David Lewis, 1972, pp. 1–55.

Seltzer, Leon F. "*Sister Carrie* and the Hidden Longing for Love: Sublimation or Subterfuge?," in *Twentieth Century Literature.* XXII (1976), pp. 192–209.

Shapiro, Charles. *Theodore Dreiser.* Carbondale: Southern Illinois University Press, 1962, pp. 1–14.

Simpson, Claude. "*Sister Carrie* Reconsidered," in *Southwest Review.* XLIV (Winter, 1959), pp. 44–53.

————. "Theodore Dreiser: *Sister Carrie,*" in *The American Novel.* Edited by Wallace Stegner. New York: Basic Books, 1965, pp. 106–116.

Taylor, Gordon O. "The Voice of Want: Frank Norris and Theodore Dreiser," in his *The Passages of Thought.* New York: Oxford University Press, 1969, pp. 136–157.

Walcutt, Charles Child. "The Divided Stream," in *Dreiser: A Collection of Critical Essays.* Edited by John Lydenberg. Englewood Cliffs, N.J.: Prentice-Hall, 1971, pp. 109–115. Also in *The Stature of Theodore Dreiser.* Edited by Alfred Kazin. Bloomington: Indiana University Press, 1976, pp. 246–269.

WALTER D. EDMONDS

Born: Boonville, New York (July 15, 1903)

Principal Works

NOVELS: *Rome Haul,* 1929; *The Big Barn,* 1930: *Erie Water,* 1933: *Drums Along the Mohawk,* 1936; *Chad Hanna,* 1940; *The Wedding Journey,* 1947; *The Musket and the Cross,* 1968.

SHORT STORIES: *Mostly Canallers,* 1934; *Young Ames,* 1941; *In the Hands of the Senecas,* 1947; *The Boyds of Black River,* 1953; *Seven American Stories,* 1970.

HISTORY: *The First Hundred Years,* 1948; *They Fought with What They Had,* 1951.

BOOKS FOR CHILDREN: *Uncle Ben's Whale,* 1955; *They Had a Horse,* 1962; *Wolf Hunt,* 1970.

Walter D(umaux) Edmonds was born on July 15, 1903, in Boonville, a small town in the heart of the upstate New York area which serves as the locale for his historical novels. His father, who operated a New York City law practice from his country farm, was a lineal descendant of the Reverend Peter Bulkeley of Concord, and his mother, Sarah Mays Edmonds, came from a family which had been involved in the witchcraft episodes around Salem. Edmonds grew up in the Erie Canal territory, and spent many hours of his boyhood listening to the colorful stories of the old canallers in the region around Boonville.

His parents sent him to St. Paul's School in Concord, New Hampshire, and then to Choate School in Wallingford, Connecticut. He later said that these years were "miserable" for him, and that it was not until he attended Harvard University that he discovered learning could be enjoyable. At Harvard, Edmonds studied with Professor Copeland and became editor of the *Harvard Advocate.* When Professor Copeland, impressed by Edmonds' work, sent one of his stories, "The End of the Towpath," to *Scribner's Magazine,* it was accepted for publication. In 1926, the year of his graduation from Harvard, he won second prize in an intercollegiate contest conducted by *Harper's.* Following his graduation, Ellery Sedgwick, then the editor of the *Atlantic Monthly,* suggested to Edmonds that he write a novel about the canal area he knew so well. The novel which he wrote during the winter of 1927–1928 was *Rome Haul,* published in 1929. It proved an immediate success, and from that time on Edmonds has concentrated his full effort on writing.

Most of his novels have been historical in character, re-creating in place and period the history of the upstate New York region. The action of *Drums Along the Mohawk* covers the years between 1776 and 1784; one of the best examples of the regional chronicle ever written in America, it tells how events on the frontier during the Revolutionary War affected the lives of settlers in the Mohawk

Valley. *Erie Water* is the story of the building of the Erie Canal between 1817 and 1825. *Rome Haul* shows the canal in the 1850's, before the railroads stripped it of romance and glory. *The Big Barn* deals with the efforts of upstate landowners, in the period of the Civil War, to preserve the large estates which united the culture of the Eastern seaboard with the crude, bluff vigor of the frontier. *Chad Hanna* is a story of circus life along the canal in its heyday. *The Boyds of Black River* presents a picture of Mohawk Valley farm life shortly after the turn of the century. *The Wedding Journey* is another story of the Erie Canal when it was a gateway to the West. Edmonds once summed up his work by saying that its purpose was "to tell, through the lives of everyday people, the story of New York State and its key periods in history."

He has also written a number of shorter books for young readers: *The Matchlock Gun* (1941), *Tom Whipple* (1942), *Wilderness Clearing* (1944), *Cadmus Henry* (1949), *Mr. Benedict's Lion* (1950), and others. In these there is the same documentary accuracy combined with atmospheric feeling that we find in his historical novels.

Edmonds has received a number of honors for the imaginative fullness and vigor of his re-creation of a segment of the American past, and the importance of his contribution has also been recognized by honorary degrees from Union College, Rutgers University, Colgate, and Harvard. He has served as a member of the Board of Overseers of Harvard University and has, in recent years, divided his time between his farm in Boonville and the academic environs of Cambridge, Massachusetts.

Bibliography

There is no full-length biography and very little criticism. Walter D. Edmonds, "How You Begin a Novel," *Atlantic Monthly*, CLVIII (1936), 189–192, is useful for information in the writer's methods of research. See also Dayton Kohler, "Walter D. Edmonds: Regional Historian," *English Journal*, XXVII (1938), 1–11; R. M. Gay, "The Historical Novel: Walter D. Edmonds," *Atlantic Monthly*, CLXV (1940), 656–658; and Lionel D. Wyld, "Canallers in *Waste Land*: Considerations of *Rome Haul*," *Midwest Quarterly*, IV (1963), 335–341.

DRUMS ALONG THE MOHAWK

Type of work: Novel
Author: Walter D. Edmonds (1903–   )
Time of plot: 1775–1783
Locale: The Mohawk Valley
First published: 1936

Set during the years of the Revolutionary War in the Mohawk Valley of Upstate New York, Drums Along the Mohawk *presents a focused rather than a sweeping view of the war years. Edmonds achieves an air of authenticity through his descriptions and his characterizations, many of which are based upon real people.*

Principal Characters

Gilbert (Gil) Martin, a young pioneer, a hard worker ambitious to have a place of his own at Deerfield and willing to continue fighting after each defeat. Senecas burn his first home and he is wounded in the ambushing of General Herkimer's militia. He works on the land and fights when needed until the valley is at last safe and he is able to return with his family to Deerfield.

Magdelana (Lana) Borst Martin, his pretty wife. She loses her first baby after the flight from Deerfield to Fort Schuyler but bears a boy, Gilly, the following spring and another boy, Joey, in August of the next year. Recovery from this birth is prolonged, but by the end of the war she has a baby girl to take to Deerfield with her husband and boys.

Mark Demooth, a captain of the militia, a small, slightly built man rather proud of himself.

John Wolff, a Tory convicted of aiding the British and sent to prison; he later escapes to Canada.

Blue Back, a friendly old Oneida Indian, dirty and paunchy, who likes Gil. He warns the Deerfield residents of a

planned raid and later serves as scout and guide for the militia. His young Indian wife is proud of his fertility despite his age.

Mrs. Sarah McKlennar, Captain Barnabas McKlennar's widow for whom Gil works as a hired hand. Her home is burned by two drunken Indians who take her bed out for her while the fire is burning.

Joseph Brant, an Indian chief who refuses to pledge neutrality in the war.

General Benedict Arnold, General Herkimer's successor appointed to reorganize the patriot army and lead it against St. Leger's camp.

Jurry McLonis, a Tory who seduces Nancy Schuyler.

Nancy Schuyler, Mrs. Demooth's maid, who bears Jurry's child and is taken by an Indian as his wife.

Hon Yost, Nancy's brother, another Tory who, when arrested, promises to spread in the British camp false reports of American strength.

Clem Coppernol,

DRUMS ALONG THE MOHAWK by Walter D. Edmonds. By permission of the author, of Harold Ober, and the publishers, Little, Brown & Co. Copyright, 1936, by Walter D. Edmonds.

The Weavers, and
The Realls, neighbors who help with the Deerfield log-rolling that is interrupted by the Seneca raid.

Mrs. Wolff, John's wife, reported missing after the Seneca raid.

General Nicholas Herkimer, commander of the Mohawk Valley patriots; he is mortally wounded when his men are ambushed and routed.

General Barry St. Leger, British general who leads a combined force of British and Indians against the patriots.

General Butler, British leader of a group of raiding and pillaging parties; he is

finally killed and his army routed.

Mrs. Demooth, a snobbish woman who so torments and frightens Nancy about her pregnancy that she leaves; Mrs. Demooth later loses her mind.

Colonel Van Schaick, leader of an attack against the Onondaga towns.

Adam Helmer and
Joe Boleo, two scouts who help Gil build a cabin after Mrs. McKlennar's house is burned.

Lt. Colonel Marinus Willett, leader of an army which pursues and attacks Butler's army, killing him and scattering his men in the wilderness.

The Story

Magdelana Borst, the oldest of five daughters, married Gilbert Martin and together they started off from her home at Fox's Mill to settle farther west in their home at Deerfield. The time was July, 1776, and the spirit of the revolution was reaching into the Mohawk Valley, where settlers who sided with the rebels had already formed a company of militia commanded by Mark Demooth. Soon after he came to his new home Gil had to report for muster day. Some Indians had been seen in the vicinity. Also, the militia had decided to investigate the home of John Wolff, suspected of being a king's man. Finding evidence that a spy had been hidden on the Wolff farm, they arrested John Wolff, convicted him of aiding the British, and sent him to the Newgate Prison at Simsbury Mines.

A few months after their arrival at Deerfield, Gil decided to have a log-rolling to clear his land for farming. The Weavers, the Realls, and Clem Coppernol all came to help with the work. When they were about half finished, Blue Back, a friendly Oneida Indian, came to warn them that a raiding party of Seneca Indians and whites was in the valley. The settlers immediately scattered for home to collect the few movable belongings which they might save, and then drove to Fort Schuyler. Lana, who was pregnant, lost her baby as a result of the wild ride to the fort. The enemy destroyed the Deerfield settlement. All the houses and fields were burned; Gil's cow was killed, and Mrs. Wolff, who had refused to take refuge with the people who had sent her husband to prison, was reported missing. Gil and Lana rented a one-room cabin in which to live through the winter. With spring coming on and needing a job to support himself and Lana, Gil became the hired man of Mrs. McKlennar, a widow. The pay was forty-five dollars a year plus the use of a two-room house and their food.

General Herkimer tried to obtain a pledge of neutrality from the Indian chief,

Joseph Brant, but was unsuccessful. At the end of the summer, word came that the combined forces of British and Indians, commanded by General St. Leger, were moving down from Canada to attack the valley. The militia was called up and set out westward to encounter this army. But the attack by the militia was badly timed and the party was ambushed. Of nearly six hundred and fifty men, only two hundred and fifty survived. The survivors returned in scattered groups. Gil received a bullet wound in the arm. General Herkimer, seriously injured in the leg, died of his wounds.

After the death of General Herkimer, General Benedict Arnold was sent out to reorganize the army and lead it in another attack—this time against General St. Leger's camp.

When Nancy Schuyler, Mrs. Demooth's maid, heard that her brother, Hon Yost, was in the neighborhood with a group of Tories, she decided to sneak out to see him. On the way she met another Tory, Jurry McLonis, who seduced her. Before she was able to see Hon, the American militia broke up the band. Hon was arrested but was later released when he agreed to go back to the British camp and spread false reports of the American strength. As a result of her meeting with Jurry McLonis, Nancy became pregnant. About that same time John Wolff escaped from the prison at Simsbury Mines and made his way to Canada to join Butler and to look for his wife.

The following spring brought with it General Butler's destructives, raiding parties that would swoop down to burn and pillage small settlements or farms. Mrs. Demooth tormented Nancy constantly because of her condition and one night frightened the girl so completely that Nancy, in terror, packed a few of her belongings in a shawl and ran away. Her only idea was to try to get to Niagara and find her brother Hon, but she had not gone far before labor pains overtook her and she bore her child beside a stream. An Indian found her there and took her with him as his wife. Lana had her child in May. The destruction by the raiding parties continued all through that summer, and the harvest was small. Mrs. McKlennar's stone house was not burned, but there was barely enough food for her household that winter. In the spring Colonel Van Schaick came to the settlement with an army, and the militia headed west once again, this time to strike against the Onondaga towns.

Lana had her second child the following August. Because of the lack of food during the winter, she was still weak from nursing her first boy, Gilly, and after the birth of her second boy it took her a long while to recover. The next winter they all had enough to eat but the cold was severe. During that winter Mrs. McKlennar aged greatly and kept mostly to her bed. The destructives continued their raids through the next spring and summer. The men never went out to their fields alone; they worked in groups with armed guards. One day, after all the men had gone to the fort, Lana took the two boys for a walk and then sat down at the edge of a clearing and fell asleep. When she awoke, Gilly was gone. Two Indians were near the house. She put the baby, Joey, into a hiding place and then searched for Gilly. She found him at last and the two of them crawled into the hiding place also. Meanwhile the two Indians had entered the house and set it on fire. Overwhelmed by Mrs. McKlennar's righteous indignation, they carried out her bed for her. They fled when men, seeing the smoke, came hurrying from the fort. Gil and the two scouts, Adam Helmer and Joe Boleo, built a cabin to house them all during the coming winter.

With the spring thaws, a flood inundated the valley. As the waters receded, Marinus Willett came into the Mohawk Valley with his army, with orders to track down and destroy the British forces under General Butler. Butler's army already was having a difficult time, for British food supplies were running out and tracking wolves killed all stragglers. The militia finally caught up with Butler, harassed his army for several miles, killed Butler, and scattered the routed army in the wilderness. The Mohawk Valley was saved.

Three years later, the war over, Gil and Lana went back to their farm at Deerfield. They now had a baby girl and Lana and Gil felt content with their hard-won security, their home, their children, and each other.

Critical Evaluation

During the 1930's the historical novel became extremely popular. Most of them followed the same pattern: they were long, had many characters, were full of action and realistic detail, and usually ended happily. *Drums Along the Mohawk* has all of these qualities, but it is one of the best of the genre. In 1936 it was on the best-seller list. Edmonds in his author's note defends the genre, noting that the life presented is not a bygone picture, for the parallel is too close to our own. The valley people faced repercussions of poverty and starvation and were plagued by unfulfilled promises and the inevitable redtape of a central government which could not understand local problems. Thus, the valley farmers, in the typically American tradition, learned to fight for themselves and for the land they had worked so hard to wrench from the wilderness and could not abandon.

Contrary to the patriotic myth, for all American soldiers the war was not a glorious fight for freedom. Many fought only because it was necessary to protect their families. They never thought of the American troops in the South and East; that was too remote, while the ever-present threat of instant disaster was too near. When Captain Demooth says to Gil, "Who gives a damn for the Stamp Tax?" Gil admits that it had not bothered him and asks the key question of most of the farmers: "Why do we have to go and fight the British at all?" The attitude of many of the men conscripted for the militia is "Damn the militia! I need to roof my barn." Yet, as the attacks upon the small settlements begin, they realize that they must band together and fight.

At times the western settlers wonder which side is the enemy. Denied food, munitions, and the protection of regular troops by the government at Albany, their seed grain commandeered, and their fences burned for firewood, the settlers of German Flats become extremely bitter at the indifferent treatment they receive. When the widowed Mrs. Reall with her many children tries to collect her husband's back pay, she is denied because he is not marked dead on the paymaster's list. Even though Colonel Bellinger swears he saw Reall killed and scalped, the money is withheld. The only alternative she is given is to file a claim before the auditor-general which must then be passed by an act of Congress. In the meantime the family must starve or rely on the charity of others who cannot really afford to help. They find that the Continental currency is practically worthless, but the climax of the colonists' disillusionment with the Congress comes when the residents receive huge tax bills for land which has been abandoned, buildings that have burned, and stock that has been killed. The incredulous settlers realize that the tax list is the one formerly used by the king.

The bestiality of what war does to men dominates the book. As the Indian raids become more ghastly, the Continentals grow more brutal. Scalps are taken by both Indian and white, and the atrocities and mutilations committed by both sides become increasingly barbarous.

Yet, in spite of the ever-present atmosphere of horror, fear, and death, Edmonds also presents the forces of life. There is fierce energy in the characters in spite of their hardships. This is seen most clearly in the character of Lana, who, though weakened by starvation, work, and fear, manages to bear and care for her two boys. There is a mystery about her as she nurses and cares for her babies. Although she deeply loves Gil, with the birth of the first child she becomes mother first. Even the rough scout Joe Boleo senses the maternal mystery she exudes. There is also beauty in life itself as seen in the human body and in reproduction. The pregnant Nancy becomes more beautiful as she carries her illegitimate child, and the marriage of young John Weaver to Mary Reall begins another generation when Mary becomes pregnant.

Edmonds' style is free flowing, and he has an excellent ear for natural folk speech. As omniscient narrator, he goes deeply into the minds of the main characters and captures their reactions to the many things going on about them. All of the main characters have individuality and the gift of life.

The praise that is often given the novel is for the realism which Edmonds achieves by minute detail; however, this is also a weakness. His accounts of the many battles and raids become repetitious, for in the interest of historical truth, he does not want to eliminate anything. Thus, the action becomes blurred because there are so many similar accounts.

Structurally the book is well handled with the exception of the last chapter, "Lana," which occurs three years after the preceeding one. It appears to have been tacked on simply to tie up a few loose ends and to give the story a happy ending. In a book which has proceeded slowly season by season for five years, the three year interval startles the reader.

The theme of the novel is the strength of the men who will endure anything to achieve the American dream. Through their own efforts they hope to earn their land, houses, animals, and the material things necessary to make life easier and more beautiful for themselves and particularly for their children. Lana and Gil begin their marriage with a cow, a few pieces of furniture, and Lana's most valued possession—a peacock feather which, with its mysterious beauty, symbolizes the beauty of the dream. All of this is lost in the war, but in the last chapter Gil realizes his ambitions. He is farming his own land, he has built a new house, and he owns a yoke of oxen. Lana has her two boys, a baby daughter, security, and even the now battered but still gorgeous peacock feather which the Indian Blue Back returns to her. She is supremely content and secure as she tells herself, "We've got this place. . . . We've got the children. We've got each other. Nobody can take those things away. Not any more."

Bibliography

Edmonds, Walter D. "A Novelist Takes Stock," in *Atlantic Monthly*. CLXXII (July, 1943), pp. 73–77.

Gay, R.M. "The Historical Novel: Walter D. Edmonds," in *Atlantic Monthly*. CLXV (May, 1940), pp. 656–658.

Kohler, Dayton. "Walter D. Edmonds: Regional Historian," in *English Journal*. XXVII (January, 1938), pp. 1–11.

McCord, David. "Edmonds Country," in *Saturday Review of Literature*. XVII (December 11, 1937), pp. 10–11.

Nyren, Dorothy. "Walter Edmonds," in *A Library of Literary Criticism; Modern American Literature*. Edited by Dorothy Nyren. New York: Frederick Ungar, 1960, pp. 154–156.

Whicher, George Frisbie. "Loopholes of Retreat," in *The Literature of the American People; An Historical and Critical Survey*. Edited by Arthur H. Quinn. New York: Appleton-Century-Crofts, 1951, pp. 890–891.

Wyld, Lionel D. "At Boyd House: Walter Edmonds' York State," in *English Record*. XX (1969), pp. 89–92.

————. "Canallers in *Waste Land*: Considerations of *Rome Haul*," in *Midwest Quarterly*. (1963), pp. 335–341.

————. "Fiction, Fact and Folklore: The World of *Chad Hanna*," in *English Journal*. LVI (May, 1967), pp. 716–719.

JAMES T. FARRELL

Born: Chicago, Illinois (February 27, 1904)
Died: Chicago (August 22, 1979)

Principal Works

NOVELS: *Young Lonigan,* 1932; *Gas-House Maginty,* 1933; *The Young Manhood of Studs Lonigan,* 1934; *Judgment Day,* 1935; *Studs Lonigan: A Trilogy,* 1935 *(Young Lonigan, The Young Manhood of Studs Lonigan, Judgment Day);* A *World I Never Made,* 1936; *No Star Is Lost,* 1939; *Father and Son,* 1940; *My Days of Anger,* 1943; *Bernard Clare,* 1946; *The Road Between,* 1949; *This Man and This Woman,* 1951; *Yet Other Waters,* 1952; *The Face of Time,* 1953; *The Silence of History,* 1963; *What Time Collects,* 1964; *Lonely for the Future,* 1966; *Invisible Swords,* 1971.

SHORT STORIES: *Calico Shoes,* 1934; *Guillotine Party,* 1935; *Can All This Grandeur Perish?* 1937; *$1000 a Week,* 1942; *To Whom It May Concern,* 1944; *When Boyhood Dreams Come True,* 1946; *The Life Adventurous,* 1947; *An American Dream Girl,* 1950; *French Girls Are Vicious,* 1956; *A Dangerous Woman, and Other Stories,* 1957: *Childhood Is Not Forever,* 1969.

ESSAYS AND STUDIES: *A Note on Literary Criticism,* 1936; *The League of Frightened Philistines,* 1945; *Literature and Morality,* 1947; *Reflections at Fifty,* 1954.

POEMS: *The Collected Poems of James T. Farrell,* 1965.

REMINISCENCES: *My Baseball Diary,* 1957.

James T(homas) Farrell remained a naturalistic writer during the 1930's at a time when the trend was toward symbolism or a highly selective realism. If he did not see life as a whole he saw it steadily, through gray-tinted glasses. He told the same story of the life of the Irish in a Chicago slum over and over again, but he retained a purly reportorial attitude on this phase of life which he knew so intimately, having been a part of it. In his fiction there is nothing that had to be invented. During the time Farrell was growing up in the Chicago South Side it was one of the harshest slums in America, and his *Studs Lonigan* trilogy (*Young Lonigan, The Young Manhood of Studs Lonigan,* and *Judgment Day*) is the story of the life of a childhood friend hardened by the environment until death saves him.

Farrell, born on the South Side on February 27, 1904, had the usual Catholic parochial education in Chicago; however, unlike most of his friends he went on to college, first to De Paul and then to the University of Chicago. Here he determined to be a writer, although his interests up to that time, except for a brief experience as reporter for a Hearst paper, were chiefly in sports; other part-time jobs had included clerking and selling. First publishing in periodicals, he gained critical attention with his early novels and achieved popular notice in 1937 when

A World I Never Made was examined by a New York court on the grounds of obscenity. The year before he had received a fellowship from the Book-of-the-Month Club for *Studs Lonigan.*

Throughout his career Farrell maintained his purpose of "exposing conditions," but his later novels, including the Danny O'Neill series which in many ways parallels his own life, did not sustain the tension of the Lonigan trilogy. He matured, however, as a socio-literary critic, and his self-assumed role of the outsider, aligned with no particular group, gave his later statements on the culture generally, and the publishing business specifically, a valuable objectivity. He died in Chicago in 1979.

Bibliography

Edgar M. Branch has prepared *A Bibliography of James T. Farrell's Writings, 1921-1957,* 1958 with two supplements bringing the list to 1967, *American Book Collector,* XI (1961) 42-48 and XVII, ix (1967), 9-19. For the only full-length study see *idem, James T. Farrell, University of Minnesota Pamphlets on American Writers,* No. 29, 1963. The best brief criticism of Farrell is Joseph Warren Beach, *American Fiction: 1920-1940,* 1941. See also Oscar Cargill, *Intellectual America,* 1941; Alfred Kazin, *On Native Grounds,* 1942; George Snell, *The Shapers of American Fiction, 1798-1947,* 1947; W. M. Frohock, *The Novel of Violence in America, 1920-1950,* 1950; Robert M. Lovett, "James T. Farrell," *English Journal,* XXVI (1937), 347-354; Calder Willingham, "A Note on James T. Farrell," *Quarterly Review of Literature,* II (1944), 120-124; and Edgar M. Branch, "Freedom and Determinism in James T. Farrell's Fiction," *Essays on Determinism in American Literature,* 1964, 79-96.

STUDS LONIGAN

Type of work: Novel
Author: James T. Farrell (1904–1979)
Time of plot: 1916–1934
Locale: Chicago
First published: 1935 (*Young Lonigan*, 1932; *The Young Manhood of Studs Lonigan*, 1934; and *Judgment Day*, 1935)

Farrell's most important work, Studs Lonigan *has been called everything from sociology to "proletarian fiction," but its honesty of depiction and its devastating vision of the degeneration of Studs Lonigan from adolescence to his death, in conjunction with the degeneration of American society from the euphoria of pre-World War I America to the despair of the Great Depression, require that the trilogy be read and criticized on equal terms with such works of literary genius as* Sherwood Anderson's Winesburg, Ohio *and William Faulkner's Snopes trilogy.*

Principal Characters

Studs Lonigan, named William. He wastes his youth carousing, drinking, and "jazzing," to prove that he is "the real stuff." He then wastes the rest of his short life trying to recapture or recall the questionable glories of his youth. His greatest ambitions in life seem to be to determine how much liquor he can drink, how many women he can handle, how many fights he can win, and how to be accepted as a leader of the disreputable group of which he is a member. He drops out of high school and goes to work for his father in order to be free to practice his particular expertise. There are times that he seems on the verge of becoming an "upright citizen," but circumstances always "force" him back to what he does best—reminiscence and raucous behavior. He ruins his health as a result of a delirious New Year's party in 1929 and from that point until his death is only a shell of "the real stuff" he was in his youth. He tries to save something of his life in his engagement to Catherine, but even in that relationship he fails: he seduces Catherine and she becomes pregnant. Studs is a stereotypical, half-educated, fiercely proud, young Irishman who disdains responsibility and the inexorable advance of time. When he dies, he has killed himself; but he is succeeded by his younger brother, "Husk" Lonigan, who seems destined to carry on the pattern of degeneration established by Studs.

Patrick Lonigan, Stud's Irish workingman father. A second generation Irish painter, he recognizes the similarities between "Bill" and himself, but feels they are human nature and cannot be changed.

Mary Lonigan, Stud's mother, who wishes, to the end, that one of her boys had the "call" to be a priest. She is an ineffectual Catholic fanatic dominated by her husband.

Frances Lonigan, Stud's eldest sister.

Loretta Lonigan, also known as "Fritzie," Stud's younger sister.

Martin Lonigan, the baby of the Lonigan family, later known as "Husk" Lonigan and portrayed as traveling the same debilitating path that kills Studs.

Lucy Scanlan, the ideal girl for Studs Lonigan. Studs opens the trilogy admitting that he loves Lucy and dies with her vision dancing through his delirium. Throughout the trilogy, Lucy is Studs's quest, his grail.

Weary Reilley, a hard-boiled lad from the same grammar school class as Studs. He is portrayed as the worst of the bad throughout. Studs licks the tough Reilley kid in the summer after graduation from grammar school and nurses his glory long after he no longer can perform such feats. Weary is, if there is one, the villain of the trilogy.

Barney Keefe, perpetually drunk, he acts as a chorus for the proceedings of Studs's gang. He is the Irish symbol who stays in the old neighborhood after the whites leave it to the blacks.

Phil Rolfe, a Jewish bookie who converts to Catholicism to gain the acceptance of the Lonigan family in order to marry Loretta.

Carroll Dowson, a "well-to-do" young man who marries Frances.

Father Gilhooley, the priest of the diocese of St. Patrick's.

Catherine Banahan, the girl Studs in engaged to. When he dies she is pregnant with his child.

Essay-Review

In much the same way that William Faulkner presents the South and Sherwood Anderson and Sinclair Lewis portray middle America, Farrell is the herald of urban Irish America. There is, critics have declared, more sociology and autobiography in the trilogy than true literature, but the chronicle of the rise and fall of Studs Lonitan is also the chronicle of the self destruction of pre-depression America and the effect of that economic disaster on Lonigan's world.

Studs Lonigan begins down the path of ruin upon his graduation from grammar school at the age of fifteen. He falls in love with Lucy Scanlan, but he is so confused by this new emotion that he renounces such nonsense. More important to Studs is that he can fight, drink, and carouse with his friends. Uninterested in high school, Studs does not attend regularly, which leads to repeated arguments with his father. Finally, they agree that he should begin to work. With the additional money he earns, Studs increases his carousing. Eventually, concerned about his failing health, Studs decides to stop drinking and become as fit as he once was. His attempts at reform fail, however, and he discovers that he has an enlarged heart. Studs watches as blacks move into the old Irish community; and like his friends and neighbors, Mr. Lonigan moves to a new area. Hit by the Depression, Mr. Lonigan's business fails. Studs, left with time on his hands, falls into reminiscence and wild parties in an attempt to regain the glory of his youth. One day while looking for work, Studs catches cold and lapses into a fatal illness. With the Depression raging, Studs dies, leaving a pregnant fiancée and a family destined to continue on the course which has led to his demise.

Farrell's style is brutal and crude. Its accuracy creates verisimilitude that encourages skepticism of its literary value. Yet the same stroke that creates the impression of reality creates a dream world in which Studs Lonigan must find himself. The dream world is bounded by the can houses and speakeasys, "gang shags" and "moon," and opens from the poolroom. This aberrant dream is the reverse of normality, that state of being which Studs flirts with but never embraces. It is the conflict of the real and the imagined, the actual and the desired, that separates the work from sociology and places it solidly in the mainstream of American literature. Farrell is crude with purpose. Amidst a group of quotations introducing *Young Lonigan*, Farrell quotes Frank Norris; "A literature that cannot be vulgarized is no literature at all and will perish." Farrell's vulgarity reflects the world he portrays. For Farrell, no manner of words or window dressing can disguise reality. Therefore, he lets us witness this reality in its own vocabulary and on its own terms.

The Irish America as represented by Studs Lonigan is, however, ambivalent at best. That ambivalence is best represented by Studs's pursuit of the ideal woman, Lucy Scanlan. Studs, from the time of his graduation from grammar school, is determined to build the mystique of "the real stuff" around himself. He is tough and untouchable. He can outdrink, outfight, and outhustle everybody on the block. But always, when he has achieved what he terms a success, Lucy enters and triggers emotions that Studs cannot understand or control. When he sits with Lucy in the oak tree in Washington Park, Studs loses his invulnerability, if only momentarily, and realizes true affection. But when his world badgers him for this weakness, he reverts to the tough mold he deems more suitable for a man in his station of life. Studs's opinion of himself and his desire go beyond his opinion towards Lucy are always at odds. Even when Studs has become a paper figure of his former self, he still dreams of Lucy and regains, again momentarily, some of his former self esteem. In the midst of a wild night in a Chicago "can house," Studs imagines himself with Lucy and reproves himself bitterly for thinking of Lucy "that way."

This quest for the unreachable and the trek through the mire following Lucy's star are the hallmarks of Studs's life, and as Studs fails, we see America failing around him. When he reaches his deathbed, we have discovered that his stocks have failed, his father's bank has failed, and that Studs, as a result of the failure of his father's business, cannot find a job in Chicago. But, even as Studs dies, Lucy dances before him through his delirious dreams.

The background of Irish Catholicism that ranges hideously behind the principals is the result of Farrell's antipathy for the religion of his youth. Lonigan's Catholicism is haphazard, fanatical, mindless, and blind. The juxtaposition of Studs's adherence to the "mother church" and Danny O'Neill's (Farrell's) educated rejection of the dogmatic church is clearly another comment on the crumbling walls of citadel America and of Studs Lonigan, himself.

The critical disdain for Farrell's work overlooks the literary merit of Farrell's view of America and sees only the strident commentary on the state of the State. The latter is, however, only a means to an end and that end is an anguished portrayal of a man walking through a tunnel who never sees the light at the end and who imagines only rarely that there might be another way. It is, more and more, a very modern allegory. Studs is the Everyman who not only does not seek, but refuses company on his trip to the grave.

Bibliography

Allen, Walter. *The Modern Novel in Britain and the United States.* New York: Dutton, 1964, pp. 148–153.

Beach, Joseph Warren. *American Fiction, 1920–1940.* New York: Russell and Russell, 1960, pp. 273–283.

Branch, Edgar M. "Destiny, Culture and Technique: *Studs Lonigan*," in *University of Kansas City Review.* XXIX (1962), pp. 103–113.

————. *James T. Farrell.* Minneapolis: University of Minnesota Press, 1963, pp. 16–22.

————. "*Studs Lonigan,* Symbolism and Theme," in *College English.* XXIII (December, 1961), pp. 191–196.

Douglas, Wallace. "The Case of James T. Farrell," in *Tri-Quarterly.* No. 2 (Winter, 1965), pp. 108–115.

Gurko, Leo. *Angry Decade.* New York: Harper & Row, 1968, pp. 119–125.

Mitchell, Richard. "*Studs Lonigan:* Research in Morality," in *Centennial Review.* VI (Spring, 1962), pp. 202–214.

Rosenthal, T.G. "*Studs Lonigan* and the Search for an American Tragedy," in *British Association for American Studies Bulletin.* VII (December, 1963), pp. 46–53.

Snell, George. *The Shapers of American Fiction, 1798–1947.* New York: Dutton, 1947, pp. 289–294.

Walcutt, Charles Child. *American Literary Naturalism, A Divided Stream.* Minneapolis: University of Minnesota Press, 1956, pp. 240–245.

WILLIAM FAULKNER

Born: New Albany, Mississippi (September 25, 1897)
Died: Byhalia, Mississippi (July 6, 1962)

Principal Works

NOVELS: *Soldiers' Pay*, 1926; *Mosquitoes*, 1927; Sartoris, 1929; *The Sound and the Fury*, 1929; As I Lay Dying, 1930; *Sanctuary*, 1931; *Light in August*, 1932; *Pylon*, 1935; *Absalom, Absalom!* 1936; *The Unvanquished*, 1938; *The Wild Palms*, 1939; *The Hamlet*, 1940; *Go Down, Moses*, 1942; *Intruder in the Dust*, 1948; *Requiem for a Nun*, 1951; A Fable, 1954; *The Town*, 1957; *The Mansion*, 1959; *The Reivers*, 1961.

SHORT STORIES: *These Thirteen*, 1931; *Doctor Martino and Other Stories*, 1934; *Knight's Gambit*, 1949; *Collected Short Stories of William Faulkner*, 1950; *Big Woods*, 1955.

POEMS: *The Marble Faun*, 1924; *A Green Bough*, 1933.

William Faulkner is a universal writer who is associated inevitably with the north Mississippi region which supplied him with most of his material. Born in New Albany, he spent most of his life in Oxford except for periodic work in New York and Hollywood, for U.S. State Department missions and European travel, and for part-time residence in Virginia during his last years. His ancestors had left Scotland in the mid-eighteenth century for America, where their most spectacular descendant, William Clark Falkner, became a Civil War colonel, wrote a popular novel, fathered a sizable family, and enlarged a regional railroad before a business rival murdered him. As a schoolboy, William Faulkner said he wanted to be a writer like his great-grandfather and had already shown a gift for storytelling, sketching, and verse-writing. But he was nearing thirty when his first book, *The Marble Faun*, was published in 1924. By that time he had continued his wide reading under the guidance of a local lawyer, Phil Stone, and had spent five months of 1918 in R.A.F. preflight training in Canada, an activity ended by the Armistice. After a series of odd jobs he attended the University of Mississippi as a special student during 1919–1920 and then quit early in his second year.

Faulkner continued to write, without commercial success, during his tenure as university postmaster from late 1921 to late 1924. Then, in early 1925 he moved into New Orleans' Vieux Carré, where Sherwood Anderson encouraged him and helped place his first novel with his publisher. Faulkner spent the second half of that year living and traveling in Europe, returning shortly before *Soldiers' Pay* appeared. This novel, like Hemingway's *The Sun Also Rises*, concerns the postwar "Lost Generation," as maimed Donald Mahon returns to Georgia to be rejected by his flapper fiancée but cherished by a war widow before his early death. Faulkner's next novel, *Mosquitoes*, was an imitative and experimental satire of New Orleans artists and aesthetes. By now he had discovered his true milieu—the life of the Deep South as he knew it—and worked on a story about aristocrats which he called *Flags in the Dust*, and another about hill men, *Father Abraham*. After a series of rejections the former appeared in January, 1929, as *Sartoris*, in which young Bayard Sartoris tries to drown his grief for his brother, killed in the war, by losing himself in carousal and finally suicide. For contrast Faulkner used the elder Sartorises (modeled on the Falkners) and other families of Yoknapatawpha County—the counterpart of Faulkner's native Lafayette County.

October of this same year saw the appearance of the first of a half-dozen major novels, all of them experimental in technique, shocking in violence and sexuality, and overwhelming in their embodiment of the dignity and indignity of man. *The Sound and the Fury* may be a tale of the Compson family's decline partly told by the idiot son Benjy, by the neurotic son Quentin, and the heartless son Jason, about an alcoholic father, a self-centered mother, and a promiscuous sister and her promiscuous daughter, but its disorder becomes a powerful parable when set against the order of the astute but faithful Negro servant Dilsey ("They endured," Faulkner wrote later). Faulkner had revised and elaborated this novel with great care. He attacked his next story with greater speed and much less concern. He would soon be married and he needed money. But the typescript of *Sanctuary* shocked even his publisher, and Faulkner resigned himself to a night job in the town power plant where, in less than two months, he did much of the work on *As I Lay Dying*. A tale of back country life, it consisted of fifty-nine short interior monologues chiefly concerning the varying relationships of husband, lover, sons, daughter, and neighbors to the dying and dead Addie Bundren. When Faulkner's publisher surprised him by sending *Sanctuary* to the printer, Faulkner insisted on rewriting from the galley proofs. He reworked the novel for a craftsman's reasons, not with the result of making its sexual, moral, and social degenerates less shocking, but apparently of investing the wild tale with a significant indictment of the evil of both hypocrisy and amorality. *Sanctuary* made its author famous, but neither the critics nor the public understood it until much later, nor did they solve the riddle of *Light in August*, whose Joe Christmas is caught in a vortex of sexual, racial, religious, and community pressures. *Pylon* was a less successful story of a *femme fatale* involved with an air circus, two lovers, and a quixotic newspaperman at Mardi Gras, but *Absalom, Absalom!* rose again to the heights. In a suspended and suspenseful sequence reconstructed by Quentin Compson, the novel concentrates on Faulkner's most tragic protagonist, Thomas Sutpen (1807–1869), who achieves his grandiose "design" of creating a great house out of nothing but fails to sustain his line because he rejects the human beings who compose it.

The Civil War was the romantic subject of most of the chapters of *The Unvanquished*, and the ravages of love in the twentieth century was the unromantic subject of *The Wild Palms*, which consists of two separate counterpointed tales (the other called *Old Man*) whose chapters alternate. *The Hamlet*, 1940, and *Go Down, Moses*, 1942, returned to the fertile earth of Yoknapatawpha. The former, taking up the saga Faulkner had envisioned in *Father Abraham*, was the first of a trilogy centering on the aggressive, amoral Flem Snopes and his odious but sometimes comic clan. It was made of linked tales, the most famous of which is the tall story masterpiece "Spotted Horses." *Go Down, Moses* looks like a collection of stories, but Faulkner saw it as a novel, and it embodies his most complex family saga, that of the McCaslin-Edmonds-Beauchamp group. This family begins with ante-bellum miscegenation and incest, proceeds through social comedy, romantic primitivism, and Christian renunciation—especially in the great novella, *The Bear*—and ends with fifth generation disintegration.

During World War II Faulkner returned to Hollywood, where he had written scenarios during two earlier prolonged stays. In 1946, when almost all his books were out of print, Malcolm Cowley's superb anthology, *The Portable Faulkner*, first demonstrated a unity as well as a variety that appealed to more than a coterie of readers. Faulkner's first novel in six years, *Intruder in the Dust*, was not so much a story of the proud Negro Lucas Beauchamp as of the teenage white boy who learns painfully how to treat him as a human being. *Knight's Gambit* was a collection of detective stories featuring Gavin Stevens, a highly articulate lawyer of Jefferson, the seat of Yoknapatawpha County. The next year, 1950, saw the publication of *Collected Stories*, which incorporated new work with stories published in two earlier volumes and showed clearly how Faulkner had ranged over the county's history from Indian times to the present. In November Faulkner was named Nobel Laureate in Literature for 1949 and reluctantly went to Stockholm, where he made the most quoted of all Nobel Prize acceptance speeches.

The new decade was a crowded one. *Requiem for a Nun* revived characters from *Sanctuary* to seek their salvation in the frame of a play with long stage directions, but in 1954 Faulkner published a totally new long novel conceived a dozen years before and set in the France of 1918. *A Fable*, which consciously allegorizes the events of the false Armistice into the events of Christ's last days, caused some confusion for the reader but won the National Book Award and the Pulitzer Prize. In the same year Faulkner made the first of a series of trips for the U.S. State Department which took him around the world. In early 1957 he stayed in the public eye as Writer-in-Residence at the University of Virginia, with which he would remain affiliated. Meanwhile he had been at work writing *The Town*, which took up the Snopes trilogy where *The Hamlet* left off. He completed this work, envisioned thirty years before, with *The Mansion*, which ended the saga as retribution finally came to Flem Snopes.

Enjoying his family, fox hunting in Albemarle County, Virginia, and writing only when he felt like it, Faulkner found that there was still another novel to be written. It was a story he had actually thought of years before, a mellow, retrospective, grandfatherly narrative of a boy's partial initiation into adulthood. Though not one of his major works, *The Reivers* was a critical and popular success when it appeared in May of 1962. He had gone to Mississippi for the summer, planning a return to Virginia in early fall, but on July 6 he died of a heart attack in a small hospital north of Oxford.

The extensive body of work he left behind him displays styles as various as Picasso's, but the most typical expression is a syntactically demanding, ornate but precise, diffuse but flowing series of long sentences, easy to parody but impossible to match—the very signal of the most original and substantial American writer of the century.

Bibliography

Michael Millgate supplies comprehensive and accurate biographical information in the first chapter of *The Achievement of William Faulkner*, 1966. Joseph Blotner's authorized biography is *Faulkner: A Biography*, 1974. Two valuable collections of early work are Carvel Collins, *William Faulkner: New Orleans Sketches*, 1958, and *William Faulkner: Early Prose and Poetry*, 1962. Useful interview volumes are *Lion in the Garden*, 1968, ed. by James B. Meriwether and Michael Millgate, and *Faulkner in the University*, 1959, ed. by Frederick L. Gwynn and Joseph Blotner. Bibliographies of the works are supplied by James B. Meriwether in *The Literary Career of William Faulkner*, 1961, and by Linton R. Massey in *William Faulkner: "Man Working, 1919–1962,"* 1968. For commentaries see Irene Lynn Sleeth, "William Faulkner: A Bibliography of Criticism," *Twentieth Century Literature*, 8 (April, 1962), 18–43, and Frederick J. Hoffman and Olga Vickery, eds., *William Faulkner: Three Decades of Criticism*, 1960. Additional bibliographies of criticism are supplied in many of the following, treating variously Faulkner's milieu, family, life, career, and works: Richard P. Adams, *Faulkner: Myth and Motion*, 1968; Melvin Backman, *Faulkner: The Major Years*, 1966; Joseph Blotner, *William Faulkner's Library—A Catalogue*, 1964; Cleanth Brooks, *William Faulkner: The Yoknapatawpha Country*, 1963, and *Toward Yoknapatawpha & Beyond*, 1978; Walter Brylowski, *Faulkner's Olympian Laugh: Myth in the Novels*, 1968; Robert Coughlan, *The Private World of William Faulkner*, 1954; Malcolm Cowley, *The Faulkner-Cowley File: Letters and Memories, 1944–1962*, 1966; John B. Cullen, with Floyd C. Watkins, *Old Times in the Faulkner Country*, 1961; Murry C. Falkner, *The Falkners of Mississippi*, 1967; John Faulkner, *My Brother Bill: An Affectionate Reminiscence*, 1963; Joseph Gold, *William Faulkner: A Study in Humanism*, 1966; John Lewis Longley, Jr., *The Tragic Mask: A Study of Faulkner's Heroes*, 1963; Irving Malin, *William Faulkner: An Interpretation*, 1957; William Van O'Connor, *The Tangled Fire of William Faulkner*, 1954; Walter J. Slatoff, *Quest for Failure: A Study of William Faulkner*, 1960; Lawrance Thompson, *William Faulkner: An Introduction and Interpretation*, 1963; Olga W. Vickery, *The Novels of William Faulkner: A Critical Interpretation*, 1959; Edmond L. Volpe, *A Reader's Guide to William Faulkner*, 1964; Hyatt H. Waggoner, *William Faulkner: From Jefferson to the World*, 1959; and James W. Webb and A. Wigfall Green, eds., *William Faulkner of Oxford*, 1965.

ABSALOM, ABSALOM!

Type of work: Novel
Author: William Faulkner (1897–1962)
Time of plot: September, 1909–January, 1910
Locale: Mississippi and Cambridge, Massachusetts
First published: 1936

Considered by many to be Faulkner's greatest work, Absalom, Absalom! *is his most comprehensive attempt to come to terms with the full implications of the Southern experience. The structure of the novel, itself an attempt by its various narrators to make some sense of the seemingly chaotic past, is indicative of the multi-faceted complexity of that experience. That Quentin's roommate at Harvard, a Canadian, is as caught up in the story as is Quentin indicates that the experience, finally, goes far beyond the regional.*

Principal Characters

Thomas Sutpen, owner of a plantation called "Sutpen's Hundred" in Yoknapatawpha County, just outside of Jefferson, Mississippi. He was born in 1807 in West Virginia and died at "Sutpen's Hundred" in 1869.

Eulalie Bon Sutpen, his first wife, a Haitian woman, the daughter of a French sugar planter, whose marriage lasted only a few years before Sutpen obtained a divorce from her immediately after their first child was born in 1831.

Charles Bon, the son of Thomas and Eulalie Sutpen. He left Haiti with his mother to live in New Orleans and later attended the university of Mississippi at Oxford. He was killed outside the gates of "Sutpen's Hundred" in 1865.

Charles Etienne Bon, son of Charles Bon and his octaroon mistress; born in New Orleans in 1859 and brought to "Sutpen's Hundred" in 1870. He died there of yellow fever in 1884.

Jim Bond, son of Charles Etienne Bon and a slave woman. He was born in 1882 and disappeared from "Sutpen's Hundred" in 1910.

Goodhue Coldfield, a merchant of Jefferson with whom Thomas Sutpen was able to make certain critical financial arrangements and whose daughter Sutpen married.

Ellen Coldfield, the daughter of Goodhue and the second wife of Thomas Sutpen. She was born in Jefferson and died at "Sutpen's Hundred" in 1862.

Rosa Coldfield, the younger sister of Ellen; born in 1845, four years after the birth of Ellen's daughter, Judith, and one of the principal voices of the narration. A few months before her death she sought out Quentin Compson on the day before he left for Harvard College.

Henry Sutpen, son of Thomas and Ellen; born in 1839 at "Sutpen's Hundred." He attended the University of Mississippi where he met Charles Etienne Bon and became his friend.

Judith Sutpen, daughter of Thomas and Ellen; born in 1841 at "Sutpen's Hundred," where she lived all her life. She was engaged for a time to Charles Etienne Bon who was killed by her brother, Henry.

"Clytie" (Clytemnestra) Sutpen, daughter of Thomas Sutpen and a slave woman. She was born in 1834 and died in 1910.

Wash Jones, squatter and handyman on the Sutpen plantation. He died there in 1869 after having murdered his granddaughter Milly, her child, and Thomas Sutpen.

Milly Jones, Wash's granddaughter, who bore a girl child for Thomas Sutpen. The infant was born and died on the same day

in 1869.

Jason Compson II, a general and owner of "Compson's Domain." He was a friend to Thomas Sutpen.

Jason Compson III, his son, a lawyer, who still lived in the house his father built on what was left of "Compson's Domain." One of the principal voices of the narration.

Quentin Compson, the son of Jason Compson III, born in 1891. A first year student at Harvard, he died there in 1910. Quentin and his friend, Shreve, try to piece together the story of Thomas Sutpen.

Shreve McCannon, a Canadian and Quentin's roommate at Harvard.

Essay-Review

Part of the Yoknapatawpha County saga, *Absalom, Absalom!* concerns five families: the Sutpens, the Compsons, the Coldfields, the Bons, and the Jones. It is a novel which could be artificially separated into a story within a story where past and present time are distinct, but, as it is constructed, past action and characters erupt into the present and the present merges with the past. Quentin Compson is not so much separated by time from Thomas Sutpen as he exists in a continuum which moves through memory, speculations, and conjectures, and it is this complex interaction which enables a reader to experience origins of the "Old South," long hidden beneath the debris of time and the machinations of history.

The framework of the novel is the experience of Quentin Compson who is on the point of leaving home for the first time to attend Harvard College, when he receives a note from Miss Rosa Coldfield asking him to call her. The novel begins in the middle of a story about Thomas Sutpen which Miss Rosa is telling Quentin. Listening, Quentin is caught up in events that had taken place forty-three years earlier. The intensity of Miss Rosa's feelings, the rage, and the hatred that she has nurtured are centered on Thomas Sutpen and the part he played in her life and in the life of her family. For three hours Quentin, listening to Miss Rosa as she grimly characterizes Sutpen, wonders why the haggard woman before him has chosen to tell him a story she has never confided to anyone else. Finally, Quentin is able to leave, promising to return with a carriage and to take her out to the old and ruined Sutpen mansion.

The next four chapters of the novel are an account of Quentin's conversation with his father, Jason III, while Quentin waits for the appointed hour when he will take Miss Rosa to the Sutpen place. The conversation between father and son continues the story of Thomas Sutpen, but where Miss Rosa had characterized Sutpen as devil, Jason III sees him as a tragic hero doomed to destruction. Quentin's father's knowledge of events has come to him principally from his own father, Jason II; and, at one point, Jason III shows Quentin a letter given to Jason II by Sutpen's daughter, Judith.

The sixth chapter of the novel finds Quentin sitting on the veranda alone, recalling and extending the stories of Thomas Sutpen which he had heard during the afternoon from Miss Rosa and his father. The next two chapters of the novel take place a few months later in Quentin's room at Harvard which he shares with Shreve and on the day Quentin has received a letter from his father telling him of Miss Rosa's death and the circumstances surrounding it. The conversation between Quentin and Shreve that takes place here brings together the different versions of the Sutpen story, revealing some information which, up to this time, has remained untold. Quentin's preoccupation with the events that had taken place so long ago and the effect that they have on him and his view that he has somehow evolved the meaning and the value of his own life emerge as he and Shreve speculate on the motives and forces which drove Sutpen and the people surrounding him. As the two young men create their own versions of the people and events of the past, the reader is given greater insight into Quentin and the reasons for his suicide, which is to occur a few months later. (The suicide is not revealed in this novel but in the earlier *The Sound and the Fury*).

The story of Thomas Sutpen emerges from recollections, speculations, conjectures, and the consciousness of the characters. Characterized by Miss Rosa as a demon in the Old Testament sense, by Jason Compson III as a latter day Agamemnon, and by Quentin as an embodiment of the South, the figure of Thomas Sutpen embraces both the truth and the legend, and his story is an exploration of the bounds of human conduct and the depths of passion and despair. The title of the novel, taken from the Biblical account of David, psalmist, warrior, King of Israel, and father to Absalom, is an expression of the intense anguish of which the human spirit is capable. It is this anguish that characterizes the entire novel, not only the South which constructed its own doom, but also the exigencies of the human condition itself.

Thomas Sutpen was born into a poor family of mountain people of Scotch-English descent. While he was still a child, his mother died and his father moved the family down to the tidewater region of Virginia. It is here that the young Sutpen encounters for the first time an economic class system that relegated all whites not rich enough to own land and slaves either into "tradespeople" or "poor white trash," the latter a condition even lower than that of slave. The encounter where Sutpen learns his place in the system is humiliating for him, and it forms the core of his resolve which carries him through his life. It is the driving force in the development of his grand design, his imperative to scale the economic ladder, to become landowner and slave owner and to perpetuate his name in a bloodline of sons who will inherit his land and his position of power.

His design carries him first to Haiti. There he not only makes money but also marries Eulalie Bon, the daughter of a sugar planter. The marriage, however, is annuled after his first child, Charles Bon, is born. Sutpen leaves Haiti, appearing later in Jefferson. The townspeople are curious about him, but he offers no explanation as to who he is or why he is there. They do learn that he has gained title to one hundred square miles of Indian land. Soon afterwards Sutpen disappears, to return later with a wagon load of slaves and an architect. Within a few years he builds a mansion on what was called "Sutpen's Hundred," marries the daughter of Goodhue Coldfield, who bears him two children, Henry and Judith, and makes friends with the men of Jefferson, especially with Jason Compson, II. Two years after the birth of Judith Sutpen to Ellen and Thomas, Ellen's sister, Rosa Coldfield, is born.

As the years pass, the plantation flourishes and the children grow into adulthood. Henry leaves to attend the University of Mississippi. There he meets Charles Bon, whom he invites home with him for the Christmas holidays. Sutpen recognizes Bon as his son, but he does not acknowledge him as such. A year later Sutpen forbids, without giving reasons, the marriage of Bon to Judith. As a result, Henry renounces his father and leaves home with Charles.

When the Civil War breaks out, Henry and Charles enlist in the same regiment. Thomas Sutpen goes off to war, also, as does Jason Compson, II. Goodhue Coldfield, however, is not sympathetic to the Southern cause, and, rather than serve in the army, he locks himself in his attic, leaving Rosa, now a young girl, to find enough food for the two of them. Eventually he dies in the attic. Ellen, for whom life with Sutpen has never been easy, dies also. Judith and Clytie, Sutpen's daughter by a black woman, manage to survive the long war and years of famine with the help of Wash Jones, a poor white man who lives in a fishing sack on the plantation and who had done odd jobs for Sutpen before the war.

When the war is over, Charles and Henry return to Jefferson. Charles had written a letter to Judith telling her that they waited long enough to be married and that he will return to her. But, at the gates of "Sutpen's Hundred," Henry shoots and kills Charles. Wash Jones is sent into town by Judith to tell Rosa of the shooting. Rosa returns with Wash to the plantation. Henry is gone, but Rosa helps with the burial of Charles Bon and then remains at the plantation with Judith and Clytie. Sutpen returns from the war an old man, but he has not given up his grand design. He sets about trying to restore the plantation, and he proposes marriage to Rosa, who accepts him. But when driven by a need for a son who will perpetuate his name, he further proposes that they postpone the wedding until she has produced a male heir; Rosa is enraged and leaves the plantation. Undaunted, Sutpen seduces the young granddaughter of Wash Jones. Her child is also a girl. When Wash realizes that Sutpen is not going to marry his granddaughter, he kills Sutpen with the nearest weapon, a rusty grass scythe. At the end of the day, when the sheriff's posse comes, Wash kills his granddaughter and her newborn baby, sets fire to the shack, and, brandishing the scythe, runs toward the posse in one final protest.

Eventually Charles Etienne Bon, the son of Charles Bon and an octaroon woman, comes to live with Judith and Clytie. He grows up, marries a slave woman and has one son, Jim Bond, a mentally retarded child. Two years later, both Judith and Charles die in a yellow fever epidemic.

Twenty-five years later, after receiving a note from Miss Rosa, Quentin calls on her and agrees to take her to "Sutpen's Hundred" because she believes that there is something hiding here. At the ruined plantation house they find Clytie, now a ninety-year-old woman, and Jim Bond. Although Clytie tries to prevent her, Miss Rosa forces her way upstairs. She returns, stumbling, her eyes wide and unseeing. Quentin, too, goes upstairs. Inside a dimly lit room, Quentin finds Henry Sutpen who reveals that Charles had Negro blood and that miscegenation and not incest had been his reason for killing Charles. The Negro blood had also been the reason for Sutpen's separation from Eulalie Bon and his abandonment of his son, Charles Bon.

The next day Quentin leaves for Harvard, and it is not until he receives a letter from his father that he learns that Miss Rosa, for reasons that can only be guessed, had sent an ambulance for Henry; but, as it approached the house, Miss Rosa seated between the driver and deputy sheriff, the old mansion was engulfed in flames. Only Jim Bond, the idiot grandson to Thomas Sutpen escaped. A few days later Miss Rosa, too, dies.

The novel ends on a cold New England night as Quentin and Shreve attempt to understand and explain Thomas Sutpen's obsessive drive to realize his grand design, Henry's reasons for killing his friend and half-brother, Charles, and Miss Rosa's hatred of Sutpen and her grim perseverance. In their attempt to give meaning to a past re-created by Quentin and Shreve from two conversations and two letters, readers are led to consider not only the past events of a small Southern town, but also a broader and more comprehensive view of history, the human condition, and the nature of reality and truth.

Although Faulkner's skillful use of a complex structure enables readers to consider abstractions, the novel's overriding sense of anguish is its pervading quality, made the more so by the heavy scent of wisteria in the Southern summer twilight which Quentin can evoke even in the dark cold night of a New England winter, an anguish that is measured by the steady ticking of the clock and announced in regular patterns by the tolling of the bell in chapel tower, a ticking that began before memory marked seasons and years.

Quentin is the recipient not only of his own family history but of the Sutpen history as well. In reconstructing Sutpen's story, Quentin realizes the substantial similarities between the Compson family and Sutpen. The first Compson had also come riding into Yoknapatawpha County with nothing but two pistols and the horse he was riding; the first Compson had also taken land from the Indians. Sutpen's story is, thus, a shorter version of not only Compson history but that of the whole South. Quentin recognizes that Sutpen, doomed from his first encounter to violence and failure, is a symbol for the South.

In Sutpen's plan, Faulkner created a paradigm for a system not only operational but so vicious in concept that even an examination of it proves disastrous. It was not a class system which most of its perpetrators were accustomed to but a structure that was based on ownership not only of land but of other human beings. It necessitated masters and slaves, and, beyond that, those who performed the services which maintained the system—the tradespeople. That left masses of the unfortunate, the unlucky, the poor, who were not only unnecessary to the system, but also incapable of maintaining it. Called "white trash," they were discarded. As such, it is fitting that Wash Jones, corrupted as much as Sutpen, at last rises up with Old Testament wrath and mystery to attempt to destroy once and for all the evil that is symbolized by Sutpen.

Goodhue Coldfield, because there is a profit, not only is willing to extend credit, but to offer his daughter as well, to Sutpen. Miss Rosa, that strange, child-like woman who had never been a child, early deprived, always cheated, hating, was willing to marry Sutpen, to accept the premises of his grand design and a position in it. Her rage against his proposal violates every notion of humaneness, but the demand that she take all the risk goes against the dictum that he who takes the risk takes the profit. Quentin's grandfather, Jason II, like Goodhue Coldfield, is a willing participant in Sutpen's scheme but for a different reason. Himself a recipient of the spoils of the same system, he cannot condemn it or Sutpen's aspirations. Quentin's father represents another perspective, another justification. Unwilling to confront the truth of the present and the reality of the past, he retreats into a romanticized and largely literary fantasy suggested by Sutpen, who saw himself as Agamemnon and had even considered calling Clytie, Cassandra. In this characterization Faulkner explores the thin veneer of the civilized Southern gentleman, who (lacking the courage to come face to face with the reality that the system, by which he and his father before him and his father's father had lived, had nothing to do with honor and courage and pride, and everything to do with simple exploitation and corruption of human beings) resorts to a glorification of the past. Not only does Jason Compson III twist Greek literature to explain and come to terms with history, but he also tries to perpetuate the myth for his son, Quentin. But he fails, as Supten fails, and as Quentin realizes, for the system is self-corrupting.

It is in the Compsons, foreshadowed by Sutpen's theatrical life and death like a little allegory set between two narratives (*The Sound and the Fury and Absalom, Absalom!*), that the past is finally realized in the present. Quentin, who dares to examine Sutpen's grand design, cannot escape the obvious implications. He is able to identify himself with Henry and, one must assume, Sutpen's idiot son with the Compson idiot son, Benjy. Quentin discovers the consequences, and, finding them, he cannot endure.

Sutpen himself, symbol that he is and corrupting and destructive as he was to the people surrounding him, is also a victim. He emerges from a wilderness with little more than his knowledge of that wilderness and his innocence to come down the mountain into the decadence of the plantation system. Unprepared by anything in his previous life for what he finds, he is immediately seduced by the system, accepts it without question, and apprehends its essentials and basic premises. Acting on these bold and terrible principles, he formulates his plan without the trappings others, less innocent, found necessary to deceive either themselves or others. It is this innocence, which he never loses, that causes him to ask: "What mistake did I make?" Unfeeling and uncaring as he is, we, nevertheless, feel that the cry "Absalom, Absalom, my son, my son" is as much for him as for other sons. Sutpen was no tragic hero, no Agamemnon, and he was no David, King of Israel, nor even a demon in Old Testament terms. He was a simple human being, a son of the earth which also will be destroyed in time by corrupt and corrupting forces.

Bibliography

Adamowski, T.H. "Children of the Idea: Heroes and Family Romance in *Absalom, Absalom!*," in *Mosaic.* X (1976), pp. 115–131.

Backman, Melvin. "Sutpen and the South: A Study of *Absalom, Absalom!*," in *PMLA.* LXXX (1965), pp. 596–604.

Behrens, Ralph. "Collapse of the Dynasty: The Thematic Center of *Absalom, Absalom!*," in *PMLA.* LXXXIX (1974), pp. 24–33.

Brooks, Cleanth. "History, Tragedy and the Imagination in *Absalom, Absalom!*," in *Yale Review.* LII (1963), pp. 340–351.

————. "The Narrative Structure of *Absalom, Absalom!*," in *Georgia Review.* XXIX (1975), pp. 366–394.

————. *William Faulkner: The Yoknapatawpha County.* New Haven, Conn.: Yale University Press, 1963, pp. 295–324.

Connolly, Thomas E. "A Skeletal Outline of *Absalom, Absalom!*," in *College English.* XXV (November, 1963), pp. 110–114.

Forrer, Richard. "*Absalom, Absalom!*: Story-telling as a Mode of Transcendence," in *Southern Literary Journal.* IX (1976), pp. 22–46.

Hoffman, A.C. "Point of View in *Absalom, Absalom!*," in *University of Kansas City Review.* XIX (Summer, 1953), pp. 233–239.

Holman, C. Hugh. "*Absalom, Absalom!*: The Historian as Detective," in *Sewanee Review.* LXXIX (1971), pp. 542–553.

Howe, Irving. *William Faulkner: A Critical Study.* New York: Vintage, 1962, pp. 71–78, 221–232.

Kartiganer, Donald M. "The Role of Myth in *Absalom, Absalom!*," in *Modern Fiction Studies.* IX (Winter, 1963–1964), pp. 357–369.

Levins, Lynn G. "The Four Narrative Perspectives in *Absalom, Absalom!*," in *PMLA.* LXXXV (1970), pp. 35–47.

Lind, Ilse Dusair. "The Design and Meaning of *Absalom, Absalom!*," in *William Faulkner: Three Decades of Criticism.* Edited by Fredrick J. Hoffman and Olga Vickery. East Lansing: Michigan State University Press, 1960, pp. 278–304.

Millgate, Michael. *The Achievement of William Faulkner.* New York: Random House, 1965, pp. 150–164.

O'Connor, William Van. *The Tangled Fire of William Faulkner.* Minneapolis: University of Minnesota Press, 1954, pp. 94–100.

Poirier, William. "Strange Gods in Jefferson, Mississippi: Analysis of *Absalom, Absalom!*," in *William Faulkner: Two Decades of Criticism.* Edited by Fredrick J. Hoffman and Olga Vickery. East Lansing: Michigan State University Press, 1951, pp. 217–243.

Putzel, Max. "What Is Gothic About *Absalom, Absalom!*," in *Southern Literary Journal.* IX (1971), pp. 3–19.

Rollyson, Carl E., Jr. "The Recreation of the Past in *Absalom, Absalom!*," in *Mississippi Quarterly.* XXIX (1976), pp. 361–374.

Stewart, David H. "*Absalom* Reconsidered," in *University of Toronto Quarterly.* XXX (October, 1960), pp. 31–44.

Swiggart, Peter. *The Art of Faulkner's Novels.* Austin: University of Texas Press, 1962, pp. 149–170.

Thompson, Lawrance. *William Faulkner: An Introduction and Interpretation.* New York: Holt, Rinehart and Winston, 1967, pp. 63–65.

Vickery, Olga. *The Novels of William Faulkner: A Critical Interpretation.* Baton Rouge: Louisiana State University Press, 1964, pp. 84–102.

Volpe, Edmond L. *A Reader's Guide to William Faulkner.* New York: Noonday Press, 1964, pp. 184–212, 387–392.

Waggoner, Hyatt H. *William Faulkner: From Jefferson to the World.* Lexington: University of Kentucky Press, 1959, pp. 148–169.

Watkins, Floyd C. "What Happens in *Absalom, Absalom!*," in *Modern Fiction Studies.* XIII (Spring, 1967), pp. 79–87.

Whan, Edgar. "*Absalom, Absalom!* as Gothic Myth," in *Perspective.* III (Autumn, 1950), pp. 192–201.

AS I LAY DYING

Type of work: Novel
Author: William Faulkner (1897–1962)
Time of plot: Early twentieth century
Locale: Mississippi
First published: 1930

Centering around the effect of Addie Bundren's death and burial on members of her family, this novel has a powerful unity not always found in Faulkner's longer works. Although his method of shifting between the multiple points of view of the different family members binds Faulkner's characters into a homogeneous unit through their common suffering, individual personalities with their special emotions and abnormalities nevertheless emerge.

Principal Characters

Anse Bundren, an ignorant poor white. When Addie, his wife, dies, he is determined to take her body to Jefferson, as he had promised, even though the town is forty miles away. In a rickety old wagon he and his sons must get across a flooding river which has destroyed most of the nearby bridges. Ostensibly, the shiftless and unlucky man is burying Addie there because of the promise. After a long trip with her unembalmed corpse, now dead more than a week, he arrives in Jefferson, pursued by a flock of buzzards which, like a grim chorus, hang apparently motionless against a sultry Mississippi sky. On reaching Jefferson, his family learns Anse's true reason for the trip: a set of false teeth and the "duck-shaped woman" whom he marries, to the surprise of his children.

Addie Bundren, Anse's overworked wife. Though dying, she wants to see her coffin finished. Anse does not know it, but she has always thought him to be only a man of words; and words, she thinks, are useless. Feeling isolated from him and her children, she has always tried to break through the wall of isola-

tion surrounding her, but despairing, she never finds any meaning in her grinding existence. To her, sexual relationship means only violation, whereas, to Anse, it means love. Before her death she knows her father's words to be true: "The reason for living was to get ready to stay dead a long time."

Darl Bundren, Addie's strange son, thought by his family to be feebleminded. Unlike the others, he seems to have the gift of second sight. Knowing the true reasons why Anse and the others are going to Jefferson, he tries to burn the barn housing his mother's body. For this act of attempted purification, his family declares him insane, and he is taken to the asylum at Jackson.

Jewel Bundren, Preacher Whitfield's illegitimate son. A violent young man, he loves only his horse, which cost him many long hours of labor at night. Although devoted to the animal, he allows Anse to trade it to Snopes for a badly needed team of mules. Like the rest of the Bundrens, he tenaciously hauls his mother on the long eventful trip, all the while cursing and raging at his brothers. When Darl tries to burn the corpse, it is Jewel who manages to save her body for burial.

Cash Bundren, Anse's son, a carpenter. While his mother is dying, he busily saws and hammers away at her coffin, just outside her window. Carefully beveling the wood (he hates shoddy work) and showing his mother each board before nailing it in place, he finishes the job shortly after Addie's death. At the flooded river he desperately tries to save his treasured tools when the wagon overturns. His leg broken on the trip, he stoically endures the pain, even after his father uses cement to plaster the swollen and infected leg.

Vardaman Bundren, Anse's son. Constantly, he repeats to himself, "My mother is a fish."

Dewey Dell Bundren, Anse's daughter. A well-developed girl of seventeen, she has a reason for going to Jefferson. She is pregnant and wants to buy drugs which she hopes will cause a miscarriage.

Dr. Peabody, a fat, seventy-year-old country doctor. During his long practice he has ministered to many poor-white families like the Bundrens. When his unpaid bills reach fifty thousand dollars, he intends to retire.

Vernon Tull, Anse's helpful neighbor. He does what he can to help Bundren on his ghoulish journey.

Cora Tull, Vernon's fundamentalist wife. Constantly praying and singing hymns, she tries to make Addie repent.

Preacher Whitfield, Addie's former lover, the father of Jewel. Hearing of her sickness, this wordy man goes to confess his sin to Anse. On the way he decides that his fight against the elements, as he crosses the flooding river, helps to expiate his sins. After she dies, he does not feel that a public confession is necessary.

Lafe, a field hand, the father of Dewey Dell's unborn child.

Mr. Gillespie, in whose barn Addie's coffin lies when Darl attempts to burn it.

The Story

Addie Bundren was dying. She lay propped up in a bed in the Bundren farm-house, looking out the window at her son Cash as he built the coffin in which she was to be buried. Obsessed with perfection in carpentry, Cash held up each board for her approval before he nailed it in place. Dewey Dell, Addie's daughter, stood beside the bed, fanning her mother as she lay there in the summer heat. In another room Anse Bundren, Addie's husband, and two sons, Darl and Jewel, discussed the possibility of the boys' making a trip with a wagonload of lumber to earn three dollars for the family. Because Addie's wish was that she be buried in Jefferson, the town where her relatives lay, Anse was afraid the boys might not get back in time to carry her body to the Jefferson graveyard. He finally approved the trip and Jewel and Darl set out.

Addie died while the two brothers were gone and before Cash could finish the coffin. When it was obvious that she was dying, a Dr. Peabody was summoned, but he came too late to help the sick woman. While Dr. Peabody was at the house, Vardaman, the youngest boy, arrived home with a fish he had caught in the river; his mother's death somehow became entangled in his mind with the death of the fish and, because Dr. Peabody was there when she died, Vardaman thought the doctor had killed her.

Meanwhile a great rainstorm came up. Jewel and Darl, with their load of lumber, were delayed on the road by a broken wagon wheel. Cash kept working through the rain, trying to finish the coffin. At last it was complete and Addie was placed in it, but the crazed Vardaman, who once had almost smothered in his crib, tried to let his mother out by boring holes through the top of the coffin.

After Jewel and Darl finally got back with the wagon, neighbors gathered at the Bundren house for the funeral service, which was conducted by Whitfield, the minister. Whitfield had once been a lover of Addie's after her marriage, and Jewel, the son whom she seemed to favor, had been fathered by the minister.

Following the service, Anse, his family, and the dead Addie started out for Jefferson, normally one hard day's ride away. The rainstorm, however, had so swollen the river that the bridge had been broken up and could not be crossed by wagon. After trying another bridge, which had also been washed out, they drove back to an old ford near the first bridge. Three of the family—Anse, Dewey Dell, and Vardaman, with the assistance of Vernon Tull, a neighboring farmer—got across the river on the ruins of the bridge. Then Darl and Cash attempted to drive the wagon across at the obliterated ford, with Jewel leading the way on his spotted horse. This horse was Jewel's one great possession; he had earned the money to purchase it by working all day at the Bundren farm and then by working all night clearing ground for a neighbor. When the wagon was nearly across, a big log floating downstream upset the wagon. As a result, Cash broke his leg and nearly died; the mules were drowned; the coffin fell out, but was dragged to the bank by Jewel; and Cash's carpenter's tools were scattered in the water and had to be recovered one by one.

Anse refused the loan of anyone's mules, insisting that he must own the team that carried Addie to the grave. He went off to bargain for mules and made a trade in which he offered, without Jewel's consent, to give the spotted horse as part payment. When Jewel found out what his father had done, he rode off, apparently abandoning the group. Later it turned out that he had put the spotted horse in the barn of Snopes, who was dickering with Anse. And so they got their new mules and the trip continued.

By the time they arrived in Mottson, a town on the way to Jefferson, Addie had been dead so long that buzzards followed the wagon. In Mottson they stopped to buy cement to strengthen Cash's broken leg. The police and citizens, whose noses were offended, insisted that the wagon move on, but they bought the cement and treated the leg before they would budge. While they were in the town, Dewey Dell left the wagon, went to a drugstore, and tried to buy medicine which would abort the illegitimate child she carried, for she had become pregnant by a man named Lafe, with whom she had worked on the farm. The druggist refused to sell her the medicine.

Addie Bundren had been dead nine days and was still not buried. The family spent the last night before their arrival in Jefferson at the house of a Mr.

Gillespie, who allowed them to put the odorous coffin in his barn. During the night Darl, whom the neighbors had always thought to be the least sane of the Bundrens, set fire to the barn. Jewel rescued the coffin by carrying it out on his back. Anse later turned Darl over to the authorities at Jefferson; they sent him to the asylum in Jackson.

Lacking a spade and shovel to dig Addie's grave, Anse stopped at a house in Jefferson and borrowed these tools. The burial finally took place. Afterward Dewey Dell again tried to buy her medicine at a drugstore. One of the clerks pretended to be a doctor, gave her some innocuous fluid, and told her to come back that night for further treatment. The further treatment took the form of a seduction in the basement of the drugstore.

Cash's broken leg, encased in cement, had by now become so infected that Anse took him to Dr. Peabody, who said that Cash might not walk for a year. Before starting on the trip home, Anse bought himself a set of false teeth that he had long needed. He then returned the borrowed tools. When he got back to the wagon he had acquired not only the new teeth but also a new Mrs. Bundren, the woman who lent him the tools.

Critical Evaluation

Considered by many contemporary critics the greatest American fiction writer, Faulkner was awarded the Nobel Prize for Literature in 1949, after a prolific career that included nineteen novels and two volumes of poetry. Although his formal education was limited, Faulkner read prodigiously in the Greek and Roman classics, the Bible, Shakespeare, the English Romantics, Conrad, Joyce, and Eliot. After relatively undistinguished early attempts in poetry and prose, Faulkner was advised by Sherwood Anderson to concentrate on his "own postage stamp of native soil." This led to the saga of Yoknapatawpha County, its partly true regional history (based on Oxford, Mississippi) merging imperceptibly into a coherent myth, that began to unravel with *Sartoris* (1929), and was continued in *The Sound and the Fury* (1929) and *As I Lay Dying* (1930.)

In the Yoknapatawpha novels Faulkner placed himself in the forefront of the avant-garde with his intricate plot organization, his bold experiments in the dislocation of narrative time, and his use of the stream-of-consciousness technique. His stylistic view of time was affected by his sense that past events continue into the present. As he once said, "There is no such thing as *was*; if *was* existed, there would be no grief or sorrow." These stylistic characteristics were undergirded by the development of a complex social structure that enabled Faulkner to explore the inherited guilt of the Southern past, the incapacity of the white aristocracy to cope with modern life, the relations between classes, and the relations between black and white.

Starkly realistic, poignantly symbolic, grotesquely comic and immensely complicated as an experiment in points of view, *As I Lay Dying* ranks with Faulkner's greatest novels: *The Sound and the Fury, Sanctuary* (1931), *Light in August* (1932) and *Absalom, Absalom!* (1936). The relative simplicity of its style, characterized by staccato-like sentences and repetitive dialogue, enhances the tragicomic effect. At the same time the prosaic quality of the narrative often renders into poetry—as when Dewey Dell becomes the symbol of heedless motherhood by wiping everything on her dress, when Darl sees stars first in the bucket then in his dipper, when Jewel's horse appears "enclosed by a glittering maze of hooves as by an illusion of wings," when the buzzards accompanying Addie's coffin are juxtaposed suddenly with the sparks that make the stars flow backward for Vardaman, or when Darl, in his visionary fashion, speculates: "It is as though the space between us were time: an irrevocable quality. It is as though time, no longer running straight before us in a diminishing line, now runs parallel between us like a looping string, the distance between the doubling accretion of the thread and not the interval between."

The novel's theme, in the very widest terms, is man's absurdly comic distinction between being and not-being. Peabody describes death as "merely a function of the mind—and that of the ones who suffer the bereavement." But the theme is stated most clearly in the single chapter narrated from Addie's viewpoint: "I could just remember how my father used to say that the reason for living was to get ready to stay dead a long time." Addie has long since considered Anse dead, because she realizes that he, like most humans, cannot distinguish between the "thin line" of words that float upward into nothingness and the terrible reality of "doing [that] goes along the earth, clinging to it." Her attitude is expressed tersely and succinctly when she comments, after allusively revealing her affair with Whitfield: "Then I found that I had Jewel. When I waked to remember to discover it, he was two months gone."

Nineteen of the fifty-nine chapters are narrated from Darl's viewpoint, making him the primary *persona* of the novel. His reference to his family's conglomerate madness sets the tone: "In sunset we fall into furious attitudes, dead gestures of dolls." The novel proceeds in a jerky, doll-like movement, as the narration passes through the viewpoints of fifteen different characters, not without occasional retrogression and hiatus. Although Darl might be called the primary narrator, whose voice is most representative of the author's own, he is not the only interesting one. Vardaman, with ten chapters, displays a mentality reminiscent of Benjy's in *The Sound and the Fury*, showing us the crazy events connected with the burial through the eyes of a confused and simple-minded child. The third chapter from his viewpoint consists of a single sentence: "My mother is a fish." Only three chapters present Anse's viewpoint; but that is enough to show that he is a bizarre combination of his sons' characteristics: Darl's imagination, Vardaman's insanity, Cash's stubborn practicality, and Dewey Dell's earthiness (which also sets her in contrast with the bitterness of Addie's outlook toward sex and motherhood).

As he does in *The Sound and the Fury,* with Jason's chapter, Faulkner achieves his greatest artistic success with the least intrinsically interesting character, Cash. The first chapter (of five) from Cash's viewpoint is an artistic *coup.* Until this point we have heard, through many different viewpoints, the steady buzzing of Cash's saw preparing his mother's coffin—a sound that provides the thread of continuity through the first half of the novel. Even through the rain and through the night, Cash will not cease his labor: "Yet the motion of the saw has not faltered, as though it and the arm functioned in a tranquil conviction that rain was an illusion of the mind." Finally we hear his own voice, in Chapter 18: "I made it on the bevel." After this statement, Cash proceeds to explain what he means as Faulkner presents the carpenter's methodological mind in a straightforward list: "1. There is more surface for the nails to grip," ending with, "13. It makes a neater job." Cash's second chapter is a nine-line warning to his impatient father and brothers that the coffin "wasn't on a balance" in the wagon. When the tragedy in the river results from their ignoring his warning, Faulkner present's Cash's third chapter in three lines, beginning with, "It wasn't on a balance," and not even mentioning the fact that Cash's leg has been broken. Cash's single-minded craftsmanship and superhuman patience become a reflection of the author's own technique. The final chapter is Cash's.

Bibliography

Bedient, Calvin. "Pride and Nakedness: *As I Lay Dying,*" in *Modern Language Quarterly.* XXIX (1968), pp. 61–76.

Bleikasten, Andre. *Faulkner's* As I Lay Dying. Bloomington: Indiana University Press, 1973.

Blotner, Joseph. "*As I Lay Dying*: Christian Love and Irony," in *Twentieth Century Literature.* III (April, 1957), pp. 14–19.

Brooks, Cleanth. *William Faulkner: The Yoknapatawpha County.* New Haven, Conn.: Yale University Press, 1963, pp. 141–166.

Cross, Barbara M. "Apocalypse and Comedy in *As I Lay Dying,*" in *Texas Studies in Literature and Language.* III (Summer, 1961), pp. 251–258.

Degenfelder, E. Pauline. "Yoknapatawphan Baroque: A Stylistic Analysis of *As I Lay Dying,*" in *Style.* VII (1973), pp. 121–156.

Detsky, John. "Faulkner's Carousel: Point of View in *As I Lay Dying,*" in *Laurel Review.* X (1970), pp. 74–85.

Franklin, R.W. "Narrative Management in *As I Lay Dying,*" in *Modern Fiction Studies.* XIII (Spring, 1967), pp. 57–65.

Goellner, Jack Gordon. "A Closer Look at *As I Lay Dying*," in *Perspective.* VII (Spring, 1954), pp. 42–54.

Hemenway, Robert. "Enigmas of Being in *As I Lay Dying*," in *Modern Fiction Studies.* XVI (1970), pp. 133–146.

Hoffman, Frederick J. *William Faulkner.* New York: Twayne, 1961, pp. 60–63.

Howe, Irving. *William Faulkner: A Critical Study.* New York: Vintage, 1962, pp. 52–56, 175–191.

Kerr, Elizabeth M. "*As I Lay Dying* as Ironic Quest," in *Wisconsin Studies in Contemporary Literature.* III (Winter, 1962), pp. 5–19.

Millgate, Michael. *The Achievement of William Faulkner.* New York: Random House, 1965, pp. 104–112.

Monaghan, David M. "The Single Narrator of *As I Lay Dying*," in *Modern Fiction Studies.* XVIII (1972), pp. 213–220.

O'Connor, William Van. *The Tangled Fire of William Faulkner.* Minneapolis: University of Minnesota Press, 1954, pp. 45–53.

Parsons, Thornton H. "Doing the Best They Can," in *Georgia Review.* XXIII (1969), pp. 292–306.

Roberts, J.L. "The Individual and the Family: Faulkner's *As I Lay Dying*," in *Arizona Quarterly.* XVI (Spring, 1960), pp. 26–38.

Ross, Stephen M. "Shapes of Time and Consciousness in *As I Lay Dying*," in *Texas Studies in Literature and Language.* XVI (1974), pp. 723–737.

Rossby, William. "*As I Lay Dying*: The Insane World," in *Texas Studies in Literature and Language.* IV (Spring, 1962), pp. 87–95.

Simon, John K. "The Scene and the Imagery of *As I Lay Dying*," in *Criticism.* VII (Winter, 1965), pp. 1–22.

Sutherland, Ronald. "*As I Lay Dying*: A Faulkner Microcosm," in *Queen's Quarterly.* LXXIII (Winter, 1966), pp. 541–549.

Swiggart, Peter. *The Art of Faulkner's Novels.* Austin: University of Texas Press, 1962, pp. 71–74, 108–130.

Vickery, Olga. "*As I Lay Dying*," in *Perspective.* III (Autumn, 1950), pp. 179–191.

———. *The Novels of William Faulkner: A Critical Interpretation.* Baton Rouge: Louisiana State University Press, 1964, pp. 50–65.

Volpe, Edmond L. *A Reader's Guide to William Faulkner.* New York: Noonday Press, 1964, pp. 126–140, 377–382.

Waggoner, Hyatt H. *William Faulkner: From Jefferson to the World.* Lexington: University of Kentucky Press, 1959, pp. 62–87.

GO DOWN, MOSES

Type of work: Novel
Author: William Faulkner (1897–1962)
Time of plot: The 1830's to about 1940
Locale: The Mississippi Delta
First published: 1942

Essay-Review

Though usually discussed as a novel, *Go Down, Moses* is both a collection of seven short stories, written and published independently, which together form a sharply detailed picture of a small region in the Mississippi Delta, and a thematically relevant, if outrageously confusing tale of the McCaslin clan. The book recapitulates the story of the American South and examines the Biblical views of human history.

"Was," which foreshadows the cruelty and injustice of later generations, and shows man treating his brother like a piece of property and gambling over human happiness, is one of the funniest stories Faulkner wrote. It opens with a pack of hounds racing through the house after a fox. A central pun of the book, "race" is the theme of the first story, which takes the form of outreageous rural comedy. Buck and Buddy, twin sons of Carothers McCaslin, chase their slave and half brother, Tomey's Turl; Turl is after his sweetheart, Tennie, a slave of Hubert and his sister Sophonsiba Beauchamp; and Sophonsiba, called Sibbey, the only woman in the whole countryside, is after Buck. Buck and Buddy must catch Turl before he catches Tennie or else Sibbey will bring Turl home, stay for a visit, and may catch Buck. When Buck arrives at Warwick, the dilapidated Beauchamp plantation which Sibbey fashions after an English estate, he is tricked into staying the night and tricked again into climbing into a bed that contains the mistress of Warwick. When he is caught by the smiling Hubert, a poker game ensues to settle once and for all whether Sibbey gets Buck, whether Turl gets Tennie, and who will buy the other slave in either event. Buddy comes to the rescue and forces Hubert's hand with a possible straight over three threes. Buck is free, Turl gets Tennie, and Hubert must buy Turl. The ending is happy, but when the hounds break into the house once again in pursuit of the fox we sense that the race is not over. And indeed it is not; Sibbey gets Buck, Ike is born, and an estate is established that will perpetuate a system of cruelty and injustice.

The story is set in a mythical past, when a man could ride for days without having to meet a woman, and when in a lifetime he did not have to dodge but one. Further, the characters are innocent. Buck and Buddy may have owned slaves, but they quartered the Negroes in the mansion and themselves in the shack. They may have locked the front door every night after putting the slaves in but they never checked the back door which became an exit as soon as the lock was turned. They may have chased a slave and half brother with dogs, they may have gambled over wedlock; but these were forms or games as silly as Sibbey's imitation of a court lady and as harmless as the episodes of a silent comedy. Although the actions of the McCaslins and the Beauchamps in this story are based on slavery, an inhuman system that will become a foundation of injustice, the individual characters are not guilty. Although their conventions are shown to be ridiculous, they are also shown to result in a humane if comic gracefulness and an idyllic equilibrium.

The story is a burlesque of the Garden of Eden, yet it is also true to the biblical form and meaning: guilt inevitably follows innocence, cruelty and destruction are inextricably bound with freedom and love. As we read further in *Go Down, Moses* we can reflect that the true focus of the opening story is not Buck, Buddy, Turl, Tennie, Sibbey, or Hubert, but Ike McCaslin. It is Ike's voice that tells the tale, although it is in his cousin Cass's idiom. Ike, past seventy, tells the story but he cannot understand it; therefore he can only repeat verbatim the words of the boy who accompanied Buck and Buddy. Perhaps this was Cass's initiation into adulthood. Ike's initiation comes later, during a bear hunt; but rather than open his eyes to the adult world with all its complexities, it seals them with blinders of fanaticism. Ike never grows beyond the self-conscious dedication of his adolescence. He can never understand the story of his older cousin because he never develops a sense of humor. While a comic view could lead to the acceptance of absurdity for fact, Ike's heroic posture can lead only to outrage and impotence—and finally to the inhumanity of what Hawthorne called the "unpardonable sin."

The next two stories universalize the situation of "Was." "The Fire and the Hearth" establishes the anguish and heroism as well as the pathos and comic dignity of Lucas Beauchamp, the son of Turl and Tennie. "Pantaloon in Black," the most tenuously connected of the stories, establishes the present condition of injustice. A powerful young Negro is driven mad by his wife's death, kills the white man who has been exploiting the black workers for years in a crooked dice game, and is finally lynched; ironically, the story is told by the sheriff, who misunderstands the Negro's motives, to his wife, who is annoyed at being kept from her picture show. "The Old People" brings us back to the main story line, describing Ike's ritual killing of his first deer, under the tutelage of Sam Fathers. "The Bear" deals with Ike's full initiation into manhood.

"The Bear" is confusing and incomprehensible out of context, for the story is told from Ike's point of view, and we tend to identify with the idealistic boy. It is only gradually that we come to see how Ike misinterprets his experience. Ike sees Sam Fathers, the bear, and the dog who is destined to catch it, as taintless and incorruptible; and he sees the woods as ideal. Sam Fathers, the illegitimate son of the Indian chief who sold the land to Carothers McCaslin, now old and the last of his line, teaches Ike humility, patience, self-reliance, and a love for the wilderness. But he fails to teach Ike, even though he baptizes the boy in the blood of his first deer, that destruction is a part of life, and that to retreat from this reality is not only suicide but an impetus to the destructive force. Ike never sees that his taintless and incorruptible bear kills farm animals and cuts a destructive path through the wilderness just like the locomotive; he never admits to himself that the hunters whom he idealizes for the rest of his life are in fact killers. He is blind to the reality of destruction even as Sam trains the dun-colored dog that will track Old Ben.

Ike can see only the wilderness of James Fenimore Cooper; he is blind to the "heart of darkness" that is all the while before him. Part IV of "The Bear," is well known for the tortured, involuted style that represents Ike's mind seeking to grasp and explain an unbelievably complex, absurd, and suppressed heritage. Ike has read through the ledgers of his father and uncle, Buck and Buddy, which burlesque the chronicles of the Old Testament and portray the South in a comic microcosm. And he has discovered that his grandfather, old Carothers McCaslin, not only violated a slave but later ordered the daughter brought to the house and had another child by her—that Tomey's Turl was a product not only of exploitation and miscegenation but of incest. Ike has come of age, and after arguing with his older cousin, Cass, he decides to repudiate a heritage founded on injustice and rapacity. Believing that Sam Fathers has set him free, he gives the land to Cass and, in imitation of Christ, becomes a carpenter.

Cass tries to explain to Ike the meaning of his responsibility. He knows that Ike is relinquishing the land for the same reason that he refused to shoot Old Ben when he had a perfect chance. The explanation is in Keats's "Ode on a Grecian Urn": Ike would forever hold the moment of his fulfillment. Cass understands that the love on the Grecian Urn had turned "Cold Pastoral," and he will accept compromise. Ike, by his attitude not only shows a possessiveness as fierce as that of the slave owner and the capitalist, but denies life, which is complex and inevitably fluid.

In "Delta Autumn" Ike, weak and nostalgic and almost eighty years of age, goes into the woods with the grandsons of the hunters who trained him. He is left in the camp while the others go off hunting, and Roth Edmonds, grandson of Cass, asks him to deliver a packet of money. A girl carrying a small child arrives in the camp while Ike is lying in bed without his glasses or trousers. Now his blindness and impotence are brought to full realization. He learns that the girl is not only part Negro but also the grand-niece of Lucas Beauchamp; the situation involves exploitation and miscegenation and incest, Carother's ancient sin all over again. Ike can only offer the girl money, the family hunting horn, and advice. His initiation, conversion, and renunciation has served only as an evasion of human responsibility. He has loved an abstraction of the past which blinded him to human necessity, although it did not finally relieve him of his responsibility. The girl recognizes that when Ike gave Cass the land, he contributed to the grandson's recklessness. She does not want money or even a husband; she knew a moment of love and is willing to recognize that it is past. All she wants is recognition. Roth evades the simple but difficult gesture by leaving camp. Ike evades it by offering empty forms and empty words. He himself has re-enacted the original sin of Carothers McCaslin, who left his illegitimate child an inheritance, recognizing that this was cheaper than saying "Son" to a Negro.

The focus of the final story, entitled "Go Down, Moses," is not on Ike, but, as Cleanth Brooks tells us, on the community. Lucas Beauchamp's grandson, Samuel, has killed a policeman in Chicago and has been electrocuted. Lucas' wife Mollie, senile and crazed by the outrage, wants the body brought home. The story shows how the leading members of the white community accept the responsibility of hiding the truth from Mollie and of bringing home the body. Sentimentality is balanced by the fine, comic characterization of Mollie.

The history of the past twenty years has dramatized the problem of leaving the race issue to the South, a position which Faulkner advocated explicitly to the press and implicitly in this story. But this is only one dimension of Faulkner's philosophy, just as it is a single facet of the story, and both are distorted in isolation. Marvin Klotz tried to establish the superiority of the original stories to their revision and collection in *Go Down, Moses*. But while the early stories may have had greater control and a finer economy, the novel that they form is far more ambitious. In a structure that combines various attitudes and perspective, Faulkner gives us a picture of the Southern situation and makes of his regional materials a metaphor of the human condition, which combines both love and destruction, which is complex and unbearable and at the same time capable of affirmation—but only when viewed from the humane vantage point that avoids fanaticism and accepts both comedy and tragedy.

Bibliography

Backman, Melvin. *Faulkner: The Major Years, A Critical Study*. Bloomington: Indiana University Press, 1966, pp. 160–174.

Gold, Joseph. *William Faulkner: A Study in Humanism from Metaphor to Discourse*. Norman: University of Oklahoma Press, 1966, pp. 49–75.

Hamilton, Gary D. "The Past in the Present: A Reading of *Go Down, Moses*," in *Southern Humanities Review*. V (1971), pp. 171–181.

Hochberg, M.R. "The Unity of *Go Down, Moses*," in *Tennessee Studies in Literature*. XXI (1977), pp. 58–65.

Howe, Irving. *William Faulkner: A Critical Study*. New York: Vintage, 1962, pp. 88–92.

Howell, Elmo. "William Faulkner and the Chickasaw Funeral," in *American Literature*. XXXVI (January, 1965), pp. 523–535.

Hunt, John W. *William Faulkner: Art in Theological Tension*. Syracuse, N.Y.: Syracuse University Press, 1965, pp. 137–168.

Hurt, Lester E. "Mysticism in *Go Down, Moses*," in *English Record.* XV (December, 1964), pp. 17–22.

Longley, John L., Jr. *The Tragic Mask: A Study of Faulkner's Heroes.* Chapel Hill: University of North Carolina Press, 1963, pp. 105–110.

Millgate, Michael. *The Achievement of William Faulkner.* New York: Random House, 1965, pp. 201–214.

Muste, John M. "The Failure of Love in *Go Down, Moses*," in *Modern Fiction Studies.* X (Winter, 1964–1965), pp. 366–378.

Nilon, Charles H. *Faulkner and the Negro.* New York: Citadel Press, 1965, pp. 13–24, 32–38, 54–59, 96–101.

O'Connor, William Van. *The Tangled Fire of William Faulkner.* Minneapolis: University of Minnesota Press, 1954, pp. 125–134.

Sultan, Stanley. "Call Me Ishmael: The Hagiography of Isaac McCaslin," in *Texas Studies in Literature and Language.* III (Spring, 1961), pp. 50–66.

Thompson, Lawrance. "A Defense of Difficulties in William Faulkner's Art," in *Carrell.* IV (December, 1963), pp. 7–19.

———. *William Faulkner: An Introduction and Interpretation.* New York: Holt, Rinehart and Winston, 1967, pp. 81–98.

Thornton, Weldon. "Structure and Theme in Faulkner's *Go Down, Moses*," in *Costerus.* III (1975), pp. 73–112.

Tick, Stanley. "The Unity of *Go Down, Moses*," in *Twentieth Century Literature.* VIII (July, 1962), pp. 67–73.

Vickery, Olga. *The Novels of William Faulkner: A Critical Interpretation.* Baton Rouge: Louisiana State University Press, 1964, pp. 124–134.

Vinson, Audrey L. "Miscegenation and Its Meaning in *Go Down, Moses*," in *College Language Association Journal.* XIV (1970), pp. 143–155.

Volpe, Edmond L. *A Reader's Guide to William Faulkner.* New York: Noonday, 1964, pp. 230–252, 393–396.

Waggoner, Hyatt H. *William Faulkner: From Jefferson to the World.* Lexington: University of Kentucky Press, 1959, pp. 199–211.

Wertenbaker, Thomas J., Jr. "Faulkner's Point of View and the Chronicle of Ike McCaslin," in *College English.* XXIV (December, 1962), pp. 169–178.

Wheeler, Otis B. "Faulkner's Wilderness," in *American Literature.* XXXI (May, 1959), pp. 127–136.

THE HAMLET

Type of work: Novel
Author: William Faulkner (1897–1962)
Time of plot: Late nineteenth century, early twentieth century
Locale: Frenchman's Bend, Yoknapatawpha County, Mississippi
First published: 1940

The first volume of Faulkner's Snopes trilogy, The Hamlet, *follows Flem Snopes, the son of a disreputable tenant farmer, as he rises financially and socially through a series of shrewd, pragmatic maneuvers. Snope's character is developed largely through episodic sequences involving other characters, and the reader views him through the eyes of the society which created him.*

Principal Characters

Will Varner, justice of the peace, election commissioner, largest landholder in the county. He owns the store, cotton gin, combined gristmill and blacksmith shop, and holds the mortgages on any good land he does not own. Judge Benbow once said of him that a milder-mannered man never bled a mule or stuffed a ballot box. As the story begins, he is age sixty, having fathered sixteen children. Will initially hires Flem Snopes to clerk at his store as a bribe to keep Ab Snopes in good spirits, but Flem soon proves himself to be very efficient, a valuable asset to Will, who rewards Flem and encourages his rise.

Jody Varner, the son of Will Varner, about thirty, a confirmed bachelor, slightly thyroidic. The ninth of sixteen children, Jody is clerk at Varner's store until Flem is hired and eventually assumes most of Jody's responsibilities. It is Jody who wants his sister Eula to attend school, and he takes her there every day.

Eula Varner, the daughter of Will Varner and youngest of his sixteen children. Incorrigibly lazy, she is slow to develop emotionally and late in learning to walk; her physical development, however, is abnormally rapid, and as a teenager she is desired by most of the men in Frenchman's Bend, though she is indifferent toward her sexuality. When she is sixteen, she becomes pregnant by Hoake McCarron (who flees the state), causing Will Varner to arrange a hasty marriage between her and Flem Snopes to save the family name.

V. K. Ratliff, a sewing-machine salesman. Ratliff relates much of the Snopes family history to the other characters; his father and Ab Snopes had rented from the same landowner, and young Ratliff accompanied Ab on his horse-trading expedition to Pat Stamper's. Though Ratliff is somewhat rational and ethical, his greed gets the better of him when he gives his half of a Jefferson restaurant to Flem in exchange for one-third interest in the old Frehchman place, which Flem has convinced Ratliff contains gold.

Ab Snopes, Flem's father, an arrogant, embittered man. According to Ratliff, Ab became soured on life through some bad experiences, having been tied up to a tree by Bayard Sartoris and Uncle Buck Mc-Caslin, shot in the heel by Colonel Sartoris, and cheated by Pat Stamper. Wherever he goes, Ab is followed by his reputation as a barn-burner.

Flem Snopes, protagonist of the novel. After Varner rents a vacant farm to Ab Snopes, he hires Ab's son Flem to clerk at his store as a bribe to keep Ab from getting angry and burning his property. Flem, his eyes the color of stagnant water, always dressed in a clean white shirt and a bowtie, runs the store efficiently and soon assumes Jody's position at the cotton gin. He helps Will Varner with his accounts, and is given virtual autonomy in his handling of the store. Flem also pursues some independent business ventures, lending money at high interest rates and opening a new blacksmith shop. When Eula becomes pregnant, Will Varner marries her to Flem and gives him the old Frenchman's place as a dowry. After a honeymoon in Texas, Flem returns with some wild horses which he manages to sell at a handsome profit. Finally, by salting the old Frenchman place with gold coins, Flem sells it to Ratliff, Armstid, and Bockwright, who believe that they have swindled Flem out of a cache of gold coins. With this last triumph, Flem Snopes feels that he has reached his limit in Frenchman's Bend and moves to Jefferson, where he expects to find a new, larger world to conquer.

Isaac Snopes (Ike), Flem's cousin, an idiot who falls in love with Jack Houston's cow, saves it from a fire, and receives it as a gift from Houston. Ike lives with the cow in Mrs. Littlejohn's barn until the animal is taken from him and destroyed.

I. O. Snopes, Flem's cousin who works in the blacksmith shop. His speech is a ridiculous combination of misquoted clichés and aphorisms. He replaces Labove as the schoolteacher and vanishes when his wife reappears with child.

Mink Snopes, Flem's cousin, a poor tenant farmer. Mink allows his cow to pasture on his neighbor Jack Houston's land for the winter. When Mink attempts to get the animal back, Houston pulls a gun and demands payment. Mink then takes the matter to court and loses. Feeling cheated, he ambushes Houston and kills him. While on trial, Mink waits for Flem to come back from Texas and assist him; however, Flem decides that helping Mink cannot produce any tangible benefit, so he avoids the trial and Mink is sent to prison.

Labove, schoolteacher at Frenchman's Bend. He is a student at the University of Mississippi when he is hired by Varner to teach school in his spare time. He becomes infatuated with Eula Varner, one of his students, and after a pathetic and unsuccessful attempt to take her by force, he leaves town in shame, though Eula never even bothers to tell Jody about Labove's advance.

Henry Armstid, a poor farmer. He breaks his leg while trying to capture one of Flem's wild horses, and later mortgages all his possessions for part interest in the old Frenchman's place. He finally goes crazy, refusing to stop digging for the nonexistent treasure, refusing to admit that he has been swindled.

The Story

In his later years Will Varner, owner of the Old Frenchman place and almost everything else in Frenchman's Bend, began to turn many of his affairs over to his thirty-year-old son Jody. One day, while Jody sat in the Varner store, he met Ab Snopes, a newcomer to town, and Ab arranged to rent one of the farms owned by the Varners. Jody then found out from Ratliff, a salesman, that Ab had been suspected of burning barns on other farms where he had been a tenant. Jody and his father concluded that Ab's unsavory reputation would do them no harm. Jody became afraid, however, that Ab might burn some of the Varner property; as a sort of bribe, he hired Ab's son, Flem, to clerk in the store.

From Ratliff came the explanation of why Ab was soured on the world. Ab's principal grievance grew out of a horse-trading deal he once made with Pat Stamper, an almost legendary trader. Ab drove a mule and an old horse to Jefferson and, before showing them to Stamper, he skillfully doctored up the old nag. Stamper swapped Ab a team of mules that looked fine, but when Ab tried to drive them out of Jefferson the mules collapsed. To get back his own mule Ab spent the money his wife had given him to buy a milk separator. Stamper also forced him to purchase a dark, fat horse that looked healthy but rather peculiar. On the way home Ab ran into a thunderstorm and the horse changed from dark to light and from fat to lean. It was Ab's old horse, which Stamper had painted and then fattened up with a bicycle pump.

Will Varner's daughter, Eula, was a plump, sensuous girl who matured early. The new schoolteacher, Labove, fell in love with her the first day she came to the schoolhouse. An ambitious young man, Labove rode back and forth between Frenchman's Bend and the University, where he studied law and played on the football team. One day he attempted to seduce Eula after school had been dismissed; he failed and later was horrified to discover that Eula did not even mention the attempt to Jody. Labove left Frenchman's Bend forever.

As she grew older Eula had many suitors, the principal one being Hoake Mc-Carron, who literally fought off the competition. When the Varners found out that Eula was pregnant, McCarron and two other suitors left for Texas. Flem Snopes then stepped in, married Eula, and went off on a long honeymoon.

The Snopes clan which had gathered in the wake of Ab and Flem began to have troubles within the family. The idiot boy, Isaac, was neglected and mistreated; when he fell in love with a cow, his behavior became a town scandal. Mink Snopes, another relative, was charged with murdering Jack Houston, who had impounded Mink's wandering cattle. Flem stayed away from town throughout this trouble. When Mink was brought to trial, Flem, who might have helped him, ignored the whole case. Mink was sent to jail for life.

Flem came back from his honeymoon accompanied by Buck Hipps, a Texan, and a string of wild, spotted horses. The Texan arranged to auction off these horses to farmers who had gathered from miles around. To start things off, the Texan gave one horse to Eck Snopes, provided that Eck would make the first bid on the next one. At this point Henry Armstid and his wife drove up. Henry, in spite of his wife's protests, bought a horse for five dollars. By dark all but three of the horses had been sold, and Henry was anxious to claim his purchase. He and his wife were almost killed in trying to rope their pony. Hipps wanted to return the Armstids' money. He gave the five dollars to Henry's wife, but Henry took the bill from her and gave it to Flem Snopes. Hipps told Mrs. Armstid that Flem would return it to her the next day.

When the other purchasers tried to rope their horses, the spotted devils ran through an open gate and escaped into the countryside. Henry Armstid broke his leg and almost died. Eck Snopes chased the horse that had been given him and ran it into a boarding-house. The horse escaped from the house and ran down the road. At a bridge it piled into a wagon driven by Vernon Tull and occupied by Tull's wife and family. The mules pulling the wagon became excited and Tull was jerked out of the wagon onto his face.

The Tulls sued Eck Snopes for the damages done to Vernon and to their wagon; the Armstids sued Flem for damages to Henry and for the recovery of their five dollars. The justice of the peace was forced to rule in favor of the defendants. Flem could not be established as the owner of the horses, and Eck was not the legal owner of a horse that had been given to him.

One day Henry Armstid told Ratliff that Flem was digging every night in the garden of the Old Frenchman place, which Flem had acquired from Will Varner. Ever since the Civil War there had been rumors that the builder of the house had buried money and jewels in the garden. Henry and Ratliff took a man named Bookwright into their confidence and, with the aid of another man who could use a divining rod, they slipped into the garden after Flem had quit digging. After locating the position of buried metal, they began digging, and each unearthed a bag of silver coins. They decided to pool their resources and buy the land in a hurry. Ratliff agreed to pay Flem an exorbitant price. At night they kept on shoveling, but they unearthed no more treasure. Ratliff finally realized that no bag could remain intact in the ground for thirty years. When he and Bookwright examined the silver coins, they found the money had been minted after the Civil War.

But Armstid, now totally out of his mind, refused to believe there was no treasure. He kept on digging, day and night. People from all over the county came to watch his frantic shoveling. Passing by on this way to Jefferson, Flem Snopes paused only a moment to watch Henry; then with a flip of the reins he drove his horses on.

Critical Evaluation

Since its publication in 1940, *The Hamlet* has come to be recognized as one of Faulkner's great achievements. Although the major Faulkner critics consider either *Absalom, Absalom!* or *The Sound and the Fury* his greatest work, *The Hamlet* is almost universally considered the most successful volume of the Snopes trilogy. Because it contains most of Faulkner's technical devices and at the same time is accessible enough to not require a separate chronology or multiple rereadings to ascertain the story, *The Hamlet* is one of the best Faulkner novels to study. *The Hamlet* is divided into four books, each focusing on different characters and employing a different tone. Book one, "Flem," introduces the reader to Frenchman's Bend, the Varners, and Ab Snopes. Ratliff tells a long story about Ab Snopes's confrontation with Major DeSpain (which was responsible for the original barn burning incident) and Pat Stamper. The rest of book one is devoted to Flem's initial successes at and eventual control of Varner's store. Book two, "Eula," tells the stories of Eula and Labove, culminating in her hasty marriage to Flem. Book two concludes with a dream sequence in which Ratliff imagines Flem in Hell. Book three, "The Long Summer," tells the stories of Ike Snopes and the cow, Jack Houston's past, Mink Snopes's murder of Houston, and Mink's imprisonment. Book four, "The Peasants," recounts Flem's sale of the wild horses, the resultant lawsuit of Tull vs. Eck Snopes, and Flem's sale of the old Frenchman place.

Since six sections of the novel were published (with varying degrees of revision) separately as stories and since many parts of the novel may be read separately from the novel and seemingly appreciated, it must be asked whether *The Hamlet* is a thrown-together book of related episodes or a unified book whose structure serves an ulterior thematic end. Careful consideration reveals the book's unity.

Flem is always central to the action even when he does not appear in a certain scene. Flem does not appear in the long section covering Eula's development; however, this section's importance is in its relationship to Flem. Eula's sensuality is so strong that it ensnares most men; Eula is described in rich, poetic terms as a Dionysian symbol, a primal earthmother. It is significant that the one man oblivious to her sensuality, Flem, is the one who marries her—for money and social stature, not for her feminine charms. Labove is ruined by his attraction to Eula; whereas, Flem has purged himself of his primal, emotional side and has used Eula's sensuality—which is responsible for her pregnancy and marriage—for his own material gain. Thus, though Flem does not appear in this section, its events ultimately play into his hands, making Flem central to the episode's meaning and function.

To understand Flem, one must understand the society that produced him. In a perfect world, Flem Snopes could not exist or would be expelled as a pariah. By detailing painful events in the pasts of Ab Snopes and Jack Houston, Faulkner portrays injustice as a partner to justice, a self-sustaining force. By contrast, Flem seems like a reflection of his society: Flem is a usurer, but so is Varner; Flem is arrogant in his business manner, but so is Ratliff when he sells Mink Snopes a sewing machine. Flem is not evil incarnate as some have claimed; rather, he exaggerates certain less-than-honorable practices to which he has been exposed.

One must also view Flem through the eyes of others. Throughout the novel, Faulkner maintains distance from Flem and never enters his mind. Instead, Flem is characterized by the reactions of others to him and by the influence of his actions on others. At the horse auction, it is Buck Hipps, Flem's surrogate, who actually sells the horses, and it is Eck Snopes and V. K. Ratliff through whom the action is filtered. The central issue, Flem's motivation and the incident's influence on his rise, is never overtly discussed by Faulkner. Yet here again, the average man's desire to get something for next to nothing is Flem's motivation. By viewing Flem as a peripheral character, Faulkner emphasizes the inevitability of a Flem Snopes—when greed exists, someone will take advantage. When read separately as "Spotted Horses," this section is merely an entertaining piece of local color; when read, as intended, in the context of *The Hamlet*, this section gives Flem's rise a tragic inevitability. Flem Snopes's success is inversely proportional to the other characters' integrity; thus, it is essential that Flem be seen from the viewpoint of those who sustain him and make him what he is.

Finally, the different episodes are intended to provide ironic contrast with one another. Book three juxtaposes three love stories, those of Ike, Mink, and Jack Houston. All three loves involve sacrifice and pain, and love has influenced the courses of all three lives. However, in contrast to Mink who finds an outlet in revenge and Houston who finds one in self-pity, Ike's love is totally altruistic and rooted in compassion—though, ironically, his bestiality is viewed as morally repugnant to society, a society which is incapable of a love so free of selfishness. In contrast with Ike's pure love and the flawed loves of other characters is Flem Snopes, who is incapable of love. Another ironic contrast is made between the cow that Ike loves and Eula. In describing both, Faulkner's writing rises to the poetic, but he complicates the relationship between the two by using feminine imagery to describe the cow and bovine imagery to describe Eula. In the eyes of the men who desire her, Eula is an animal to be conquered as a cow is slain; in the eyes of Ike Snopes, his cow is a goddess to be revered. Is a society that is incapable of love capable of sanctioning one form and forbidding another? Through juxtaposition of diverse sections of narrative, Faulkner is able to present these thematic concerns; viewed in isolation, Eula's section is hyperbolic, and Ike's section is prurient.

As in all of Faulkner's major works, the novel's form is a vehicle through which meaning is developed. In *The Hamlet*, each divergent episode or detail either provides a background for understanding context or is unified by Flem's implicit presence.

The creation of a complex novelist, Flem Snopes is of course a complex character. Whether he is viewed as a symbol of the South's acquiescence to mercantilism, a mirror of a selfish and amoral society, or a symbol of the impotence of twentieth-century affluence, Flem is not a stock villain from the melodrama of the last century. He should be compared and contrasted with F. Scott Fitzgerald's Jay Gatsby and Theodore Dreiser's Frank Cowperwood. The self-made man is a part of both our national history and our national mythology. Whether a composite of actual characters from the turn of the century or an archetypal creation, Flem Snopes is a dynamic, complex, and realistic character—significant in both

Faulkner's canon and American fiction of this century.

In *The Hamlet*, Faulkner makes Yoknapatawpha County as timeless, exuberant, and detailed as the London of late Dickens novels; simultaneously, his archetypal characters and situations are relevant to and still recurrent in today's world. This combination should guarantee *The Hamlet* interested readers and critics for as long as great novels are read and studied.

Bibliography

See **The Snopes Trilogy**, page 209.

LIGHT IN AUGUST

Type of work: Novel
Author: William Faulkner (1897–1962)
Time of plot: 1930
Locale: Mississippi
First published: 1932

Light in August *is a study of the race problem in the South and of the psychological obsession with the Civil War which lingers there. A fascinating narrative with little regard for strict time sequence, the novel is important for its vivid treatment of a theme of wide social significance and for the intensity of Faulkner's moral vision.*

Principal Characters

Joe Christmas, a mulatto. Placed in an orphan home by his demented grandfather, he is to lead a tortured life of social isolation, as he belongs neither to the white nor to the colored race; in fact, he prefers this kind of existence. After staying with the fanatical Calvin McEachern during his boyhood, Joe knocks his foster father unconscious and strikes out on his own, rejecting any friendly overtures. At last, he is driven to his final desperate act: he kills his benefactress, Joanna Burden, and faces death at the hands of merciless Percy Grimm.

Joanna Burden, Joe Christmas' mistress, the descendant of a New England family. Rejected by many of her neighbors, she is the friend of Negroes and interested in improving their lot. In her efforts to make Joe useful to the world, she also tries to possess and dominate him sexually, and so meets her death.

Calvin McEachern, Joe's foster father. A ruthless, unrelenting religious fundamentalist, McEachern, without real animosity, often beats the boy savagely for trifling misdemeanors and tells him to repent. He demands that "the Almighty be as magnanimous as himself."

Eupheus Hines (Doc), Joe Christmas' grandfather. Always a hot-tempered little man, he is often in fights. When he learns that his daughter Milly has a mulatto lover, the fiery old man kills him. Later he allows Milly to die in childbirth, unaided by a doctor. Soon after her death he places the baby in an orphanage. Years later, learning of Joe's imprisonment, Doc Hines demands that his grandson be lynched. Prior to this time, the old man has devoted much effort to preaching to bemused Negroes about white supremacy.

Gail Hightower, a minister. Most of Hightower's life has been devoted to a dream. Long before, his grandfather had died while serving with a troop of Confederate cavalry. Because of his grandfather he becomes obsessed with the Civil War. Now an outcast, he has driven his wife to her death because of this obsession; in the process he is forced from his church by his outraged congregation.

Joe Brown (Lucas Burch), Lena Grove's

lover and the unwilling father of her child. A loudmouthed, weak man, he deserts Lena and finds work in another town. After meeting Joe Christmas, he becomes a bootlegger and lives with Joe in a cabin behind Joanna Burden's house. When Christmas is captured, Brown, hoping for a large reward, tells the sheriff that Joe has murdered Miss Burden. Unable to face responsibilities, he hops a freight train in order to avoid Lena.

Lena Grove, a country girl seduced and deserted by Joe Brown. Ostensibly, this simple-hearted, fecund young woman pursues her lover because he is the father of her child; actually, she continues looking for him so that she can see different parts of the South.

Milly Hines, Doc Hines' daughter. She dies in childbirth because her enraged father refuses to let a doctor deliver a mulatto child.

Byron Bunch, a worker at the sawmill. Although he loves Lena, this good man helps her look for Joe Brown.

Mrs. Hines, Joe Christmas' grandmother. Always loving Joe, she tries to get Hightower to say that Joe was elsewhere when the murder was committed.

Mrs. McEachern, Calvin McEachern's long-suffering, patient wife. Like the other women, she is rebuffed when she tries to help Joe Christmas.

Percy Grimm, a brutal National Guard captain. He hunts Joe down after the latter escapes from a deputy. Not satisfied with shooting Christmas, Grimm also mutilates the injured man.

The Story

Joe Christmas was the illegitimate son of a dark-skinned circus trouper who was thought to be of Negro blood and a white girl named Milly Hines. Joe's grandfather, old Doc Hines, killed the circus man, let Milly die in childbirth, and put Joe—at Christmas time; hence his last name—into an orphanage, where the children learned to call him "Nigger." Doc Hines then arranged to have Joe adopted by a religious and heartless farmer named McEachern, whose cruelties to Joe were met with a matching stubbornness that made of the boy an almost subhuman being.

One day in town McEachern took Joe to a disreputable restaurant, where he talked to the waitress, Bobbie Allen. McEachern told the adolescent Joe never to patronize the place alone. But Joe went back. He met Bobbie at night and became her lover. Night after night, while the McEacherns were asleep, he would creep out of the house and hurry to meet her in town.

One night McEachern followed Joe to a country dance and ordered him home. Joe reached for a chair, knocked McEachern unconscious, whispered to Bobbie that he would meet her soon, and raced McEachern's mule home. There he gathered up all the money he could lay his hands on and went into town. At the house where Bobbie stayed he encountered the restaurant proprietor and his wife and another man. The two men beat up Joe, took his money, and left for Memphis with the two women.

Joe moved on. Sometimes he worked. More often he simply lived off the money women would give him. He slept with many women and nearly always told them he was of Negro blood.

At last he went to Jefferson, a small town in Mississippi, where he got work shoveling sawdust in a lumber mill. He found lodging in a long-deserted Negro cabin near the country home of Miss Joanna Burden, a spinster of Yankee origin who had few associates in Jefferson because of her zeal for bettering the lot of the Negro. She fed Joe and, when it appeared that he was of Negro blood, planned to send him to a Negro school. Joe was her lover for three years. Her reactions ranged from sheer animalism to evangelism, in which she tried to make Joe repent his sins and turn Christian.

A young man who called himself Joe Brown came to work at the sawmill, and Joe Christmas invited Brown to share his cabin with him. The two began to sell bootleg whiskey. After a while Joe told Brown that he was part Negro; before long Brown discovered the relations of Joe and Miss Burden. When their bootlegging prospered, they bought a car and gave up their jobs at the lumber mill.

One night Joe went to Miss Burden's room half-determined to kill her. That night she attempted to shoot him with an antiquated pistol that did not fire. Joe cut her throat with his razor and ran out of the house. Later in the evening a fire was discovered in Miss Burden's house. When the townspeople started to go upstairs in the burning house, Brown tried to stop them. They brushed him aside. They found Miss Burden's body in the bedroom and carried it outside before the house burned to the ground.

Through a letter in the Jefferson bank, the authorities learned of Miss Burden's New Hampshire relatives, whom they notified. Almost at once word came back offering a thousand dollars reward for the capture of the murderer. Brown tried to tell the story as he knew it, putting the blame on Joe Christmas, so that he could collect the money. Few believed his story, but he was held in custody until Joe Christmas could be found.

Joe Christmas remained at large for several days, but at last with the help of bloodhounds he was tracked down. Meanwhile old Doc Hines had learned of his grandson's crime and he came with his wife to Jefferson. He urged the white people to lynch Joe, but for the most part his rantings went unheeded.

. On the way to face indictment by the grand jury in the courthouse, Joe, handcuffed but not manacled to the deputy, managed to escape. He ran to a Negro cabin and found a gun. Some volunteer guards from the American Legion gave chase, and finally found him in the kitchen of the Reverend Gail Hightower, a one-time Presbyterian preacher who now was an outcast because he had driven his wife into dementia by his obsession with the gallant death of his grandfather in the Civil War. Joe had gone to Hightower at the suggestion of his grandmother, Mrs. Hines, who had had a conference with him in his cell just before he escaped. She had been advised of this possible way out by Byron Bunch, Hightower's only friend in Jefferson. The Legionnaires shot Joe down; then their leader mutilated him with a knife.

Brown now claimed his reward. A deputy took him out to the cabin where he had lived with Joe Christmas. On entering the cabin, he saw Mrs. Hines holding a new-born baby. In the bed was a girl, Lena Grove, whom he had slept with in a town in Alabama. Lena had started out to find Brown when she knew she was going to have a baby. Traveling most of the way on foot, she had arrived in Jefferson on the day of the murder and the fire. Directed to the sawmill, she had at once seen that Byron Bunch, to whom she had been sent, was not the same man as Lucas Burch, which was Brown's real name. Byron, a kindly soul, had fallen in love with her. Having identified Brown from Byron's description, she was sure that in spite of his new name Brown was the father of her child. She gave birth to the baby in Brown's cabin, where Byron had made her as comfortable as he could, with the aid of Mrs. Hines.

Brown jumped from a back window and ran away. Byron, torn between a desire to marry Lena and the wish to give her baby its rightful father, tracked Brown to the railroad grade outside town and fought with him. Brown escaped aboard a freight train.

Three weeks later Lena and Byron took to the road with the baby, Lena still searching for Brown. A truck driver gave them a lift. Byron was patient, but one night tried to compromise her. When she repulsed him, he left the little camp where the truck was parked. But next morning he was waiting at the bend of the road, and he climbed up on the truck as it made its way toward Tennessee.

Critical Evaluation

Faulkner was thirty-five when he wrote *Light in August* as the final explosive creation of the richest part of his artistic career that saw the production of *Sartoris* (1929), *The Sound and the Fury* (1929), *As I Lay Dying* (1930), and *Sanctuary* (1931). Only *Absalom, Absalom!* (1936) would approach again the intensity and splendid richness of this, his tenth book published and the seventh in the series about Yoknapatawpha County. Armstid, who appears in the novel's first chapter, is the same farmer of *As I Lay Dying;* and Joanna Burden mentions Colonel Sartoris in her account of her own family's blood-spattered history. *Light in August* is Faulkner's longest work, his most varied "in mood and character" (as Richard H. Rovere points out), and perhaps equaled only by *The Sound and the Fury* as a penetrating and compelling analysis of Southern society.

The style of this novel has often been criticized for its inconsistency, often pointed to as an example of Faulkner's "undisciplined genius." Indeed, its stylistic characteristics are manifold and complex: sudden changes of narrative tense, from present to past and back again; abrupt shifts in point of view, ranging from the viewpoints of the major characters to viewpoints of characters who apparently have no part in the main action at all; occasional use of the stream-of-consciousness technique based on the Proustian obsession with key images, or on what Joyce termed "radiating imagery"; the frequent use, also Joycean, of run-together words like "womanpinksmelling," "August-tremulous," "stillwinged," "womanshenegro"; the appearance of Joycean epiphanies, as when Chapter 16 ends with Hightower's "extended and clenchfisted arms lying full in the pool of light from the shaded lamp" or Joe Christmas caught in the glare of headlamps after the murder; the suggestion of Eliot's emphasis on all the senses—"an odor, an attenuation, an aftertaste"; and the use of Frost's simplicity of imagery, mixed with the kind of flamboyant poetic diction characteristic of Wallace Stevens—with the repetition of implicit interrogatives, and phrases such as "grown heroic at the instant of vanishment" and the "two inescapable horizons of the implacable earth." There is, in fact, awkwardly repetitious use of manneristic expressions such as "by ordinary," "terrific," and the adverb "quite" (as in "quite calm, quite still") that seem to support the argument that the composition of this admitted masterpiece was at times hurried and even heedless.

But the last two chapters of the novel—Hightower's rambling retrogression into Civil War history, and the resumption of Lena's travels (this time with Byron) as told by the unnamed furniture dealer who has nothing to do with the plot—achieve a sense of open-ended comprehensiveness that indicates Faulkner's epic concept of his novel. And it is the universality of the epic genre that may account for the apparently arbitrary concatenation of stylistic elements. Every angle of insight, every avenue of perspective, every mode of entry is used by the author to compel the reader into the world of the novel—a world complete with its own dimensions, of time as well as of space, of emotions and events. As an epic, *Light in August* falls into the genre of "search epics" that began with Homer's *Odyssey*. Joe is searching for a light that will give meaning to his existence, exploring, in turn, the light of McEachern's "home," the light of his adolescent town, the lamp of Bobbie Allen's room, the inordinate street—and room-lights of nameless Negro ghettos, the light of Joanna's candle and, finally, the light of the flames of Joanna's burning house—the "light in August" around whose central, sinister radiance all the main characters' lives resolve. For that burning light brings their identities into momentary and terrible focus: disillusioning Lena of her dreams of trust and security, forcing Lucas Burch and Gail Hightower to confront their cowardice, coercing Byron Bunch to throw his lot irrevocably with his love, ending Joanna's ambiguously introverted life in perverted horror, and, with supreme irony, ultimately identifying Christmas through the reaction of the outraged town and, through the identification, ending his search in death.

The novel is also epic in its thematic scope, a scope embodied in the ambivalence of Christmas himself who, like Homer's Helen, is tragically made to straddle, through no fault of his own, two worlds—neither of which will accept him because of his relations to the other, neither of which he will accept because of his inherent inability to be singularly defined. The two worlds, as Faulkner steeps them through the very fiber of his novel, may be described as a kind of movable equation—an equation generally defined by the Jungian distinction betwen the *anima* and the *animus,* and also by the racial distinction between black and white. On one side Christmas confronts his (possible) Negro blood, death (as stasis), darkness or artificial light, evil, fire, the female, sleeping, insanity, sin, savageness, violence, secrecy, cunning and deceit, softness, the fugitive state, belief, and passivity. Opposed to these elements, but also mingling and combining with them in unpredictable and unmanageable (for Christmas) patterns, are his white skin, life (as kinesis and fluid movement), light, good, the sun, the male, being awake and aware, control, righteousness, calm, openness, durability and determination, domestic security, knowing, and activity. "He never acted like either a nigger or a white man," one of his murderers comments at the end. Because Christmas could not find himself on either side of the equation, because his entire life was a confusion between the two sides, his epic quest ends in his own individual death and in the symbolic death of the community of Jefferson.

It is because Faulkner envisioned Christmas as an epic hero that he identified him with Christ—not only in name, but also in his peculiar silences; his master-disciple relationship with Brown; his capture on a Friday; the nurse who offers him a silver dollar bribe; Joanna's resemblance to both Mary Magdalene and the Virgin Mary; his thirty years of private life (about which the narrator tells of nothing specific); his refusal to complain when beaten at the end; and the town's final comment that "it was as though he had set out and made his plans to passively commit suicide." But *Light in August* is Christological only in the sense that it draws upon the Christian myth to complicate and deepen the essentially secular, sociological myth Faulkner constructs consistently in all the saga of Yoknapatawpha County. *Light in August* professes only the religion of man, a religion that must function in a world "peopled principally by the dead," as Hightower, the rejected minister, remarks. This is a novel of "mighty compassion."

Bibliography

Baldanza, Frank. "The Structure of *Light in August,*" in *Modern Fiction Studies.* XIII (Spring, 1967), pp. 67–78.

Borden, Caroline. "Characterization in Faulkner's *Light in August,*" in *Literature and Ideology.* XIII (1972), pp. 41–50.

Brooks, Cleanth. *William Faulkner: The Yoknapatawpha County.* New Haven, Conn.: Yale University Press, 1963, pp. 47–74.

Collins, R.G. "*Light in August*: Faulkner's Stained Glass Triptych," in *Mosaic.* VII (1973), pp. 97–157.

Cottrell, Beekman W. "Christian Symbols in *Light in August*," in *Modern Fiction Studies*. II (Winter, 1956), pp. 207–213.

Fowler, D.F. "Faith as a Unifying Principle in Faulkner's *Light in August*," in *Tennessee Studies in Literature*. XXI (1977), pp. 49–57.

Howe, Irving. *William Faulkner: A Critical Study*. New York: Vintage, 1962, pp. 61–70, 200–214.

Kazin, Alfred. "The Stillness of *Light in August*," in *William Faulkner: Three Decades of Criticism*. Edited by Frederick J. Hoffman and Olga Vickery. East Lansing: Michigan State University Press, 1960, pp. 247–265.

Lamont, William H.F. "The Chronology of *Light in August*," in *Modern Fiction Studies*. III (Winter, 1957–1958), pp. 360–361.

Langston, Beach. "The Meaning of Lena Grove and Gail Hightower in *Light in August*," in *Boston University Studies in English*. V (September, 1961), pp. 46–63.

Longley, John L., Jr. *The Tragic Mask: A Study of Faulkner's Heroes*. Chapel Hill: University of North Carolina Press, 1963, pp. 50–62, 192–205.

McElderry, B.R., Jr. "The Narrative Structure of *Light in August*," in *College English*. XIX (February, 1958), pp. 200–207.

Millgate, Michael. *The Achievement of William Faulkner*. New York: Random House, 1965, pp. 124–137.

Minter, David L., Editor. *Twentieth Century Interpretations of* Light in August. Englewood Cliffs, N.J.: Prentice-Hall, 1969.

Mulquien, James E. "*Light in August*; Motion, Eros, and Death," in *Notes on Mississippi Writers*. VIII (1975), pp. 91–98.

Neufeldt, Leonard. "Time and Man's Possibilities in *Light in August*," in *Georgia Review*. XXV (1971), pp. 27–40.

Nilon, Charles H. *Faulkner and the Negro*. New York: Citadel Press, 1965, pp. 73–93.

Pearce, Richard. "Faulkner's One Ring Circus," in *Wisconsin Studies in Contemporary Literature*. VII (1966), pp. 270–283.

Pitavy, Francois L. *Faulkner's* Light in August. Bloomington: Indiana University Press, 1973.

Porter, Carolyn. "The Problem of Time in *Light in August*," in *Rice University Studies*. LXI (1975), pp. 107–125.

O'Connor, William Van. *The Tangled Fire of William Faulkner*. Minneapolis: University of Minnesota Press, 1954, pp. 72–87.

Slatoff, Walter J. *Quest for Failure: A Study of William Faulkner*. Ithaca, N.Y.: Cornell University Press, 1960, pp. 173–198.

Swiggart, Peter. *The Art of Faulkner's Novels.* Austin: University of Texas Press, 1962, pp. 41–48, 131–148.

Thompson, Lawrance. *William Faulkner: An Introduction and Interpretation.* New York: Holt, Rinehart and Winston, 1967, pp. 66–80.

Vickery, Olga. *The Novels of William Faulkner: A Critical Interpretation.* Baton Rouge: Louisiana State University Press, 1964, pp. 66–83.

Volpe, Edmond L. *A Reader's Guide to William Faulkner.* New York: Noonday, 1964, pp. 151–174.

THE MANSION

Type of work: Novel
Author: William Faulkner (1897–1962)
Time of plot: 1908–1946
Locale: Yoknapatawpha County, Mississippi
First published: 1959

Essay-Review

It is within the power of some writers to hit upon the illuminating figure of, speech, sentence, or brief passage that echoes through the total body of their work like a meaningful refrain. Offhand, one thinks of Melville's "Call me Ishmael" at the opening of *Moby Dick*, Walt Whitman's declaration, "I was the man, I suffer'd, I was there," and Fitzgerald's penetration deep into the heart of the great middle-class illusion which lights up his legend of the Twenties, his innocent belief that the very rich are different from the rest of us. A passage of similar import comes at the close of William Faulkner's *Absalom, Absalom!* after Quentin Compson has related to his Canadian roommate at Harvard the long, violent chronicle of Sutpen's innocence and guilt. At the end Shreve McCannon has one more question to ask. Why does Quentin hate the South? And Quentin's repeated violent, almost desperate reply is that he doesn't hate it.

Quentin's agonized reply betrays something of Faulkner's own ambivalence, the mixed sense of love and guilt in his attitude toward his Mississippi homeland, as well as the ambiguities of character and conduct in his vision of ruin and decay within the Yoknapatawpha County scene. Almost everything he has written has been an attempt to define the nature and meaning of his moral history of the human effort and its limitations, and he had the habit of reworking his material, of retelling old stories and presenting familiar characters in a different light, in order to extract fresh meanings and deeper understanding—for himself, it seems as much as for his readers. In the process, over the years, he was engaged in filling in the details of an elaborate design, one part here, another part there, a new detail somewhere else, with each story adding to the totality of the human situation which most readers expected would be fully revealed when the Yoknapatawpha saga was complete. *The Mansion* rounds out one pattern in his complex overall design, completing *Snopes*, a trilogy begun in *The Hamlet* in 1940 and continued in *The Town*, published in 1957.

To readers who know the whole body of Faulkner's writing, his habit of going back to or recombining earlier themes and events is not a matter of great importance. Since all his books lead inevitably into one another, the reappearance of old characters, the telling of a new story in a familiar setting, or the conclusion of an episode begun in some other novel or short story merely adds to our sense of familiarity with his people and his region. No one should be surprised, then, to find in *The Mansion* a second and more revealing account of Mink Snopes's murder of Jack Houston (first told in *The Hamlet*), to discover at last why Flem Snopes framed Montgomery Ward Snopes, the pornographer, with planted moonshine whiskey and made him an agent in getting Mink's prison term extended another twenty years, or to learn new facts about Gavin Stevens' strange, detached love for Flem's wife Eula, an earthy fertility goddess from a crossroads community, and the even stranger relationship between the middle-aged lawyer and Eula's daughter Linda.

If discrepancies developed between the earlier novels and *The Mansion*, Faulkner had an answer for their presence: In a brief foreward he informed the reader that he himself had discovered more contradictions and discrepancies than he hoped his readers would find. He explained that such discrepancies existed because during the thirty-four years he had worked on the Snopes saga he had learned more about man's perplexities and conflicts and more about the people in his chronicle.

Members of the grasping Snopes clan came into Faulkner's fiction as early as *Sartoris*, but he did not give them a book of their own until *The Hamlet* appeared in 1940. That novel, rich in folk comedy, grotesque in its horrors, sharp in social criticism, tells how Ab Snopes, ex-bushwacker, horse trader, and sharecropper won immunity in Frenchman's Bend because of his reputation as a barn burner and how his son Flem became a clerk in Will Varner's store. Before long other members of the family descend like swarming locusts on the village, nibbling away at its social, economic, and moral life until they have picked it as clean as a ham bone at a Sunday School barbecue. Led by Flem, who has set himself up in the world by marrying Eula Varner when she was pregnant with another man's child, they then move on to Jefferson, the county seat.

There, in *The Town*, Flem sets respectability and wealth as his goals, and by following a career of chicanery, conniving, double-dealing, and playing the willing cuckold for years, he ends up as the president of the bank Bayard Sartoris had founded. In the meantime he has cleared his coattails of the more disreputable members of his family—Mink Snopes, the murderer; I. O. Snopes, the bigamist; Montgomery Ward Snopes, a dealer in pornography; and even his wife, who commits suicide as a way of escape from Flem's maneuverings to possess her daughter's inheritance, ruin her lover, and take over the bank.

Presented as a series of episodes narrated by such familiar Faulkner characters as Gavin Stevens, the lawyer; his nephew, Charles Mallison; and V. K. Ratliff, the wry-humored, compassionate, observing sewing-machine salesman, *The Mansion* covers a time span linking Jack Houston's murder with Flem's violent death at the hands of Mink Snopes thirty-eight years later. In this novel, however, much of Flem's trickery and greed for money and power fade into the background and Linda, Eula's daughter, becomes the central figure. After Gavin Stevens has aided her in her escape from Flem at the time of her mother's death, she goes to New York, marries a Jewish sculptor, Barton Kohl, joins the Communist Party to which her husband belongs, and goes with him to Spain during the Spanish Civil War. Kohl and Linda are both casualties of the war. He is killed while flying for the Loyalists and she is deafened when the ambulance she is driving detonates a mine, bursting her eardrums in the explosion. Living in a world of silence, unable to hear her own harsh toneless voice, she returns to Jefferson and settles in the old mansion Flem has remodeled.

Gavin Stevens, who had been in love with Eula Snopes, though never her lover, has already transferred his affections to Linda, who is some sixteen years his junior. Their association never passes the bounds of friendship, however, and in the end it is Linda who brings about his marriage to another woman. In the course of this novel Charles Mallison grows up and becomes a participant in rather than an observer of the life of Jefferson. V. K. Ratliff continues to ponder the unpredictable, and generally cussed, ways of man. And Flem goes on his Snopesian way until Mink Snopes, released from prison through Linda's efforts, commits the second murder for which he has waited almost forty years. The final irony is that an ignorant, vindictive cousin brings Flem to the end he deserves, but there are many in Jefferson—among them Lawyer Stevens and shrewd, humane Ratliff—who see Flem's death as an act of retribution which the decent people of the town were powerless to administer.

In *The Hamlet* and in the opening sections of *The Town*, Flem Snopes gave every promise of becoming one of Faulkner's great grotesques—a dehumanized, inscrutable, almost sexless, but implacable force of rapacity and greed. As a symbol of the upward climb of predatory Snopeses from mule trading and storekeeping to become the bankers and suspender-snapping politicians of the new South he exhibited those traits of the grotesque and the comic which Faulkner handled with superb ease. But as a respectable member of the social community he is less effective; he remains a background figure, even though we are always conscious that, as Ratliff says, there is no limit to which he will not go, nothing which he will not use to his selfish ends, nobody not likely to suffer or grieve because of him.

Instead, it is his cousin Mink who dominates this novel. In *The Hamlet* he is a creature of pure malice, sly as a weasel, deadly as a rattlesnake. But in *The Mansion* we learn that the killing of Houston was motivated by more than revenge for failure to get free winter grazing for his cow. The killing, as Faulkner now reveals, was a desperate, violent attempt to retain some measure of human dignity denied him by the moods of nature and the ways of men. It is the same with his hatred for Flem. According to Mink's simple code, a kinsman must stand by his kin. When Flem fails to appear at the time of Mink's trial, Mink sees the killing of his cousin as a simple act of justice. Flem's use of Montgomery Ward Snopes to maneuver Mink into an attempt to escape and thus double his sentence convinces Mink that it is Old Moster's will that he rid the world of his betrayer. The story of Mink's return from the prison at Parchman, his encounter with J. C. Goodyhay, an ex-Marine sergeant turned evangelist, the buying of the gun, the shooting while Flem sits chewing silently, his eyes fixed on the hammer of Mink's gun as it goes off—these scenes show Faulkner at his best.

Unfortunately, not all of the novel is of this quality. *The Mansion* is a discursive, uneven work that is earthily humorous, ironic, violent, and compassionately reflective at times, but rambling and even dull at others. Like most of Faulkner's writing, it has a sound substructure in social morality, and although it lacks much of the dramatic intensity and impassioned rhetoric of this writer at the top of his bent, it is nevertheless, despite its lapses, a richly imagined and somberly moving story. No one has isolated to better advantage the nature of Snopesism, the relentless, dehumanized drive of greed and gain in our materialistic society. These matters moved Faulkner to indignation, and when he was aroused he generated in his fiction a kind of wild, brooding poetry of primitive vision, elemental power, and deep moral insights. Certainly the idea of man's mortality has seldom been presented more simply or beautifully than in the final pages of this novel, as Mink prepares to return his body to the waiting earth.

Bibliography

The Snopes Trilogy

Adams, Percy G. "Humor as Structure and Theme in Faulkner's Trilogy," in *Wisconsin Studies in Contemporary Literature*. V (Autumn, 1964), pp. 205–212.

Arpad, Joseph J. "William Faulkner's Legendary Novels: The Snopes Trilogy," in *Mississippi Quarterly*. II (1969), pp. 214–225.

Backman, Melvin. *Faulkner: The Major Years, A Critical Study*. Bloomington: Indiana University Press, 1966, pp. 139–159.

Beck, Warren. *Man in Motion: Faulkner's Trilogy*. Madison: University of Wisconsin Press, 1961.

Bigelow, Gordon E. "Faulkner's Snopes Saga," in *English Journal*. XLIX (December, 1960), pp. 595–605.

Brooks, Cleanth. *William Faulkner: The Yoknapatawpha County*. New Haven, Conn.: Yale University Press, 1963, pp. 167–243.

Dirksen, Sherland N. "William Faulkner's Snopes Family: *The Hamlet, The Town*, and *The Mansion*," in *Emporia State Research Studies*. XI (December, 1962), pp. 5–45.

Farmer, Norman, Jr. "The Love Theme: A Principal Source of Thematic Unity in Faulkner's Snopes Trilogy," in *Twentieth Century Literature*. VIII (January, 1963), pp. 111–123.

Gold, Joseph. *William Faulkner: A Study in Humanism from Metaphor to Discourse*. Norman: University of Oklahoma Press, 1966, pp. 148–173.

Hoffman, Frederick J. *William Faulkner*. New York: Twayne, 1961, pp. 85–95.

Kerr, Elizabeth M. "Snopes," in *Wisconsin Studies in Contemporary Literature*. I (Spring–Summer, 1960), pp. 66–83.

Lawson, Lewis A. "The Grotesque-Comic in the Snopes Trilogy," in *Literature and Psychology*. XV (Spring, 1965), pp. 92–106.

Leibowitz, Herbert A. "The Snopes Dilemma and the South," in *University of Kansas City Review*. XXVIII (Summer, 1962), pp. 273–284.

Levine, Paul. "Love and Money in the Snopes Trilogy," in *College English*. XXIII (December, 1961), pp. 192–203.

Longley, John L., Jr. *The Tragic Mask: A Study of Faulkner's Heroes*. Chapel Hill: University of North Carolina Press, 1963, pp. 63–78, 150–164.

Marcus, Steven. "Snopes Revisited," in *William Faulkner: Three Decades of Criticism*. Edited by Frederick J. Hoffman and Olga Vickery. East Lansing: Michigan State University Press, 1960, pp. 382–391.

Millgate, Michael. *The Achievement of William Faulkner*. New York: Random House, 1965, pp. 180–200, 235–252.

Norris, Nancy. "*The Hamlet, The Town,* and *The Mansion*: A Psychological Reading of the Snopes Trilogy," in *Mosaic*. VII (1973), pp. 213–235.

O'Connor, William Van. *The Tangled Fire of William Faulkner*. Minneapolis: University of Minnesota Press, 1954, pp. 111–124.

Payne, Ladell. "The Trilogy: Faulkner's Comic Epic in Prose," in *Studies in the Novel*. I (1969), pp. 27–37.

Roberts, James L. "Snopeslore: *The Hamlet, The Town, The Mansion,*" in *University of Kansas City Review*. XXVIII (October, 1961), pp. 65–71.

Swiggart, Peter. *The Art of Faulkner's Novels*. Austin: University of Texas Press, 1962, pp. 48–51, 195–206.

Thompson, Lawrance. *William Faulkner: An Introduction and Interpretation*. New York: Holt, Rinehart and Winston, 1967, pp. 133–158.

Vickery, Olga. *The Novels of William Faulkner: A Critical Interpretation*. Baton Rouge: Louisiana State University Press, 1964, pp. 167–208.

Volpe, Edmond L. *A Reader's Guide to William Faulkner*. New York: Noonday, 1964, pp. 304–343, 401–403.

Waggoner, Hyatt H. *William Faulkner: From Jefferson to the World*. Lexington: University of Kentucky Press, 1959, pp. 183–193, 232–237.

Watson, James G. *The Snopes Dilemma: Faulkner's Trilogy*. Coral Gables, Fla.: University of Miami Press, 1970.

THE REIVERS

Type of work: Novel
Author: William Faulkner (1897–1962)
Time of plot: May, 1905
Locale: Yoknapatawpha County, Mississippi; Memphis and Parsham, Tennessee
First published: 1962

Essay-Review

Subtitled "A Reminiscence," *The Reivers* begins on a note of action recalled in memory, and about a fourth of the way through the novel, posthumously awarded the 1963 Pulitzer Prize for fiction, we come upon one of William Faulkner's most engaging yarns.

In 1905 eleven-year-old Lucius Priest; Boon Hogganbeck, tough, faithful, but completely unpredictable and unreliable part-Chickasaw Indian mad about machinery; and freeloading Ned William McCaslin, the Priests' colored coachman and handyman, are on their way to Memphis in the Winton Flyer owned by young Lucius' grandfather and "borrowed" for the excursion without the owner's permission or knowledge. Because of the condition of the roads the truants are forced to make an overnight stop at Miss Ballenbaugh's, a small country store with a loft above it containing shuck mattresses for the convenience of fishermen and fox or coon hunters. The next morning, after one of the breakfasts for which Miss Ballenbaugh is famous, they start out early and soon reach Hell Creek bottom, the deepest, miriest mudhole in all Mississippi. There is no way around it: started in one direction, the travelers would end up in Alabama; head in the other, and they would fall into the Mississippi. Of course the automobile becomes mired and remains stuck in spite of their labors with shovel, barbed wire, block and tackle, and piled branches. Meanwhile on the gallery of a paintless cabin nearby, his two mules already harnessed in plow gear, a barefooted redneck watches and waits. This backwoods opportunist remarks that mud is one of the best crops in the region when the three give up in exasperation and he appears to pull the car out of the slough. Then follows some stiff bargaining. Boon claims that six dollars is too much for the job, all the more so because one of his passengers is a boy and the other is black. The man's only answer is that his mules are color-blind.

This is the tall-story idiom and spirit of Huck Finn brought forward in time, but its presence in *The Reivers* is not so much a matter of imitation as of a common source. For there is a sense in which Faulkner stands at the end of a literary tradition rather than, as many of his admirers claim, at the beginning of a new one. Through all of his writing runs a strain of broad folk humor and comic invention going back through Mark Twain to A. B. Longstreet's *Georgia Scenes* and George W. Harris' *Sut Lovingood's Yarns*, and beyond them to the Davy Crockett almanacs and the anonymous masters of the oral anecdote who flourished in the old Southwest. The early American was by nature a storyteller. The realities of frontier life and his own hard comic sense created a literature of tall men and tall deeds repeated in the trading post, the groggery, the rafters' camp, wherever men met on the edge of the wilderness. These stories, shaped by the common experience and imagination, had a geography, a mythology, and a lingo of their own. Some were streaked with ballad sentiment. Others guffawed with bawdy humor. But mostly these tales were comic elaborations of charater, of fantastic misadventures in which the frontiersman dramatized himself with shrewd appraisal and salty enjoyment. Through them goes a raggle-taggle procession of hunters, peddlers, horse traders, horse thieves, eagle orators, prophets, backwoods swains, land speculators, settlers—a picture of the country and the times.

Faulkner's Yoknapatawpha County lies, after all, in the same geographical belt with the Mississippi River and the Natchez Trace, and these are regions of history, folklore, and fantasy revealed in tall-story humor. This humor came into Faulkner's fiction as early as *Mosquitoes*, in the account of Old Hickory's descendant who tried raising sheep in the Louisiana swamps and eventually became so much at home in the water that he turned into a shark. It contributes to effects of grotesque outrage and exaggeration in *As I Lay Dying*, gives *Light in August* a warming pastoral glow, adds three episodes of pure comedy to *The Hamlet*, and provides illuminating comment on the rise and fall of Flem Snopes. Faulkner's habit in the past, however, was to subordinate his racier effects to the more serious concerns of man's mortality and the disorder of his moral universe. Not until he wrote *The Reivers* did he give free play to his talent for comedy of character and situation and, like Mark Twain in *Huckleberry Finn*, make it the master bias of structure and theme.

Other parallels with Twain's novel are not lacking. One is the unmistakable flavor of a style derived from the drawled tones of reminiscence. If we turn back to the nineteenth chapter of *Huckleberry Finn* we see how this style was being shaped to reveal habits of thought and feeling in art, a truly colloquial style, marvelously tuned in pulse and improvisation, with the incorrectness of folk speech in its idiom as Lucius Priest tells his story to his grandson. In *The Reivers* it is made to support both a burden of feeling within a boy's range of response and an old man's accumulation of a lifetime's reflections; and it can record sensory impressions with poetic finality.

Like *Huckleberry Finn*, too, *The Reivers* is a story of initiation, of innocence corrupted and evil exorcised. Both show the world through the eyes of childhood, an effective device when employed as a freshener of experience or a corrective of judgment, but between the two novels there is this important difference: Huck is protected by the earthy nonchalance of his own native shrewdness and resourcefulness from the contamination of the shore. Young Lucius Priest lives by the code of his class, the code of a gentleman, and he brings its values to the bordello and the racetrack. The true test is not innocence itself but what lies behind the mask of innocence. Grandfather Priest claims that when adults speak of childish innocence, they really mean ignorance. Actually, children are neither, in his opinion, for an eleven-year-old can envision any crime. If he possesses innocence, it is probably lack of appetite, just as his ignorance may be a lack of opportunity or ability.

So young Lucius Priest had only the gentleman's code to protect him when his grandfather, the president of a Jefferson bank and the owner of the second automobile ever seen in the county, goes to Louisiana to attend a funeral and Boon Hogganbeck tempts the boy with a proposal that they drive the Winton Flyer to Memphis during its owner's absence. Lucius proves vulnerable to Boon's proposal and after considerable conniving they set out. On the way they discover Ned William McCaslin hidden under a tarpaulin on the back seat. Having passed Hell Creek bottom, they arrive in Memphis, but instead of going to the Gayoso Hotel, as Lucius expected (the McCaslins and Priests always stayed at the Gayoso because a distant member of the family had in Civil War times galloped into the lobby in an effort to capture a Yankee general), Boon drives his passengers to Miss Reba's house on Catalpa Street. (This is the same Miss Reba, grown older, who figures in *Sanctuary*.) Boon has his reasons; Miss Corrie, one of Miss Reba's girls, shares with the Winton Flyer the affections of his crude but open and innocent heart. That night Ned, a master of indirection and a reckless gambling man, trades the stolen automobile for a stolen racehorse never known to run better than second. Before the three can return to Jefferson it is necessary for young Lucius to turn jockey and win a race against a better horse, Colonel Linscomb's Acheron. Meanwhile he has fought with Otis, the vicious nephew who slurred Miss Corrie, and his chivalric gesture restores her self-respect. Boon and Ned become involved in difficulties with the law as represented by Butch Lovemaiden, a corrupt deputy sheriff; it is discovered that Otis has stolen the gold tooth prized by Minnie, Miss Reba's maid; and Boon finds, and fights, rivals for Miss Corrie's charms. As the result of all this. Lucius, forced to assume a gentleman's responsibilities of courage and conduct, has lost the innocence of childhood before his grandfather appears to set matters straight. At times the boy is close to despair but he realizes that he has come too far, that to turn back now would not be homesickness but shame.

Lucius survives his ordeal, but at considerable cost to his conscience and peace of mind. Grandfather Priest has the final work on his escapade. When the boy asks how he can forget his folly and guilt, his grandfather tells him that he cannot because nothing in life is ever forgotten or lost. Lucius wants to know what he can do. His grandfather says that he must live with it. To the weeping boy's protests he replies that a gentleman can live through anything because he must always accept the responsibility of his actions and the weight of their consequences. Grandfather Priest ends by telling Lucius to go wash his face; a gentleman may cry, but he washes his face afterward.

From these examples it will be seen that under its surface of fantastic invention and tall-story humor *The Reivers* is another moral fable in the Faulknerian man-

214 *The Reivers* / FAULKNER

ner. Yet it is quite different in effect from the earlier, darker studies of manners and morals. In tragedy, and Faulkner was a great tragic artist, the soul of man stands naked before God, and He is not mocked. In comedy it is not the possible man that is to be revealed but the probable in conduct or belief. Thus, man in comedy is viewed in relation to some aspect of his society. In *The Reivers*—the title means plunderers or freebooters—a master of comedy was at work testing young Lucius Priest by the behavior of a gentleman in a world of evasion and deceit where it is easier to run from one's responsibilities than to stand up and face them.

In setting these matters straight, the triumph of the novel is in the manner of the telling. *The Reivers* is a story about a boy, but it is told by a man grown old enough and wise enough through the years of accumulated experience to look back on his adventure, relish it in all its qualities of adventure and fantasy, and at the same time pass judgment on it. This judgment is never harsh. Lucius Priest, telling the story to *his* grandson, is revealed as a person of tolerance and understanding of much that is so deeply and irrevocably ingrained in the eternal condition of man, and his point of view gives the novel added depth and dimension.

Put beside the novels of his great period, *The Reivers* is minor Faulkner. At the same time it is a good yarn in the tall-story tradition, skillfully told, comic in effect, shrewd in observation on manners, morals, politics, and the general cussedness and downright foolishness of mankind. More to the point, it broadens even if it does not deepen our knowledge of Faulkner's legendary Mississippi country.

Bibliography

Bradford, M.E. "What Grandfather Said: The Social Testimony of Faulkner's *The Reivers*," in *Occasional Review*. I (1974), pp. 5–15.

Brooks, Cleanth. *William Faulkner: The Yoknapatawpha County*. New Haven, Conn.: Yale University Press, 1963, pp. 349–368.

Gold, Joseph. *William Faulkner: A Study in Humanism from Metaphor to Discourse*. Norman: University of Oklahoma Press, 1966, pp. 174–187.

Kerr, Elizabeth M. "*The Reivers*: The Golden Book of Yoknapatawpha County," in *Modern Fiction Studies*. XIII (Spring, 1967), pp. 95–113.

Mellard, J.M. "Faulkner's 'Golden Book': *The Reivers* as Romantic Comedy," in *Bucknell Review*. XIII (December, 1965), pp. 19–31.

Millgate, Michael. *The Achievement of William Faulkner*. New York: Random House, 1965, pp. 253–258.

Moses, Edwin. "Faulkner's *The Reivers*: The Art of Acceptance," in *Mississippi Quarterly*. XXVII (1974), pp. 307–318.

Rossky, William. "*The Reivers*: Faulkner's *Tempest*," in *Mississippi Quarterly*. XVIII (Spring, 1965), pp. 82–93.

Swiggart, Peter. *The Art of Faulkner's Novels.* Austin: University of Texas Press, 1962, pp. 207–214.

Vickery, Olga. *The Novels of William Faulkner: A Critical Interpretation.* Baton Rouge: Louisiana State University Press, 1964, pp. 228–239.

Volpe, Edmond L. *A Reader's Guide to William Faulkner.* New York: Noonday, 1964, pp. 343–349.

Vorpahl, Ben M. "Moonlight at Ballenbaugh's: Time and Imagination in *The Reivers*," in *Southern Literary Journal.* I (1969), pp. 3–26.

SANCTUARY

Type of work: Novel
Author: William Faulkner (1897–1962)
Time of plot: 1929
Locale: Jefferson and Oxford, Mississippi; Memphis, Tennessee
First published: 1931

William Faulkner's Sanctuary—*a sensationalistic saga of rape, murder, bootlegging, and wayward justice which Faulkner claimed to have written to make money—horrified critics but titillated the reading public, who made the novel a bestseller; the novel is not merely a potboiler, however, but constitutes an important segment of Faulkner's Yoknapatawpha mythology.*

Principal Characters

Temple Drake, as her name suggests, is a woman on a pedestal, a Southern belle, a foolish virgin who believes she will always be protected by chivalry. Her resultant dependence makes her an ideal victim. A coltish redhead who has been bred for flirtation, a vestal virgin set up to be violated, she—out of boredom and other deprivations—learns to live for sexual encounters. Her revenge is aggression.

Horace Benbow, a lawyer who still believes in justice. He leaves his wife on the eve of the story, disillusioned with marriage and losing his illusions about women. He is disgusted with the state of things and the state of Mississippi. Literary and intellectual—Popeye calls him the "professor"—he becomes involved in the sordid affairs of a bootlegger and his common-law wife, a Memphis gangster and a fallen Mississippi belle.

Ruby Lamar, a "ruby in the dust," a former prostitute with a heart of gold. The common-law wife of Lee Goodwin, the bootlegger, she is willing to fight for her man but resigned to the *status quo* of life in the South. Excessively mothering, her mothering seems to be smothering her baby.

Popeye, the unnatural man. Frightened of owls and dense woods, paranoid, "skeered of his own shadow" in the words of Tommy, his appearance is compared to stamped tin and a modernistic lampstand. He is the black man (he always wears a tight black suit), a syphilitic incapable of performing the sex act, always armed, and a murderer. He rapes Temple by means of a corn cob and murders the lover he provided for her.

Lee Goodwin, a "real man." A bootlegger, he is apparently humane in that he cares for the mysterious "Pap" and is concerned about the fate of Ruby and his child. Watchful of Temple—but a relatively undeveloped character—he is innocent of the murder of Tommy, but many critics suggest that he is at least guilty in his mind of the rape of Temple.

Gowan Stevens, a Southern gentleman who learned "how to drink" at Virginia. Narcissa's rejected suitor, he is one of Temple's beaus. Like Narcissa, he cares for appearances—when they get too bad to be kept up, he evades them.

Narcissa Benbow Sartoris, Benbow's widowed sister. She is indolent, self-centered and self-serving, as her name indicates. A Southern Christian lady, she cares only for appearances. She works against her brother in his defense of Ruby and Goodwin in order to maintain her position in Jefferson, which is partly dependent on her brother's returning to his wife. In no need of love, as she has already had one child, she rejects Gowan Stevens' proposal.

Tommy, an innocent, humorous, half-witted "old boy" who assists Goodwin in his bootlegging operation. Surprisingly perceptive in his judgments of Popeye, he is Temple's protector. He is murdered by Popeye.

Reba Rivers, the madam of a Memphis whore house. She is sentimental in the extreme, still mourning over the death of her lover Mr. Binford. She finally recognizes the unnaturalness of Popeye and Temple's plight.

Senator Clarence Snopes, the stupid, back-slapping, corrupt, cheap, and money-grubbing local politician. He sells information to Benbow about Temple's whereabouts, then suggests an alternative whore house to Benbow, perhaps with future blackmail in mind. He is insulted when the Jewish lawyer from Memphis will not buy the same information.

Virgil Snopes and **Fonzo,** Senator Snopes's naïve nephew and his friend who, on arriving in Memphis to attend Barber School, mistake Miss Rivers' house for a boarding house.

Pap, a blind and deaf old man. His existence is perhaps only to intensify the Gothic effect of the novel. Benbow imagines that he was first the ward of the "Old Frenchman." He is more horrifying to Temple than any of the men who pose a real threat to her. He is never mentioned again after Goodwin is brought to town for trial.

The Story

Horace Benbow, having decided to leave his wife, was on his way to Jefferson one afternoon in May when he stopped to drink from a spring on the Old Frenchman place. There he encountered Popeye, an undersized man in a black suit. Popeye had a gun in his pocket and suspected the same of Benbow. After two hours of watching one another, Popeye was satisfied that Benbow was not a revenue officer and led him to the ruined plantation house.

That night Benbow had dinner with Popeye, Lee Goodwin, and several other moonshiners, including Tommy and a blind and deaf old man known only as "Pap." They were fed by Ruby, Goodwin's common-law wife. Under the influence of moonshine whiskey, Benbow revealed that he had left his wife. After dinner he talked with Ruby and promised to send her an orange stick from town. Benbow was then given a lift to town on a truck loaded with whiskey on its way to Memphis.

The next afternoon, at the home of Narcissa, his widowed sister, Benbow watched her walking in the garden with Gowan Stevens. Stevens left after dinner to keep his date with Temple Drake, a co-ed at the State University.

After the dance, Stevens got drunk and passed out, awakening the next morning in the Oxford railroad station where he saw Temple's name on the men's bathroom wall. Having promised to pick Temple up at the train station, Stevens raced to the next town to catch up with the special train taking students to a baseball game. Temple got off the train but was disgusted at Stevens' disheveled state. Stevens persuaded her that he was all right, and she got into his car only after he assured her that he would drive her back to the university. On the way there, Stevens stopped several times to get more whiskey, finally deciding to stop at the Old Frenchman place. He was unaware that Popeye had felled a tree across the road, and he wrecked his car. Popeye and Tommy were watching and led Temple and Stevens to the house. Temple was immediately frightened by the atmosphere of the place and especially frightened by the sight of Pap. Stevens was drinking again and refused to help Temple. When she asked Popeye for a ride into town, he also refused her. Ruby warned her to leave as soon as possible, suggesting that she walk, but Temple was too frightened and unaccustomed to action.

When Temple went into the dining room to eat, one of the bootleggers, Van, tried to grab her, and she fled from the house. Tommy brought her a plate of food, but when she heard the other men coming she ran away again. The men—Van, Goodwin, and Stevens—began fighting over Temple. Stevens was finally knocked unconscious and carried into the bedroom where Temple was waiting. In the bedroom Van and Popeye both molested Temple until Goodwin stopped them.

Then began a series of comings and goings in the bedroom. Ruby came to stand quietly in the darkness. Later Goodwin entered to claim a raincoat in which Temple had wrapped herself. Popeye came in, followed silently by Tommy, who squatted in the dark beside Ruby. When the men finally left the house to load the truck for its run to Memphis, Ruby took Temple out to the corncrib in the barn and stayed with her until daylight.

Stevens awoke early the next morning and felt too ashamed to face Temple. He started out for the nearest house to hire a car to pick her up; he would hitch a ride into town. Learning that Stevens had already gone, Temple talked to Ruby. Outside she saw a man watching her from behind the barn. She ran to the house but saw Goodwin coming toward her. She ran to the barn again, falling through a loose board in the loft into the corncrib. Tommy came into the barn, and Temple asked him to guard the door to the corncrib.

Ruby decided to take her baby and to leave the house. She walked to the spring, where she met Popeye, who said he was going to Memphis. Popeye went back to the house, where he saw Goodwin watching the barn. Popeye crept into the barn and saw Tommy guarding the door of the corncrib. Popeye climbed into the loft and down into the corncrib and asked Tommy to open the door; he then shot Tommy and raped Temple. Ruby, on her way back to the house, saw Popeye and Temple drive away. At the house, Goodwin told her that there had been a shooting and to go for the sheriff.

In Jefferson, Benbow stayed with his sister for two days and then moved into the old family house. When Goodwin was brought in for the murder of Tommy, Benbow agreed to defend the prisoner. Goodwin, afraid of Popeye, claimed only that he had not shot Tommy. Later Ruby told Benbow about Temple leaving with Popeye.

Benbow visited the State University at Oxford in an attempt to trace Temple's whereabouts. Senator Snopes, whom he met on the return train, told him that Judge Drake's daughter was supposed to be visiting an aunt in Michigan after an attempted runaway marriage.

In Memphis Temple lived at Miss Rivers' whore house where Popeye brought a speakeasy bouncer named Red to visit her. Virgil Snopes and his friend Fonzo, who were attending Barber School in Memphis, had mistaken Miss Rivers' establishment for a boarding house and were living there. Senator Snopes found them there and saw Temple. Snopes contacted Benbow in order to sell him this information. Benbow visited Temple at Miss Rivers' bawdy house. She confirmed his suspicions about the circumstances surrounding the murder of Tommy.

One morning following Benbow's visit, Temple bribed Reba Rivers' servant, Minnie, to let her out of the house to make a phone call. That evening she managed to sneak out again, just as a car with Popeye in it pulled up at the curb. When she refused to go back to her room, he took her to the Grotto, where she had arranged to meet Red. Temple got drunk, and two of Popeye's henchmen drove her home; as they pulled away from the nightclub, Temple saw Popeye sitting in a parked car, waiting for Red. Red's funeral was held in the Grotto. Miss Reba and her friends attended. For the occasion the tables had been draped in black and a band had been hired to play hymns. Drinks were on the house.

The night before the trial Benbow phoned Reba Rivers and learned that Popeye and Temple had left. On June 20, the trial opened and Ruby testified in her husband's defense. That night Ruby and Benbow spent the night in the jail cell with Goodwin, who was still afraid that Popeye might shoot him. The next day Temple appeared at the trial and testified that Goodwin had raped her and murdered Tommy. The District Attorney placed the corn cob (with which Popeye had raped Temple) in evidence. That night Goodwin was dragged from the jail and burned by the angry mob.

Benbow returned to his wife in Kinston. Popeye, on his way to Pensacola to visit his mother, was arrested for committing a murder which occurred at the same time he had actually murdered Red. He was convicted and executed for this murder which he did not commit. Judge Drake took Temple to Paris.

Critical Evaluation

When *Sanctuary* was first published, Faulkner's usual admirers condemned the novel as sensationalistic and unnecessarily vicious, but the reading public of the 1930's enjoyed the hard-boiled fiction which was then in vogue and made

Faulkner a best-selling author for the first time in his career. The novel has much in common with the works of James M. Cain, Dashiell Hammett, Raymond Chandler, and others: it tells a story of degradation and corruption and presents as hero a disillusioned man who still clings to certain knightly values, who still attempts to rescue fair maidens in distress only to discover that they are neither truly fair nor in actual need of rescue. The novel fulfilled the fantasies of the depression-era audience and was subsequently rewritten by Faulkner as a screenplay, *The Story of Temple Drake*, which was filmed with Joan Crawford in the title role.

Although the rich and complex symbolism which one associates with Faulkner's work is also found, to a lesser degree, in the hard-boiled novels of the 1930's, *Sanctuary* does not adhere to the formulaic style of hard-boiled fiction. The plot of *Sanctuary* is not episodic and is never fully unravelled; the complex plot structure is itself the vehicle of suspense. For example, the reader does not learn that Popeye has raped Temple by means of a corn cob until Chapter 28 (the fourth from the last) when the District Attorney presents this information as evidence at Goodwin's trial. A summation of all the events involved in the crime is never presented; the reader must do this work for himself. The plot presents many difficulties: it is not presented chronologically, rather each chapter consists of a discrete unit in time. Some chapters are flashbacks (for example, Chapter 18 continues Temple's story from Chapter 13); others seem to leap ahead in time (the events in Chapter 24 occur at least a week after Benbow visits Temple at Miss Reba's, which is described in Chapter 23). As well, there are some inconsistencies and omissions in the plot: in Chapter 10 Gowan Stevens engages Mr. Tull to fetch Temple from the Old Frenchman place, but this mission is apparently never fulfilled; Pap, the blind and deaf old man whose presence among the bootleggers is never explained, is not mentioned again after Goodwin is brought into Jefferson; Benbow leaves his pipe at home when he takes the train to Oxford (Chapter 19), but when he makes the return journey he is in possession of his pipe.

The presence of Pap in the novel may be justified as a device to heighten the Gothic atmosphere of the events which occur at the Old Frenchman place. Having to spend the night in a ruined antebellum mansion, Temple reacts with unreasoning terror at the vision of the old man—who is ironically incapable of harming her—while she is somewhat less frightened of those who pose a real threat to her; she taunts Popeye when he rejects her request for a ride into town: "What river did you fall in with that suit on? Do you have to shave it off at night?" Pap seems to function merely as a frightening detail, like the rats in the corncrib. André Malraux, one of the first critics to reconsider *Sanctuary* as a serious work, believed the novel to be in the Gothic tradition of Poe.

Sancutary is now generally considered to be an important work, forming part of Faulkner's Yoknapatawpha County mythology and containing many of the themes which are central to Faulkner's work as a whole. Faulkner continues the story of two of the major characters, Temple Drake and Gowan Stevens, in *Requim for a Nun* (1951). Some critics view *Sanctuary* as Faulkner's most pointed statement of the wasteland theme, suggesting that Temple is symbolic of the old South, raped by Modern Industry in the form of Popeye.

Generally, *Sanctuary* has been viewed as Horace Benbow's story (failed idealism) or as the depiction of the conflict between Popeye and Benbow (modern cynicism, opportunism, and corruption *vs.* idealism and justice), but these views of the novel do not account for its complexity. In these analyses, it is always pointed out that Popeye is ill at ease with nature: he is both ignorant of and frightened by nature as it manifests itself at the Old Frenchman place; he is described as "all angles, like a modernistic lampstand." However, Benbow also feels at odds with nature: "Nature is 'she' and Progress is 'he,' " according to Benbow, and both nature and women horrify him, seem to him hypocritical—the spring lasts too long, making one think it had some purpose (Chapter 24) and he finds a rag with rouge on it tucked behind the mantle (Chapter 2)—and obscene—he sees his step-daughter, Little Belle, as in "seething sympathy with the blossoming grape" and as "older in sin than he would ever be" (Chapter 19).

Because of the portrayal of women in the novel and because of the subject of rape, *Sanctuary* is of particular interest to the contemporary reader. *Sanctuary* is not the story of failed idealism—Benbow is already disillusioned at the outset; it depicts instead how certain kinds of idealism—in particular, the ideal of chaste Southern womanhood—necessarily lead to corruption. In revising the original galley proofs of *Sanctuary*, Faulkner systematically played down those portions of the novel which focus on the character of Benbow and enhanced the story of Temple Drake so that it emerges as central to the novel.

Temple Drake has been viewed in various ways. Leslie Fiedler sees her as the Fair Lady of the American Romance tradition—the descendant of the fictional Charlotte Temple or Maggie Verver—who has toppled from her pedestal and who, because of her betrayal of the traditional passive feminine role, evokes Faulkner's revulsion. David Williams sees her as the embodiment of Draconian justice, bringing judgment in its more violent form to bear on the men who have betrayed her (and all women) and who have perverted true justice. Temple is, as well, a Southern belle trying to function in a modern world while believing in the protection of an outdated chivalry.

The most that is known of her background is that her father is a judge and her youngest brother has promised to beat her if she is ever "caught . . . with a drunk man." At the Old Frenchman place, in her terror, she prays to her father the judge, rather than to her Heavenly Father, for protection. Temple discovers, too late, that she cannot rely on chivalry: Gowan, the Southern gentleman, gets too drunk to defend her and no one will drive her to town. Her dependence prevents her from running away, although Ruby suggests this to her; when she awaits her would-be attackers in the dark bedroom she imagines herself turning into a boy, being locked into a chastity belt, being dead, and finally being a formidable elderly schoolteacher, thinking that in any of these forms she would be immune from rape.

Ruby Lamar, who has never been protected by men, views the world more realistically than Temple, but she is equally dependent on men. The antagonism between the two women is also due to Ruby's sympathy and fear for Temple—she doesn't want her to become the victim of a "real man." Ironically, Ruby becomes a prostitute due to the role her father and brother have played in her life; they kill her first lover and force her to leave home. On hearing Ruby's story, Temple responds that she, too, has been called a whore. Ruby criticizes "good women" like Temple who she sees as "cheap sports," "giving nothing," and incapable of love; but she stands guard over Temple in the house and spends the night with her in the corncrib.

Another "good woman" is Horace Benbow's widowed sister, Narcissa Sartoris. Narcissa is the fulfilled Southern belle—she has had one child, does not wish to remarry, but enjoys suitors as the tribute she is due, and spends her life maintaining appearances, even to the point of betraying her brother. Her excuse for her callous behavior with regard to Ruby is her own womanhood: "I live here, in this town. I'll have to stay here. But you're a man. It doesn't matter to you. You can go away."

In Benbow's mind Temple is related to his stepdaughter, Little Belle. They are of the same age and have similar backgrounds. Little Belle might also be the victim of rape; but more horrible to Benbow is the suspicion of Little Belle's sexuality. After interviewing Temple and hearing her recount the events of the night she spent at the Old Frenchman place "with actual pride, a sort of naïve and impersonal vanity," Benbow looks at Little Belle's photograph and, confusing the two women, becomes nauseated. Benbow sees Little Belle as "older in sin than he would ever be," but Temple's schoolmate's story gives a feminist version of the fall of man: "boys thought all girls were ugly except when they were dressed. She said the Snake had been seeing Eve for several days and never noticed her until Adam made her put on the fig leaf." Man, who invented Progress (again, according to Benbow), feels threatened by nature and by women; sex in the masculine modern world of *Sanctuary* is sterile and intellectual, involving surrogates and prostitution.

Benbow distrusts feminity; Goodwin has killed a man over a "nigger woman," has never married Ruby; Tommy, Van, Stevens, and Goodwin all long to violate Temple; Popeye accomplishes her rape by means of a corn cob; and a traveling salesman, on the night Goodwin is burned by the outraged townspeople, remarks "Jeez, I wouldn't have used no cob." Popeye himself might be viewed as one result of the betrayal of woman—his father bequeathed him syphilis and deserted his mother.

All of the men in *Sanctuary* are guilty and receive a kind of delayed justice. In the novel, woman has her revenge: Benbow loses his case, Goodwin is executed by the mob, and Popeye—on the way to visit his mother—is arrested for a murder he did not commit and sentenced to death. Woman does not triumph, however; she has been perverted for too long by the masculine world. In the final paragraph of *Sanctuary*, Temple is seen sitting with her father in the Luxembourg Gardens. She is "sullen and discontented and sad" as she gazes at the statues of "dead and tranquil queens in stained marble"—images of women artificially maintained on the pedestals men have erected for them.

Bibliography

Brooks, Cleanth. "Faulkner's *Sanctuary*: The Discovery of Evil," in *Sewanee Review.* LXXI (1963), pp. 1–24.

———. *William Faulkner: The Yoknapatawpha County.* New Haven, Conn.: Yale University Press, 1963, pp. 116–138.

Brown, James. "Shaping the World of *Sanctuary*," in *University of Kansas City Review.* XXV (Winter, 1958), pp. 137–142.

Cole, Douglas. "Faulkner's *Sanctuary*: Retreat from Responsibility," in *Western Humanities Review.* XIV (Summer, 1960), pp. 291–298.

Creighton, Joanne V. "Self-Destructive Evil in *Sanctuary*," in *Twentieth Century Literature.* XVIII (1972), pp. 259–270.

Cypher, James R. "The Tangled Sexuality of Temple Drake," in *American Imago.* XIX (Fall, 1962), pp. 243–252.

Flynn, Robert. "The Dialectic of *Sanctuary*," in *Modern Fiction Studies.* II (Autumn, 1956), pp. 109–113.

Frazier, David L. "Gothicism in *Sanctuary*: The Black Pall and the Crap Table," in *Modern Fiction Studies.* II (Autumn, 1956), pp. 114–124.

Gold, Joseph. "No Refuge: Faulkner's *Sanctuary*," in *University Review.* XXXIII (Winter, 1966), pp. 129–135.

Graham, Philip. "Patterns in *Sanctuary* and *Requiem for a Nun*," in *Tennessee Studies in Literature.* VIII (1963), pp. 39–46.

Guerard, Albert J. "The Misogynous Vision as High Art," in *Southern Review.* XII (1976), pp. 215–231.

Hamblen, Abigail Ann. "Faulkner's Pillar of Endurance: *Sanctuary* and *Requiem for a Nun*," in *Midwest Quarterly.* VI (July, 1965), pp. 369–375.

Howe, Irving. *William Faulkner: A Critical Study.* New York: Vintage, 1962, pp. 57–61, 192–199.

Howell, Elmo. "The Quality of Evil in Faulkner's *Sanctuary*," in *Tennessee Studies in Literature.* IV (1959), pp. 99–107.

Kubie, Lawrence S. "William Faulkner's *Sanctuary*: An Analysis," in *Faulkner: A Collection of Critical Essays.* Edited by Robert Penn Warren. Englewood Cliffs, N.J.: Prentice-Hall, 1966, pp. 137–146.

Lisca, Peter. "Some New Light on Faulkner's *Sanctuary*," in *Faulkner Studies*. II (Spring, 1953), pp. 5–9.

Millgate, Michael. *The Achievement of William Faulkner*. New York: Random House, 1965, pp. 113–123.

Monteiro, George. "Initiation and the Moral Sense in Faulkner's *Sanctuary*," in *Modern Language Notes*. LXXIII (November, 1958), pp. 500–504.

O'Connor, William Van. *The Tangled Fire of William Faulkner*. Minneapolis: University of Minnesota Press, 1954, pp. 55–64.

Rossky, William. "The Pattern of Nightmare in *Sanctuary*: or Miss Reba's Dogs," in *Modern Fiction Studies*. XV (1969), pp. 503–515.

Schmuhl, Robert. "Faulkner's *Sanctuary*: The Last Laugh of Innocence," in *Notes on Mississippi Writers*. VI (1974), pp. 73–80.

Tate, Allen. "Faulkner's *Sanctuary* and the Southern Myth," in *Virginia Quarterly Review*. XLIV (1968), pp. 418–427.

Thompson, Lawrance. *William Faulkner: An Introduction and Interpretation*. Holt, Rinehart and Winston, 1967, pp. 99–116.

Vickery, Olga. *The Novels of William Faulkner: A Critical Interpretation*. Baton Rouge: Louisiana State University Press, 1964, pp. 103–114.

Volpe, Edmond L. *A Reader's Guide to William Faulkner*. New York: Noonday, 1964, pp. 140–151, 383–387.

Waggoner, Hyatt H. *William Faulkner: From Jefferson to the World*. Lexington: University of Kentucky Press, 1959, pp. 88–100, 118–120.

SARTORIS

Type of work: Novel
Author: William Faulkner (1897–1962)
Time of plot: 1919–1920
Locale: Jefferson, Yoknapatawpha County, Mississippi
First published: 1929

Essay-Review

Sartoris is the third of Faulkner's novels but the first in which he established the family of Sartoris and the fictional Mississippian town of Jefferson, seat of Yoknapatawpha County, which remained his locale in most of the novels he wrote afterwards. The principal character in the novel is Bayard Sartoris, a young man of twenty-six who has just returned from service with the British Royal Air Force in World War I. In a series of actions which reveal a compulsive, self-destructive lust for violence, the young veteran turns his homecoming into tragedy. He begins by purchasing a high-powered new car which he drives at a fanatical speed about the countryside, terrifying pedestrians and wagon drivers; he gashes his head in an attempt to ride bareback on an untrained stallion; he overturns the car into a creek and fractures his ribs in the process. After his bones are mended, he resumes his reckless driving habits, and on one wild ride he plunges over a cliff, causing the death of his grandfather. He flees abruptly from home and finally meets his own end as a test pilot, when he dies in the crash of a crackpot's experimental airplane.

This skeleton of the action in the novel can barely suggest the range and depth of its implications. Much of its power derives from an elaborate counterpoint between past and present. Bayard Sartoris' hunger for violence and recklessness is part of his ancestral inheritance, a kind of inborn fever that courses through his blood. At the beginning of the novel, we learn that Bayard's wife has died in childbirth and that the war had recently taken his twin brother John, who was shot down in a plane while fighting the Germans. But John's death, consequence of an action which Bayard himself thought foolhardy, is only a symptom of the desperate carelessness with which the Sartoris men have always lived. Young Bayard returns to a house that is still haunted by the ghosts of his great-grandfather, Colonel John Sartoris, and of his great-great uncle, who was also named Bayard Sartoris. The memory of Bayard is kept alive by young Bayard's great-great aunt Jenny, sister of the dead Colonel John, who never tires of telling with romantic (and unconsciously ironic) reverence the story of how her brother Bayard "gallantly" gave his life at the age of twenty-three during the Civil War; he was killed when he acted on a chance word from General Jeb Stuart and attempted to steal anchovies from a Federal encampment. On the other hand, the ghost of the dead Colonel John perserveres in the tireless recollections of Will

Falls, an impoverished nonagenarian who subsists on regular handouts from young Bayard's grandfather, old Bayard, who is president of the local bank. In return for the banker's generosity, Falls sometimes provides a backwoods brand of medical care (he successfully removes a wen from old Bayard's face with an Indian salve considered wholly unacceptable by three doctors), but more often he brings stories of Colonel John, old Bayard's father and Fall's contemporary. Falls recounts Colonel John's exploits in the Civil War, and he also tells us how the colonel calmly shot two Yankee carpetbaggers who had tried to gain voting rights for Negroes. It is Falls, too, who adverts to Colonel John's death at the hands of a man named Redlaw. One evening, without apparent provocation, Redlaw shot the colonel in cold blood in the public square of Jefferson.

But the Sartoris clan is distinguished, putatively, at least, for more than recklessness and violence. Through the history of its generations, transmuted into the shining gold of legend by the alchemy of Falls's admiration and Aunt Jenny's romantic imagination, we find a powerful strain of heroism, grandeur, nobility, and aristocratic elegance. This is the magnificent myth; and in spite of the fact that the Sartoris men so often live violently and die absurdly, the myth survives. Young Bayard must somehow sustain the would-be tradition in a time of peace, and his extravagant exhibitionism with the wild stallion and the high-powered car is only his peculiar way of expressing an inherited compulsion. Indeed, even though Aunt Jenny and old Bayard repeatedly warn him against the dangers of speeding, his wildness with the car becomes a kind of heroism in the eyes of Narcissa Benbow. She is a frail, quiet, frigidly self-conscious young woman (her name is a clue to her character) who still adores the memory of young John, but who gradually transfers her love to young Bayard. During his bedridden convalescence after he fractures his ribs in the automobile crash, she visits him faithfully, reads to him, and gently penetrates the hard surface of his bitter obsession with violence and with the only person he has ever loved, his dead brother John. Gradually and delicately, she wins enough of Bayard's attention to become his second wife.

Seemingly, his marriage to Narcissa invests young Bayard's life with a kind of gentleness, dignity, and purpose. For a time at least, she is distinctly a stabilizing influence; she exacts from him a promise that he will curb his reckless driving. But Narcissa brings to Bayard her own pale shadow of sordidness, one that constantly threatens the tranquil elegance of the Sartoris home. Before her marriage, she had been receiving unsigned, semi-literate, indecent love letters which she had kept. The letters came from a man called Byron Snopes (again the Christian name is significant, this time ironically so), whose surname in the later novels of Faulkner comes to epitomize the crass rootlessness of a family that is the antithesis of the Sartoris clan. In addition, the end of the war has brought home Narcissa's beloved brother Horace, who lives ostensibly in a world of poetry, fine-spun rhetoric, and exquisite glass-blowing (he produces lovely vases from time to time), but who actually is conducting a rather sterile love affair with Belle

Mitchell, the wife of his friend and neighbor, Harry Mitchell. Neither Horace Benbow's passion for Belle nor Byron's desperate yearning for Narcissa is satisfactorily resolved in this novel, nor does either man emerge here as a fully developed character. (Faulkner takes them both much further in his later work.) But we see enough of these men to understand the forces which mysteriously menace the apparent serenity of Narcissa's marriage to Bayard.

In spite of its occasional violence, *Sartoris* is not so terrifying or tragic in impact as several of Faulkner's greater novels, *The Sound and the Fury*, for example, or *Light in August*. His portrayal of the Negro characters who decorate the canvas of his tale in such rich abundance is witty, deft, and buoyant. Early in the novel we meet Simon Strother, the garrulous and superannuated family retainer, when he comes in a horse-drawn carriage to pick up old Bayard at the bank. Simon is filled with a sense of his own importance as the driver for the most aristocratic family in town, and he manages to give a kind of theatrical majesty to so prosaic an action as the departure of the carriage with the master inside. We learn, however, that Simon is just as venal and parasitical as many another Negro in the town, for we discover later that he has misappropriated the money entrusted to him by elders of the local Negro church. Claiming that he has lost the money in a bad investment, he succeeds in persuading old Bayard to pay off the church elders; but he has actually used their money to keep a young mistress. One day his body is found in her cabin, his head battered by an unknown assailant. He is a lesser victim of the violence that pervades the novel.

But for all his inconsequence, what happens to Simon is a good example of what happens to the entire world of Sartoris, to the legend of heroism and majesty. With her brusque and candid insight, Aunt Jenny, herself the repository of the legend, knows only too well the disparity between the romantic ideals inherited from the past and the futile destructiveness of the present. Narcissa marries young Bayard in an atmosphere bright with peace and promise, and shortly afterward she conceives his child. But marriage is not enough for Bayard; he reverts to his savagery behind the wheel of his newly repaired automobile, kills his grandfather when the car tumbles over a cliff, and promptly abandons his new wife. He seeks escape for a time in the company of the MacCallums, a country family with whom he and Johnny used to go hunting. But there is only pain in their talk of his grandfather or of old hunting days with Johnny, and soon he must be on his lonely way. Later Narcissa learns of his death in the airplane crash. The fatal accident seems to finish the Sartoris line.

But the death of young Bayard is robbed of its finality by the almost simultaneous birth of his child, an event which lends a typical Faulknerian ambiguity to the conclusion of the novel. The Sartoris family has not yet succeeded in destroying itself wholly; in the birth of the child, a boy, there is hope for future generations of the line. Yet before he is born the young boy's future is overshadowed by a fate that comes out of the past. Narcissa wants to christen him Benbow, but Aunt Jenny calls him Johnny while he is still in the womb, a name recalling the impulsive recklessness of the two John Sartorises who came before him. The final scene is ostensibly a peaceful one, with Narcissa softly and gently playing the piano for Aunt Jenny on a calm, windless night. But the ghosts of past generations still linger in the house, and through its rooms and hallways we continue to hear the dark whisperings of disaster and fatality that have always intermingled themselves with the legendary glamor of the Sartoris name.

Indeed, in *Sartoris*, as in the great novels that follow it, no member of the mythic family dies an absolute death. His ghost remains, his spirit fills the bones and bloodstream of each of his descendants. The novel in which Faulkner introduces this family is far from perfect; it is flawed with broken pieces and unassimilated parts, like the characters of Horace Benbow and Byron Snopes, or the visit of young Bayard to the MacCallums. But in *Sartoris* Faulkner established the materials of his fictional world, and out of these materials, molded, shaped, and transformed into the shapes of his great novels, he created the work on which his reputation stands.

Bibliography

Brooks, Cleanth. *William Faulkner: The Yoknapatawpha County.* New Haven, Conn.: Yale University Press, 1963, pp. 100–115.

Hoffman, Frederick J. *William Faulkner.* New York: Twayne, 1961, pp. 44–48.

Howe, Irving. *William Faulkner: A Critical Study.* New York: Vintage, 1962, pp. 33–41.

Howell, Elmo. "Faulkner's *Sartoris* and the Mississippi Country People," in *Southern Folklore Quarterly.* XXV (June, 1961), pp. 136–146.

Millgate, Michael. *The Achievement of William Faulkner.* New York: Random House, 1965, pp. 76–85.

Page, Ralph. "John Sartoris: Friend or Foe," in *Arizona Quarterly.* XXIII (Spring, 1967), pp. 27–33.

Scholes, Robert E. "Myth and Manners in *Sartoris,*" in *Georgia Review.* XVI (Summer, 1962), pp. 195–201.

Stevens, Lauren G. "*Sartoris*: Germ of the Apocalypse," in *Dalhousie Review.* XLIX (1969), pp. 80–87.

Vickery, Olga. *The Novels of William Faulkner: A Critical Interpretation.* Baton Rouge: Louisiana State University Press, 1964, pp. 15–27.

Volpe, Edmond L. *A Reader's Guide to William Faulkner.* New York: Noonday, 1964, pp. 66–76.

Waggoner, Hyatt H. *William Faulkner: From Jefferson to the World.* Lexington: University of Kentucky Press, 1959, pp. 20–33.

Walker, Ronald G. "Death in the Sound of Their Name: Character Motivation in Faulkner's *Sartoris*," in *Southern Humanities Review*. VII (1973), pp. 271–278

THE SOUND AND THE FURY

Type of work: Novel
Author: William Faulkner (1897–1962)
Time of plot: 1910–1928
Locale: Mississippi
First published: 1929

A stunning example of Faulkner's skill, The Sound and the Fury *is an involved and difficult but a compelling study of the dissolution of an old Southern family. It is a novel not primarily of cause and effect but rather of character and attitudes, and while a chronological sequence of events can be deduced, the "time" of the novel is that complex and subtle time of memory which overshadows and shapes events and meaning, and which meshes past and present, reality and illusion, the conscious and the subconcious.*

Principal Characters

Jason Lycurgus Compson (III), grandson of a Mississippi governor, son of a Confederate general, and father to the last of the Compsons. Like his illustrious ancestors, his name suggested his passion, the classics. Unlike his forbears, he is unable to make a living or to fulfill his deepest ambition, the study of the Greek and Latin epigrammatists, but his stoic philosophy, culled from his reading, stands him in good stead. He speaks wisely, does little, drinks much, and is weary of his complaining wife, his wayward daughter, and his bickering sons.

Caroline Bascomb Compson, his wife, who resents the Compson lineage and feels that hers is more glorious. A neurotic woman with psychosomatic symptons, she complains constantly of her grievances and ills. Reluctant to face reality and rejoicing that she was not born a Compson, she indulges her fancies and pretends to be an antebellum Southern gentlewoman. Her fortitude in tragedy is even more remarkable for all her complaining, but she victimizes her children and devoted servants to maintain her resentment and illnesses.

Candace Compson, their only daughter, affectionate, loyal, libido-driven. Called **Caddy,** a name which results in great confusion for her idiot brother whose playground is the pasture sold to a golf course where he hears her name. She herself is doomed, though devoted to her dead brother, her weak-minded brother, her own illegitimate daughter, her living father. She is at odds with her mother, her vengeful brother Jason, and several husbands. So promiscuous is she, even urging her sensitive brother Quentin to abortive intercourse, that she does not really know the father of her child. As an adventuress she travels widely, and in the postlude to the novel appears as the consort of a Nazi officer in Paris.

Quentin Compson, her beloved brother for whom she names her child even before the baby's birth. Obsessed by a sense of guilt, doom, and death, he commits suicide by drowning in June, 1910, two months after his sister's marriage to a man he calls a blackguard. Because he is deeply disturbed by family affairs—the selling of a pasture to pay for his year at Harvard, the loss of his sister's honor, the morbid despair he feels for his idiot brother, his hatred of the family vices of pride and snobbishness—his death is predictable, unalterable.

Jason Compson (IV), the only son to stay on in the Old Compson place, loyal to his weak querulous mother, determined to gain his full share of his patronage, bitter over his deep failures. His tale is one of petty annoyances, nursed grievances, and egotistic aggressiveness in his ungenerous and self-assertive mastery of his niece and the colored servants. This descendant of aristocrats is more the type of small-town redneck, wily, canny, cunning, and deceitful. Not without his reasons for bitterness, he finally rids himself of his enervating responsibilities for a dying line by himself remaining a bachelor and having his idiot brother castrated.

Quentin, the daughter of Candace and her mother's own child. Reared by Dilsey, the colored cook, Quentin is the last of anything resembling life in the old Compson house. As self-assertive as her uncle, she steals money he calls his but which is rightfully hers, and elopes with a carnival pitchman. Beautiful in the wild way of her mother, she has never had affection from anyone except her morbid old grandmother and a broken-hearted servant.

Dilsey Gibson, the bullying but beloved black family retainer, cook, financier (in petty extravagances), and benefactress who maintains family standards that no longer concern the Compsons. Deeply con-

cerned for them, she babies the thirty-year-old Benjamin, the unfortunate Quentin, the querulous old "Miss Cahline," though she resists the egocentric Jason. A woman whose wise understanding nature is beyond limits of race or color, she endures for others and prolongs the lives of those dependent on her shrewdness and strength.

Benjamin Compson, called **Benjy,** at first named Maury after his mother's brother. He is an idiot who observes everything, smells tragedy, loves the old pasture, his sister Caddy, firelight, but cannot compose his disordered thoughts into any coherent pattern of life or speech. Gelded by his brother Jason, he moans out his pitiful existence and is finally sent to the state asylum in Jackson.

Maury L. Bascomb, Mrs. Compson's brother. A bachelor, a drunkard, and a philanderer, he is supported by the Compsons. Benjy Compson was christened Maury, after his uncle.

Roskus, the Compsons' black coachman when the children were small.

T.P., a black servant who helps to look after Benjy Compson. He later goes to Memphis to live.

Luster, a fourteen-year-old black boy who is thirty-three-old Benjy Compson's caretaker and playmate.

Frony, Dilsey's daughter.

Sydney Herbert Head, a young banker, Caddy Compson's first husband. He divorces her after he realizes that her daughter Quentin is not his child. The divorce ends young Jason Compson's hope of getting a position in Head's bank.

Shreve McCannon, Quentin Compson's Canadian roommate at Harvard.

Essay-Review

After early undistinguished efforts in verse (*The Marble Faun*, 1924) and fiction (*Soldier's Pay*, 1926; *Mosquitoes*, 1927), William Faulkner moved suddenly into the forefront of American literature in 1929 with the appearance of *Sartoris* and *The Sound and the Fury*, the first installments in the artistically complex and subtly satirical saga of Yoknapatawpha County that would be spun out further in *As I Lay Dying* (1930), *Light in August* (1932), *Absalom, Absalom!* (1936), *Go Down, Moses* (1942), *The Unvanquished* (1938), *Intruder in the Dust* (1948), The *Hamlet-Town-Mansion* trilogy (1940, 1957, 1959), and *Requiem for a Nun* (1951)—the last an extension of materials in *Sanctuary* (1931). Chiefly in recognition of the monumental literary importance of the Yoknapatawpha Saga, Faulkner was awarded the Nobel Prize in 1949.

The Sound and the Fury marked the beginning of the most fertile period of Faulkner's creativity, when he was in his early thirties. Yet both for its form and for its thematic significance this novel may well be considered Faulkner's masterpiece. Never again would his work demonstrate such tight, precise structure, combined with the complexities of syntax and punctuation that became his most characteristic stylistic trait. Furthermore, the themes recorded in his simple but elegant Nobel Prize speech—"love and honor and pity and pride and compassion and sacrifice"—are already present in this novel with a forcefulness of characterization that could hardly be improved upon. It was in this novel that Faulkner found a way of embodying his peculiar view of time in an appropriate style, a style much influenced by Joycean stream-of-consciousness, and by Faulkner's own stated desire ultimately to "put all of human experience between one Cap and one period." That concept of time, most emphatic in Quentin's section, can be summarized by Faulkner's statement that "there is no such thing as *was*; if *was* existed there would be no grief or sorrow." The continuation of the past into the present, as a shaping influence that cannot be avoided, is the larger theme of Faulkner's life work.

In this novel, that theme is embodied specifically in the history of the decline of the once-aristocratic Compson family. Nearly twenty years after the original publication of the novel, at the instigation of his publisher Malcolm Cowley, Faulkner wrote the background history of the Compsons as an "Appendix" that appears at the front of the book, beginning with Quentin McLachan Compson, the son of a Glasgow printer, who fled Scotland to the Carolinas in America. It was his grandson Jason Lycurgus who came to Mississippi in 1811 and in exchange for a fast running horse got a square mile of forest land from a Chicksaw chief, Ikemotubbe. At first a clerk in the Indian Agency which was actually a well stocked store, Jason became a partner within twelve years; and in twenty years' time, he was able to transform the square mile of forest into a park with pavillions and promenades, a large house and slave quarters, stables and kitchen gardens. In the meantime, not only the town of Jefferson but a whole county had grown up around the square mile which was still intact and remained so until

1866, being known as the Compson domain. Jason's son, Quentin, became Governor and was the "last Compson who would not fail at everything he touched save longevity and suicide." Quentin was followed by Brigadier Jason Lycurgus II, who was not only a failed soldier but who also put the first mortgage on the original square mile and spent the rest of his life selling off small pieces of it to keep up the mortgage payments on the rest. He died in 1900. His son was Jason III, who married Caroline Bascomb. Their children, Quentin III, Candace (Caddy), Jason IV, and Benjamin are the last of the Compson line.

Faulkner presents terse but invaluable insight into the chief characters of *The Sound and the Fury*: Candace, who knew she was doomed, who regarded her virginity as no more than a "hangnail," and whose promiscuity represents the moral sterility of the family; Quentin III, who "identified family with his sister's membrane," convinced himself he had committed incest with her, but really loved only death—in his sublimation of emotions into a kind of latterday courtly love mystique—and found his love in June, 1910, by committing the physical suicide which the destruction of his grandfather's watch symbolized; Benjy, the "idiot" whose "tale" forms the remarkable first section of the novel, and who "loved three things: the pasture . . . his sister Candace (who 'smelled like trees'), and firelight" and who symbolizes both the mental deterioration of the family and, through his castration, its physical sterility; Jason IV, "the first sane Compson since before Culloden and (a childless bachelor) hence the last," who commits Benjy to an asylum, sells the house, and displays the pathetically mediocre intelligence that alone is able to cope with the incursions of the modern world symbolized by the Snopes family; and Quentin IV, the child of Candace, "already doomed to be unwed from the instant the dividing egg determined its sex," who is the last Compson and the final burden destined for Mrs. Compson, the personification, to Jason, of all the evil and insanity of his decaying, decadent family.

The first section of the novel is dated April 7, 1928 and is comprised of the flow of thoughts of Benjamin (Benjy), thirty-three years old but with the mind of a child. He is not capable of speech but moans when he is sad and bellows when he is frustrated. Within this section most of the events of the other sections take place filtered through Benjy's infant mind. Thus there is little to distinguish one time from another since Benjy's thoughts flow by means of association. A great deal is revealed, however, both about events and characters. Benjy's parents, brothers, sister, and the black servants are shown in interaction with Benjy and with one other. The father is preoccupied; the mother is neurotic and sickly. Jason is a loner, attached only to his mother. Quentin is never seen except attached to Caddy. Caddy, whom Benjy loves above all else, accepts responsibility even at an early age for his well being. Dilsey, the black cook, is strong, sensitive and loving. Other characters emerge: a female Quentin, seen sometimes as an infant and sometimes as a young woman; an uncle and a series of black servants: Roskus, Versh, Frony, T. P., and Luster.

This section is written with incredibly delicate perception, pronouncing the lucidity of a simple-minded innocence that can yet be accompanied by a terrible sharpness and consistency of memory. In its confusion of his father's funeral with Candace's wedding, in its constant painful reactivation by the sound of the golfers crying "caddie" to cause him to bellow out his hollow sense of his sister's loss, Benjy's mind becomes the focus of more cruelty, compassion, and love than anyone but Dilsey imagines.

Part Two is dated June 2, 1910. Told through Quentin's point of view it is an account of how he spends the day before he commits suicide. It is also the last day of his first year at Harvard. His father had sold a piece of land called Benjy's pasture in order that Quentin might attend Harvard for at least one year. Through Quentin's unfolding memories, his early attachment to Caddy is shown to have grown into an obsession. Throughout the day as he wanders around town, alone most of the time, his mind is filled with memories of Caddy: his response to her when she has her first affair with Dalton Ames, a stranger in town: his desperate need of her that drives him to tell their father a lie—that he and Caddy have committed incest—in hopes that they would be sent away together. Many of the events narrated in Benjy's section are replayed here but this time through Quentin's consciousness, thus giving them a different perspective; and many of the events only alluded to in Benjy's section are developed more fully. Quentin's anguish is deep; his despair is real, but ironically he waits to kill himself until the last day of his classes so that the selling of Benjy's pasture will not have been in vain.

Quentin III's section is one of the most sustained lyrical passages of twentieth century prose. The concentration of Quentin's stream-of-consciousness around the broken, handless watch is one of Faulkner's greatest achievements. Just as the leitmotiv of Benjy's section was the smell of trees associated with Caddy's loss, the recurring refrain of Quentin's is the desperate rhetorical question, "Did you ever have a sister?"

The third section, dated April 6, 1928, is told through Jason's point of view. Now a grown man and head of the family since the death of his father and older brother, Jason lives with his mother, who is still a complaining invalid cared for by a seemingly tireless Dilsey, his brother Benjy who is now cared for by Luster, Frony's son and Dilsey's grandson, and with Quentin, Caddy's daughter, conceived before her marriage to Sidney Herbert Read in 1910. Forbidden to return home by her parents, Caddy nevertheless has given Quentin into her parent's care.

Jason is a bitter man, sadistic and unloving. He works as a clerk at a store in town to support the family and blames all of his misfortunes on Caddy. The money that came from the sale of Benjy's pasture having gone to pay tuition at Harvard for Quentin and the rest for Caddy's wedding, Jason's future had been tied to a promise made by Caddy's husband that he would find a place for Jason in his bank, a position not realized when Read divorced Caddy. Quentin, at the age of seventeen, is the target for most of Jason's anger. She is rebellious, bitter, and unhappy. Locked in her room every night by her grandmother, taunted and threatened by Jason, her one desire is escape.

During the course of Jason's day it is revealed that he has been systematically robbing Quentin of money sent by her mother, that he is gambling on the cotton market, and that he is paranoid in his relations to everyone. He is afraid of Dilsey, and he has tried unsuccessfully to get rid of her. He has succeeded in having Benjy castrated. Other events, shadowy and puzzling in Benjy's section, are brought more clearly into focus. The original square mile has been reduced to the house and Dilsey's cabin. The pasture and creek where Benjy had loved to play is a golf course. The only close relationship that Jason has, or has ever had, is with a whore in Memphis.

On the morning of April 6, 1928, Jason has attempted to beat Quentin for cutting her classes, but Dilsey intervenes. In order to make sure that she gets to school, Jason drives Quentin into town. There is a traveling show in town on this day, and in the afternoon, when Quentin is supposed to be in school, Jason sees her with a man whom Jason immediately identifies as a pitchman with the traveling show. Quentin does not return home until after dinner. She goes straight to her room. Mrs. Compson locks Quentin's door, as she is accustomed to doing. That night Jason counts the money in the strongbox which he keeps hidden in his room. Jason's theme is hate, a hate as pitiful as is the diminution of Compson pride into pathetic vanity; and this third section of the novel may be the greatest for its evocation of deep, moving passions from even the most mediocre.

The fourth section of the novel is dated April 8, 1928. It is told in the third person and focused on Dilsey, who "seed de first en de last" and who represents, to Faulkner, the only humanity that survives the fall of the house of Compson. She is old and almost incapable of going up and down the stairs in response to the demands of Mrs. Compson. Luster takes care of Benjy, who has to be fed, dressed, and attended by someone every minute of his waking hours. It is not until breakfast is ready and Jason insists that Quentin come downstairs that they discover that she has gone. Not only has she escaped, but Jason discovers to his horror that she has broken into his room and robbed the cash box not only of three thousand dollars of his own savings but also of four thousand dollars of the money that Caddy had sent through the years for Quentin.

The Appendix continues the cause and effect sequence. As soon as his mother died in 1933, Jason had Benjy committed to the state asylum at Jackson. He then sold the Compson house to a man who operated it as a boarding house. Jason remained unwed and childless, the last of the Compsons. Caddy, divorced by her first husband in 1911, married again in 1920 in Hollywood, California, to a minor moving picture magnate and was divorced in Mexico in 1928. She went to Paris, where she disappeared after the invasion of 1940. In 1943 the librarian in Jefferson saw a color photograph in a magazine of Caddy, beautiful still, dressed in a fur coat and seated in an expensive sports car with a middle-aged and decorated German staff general. Quentin, the last born of the Compsons, escaped altogether. Jason, unable to prosecute her for the theft of his money without revealing his own embezzlement, is left with no alternative but to allow her to do the one thing she has always wanted—to leave and escape from him and the town of Jefferson.

Bibliography

Backman, Melvin. *Faulkner: The Major Years, A Critical Study.* Bloomington: Indiana University Press, 1966, pp. 13–40.

Bleikasten, Andre. *The Most Splendid Failure: Faulkner's* The Sound and the Fury. Bloomington: Indiana University Press, 1976.

Brooks, Cleanth. *William Faulkner: The Yoknapatawpha County.* New Haven, Conn.: Yale University Press, 1963, pp. 325–348.

Collins, Carvel. "The Interior Monologues of *The Sound and the Fury*," in *English Institute Essays, 1952.* New York: Columbia University Press, 1954, pp. 29–55.

————. "William Faulkner's *The Sound and the Fury*," in *The American Novel from James Fenimore Cooper to William Faulkner.* Edited by Wallace Stegner. New York: Basic Books, 1965, pp. 219–228.

Cowan, Michael H., Editor. *Twentieth Century Interpretations of* The Sound and the Fury. Englewood Cliffs, N.J.: Prentice-Hall, 1968.

Edel, Leon. "How to Read *The Sound and the Fury*," in *Varieties of Literary Experience: Eighteen Essays in World Literature.* Edited by Stanley Burnshaw. New York: New York University Press, 1962, pp. 241–257.

England, Martha Winburn. "Quentin's Story: Chronology and Explication," in *College English.* XXII (January, 1961), pp. 225–235.

Gross, Beverly. "Form and Fulfillment in *The Sound and the Fury*," in *Modern Language Quarterly.* IX (1968), pp. 439–449.

Handy, William J. "*The Sound and the Fury*: A Formalist Approach," in *North Dakota Quarterly.* XLIV (1976), pp. 71–83.

Hoffman, Frederick J. *William Faulkner.* New York: Twayne, 1961, pp. 49–60.

Hornback, Vernon T., Jr. "The Uses of Time in Faulkner's *The Sound and the Fury*," in *Papers on English Language and Literature.* I (Winter, 1965), pp. 50–58.

Howe, Irving. *William Faulkner: A Critical Study.* New York: Vintage, 1962, pp. 46–52, 124–136, 157–174.

Humphrey, Robert. "Form and Function in William Faulkner's *The Sound and the Fury*," in *University of Kentucky Review.* XIX (Autumn, 1952), pp. 34–40.

Longley, John L., Jr. "Who Never Had a Sister: A Reading of *The Sound and the Fury*," in *Mosaic*. VII (1973), pp. 35–53.

Lowrey, Perrin. "Concepts of Time in *The Sound and the Fury*," in *English Institute Essays, 1952*. New York: Columbia University Press, 1954, pp. 57–82.

Meriwether, James B., Editor. *Studies in* The Sound and the Fury. Columbus, Oh.: Charles E. Merrill, 1970.

Millgate, Michael. *The Achievement of William Faulkner*. New York: Random House, 1965, pp. 86–103.

Stewart, George R. and Joseph M. Backus. " 'Each in its Ordered Place': Structure and Narrative in 'Benjy's Section' of *The Sound and the Fury*," in *American Literature*. XXIX (January, 1958), pp. 440–456.

Swiggart, Peter. *The Art of Faulkner's Novels*. Austin: University of Texas Press, 1962, pp. 61–70, 87–107.

Thompson, Lawrance. *William Faulkner: An Introduction and Interpretation*. New York: Holt, Rinehart and Winston, 1967, pp. 29–52.

Vickery, Olga. *The Novels of William Faulkner: A Critical Interpretation*. Baton Rouge: Louisiana State University Press, 1964, pp. 28–49.

Volpe, Edmond L. *A Reader's Guide to William Faulkner*. New York: Noonday, 1964, pp. 87–126, 353–377.

Waggoner, Hyatt H. *William Faulkner: From Jefferson to the World*. Lexington: University of Kentucky Press, 1959, pp. 34–61.

Wall, Carey. "*The Sound and the Fury*: The Emotional Center," in *Midwest Quarterly*. XI (1970), pp. 371–387.

Young, James Dean. "Quentin's Maundy Thursday," in *Tulane Studies in English*. X (1960), pp. 143–151.

THE TOWN

Type of work: Novel
Author: William Faulkner (1897–1962)
Time of plot: 1909–1927
Locale: Jefferson, Yoknapatawpha County, Mississippi
First published: 1957

A *continuation of* The Hamlet, *this novel treats both with wild comedy and savage indignation the further adventures of the degenerate Snopes clan, especially Flem's rise from restaurant owner to bank president, symbolic of the disintegrating values of the Old South.*

Principal Characters

Flem Snopes, the shrewdest of the materialistic Snopes clan. After successfully taking over the hamlet of Frenchman's Bend, Flem lets his desire for respectability master his voracious thirst for money and he begins a systematic rise from restaurant owner to bank president in Jefferson. He marries Eula to secure Will Varner as an ally and permits an affair between Manfred de Spain and his wife in order to secure de Spain's aid in his rise. When the proper time arrives, he uses this affair to remove de Spain and take his place as president of the bank.

Manfred de Spain, the mayor of Jefferson. When a vacancy occurs, de Spain resigns as mayor and becomes president of the bank; he makes Flem vice president. After his eighteen-year affair becomes common knowledge, de Spain sells his bank stock and leaves the presidency vacant for Flem.

Eula Varner Snopes, Flem's wife. Already pregnant by Hoake McCarron, Eula is married to impotent Flem Snopes in order to save the family name. She has a long affair with Manfred de Spain but refuses to leave Jefferson with him. After exacting a promise from Gavin Stevens that he will marry Linda, she commits suicide.

Linda Snopes, Eula's daughter.

Gavin Stevens, a verbose county attorney. In his role as the conscience of Jefferson, Stevens attempts to reform Eula and later promises to marry Linda, if necessary, to protect her from Flem's schemes.

V. K. Ratliff, a garrulous, likable country sewing machine salesman, a narrator.

Charles Mallison, Gavin Stevens' nephew, one of the narrators.

Will Varner, Eula's father.

I. O. Snopes,
Byron Snopes,
Montgomery Ward Snopes,
Mink Snopes, and
Eck Snopes, Flem's worthless cousins, whom he abandons as he rises.

Ab Snopes, Flem's father, a horse thief and barn burner.

Wallstreet Panic Snopes, Flem's successful cousin.

The Story

The Snopes family, which came out of nowhere after the Civil War, had successfully completed the invasion of Frenchman's Bend. Now Flem Snopes, son of Ab Snopes, a bushwacker, sharecropper, and horse thief, was ready for the next goal, the domination of Jefferson, county seat of Yoknapatawpha County.

Flem Snopes was ruthless, shrewd, uneducated, and possessed of a fanatic belief in the power of money. The townspeople, who had seen him when he took over Frenchman's Bend and then left it under control of other family members, were wondering about Flem's next move. Among those interested were Gavin Stevens, a young lawyer educated in Heidelberg, and V. K. Ratliff, a good-natured sewing machine salesman, who made up for his lack of education with a great measure of common sense. Stevens felt a moral responsibility to defend the town against the Snopeses, and Ratliff was once the victim of Snopeism when, thinking that it contained a buried treasure, he bought worthless property from Flem for a high price. Another who became an assistant in the fight against Snopes infiltration was Stevens' nephew, Charles Mallison, who watched the Snopes invasion from his childhood through adolescence.

Flem Snopes realized that more subtle methods for conquering Jefferson were necessary than those he had used in Frenchman's bend. The greatest advantage for him was his marriage with Eula Varner, daughter of Will Varner, chief property owner in that community. When Eula was pregnant, impotent Flem had married her after making a profitable deal with Varner, who despised Snopes but wanted to save his daughter's honor.

In a small rented house Flem and his wife made a modest beginning in Jefferson by operating a small restaurant of which Ratliff had been a partner before he lost his share in the business deal with Flem. Later the restaurant was transformed into a hotel. The first hint that Flem was aiming even higher came when he was appointed superintendent of the local power plant, before the people even knew that such a position existed.

As the new mayor of Jefferson, Manfred de Spain was not in favor with the town conservatives, but he had won the election in a landslide when he declared himself against an automobile ban imposed by the former mayor. Soon it became known in the town that Eula Snopes and the new mayor were lovers. No one had seen anything, but everybody seemed to know about the affair except her husband.

Shortly after the war, during which Gavin Stevens served overseas, the president of Jefferson's oldest bank was killed in an auto accident. De Spain, named president on account of the bank stock he had inherited, resigned as mayor. The election of a new president made necessary a routine check by government auditors, who uncovered the theft of a large sum of money by a defaulting clerk, Byron Snopes, who fled to Mexico. Announcement was made that the money had been replaced by the new president and that Mr. Flem Snopes had been made a vice president of the bank. Flem's appointment indicated to his opponents a new phase of Snopesism: the search for money power was now overshadowed by Flem's desire for respectability. This new tactic also became apparent when he rid himself and Jefferson of some undesirable kinsmen, like Montgomery Ward Snopes, who might have destroyed his efforts to make the name Snopes respectable. Montgomery Ward Snopes had returned from the war in France with a rich supply of pornographic pictures. A short time later he opened a photographic studio and gave nightly slide shows for a large part of the male population of Yoknapatawpha County. Flem, not wishing to have his name associated with this shady enterprise, put bootleg whiskey in Montgomery Ward's studio to assure his arrest. When another Snopes, Mink, was jailed for murder, Flem failed to give him any assistance. There was also Eck Snopes, who did not fit into the Snopes pattern on account of his weak intelligence. Flem had no need to bring about his removal, for Eck removed himself. He had been hired to watch an oil tank. While a search was being made for a lost child, Eck, trying to make sure that the child had not climbed into his oil tank, took a lantern and went to look inside the tank. After the explosion only Eck's metal neck brace was available for burial. Meanwhile, the child was found safely somewhere along the road.

Flem's new desire for respectability also made him forget Wallstreet Panic Snopes, who had dared to become a self-made man without his kinsman's help. Wallstreet Panic, a successful grocer, introduced the first self-service store in Jefferson. Flem also disliked the outcome of one of his family projects with I. O. Snopes, who was trained to tie mules to the railroad track in order to collect money from damage law suits against the railroad. When I. O. Snopes was killed during one of these operations, Flem hoped to collect the indemnity. But I. O's stubborn wife kept all the money and Flem, in order to avoid complications, was forced to pay off the man who had supplied the mules. Flem also tried to live up to his new social standing by letting a professional decorator furnish his house.

In the meantime Gavin Stevens, who had never been able to rid himself of the attraction Eula Snopes held for him, concentrated his reform efforts on Linda, Eula's daughter. Linda, now in high school, did not know that Flem was not her real father. The lawyer loved Linda and tried to influence her to attend a northern college far away from Snopesism. But Flem, needing a front of outwardly solid family life for his show of respectability, was opposed to the possibility of losing his control of Linda, especially since a will existed which gave the girl a great deal of Will Varner's estate. So Flem disregarded the pleas of his daughter because he still had one more step ahead of him to achieve the position he desired in Jefferson: his scheme to replace de Spain as president of the bank. When he failed in his first attempt to ruin the bank by instigating a run on it, he decided that the time had come to use his knowledge of his wife'a adultery as a weapon. Acting as if had just learned of the eighteen-year-old affair, and armed with a declaration from Linda that she would leave her part of her inheritance to her father, he visited Will Varner. Once more, in order to save the honor of his daughter and in return for Flem's promise to destroy Linda's note about the inheritance, Varner helped Flem to get rid of de Spain and Flem became president of the bank. Hoping Eula would run away with him, de Spain sold his bank stock, but Eula, hoping to keep her duaghter from ever learning of her affairs, remained in Jefferson. She committed suicide after securing from Gavin Stevens a promise that he would marry Linda.

Flem, having reached his goal, agreed to let Linda leave Jefferson. But for a short interval the ghost of old Snopesism came back to Jefferson, when bank thief Byron Snopes sent his four half-Indian children to stay with his kinsfolk. After a series of incidents in which the children terrorized Jefferson and Frenchman's Bend, Flem himself made sure that these last reminders of primitive Snopesism were sent back to Mexico. Meanwhile, he had bought the de Spain house, and workers were busy transforming it into a mansion suitable to Flem Snopes, president of the Bank of Jefferson.

Critical Evaluation

It was in the 1920's that William Faulkner first conceived of the Snopes Saga: a clan of crude, avaricious, amoral, unfeeling, but energetic and hard-driving individuals who would move into the settled, essentially moral society of the Old South and gradually, but inevitably, usurp the old order. To Faulkner the Snopeses were not a special Mississippi phenomenon, but a characteristic evil of the mechanized, dehumanized twentieth century which filled the void left by the collapse of the agrarian pre-Civil War South. Flem Snopes is the supreme example of the type, and the Snopes Trilogy is primarily a chronicle of his career and its implications.

However, it was 1940 before Faulkner finished *The Hamlet,* the first book in the series (although several short stories appeared earlier), and not until the 1950's that he completed the trilogy with *The Town* and *The Mansion.* In the intervening time Faulkner's vision of human morality and society had become more complex and, although the original design remained intact, the quest of the Snopes Clan became more devious and complicated, and "Snopesism" took on increasingly ambiguous meanings.

At the beginning of *The Town,* Flem arrives in Jefferson fresh from his triumphs in Frenchman's Bend, but with only a wagon, a new wife, Eula Varner Snopes, and their baby daughter, Linda. The book traces his rise in short order from restaurant owner to hotel owner, to power plant supervisor, to bank vice-president, and finally to bank president, church deacon, and grieving widower. The book also describes the life of his wife, Eula, her lengthy affair with Manfred de Spain, her relations to the community, and her efforts for her daughter—all of which leads her, at last, to suicide.

If Flem is the embodiment of ruthless, aggressive inhumanity and devitalized conformity, Eula is the essence of warmth, emotional involvement, sexuality, and freedom. Although their direct confrontations are muted, *The Town* is basically about the struggle between these two characters and the contrasting approaches to life that they represent.

The story is told by three anti-Snopesean citizens: V. K. Ratliff, the sewing machine salesman who previously tangled with Flem in Frenchman's Bend; Gavin Stevens, Heidelberg and Harvard educated County Attorney; and Charles Mallinson, Stevens' young nephew. Although they confirm the essential facts, each speaker has a separate interpretation of the events. Thus, the reader must sift through their different attitudes and conclusions to arrive at the "truth" of the book. Frequently it is the ironical distance between the events and the characters' interpretations of them that gives the book its bite and message—as well as its humor.

Mallinson, who saw the events as a child but recounts them as an adult, is probably the most detached of the narrators. Ratliff is sardonic and realistic, but his bitter experiences with the Snopeses somewhat color his accounts. Gavin Stevens is the primary narrator and chief enemy of Flem, but the reliability of his statements is jeopardized by his lengthy, emotional, somewhat confused involvements with both Eula and Linda.

Stevens is a well-educated, sophisticated modern man who understands the complexities and difficulties of human relationships; but, at the same time, he is an old-fashioned Southern Gentleman who clings to old attitudes and traditions. When Eula offers herself to him, it is not morality, but romanticism coupled with self-doubt that stimulates his refusal. He insists on viewing her through a romantic haze which prevents him from reacting realistically in the most critical situations. "What he was doing was simply defending forever with his blood the principle that chastity and virtue in women shall be defended whether they exist or not."

The same kinds of assumptions determine his relationship to Linda Snopes. Since he is nearly twice her age, he cannot imagine a sexual or marital arrangement between them in spite of the fact that he loves her and is encouraged by her mother. So, in the role of father protector and educator, Stevens reads poetry to Linda over sodas and feeds her dreams with college catalogs. Thus, because of his intense emotions, sense of morality, and traditional assumptions, Gavin Stevens is unable to deal either with Eula's simple sensuality or Flem Snopes' one-dimensional inhumanity.

In the final conflict between these two forces, Flem's ruthless rationality easily overcomes Eula's passionate free spirit. Being both physically and spiritually impotent, Flem can coldly and callously manipulate the sexual and emotional drives in others. Not only does he do so to thwart Stevens' anti-Snopes efforts, but more importantly to his plans, he also uses them to gain control over his primary Jefferson rival, Manfred de Spain.

Flem learns of his wife's affair with de Spain soon after his arrival in Jefferson, but he chooses to ignore it as long as it is profitable. It is even suggested that the two men work out a tacit agreement whereby Flem overlooks the affair in return for an appointment to the newly created job of power plant superintendent. De Spain's influence is later instrumental in securing Flem the vice-presidency of the Sartoris Bank. After eighteen years, however, when Flem decides to make his move for the bank presidency, he suddenly becomes the outraged husband. He uses the threat of scandal to provoke Will Varner to action, to drive de Spain from the bank, to push Eula to suicide, and to coerce Stevens into unwilling complicity. Neither integrity nor sensuality can stop Snopesism.

However, as Flem succeeds in his drive to monetary wealth another goal becomes predominant—"respectability." He learns from de Spain that in Jefferson one can become respectable without being moral—if one has the necessary money. So Flem systematically acquires all the requisite signs of success and they, in turn, provide him with access to respectability. Only one last obstacle remains between Flem and complete social acceptance—the other Snopeses.

Consequently, it is Flem, himself, who finally rids Jefferson of the Snopeses. Using the same callous attitude and devious strategy on his kin that he used on other victims, he eliminates all of the lesser Snopeses who might pose a threat to his new status: Mink, Byron, Montgomery Ward, I.O., and, finally, Byron's brood of wild, half-breed children, "The last and final end of Snopes out-and-out unvarnished behavior in Jefferson."

So Flem becomes respectable. Faulkner's final question to the reader is this: has Flem's drive to social acceptance weakened and narrowed him to the point where he is vulnerable, if not to the morality of the Ratliffs, Stevenses, and Mallinsons, then to the latent vengeances of Snopesism? Faulkner answers that question in *The Mansion*.

Bibliography

See **The Snopes Trilogy**, page 209.

THE UNVANQUISHED

Type of work: Novel
Author: William Faulkner (1897–1962)
Time of plot: 1863–1874
Locale: Jefferson, Yoknapatawpha County, Mississippi
First published: 1938

Essay-Review

Most of William Faulkner's novels have an individual and unconventional form, but two share a common formal distinction: *Go Down, Moses* and *The Unvanquished* appear at first glance to be collections of short stories. The chronology in both, like that of the conventional novel, is strictly observed; but the exact order of composition of the episodes, first published as separate short stories, has not been determined.

At least three stages appear to have occurred in creating the novel from the stories. First, Faulkner's imagination played freely on real and remembered incidents which became a set of anecdotes about the adventures of the Sartoris women and children during the Civil War. Next, these were arranged in order to provide a family chronicle from the moment the first Union troops appeared near Jefferson, with resulting disruption of Sartoris family life, until its tentative reestablishment at the Sartoris home during the Reconstruction. Last, the chronicle was given both the perspective and larger meaning a novel offers by writing a new story, "An Odor of Verbena," set some years later than the rest, in which the role of Bayard is clarified as "the unvanquished." This concluding story was necessary because there is no separate story or chapter so called in the book, though the story "Riposte in Tertio" originally bore that title. Five of the stories were published in chronological order in *The Saturday Evening Post* between September, 1934, and December, 1936; "Skirmish at Sartoris" appeared in *Scribner's Magazine* during that period. Very few changes in text were made between periodical and book publication. "An Odor of Verbena" was printed for the first time in the novel.

The Unvanquished is, therefore, an interesting example of how Faulkner could mine his Sartoris material for a number of anecdotes which, as they were gradually assembled, he shaped into a novel by writing a conclusion that would transfer the attention from Granny Millard (who with Ringo dominates the first four stories) to Bayard, who completed Granny's history in the fifth story. At the same time Faulkner explored the whole Southern code and in the new story he wrote came up with a different ending to the series of episodes. The imposition of this conclusion is Faulkner's clearest statement about the origins and foundations of the Southern code and this fact makes *The Unvanquished* not only the best introduction to his work and the earliest in the Yoknapatawpha saga, but also the most important to an understanding of all his writings.

At the start of the novel the "unvanquished" are three of the four recognized constituents of a Southern Civil War novel: Southern men, women, children, and Negroes. In turn the first two are vanquished not by the Union but by inherent weakness in the Southern code; the child grown into a man remains unvanquished by North or South; the Negro looks on and survives. Certain unifying features bring out these distinctions. All seven stories or chapters are told in the first person by Bayard, so that the book could be considered a child's testament to the War; the setting is held to Jefferson as much as possible, but the homestead serves largely as a point of departure and return; even when the house has been burned to the ground the chimneys will not fall and the cabins are used for shelter. The events take place between the fall of Vicksburg in 1863, when Bayard is twelve, and 1874, when he is twenty-four. The first six stories, however, take place in the three years after the novel opens; "An Odor of Verbena," separated by more than time from the others, serves as an epilogue to the volume.

The progression of events leading to the last story is based on shootings and deaths; at the end of the fourth story, "Riposte in Tertio," Granny has been shot by Major Grumby, a renegade Southerner and leader of Grumby's Independents, with the apparent connivance of Ab Snopes, historically the first of the Snopes in Yoknapatawpha County. At the end of the fifth story, "Vendée," Grumby has been shot in revenge by Bayard; before the beginning of the last story Colonel Sartoris has been shot by Benjamin J. Redmond, his former partner in a railroad-building venture. The structure of the novel depends on a similar parallelism of characters, situations, and events, with the movement of the Union troops precipitating most of the action. Bayard, for example, is accompanied or paralleled by Ringo; the action of the first four stories is based on the struggle between Union troops and Confederate raiding parties, such as that of Colonel Sartoris, to hold or control Mississippi, but for every triumph of the former, the populace in that section of Mississippi, led by Granny Millard, score a victory over the invaders. When that struggle concludes another begins between Granny and the harsh conditions of the Reconstruction: her death at the hands of Major Grumby and Ab Snopes causes the death of Grumby at the hands of Bayard and Ringo. A third struggle between the returned Southerners and the carpetbaggers begins in the sixth story, "Skirmish at Sartoris." The last confrontation, between Bayard and the Southern code, is the final story.

This is also a progression from the high comedy of the two boys, Bayard and Ringo, blindly shooting at Yankees in the first story, through the various shooting and killings until Bayard is grimly face to face with Redmond in the last story; Redmond, like Grumby, shoots twice at Bayard, misses, and leaves town. Bayard, unarmed, has brought the cycle of violence, initiated by his own act in shooting at the Yankees, to a Christian close. Accompanied by Ringo, escorted by the colonel's old troop, challenged by Drusilla, Bayard manages to withstand all these encouragements to violence, thus gaining the approval of his father's sister, Aunt

Jenny Sartoris, who takes the place of dead Granny Millard as the voice of good conduct. Granny Millard was killed because she had been compelled to violate her own standards: in the first story, "Ambuscade," she lies to Colonel Dick to protect Bayard and Ringo; in the second, "Retreat," she swears as the Union troops burn the Sartoris house; in the third "Raid," she steals from the Union troops by forging copies of the official order generous Colonel Dick gave her to make up for her original loss of slaves, mules, and silver. Her habit had been to punish the boys for such transgressions and she tried to keep up such a code of punishments, but at the end Bayard and Ringo were unable to stop her trying one last theft and lie. In the fourth story she meets worse liars and robbers in Ab Snopes and Grumby; to these crimes they add murder.

The accretion of parallel events and the final moral decision confronting Bayard—whether to shoot Redmond as Redmond shot his father—give the novel both epic and ethical dimensions. The epic dimension is shown in the way Granny Millard comes to stand for all Southern womanhood fighting with wit and grit apparently overwhelming forces, and winning. Most of the exciting passages, such as the great river of freed slaves "going to Jordan" or the trailing of Major Grumby are associated with the epic of Granny Millard and Ringo, in which Bayard is largely a bystander. The ethical dimension comes from the three occasions on which Bayard handles a gun: first when he shoots at the Yankees; second, when he kills Grumby; third, when Drusilla presses on him the duelling pistols with which she intends he shall shoot Redmond. But greater than the courage of pistols is the courage of endurance, which must be the total meaning of the Civil War to the South. The power of the pistol failed, but the power to endure carried the South on. This latter power is represented as "the odor of verbena," and in the last story so named Drusilla, the toughest battler of them all, comes to recognize that Bayard deserves this accolade.

Although Colonel Sartoris was eventually vanquished by Northern arms and even more by the triumph of total war as practiced by Sherman, and although Granny was eventually vanquished by the desire to loot, but for the highest and most unselfish motives, Bayard has been able to escape the fever of killing, break the chain of shootings, and in doing so offer a way of escape to the South and from the past. He could not do so without the example of Granny and his father. He is "unvanquished" because he did not allow the Southern code to negate the universal law against killing. The tragedy of the South, as Faulkner explores it in his work, is that it could not see that Bayard, the Christ-figure, had come to redeem the South from itself.

Bibliography

Backman, Melvin. *Faulkner: The Major Years, A Critical Study*. Bloomington: Indiana University Press, 1966, pp. 113–126.

Brooks, Cleanth. *William Faulkner: The Yoknapatawpha County.* New Haven, Conn.: Yale University Press, 1963, pp. 75–99.

Howe, Irving. *William Faulkner: A Critical Study.* New York: Vintage, 1962, pp. 41–45.

Knoll, Robert E. *"The Unvanquished* for a Start," in *College English.* XIX (May, 1958), pp. 338–343.

Longley, John L., Jr. *The Tragic Mask: A Study of Faulkner's Heroes.* Chapel Hill: University of North Carolina Press, 1963, pp. 177–191.

Millgate, Michael. *The Achievement of William Faulkner.* New York: Random House, 1965, pp. 165–170.

Nilon, Charles H. *Faulkner and the Negro.* New York: Citadel Press, 1965, pp. 59–66.

Trimmer, Joseph F. *"The Unvanquished*: The Teller and the Tale," in *Ball State University Forum.* X (1969), pp. 35–42.

Volpe, Edmond L. *A Reader's Guide to William Faulkner.* New York: Noonday, 1964, pp. 76–87.

Waggoner, Hyatt H. *William Faulkner: From Jefferson to the World.* Lexington: University of Kentucky Press, 1959, pp. 170–183.

Walker, William E. *"The Unvanquished*: The Restoration of Tradition," in *Reality and Myth: Essays in American Literature in Memory of Robert Croom Beatty.* Nashville, Tenn.: Vanderbilt University Press, 1964, pp. 275–297.

THE WILD PALMS

Type of work: Novel
Author: William Faulkner (1897–1962)
Time of plot: 1927 and 1937
Locale: The United States
First published: 1939

Essay-Review

Often considered to be an inferior novel even by Faulkner's better critics, *The Wild Palms* has had a curious history, for it has most often been reprinted as two short novels (*Wild Palms* and *Old Man*), sometimes in the same volume and even more often as two separate books. That it has been so casually treated is unfortunate, for it is structurally perhaps the most subtle and demanding of Faulkner's novels, and it is also his best approach to the comically absurd world of male-female relationships.

Most of the misunderstanding of the novel grows from its unique structure. The two short novels, either of which appears to be able to stand alone, are presented in alternating chapters in the novel. Their plots never cross nor relate directly to each other; but they are so deeply involved in theme and symbolic and imagistic texture that apart each seems almost a thematic contradiction of the other. Together, however, they form an organic unit in which contrasts form parallels and contradiction becomes paradox. The novel demands of its readers an imaginative commitment beyond that of a more conventionally constructed novel, for its paradox, of both meaning and structure, must be solved by the reader willing to read the book with the attention to rhythm and form that he would normally give to a piece of music and the attention to images and words that he would normally give to a poem.

The pattern of events of the two parts of the novel are relatively simple. "Wild Palms" takes place in 1937, in the heart of the depression, and is the love story of Harry Wilbourne and Charlotte Rittenmeyer. Charlotte leaves her husband for Harry who, not having finished his internship, is incapable of gaining any steady work. They wander from New Orleans to Chicago to Wisconsin and even to a remote mining camp in Utah until Charlotte becomes pregnant accidentally; their journeys, too, have carried them deeper into squalor and their love from romance into the physically sordid. Urged by Charlotte, Harry performs an unsuccessful abortion which results in her death; but in prison he refuses suicide, choosing grief to nothing.

The events in "Old Man" take place ten years earlier during the great Mississippi River flood of 1927, and they compose the chronicle of a comic hero in a physical world gone quite as mad as the social world of the depression in "Wild Palms." A young convict is sent out onto the flooded Mississippi in a skiff with another convict to rescue a woman stranded in a tree and a man on a cottonhouse. He loses the other convict, rescues the woman who proves to be very pregnant, and is carried downstream by a wild flood. Battered by gigantic waves, he is offered three temptations for escape, but after a time killing alligators with a group of Cajuns he returns the boat and the woman with her safely born child and is given an additional ten-year sentence for attempted escape.

Neither of these brief descriptions even approaches the complexities of the two stories, separately or as a unit, for theirs is an artistic value of reflection and texture in which event is but an item of form, and form a vehicle for imaginative idea. "Wild Palms" is a tragicomedy, a parody of Hemingway's romantic "antiromantic" ideas (particularly those in *A Farewell to Arms*), a parable of a fallen world in which *agape* is lost to an *eros* made perverse by the forces of a society built on money and sexually inverted by the "freeing" of woman. "Old Man" is also a bitter comedy, but one in which the comic hero, God's fool, bears the burdens of the world and finds his victory in seeming defeat, his reward in the last ironic slap of "risible nature." "Wild Palms" resolves itself in onanistic frustration, and "Old Man" discovers the rewards of struggle in this life to be only the peace of being allowed out of life. The novel is a product, then, of the same era which produced *The Waste Land*, but its Chaucerian comic sense makes it more than an existential lament for a meaningless world, transforms its madness and ugliness into a Christian comedy of human folly which shows man at his worst, only to remind him of the necessity of striving toward his best. The novel is not a moral allegory, although "Old Man" often seems to be, but a parable of the vanity of human wishes and the follies of this earth.

The primary themes of both parts of the novel are those of human folly: the tragic consequences of romantic but earthly ideals and the failure of sex as the essential element of human fulfillment. Both Harry and the convict are victims of romantic ideals: the convict was sent to prison for an attempted train robbery inspired by reading dime novels, and intended to impress a girl; Harry was betrayed into his affair with Charlotte by his ascetic student's life and his belief (fostered by Charlotte) in physical love and the value of physical permanence in a spirtless world.

If the heroes of both stories are innocents in a confusing world, women offer them little aid or solace. The women in the novel represent the two emasculating extremes of the female character, isolated with the simplicity of parable. Charlotte is the de-feminized female artist of masculine mind and manner, the aggressor in the sexual act and in life; the woman in "Old Man" is simple nearly to mindlessness, for she is the mother, the primitive force of life to be borne by man as the weight of his duty. Charlotte is destroyed by the sex which she attempts to use as a man uses his, but cannot because she is what she wishes to deny—a woman, a vessel and bearer of man's seed and progeny. The woman in "Old Man" realizes and fulfills her proper role as mother, but in this comic world fails as a romantic sexual figure even as she succeeds; she lives on but without her man, the convict who had complained that she, of all the women in the world, is the one with whom he has been thrown by chance.

The men are innocents; the women are failures with them. "Old Man" ends with the convict's brief, violent summation of his feelings about the world of sex and women. "Wild Palms" ends with Harry's refusal to kill himself only because in his grief he can find the onanistic solace of the memory of Charlotte's flesh. Both stories end in hollowness and ugliness. Each, taken by itself, presents a vision of frustration and despair, yet the novel itself has no such effect.

The two stories present opposing accounts of the nature of failure and comic success which, if seen in the perspective which their juxtaposition in an organic whole imposes upon the reader (a perspective similar to that formed by the shifting points of view in *As I Lay Dying*), cancel each other out. This is a vision which causes the reader to apply his own norms to the events and see the exact nature of the folly of both extremes, of sex and sexlessness, or romantic and anti-romantic ideals shattered. The world of *The Wild Palms* is a mad world, but its madness casts bright light upon our own world, mad in its own right but alive with balances which may be found with comic and artistic perspective.

Faulkner does not explicitly offer his reader the moral of his novel but it is there to be drawn. That the reader can find it by an imaginative and creative act of his own synthesis is the true power of the novel. When man can laugh for joy even as he weeps in sorrow, he can survive and prevail. Such was the intention of this novel which, for all its difficulty, is an extraordinary example of the variety of Faulkner's ability, of his artistic genius.

Bibliography

Backman, Melvin. *Faulkner: The Major Years, A Critical Study.* Bloomington: Indiana University Press, 1966, pp. 127–138.

Feaster, John. "Faulkner's *Old Man*: A Psychoanalytic Approach," in *Modern Fiction Studies.* XIII (Spring, 1967), pp. 89–93.

Galharn, Carl. "Faulkner's Faith: Roots from *The Wild Palms*," in *Twentieth Century Literature.* I (October, 1955), pp. 139–160.

Howe, Irving. *William Faulkner: A Critical Study.* New York: Vintage, 1962, pp. 233–242.

Longley, John L., Jr. *The Tragic Mask: A Study of Faulkner's Heroes.* Chapel Hill: University of North Carolina Press, 1963, pp. 29–33.

McHaney, Thomas L. *William Faulkner's* The Wild Palms: *A Study.* Oxford: University Press of Mississippi, 1975.

Millgate, Michael. *The Achievement of William Faulkner.* New York: Random House, 1965, pp. 171–179.

Moldenhauer, Joseph J. "Unity of Structure and Theme in *The Wild Palms*," in *William Faulkner: Three Decades of Criticism.* Edited by Frederick J. Hoffman and Olga Vickery. East Lansing: Michigan State University Press, 1960, pp. 305–322.

Moses, W.R.   "The Unity of *The Wild Palms,*" in *Modern Fiction Studies.* II (Autumn, 1956), pp. 125–131.

O'Connor, William Van.   *The Tangled Fire of William Faulkner.* Minneapolis: University of Minnesota Press, 1954, pp. 105–110.

Reed, John Q.   "Theme and Symbol in Faulkner's *Old Man,*" in *Educational Leader.* XXI (January, 1958), pp. 25–31.

Reeves, Carolyn H.   "*The Wild Palms*: Faulkner's Chaotic Cosmos," in *Mississippi Quarterly.* XX (1967), pp. 148–157.

Swiggart, Peter.   *The Art of Faulkner's Novels.* Austin: University of Texas Press, 1962, pp. 51–57.

Vickery, Olga.   *The Novels of William Faulkner: A Critical Interpretation.* Baton Rouge: Louisiana State University Press, 1964, pp. 156–166.

Volpe, Edmond L.   *A Reader's Guide to William Faulkner.* New York: Noonday, 1964, pp. 212–230.

Waggoner, Hyatt H.   *William Faulkner: From Jefferson to the World.* Lexington: University of Kentucky Press, 1959, pp. 132–147.

F. SCOTT FITZGERALD

Born: St. Paul, Minnesota (September 24, 1896)
Died: Hollywood, California (December 21, 1940)

Principal Works

NOVELS: *This Side of Paradise,* 1920; *The Beautiful and Damned,* 1922; *The Great Gatsby,* 1925; *Tender Is the Night,* 1934; *The Last Tycoon,* 1941.

SHORT STORIES: *Flappers and Philosophers,* 1920; *Tales of the Jazz Age,* 1922; *All the Sad Young Men,* 1926; *Taps at Reveille,* 1935; *The Stories of F. Scott Fitzgerald,* 1951.

F. Scott Fitzgerald achieved early success with the publication of his first novel when he was twenty-four. He was acclaimed as the laureate of the jazz age; but when that era became unfashionable, the epithet was converted to stigmatize Fitzgerald as the playboy of American literature. Then, after his death, his reputation was gradually re-established on the basis of a fair assessment of his achievements. His writing was intensely autobiographical: not so much in the sense that he actually reported events in his life, but rather that he applied his work to interpret his career and evaluate the hectic time in which he lived.

Francis Scott Key Fitzgerald was born in St. Paul, Minnesota, on September 24, 1896. During his boyhood in that city he developed strong feelings about youth, romantic love, wealth, and success. These glamorous ideas were carried east to prep school and then to Princeton University. At Princeton he neglected his studies for literary activities, and dropped out of college to join the army in World War I. While stationed in Alabama he fell desperately in love with Zelda Sayre but lacked the means to marry her. When he became convinced after demobilization that the conventional road to success was too long, Fitzgerald quit his job to rewrite the novel he had been working on since college.

This Side of Paradise won immediate success with its blend of *Weltschmerz* and wild college life. The author-celebrity married his Southern belle and plunged into expensive living. For the rest of his life Fitzgerald was to be involved in a cycle of extravagant expenditure and writing himself out of debt. The novel was followed by *Flappers and Philosophers,* a collection of short stories. Fitzgerald's story output was very high—it eventually amounted to 160—for stories supplied him with money to meet his expenses while working on novels. Although he wrote stories primarily to earn money quickly, Fitzgerald's body of truly fine stories places him as one of the chief American short story writers.

The Beautiful and Damned, a novel dealing with the emotional and spiritual collapse of a wealthy young man during as unstable marriage, was less successful than Fitzgerald's first novel. The second novel was followed by *Tales of the Jazz Age,* a collection which included "May Day." An attempt to repair his finances with a play, *The Vegetable, or From President to Postman* (1923), proved unsuccessful.

The rich promise of Fitzgerald's earlier work was abundantly fulfilled by *The Great Gatsby*. In this novel treating a romantic racketeer's deep love for a rich and selfish married woman, the writing is perhaps unequalled for its lucidity and euphony. *All the Sad Young Men*, Fitzgerald's next collection, included "The Rich Boy" and "Absolution."

Following the critical success of *The Great Gatsby*, Fitzgerald's personal difficulties began to close in on him. In addition to the ever-present financial problems, his heavy drinking and his wife's mental breakdown forestalled work on the next novel. After several false starts, *Tender Is the Night* was completed at an inauspicious time. Although many critics now judge this study of a brilliant young doctor's disintegration to be Fitzgerald's finest work, the depression-ridden 1930's were unenthusiastic about a novel dealing with rich expatriates. *Taps at Reveille*, Fitzgerald's last story collection, included the Basil stories and "Babylon Revisited."

Fitzgerald then turned to screenwriting, and was engaged in a novel about a Hollywood producer when he died in that town on December 21, 1940. This unfinished novel, *The Last Tycoon*, was well-received; some critics felt that the prose style showed an even greater power and grace than that of *The Great Gatsby*. A final Fitzgerald volume, *The Crack-Up* (1945), edited by Edmund Wilson, gathered together autobiographical pieces, letters, notebook selections, and critical tributes.

After a period of neglect, F. Scott Fitzgerald was the subject of a remarkable literary revival in the 1950's. He now appears to be firmly established in the very first rank of American writers.

Bibliography

The definitive biography is Andrew Turnbull, *Scott Fitzgerald*, 1962, supplemented by *The Letters of F. Scott Fitzgerald*, Turnbull, ed., 1963. Also important is Arthur Mizener, *The Far Side of Paradise*, 1951. Representative critical studies have been reprinted in a volume edited by Alfred Kazin, *F. Scott Fitzgerald: The Man and His Work*, 1951. See also Paul Rosenfeld, "F. Scott Fitzgerald" in *Men Seen*, 1925; Maxwell Geismar, *The Last of the Provincials*, 1947; J. W. Aldridge, *After the Lost Generation*, 1951; John Berryman, "F. Scott Fitzgerald," *Kenyon Review*, VIII (1946), 103–112; Anon., "Power Without Glory," *London Times Literary Supplement*, XLIX (1950), p. 40; Henry D. Piper, "Fitzgerald's Cult of Disillusion," *American Quarterly*, III (1951), 69–80; Edwin Fussell, "The Stature of Scott Fitzgerald," *Kenyon Review*, XIII (1951), 530–534; William Barrett, "Fitzgerald and America," *Partisan Review*, XVIII (1951), 345–353; Tom Burnam, "The Eyes of Dr. Eckleburg: A Re-examination of *The Great Gatsby*," *College English*, XIV (1952), 7–12; Marius Bewley, "Scott Fitzgerald's Criticism of America," *Sewanee Review*, LXII (1954), 223–246; and R. W. Stallman, "Gatsby and the Hole in Time," *Modern Fiction Studies*, I (November, 1955), 2–16. See also Arthur Mizener, ed., *F. Scott Fitzgerald: A Collection of Critical Essays*, 1963; and Nancy Milford, *Zelda*, 1970.

The Crack-Up, edited by Edmund Wilson, 1945, contains autobiographical sketches, letters, and selections from Fitzgerald's notebooks. *The Disenchanted*, by Budd Schulberg, 1951, is a novel based on Fitzgerald's career and personality.

THE GREAT GATSBY

Type of work: Novel
Author: F. Scott Fitzgerald (1896–1940)
Time of plot: 1922
Locale: New York City and Long Island
First published: 1925

Jay Gatz changes his name to Gatsby and amasses great wealth by dubious means solely to please Daisy, a socialite. Wooed earlier by the penniless Gatsby, Daisy had rejected him for her social equal, Tom Buchanan. Yet no matter how high Gatsby rises, he is doomed, for the wealthy Buchanans are not worthy of Gatsby's sincerity and innocence. Though Gatsby plans to take the blame for a hit-and-run murder committed by Daisy, Tom Buchanan tells the victim's husband that Gatsby was driving, and the husband murders Gatsby. The Buchanans retreat into the irresponsibility their wealth allows them.

Principal Characters

Nick Carraway, the narrator. A young Midwesterner who was dissatisfied with his life at home, he was attracted to New York and now sells bonds there. He is the most honest character of the novel and because of this trait fails to become deeply fascinated by his rich friends on Long Island. He helps Daisy and Jay Gatsby to renew a love they had known before Daisy's marriage, and he is probably the only person in the novel to have any genuine affection for Gatsby.

Jay Gatsby, a fabulously rich racketeer whose connections outside of the law are only guessed at. He is the son of poor parents from the Middle West. He has changed his name from James Gatz and becomes obsessed with a need for making more and more money. Much of his time is spent in trying to impress, and become accepted by, other rich people. He gives lavish parties for people he knows nothing about and most of whom he never meets. He is genuinely in love with Daisy Buchanan and becomes a sympathetic character when he assumes the blame for her hit-and-run accident. At his death he has been deserted by everyone except his father and Nick.

Daisy Buchanan, Nick's second cousin. Unhappy in her marriage because of Tom Buchanan's deliberate unfaithfulness, she has the character of a "poor little rich girl." She renews an old love for Jay Gatsby and considers leaving her husband, but she is finally reconciled to him. She kills Tom's mistress in a hit-and-run accident after a quarrel in which she defends both men as Tom accuses Gatsby of trying to steal her from him; but, she allows Gatsby to take the blame for the accident and suffers no remorse when he is murdered by the woman's husband.

Tom Buchanan, Daisy's husband. The son of rich Midwestern parents, he reached the heights of his career as a college football player. Completely without taste, culture, or sensitivity, he carries on a rather sordid affair with Myrtle Wilson. He pretends to help George Wilson, her husband, but allows him to think that Gatsby was not only her murderer but also her lover.

Myrtle Wilson, Tom Buchanan's mistress. She is a fat, unpleasant woman who is so highly appreciative of the fact that her lover is a rich man that she will suffer almost any degradation for him. While she is with Tom, her pretense that she is rich and highly sophisticated becomes ludicrous.

George Wilson, Myrtle's husband, and a rather pathetic figure. He runs an auto repair shop and believes Tom Buchanan is really interested in helping him. Aware that his wife has a lover, he never suspects who he really is. His faith in Tom makes him believe what Buchanan says, which, in turn, causes him to murder

Gatsby and then commit suicide.

Jordan Baker, a friend of the Buchanans, a golfer. Daisy introduces Jordan to Nick and tries to throw them together, but when Nick realizes that she is a cheat who refuses to assume the elementary responsibility of the individual, he loses all interest in her.

Meyer Wolfshiem, a gambler and underworld associate of Gatsby.

Catherine, Myrtle Wilson's sister, who is obviously proud of Myrtle's rich connection and unconcerned with the immorality involved.

Mr. and Mrs. McKee, a photographer and his wife who try to use Nick and Tom to get a start among the rich people of Long Island.

Mr. Gatz, Jay Gatsby's father who, being unaware of the facts of Jay's life, thought his son had been a great man.

The Story

Young Nick Carraway decided to forsake the hardware business of his family in the Middle West in order to sell bonds in New York City. He took a small house in West Egg on Long Island and there became involved in the lives of his neighbors. At a dinner party at the home of Tom Buchanan he renewed his acquaintance with Tom and Tom's wife, Daisy, a distant cousin, and he met an attractive young woman, Jordan Baker. Almost at once he learned that Tom and Daisy were not happily married. It appeared that Daisy knew her husband was deliberately unfaithful.

Nick soon learned to despise the drive to the city through unkempt slums; particularly, he hated the ash heaps and the huge commercial signs. He was far more interested in the activities of his wealthy neighbors. Near his house lived Jay Gatsby, a mysterious man of great wealth. Gatsby entertained lavishly, but his past was unknown to his neighbors.

One day Tom Buchanan took Nick to call on his mistress, a dowdy, overplump, married woman named Myrtle Wilson, whose husband, George Wilson, operated a second-rate auto repair shop. Myrtle, Tom, and Nick went to the apartment Tom kept, and there the three were joined by Myrtle's sister Catherine and Mr. and Mrs. McKee. The party settled down to an afternoon of drinking, Nick unsuccessfully doing his best to get away.

A few days later Nick attended another party, one given by Gatsby for a large number of people famous in speak-easy society. Food and liquor were dispensed lavishly. Most of the guests had never seen their host before.

At the party Nick met Gatsby for the first time. Gatsby, in his early thirties, looked like a healthy young roughneck. He was offhand, casual, eager to entertain his guests as extravagantly as possible. Frequently he was called away by long-distance telephone calls. Some of the guests laughed and said that he was trying to impress them with his importance.

That summer Gatsby gave many parties. Nick went to all of them, enjoying each time the society of people from all walks of life who appeared to take advantage of Gatsby's bounty. From time to time Nick met Jordan Baker there and when he heard that she had cheated in an amateur gold match his interest in her grew.

Gatsby took Nick to lunch one day and introduced him to a man named Wolfshiem, who seemed to be Gatsby's business partner. Wolfshiem hinted at some dubious business deals that betrayed Gatsby's racketeering activities and Nick began to identify the sources of some of Gatsby's wealth.

Jordan Baker told Nick the strange story of Daisy's wedding. Before the bridal dinner Daisy, who seldom drank, became wildly intoxicated and kept reading a letter that she had just received and crying that she had changed her mind. However, after she had become sober she went through with her wedding to Tom without a murmur. Obviously the letter was from Jay Gatsby. At the time he was poor and unknown; Tom was rich and influential.

But Gatsby was still in love with Daisy, and he wanted Jordan and Nick to bring Daisy and him together again. It was arranged that Nick should invite Daisy to tea the same day he invited Gatsby. Gatsby awaited the invitation nervously.

On the eventful day it rained. Determined that Nick's house should be presentable, Gatsby sent a man to mow the wet grass; he also sent over flowers for decoration. The tea was a strained affair at first, both Gatsby and Daisy shy and awkward in their reunion. Afterward they went over to Gatsby's mansion, where he showed them his furniture, clothes, swimming pool, and gardens. Daisy promised to attend his next party.

When Daisy disapproved of his guests, Gatsby stopped entertaining. The house was shut up and the bar-crowd turned away.

Gatsby informed Nick of his origin. His true name was Gatz, and he had been born in the Middle West. His parents were poor. But when he was a boy he had become the protégé of a wealthy old gold miner and had accompanied him on his travels until the old man died. He had changed his name to Gatsby and was daydreaming of acquiring wealth and position. In the war he had distinguished himself. After the war he had returned penniless to the States, too poor to marry Daisy, whom he had met during the war. Later he became a partner in a drug business. He had been lucky and had accumulated money rapidly. He told Nick that he had acquired the money for his Long Island residence after three years of hard work.

The Buchanans gave a quiet party for Jordan, Gatsby, and Nick. The group drove into the city and took a room in a hotel. The day was hot and the guests uncomfortable. On the way, Tom, driving Gatsby's new yellow car, stopped at Wilson's garage. Wilson complained because Tom had not helped him in a projected car deal. He said he needed money because he was selling out and taking his wife, whom he knew to be unfaithful, away from the city.

At the hotel Tom accused Gatsby of trying to steal his wife and also of being dishonest. He seemed to regard Gatsby's low origin with more disfavor than his interest in Daisy. During the argument, Daisy sided with both men by turns.

On the ride back to the suburbs Gatsby drove his own car, accompanied by Daisy, who temporarily would not speak to her husband.

Following them, Nick and Jordan and Tom stopped to investigate an accident in front of Wilson's garage. They discovered an ambulance picking up the dead body of Myrtle Wilson, struck by a hit-and-run driver in a yellow car. They tried in vain to help Wilson and then went on to Tom's house, convinced that Gatsby had struck Myrtle Wilson.

Nick learned that night from Gatsby that Daisy had been driving when the woman was hit. However, Gatsby was willing to take the blame if the death should be traced to his car. He explained that a woman had rushed out as though she wanted to speak to someone in the yellow car and Daisy, an inexpert driver, had run her down and then collapsed. Gatsby had driven on.

In the meantime George Wilson, having traced the yellow car to Gatsby, appeared on the Gatsby estate. A few hours later both he and Gatsby were discovered dead. He had shot Gatsby and then killed himself.

Nick tried to make Gatsby's funeral respectable, but only one among all of Gatsby's former guests attended along with Gatsby's father, who thought his son had been a great man. None of Gatsby's racketeering associates appeared.

Shortly afterward Nick learned of Tom's part in Gatsby's death. Wilson had visited Tom and with the help of a revolver forced him to reveal the name of the owner of the hit-and-run car. Nick vowed that his friendship with Tom and Daisy was ended. He decided to return to his people in the Middle West.

Critical Evaluation

F. Scott Fitzgerald, the prophet of the jazz age, was born in St. Paul, Minnesota, to the daughter of a self-made Irish immigrant millionaire. His father was a ne'er-do-well salesman who had married above his social position. From his mother, Fitzgerald inherited the dream that was America—the promise that any young man could become anything he chose through hard work. From his father he inherited the propensity for failure. This antithesis pervaded his own life and most of his fiction. Educated in the East, Fitzgerald was overcome with the glamour of New York and Long Island. To him it was the "stuff of old romance," "the source of infinite possibilities."

His fiction focused primarily on the lives of the rich. With the family fortune depleted by his father, Fitzgerald found himself in his early twenties an army officer in love with a southern belle, Zelda Sayre, who was socially above him. She refused his first proposal of marriage because he was too poor. Fitzgerald was determined to have her. He wrote and published *This Side of Paradise* (1920), on the basis of which Zelda married him.

Their public life for the next ten years epitomized the dizzy spiral of the 1920's—wild parties, wild spending, and wild cars—and following the national pattern, they crashed just as spectacularly in the 1930's. Zelda went mad and was committed finally to a sanitarium. Fitzgerald became a functional alcoholic. From his pinnacle in the publishing field during the 1920's when his short stories commanded as much as $1500, he fell in the 1930's to writing luke-warm Hollywood scripts. He died in Hollywood in 1940, mostly forgotten and with most of his work out of print. Now back in academic vogue, Fitzgerald's place in American letters has been affirmed by a single novel—*The Great Gatsby*.

Fitzgerald once said, "America's great promise is that something's going to happen, but it never does. America is the moon that never rose." This indictment of the American Dream could well serve as an epigraph for *The Great Gatsby*. Jay Gatsby pursues his dream of romantic success without ever understanding that it has escaped him. He fails to understand that he cannot recapture the past (his fresh, new love for Daisy Buchanan) no matter how much money he makes, no matter how much wealth he displays.

The character of Gatsby was never intended by Fitzgerald to be a realistic portrayal; he is a romantic hero, always somewhat unreal, bogus and absurd. No matter the corrupt sources of his wealth such as bootlegging and gambling (and these are only hinted at) he stands for hope, for romantic belief—for innocence. He expects more from life than the other characters who are all more or less cynical. He is an eternal juvenile in a brutal and corrupt world.

To underscore the corruption of the Dream, Fitzgerald's characters all are finally seen as liars. Buchanan's mistress lies to her husband. Jordan Baker is a pathological liar who cheats in golf tournaments. Tom Buchanan's lie to his mistress Myrtle's husband results in the murder of Gatsby. Daisy, herself, is basically insincere; she lets Gatsby take the blame for her hit-and-run accident. Gatsby's whole life is a lie: he lies about his past and his present. He lies to himself. Nick Carraway, the Midwestern narrator, tells us that he is the only completely honest person he knows. However, he panders for Gatsby, and in the end he turns away from Tom Buchanan, unable to force the truth into the open. He knows the truth about Gatsby but is unable to tell the police. His affirmation of Gatsby at the end is complex; he envies Gatsby's romantic selflessness and innocence at the same time that he abhors his lack of self-knowledge.

The Great Gatsby incorporates a number of themes and motifs that unify the novel and contribute to its impact. The initiation theme governs the narrator Nick Carraway, who is a young man come East to make his fortune in stocks and bonds and who returns to the Midwest sadly disillusioned. The frontier theme is also present. Gatsby believes in the "green light," the ever-accessible future in which one can achieve what one has missed in the past. The final paragraphs of the novel state this important theme as well as it has ever been stated. Class issues are very well presented. Tom and Daisy seem accessible but when their position is threatened they close the doors, retreating into their wealth and carelessness, letting others like Gatsby pay the vicious price in hurt and suffering. The carelessness of the rich and their followers is seen in the recurring motif of the bad driver.

Automobile accidents are ubiquitous. At Gatsby's first party there is a smash-up with drunk drivers. Jordan Baker has a near accident after which Nick calls her "a rotten driver." Gatsby is stopped for speeding but is able to fix the ticket by showing the cop a card from the mayor of New York. Finally, Myrtle Wilson is killed by Daisy, driving Gatsby's car. Bad driving becomes a moral statement in the novel.

Settings in the novel are used very well by Fitzgerald, from the splendid mansions of Long Island through the wasteland of the valley of ashes presided over by the eyes of Dr. T. J. Eckleburg (where the Wilsons live) to the New York of the Plaza Hotel or Tom and Myrtle Wilson's apartment. In each case a variety of texture and social class is presented to the reader. Most important, however, is Fitzgerald's use of Nick as a narrator. Like Conrad before him—and from whom he learned his craft—Fitzgerald had a romantic sensibility which controlled fictional material best through the lens of a narrator. As with Marlow in Conrad's *Heart of Darkness,* Nick relates the story of an exceptional man who fails in his dream. He is both attracted and repelled by a forceful man who dares to lead a life he could not sustain. Like Marlow, he pays tribute to his hero who is also his alter-ego. Gatsby's tragedy is Nick's education. His return to the Midwest is a moral return to the safer, solider values of the heartland. Fitzgerald himself was unable to follow such a conservative path but he clearly felt that the American Dream should be pursued with less frantic, orgiastic, prideful convulsions of energy and spirit. It is a lesson we are still learning.

Bibliography

Bewley, Marcus. "Scott Fitzgerald's Criticism of America," in *Sewanee Review.* LXII (Spring, 1954), pp. 223–246.

Chase, Richard. The Great Gatsby: *The American Novel and Its Traditions.* New York: Doubleday, 1957, pp. 162–167. Reprinted in The Great Gatsby: *A Study.* Edited by Frederick J. Hoffman. New York: Scribner's, 1962, pp. 297–302.

Cowley, Malcolm. "The Romance of Money," in *Three Novels of F. Scott Fitzgerald*. Edited by Malcolm Cowley. New York: Scribner's, 1953, pp. ix–xx. Reprinted in *Fitzgerald's* The Great Gatsby: *The Novel, the Critics, the Background*. Edited by Henry Dan Piper. New York: Scribner's, 1970, pp. 133–140.

Cross, K.G.W. *F. Scott Fitzgerald*. New York: Grove, 1964, pp. 51–68.

Dyson, A.E. "*The Great Gatsby*: Thirty-six Years After," in *Modern Fiction Studies*. VII (Spring, 1961), pp. 37–48. Reprinted in *F. Scott Fitzgerald: A Collection of Critical Essays*. Edited by Arthur Mizener. Englewood Cliffs, N.J.: Prentice-Hall, 1963, pp. 112–124.

Eble, Kenneth. *F. Scott Fitzgerald*. New York: Twayne, 1977, pp. 86–107.

Foster, Richard. "The Way to Read *Gatsby*," in *Sense and Sensibility in Twentieth Century Writing*. Edited by Brom Weber. Carbondale: University of Southern Illinois Press, 1970, pp. 94–108.

Fussell, Edwin. "Fitzgerald's Brave New World," in *English Literary History*. XIX (December, 1952), pp. 291–306. Reprinted in The Great Gatsby: *A Study*. Edited by Frederick J. Hoffman. New York: Scribner's, 1962, pp. 244–262. Also reprinted in *F. Scott Fitzgerald: A Collection of Critical Essays*. Edited by Arthur Mizener. Englewood Cliffs, N.J.: Prentice-Hall, 1963, pp. 43–56.

Hanzo, Thomas A. "The Theme and Narrator of *The Great Gatsby*," in *Modern Fiction Studies*. II (Winter, 1956–1957), pp. 183–190. Reprinted in The Great Gatsby: *A Study*. Edited by Frederick J. Hoffman. New York: Scribner's 1962, pp. 286–296. Also reprinted in *Twentieth Century Interpretations of* The Great Gatsby. Edited by Ernest H. Lockridge. Englewood Cliffs, N.J.: Prentice-Hall, 1968, pp. 61–69.

Hoffman, Frederick J. "Introduction," in The Great Gatsby: *A Study*. Edited by Frederick J. Hoffman. New York: Scribner's, 1962, pp. 1–18.

Lahau, Richard D. *F. Scott Fitzgerald and the Craft of Fiction*. Carbondale: University of Southern Illinois Press, 1966, pp. 91–122.

Lockridge, Ernest H. "Introduction," in *Twentieth Century Interpretations of* The Great Gatsby. Edited by Ernest H. Lockridge. Englewood Cliffs, N.J.: Prentice-Hall, 1968, pp. 1–18.

Mencken, H.L. "*The Great Gatsby*," in *Baltimore Evening Sun* (May 2, 1925), p. 9. Reprinted in *Fitzgerald's* The Great Gatsby: *The Novel, the Critics, the Background*. Edited by Henry Dan Piper. New York: Scribner's, 1970, pp. 121–123.

Miller, James E., Jr. "Fitzgerald's *Gatsby*: The World as Ash Heap," in *The Twenties*. Edited by Warren French. DeLand, Fla.: Everett/Edwards, 1975, pp. 181–202.

————. *F. Scott Fitzgerald: His Art and His Technique.* New York: New York University Press, 1964, pp. 98–126. Reprinted in *Twentieth Century Interpretations of* The Great Gatsby. Edited by Ernest H. Lockridge. Englewood Cliffs, N.J.: Prentice-Hall, 1968, pp. 19–36.

Mizener, Arthur. *The Far Side of Paradise.* Boston: Houghton Mifflin, 1951, pp. 169–178. Reprinted in *Fitzgerald's* The Great Gatsby: *The Novel, the Critics, the Background.* Edited by Henry Dan Piper. New York: Scribner's, 1970, pp. 127–132.

Moseley, Edwin M. *F. Scott Fitzgerald: A Critical Essay.* Grand Rapids, Mich.: Eerdmans, 1967, pp. 22–35.

Perosa, Sergio. *The Art of F. Scott Fitzgerald.* Ann Arbor: University of Michigan Press, 1965, pp. 60–82.

Raleigh, John H. "F. Scott Fitzgerald's *The Great Gatsby*," in *University of Kansas City Review.* XXIV (Autumn, 1957), pp. 55–58. Reprinted in *F. Scott Fitzgerald: A Collection of Critical Essays.* Edited by Arthur Mizener. Englewood Cliffs, N.J.: Prentice-Hall, 1963, pp. 99–103. Also reprinted in *Fitzgerald's* The Great Gatsby: *The Novel, the Critics, the Background.* Edited by Henry Dan Piper. New York: Scribner's, 1970, pp. 141–144.

Samuels, Charles Thomas. "The Greatness of *Gatsby*," in *Massachusetts Review.* VII (Autumn, 1966), pp. 783–794. *Fitzgerald's* The Great Gatsby: *The Novel, the Critics, the Background.* Edited by Henry Dan Piper. New York: Scribner's, 1970, pp. 151–159.

Scrimgeour, Gary J. "Against *The Great Gatsby*," in *Criticism.* VIII (Winter, 1966), pp. 75–86. Reprinted in *Twentieth Century Interpretations of* The Great Gatsby. Edited by Ernest H. Lockridge. Englewood Cliffs, N.J.: Prentice-Hall, 1968, pp. 70–81.

Shain, Charles E. *F. Scott Fitzgerald.* Minneapolis: University of Minnesota Press, 1961, pp. 32–35.

Sklar, Robert. *F. Scott Fitzgerald: The Last Laocoön.* New York: Oxford University Press, 1967, pp. 135–196.

Stern, Milton R. *The Golden Moment: The Novels of F. Scott Fitzgerald.* Urbana: University of Illinois Press, 1970, pp. 161–288.

Trilling, Lionel. *F. Scott Fitzgerald: The Liberal Imagination.* New York: Viking, 1950, pp. 243–254. Reprinted in The Great Gatsby: *A Study.* Edited by Frederick J. Hoffman. New York: Schribner's, 1962, pp. 232–243. Also reprinted in *F. Scott Fitzgerald: A Collection of Critical Essays.* Edited by Arthur Mizener. Englewood Cliffs, N.J.: Prentice-Hall, 1963, pp. 11–19.

THE LAST TYCOON

Type of work: Novel
Author: F. Scott Fitzgerald (1896–1940)
Time of plot: The 1930's
Locale: Hollywood
First published: 1941

This unfinished novel is perhaps the most highly regarded fragment in American literature, for in it, Fitzgerald's prose is said to have achieved its greatest power, flexibility, and economy. The heart of the novel is the love affair of Hollywood producer Monroe Stahr with the girl Kathleen, who resembles his dead wife.

Principal Characters

Monroe Stahr, a brilliant, young film producer, as much interested in the artistic value of motion pictures as in making money. Having lost his wife whom he had loved deeply, he now courts death through overwork. He is extremely interested in the welfare of his employees, although he is not always appreciated by them. His short but passionate affair with Kathleen seems to be at the center of this unfinished novel.

Kathleen Moore, Stahr's mistress, who reminds him of his dead wife. She later marries another man out of a sense of obligation but continues her affair with Stahr.

Pat Brady, Stahr's partner. Interested only in making money, Brady is a cold and calculating man. He often opposes Stahr's policies although he understands almost nothing of the technical end of the industry.

Cecilia Brady, Pat's daughter and the narrator of the story. She falls in love with Stahr but he pays no attention to her. After an affair with another man she suffers a complete breakdown and relates the story from a tuberculosis sanitarium.

Wylie Whyte, a screenwriter who tries to marry Cecilia and thus gain her father's influence.

Pete Zavras, a cameraman whom Stahr helps to find work. He later helps Stahr when Kathleen's husband finds out she is having an affair.

Schwartz, a ruined producer who commits suicide.

The Story

Cecilia Brady was flying to California for a summer vacation from college. On the plane she met Wylie White, an alcoholic screenwriter, and Schwartz, a ruined producer. Monroe Stahr, the partner of Cecilia's father, was also aboard, though traveling as Mr. Smith. When the plane was grounded at Nashville, Schwartz sent a note to Stahr, warning him about Pat Brady, Cecilia's father. When the plane took off again, Schwartz stayed behind and committed suicide.

Stahr had been the boy wonder of the film industry. He had been in charge of the studio in his twenties, almost dead from overwork at thirty-five. Indeed, he was half in love with death for the sake of his dead wife, Minna Davis, a great star with whom he had been deeply in love. Since her death he had increased his work load, often remaining in his office around the clock. In contrast to Stahr's highly developed sense of responsibility, Brady was mean and selfish. Lacking taste and understanding little of the technical end of the industry, Brady had acquired his share of the studio through luck and had retained it through shrewdness.

One night, while Cecilia was visiting the studio, there was an earthquake. Stahr, working with his trouble-shooter, Robinson, to clear away the mess, saw a sightseer perched on top of a floating idol. The girl reminded him of his dead wife, and he tried to discover her identity. That night Cecilia also fell in love with Stahr, but she felt that her attachment was hopeless.

A self-made, paternalistic employer, Stahr personally managed almost every detail at the studio, from picking the stories to passing on the rushes. Though not an educated man, he had raised the artistic level of the movies and did not hesitate to make good pictures that would lose money. As a result he had incurred the distrust of the stockholders, exploiters who saw the movies only as a business. Their distrust, however, was mixed with a genuine respect for the producer's many abilities. In addition to the opposition of the stockholders, Stahr was concerned because Communists were trying to organize the writers; he worked closely with his writers and wanted them to trust him. Wylie White, in particular, enjoyed his favor, although White resented him. At this time White hoped to marry Cecilia for the sake of her father's influence. Typical of Stahr's interest in his employees was his investigation of the attempted suicide of a cameraman, Pete Zavras. Stahr learned that Zavras had been unable to find work because of a rumor that he was going blind. Stahr was able to scotch the rumor by providing Zavras with a statement from an oculist.

By this time Stahr had succeeded in locating the girl who resembled his wife. She was Kathleen Moore. Though she was at first reluctant to meet him, they later had a brief, passionate affair. Stahr learned that she had been the mistress of a deposed monarch who had undergone a personality deterioration and that now she was about to marry an American who had rescued her from that situation. Stahr realized that marriage to Kathleen could give him the will to go on living. While he hesitated, her fiancé arrived ahead of schedule, and she went through with the marriage from a sense of obligation.

Cecilia, knowing nothing of these matters, was still desperately hoping to attract Stahr, her pull toward him increased by a break with her father after she had discovered him with his nude secretary. At Stahr's request she arranged a meeting with a Communist organizer. Then Stahr got drunk and tried to beat him up.

At this point the manuscript ends, but the rest of the story may be pieced together from the author's notes. Because the studio had been in financial difficulties, Brady had tried to push through a wage cut. Stahr, opposing this plan, had gone east to convince the other stockholders to postpone the wage slash. Brady cut the salaries and betrayed the writers while Stahr was sick in Washington. Although he broke with Brady after that, Stahr agreed to go along with Brady's plan for a company union, chiefly because Stahr felt personally responsible for the welfare of his employees. Wylie White had also turned on Stahr.

In the meantime Kathleen and Stahr resumed their relationship. When Brady tried to blackmail Stahr, the producer threatened him with some information about the death of Brady's wife. At one time Fitzgerald had considered having Brady persuade Robinson to undertake Stahr's murder; however, Fitzgerald rejected this idea in favor of having Brady inform Kathleen's husband, a movie technician involved with the union organizers, of Kathleen's affair with Stahr. An alienation-of-affection suit resulted from that, but Stahr was somehow saved by Zavras, the cameraman.

Stahr became alienated from Kathleen and was no longer able to dominate his associates at the studio. Nevertheless, he continued to oppose Brady. Finally, Stahr felt that he had to eliminate Brady before Brady had him killed. After hiring gangsters to murder Brady, Stahr flew east to provide himself with an alibi; but he changed his mind on the plane and decided to call off the killers at the next airport. The plane crashed before he could carry out his intention.

Fitzgerald was uncertain about including an episode in which the plane's wreckage was plundered by three children who discovered it, the idea being that each child's personality was reflected by the items he stole. Stahr's funeral would have been a powerful, detailed, ironic arraignment of Hollywood sham. It would have included the incident of a has-been cowboy actor who was invited to be a pallbearer by mistake and consequently enjoyed a return of good fortune.

Cecilia later had an affair, probably with Wylie White, and then suffered a complete breakdown. At the end of the novel the reader was to learn that she was telling the story while a patient in a tuberculosis sanitarium.

Critical Evaluation

After the overwhelming success of his autobiographical novel, *This Side of Paradise* (1920), and *Tender Is the Night* (1934), describing the precipitation of what he later termed "emotional bankruptcy," F. Scott Fitzgerald settled in Hollywod. There, he died in 1941 while pursuing a fruitless career as a screenwriter. *The Last Tycoon,* Fitzgerald's last and unfinished novel, is a sobering picture of society written by a man who had experienced both ends of prosperity's spectrum.

Although Fitzgerald intended this novel to be ". . . an escape into a lavish, romantic past that perhaps will not come again in our time," the fragmentary novel has at least two qualities that transcend its nostalgia: the manner in which the narrative is handled and the characters' views of society. Cecilia Brady functions as both narrator and character and is able to piece the story together by collecting fragments from people involved in various incidents. However, by means of a retrospective device revealed in the novel's projected outline, she is shown to be as limited in her view of American society as anyone else in the novel connected with the motion picture industry. It is this limited viewpoint that gives unity between plot and theme to the novel as well as credibility to the characters.

Fitzgerald's decision to use Cecilia Brady instead of a detached narrator allows him to reveal only those elements of reality that he deems thematically essential. Reality is filtered through life in Hollywood; Hollywood, in turn, is revealed only in relation to Stahr; and Cecilia reveals only the aspects of Stahr's life that she finds interesting. The narrator functions as a personification of the illnesses of Hollywood life; the illnesses physically manifest themselves in the form of her tuberculosis.

The major significance of this unfinished novel is the evidence in its stylistic daring and social criticism that Fitzgerald was far from through as a novelist. The moral subtleties of Stahr's characterization recall Fitzgerald's greatest achievement: *The Great Gatsby*. Like the hero of that novel, Stahr is involved with the underworld in order to preserve a dream. The difference between Gatsby's illusion of Daisy and Stahr's professional integrity is the measure of Fitzgerald's own hardwon maturity as a writer and man.

Bibliography

Allen, Joan M. *Candles and Carnival Lights: The Catholic Sensibility of F. Scott Fitzgerald.* New York: New York University Press, 1978, pp. 137–141.

Benét, Stephen Vincent. *"The Last Tycoon,"* in *F. Scott Fitzgerald: The Man and His Work.* Edited by Alfred Kazin. Cleveland: World, 1951, pp. 130–132.

Bruccoli, Matthew. *The Last of the Novelists: F. Scott Fitzgerald and* The Last Tycoon. Carbondale: Southern Illinois University Press, 1977.

Cross, K.G.W. *F. Scott Fitzgerald.* New York: Grove, 1964, pp. 97–110.

Dos Passos, John. "A Note on Fitzgerald," in *The Crack Up* by F. Scott Fitzgerald. Edited by Edmund Wilson. Norfolk, Conn.: New Directions, 1945, pp. 338–343. Reprinted in *The Idea of an American Novel.* Edited by Louis D. Rubin, Jr. and John Rees Moore. New York: Thomas Y. Crowell, 1961, pp. 325–330.

Eble, Kenneth. *F. Scott Fitzgerald.* New York: Twayne, 1963, pp. 148–151.

Fahey, William A. *F. Scott Fitzgerald and the American Dream.* New York: Thomas Y. Crowell, 1973, pp. 119–134.

Gross, Barry. "Scott Fitzgerald's *The Last Tycoon*: The Great American Novel?" in *Arizona Quarterly.* XXVI (Autumn, 1970), pp. 197–216.

Hart, John E. "Fitzgerald's *The Last Tycoon*: A Search for Identity," in *Modern Fiction Studies.* VII (Spring, 1961), pp. 63–70.

Hindus, Milton. *F. Scott Fitzgerald: Introduction and Interpretation.* New York: Barnes & Noble, 1968, pp. 70–86.

Lehan, Richard D. *F. Scott Fitzgerald and the Craft of Fiction.* Carbondale: University of Southern Illinois Press, 1968, pp. 153–163.

Margolies, Alan. "The Dramatic Novel, *The Great Gatsby*, and *The Last Tycoon*," in *Fitzgerald/Hemingway Annual 1971*, pp. 159–172.

Maurer, Robert E. "F. Scott Fitzgerald's Unfinished Novel, *The Last Tycoon*," in *Bucknell University Studies.* III (May, 1952), pp. 139–156.

Miller, James E., Jr. *F. Scott Fitzgerald: His Art and His Technique.* New York: New York University Press, 1964, pp. 148–158.

Millgate, Michael. *American Social Fiction.* New York: Barnes & Noble, 1965, pp. 120–127, 156–159, 162–165. Reprinted in *F. Scott Fitzgerald: A Collection of Criticism.* Edited by Kenneth Eble. New York: McGraw-Hill, 1973, pp. 127–134.

Mizener, Arthur. *The Far Side of Paradise.* Boston: Houghton Mifflin, 1951, pp. 291–297.

Moseley, Edwin M. *F. Scott Fitzgerald: A Critical Essay.* Grand Rapids, Mich.: Eerdmans, 1967, pp. 42–44.

Perosa, Sergio. *The Art of F. Scott Fitzgerald.* Ann Arbor: University of Michigan Press, 1965, pp. 152–178.

Piper, Henry Dan. *F. Scott Fitzgerald: A Critical Portrait.* New York: Holt, Rinehart and Winston, 1965, pp. 258–286.

Rodda, Peter. "*The Last Tycoon*," in *English Studies in Africa.* XIV (March, 1971), pp. 49–71.

Shain, Charles E. *F. Scott Fitzgerald.* Minneapolis: University of Minnesota Press, 1961, pp. 44–45.

Sklar, Robert. *F. Scott Fitzgerald: The Last Laocoön.* New York: Oxford University Press, 1967, pp. 329–341.

Wilson, Edmund. "Foreword," in *The Last Tycoon.* New York: Scribner's, 1941, pp. ix–xi. Reprinted in *Classics and Commercials.* New York: Farrar, Straus, 1950, pp. 50–51.

TENDER IS THE NIGHT

Type of work: Novel
Author: F. Scott Fitzgerald (1896–1940)
Time of plot: The 1920's
Locale: Europe
First published: 1934

This important psychological novel is also a roman à clef *in which a number of characters have been identified with real people. Fitzgerald describes the disintegrating social world of mostly affluent Americans wandering from one diversion to another in Europe and the United States.*

Principal Characters

Dick Diver, a brilliant young psychiatrist who inspires confidence in everyone. As a young man he met and married a patient of his and devoted most of his time during the next several years to helping her regain a certain normality. But in the process of helping his wife he loses his own self-respect, alienates most of his friends, and drowns his brilliance in alcohol. His professional position deteriorates to that of a general practitioner in successively smaller towns across the United States.

Nicole Warren Diver, Dick's wife, a fabulously rich American. As a young girl she had an incestuous relationship with her father and subsequently suffered a mental breakdown. She marries Dick while still a patient and is content to let him guide her in all things for several years. When he begins to drink heavily and make scenes in public, she tries to stop him; in doing so she begins to gain some moral strength of her own. In a short time she no longer needs Dick, has a brief affair, and divorces Dick to marry her lover. Apparently aware of her part in Dick's downfall, she continues to be somewhat concerned for him.

Rosemary Hoyt, a beautiful young American movie actress. Having fallen in love with Dick, who is several years her senior, on their first meeting, she later has a brief affair with him. When she finally recognizes the decline in him, she is powerless to do anything about it. Although she retains her devotion to both of the Divers, she has never really grown up herself and is incapable of acting positively without direction.

Tommy Barban, a war hero and professional soldier. Typically cold and unfeeling where most people are concerned, he spends much of his time fighting in various wars. He eventually becomes Nicole's lover and then her second husband.

Beth Evan (Baby) Warren, Nicole's older sister. Knowing nothing of the real nature of Nicole's illness, she feels that the family should buy a doctor to marry and care for her. She never fully approves of Dick because her snobbery makes her feel superior to him. After a succession of quiet, well-mannered affairs, she remains without roots or direction in her life.

Mrs. Elsie Speers, Rosemary Hoyt's

mother. She devotes her life to making Rosemary a successful actress. She also tries to make her an individual but fails to achieve this goal.

Abe North, an unambitious musician. An early friend of the Divers, he goes consistently downhill and is finally murdered.

Mary North, Abe's wife. She is an ineffectual person while married to Abe; later she makes a more advantageous marriage and fancies herself one of the queens of the international set.

Collis Clay, a young American friend of Rosemary. Fresh from Yale, he is now studying architecture in Europe and despairs of ever having to go back to Georgia to take over the family business.

Franz Gregorovious, a Swiss psychiatrist who becomes Dick Diver's partner in a clinic they establish with Nicole's money.

Kaethe, his wife, a tactless woman who is jealous of Americans and their money.

Gausse, the proprietor of a small hotel on the Riviera where the Divers and their friends often spend their summers.

Mr. and Mrs. McKisco, an American novelist and his wife who, after achieving financial success, lose their sense of inferiority and gain the superiority and snobbishness typical of the moneyed Americans in the Diver set.

Lady Caroline Sibly-Biers, an English friend of Mary North after her second marriage. She typifies the overbearing attitude of her class.

The Story

Rosemary Hoyt was just eighteen, dewy fresh and giving promise of beautiful maturity. In spite of her youth, she was already a famous actress, and her movie, *Daddy's Girl*, was all the rage. She had come to the south of France with her mother for a rest. Rosemary needed relaxation, for she had been very ill after diving repeatedly into a Venetian canal during the shooting of her picture.

At the beach she met Dick Diver, and suddenly she realized that she was in love. After she became well acquainted with the Divers, she liked Diver's wife Nicole, too. Nicole was strikingly beautiful and her two children complemented her nicely. Rosemary's mother also approved of Dick. When Rosemary attended one of the Divers' famous parties, she told Dick outright that she loved him, but he made light of her declaration.

During the party a Mrs. McKisco saw Nicole behaving hysterically in the bathroom, and on the way home she tried to tell about it. Tommy Barban, a war hero, made her keep silence. Resenting Tommy's interference, Mr. McKisco provoked a quarrel with him. The quarrel ended in a duel in which several shots were exchanged but no one was hurt. Rosemary was greatly moved by the occurrence.

Rosemary traveled to Paris with the Divers and went on a round of parties and tours with them. Often she made advances to Dick. He refused, apathetically, until one day a young college boy told of an escapade in which Rosemary had been involved, and then Dick began to desire the young girl. Although their brief love affair was confined to furtive kisses in hallways, Nicole became suspicious.

Abe North, a brawling composer, offended two Negroes and involved a third.

While Dick was in Rosemary's hotel room, Abe brought one of the Negroes to ask Dick's help in straightening up the mess. When Dick took Abe to his own room, the Negro stayed in the corridor. The two other Negroes killed him and laid the body on Rosemary's bed. When the body was found, Dick carried it into the hall and took Rosemary's spread into his bathtub to wash it out. Seeing the bloody spread, Nicole broke down and in an attack of hysteria accused Dick of many infidelities. Her breakdown was like the one Mrs. McKisco had previously seen in the bathroom at the party.

Some years before Dick had been doing research in advanced psychology in Zurich. One day in the clinic he had met a pathetic patient, beautiful young Nicole Warren. Attracted to her professionally at first, he later learned the cause of her long residence in the clinic.

Nicole came from a wealthy Chicago family. When she was eleven her mother died, and her father became very close to her. After an incestuous relationship with him, she suffered a breakdown. Her father, too cowardly to kill himself as he had planned, had put her in the clinic at Zurich. For many reasons Dick became Nicole's tower of strength; with him she was almost normal. Finally, motivated by pity and love, Dick married her. For a time he was able to keep her from periodic schizophrenic attacks and the marriage seemed to be a success, aided by the fact that Nicole's family was rich, so rich that Nicole's older sister was able to buy Dick a partnership in the clinic where Dick had first met Nicole.

For some time after the episode involving Rosemary, Nicole was quite calm, but too withdrawn. Then a neurotic woman wrote her a letter accusing Dick of misdeeds with his women patients. The letter was the working of a diseased mind, but Nicole believed what the writer said and had another relapse. She left her family at a country fair and became hysterical while riding on the ferris wheel.

At one time Dick had shown great promise as a writer and as a psychologist. His books had become standard and among his colleagues he was accounted a genius. It seemed, however, that after Nicole's hysterical fit on the ferris wheel he could do little more real work. For one thing, Nicole was growing wealthier all the time; her husband did not have to work. At thirty-eight, he was still a handsome and engaging man, but he began to drink heavily.

On several occasions Nicole was shamed by her husband's drunken behavior. She did her best to make him stop, and in so doing she began to gain a little moral strength of her own. For the first time since the long stay at the clinic she gradually came to have an independent life outside of Dick's influence.

Dissatisfied with the life he was leading, Dick decided to go away by himself for a while. He ran into Tommy Barban, still a reckless, strong, professional soldier. Tommy had just had a romantic escape from Russia. While still absent from his wife, Dick received word that his father had died.

Going back to America was for him a nostalgic experience. His father had been a gentle clergyman, living a narrow life; but his life had had roots, and he was buried among his ancestors. Dick had been away so long, had lived for so many years a footless, unfettered life, that he almost determined to remain in America.

On the way back to meet his family Dick stopped in Naples. In his hotel he met Rosemary again. She was making another picture, but she managed to find time to see him. Not so innocent now, she proved an easy conquest. Dick also met Nicole's older sister in Naples.

One night Dick drank far too much and became embroiled with a chiseling taxi driver. When he refused to pay an exorbitant fee, a fight broke out and Dick was arrested. The police captain unfairly upheld the taxi driver. Blind with rage, Dick struck a policeman and in return was severely beaten by the Fascist carabinieri. Thinking his eye had been gouged out, Dick got word to Nicole's sister, who brought all her influence to bear upon the consul to have her brother-in-law released.

Back in Zurich, Dick was busy for a time at the clinic. On a professional visit to Lausanne, he learned to his surprise that Nicole's father was there, very near death. When the dying man expressed a wish to see his daughter again, Dick sent for Nicole. Strangely enough, the weakened father still could not face his daughter. In a despairing frenzy he escaped from the hospital and disappeared.

Dick continued to go downhill. He always drank too much. A patient, objecting to the liquor on his breath, created a scene. At last Dick was forced to surrender his partnership in the clinic.

With no job, Dick wandered about restlessly. He and his wife, he realized, had less and less in common. At last, after Dick had disgraced his family many times in drunken scenes, Nicole began to welcome the attentions of Tommy Barban. She confidently looked forward to an independent life with Tommy. She no longer needed Dick.

After the divorce Dick moved to America. Nicole heard of him occasionally. He moved several times to successively smaller towns, an unsuccessful general practitioner.

Critical Evaluation

In all his literary work, F. Scott Fitzgerald proves to be a retrospective oracle. He describes an age of individuals who came on the scene and burned themselves out even before they were able to conceptualize themselves. His first published novel, *This Side of Paradise* (1920) is autobiographical and describes the early "Jazz Age" with its vague values of money, beauty, and a distorted sense of social propriety. His masterpiece, *The Great Gatsby,* came in 1925, and *Tender Is the Night* (1934) fictionalizes the personal and social disintegration that followed the success which *The Great Gatsby* brought Fitzgerald.

In addition to the glamor, the excitement, the frenetic pursuit of the good life between two world wars described in *Tender Is the Night,* the novel also contains a masterful attempt at thematic telescoping. The character of Dick Diver functions in a triple capacity: he is, on the largest scale, a contemporary American equivalent of the tragic hero; also, he signifies the complex disintegration of the American during this precarious point in time; and, by the close of the novel, the reader's attention is ultimately focused on Diver as a fictional character.

In many ways, Diver's fall follows Aristotle's formula for classical tragedy: he is an isolated hero upon whom an entire community of individuals depends for necessary form to their lives; he has a tragic flaw, since he is told by a classmate, "That's going to be your trouble—judgment about yourself . . . ," that is, he lacks perspective and introspection; he is a representative individual in that he is a psychiatrist expected to understand human motivation; he is at the mercy of fate, since the precipitating element, Nicole's case, "drifted into his hands"; and, his fall is monumental, from an elevated position in life into failure and anonymity. But most significant of all, Diver has a true sense of his own tragic importance; he realizes that he is losing his grip on situations, and, even though he recognizes some of the possible consequences of his actions, he is not equipped psychologically to combat them.

However, Dick Diver is not the strictly tragic figure prescribed in *The Poetics*. Rather, he is at most the sort of tragic hero that America would allow in the 1920's, and it is in this capacity that Diver serves to describe the gradual disintegration of the American character. Dick is not simply symbolic of an American; his character is instead individualized to represent what an American with his exemplary vulnerabilities could become in a special set of circumstances. Diver and his companions create their own mystique to avoid the realities of a world thrown into, and later extracting itself from, war. Their frenetic rites and the aura in which the compatriots hide ultimately form the confusion that grows larger than Diver, unleashing itself and swallowing him. For, Diver and the American character at this time are incomplete; each is detrimentally eclectic and at the mercy of the props, such as music, money, and material possessions, upon which it depends for support. Incompleteness nourishes Diver's paternalistic assimilation of portions of the personalities that surround him and depend on him. But his need to be needed causes him to assimilate weaknesses more often than strengths; and the organic process is abortive. For the American character is a limited one, a possessive one, and there is a sense of something existing beyond Diver's intellectual and emotional reach that could have proved to be his salvation. Fitzgerald emphasizes the eclectic and incomplete nature of the American during this era by interweaving elements of the romantic, the realistic, and the didactic when describing actions and motivations of his characters. The result presents a severely realistic emotional conflict that sporadically explodes several characters, including Dick Diver, into psychological chaos.

Finally, Diver functions most specifically as the pivotal character of the plot itself. Given the demands of a novel of such scope, Fitzgerald relays Diver's decline quite convincingly. He succeeds by providing the reader subliminally with the correct formula for observing Diver's actions and their consequences. Within the first three chapters of the novel, the reader is taught, through Nicole's exemplary case, to appreciate the importance of psychological analysis and to isolate the "precipitating factor" in a character's development, and then to consider that factor's influence in subsequent actions. The reader is thereby equipped to transfer these premises to his observations of Diver. Throughout the duration of the novel the reader realizes that Dick Diver is driven by a need to be needed; and it is this aspect of his personality that leads him increasingly into circumstances that involve him directly, causing him almost voluntarily to allow his energy to be sapped from him.

Tender Is the Night is above all a psychological novel that is more successful than most novels of its type. The device upon which the success of the novel depends is Fitzgerald's handling of time. Here, time serves both a horizontal and a vertical purpose. Horizontally, time is chronological, for chronological observation is an advantage the reader has—that Diver does not have—throughout the duration of the novel (this fact was not so in earlier drafts of the novel). The reader knows that Diver grows older; knows that Rosemary matures and finds other interests; knows that Nicole eventually recovers from her illness. But these are circumstances of which Diver is ignorant. For him, time is merely a psychological abstraction; only major events determine whether or not one is in stasis. Yet time also functions vertically, making the notion of thematic telescoping possible. Diver is not cognizant of the passing of time until his plunge is in its advanced stages. So as Diver's gradual acknowledging of time and of the vast gap between his "heroic period" and his encroaching anonymity becomes increasingly important, one's awareness of Diver's thematic function passes from the purely tragic figure, through the import of the national character, and, toward the close of the novel, rests ultimately on the individual Dick Diver and his acceptance of his situation.

Bibliography

Cross, K.G.W.   *F. Scott Fitzgerald.* New York: Grove, 1964, pp. 78–90.

Doherty, William E.   *"Tender Is the Night* and 'Ode to a Nightingale,' " in *Explorations of Literature.* Edited by Rima Drell Reck. Baton Rouge: Louisiana State University Press, 1966, pp. 100–114. Reprinted in Tender Is the Night: *Essays in Criticism.* Edited by Marvin J. LaHood. Bloomington: Indiana University Press, 1969, pp. 190–206. Also reprinted in *F. Scott Fitzgerald: A Collection of Criticism.* Edited by Kenneth Eble. New York: McGraw-Hill, 1973, pp. 112–126.

Eble, Kenneth. *F. Scott Fitzgerald.* New York: Twayne, 1977, pp. 132–140.

Ellis, James. "Fitzgerald's Fragmented Hero: Dick Diver," in *University Review.* XXXII (October, 1965), pp. 43–49. Reprinted in Tender Is the Night: *Essays in Criticism.* Edited by Marvin J. LaHood. Bloomington: Indiana University Press, 1969, pp. 127–137.

Fahey, William A. *F. Scott Fitzgerald and the American Dream.* New York: Thomas Y. Crowell, 1973, pp. 94–114.

Greiff, Louis K. "Perfect Marriage in *Tender Is the Night*: A Study in the Progress of a Symbol," in *Fitzgerald/Hemingway Annual 1974*, pp. 63–73.

Hall, William F. "Dialogue and Theme in *Tender Is the Night*," in *Modern Language Notes.* LXXVI (November, 1961), pp. 616–622. Reprinted in Tender Is the Night: *Essays in Criticism.* Edited by Marvin J. LaHood. Bloomington: Indiana University Press, 1969, pp. 144–150.

Hindus, Milton. *F. Scott Fitzgerald: An Introduction and Interpretation.* New York: Barnes & Noble, 1968, pp. 50–69.

Kinaham, Frank. "Focus on F. Scott Fitzgerald's *Tender Is the Night*," in *American Dreams, American Nightmares.* Edited by David Madden. Carbondale: University of Southern Illinois Press, 1970, pp. 115–128.

Kreuter, Kent and Gretchen Kreuter. "The Moralism of the Later Fitzgerald," in *Modern Fiction Studies.* VII (Spring, 1961), pp. 71–81. Reprinted in Tender Is the Night: *Essays in Criticism.* Edited by Marvin J. LaHood. Bloomington: Indiana University Press, 1969, pp. 48–60.

Kuehl, John. "Scott Fitzgerald: Romantic and Realist," in *Texas Studies in Literature and Language.* I (Autumn, 1959), pp. 412–426. Reprinted in Tender Is the Night: *Essays in Criticism.* Edited by Marvin J. LaHood. Bloomington: Indiana University Press, 1969, pp. 1–19.

LaHood, Marvin J. "Sensuality and Asceticism in *Tender Is the Night*," in Tender Is the Night: *Essays in Criticism.* Edited by Marvin J. LaHood. Bloomington: Indiana University Press, 1969, pp. 151–155.

Lehan, Richard D. *F. Scott Fitzgerald and the Craft of Fiction.* Carbondale: University of Southern Illinois Press, 1966, pp. 123–148. Reprinted in Tender Is the Night: *Essays in Criticism.* Edited by Marvin J. LaHood. Bloomington: Indiana University Press, 1969, pp. 61–85.

Miller, James E., Jr. *F. Scott Fitzgerald: His Art and His Technique.* New York: New York University Press, 1964, pp. 132–148. Reprinted in Tender Is the Night: *Essays in Criticism.* Edited by Marvin J. LaHood. Bloomington: Indiana University Press, 1969, pp. 86–101.

Mizener, Arthur. *Twelve Great American Novels.* New York: New American Library, 1967, pp. 104–119. Reprinted in Tender Is the Night: *Essays in Criticism.* Edited by Marvin J. LaHood. Bloomington: Indiana University Press, 1969, pp. 102–116.

Moseley, Edwin M.   *F. Scott Fitzgerald: A Critical Essay.* Grand Rapids, Mich.: Eerdmans, 1967, pp. 36–41.

Perosa, Sergio.   *The Art of F. Scott Fitzgerald.* Ann Arbor: University of Michigan Press, 1965, pp. 102–130.

Piper, Henry Dan.   *F. Scott Fitzgerald: A Critical Portrait.* New York: Holt, Rinehart and Winston, 1965, pp. 205–228.

Shain, Charles E.   *F. Scott Fitzgerald.* Minneapolis: University of Minnesota Press, 1961, pp. 38–42.

Sklar, Robert.   *F. Scott Fitzgerald: The Last Laocoön.* New York: Oxford University Press, 1967, pp. 249–292.

Stanton, Robert.   " 'Daddy's Girl': Symbol and Theme in *Tender Is the Night,*" in *Modern Fiction Studies.* IV (June, 1958), pp. 136–142. Reprinted in Tender Is the Night: *Essays in Criticism.* Edited by Marvin J. LaHood. Bloomington: Indiana University Press, 1969, pp. 156–164.

Steinberg, Abraham H.   "Fitzgerald's Portrait of a Psychiatrist," in *University of Kansas City Review.* XXI (March, 1955), pp. 219–222.

Stern, Milton R.   *The Golden Moment: The Novels of F. Scott Fitzgerald.* Urbana: University of Illinois Press, 1970, pp. 289–462.

Trachtenberg, Alan.   "The Journey Back: Myth and History in *Tender Is the Night,*" in *Experience in the Novel.* Edited by Roy Harvey Pearce. New York: Columbia University Press, 1968, pp. 133–162.

White, Eugene.   "The 'Intricate Destiny' of Dick Diver," in *Modern Fiction Studies.* VII (Spring, 1961), pp. 55–62. Reprinted in Tender Is the Night: *Essays in Criticism.* Edited by Marvin J. LaHood. Bloomington: Indiana University Press, 1969, pp. 117–126.

ELLEN GLASGOW

Born: Richmond, Virginia (April 22, 1874)
Died: Richmond (November 20, 1945)

Principal Works

NOVELS: *The Voice of the People,* 1900; *The Battle-Ground,* 1902; *The Deliverance,* 1904; *The Wheel of Life,* 1906; *The Ancient Law,* 1908; *The Romance of a Plain Man,* 1909; *The Miller of Old Church,* 1911; *Virginia,* 1913; *Life and Gabriella,* 1916; *The Builders,* 1919; *One Man in His Time,* 1922; *Barren Ground,* 1925; *The Romantic Comedians,* 1926; *They Stooped to Folly,* 1929; *The Sheltered Life,* 1932; *Vein of Iron,* 1935; *In This Our Life,* 1941.

SHORT STORIES: *The Shadowy Third and Other Stories,* 1923.

POEMS: *The Freeman and Other Poems,* 1902.

ESSAYS: *A Certain Measure,* 1943.

AUTOBIOGRAPHY: *The Woman Within,* 1954.

By birth and tradition Ellen Glasgow was as deeply involved as John Esten Cooke or Thomas Nelson Page in the historical situation and society of her region, but from the beginning her path cut straight across the elegiac romanticism of the plantation school of fiction. That literature, which came into being partly to redeem the pride of a defeated people, served its purpose for the age in which it was written, and its nostalgic recapture of the past held a certain dignity and grace. Too often, however, it was true to ideals which were in turn false to practice in human conduct. As an apprentice novelist, Ellen Glasgow was forced to look elsewhere for the lessons of experience.

Born in Richmond, Virginia, on April 22, 1874, Ellen (Anderson Gholson) Glasgow grew up in a society which had emerged from the Civil War with its principles, if not its property, almost intact. Her mother came from an aristocratic family of the Tidewater; her father, descended from Scotch-Irish pioneers who had settled west of the Blue Ridge, was the manager of an ironworks which had manufactured cannon for the Confederacy. Perhaps it was her good fortune that as a child she was too delicate for formal education. Her real teachers—John Stuart Mill, Hume, Voltaire, Plato, Darwin, Huxley, Adam Smith—she found in the books in her father's library; no university in the South could have provided a more liberal education at the time. Although the University of Virginia did not admit women, she read for, and passed the honors examination in political economy. These studies prepared her for lifelong revolt against an apathy of war memories and a code of evasive idealism whose only meaning lay in a backward look toward glory. Although writers of an earlier generation spoke eloquently for the tradition uprooted at Appomattox, their sentiments were too cloying for a girl who had read literary masterpieces as well as the great scientists and philosophers.

More personally, as she told in her posthumous autobiography, *The Woman Within*, domestic tensions and the experience of a love doomed to unfulfillment helped to shape a philosophy of life that was essentially tragic and gave her deeper insight into the gap between appearance and reality. Skepticism became the natural habit of her mind, flowering eventually in the novel of manners and reflecting with indulgent irony the final disenchantment of a society caught in the entanglement of its social and moral code.

Few writers have revealed more candidly the influences contributing to the development of a point of view and a literary method. Fielding gave her the model of his comic epic in prose. Tolstoy showed that a writer may remain provincial and yet fasten on universals. Jane Austen provided a depth of critical penetration and an illuminating irony which sets everything in its proper place within a small conservative society. The novels of Balzac and Zola demonstrated a method for tracing patterns of change through whole social groups. Her apprenticeship began early. By the time she was eighteen she had secretly written and destroyed her first novel. She then began to write *The Descendant*, but because of grief and shock at the time of her mother's death it was not published until 1897. This novel was followed a year later by *Phases of an Inferior Planet*. These are minor works on a minor theme, the escape of the Virginian to New York; in them Glasgow had not yet found the proper subject for her method and style. That moment came with *The Voice of the People* in 1900, the story of Nick Burr and his climb from the poverty and misery of a poor dirt-farmer's family to become governor of Virginia. This was the first of her novels written, as she said later, out of her determination to write of the South not sentimentally, as a stricken province or a lost, romantic legend, but as part of the larger human world.

In the Virginia Edition of her works, for which she wrote the series of critical prefaces later reprinted in *A Certain Measure*, Glasgow divided her best novels into three groups. The first of these is a cycle designed as a social history of the Commonwealth, beginning with a picture of plantation society and the war years in *The Battle-Ground* and ending, in *Virginia* and *Life and Gabriella*, with ironic studies of woman's place in the traditional code of gentility. In her novels of the Reconstruction period—*The Deliverance*, *The Voice of the People*, and *The Romance of a Plain Man*—Glasgow tells of the rise of a new middle class, the sturdy, honest, hard-working Scotch-Irish families who have given the South its real backbone running like a "vein of iron" beneath surface pleasantries of custom and tradition. Closely associated with these "Novels of the Commonwealth" are her three "Novels of the Country." *The Miller of Old Church*, rich in its atmosphere of the Virginia countryside, sustains much of its action in a pastoral mood, but without sentimentality or the limitations of local color quaintness. Always at her best in her portrayal of women, Glasgow created her best character in Dorinda Oakley of *Barren Ground*, in which the plot, characterization, and mood combine to make this story of rural change one of the wisest and most compelling of modern American novels. *Vein of Iron* presents another notable heroine, Ada Fincastle, in a novel which spans the course of Virginia history from a grandmother's memories of the mountain frontier to the depression years of the 1930's.

The "Novels of the City," are three brilliant comedies of manners which relate Glasgow's fiction not only to the history of her state but also to the history of literature. Her skepticism and wit have full play in *The Romantic Comedians*, a novel dissecting the heart and mind of the traditionally gallant Southern gentleman, and in *They Stooped to Folly*, slyly malicious in its picture of a "perfect" marriage set against a background of changing moral standards. *The Sheltered Life* presents the last act in a long drama of sentimentality and sham. *In This Our Life*, her last novel, closer to the social histories than the comedies of manners, brings Glasgow's study of Virginia society down to the summer of 1939. In the story of the Timberlake family she shows on a domestic level and against an urban background a world falling apart in loneliness and cruelty and fear. This is the most pessimistic of her novels; its mood of deep despair is scarcely leavened by the bright quality of her wit.

Ellen Glasgow's fiction is of one piece, a prescription of the "blood and irony" that she recommended for the South in 1925. After years of "benevolent neglect" many honors came to her toward the end of her career. Elected to the American Academy of Arts and Letters in 1938, she was awarded the Howells Medal in 1940 and in the same year the *Saturday Review of Literature* plaque for distinguished service to American letters. She received the Southern Authors' Prize in 1941 and *In This Our Life* was named for the Pulitzer Prize in 1942. She died at her home in Richmond on November 20, 1945.

Bibliography

Ellen Glasgow's representative novels have been collected in two editions, neither definitive: the Old Dominion Edition, 8 vols., 1929–1933, and the limited Virginia Edition, 12 vols., 1938. Both contain the prefaces republished in *A Certain Measure*, 1943, to which the author added a thirteenth essay on *In This Our Life*. *The Collected Stories* were edited by Richard K. Meeker, 1963. For biographical material the best source is *The Woman Within*, 1954, and for discussion of her theories of the art of fiction the essays in *A Certain Measure*.

For brief studies in books or pamphlets see Louise Maunsell Field, *Ellen Glasgow: Novelist of the Old and the New South*, 1923; Stuart P. Sherman, *Critical Woodcuts*, 1926; Dorothea L. Mann, *Ellen Glasgow*, 1927, with additional sketches by James Branch Cabell, Joseph Collins, and Carl Van Vechten; James Branch Cabell, *Some of Us*, 1930; Emily Clark, *Innocence Abroad*, 1931; Friedrich Brie, *Ellen Glasgow*, 1931; Arthur H. Quinn, *American Fiction*, 1936; N. Elizabeth Monroe, *The Novel and Society*, 1941, and "Ellen Glasgow: Ironist of Manners," in *Fifty Years of the American Novel*, edited by Harold C. Gardiner, S.J., 1951; Alfred Kazin, *On Native Grounds*, 1942; Frederick J. Hoffman, *The Modern Novel in America, 1900–1950*, 1951; Edward Wagenknecht, *Cavalcade of the American Novel*, 1952; Maxwell Geismar, *Rebels and Ancestors: The American Novel, 1890–1915*, 1953; and John Edward Hardy, "Ellen Glasgow," in *Southern Renascence*, edited by Louis D. Rubin, Jr., and Robert D. Jacobs, 1953. See also Frederick P. W. McDowell, *Ellen Glasgow and the Ironic Art of Fiction*, 1960; Louis D. Rubin, Jr., *No Place on Earth: Ellen Glasgow, James Branch Cabell, and Richmond-in-Virginia*, 1960; Joan Foster Santas, *Ellen Glasgow's American Dream*, 1965; and C. Hugh Holman, *Three Modes of Modern Southern Fiction: Glasgow, Faulkner, Wolfe*, 1966.

BARREN GROUND

Type of work: Novel
Author: Ellen Glasgow (1874–1945)
Time of plot: Late nineteenth and early twentieth centuries
Locale: Rural Virginia
First Published: 1925

In this realistic novel of the South, Glasgow portrays the struggle of an aristocratic class to maintain high living standards in the face of humiliating economic facts. Dorinda, the heroine, is contrasted in her strength and vitality to her weak-willed lover Jason.

Principal Characters

Dorinda Oakley, the daughter of a poor white Virginia farmer. Tall, dark-haired, radiant-eyed, she is not pretty, but when she smiles her eyes and mouth reveal an inner warmth. A vein of iron in her enables her to survive Jason's desertion of her, his marriage to Geneva Ellgood, her own attempt to kill him, the loss of her baby in a New York accident, the deaths of her parents and of Nathan, and the years of hard work necessary to maintain and improve her dairy farm. Dorinda, one of Ellen Glasgow's self-admitted favorite characters, is among the most impressive rural heroines in modern American fiction. She may be compared with Willa Cather's Alexandra Bergson and Ántonia Shimerda.

Josiah Oakley, her brother, a personification of futility who seems to Dorinda to ooze failure from the pores of his skin.

Rufus Oakley, another brother who, accused of murdering a neighboring farmer, is saved by his mother's lying statement that he was at home when the shooting occurred.

Jason Greylock, the last member of an old Virginia family. Red-haired, chinkapin-eyed, and slightly freckled, he is charm-ing when he smiles; and young Dorinda is charmed. An inner weakness leads him to desert the pregnant Dorinda and marry Geneva. The same weakness takes him on the road his father has followed, a road to death through drink.

Geneva Ellgood, later Jason's wife. She ages rapidly from living with Jason, her mind begins to fail, and she eventually drowns herself.

Nathan Pedlar, a country farmer and merchant. A tall, lank, homely man of unimpressive personality, Nathan has an instinctive knowledge of intelligent farm practices which conserve land instead of wearing it out. He wisely advises Dorinda in the development of her dairy farm and later marries her. He is killed while trying to save the lives of passengers in a train wreck and is given a hero's funeral.

Dr. Greylock, Jason's father. Formerly a man of prominence and owner of a fine farm, he has been for some years drinking his life away and letting the farm go to ruin.

Eudora Abernethy Oakley, Dorinda's mother, who after her husband's death

BARREN GROUND by Ellen Glasgow. By permission of the publishers, Harcourt, Brace & Co., Inc. Copyright, 1925, 1933, by Ellen Glasgow.

reveals a suppressed religious mania. After her lie saves Rufus, her conscience drives her insane. She dies in her sleep.

Dr. Faraday, a physician who saves Dorinda's life after an accident in New York. He later hires her to look after his office and his children.

Aunt Mehitable Green, an old Negro conjure woman and midwife in whose home Dorinda becomes ill and learns she is pregnant.

Elvira Oakley, Josiah's wife, a scold who is as much a failure as her husband.

John Abner Pedlar, Nathan's crippled

son, who helps Dorinda farm and toward whom she feels almost as close as if he were her own son.

Matthew Fairlamb, a retired carpenter, a still vigorous and talkative old man.

James Ellgood, the owner of Green Acres, a flourishing stock farm.

Joshua Oakley, Dorinda's father, a good and industrious but ineffectual man.

Rose Milford, Nathan's sick wife, a former schoolteacher who faces death by pretending it is not near.

The Story

Late one cold winter day Dorinda Oakley started to walk the four miles between Pedlar's Mill and her home at Old Farm. The land was bleak and desolate under a gray sky, and a few flakes of snow were falling. For almost a year she had worked in Nathan Pedlar's store, taking the place of his consumptive wife. Her brisk walk carried her swiftly over the rutted roads toward her father's unproductive farm and the dilapidated Oakley house. On the way she passed Green Acres, the fertile farm of James Ellgood, and the run-down farm of Five Oaks, owned by dissolute old Doctor Greylock, whose son, Jason, had given up his medical studies to take over his father's practice and to care for his drunken father.

As she walked, Dorinda thought of young Jason Greylock. Before she reached Old Farm, Jason overtook her in his buggy. During the ride to her home she remembered the comment of old Matthew Fairlamb, who had told her that she ought to marry Jason. The young doctor was handsome. He represented something different from the drab, struggling life Dorinda had always known. Her father and mother and her two brothers were all unresponsive and bitter people. Mrs. Oakley suffered from headaches and tried to forget them in a ceaseless activity of work. At Old Farm, supper was followed by prayers and prayers by sleep.

Dorinda continued to see Jason. Taking the money she had been saving to buy a cow, she ordered a pretty dress and a new hat to wear to church on Easter Sunday. But her Easter finery brought her no happiness. Jason sat in church with the Ellgoods and their daughter, Geneva, and afterward he went home with them to dinner. Dorinda sat in her bedroom that afternoon and meditated on her unhappiness.

Later, Jason proposed unexpectedly, confessing that he too was lonely and unhappy. He spoke of his attachment to his father which had brought him back to

Pedlar's Mill, and he cursed the tenant system which he said was ruining the South. He and Dorinda planned to be married in the fall. When they met during the hot, dark nights that summer, he kissed her with half-angry, half-hungry violence.

Meanwhile Geneva Ellgood told her friends that she herself was engaged to Jason Greylock. Late in September Jason left for the city to buy surgical instruments. When he was overlong in returning, Dorinda began to worry. At last she visited Aunt Mehitable Green, an old Negro conjure woman, in the hope Aunt Mehitable would have heard from the Greylock servants some gossip concerning Jason. There Dorinda became ill and learned that she was to have a child. Distressed, she went to Five Oaks and confronted drunken old Dr. Greylock, who told her, as he cackled with sly mirth, that Jason had married Geneva Ellgood in the city. The old man intimated that Jason was white-livered and had been forced into the marriage by the Ellgoods. He added, leering, that Jason and his bride were expected home that night.

On the way home Dorinda saw, herself unseen, the carriage which brought Jason and Geneva to Five Oaks. Late that night she went to the Greylock house and attempted to shoot Jason. Frightened, Jason begged for pity and understanding. Despising him for his weakness and falseness, she blundered home through the darkness. Two days later she packed her suitcase and left home. By accident she took the northbound train rather than the one to Richmond, and so she changed the course of her later life.

Dorinda arrived in New York in October, frightened, friendless, with no prospects of work. Two weeks later she fortunately met a kindly middle-aged woman who took her in and gave her the address of a dressmaker who might hire her. But on the way to the shop Dorinda was knocked down by a cab. She awoke in a hospital. Dr Faraday, a surgeon who had seen the accident, saved her life, but she lost her baby. Dr. Faraday hired her to look after his office and children.

Dorinda lived in New York with the Faradays for two years. Then her father had a stroke and she returned home. Her brother Josiah was married; Mrs. Pedlar was dead. Dorinda had become a woman of self-confidence and poise. She saw Geneva Greylock, who already looked middle-aged, and had only pity for the woman who had married Jason. Her brother Rufus said Jason was drinking heavily and losing all his patients. Five Oaks farm looked more run-down than ever. Determined to make the Oakley land productive once more, Dorinda borrowed enough money to buy seven cows. She found Nathan Pedlar helpful in many ways, for he knew good farming methods and gave her advice. When she saw Jason again, she wondered how she could ever have yielded herself to the husk of a man that Jason was.

After her father's death, Josiah and his wife Elvira went to live on their own land. Rufus, who hated the farm, planned to go to the city. Before he left the farm, however, Rufus was accused of murdering a neighboring farmer. Dorinda was sure that he had committed the murder, but Mrs. Oakley swore under oath

that her son had been at home with her at the time of the shooting. Her lie saved
Rufus. Mrs. Oakley's conscience began to torment her because of the lie she had
told, and she took to her bed. Her mind broken, she lived in dreams of her youth.
When she died in her sleep, Dorinda wept. To her it seemed that her parents' lives
had been futile and wasted.

During the next ten years Dorinda worked hard. She borrowed more money to
improve the farm and she saved and scrimped, but she was happy. Geneva
Greylock was losing her mind. One day she told Dorinda that she had borne a
child but that Jason had killed it and buried it in the garden. Geneva drowned
herself the same day that Nathan Pedlar asked Dorinda to marry him.

Together Dorinda and Nathan prospered. She was now thirty-eight and still
felt young. John Abner Pedlar, Nathan's crippled son, looked to her for help and
she gave it willingly. Nathan's other children meant less to her, and she was glad
when they married and moved away. When Five Oaks was offered for sale, Dorinda and Nathan bought it for six thousand dollars. As Jason signed over the
papers to her, Dorinda noticed that he was his dirty, drunken old father all over
again.

The next few years Dorinda devoted to restoring Five Oaks. John Abner was
still her friend and helper. There were reports that Jason was living in an old
house in the pine woods and drinking heavily. Dorinda, busy with her house and
dairy farm, had little time for neighborhood gossip.

One day Nathan took the train to the city to have a tooth pulled and to attend
a lawsuit. The train was wrecked, and Nathan was killed while trying to save the
lives of the other passengers. He was given a hero's funeral.

The years following Nathan's death were Dorinda's happiest, for as time
passed she realized that she had regained, through her struggle with the land, her
own integrity and self-respect.

One day some hunters found Jason sick and starving in the woods, and her
neighbors assumed Dorinda would take him in. Unwillingly, she allowed him to
be brought to Old Farm, where she engaged a nurse to look after him. In a few
months Jason died. Many of the people at the funeral came only out of curiosity,
and a pompous minister said meaningless things about Jason, whom he had never
known. Dorinda felt nothing as she stood beside the grave, for her memories of
Jason had outlived her emotions. She sensed that for good or ill the fervor and
fever of her life were ended.

Critical Evaluation

Barren Ground is a disturbing novel because it represents the ways life can
be lived under the most harrowing of circumstances. Glasgow writes about
farmers who are faced with the difficulties of making an unwilling earth— a
waste land in fact—yield. A few triumph against the odds; some do their
best and barely survive; others give up and die early. All except those in the

last category work exceedingly hard. Glasgow believes, as she says in the 1933 Preface to *Barren Ground,* that "the novel is experience illumined by imagination." In this novel, she is faithful to her own experience in her native Virginia, but, as in much of her work, she colors that experience with a dark imagination, an imagination that views human life as a constant struggle in which even the strong do not always survive. And those who do survive must adjust their idealism to fit reality.

The main theme of the novel is stated by its main character, Dorinda Oakley, who thinks that for the majority life is "barren ground where they have to struggle to make anything grow." Dorinda has more than the soil of rural Virginia to make her feel this way. At the age of twenty she has the seed of love planted in her heart only to have it uprooted by her lover's weakness: he marries Geneva Ellgood under the duress of her brothers. Henceforward her heart is indeed barren ground where passion is concerned. And, Glasgow seems to suggest, Dorinda's life is also barren ground as far as happiness is concerned. To women, Glasgow writes, "love and happiness [are] interchangeable terms." After Jason jilts her, Dorinda spends a lifetime distrusting men and building up emotional, mental, physical, and financial walls in order to protect herself from them. She permits herself to marry Nathan Pedlar only because she fears loneliness and because he is submissive to her and is willing to live without any physical intimacy with her. Dorinda becomes a cynic about love and marriage, believing that they seldom, if ever, go together; and even when they do the love does not endure.

Dorinda, like the characters of Thomas Hardy, is driven by forces beyond her control, by the "eternal purpose." She feels that the trivial incidents in life are the crucial ones. One of these trivial incidents was Nathan's train trip, which resulted in his heroic death. That incident

> was apparently as trivial as her meeting with Jason in the road, as the failure of her aim when the gun had gone off, as the particular place and moment when she had fallen down in Fifth Avenue. These accidents had changed the course of her life. Yet none of them could she have foreseen and prevented; and only once, she felt, in that hospital in New York, had the accident or the device of fortune been in her favour.

Much like Dreiser's Carrie Meeber or Hurstwood, Dorinda is "a straw in the wind, a leaf on a stream."

But Glasgow, as she says in her Preface, believes that "character is fate," so that the individual destinies of her characters are partly determined by the nature they inherit, by, that is, their blood: destiny is in the genes. The "vein of iron" that keeps Dorinda struggling (and that helps her to succeed) is a product of the "sense" of her great-grandfather, a member of the Southern upper class, and the physical strength of her father, a member of the "poor white" class. Jason fails, like his father had, because of "bad blood." Even though unforeseen events control our destinies, our characters determine what we do under the unasked-for circumstances.

Archetypally, Dorinda is at first Medea, who falls in love with a Jason who will forsake her for another. But she becomes an Artemis or an Atalanta, the devouring female who remains estranged physically and psychologically, from the male. (In the last analysis, Glasgow shows that each individual is always isolated from his fellow creatures.) She is also, paradoxically, an Earth Mother, who causes the soil to be productive and who keeps the best cows in the state. Her maternal instinct is satisfied by this bond with the soil as well as by her adoption through marriage of Nathan's children, John Abner in particular.

Though she is never a whole person psychologically, Dorinda does the best she can, given her character and experience. She achieves a wholeness that most never achieve. Though a woman, she farms better than most of the men in her rural community. Her black hair symbolizes her relationship with the earth and combines with its opposite, the sky, in her blue eyes. Her experiences are much like her mother's (an early separation from a lover, a loveless marriage), but she manages to combine her mother's hard-work habits with a contentment—if not a happiness—that her morally repressed mother never had. Jason goes away to New York and comes back to a dying father just as Dorinda is to do. But Jason allows the interminable broomsedge to conquer him. Dorinda does not.

Bibliography

Auchincloss, Louis. *Ellen Glasgow.* Minneapolis: University of Minnesota Press, 1964, pp. 27–29.

Cabell, James Branch. "The Last Cry of Romance," in *Literary Biographies.* IV (1928), pp. 26–31.

Collins, Joseph. "Realism in a Southern Novel," in *Literary Biographies.* IV (1928), pp. 32–38.

Geismar, Maxwell. *Rebels and Ancestors: The American Novel, 1890–1915.* Boston: Houghton Mifflin, 1953, pp. 258–263.

Godbold, E. Stanly, Jr. *Ellen Glasgow and the Woman Within.* Baton Rouge: Louisiana State University Press, 1972, pp. 137–150.

Jessup, Josephine Lurie. *The Faith of Our Feminists: A Study in the Novels of Edith Wharton, Ellen Glasgow, Willa Cather.* New York: Richard R. Smith, 1950, pp. 34–53.

McDowell, Frederick P.W. *Ellen Glasgow and the Ironic Art of Fiction.* Madison: University of Wisconsin Press, 1960, pp. 146–160.

Mann, Dorothea Lawrance. "Ellen Glasgow," in *Literary Biographies.* IV (1928), pp. 18–19.

Marshall, George O., Jr. "Hardy's *Tess* and Ellen Glasgow's *Barren Ground*," in *Texas Studies in Literature and Language*. I (Winter, 1960), pp. 517–521.

Murr, Judy Smith. "History in *Barren Ground* and *Vein of Iron*: Theory, Structure, and Symbol," in *Southern Literary Journal*. VIII (1975), pp. 39–54.

Raper, J.R. *Without Shelter: The Early Career of Ellen Glasgow*. Baton Rouge: Louisiana State University Press, 1971, pp. 149–173.

Rouse, Blair. *Ellen Glasgow*. New York: Twayne, 1962, pp. 86–97.

Santas, Joan Foster. *Ellen Glasgow's American Dream*. Charlottesville: University Press of Virginia, 1965, pp. 138–163.

THE ROMANTIC COMEDIANS

Type of work: Novel
Author: Ellen Glasgow (1874–1945)
Time of plot: 1920's
Locale: Richmond, Virginia
First published: 1926

The Romantic Comedians *presents the age-old problem of an old man who marries a young girl. More particularly, Glasgow symbolizes in her two main characters the struggle between two diverse eras in American culture. Judge Gamaliel Bland Honeywell stands for the faded Victorianism of the American South in the last third of the nineteenth century, while Annabel represents the first Southern generation after World War I.*

Principal Characters

Judge Gamaliel Bland Honeywell, a wealthy widower of sixty-five. He is tall, dignified, and well preserved, but spindle-legged. His hair and beard are silvery; his moustache is dark; his eyebrows are beetling; his nose is Roman. His views are conservative, Southern, nineteenth century ones. Especially interested in young women, he is chivalrous toward all women. Unless careful of his diet he suffers from dyspepsia. Retired from the bench, he now practices law and enjoys respect for his legal ability. Lacking a common-sense knowledge of human nature, he enters a marriage which is doomed from its beginning. Though kind and generous to Annabel, he is nonetheless chained to his habits and his enjoyment of physical comfort, and he is unable to perceive her urgent need for the kind of love he cannot give. He accepts the blame for Annabel's leaving him since, as he says, he is older and should have known that marriage to him would not be enough for her.

Annabel, his second wife, a girl of twenty-three. Appealingly fragile in body, she has a freckled, heart-shaped face, nut-brown hair with coppery glints, and gray-green eyes. She is a frank and somewhat selfish realist but much more naïve than she thinks. Bitter and filled with hatred over Angus Blount's deserting her, she resents the genteel poverty in which she and her mother live, and she accepts the judge partly to forget Angus and partly to escape the atmosphere of her home. Vivacious, impulsive, and extravagant, she is cold and hardly appreciative of what the judge does for her. The judge is drawn by her elusive charm, but he cannot conquer her aversion to him, her fear and resentment of his being affectionate. Insisting that she has no desire to live without love, she is determined to attain her goal regardless of consequences.

Mrs. Bella Upchurch, Annabel's mother, a widow, brisk, cheerful, plump, pretty, and talkative.

Edmonia Bredalbane, the judge's twin sister, large, raw-boned, heavy-bosomed, a woman of liberal views and unorthodox behavior, the mate of four husbands and reputedly (though she denies it) the mistress of many rich lovers. She is a gaudy dresser with tinted brown hair. To the judge she appears to flaunt her past instead of being ashamed of it. Having more worldly perception than her brother, Edmonia attempts to keep him from making a fool of himself and vainly tries to promote a marriage to Amanda.

Amanda Lightfoot, the judge's childhood sweetheart, fifty-eight, unmarried, handsome, tall, willowy, regal, blue-eyed, and silver-haired. She dresses in an old-fashioned manner in the colors that Gamaliel used to like on her many years earlier. She has accepted her plight in an excessively ladylike manner, remaining pious and chaste through the years,

tediously faithful to the man she lost but never ceased to love.

Dabney Birdsong, Annabel's childhood playmate, now a successful architect. He becomes her lover and she deserts the judge for him.

Angus Blount, Annabel's false lover, who married a French girl after deserting Annabel.

Dr. Buchanan, the judge's physician.

[Cordelia Honeywell, the judge's deceased first wife to whom he was peacefully and unexcitingly married for thirty-six years. He continually remembers Cordelia's tastes and ways and contrasts them with Annabel's.]

The Story

As Judge Honeywell walked home from church on the first Easter morning after his wife's death, he was surprised by his own reactions to the Virginia springtime. He felt quite young, for sixty-five, and life with his wife, now dead, seemed so remote as never to have happened. In fact, he felt relieved, for his first wife had seldom let him lead an existence of his own.

The judge looked after Mrs. Upchurch and her daughter Annabel in a friendly way because they were kinswomen of his late wife. But shortly after that memorable Easter morning he began to think of twenty-three-year old Annabel in quite another way. His changed attitude began because he was secretly sorry for her. She had been engaged to a young man who had left her almost at the altar. It had hurt her bitterly, as the judge and her mother knew.

As time passed the judge found himself thinking more and more of Annabel Upchurch and of Amanda Lightfoot, his childhood sweetheart. Unfortunately, the judge's sister, Mrs. Bredalbane, tried to convince him that falling in love with Amanda would be the sensible thing for him to do. The judge, like most men, promptly closed his mind to Amanda and began thinking more of Annabel, who had asked the judge if he would help her to open a flower shop.

Soon the judge had purchased a house with a large garden for Mrs. Upchurch and her daughter, so that Annabel might practice landscape gardening. When he told the girl, he added that he only expected the reward of seeing her happy. But when she left, he kissed her.

By the time that Mrs. Upchurch and Annabel were settled in their new home, the judge knew he was in love with the girl, who was more than forty years younger than he. He bought new clothes and had his hair and beard trimmed to lessen the amount of gray which had appeared. He felt that he could give Annabel everything she needed—love, tenderness, security, and wealth.

The number and quality of the judge's gifts soon made apparent to Annabel and her mother what was in the old man's mind. Annabel thought at first that it would be more suitable for him to marry her mother. But, as she informed her mother, marrying an older man was certainly better than living in an atmosphere of shabby gentility. Annabel decided to visit Amanda Lightfoot. Knowing that Amanda had never married because she had been in love with the judge, Annabel wished to find out if the older woman still loved him. If she did not, Annabel decided, she herself would marry him. But the older woman almost refused to say anything at all. Annabel was disappointed but secretly relieved. When she arrived home, Judge Honeywell was waiting with a present for her, a sapphire bracelet. Before he left the house he told her he loved her, and she accepted him.

After the marriage the judge and Annabel traveled in Europe and in England. The judge felt that he was as fine a man as he had been at thirty-five, although his nerves were jarred a little when someone occasionally referred to Annabel as his daughter. That she often danced with young men did not bother him. He felt no envy of their youth; after all, she was his wife.

The judge was glad to be back in his home in Virginia after the honeymoon. His dyspepsia soon disappeared after he began to eat familiar cooking once more, and he felt at peace to be living in the familiar old house which had not been refurnished in over thirty years.

The couple dined out frequently and went to many dances. The judge, after noting how silly his contemporaries appeared on the dance floor, abstained from any dancing, but he encouraged Annabel to enjoy herself. He always went with her, not from jealousy but because he felt that he had to keep up with her life. It cost him a great deal of effort, for on those evenings he sometimes thought that he had never before known what fatigue was really like.

At home, Annabel had brought changes into the house. While he did not approve, the judge said nothing until she tried to change the furniture in his own room. She learned then, although it cost him a ring she had admired, that he would not let her meddle with his own privacy.

When the judge came down with bronchitis, Annabel proved an able and attentive nurse. During his convalescence, however, she found it difficult to remain at home reading night after night. He, noticing her restlessness, told her to begin going out again, even though he could not go with her. When Annabel went out, her mother or the judge's sister would come to have dinner and stay with him during the evening.

The passing weeks brought in Annabel a change which many people noticed. Noted for her boisterous spirits and lack of reticence, she surprised them by becoming more vague about her comings and goings. At the same time they complimented the judge on how happy she seemed. The compliments made the old gentleman content, for, as he said, Annabel's happiness was what he wanted most.

Slowly the judge began to feel that all was not right in his home. Annabel was distant in her manner. When he talked with his sister and Annabel's mother, both reassured him of the girl's devotion. Still, he knew something was not right. He received proof one day when he found Annabel kissing a young man. Dabney Birdsong belonged to an old family in the community. Annabel had resolved to have him, cost what it might. To the judge, his greatest sorrow was that it might be only an infatuation which would not make Annabel happy. The girl, on the other hand, thought if she did not have Dabney she would die.

Annabel and her lover ran away and went to New York. The judge followed them to the city. Unable to understand his young wife, he felt sorry for her because she defied convention, and he thought that he himself was to blame for what had happened. After a talk with Annabel he left New York, defeated, to return to Virginia.

The rain and the draughty train gave the judge a cold which turned into influenza, and he was in bed for several weeks in a serious condition. During his convalescence he discovered that spring had once more arrived. With the stirring in nature, he felt a resurgence of life in his weary body. Like many an old man before him, the season of freshness and greenery gave him the feeling of youth that he had had on the previous Easter Sunday morning. He found himself beginning to look with new, eager interest at the young nurse who was attending him during his illness.

Critical Evaluation

Ellen Glasgow has been largely overlooked by students of American literature. Her output was prodigious, and her penetrating analysis of the social history of Virginia from 1850 to 1930, her insight into the position of women, her brilliant use of ironic characterization are qualities that set her apart from the mass of popular novelists of the first third of the century and necessitate a reevaluation of her work.

It was Glasgow's colleague, James Branch Cabell, who first called her a social historian; reviewing *Barren Ground,* he said that her books, taken collectively, were a "portrayal of all social and economic Virginia since the War Between the States." Other critics and Glasgow herself accepted the label; despite its accuracy, the phrase "social historian" is too narrow for the wide range of Glasgow's talents and has been partially responsible for the present neglect of her work. She has also suffered from commentary by antagonistic male critics. Never one to accept a "woman's role," Glasgow often attacked those whose writing or person she did not admire. This penchant, as well as her creation of less-than-admirable male characters, has led to some highly questionable commentary about both her life and work.

As late as 1971, one critic commented on her "anti-maleness," and then went on to contradict himself: "She continued to pursue the male of her own species with glee." Such unmeasured statements have not helped Glasgow's literary reputation.

Properly, Glasgow should be seen as an early member of the Southern Literary Renaissance. In 1931 she helped to organize a conference of Southern writers at the University of Virginia, attended by William Faulkner, Sherwood Anderson, and Allen Tate, among others. She was always interested in her native Virginia and wrote perceptively about various epochs and social classes. If her view is often an ironic one, it nevertheless helps the reader to see the love-hate relationship that she had with the South. She judges, but with a sympathetic voice.

The Romantic Comedians comes just after the more famous *Barren Ground* and is, like Glasgow's succeeding work (*They Stooped to Folly*), a novel of manners. Like all such works, *The Romantic Comedians* depends for much of its impact on tone and point of view, for neither plot nor characters are unique. The novel relies on the reader's knowledge of similar situations and characters in making its ironic commentary. From the outset, the narrator directs the reader's attitudes. Characters' names satirically reveal inner traits: "Bland Honeywell," "Upchurch," "Bredalbane," "Lightfoot." We see the Judge as a slightly ridiculous figure, interested in the outward demonstration of his grief and unable to understand correctly his own emotions: " 'I am a bird with a broken wing,' he sighed to himself. . . ." This romantic outward show of grief over his dead wife lacked sincerity, for simultaneously, he ". . . felt an odd palpitation . . . where his broken wing was helplessly trying to flutter." The narrator's voice is unmistakable, and Glasgow shows herself to be in the great tradition of Jane Austen and George Eliot, two other ironic critics of society.

Judge Honeywell is portrayed as a man of a bygone era, unable to understand or adjust to new ideas, yet somewhat naïvely excited by the prospect of Annabel's youth and beauty. He has firm beliefs which nevertheless do not alter his self-interested actions. His most endearing characteristic is his willingness to forgive Annabel, but this too he carries to excess, needlessly accepting the guilt for her unhappiness.

But not only Judge Honeywell is satirized; all of the characters are shown to be romantic or a bit ridiculous. Annabel is deluded by imagining that ultimate personal happiness is attainable and of primary importance. Her amoral attitude does, however, cut through the hypocrisy and moral sham of people like her mother and Amanda Lightfoot. Annabel asserts that perfect ladies "lie as perfectly as they behave." Edmonia Bredalbane carries her "scandalous" behavior to an extreme which, even in its refreshing lack of convention, is shown to be silly. Glasgow reverses the generally accepted roles in the relationship of the Judge and his twin sister; here the woman is emancipated and the man tied by convention.

The theme of the novel is voiced by Mrs. Upchurch who muses on "the popular supersitition that love and happiness are interchangeable terms." She notes that both old and young, old-fashioned and modern, are "enslaved" by this illusion. The Judge, Amanda, Annabel, Dabney—"all this company of happiness-hunters appeared to be little better than a troupe of romantic comedians." This attitude seems to be the view of the narrator as well, but Mrs. Upchurch is not always the narrator's mouthpiece. In fact, Mrs. Upchurch's pragmatic morality, which shifts radically depending on the situation, is as often laughed at as the Judge's unyielding system. But Mrs. Upchurch has a more realistic view of life than any other character.

Glasgow displays skill not only in the consistency of her tone but also in her use of images to suggest character. The Judge always thinks of Annabel in terms of nature—"fields and streams," "tall wind-blown grasses," the "April mist" in her eyes. But these very qualities in Annabel—her "natural" freedom and amorality—doom their marriage; wild nature cannot become domestic and maternal. As their relationship deteriorates, he begins to think of her in terms of images of light without heat: she lacks the warmth he craves. She is like "the fire at the heart of an opal"; her head is like "November leaves in the sunlight"; after she runs off with Dabney she looks alive "not as a flower, but as a jewel."

Although the point of view is most often centered in Judge Honeywell's consciousness, the narrator sometimes inserts commentary to make her attitude more obvious. Usually this is unobtrusive but occasionally it becomes an affectation of style or a violation of the convention already established. An example would be the phrase, "like most lawyers and all vestrymen" in beginning a comment on the Judge. In general, though, Glasgow's ironic tone is consistent, pungent, and entertaining. The female characters—including the dead Cordelia—each represent a distinctive way of dealing with the role assigned to women in the South of the 1920's. These aspects make Glasgow more than a social historian and suggest a higher place for her in the hierarchy of American letters.

Bibliography

Auchincloss, Louis. *Ellen Glasgow*. Minneapolis: University of Minnesota Press, 1964, pp. 29–31.

Godbold, E. Stanly, Jr. *Ellen Glasgow and the Woman Within*. Baton Rouge: Louisiana State University Press, 1972, pp. 161–164.

Holman, C. Hugh. "The Comedies of Manners," in *Ellen Glasgow: Centennial Essays*. Edited by M. Thomas Inge. Charlottesville: University Press of Virginia, 1976, pp. 111–128.

Jessup, Josephine Lurie. *The Faith of Our Feminists: A Study in the Novels of Edith Wharton, Ellen Glasgow, Willa Cather.* New York: Richard R. Smith, 1950, pp. 34–53.

McDowell, Frederick P.W. *Ellen Glasgow and the Ironic Art of Fiction.* Madison: University of Wisconsin Press, 1960, pp. 161–171.

Mann, Dorothea Lawrance. "Ellen Glasgow," in *Literary Biographies.* IV (1928), pp. 23–25.

Rouse, Blair. *Ellen Glasgow.* New York: Twayne, 1962, pp. 97–102.

Santas, Joan Foster. *Ellen Glasgow's American Dream.* Charlottesville: University Press of Virginia, 1965, pp. 164–173.

Van Vechten, Carl. "A Virginia Lady Dissects a Virginia Gentleman," in *Literary Biographies.* IV (1928), pp. 39–42.

DASHIELL HAMMETT

Born: St. Mary's County, Maryland (May 27, 1894)
Died: New York, N. Y. (January 10, 1961)

Principal Works

NOVELS: *The Maltese Falcon*, 1930; *The Glass Key*, 1931; *The Thin Man*, 1932; *Secret Agent X-9*, 1935.

SHORT STORIES: *Adventures of Sam Spade, and Other Stories*, 1945; *The Continental Operator*, 1945; *The Creeping Siamese*, 1950.

(Samuel) Dashiell Hammett was the successful innovator of a form of detective fiction that dominates the genre today, the mystery novel in which the detective is as tough as the quarry he pursues and sometimes as immoral. Hammett's list of works is shorter than that of many writers of detective fiction, but his two most famous detectives, Sam Spade and Nick Charles, are the ancestors of the hard-drinking, hard-knuckled, and saturnine heroes of the novels of Raymond Chandler, Mickey Spillane, and others.

Born in Southern Maryland on May 27, 1894, Hammett was educated at the Baltimore Polytechnic Institute. Shortly after he left school he went through a variety of occupations as newsboy, messenger boy, clerk, stevedore, and private detective, occupations that were very useful to him as a writer. He developed his method of horror and shock in *Red Harvest* (1929) and *The Dain Curse* (1929) but failed to win popular favor until he published *The Maltese Falcon* in 1930. In 1946–1947 he was an instructor in the Jefferson School of Social Science in New York. Hammett was active in both wars, and later he was touched by several investigations into Communist front organizations.

Hammett's success as a writer was for some years overshadowed by the almost independent life which two of his characters, Nick and Nora Charles, achieved in a series of motion pictures and radio and television programs. Hammett was buried in Arlington National Cemetery.

Bibliography

There is no extended biographical study or criticism. See William F. Nolan, *Dashiell Hammett: A Casebook*, 1969. For a brief sketch see Elizabeth Sanderson, "Ex-detective Hammett," *Bookman*, LXXIV (1932), 516–518.

THE GLASS KEY

Type of work: Novel
Author: Dashiell Hammett (1894–1961)
Time of plot: 1930's
Locale: New York area
First published: 1931

This novel is an excellent example of the school of hard-boiled realism. In the course of tracking down a murderer, the detective-hero also breaks up a bootlegging operation and finds himself embroiled in a bitter political power play. As in most good detective novels, the culprit turns out to be the least suspected character; and since this is a modern form of the genre, the hero has a love interest.

Principal Characters

Ned Beaumont, a tall, lean, narrow-eyed, mustached, cigar-smoking, tough gambler and amateur detective. He finds Taylor Henry's body, collects the money Bernie owes him, is tortured by O'Rory, disbelieves Madvig's confession, witnesses O'Rory's murder, receives Senator Henry's confession, and gets the girl Janet.

Paul Madvig, his blond, heavy-set, ruddily handsome friend and the city's political boss, in love with Janet. Though innocent, he confesses to Taylor's murder.

Senator Henry, Madvig's distinguished, patrician-faced candidate for reëlection; the real murderer of his son Taylor during a violent quarrel.

Janet Henry, his brown-eyed daughter who hates Madvig and falls in love with Ned.

Shad O'Rory, Madvig's rival, a gangster and ward boss who has Ned brutally beaten for refusing to help frame Paul. He is killed by Jeff.

Opal Madvig, Madvig's blue-eyed, pink-skinned daughter who had been meeting Taylor secretly. She attempts suicide.

Bernie Despain, a gambler Ned suspects of having murdered Taylor. He owes Ned money which he finally pays.

Taylor Henry, Senator Henry's son, found dead in the street.

Jack Rumsen, a private detective hired by Ned to trail Bernie.

Michael Joseph Farr, the district attorney, stout, florid, pugnacious.

Jeff, O'Rory's apish bodyguard who beats Ned and later strangles O'Rory.

The Story

Ned Beaumont reported to his friend, Paul Madvig, the political boss of the city, that he had found the dead body of Taylor Henry in the street. Taylor was the son of Senator Henry, Madvig's candidate for reëlection. When Madvig failed to show much interest, Ned told his story to the police. Next day he went to collect from Bernie Despain the thirty-two hundred and fifty dollars that he had won on a horse race and found that Bernie had vanished, leaving behind twelve hundred dollars worth of Taylor's I.O.U.'s. Ned had himself appointed special investigator in the district attorney's office so that he could work on Taylor Henry's case. What he really wanted to do was to find Bernie and get his money.

His first step was to get the help of Madvig's daughter Opal, who had been meeting Taylor secretly. Ned had found no hat on Taylor the night of the murder. Opal got one for him from the room she and Taylor had rented. Then Ned went to New York to a speakeasy that Bernie frequented. Bernie came in accompanied by a burly bodyguard who, when Ned asked for his money, struck Ned a terrific blow. With the help of Jack Rumsen, a private detective, Ned trailed Bernie from the hotel where he was staying to a brownstone house on Forty-ninth Street. There he told Bernie that he had planted Taylor's hat behind a sofa cushion in Bernie's hotel room and would leave it there for the police to find if Bernie did not pay him the money. Bernie paid off.

Back from New York, Ned went to see Farr, the district attorney. Farr showed Ned an envelope enclosing paper on which were typed three questions implicating Madvig in Taylor's murder. Meanwhile Madvig had decided to have the police close down several speak-easies belonging to Shad O'Rory, gangster and ward boss. O'Rory reopened the Dog House, where Ned went to get information. O'Rory had him tortured for several days. Finally he escaped. He was taken to a hospital.

There he had many callers, including Madvig and Janet Henry, Taylor's sister. Opal Madvig went to tell Ned she was sure her father had killed Taylor. Ned assured her he did not believe Madvig had committed the murder. Partly recovered, he left the hospital against orders.

Shortly afterward Ned and Madvig dined with Senator Henry and his daughter Janet. Ned made Janet admit that she secretly hated Madvig, who was in love with her.

Ned went to see Madvig and told him that even his henchmen were beginning to betray him because they thought he had committed the murder. Madvig admitted Taylor had followed him out of the Henry house that night, that they had quarreled, and that he killed Taylor with a brown, knobby cane which Taylor had been carrying. Madvig claimed that he had then carried the cane away under his coat and burned it. Ned later asked Janet to look for the cane. She said it was with some others in the hall of their home. She also told him of a dream in which she and Ned had found a house with a banquet spread inside; they had to unlock the door and let out a great many snakes before they could go in to enjoy the food.

Ned went next to Farr's office and signed an affidavit telling of Madvig's confession. Then he went to a bar where he found Jeff, O'Rory's bodyguard. In a private room upstairs he accused Jeff of a gangster killing planned by O'Rory.

O'Rory walked in on them and in the ensuing quarrel Jeff strangled O'Rory. Ned had a waiter call the police to the scene.

Ned went to the Madvig home, where Madvig's mother said that Madvig was nowhere to be found and that Opal had unsuccessfully attempted to commit suicide. Next morning Ned went to Senator Henry's house and told the senator that Madvig had confessed. It was all Janet and Ned could do to keep the senator from rushing out to kill Madvig. The senator asked Janet to leave him alone with Ned. Ned told him that Janet hated Madvig. The senator insisted he was not going to permit the murderer of his son to go unpunished. Then Ned accused the senator of killing Taylor, of wanting to kill Madvig so that he would not testify against him, of caring more of his own reëlection than for the life of his son. The senator confessed that he had interfered in a street quarrel between Taylor and Madvig and had asked the political boss to leave him with his son. Madvig had done so after giving him the cane Madvig had taken away from Taylor. The senator, angry with his son because of the quarrel he had forced upon Madvig, had angrily struck Taylor with the cane and killed him. He had then carried home the cane. After hearing the old man's confession, Ned refused to leave him alone because he feared the senator would kill himself before the police arrived.

Next day Janet begged Ned to let her go with him to New York. She said the key to the house in her dream had been of glass and had shattered just as they opened the door because they had had to force the lock. When Madvig came in, he learned that he had lost Janet, that she was going away with Ned Beaumont.

Critical Evaluation

The Glass Key was Dashiell Hammett's personal favorite among his novels and may well be, in the words of critic-novelist Julian Symons, "the peak of Hammett's achievement, which is to say, the peak of the crime writer's art in the twentieth century."

Although Ned Beaumont has much in common with Hammett's other "hard-boiled" heroes, Sam Spade and Continental Op, he is not simply a professional detective hired to solve a crime but a man involuntarily thrust into the center of a violent and puzzling situation. The fate of his employer and best friend, Paul Madvig—and ultimately of himself—is dependent on his ability to solve the murder of Henry Taylor. Beaumont's search for the murderer becomes, moreover, not only a problem in detection but also an exploration of the social mores and political forces operative in the America of 1931. And as Ned pursues his quest, he also comes to understand his own relationship to that social and political system.

Hammett's picture of big-city politics has little to do with electoral niceties. Favors are bought and sold. Survival and power go to the fittest; that is, to those most willing and able to manipulate the power factions as they vie to maintain and expand their own self interests. Paul Madvig is no more honest than his rival Shad O'Rory, only a bit more adroit and likeable. Holding on to power is a matter of keeping a delicate balance of contending factions; the slightest mistake can topple one from the pinnacle all the way down. Those not at the center of the struggle, from District Attorney Farr down to the bartender at the speakeasy where O'Rory is murdered, are loyal only to themselves and switch sides at the slightest indication that power relationships are changing. Thus, to everyone except his sister Janet, the murder of Henry Taylor matters only as a dangerous variable in this struggle for political dominance. The most "respectable" member of the establishment, old Senator Henry, turns out to be the most corrupt. He kills his own son in a fit of temper and is willing to kill again to keep the truth concealed.

Ned Beaumont accepts and even participates in this system of institutionalized corruption. But his loyalty to Paul, to Janet, and to the "job" he has to do, suggests another possible "morality" in the book based on personal relationships rather than on adherence to particular institutions or abstract principles. Although Beaumont fights with Madvig, leaves him at one point, and finally goes off with his girl, he maintains throughout the book a dogged loyalty to his boss and friend, even in the face of nearly fatal tortures and beatings. If the system is corrupt, Hammett seems to be saying, it is still possible for a man to retain his moral integrity by holding fast to his own sense of self, his personal "code," and those commitments, to self and others, that are the product of that "code."

The book ends on an optimistisc note. Ned and Janet are about to leave together. Paul accepts the new arrangement with equanimity and promises to use his expertise and power to do a "housecleaning." But this final optimism is unconvincing. The image of the "American Dream" that remains in the mind is that of Janet's dream which gives the book its title: a delicious banquet apparently free for the taking, but guarded by hidden snakes that swarm over the unwary who dare to unlock the door with a glass key.

THE MALTESE FALCON

Type of work: Novel
Author: Dashiell Hammett (1894–1961)
Time of plot: Twentieth century
Locale: San Francisco
First published: 1930

A detective novel of the hardboiled school, The Maltese Falcon's *distinction lies in the fact that the detective himself becomes involved in crime. Written in racy, colloquial language, the book pretends to be no more than entertainment, but it is a classic example of its type and has influenced many subsequent writers, both in and out of the detective genre.*

Principal Characters

Sam Spade, a tall, blond, pleasantly satanic-looking, hard-boiled private detective suspected of having killed Thursby and of having also killed Miles Archer in order to marry Iva. He at last discovers how he has been used in the plot to get the Maltese falcon; he discovers the murderers of Miles and Thursby, and he turns Brigid over to the police.

Brigid O'Shaughnessy, his tall, attractive, auburn-haired, deceitful client, who first masquerades as a Miss Wonderly, then shoots Miles, double-crosses her associates, and finally attempts in vain to seduce Sam into letting her go free of a murder charge.

Casper Gutman, her fat, tough employer, who is attempting to get hold of the Maltese falcon. He is shot by Wilmer Cook.

Wilmer Cook, Gutman's young bodyguard, murderer of Thursby, Jacobi, and Gutman.

Joel Cairo, Gutman's dark-skinned, flashily dressed one-time agent.

Miles Archer, Spade's middle-aged partner, solidly built, wide-shouldered, red-faced. He is shot and killed by Brigid.

Floyd Thursby, Brigid's murdered accomplice.

Iva Archer, Miles's wife, a voluptuous, still pretty blonde in her thirties; in love with Sam.

Kemidov, a Russian in Constantinople who has substituted a lead imitation for the genuine Maltese falcon.

Jacobi, captain of the ship "La Paloma"; killed by Wilmer.

Effie Perine, Sam's lanky, boyish-faced, suntanned secretary.

Rhea Gutman, daughter of Gutman.

THE MALTESE FALCON by Dashiell Hammett. By permission of the publishers, Alfred A. Knopf, Inc. Copyright, 1929, 1930, by Alfred A. Knopf, Inc.

The Story

Brigid O'Shaughnessy went to the office of Sam Spade and Miles Archer, detectives, to ask them to trail a Floyd Thursby. Archer, who undertook the job, was killed the first night. About an hour later Thursby himself was killed in front of his hotel. The police were inclined to suspect Spade of the murder of his partner, for it was known that Iva Archer had been wanting a divorce so that she could marry Spade.

Brigid left word at Spade's office that she wanted to see him. She had changed hotels because she was afraid. She said she could not tell Spade the whole story, but that she had met Thursby in the Orient and that they had arrived in San Francisco the week before. She said she did not know who killed Thursby.

When Spade returned to his office, Joel Cairo was waiting for him. He asked Spade where the statuette of the black bird was and offered five thousand dollars for the recovery of the ornament. That night Spade was trailed by a small young man in a gray overcoat and cap. Spade eluded his pursuer long enough to slip into Brigid's hotel unseen. There he learned that Brigid was connected in some way with a mysterious black bird, an image of a falcon. Later she went with Spade to his apartment, to meet Cairo. She told Cairo that she did not have the prize, that he would have to wait possibly a week for its return.

When the police arrived to question Spade about his relations with Iva, they discovered Cairo and Brigid in the apartment. Spade introduced Brigid as an operator in his employ and explained that he had been questioning Cairo about the murders of Archer and Thursby. After Cairo and the police had gone, Brigid told Sam that she did not know what made the falcon so important. She had been hired to get it away from a Russian named Kemidov in Constantinople.

Next morning, before Brigid was awake, Spade went out to get groceries for breakfast and incidentally to search her hotel room for the falcon, which he failed to find. He was certain that Brigid knew where the falcon was. Brigid was afraid of what Cairo might do, however, and Spade arranged for her to stay a few days at the home of his secretary.

Because, in explaining to Cairo how Thursby was killed, Brigid had outlined the letter G in the air, Spade knew that there was some special significance attached to the letter. He again saw the young man trailing him in the corridor of a hotel and went up to him. Spade said that someone would have to talk, and G might as well know it. Shortly afterward a Mr. Gutman called and asked Spade to go see him. Spade told him that Cairo was offering him ten thousand dollars, not five, for the return of the falcon. Gutman laughed derisively; the bird was obviously worth an enormous fortune. Angry because Gutman would tell him no more, Spade left, saying he would give Gutman until five-thirty to talk.

From a taxi driver Spade learned that Brigid had gone to the Ferry Building and not to his secretary's house and that she had stopped on the way to buy a newspaper. When he returned to Gutman's hotel, he learned that the falcon was an old ornament, made in Malta, encrusted with precious gems and covered with black enamel for protection. Gutman had traced it to the Constantinople home of Kemidov, where Gutman's agents had got it. Now Gutman was wondering where it was.

Next day Spade searched Cairo's hotel room and found that the ships' schedules had been torn out of a newspaper of the day before. He bought a copy of the paper and saw that the ship *La Paloma* had arrived from Hong Kong. Remembering that Brigid had mentioned the Orient, he associated her going to the Ferry Building with the arrival of the ship. Later he learned that Cairo, the strange young man, and Brigid had had a long conference with Jacobi, the captain.

While Spade was telling his secretary of his discoveries, a man came in, held out a bundle to Spade, and dropped over dead. Spade opened the package and discovered the falcon. Spade was sure that the man was Jacobi. He had his secretary call the police while he checked the package in a station nearby. The key he mailed to his post-office box. He then went to answer a distress call from Brigid, but she was not in her room. Instead, Spade found Gutman's daughter, who sent him to the suburbs on a wild-goose chase. When he returned to his apartment, he met Brigid waiting outside, obviously frightened. Opening the door, he found Gutman, the young man, and Cairo waiting for him.

Spade realized that his wild-goose chase had been planned to get him out of the way long enough to give these people a chance to find Jacobi before he returned. Since they were all together, Spade said he would give them the falcon in return for ten thousand dollars and someone on whom to blame the murders. He suggested the young man, whose name was Wilmer, as the suspect. Spade explained that if Wilmer were hanged for the murder of Thursby, the district attorney would drop the case, taking it for granted that Jacobi had been murdered by the same person. Gutman, sure that Thursby had killed Archer, finally consented to make Wilmer the victim.

Gutman produced ten one-thousand-dollar bills. Then Spade called his secretary and asked her to get the claim check from the post-office and redeem the falcon. After she had delivered the package to Spade's apartment, Gutman untied it and, to make sure he had the genuine falcon, began to scratch away the enamel. The falcon was a lead imitation. Kemidov had tricked him. Spade gave back nine thousand dollars. Then he called the police and told them that Wilmer had killed Jacobi and Thursby.

Knowing that Gutman would tell about his and Brigid's part in the plot, Spade made Brigid confess to him that she had drawn Archer into an alley that first night and had killed him with a pistol borrowed from Thursby. He told Brigid that he intended also to turn her over to the police. He had to clear himself of suspicion of killing his partner, and he could not let a woman stand in his way.

Critical Evaluation

The Maltese Falcon introduces the detective Sam Spade, a rough, crude, unassuming, and peculiarly unattractive private eye. His appearance is anything but that of a hero's: he lacks wavy hair, a charming smile, or an athletic physique. An antihero, a negative character cast in a positive role, his success, however, is directly related to his nonheroic qualities. Since his world is the underside of respectability, the seedy areas of San Francisco in which he is usually employed in some sort of marital espionage, Spade must adopt his methods to the environment in order to survive. Indeed what finally comes clear is that the detective is the only truly sane and perhaps just man in the novel. He deals with the evil and treacherous, those like the satanic Gutman, as well as the police, who are for the most part stupid or only intent upon making an arrest, the matter of justice being of no large consequence.

Spade's role as the isolated antihero who brings justice to a corrupt world is a familiar figure in American folklore and literature. *The Maltese Falcon* is in some sense a modern, urban staging of the traditional Western story with Spade as the lone gunman, without credentials, combating the greed of the adventurers in their pursuit of wealth (in the Western, it was gold, here it is the falcon). Notably different, however, is the fact that the heroine in Hammett's novel, Brigid O'Shaughnessy, unlike the Western heroine, is herself treacherous and guilty; and Spade, for all his virtue, is not above dishonest gain. For all the similarities, then, we are in a radically different world in *The Maltese Falcon,* one of lost innocence, where heroism is impossible and trust and affection have disappeared. The whole is unsavory and decayed.

Bibliography

Bazelon, D.T. "Dashiell Hammett's 'Private Eye'; No Loyalty Beyond the Job," in *Commentary.* VII (May, 1949), pp. 467–472.

Ednebaum, Robert. "The Poetics of the Private Eye: The Novels of Dashiell Hammett," in *Tough Guy Writers of the Thirties.* Edited by David Madden. Carbondale: Southern Illinois University Press, 1968, pp. 80–102.

Greela, G. "The Wings of the Falcon and the Maltese Dove," in *A Question of Quality: Popularity and Value in Modern Creative Writing.* Edited by Louis Filler. Bowling Green, Oh.: Bowling Green University Press, 1976, pp. 108–114.

Haycraft, Howard. *Art of the Mystery Story.* New York: Simon and Schuster, 1946, pp. 417–422.

Hully, Kathleen. "From the Crystal Sphere to Edge City; Ideology in the Novels of Dashiell Hammett," in *Myth and Ideology in American Culture.* Edited by Regis Durard. Lille, France: l'Universit'e de Lille, 1976, pp. 111–127.

Malin, Irving. "Focus on the *Maltese Falcon*: The Metaphysical Falcon," in *Tough Guy Writers of the Thirties.* Edited by David Madden. Carbondale: Southern Illinois University Press, 1968, pp. 104–109.

Reilly, John M. "The Politics of Tough Guy Mysteries," in *University of Dayton Review.* X (1973), pp. 25–31.

Ruehlmann, Williams. *Saint with a Gun.* New York: New York University Press, 1974, pp. 73–75.

Sanderson, E. "Ex Detective Hammett," in *Bookman.* LXXIV (January, 1932), pp. 516–518.

Thompson, George J. "The Problem of Moral Vision on Dashiell Hammett's Detective Novels, Part IV: The *Maltese Falcon*," in *Armchair Detective.* VII (1974), pp. 178–192.

ERNEST HEMINGWAY

Born: Oak Park, Illinois (July 21, 1899)
Died: Ketchum, Idaho (July 2, 1961)

Principal Works

NOVELS: *The Torrents of Spring*, 1926: *The Sun Also Rises*, 1926; *A Farewell to Arms*, 1929; *To Have and Have Not*, 1937; *For Whom the Bell Tolls*, 1940; *Across the River and into the Trees*, 1950; *The Old Man and the Sea*, 1952; *Islands in the Stream*, 1970 (Written 1951).

SHORT STORIES: *Three Stories and Ten Poems*, 1923; *In Our Time*, 1924 (enlarged edition, New York, 1925); *Men Without Women*, 1927; *Winner Take Nothing*, 1933; *The Fifth Column and the First Forty-nine Stories*, 1938.

SPORT AND TRAVEL SKETCHES: *Death in the Afternoon*, 1932; *Green Hills of Africa*, 1935.

MEMOIR: *A Moveable Feast*, 1964.

JOURNALISM: *The Wild Years* (edited by Gene Z. Hanrahan), 1962; *By-line* (edited by William White), 1967.

Oak Park, Illinois, seems as unlikely a birthplace for Ernest Hemingway as does Hailey, Idaho, for Ezra Pound; but it was in Oak Park—a quiet, middle-class, somewhat puritanical suburb of Chicago—that the boy who was to become the champion, in his bare-bones prose, of the hard-drinking, hard-loving, hard-fighting life was born on July 21, 1899. His father, a doctor, took him on hunting and fishing trips to Horton Bay, Michigan, and his experiences there, rather than in Oak Park, gave him the material for short stories (such as "Big Two-Hearted River" and "Indian Camp") that appeared in *In Our Time*. In Oak Park young Hemingway contributed to *Trapeze*, his high school newspaper, and wrote the class prophecy for the 1917 yearbook, but not until he worked for the *Kansas City Star* as a reporter did he begin to develop (aided by the *Star*'s fine editorial staff) the style which eventually became as distinctive as Shakespeare's and which has influenced scores of contemporary writers.

Hemingway wanted to get into the First World War. When he was turned down by the army because of poor eyesight, he joined an American ambulance unit, later transferred to the Italian Arditi; after only seven days on the front lines he was seriously wounded. But war's fascination had taken hold of him: he covered the Greco-Turkish War in 1920, the civil war in Spain in 1937, and the Allied invasion of Europe in 1944. War and death comprise a major part of his subject matter, from the vignettes of *In Our Time* to *Across the River and into the Trees*.

After the Armistice, Hemingway came back to the United States and married Hadley Richardson, a childhood Michigan friend. She was the first of four wives. (The others, with the dates of his marriages, were Pauline Pfeiffer, a Paris fashion writer for *Vogue*, 1927; Martha Gellhorn, a writer, 1940; and Mary Welsh, a correspondent for *Time*, 1944.) Hemingway tried newspaper work again, this time in Toronto, but a restless postwar disillusionment came upon him, his editor proved grimly unsympathetic, and so Hemingway left for Europe to become, after the Greco-Turkish War interlude, a part of Paris and "the lost generation." That name was created by Gertrude Stein; and she, Ezra Pound, and Sherwood Anderson had the greatest "literary" influence on his early writing. In 1923 he published *Three Stories & Ten Poems* in Dijon. One of these stories, "My Old Man" is very Andersonian, but the books that followed this modest volume—*In Our Time*; *The Torrents of Spring*, a burlesque of Anderson's style; *The Sun Also Rises*, a novel that is really a long, sparkling short story; and *Men Without Women*, another collection of brilliant short stories—show that Hemingway had absorbed his influences and become a craftsman whose ear for dialogue was flawless and a taster of life who savored emotions by rolling them, as it were, on his tongue.

Financial success came in 1929 with *A Farwell to Arms*. Although this novel lacks the sparkle of *The Sun Also Rises*, its emotional impact is greater and its war scenes are raw, vivid, and true.

Between wars and books, Hemingway occupied himself with many virile sports, and sport provided him with some of his best material. An accomplished amateur boxer in his youth, he used the prize-ring background in the stories "Fifty Grand" and "The Battler." His absorption with bullfighting appears in *The Sun Also Rises*, in short stories like "The Undefeated," and, of course, in that clever compendium of bullfighting and literary philosophy, *Death in the Afternoon*. In 1934 he went on an African safari; the following year he published *The Green Hills of Africa*, chiefly concerned with big-game hunting. Another trophy of this trip was the much-anthologized story, "The Snows of Kilimanjaro." Hemingway also liked to fish, and though the size of the catch increased from the trout of "Big Two-Hearted River" to the giant marlin of *The Old Man and the Sea*, the thrill of the strike is the same.

War came again in the late 1930's. With the outbreak of the fighting in Spain, Hemingway raised money to buy ambulances for the Madrid Loyalists; in February, 1937, he sailed for Spain to cover the war for the North American Newspaper Alliance and to collect the material that was to become in 1940, *For Whom the Bell Tolls*, his own favorite of his novels, and a book that is certainly more mature, because of its concern with moral values, than anything he had previously published. From Spain he returned to Key West, Florida, but he continued his interest in the fight against fascism. When the United States entered World War II, Hemingway for a while helped the Navy spot submarines in the Caribbean, then covered the land fighting in Europe, where he was nicknamed "Papa" by the new generation of fighting men. After the war he wrote a novel about an aging soldier, *Across the River and into the Trees*, a disappointing effort in which many critics have detected two flaws rarely found in Hemingway—the banal and the phoney. But with *The Old Man and the Sea* he quickly bounded back into favor, and the warmth and humanity of this story (though it seems strangely repetitious) probably did more than anything else to win for him the 1953 Nobel Prize as well as the Pulitzer Prize in the same year.

Following another African hunting trip on which he was once reported dead after a series of airplane crashes, Hemingway settled down with his wife Mary on a sprawling ranch in Cuba. But the advent of the Castro regime forced him to leave, and with his wife he returned to the United States in the summer of 1960. During the next year he underwent frequent treatments for hypertension. There was increasing mental disorder, which culminated in his suicide on July 2, 1961.

As Hemingway mellowed during his later years, many acclaimed him as the greatest living writer. This judgment can be disputed: he is an unquestioned master of the short story, but his novels lend themselves to fragmentation so well that the reader wonders if these too might not have been better as a series of stories. In spite of his obvious drumbeats (on the chest) for an over-glamorized masculinity, Hemingway stands as a stylist whose words ring clean and true and whose touch with love and hate and courage is as gentle-firm as that of a doctor's fingers, probing, trying to find the strength and the sickness in our times.

Bibliography

The definitive biography is Carlos Baker, *Hemingway: The Writer as Artist* (3rd, revised edition) 1964. Biographical and critical materials are contained in the following: Carlos Baker, *Hemingway: The Writer as Artist*, 1952; Philip Young, *Ernest Hemingway*, 1952; Charles A. Fenton, *The Apprenticeship of Ernest Hemingway*, 1954. The best short study is Earl Rovit, *Ernest Hemingway*, 1963. Other studies are H. J. Muller, *Modern Fiction: A Study in Values*, 1937; Maxwell Geismar, *Writers in Crisis*, 1942; Alfred Kazin, *On Native Grounds*, 1942; E. B. Burgum, *The Novel and the World's Dilemma*, 1947; W. M. Frohock, *The Novel of Violence in America, 1900–1950*, 1950; F. J. Hoffman, *The Modern Novel in America, 1900–1950*, 1951; R. B. West, Jr., *The Short Story in America, 1900–1950*, 1951; and Philip Young, *Ernest Hemingway: A Reconsideration*, 1966.

John K. M. McCaffery, Jr., has edited an important collection of critical studies, *Ernest Hemingway: The Man and His Work*, 1950. Carlos Baker has also edited *Hemingway and His Critics: An International Anthology*, 1961, and *Ernest Hemingway: Critiques of Four Major Novels*, 1962. See also David Daiches, "Ernest Hemingway," *College English*, II (1941), 725–736; Malcolm Cowley, "Hemingway at Midnight," *New Republic*, CXI (1944), 190–195; *idem*, "Hemingway and the Hero," *New Republic*, CXI (1944), 754–758; Robert Penn Warren, "Ernest Hemingway," *Kenyon Review*, IX (1947), 1–28 (reprinted in enlarged version as introduction to Modern Standard Authors edition of *A Farewell to Arms*, 1949); Melvin Backman, "The Matador and the Crucified," *Modern Fiction Studies*, I (August, 1955), 2–11; B. S. Oldsey, "Hemingway's Old Men," *Modern*

Fiction Studies, I (August, 1955), 31–35; Warren Beck, "The Shorter Happy Life of Mrs. Macomber," *Modern Fiction Studies*, I (November, 1955), 28–37; Robert C. Hart, "Hemingway on Writing," *College English*, XVIII (1957), 314–320.

The Ernest Hemingway Number of *Modern Fiction Studies*, I (August, 1955), contains a selected checklist of criticism of Hemingway with an index to studies of his separate works, 36–45.

A FAREWELL TO ARMS

Type of work: Novel
Author: Ernest Hemingway (1899–1961)
Time of plot: World War I
Locale: Northern Italy and Switzerland
First published: 1929

This story of a tragic love affair is set on the Italian front during World War I. Hemingway tells his tale with an abundance of realistic detail. Rather than a celebration of the "Triumph of victory and the agony of defeat," the author's vision is uncompromisingly disillusioned. Not only is war useless, but efforts to maintain any meaningful relationship with individuals in the modern world are equally doomed.

Principal Characters

Lieutenant Frederic Henry, an American who has volunteered to serve with an Italian ambulance unit during World War I. Like his Italian companions, he enjoys drinking, trying to treat the war as a joke, and (it is implied) visiting brothels. Before the beginning of a big offensive he meets Catherine Barkley, one of a group of British nurses assigned to staff a hospital unit. Henry begins the prelude to an affair with her but is interrupted by having to go to the front during the offensive; he is wounded, has an operation on his knee, and is sent to recuperate in Milan, where he again meets Miss Barkley, falls in love with her, and sleeps with her in his hospital room. When Henry returns to the front, he knows Catherine is pregnant. In the retreat from Caporetto, Henry is seized at a bridge across the Tagliamento River and realizes he is about to be executed for deserting his troops. He escapes by swimming the river. At Stresa he rejoins Catherine and, before he can be arrested for desertion, the two lovers row across Lake Como to Switzerland. For a few months they live happily at an inn near Montreux—hiking, reading, and discussing American sights (such as Niagara Falls, the stockyards, and the Golden Gate) that Catherine must see after the war. Catherine is to have her baby in a hospital. Her stillborn son is delivered by Caesarian section and that same night Catherine dies. Lieutenant Henry walks back to his hotel through darkness and rain. As developed by Hemingway, Henry is a protagonist who is sensitive to the horrors and beauties of life and war. Many of his reactions are subtly left for the reader to supply. At the end of the novel, for instance, Henry feels sorrow and pity for the dead baby strangled by the umbilical cord, but the full, unbearable weight of Catherine's death falls upon the reader.

Catherine Barkley, the nurse whom Frederic Henry nicknames "Cat." She had been engaged to a childhood sweetheart killed at the Somme. When she falls in love with Henry she gives herself freely to him. Although they both want to be married, she decides the ceremony would not be a proper one while she is pregnant; she feels they are already married. Catherine seems neither a deep thinker nor a very complex person; but she enjoys life, especially good food, drink, and love. She has a premonition that she will die in the rain; the premonition is tragically fulfilled at the hospital in Lausanne.

Lieutenant Rinaldi, Frederick Henry's jokingly cynical friend. Over many bottles they share their experiences and feelings. Although he denies it, Rinaldi is a master of the art of priest-baiting. He is very fond of girls, but he teases Henry about Catherine, calling her a "cool goddess."

The Priest, a young man who blushes easily but manages to survive the oaths and obscenities of the soldiers. He hates the war and its horrors.

Piani, a big Italian soldier who sticks by Henry in the retreat from Caporetto after the others in the unit have been killed

or have deserted. With other Italian soldiers he can be tough but with Henry he is gentle and tolerant of what men suffer in wartime.

Helen Ferguson, a Scottish nurse who is Catherine Barkley's companion when Frederic Henry arrives in Stresa. She is harsh with him because of his affair with Catherine.

Count Greffi, ninety-four years old, a contemporary of Metternich and a former diplomat with whom Frederic Henry plays billiards at Stresa. A gentle cynic, he says that men do not become wise as they grow old; they merely become more careful.

Ettore Moretti, an Italian from San Francisco serving in the Italian army. Much decorated, he is a professional hero whom Frederic Henry dislikes and finds boring.

The Story

Lieutenant Frederic Henry was a young American attached to an Italian ambulance unit on the Italian front. An offensive was soon to begin, and when Henry returned to the front from leave he learned from his friend, Lieutenant Rinaldi, that a group of British nurses had arrived in his absence to set up a British hospital unit. Rinaldi introduced him to nurse Catherine Barkley.

Between ambulance trips to evacuation posts at the front, Henry called on Miss Barkley. He liked the frank young English girl in a casual sort of way, but he was not in love with her. Before he left for the front to stand by for an attack, she give him a St. Anthony medal.

At the front, as Henry and some Italian ambulance drivers were eating in a dugout, an Austrian projectile exploded over them. Henry, badly wounded in the legs, was taken to a field hospital. Later he was moved to a hospital in Milan.

Before the doctor was able to see Henry in Milan, the nurses prohibited his drinking wine, but he bribed a porter to bring him a supply which he kept hidden behind his bed. Catherine Barkley came to the hospital and Henry knew that he was in love with her. The doctors told Henry that he would have to lie in bed six months before they could operate on his knee. Henry insisted on seeing another doctor, who said that the operation could be performed the next day. Meanwhile, Catherine managed to be with Henry constantly.

After his operation, Henry convalesced in Milan with Catherine Barkley as his attendant. Together they dined in out of the way restaurants, and together they rode about the countryside in a carriage. Henry was restless and lonely at nights and Catherine often came to his hospital room.

Summer passed into autumn. Henry's wound had healed and he was due to take convalescent leave in October. He and Catherine planned to spend the leave together, but he came down with jaundice before he could leave the hospital. The head nurse accused him of bringing on the jaundice by drink, in order to avoid being sent back to the front. Before he left for the front, Henry and Catherine stayed together in a hotel room; already she had disclosed to him that she was pregnant.

Henry returned to the front with orders to load his three ambulances with hospital equipment and go south into the Po valley. Morale was at low ebb. Rinaldi admired the job which had been done on the knee and observed that Henry acted like a married man. War weariness was all-pervasive. At the front, the Italians, having learned that German divisions had reinforced the Austrians, began their terrible retreat from Caporetto. Henry drove one of the ambulances loaded with hospital supplies. During the retreat south, the ambulance was held up several times by wagons, guns, and trucks which extended in stalled lines for miles. Henry picked up two straggling Italian sergeants. During the night the retreat was halted in the rain for hours.

At daybreak Henry cut out of the long line and drove across country in an attempt to reach Udine by side roads. The ambulance got stuck in a muddy side road. The sergeants decided to leave, but Henry asked them to help dislodge the car from the mud. They refused and ran. Henry shot and wounded one; the other escaped across the fields. An Italian ambulance corpsman with Henry shot the wounded sergeant through the back of the head. Henry and his three comrades struck out on foot for Udine. On a bridge, Henry saw a German staff car and German bicycle troops crossing another bridge over the same stream. Within sight of Udine, one of Henry's group was killed by an Italian sniper. The others hid in a barn until it seemed safe to circle around Udine and join the main stream of the retreat toward the Tagliamento River.

By that time the Italian army was nothing but a frantic mob. Soldiers were throwing down their arms and officers were cutting insignia of rank from their sleeves. At the end of a long wooden bridge across the Tagliamento military carabiniere were seizing all officers, giving them drumhead trials, and executing them by the river bank. Henry was detained, but in the dark of night he broke free, plunged into the river, and escaped on a log. He crossed the Venetian plain on foot, then jumped aboard a freight train and rode to Milan, where he went to the hospital in which he had been a patient. There he learned that the English nurses had gone to Stresa.

During the retreat from Caporetto Henry had made his farewell to arms. He borrowed civilian clothes from an American friend in Milan and went by train to Stresa, where he met Catherine, who was on leave. The bartender of the hotel in which Henry was staying warned Henry that authorities were planning to arrest him for desertion the next morning; he offered his boat by means of which Henry and Catherine could escape to Switzerland. Henry rowed all night. By morning his hands were so raw that he could barely stand to touch the oars. Over his protests, Catherine took a turn at the rowing. They reached Switzerland safely and were arrested. Henry told the police that he was a sportsman who enjoyed rowing and that he had come to Switzerland for the winter sports. The valid passports and the ample funds that Henry and Catherine possessed saved them from serious trouble with the authorities.

During the rest of the fall and the winter the couple stayed at an inn outside Montreux. They discussed marriage, but Catherine would not be married while she was with child. They hiked, read, and talked about what they would do together after the war.

When the time for Catherine's confinement approached, she and Henry went to Lausanne to be near a hospital. They planned to return to Montreux in the spring. At the hospital Catherine's pains caused the doctor to use an anaesthetic on her. After hours of suffering she was delivered of a dead baby. The nurse sent Henry out to get something to eat. When he went back to the hospital, he learned that Catherine had had a hemorrhage. He went into the room and stayed with her until she died. There was nothing he could do, no one he could talk to, no place he could go. Catherine was dead. He left the hospital and walked back to his hotel in the dark. It was raining.

Critical Evaluation

Ernest Hemingway once referred to *A Farewell to Arms* as his *Romeo and Juliet*. Without insisting on a qualitative comparison, several parallels are obvious. Both works are about "star-crossed" lovers; both show erotic flirtations that rapidly develop into serious, intense, mature love affairs; and both describe the romances against a backdrop of social and political turmoil. Whether or not *A Farewell to Arms* finally qualifies as "tragic" is a matter of personal opinion, but it certainly represents, for Hemingway, an attempt to broaden his concerns from the aimless tragicomic problems of the expatriates in *The Sun Also Rises* (1926) to the fundamental question of life's meaning in the face of human mortality.

Frederic Henry begins the affair as a routine wartime seduction, "a game, like bridge, in which you said things instead of playing cards." He feels mildly guilty, especially after learning about Catherine's vulnerability because of the loss of her lover in combat, but he still foresees no complications from the temporary arrangement. It is not until he is wounded and sent to her hospital in Milan that their affair deepens into love—and from that point on they struggle to free themselves in order to realize it. But they are constantly thwarted, first by the impersonal bureaucracy of the military effort, then by the physical separation imposed by the war itself, and, finally, by the biological "accident" that kills Catherine at the point where their "separate peace" at last seems possible.

As Henry's love for Catherine grows, his disillusionment with the war also increases. From the beginning of the book Henry views the military efforts with ironical detachment, but there is no suggestion that, prior to his meeting with her, he has had any deep reservations about his involvement. Hemingway's attitude toward war was always an ambiguous one. He questioned the rationales for fighting them and the slogans offered in their defense. Like Henry, he felt that "abstract words such as glory, honor, courage, or hallow were obscene." But for the individual, war could be the necessary test. Facing imminent death in combat, one either demonstrated "grace under pressure" and did the "one right thing" or one did not; one either emerged from the experience as a whole person with self-knowledge and control or one came out of it lost and broken.

But there is little heroism in this war as Henry describes it. The hero's disengagement from the fighting is made most vivid in the extended "retreat from Caporetto," generally considered one of the great sequences in modern fiction. The retreat begins in an orderly, disciplined, military manner. But as it progresses, authority breaks down, emotions of self-preservation supersede loyalties and the neat military procession gradually turns into a panicking mob. Henry is caught up in the momentum and carried along with the group in spite of his attempts to keep personal control and fidelity to the small band of survivors he travels with. Upon reaching the Tagliamento River, Henry is seized, along with all other identifiable officers, and held for execution. After he escapes by leaping into the river—an act of ritual purification as well as physical survival—he feels that his "trial" has freed him from any and all further loyalty to the Allied cause.

Henry then rejoins Catherine, and they complete the escape together. In Switzerland, they seem lucky and free at last. Up in the mountains they hike, ski, make love, prepare for the baby, and plan for their postwar life together. Yet even in their most idyllic times there are ominous hints; they worry about the baby; Catherine jokes about her narrow hips; she becomes frightened by a dream of herself "dead in the rain."

Throughout the novel Hemingway associates the "plains" and "rain" with death, disease, and sorrow; the "mountains" and the "snow" with life, health, and happiness. Catherine and Frederic are safe and happy in the mountains, but it is impossible to remain their indefinitely. Eventually everyone must return to the plains. When Catherine and Henry descend to the city it is, in fact, raining, and she does, in fact, die.

Like that of Romeo and Juliet, the love between Catherine and Henry is not destroyed by any moral defect in their own characters. Henry muses that Catherine's fate is the "price" paid for the "good nights" in Milan, but such a price is absurdly excessive. Nor, strictly speaking, is the war responsible for their fate, any more than the Montague-Capulet feud directly provokes the deaths of Shakespeare's lovers. Yet the war and the feud provide the backdrop of violence and the accumulation of pressures that coerce the lovers into actions that contribute to their doom. But, in the final analysis, both couples are defeated by bad luck—the illness that prevents the friar from delivering Juliet's note to Romeo, the accident of Catherine's anatomy that prevents normal childbearing. Thus, both couples are "star-crossed." But if a "purpose" can be vaguely ascertained in Shakespeare's version—the feud is ended by the tragedy—there is no metaphysical justification for Catherine's death; it is, in her own words, "a dirty trick"—and nothing more.

Hemingway does not insist that the old religious meanings are completely invalid, only that they do not work for his people. Henry would like to visit with the priest in his mountain village, but he cannot bring himself to do it. His friend Rinaldi, a combat surgeon, proclaims atheism, hedonism, and work as the only available meanings. Count Greffi, an old billiard player Henry meets in Switzerland, offers good taste, cynicism, and the fact of a long, pleasant life. Catherine and Henry have each other: "You are my religion," she tells him.

But all of these things fail in the end. Religion is only for others, patriotism is a sham, hedonism becomes boring, culture is a temporary distraction, work finally fails (the operation on Catherine was "successful"), even love cannot last (Catherine dies; they both know, although they won't admit it, that the memory of it will fade).

All that remains is a stoic acceptance of the above facts with dignity and without bitterness. Life, like war, is absurd. Henry survives because he is lucky; Catherine dies because she is unlucky. But there is no guarantee that the luck ever balances out and, since everyone ultimately dies, it probably does not matter. What does matter is the courage, dignity, and style with which one accepts these facts as a basis for life and, more importantly, in the face of death.

Bibliography

Anderson, Charles R. "Hemingway's Other Style," in *Modern Language Notes*. LXXVI (May, 1961), pp. 434–442. Reprinted in *Ernest Hemingway: Critiques of Four Major Novels*. Edited by Carlos Baker. New York: Scribner's, 1962, pp. 41–46.

Baker, Carlos. *Hemingway: The Writer as Artist*. Princeton, N.J.: Princeton University Press, 1963, pp. 94–116. Reprinted in *Ernest Hemingway: Critiques of Four Major Novels*. Edited by Carlos Baker. New York: Scribner's, 1962, pp. 47–60.

Baker, Sheridan. *Ernest Hemingway*. New York: Holt, Rinehart, and Winston, 1967, pp. 66–73.

Beach, Joseph Warren. *American Fiction, 1920–1940.* New York: Macmillan, 1941, pp. 84–89.

Benson, Jackson J. *Hemingway: The Writer's Art of Self-Defense.* Minneapolis: University of Minnesota Press, 1969, pp. 81–112.

Fetterly, J. *"A Farewell to Arms*: Ernest Hemingway's 'Resentful Cryptogram,'* " in *The Authority of Experience: Essays in Feminist Criticism.* Edited by Arlyn Diamond and Lee R. Edwards. Amherst: University of Massachusetts Press, 1977, pp. 257–273.

Ford, Ford Madox. "Introduction," in *A Farewell to Arms.* New York: Modern Library, 1932.

Gelfant, Blanche. "Language as a Moral Code in *A Farewell to Arms,*" in *Modern Fiction Studies.* IX (Summer, 1963), pp. 173–176.

Glasser, William. *"A Farewell to Arms,*" in *Sewanee Review.* LXXIV (Spring, 1966), pp. 453–469.

Gurko, Leo. *Ernest Hemingway and the Pursuit of Heroism.* New York: Crowell, 1968, pp. 81–109.

Hardy, John Edward. *Man in the Modern Novel.* Seattle: University of Washington Press, 1964, pp. 123–136.

"Hemingway's *A Farewell to Arms,*" in *Explicator.* III (November, 1944), item 11.

Killinger, John. *Hemingway and the Dead Gods: A Study in Existentialism.* Lexington: University of Kentucky Press, 1960, pp. 46–48. Reprinted in *Twentieth Century Interpretations of* A Farewell to Arms. Edited by Jay Gellens. Englewood Cliffs, N.J.: Prentice-Hall, 1970, pp. 103–105.

Lewis, Robert W., Jr. *Hemingway on Love.* Austin: University of Texas Press, 1965, pp. 39–54. Reprinted in *Twentieth Century Interpretations of* A Farewell to Arms. Edited by Jay Gellens. Englewood Cliffs, N.J.: Prentice-Hall, 1970, pp. 41–53.

Light, James F. "The Religion of Death in *A Farewell to Arms,*" in *Modern Fiction Studies.* VII (Summer, 1961), pp. 169–172. Reprinted in *Ernest Hemingway: Critiques of Four Major Novels.* Edited by Carlos Baker. New York: Scribner's, 1962, pp. 37–40.

Rovit, Earl. *Ernest Hemingway.* New York: Twayne, 1963, pp. 98–106. Reprinted in *Twentieth Century Interpretations of* A Farewell to Arms. Edited by Jay Gellens. Englewood Cliffs, N.J.: Prentice-Hall, 1970, pp. 33–40.

Russell, H.K. "The Catharsis in *A Farewell to Arms,*" in *Modern Fiction Studies.* I (August, 1955), pp. 25–30.

Sanderson, Stewart. *Hemingway.* New York: Grove, 1961, pp. 51–61.

Savage, D.S. *The Withered Branch: Six Studies in the Modern Novel.* London: Eyre and Spottiswoode, 1950, pp. 32–36. Reprinted in *Twentieth*

Century Interpretations of A Farewell to Arms. Edited by Jay Gellens. Englewood Cliffs, N.J.: Prentice-Hall, 1970, pp. 91–102.

Schneider, Daniel J. "Hemingway's *A Farewell to Arms*: The Novel as Pure Poetry," in *Modern Fiction Studies.* XIV (Autumn, 1968), pp. 283–296. Reprinted in *Ernest Hemingway: Five Decades of Criticism.* Edited by Linda W. Wagner. East Lansing: Michigan State University Press, 1974, pp. 252–266.

Waldhorn, Arthur. *A Reader's Guide to Ernest Hemingway.* New York: Noonday, 1972, pp. 113–130.

Warren, Robert Penn. "Introduction," in *A Farewell to Arms.* New York: Scribner's, 1949. Reprinted in *Selected Essays.* New York: Random House, 1958. Also reprinted in *Literary Opinion in America.* Edited by Morton Dauwen Zabel. New York: Harper, 1952, pp. 444–463.

West, Ray B., Jr. "*A Farewell to Arms*," in his and R.W. Stallman's *The Art of Modern Fiction.* New York: Rinehart, 1949, pp. 622–633. Reprinted in *Ernest Hemingway: Critiques of Four Major Novels.* Edited by Carlos Baker. New York: Scribner's, 1962, pp. 28–36. Also reprinted in *Hemingway: A Collection of Critical Essays.* Edited by Robert Weeks. Englewood Cliffs, N.J.: Prentice-Hall, 1962, pp. 139–151. Also reprinted in *Twentieth Century Interpretations of* A Farewell to Arms. Edited by Jay Gellens. Englewood Cliffs, N.J.: Prentice-Hall, 1970, pp. 15–27.

Wylder, Delbert E. *Hemingway's Heroes.* Albuquerque: University of New Mexico Press, 1969, pp. 66–95.

Young, Philip. *Ernest Hemingway.* New York: Rinehart, 1952, pp. 60–66. Reprinted in *Twentieth Century Interpretations of* A Farewell to Arms. Edited by Jay Gellens. Englewood Cliffs, N.J.: Prentice-Hall, 1970, pp. 28–32.

FOR WHOM THE BELL TOLLS

Type of work: Novel
Author: Ernest Hemingway (1899–1961)
Time of plot: 1937
Locale: Spain
First published: 1940

The novel's title, an allusion to lines from John Donne's poem, "No Man Is An Island," tells the story of a young American, fighting voluntarily against Franco's fascist forces in Spain, who leads a band of guerrillas in what turns out to be a totally useless military exploit. The entire novel encompasses only a seventy-two-hour time period during which Robert Jordan loses his comrades in battle, falls in love, is wounded too badly to continue, and finally prepares to make a suicidal stand for his cause.

Principal Characters

Robert Jordan, an American expatriate school teacher who has joined the Loyalist forces in Spain. Disillusioned with the world and dissatisfied with his own country, Jordan has come to Spain to fight and die, if necessary, for a cause he knows is vital and worth while, that of the native, peasant, free soul against the totalitarian cruelty of Franco and his Fascists. He is, however, aware of the contrast between his ideals and the realities he has found among narrow, self-important, selfish, bloodthirsty men capable of betrayal and cruelty as well as courage. He also finds love, devotion, generosity, selflessness in the persons of Anselmo, Pilar, and especially Maria. The latter he loves with the first true selflessness of his life, and he wishes to avenge her cruel suffering and someday make her his wife in a land free of oppression and cruelty. With bravery, almost bravado, he carries out his mission of blowing up a bridge and remains behind to die with the sure knowledge that in Maria and Pilar his person and ideals will survive. Successful for the first time

in his life, in love and war, he awaits death as an old friend.

Maria, a young and innocent Spanish girl cruelly ravaged by war and men's brutality. Befriended by Pilar, a revolutionary, Maria finds a kind of security in the guerrilla band and love in her brief affair with Robert Jordan. As his common-law wife almost all memory of her rape and indignities disappear, and at a moment of triumph for their forces it looks as if they will live to see their dreams of the future fulfilled. Elemental in her passions and completely devoted to her lover, she refuses to leave him and must be forced to go on living. The embodiment of Jordan's ideals, she must live.

Pilar, the strong, almost masculine leader of the guerrilla group with whom Jordan plans to blow up the bridge. Although a peasant and uneducated, Pilar has not only deep feeling but also a brilliant military mind; she is somewhat a Madame Defarge of the Spanish Civil War. Her great trial is her murderous, traitorous husband whom she loves but could kill. Without fear for herself, she has sensitive feelings for Maria, who is suffering from her traumatic experiences as the victim of Fascist lust and cruelty behind the lines. Greatly incensed by inhumanities, Pilar valorously carries out her mission in destroying the bridge, the symbol of her vindictiveness.

Pablo, Pilar's dissolute, drunken, treacherous husband, a type of murderous peasant for whom nothing can be done but without whom the mission cannot be successfully carried out. A hill bandit, Pablo feels loyalty only to himself, kills and despoils at random, is given to drinking and whoring at will. Nevertheless he displays a kind of generosity, even after he has stolen the detonators and peddled them to the enemy, when he comes back to face almost certain death and to go on living with the wife whom he loves and fears. This admixture of cunning, cruelty, and bravado finally leads the band to safety. Pablo represents that irony of ways and means which war constantly confuses.

Anselmo, the representative of peasant wisdom, devotion to duty, high-minded, selfless love for humanity, and compassion for the human condition. Hating to kill but not fearing to die, Anselmo performs his duty by killing when necessary, but without rancor and with a kind of benediction, and dies as he lived, generously and pityingly. While the others of the guerrilla band are more of Pablo's persuasion, brutally shrewd and vindictive in loyalty, Anselmo tempers his devotion to a cause with a larger view. Aligned with Pilar and Jordan in this larger vision, he displays disinterested and kindly loyalty that is almost pure idealism, all the more remarkable for his age, background, and experience. The benignant, almost Christ-like Anselmo dies that others may live and that Robert Jordan may know how to die.

El Sordo, a Loyalist guerrilla leader killed in a Fascist assault on his mountain hideout.

General Golz, the Russian officer commanding the Thirty-fifth Division of the Loyalist forces.

Karkov, a Russian journalist.

Andrés, a guerrilla sent by Robert Jordan with a dispatch for General Golz.

André Marty, the commissar who prevents prompt delivery of the dispatch intended for General Golz.

Rafael, a gipsy,

Agustín,
Fernando,
Primitivo, and
Eladio, other members of the guerrilla band led by Pablo and Pilar.

The Story

At first nothing was important but the bridge, neither his life nor the imminent danger of his death —just the bridge. Robert Jordan was a young American teacher who was in Spain fighting with the Loyalist guerrillas. His present and most important mission was to blow up a bridge which would be of great strategic importance during a Loyalist offensive three days hence. Jordan was behind the Fascist lines, with orders to make contact with Pablo, the leader of a guerrilla band, and with his wife Pilar, who was the really strong figure among the partisans. While Pablo was weak and a drunken braggart, Pilar was strong and trustworthy. She was a swarthy, raw-boned woman, vulgar and outspoken, but she was so fiercely devoted to the Loyalist cause that Jordan knew she would carry out her part of the mission regardless of her personal danger.

The plan was for Jordan to study the bridge from all angles and then to make final plans for its destruction at the proper moment. Jordan had blown up many bridges and three trains, but this was the first time that everything must be done on a split-second schedule. Pablo and Pilar were to assist Jordan in any way they could, even to rounding up other bands of guerrillas if Jordan needed them to accomplish his mission.

At the cave hideout of Pablo and Pilar, Jordan met a beautiful young girl named Maria, who had escaped from the Fascists. Maria had been subjected to every possible indignity that a woman could suffer. She had been starved and tortured and raped, and she felt unclean. At the camp Jordan also met Anselmo, a loyal old man who would follow orders regardless of his personal safety. Anselmo hated having to kill but, if he were so ordered, faithful Anselmo would kill.

Jordan loved the brutally shrewd, desperate, loyal guerrillas, for he knew their cruelties against the Fascists stemmed from poverty and ignorance. But the Fascists' cruelty he abhorred, for the Fascists came largely from the wealthy, ambitious people of Spain. Maria's story of her suffering at their hands filled him with such hatred that he could have killed a thousand of them, even though he, like Anselmo, hated to kill.

The first night he spent at the guerrilla camp destroyed his cold approach to the mission before him, for he fell deeply in love with Maria. She came to his sleeping bag that night, and although they talked but little, he knew after she left that he was no longer ready to die. He told Maria that one day they would be married, but he was afraid of the future. And fear was dangerous for a man on an important mission.

Jordan made many sketches of the bridge and laid his plans carefully. There his work was almost ruined by Pablo's treachery. On the night before the blowing up of the bridge Pablo deserted after stealing and destroying the explosives and the detonators hidden in Jordan's pack. Pablo returned, repentant, on the morning of the mission, but the damage had been done. The loss of the detonators and the explosives meant that Jordan and his helper would have to blow the bridge with hand grenades, a much more dangerous method. Pablo had tried to redeem himself by bringing with him another small guerrilla band and their horses. Although Jordan despised Pablo by that time, he forgave him, as did Pilar.

At the bridge Jordan worked quickly and carefully. Each person had a specific job to do, and each did his work well. First Jordan and Anselmo had to kill the sentries, a job Anselmo hated. Pablo and his guerrillas attacked the Fascist lines approaching the bridge, to prevent their crossing before the bridge was demolished. Jordan had been ordered to blow up the bridge at the beginning of a Loyalist bombing attack over the Fascist lines. When he heard the thudding explosions of the bombs, he pulled the pins and the bridge shot high into the air Jordan got to cover safely, but Anselmo was killed by a steel fragment from the bridge. As

Jordan looked at the old man and realized that he might be alive if Pablo had not stolen the detonators, he wanted to kill Pablo. But he knew that his duty was otherwise, and he ran to the designated meeting place of the fugitive guerrillas.

There he found Pablo, Pilar, Maria, and the two remaining gipsy partisans. Pablo, herding the extra horses, said that all the other guerrillas had been killed. Jordan knew that Pablo had ruthlessly killed the other men so that he could get their horses. When he confronted Pablo with this knowledge, Pablo admitted the slaughter, but shrugged his great shoulders and said that the men had not been of his band.

The problem now was to cross a road which could be swept by Fascist gunfire, the road that led to safety. Jordan knew that the first two people would have the best chance, since probably they could cross before the Fascists were alerted. Because Pablo knew the road to safety, Jordan put him on the first horse. Maria was second, for Jordan was determined that she should be saved before the others. Pilar was to go next, then the two remaining guerrillas, and last of all Jordan. The first four crossed safely, but Jordan's horse, wounded by Fascist bullets, fell on Jordan's leg. The others dragged him across the road and out of the line of fire, but he knew that he could not go on; he was too badly injured to ride a horse. Pablo and Pilar understood, but Maria begged to stay with him. Jordan told Pilar to take Maria away when he gave the signal, and then he talked to the girl he loved so much. He told her that she must go on, that as long as she lived, he lived also. But when the time came, she had to be put on her horse and led away.

Jordan, settling down to wait for the approaching Fascist troops, propped himself against a tree, with his submachine gun across his knees. As he waited, he thought over the events that had brought him to that place. He knew that what he had done was right, but that his side might not win for many years. But he knew, too, that if the common people kept trying, kept dying, someday they would win. He hoped they would be prepared when that day came, that they would no longer want to kill and torture, but would struggle for peace and for good as they were now struggling for freedom. He felt at the end that his own part in the struggle had not been in vain. As he saw the first Fascist officer approaching, Robert Jordan smiled. He was ready.

Critical Evaluation

In 1940 Ernest Hemingway published *For Whom the Bell Tolls* to wide critical and public acclaim. The novel became an immediate best seller, erasing his somewhat flawed performance in *To Have and Have Not* (1937). During the 1930's Hemingway enjoyed a decade of personal publicity that put most American authors in his shade. These were the years of his African safari which produced *Green Hills of Africa* (1935) and his *Esquire* column (1933-1936). Wherever he went he was news. In 1940 he was divorced by his second wife, Pauline Pfeiffer, and then married

Martha Gellhorn. He set fishing records at Bimini in marlin tournaments. He hunted in Wyoming and fished at Key West where he bought a home. In 1937 when the Spanish Civil War broke out, Hemingway went to Spain as a correspondent with a passionate devotion to the Spain of his early years. Not content merely to report the war, he became actively involved with the Loyalist Army in its fight against Franco and the generals. He wrote the script for the propaganda film *The Spanish Earth* (1937) which was shown at the White House at a presidential dinner. The proceeds of the film were used to buy ambulances for the Loyalists. In 1939, with the war a lost cause, Hemingway wrote *For Whom the Bell Tolls* just as World War II was beginning to destroy Europe.

Even more than in *A Farewell to Arms,* Hemingway here has focused the conflict of war on a single man. Like Frederic Henry, Robert Jordan is an American in a European country fighting for a cause that is not his by birth. Frederic, however, just happened to be in Italy when World War I broke out; he had no ideological commitment to the war. Robert Jordan has come to Spain because he believes in the Loyalist cause. Although the Loyalists have communist backing, Jordan is not a communist. He believes in the land and the people, and ultimately this belief costs him his life. Jordan's death is an affirmation. One need only compare it with the earlier novels to see this novel as a clear political statement of what a man must do under pressure.

For Whom the Bell Tolls is a circular novel. It begins with Robert Jordan belly-down on a pine forest in Spain observing a bridge he has been assigned to destroy. At the conclusion, Jordan is once again belly-down against the Spanish earth; this time snow covers the pine needles and he has a broken leg. He is carefully sighting on an enemy officer approaching on horseback, and "he could feel his heart beating against the pine needle floor of the forest." Between the opening and closing paragraphs, two hundred thousand words have passed covering a time period of only seventy hours. At the center of all the action and meditation is the bridge. It is the focal point of the conflict to which the reader and the characters are drawn back again and again.

In what was his longest novel to that point, Hemingway forged a tightly unified plot: a single place, a single action, and a brief time—the old Greek unities. Jordan's military action takes on other epic qualities associated with the Greeks. His sacrifice is not unlike that of Leonidas at the crucial pass, Thermopylae, during the Persian Wars. There, too, heroic action was required to defend an entry point, and there, too, the leader died in an action which proved futile in military terms but became a standard measure of courage and commitment.

Abandoning somewhat the terse, clipped style of his earlier novels, Hemingway makes effective use of flashbacks to delineate the major characters.

Earlier central characters seemed to exist without a past. But if Robert Jordan's death was to "diminish mankind," then the reader had to know more about him. This character development takes place almost within suspended time. Jordan and Maria try to condense an entire life into those seventy hours. The reader is never allowed to forget time altogether, for the days move, light changes, meals are eaten, snow falls. Everything moves toward the time when the bridge must be blown, but this time frame is significant only to Jordan and the gipsy group. It has little reference to the rest of the world. Life, love, and death are compressed into those seventy hours, and the novel becomes a compact cycle suspended in time.

The novel has more fully developed characters than the earlier Hemingway novels. In the gipsy camp each person becomes important. Pilar is often cited as one of Hemingway's better female characters, just as Maria is often criticized as being unbelievable. However, Maria's psychological scars are carefully developed. She has been raped by the Fascists, and has seen her parents and village butchered. She is just as mentally unstable as were Brett Ashley and Catherine Barkley. Jordan, too, is a wounded man. He lives with the suicide of his father and the killing of his fellow dynamiter. The love of Jordan and Maria makes each of them whole again.

The bridge is destroyed on schedule, but, through no fault of Jordan's, its destruction is meaningless in military terms. Seen in the context of the military and political absurdities, Jordan's courage and death were wasted. However, the bridge was more important for its effect upon the group. It gave them a purpose and a focal point; it forged them into a unity, a whole. They can take pride in their accomplishment in spite of its cost. Life is ultimately a defeat no matter how it is lived; what gives defeat meaning is the courage that a man is capable of forging in the face of death's certainty. One man's death does diminish the group, for they are involved together. Jordan's loss is balanced by the purpose he has given to the group.

Just as the mountains are no longer a safe place from the Fascists with their airplanes, Hemingway seems to be saying that no man and no place are any longer safe. It is no longer possible to make a separate peace as Frederic Henry did with his war. When fascist violence is loose in the world, a man must take a stand. Jordan does not believe in the communist ideology that supports the Loyalists, but he does believe in the earth and its people. He is essentially the nonpolitical man caught in a political conflict which he cannot avoid. He does the best he can with the weapons available to him.

Bibliography

Adler, Jack. "Theme and Character in Hemingway: *For Whom the Bell Tolls*," in *University Review.* XXX (June, 1964), pp. 293–299.

Aldridge, John W.   *After the Lost Generation.* New York: McGraw-Hill, 1951, pp. 34–38.

Atkins, John.   *The Art of Ernest Hemingway: His Work and Personality.* London: Peter Nevill, 1952, pp. 27–45.

Baker, Carlos.   *Hemingway: The Writer as Artist.* Princeton, N.J.: Princeton University Press, 1963, pp. 223–263. Reprinted in *Ernest Hemingway: Critiques of Four Major Novels.* Edited by Carlos Baker. New York: Scribner's, 1962, pp. 108–130.

Baker, Sheridan.   *Ernest Hemingway.* New York: Holt, Rinehart, and Winston, 1967, pp. 109–118.

Beach, Joseph Warren.   *American Fiction, 1920–1940.* New York: Macmillan, 1941, pp. 89–93, 112–119.

Benson, Jackson J.   *Hemingway: The Writer's Art of Self-Defense.* Minneapolis: University of Minnesota Press, 1969, pp. 153–168.

Bessie, Alvah.   "Hemingway's *For Whom the Bell Tolls*," in *New Masses.* XXXVII (November 5, 1940), pp. 25–29. Reprinted in *Ernest Hemingway: Critiques of Four Major Novels.* Edited by Carlos Baker. New York: Scribner's, 1962, pp. 90–94.

Brooks, Cleanth.   *The Hidden God: Studies in Hemingway, Faulkner, Yeats, Eliot, and Warren.* New Haven, Conn.: Yale University Press, 1963, pp. 16–20.

Cooperman, Stanley.   "Hemingway's Blue-Eyed Boy: Robert Jordan and 'Purging Ecstasy,' " in *Criticism.* VIII (Winter, 1966), pp. 87–96.

Frankenberg, Lloyd.   "Themes and Characters in Hemingway's Latest Period," in *Southern Review.* VII (Spring, 1942), pp. 776–788.

French, Warren.   *The Social Novel at the End of an Era.* Carbondale: Southern Illinois University Press, 1966, pp. 87–124.

Geismar, Maxwell.   *Writers in Crisis: The American Novel Between Two Wars.* Boston: Houghton Mifflin, 1942, pp. 79–84.

Gurko, Leo.   *Ernest Hemingway and the Pursuit of Heroism.* New York: Crowell, 1968, pp. 110–136.

Guttmann, Allen.   "Mechanized Doom: Ernest Hemingway and the Spanish Civil War," in *Massachusetts Review.* I (May, 1960), pp. 541–561. Reprinted in *Ernest Hemingway: Critiques of Four Major Novels.* Edited by Carlos Baker. New York: Scribner's, 1962, pp. 95–107.

Lewis, Robert W., Jr.   *Hemingway on Love.* Austin: University of Texas Press, 1965, pp. 143–178.

Rovit, Earl.   *Ernest Hemingway.* New York: Twayne, 1963, pp. 74–76, 136–146.

Sanderson, Stewart. *Hemingway.* New York: Grove, 1961, pp. 89–102.

Savage, D.S. *The Withered Branch: Six Studies in the Modern Novel.* London: Eyre and Spottiswoode, 1950, pp. 36–43.

Sickels, Eleanor M. "Farewell to Cynicism," in *College English.* III (October, 1941), pp. 31–38.

Snell, George. *Shapers of American Fiction: 1798–1947.* New York: Dutton, 1947, pp. 166–171.

Trilling, Lionel. "An American in Spain," in *The Partisan Reader.* Edited by William Phillips and Philip Rahv. New York: Dial, 1946, pp. 639–644. Reprinted in *Ernest Hemingway: Critiques of Four Major Novels.* Edited by Carlos Baker. New York: Scribner's, 1962, pp. 78–81.

Waldhorn, Arthur. *A Reader's Guide to Ernest Hemingway.* New York: Noonday, 1972, pp. 163–177.

Wylder, Delbert E. *Hemingway's Heroes.* Albuquerque: University of New Mexico Press, 1969, pp. 127–164.

Young, Philip. *Ernest Hemingway.* New York: Rinehart, 1952, pp. 75–86.

THE OLD MAN AND THE SEA

Type of work: Novelette
Author: Ernest Hemingway (1899–1961)
Time of plot: Mid-twentieth century
Locale: Cuba and the Gulf Stream
First published: 1952

On the surface an exciting but tragic adventure story, The Old Man and the Sea *enjoys near-perfection of structure, restraint of treatment, and evocative simplicity of style. On a deeper level, the book is a fable of the unconquerable spirit of man, a creature capable of snatching spiritual victory from circumstances of disaster and apparent defeat; on yet another level, it is a religious parable which unobtrusively utilizes Christian symbols and metaphors.*

Principal Characters

Santiago, an old Cuban fisherman. After more than eighty days of fishing without a catch, the old man's patient devotion to his calling is rewarded. He catches a marlin bigger than any ever brought into Havana harbor. But the struggle to keep the marauding sharks from the fish is hopeless, and he reaches shore again with only a skeleton, worthless except as a symbol of his victory.

Manolin, a young Cuban boy devoted to Santiago, with whom he fishes until forbidden by his father after Santiago's fortieth luckless day. He begs or steals to make sure Santiago does not go hungry.

The Story

For eighty-four days old Santiago had not caught a single fish. At first a young boy, Manolin, had shared his bad fortune, but after the fortieth luckless day the boy's father told his son to go in another boat. From that time on Santiago worked alone. Each morning he rowed his skiff out into the Gulf Stream where the big fish were. Each evening he came in empty-handed.

The boy loved the old fisherman and pitied him. If Manolin had no money of his own, he begged or stole to make sure that Santiago had enough to eat and fresh baits for his lines. The old man accepted his kindness with humility that was like a quiet kind of pride. Over their evening meals of rice or black beans they would talk about the fish they had taken in luckier times or about American baseball and the great DiMaggio. At night, alone in his shack, Santiago dreamed of lions on the beaches of Africa, where he had gone on a sailing ship years before. He no longer dreamed of his dead wife.

On the eighty-fifth day Santiago rowed out of the harbor in the cool dark before dawn. After leaving the smell of land behind him, he set his lines. Two of his baits were fresh tunas the boy had given him, as well as sardines to cover his hooks. The lines went straight down into deep dark water.

As the sun rose he saw other boats in toward shore, which was only a low green line on the sea. A hovering man-of-war bird showed him where dolphin were chasing some flying fish, but the school was moving too fast and too far away. The bird circled again. This time Santiago saw tuna leaping in the sunlight. A small one took the hook on his stern line. Hauling the quivering fish aboard, the old man thought it a good omen.

Toward noon a marlin started nibbling at the bait which was one hundred fathoms down. Gently the old man played the fish, a big one, as he knew from the weight on the line. At last he struck to settle the hook. The fish did not surface. Instead, it began to tow the skiff to the northwest. The old man braced himself, the line taut across his shoulders. Although he was alone and no longer strong, he had his skill and knew many tricks. He waited patiently for the fish to tire.

The old man shivered in the cold that came after sunset. When something took one of his remaining baits, he cut the line with his sheath knife. Once the fish lurched suddenly, pulling Santiago forward on his face and cutting his cheek. By dawn his left hand was stiff and cramped. The fish had headed northward; there was no land in sight. Another strong tug on the line sliced Santiago's right hand. Hungry, he cut strips from the tuna and chewed them slowly while he waited for the sun to warm him and ease his cramped fingers.

That morning the fish jumped. Seeing it leap. Santiago knew he had hooked the biggest marlin he had ever seen. Then the fish went under and turned toward the east. Santiago drank sparingly from his water bottle during the hot afternoon. Trying to forget his cut hand and aching back, he remembered the days when men had called him *El Campéon* and he had wrestled with a giant Negro in the tavern at Cienfuegos. Once an airplane droned overhead on its way to Miami.

Close to nightfall a dolphin took the small hook he had rebaited. He lifted the fish aboard, careful not to jerk the line over his shoulder. After he had rested, he cut fillets from the dolphin and kept also the two flying fish he found in its maw. That night he slept. He awoke to feel the line running through his fingers as the fish jumped. Feeding line slowly, he tried to tire the marlin. After the fish slowed its run, he washed his cut hands in sea water and ate one of the flying fish. At sunrise the marlin began to circle. Faint and dizzy, he worked to bring the big fish nearer with each turn. Almost exhausted, he finally drew his catch alongside and drove in the harpoon. He drank a little water before he lashed the marlin to bow and stern of his skiff. The fish was two feet longer than the boat. No catch like it had ever been seen in Havana harbor. It would make his fortune, he thought, as he hoisted his patched sails and set his course toward the southwest.

An hour later he sighted the first shark. It was a fierce Mako, and it came in fast to slash with raking teeth at the dead marlin. With failing might the old man struck the shark with his harpoon. The Mako rolled and sank, carrying the harpoon with it and leaving the marlin mutilated and bloody. Santiago knew the scent would spread. Watching, he saw two shovel-nosed sharks closing in. He struck at one with his knife lashed to the end of an oar and watched the scavenger sliding down into deep water. The other he killed while it tore at the flesh of the marlin. When the third appeared, he thrust at it with the knife, only to feel the blade snap as the fish rolled. The other sharks came at sunset. At first he tried to club them with the tiller from the skiff, but his hands were raw and bleeding and there were too many in the pack. In the darkness, as he steered toward the faint glow of Havana against the sky, he heard them hitting the carcass again and again. But the old man thought only of his steering and his great tiredness. He had gone out too far and the sharks had beaten him. He knew they would leave him nothing but the stripped skeleton of his great catch.

All lights were out when he sailed into the little harbor and beached his skiff. In the gloom he could just make out the white backbone and the upstanding tail of the fish. He started up the shore with the mast and furled sail of his boat. Once he fell under their weight and lay patiently until he could gather his strength. In his shack he fell on his bed and went to sleep.

There the boy found him later that morning. Meanwhile other fishermen, gathered about the skiff, marveled at the giant marlin, eighteen feet long from nose to tail. When Manolin returned to Santiago's shack with hot coffee, the old man awoke. The boy, he said, could have the spear of his fish. Manolin told him to rest, to make himself fit for the days of fishing they would have together. All that afternoon the old man slept, the boy sitting by his bed. Santiago was dreaming of lions.

Critical Evaluation

Hemingway began his career as a journalist with the *Kansas City Star* in 1917, and later was a wartime foreign correspondent for the *Toronto Star*. His first important collection of short stories, *In Our Time,* appeared in 1925, to be followed, in 1926, by what many consider to be his finest novel, *The Sun Also Rises.* During his long stay among other American expatriates in Paris, Hemingway was influenced by Gertrude Stein, Ezra Pound, and James Joyce. From their models, from his own journalistic background, and from his admiration for Mark Twain, Hemingway developed his own characteristic style—a style so idiosyncratic that it precluded imitation and, eventually, strangled Hemingway's own artistic development. The Hemingway style, further expressed in *A Farewell to Arms* (1929), then gradually sinking toward stereotypical stylization in *Death in the Afternoon* (1932), *The Green Hills of Africa* (1935), and *For Whom the Bell Tolls* (where it reaches its lowest point of self-caricature, undermining his most ambitious novel), is marked by consistent elements: understatement created by tersely realistic dialogue; use of everyday speech and simple vocabulary; avoidance of the abstract; straightforward sentence structure and paragraph development; spare and specific imagery; objective, reportorial viewpoint; and emphasis on "the real thing, the sequence of emotion and fact to make the emotion." This last, Wordsworthian, technique accounts for Hemingway's position as the most gifted of the "Lost Generation" writers.

Accompanying these stylistic traits is a set of consistent thematic concerns that have become known as the Hemingway "code": obsession with all outdoor pursuits and sports; identification with the primitive; constant confrontation with death; fascination with violence, and with the skillful control of violence; what he calls "holding the purity line through the maximum of exposure." The typical Hemingway hero, existential in a peculiarly American way, faces the sterility and failure and death of his contemporary world with steady-handed courage and a stoical resistance to pain that allows him a fleeting, but essentially human, nobility and grace.

After a decade of silence, while Hemingway was preoccupied with the turmoil of World War II, he published *Across the River and into the Trees* (1950)—an inferior book that led many to believe his genius had dried up. But two years later, drawn from his experiences in Cuba, *The Old Man and the Sea* appeared—to be awarded the Pulitzer Prize, and to lead to a Nobel Prize for Literature (1954) for his "mastery of the art of modern narration." As a kind of ultimate condensation of the Hemingway code, this novelette attains an austere dignity from its extreme simplicity of imagery, symbolism, setting, and character. As such it is in stark contrast with Melville's sprawling epic masterpiece with which it has much in common: *Moby Dick*.

Hemingway displays his genius of perception by using, without apology, the most obvious symbolic imagery; in fact, he creates his desired impact by admitting the ordinary (in the way of Robert Frost, whose "An Old Man's Winter's Night" resembles this book). An example is the statement that the old man's furled sail each evening "looked like a flag of permanent defeat." Here the admission of the obvious becomes ironic, since the old man is not, as he himself declares, *defeated*—although he is "destroyed." Aside from the two overt image-symbols of the lions on the beach and of "the great Di Maggio" ("who does all things perfectly even with the pain of the bone spur in his heel"), the implicit image of Christ stalks through the work until the reader understands that it is not, after all, a religious symbol, but a secular one that affirms that each man has his own agonies and crucifixion. As for setting, three elements stand out: the sea itself, which the old man regards as feminine—not as an enemy but as the *locus* in which man plays his little part with security and serenity derived from acceptance of her inevitable capriciousness; the intrusions of the outside world, with the jet plane high overhead and the tourist woman's ignorant comment at the end that shows total insensitivity to the common man's capacity for tragedy; and the sharks, which make "everything wrong" and stand for the heroic absurdity of human endeavors.

The old man's character is revealed to us in two ways: by the observations of the narrator, and by his own monologue. The latter device might seem theatrical and out of place if Hemingway had not taken pains to set up its employment openly: "He did not remember when he had first started to talk aloud when he was by himself." But the words he says to no one but himself reveal the old man's mind as clearly as, and even more poignantly than, the narrator's knowledge of his thoughts. We see him as the unvanquished (whose eyes are as young as the sea); with sufficient pride to allow humility; with unsuspected, though simple, introspection ("I am a strange old man"); with unquestioning trust in his own skills and in the folklore of his trade; with almost superhuman endurance; and with a noble acceptance of the limitations forced upon him by age. Before the drama is over, the old man projects his own qualities into the fish—his strength, his wisdom—until his initial hunter's indifference turns to pity and the fish becomes "friend" and "brother." "But I must kill him," the old man says, stating Hemingway's consciousness of naturalistic realism: "I am glad we do not have to try to kill the stars. . . . It is enough to live on the sea and kill our true brothers." Killing with dignity, as it is done also in the bullring, is an accepted part of the human condition. Only the graceless, undignified sharks (like the hyenas in "The Snows of Kilimanjaro") are abhorrent and diminish the tragic grandeur of the human drama.

The Old Man and the Sea is a direct descendant of *Moby Dick*. The size, strength, and mystery of the great marlin recall the presence of the elusive white whale; similarly, the strength, determination (like Ahab, the old man does not bother with eating or sleeping), and strangeness of Hemingway's hero may be compared to the epic qualities of Melville's. But the differences are as important as the similarities. In Melville, both the whale and Ahab have sinister, allusive, and unknown connotations that they seem to share between them and that are not revealed clearly to the reader—in the fashion of romanticism. Hemingway's realism does not present the struggle as a pseudo-sacred cosmic one between forces of darkness but as an everyday confrontation between the strength of an ordinary man and the power of nature. Hemingway's fish is huge, but he is not solitary and unique; the old man is not the oldest, nor the greatest, fisherman. Finally, neither the old man, nor the fish, is completely victorious. The fish does not kill the old man, nor does it make him older or wiser; it only makes him very tired.

Bibliography

Aldridge, John W.   *Time to Murder and Create: The Contemporary Novel in Crisis.* New York: David McKay, 1966, pp. 185–191.

Backman, Melvin.   "Hemingway: The Matador and the Crucified," in *Modern Fiction Studies.* I (August, 1955), pp. 2–11. Reprinted in *Hemingway and His Critics: An International Anthology.* Edited by Carlos Baker. New York: Hill and Wang, 1961, pp. 245–258. Also reprinted in *Ernest Hemingway: Critiques of Four Major Novels.* Edited by Carlos Baker. New York: Scribner's, 1962, pp. 135–143.

Baker, Carlos.   *Hemingway: The Writer as Artist.* Princeton, N.J.: Princeton University Press, 1963, pp. 289–328. Reprinted in *Ernest Hemingway: Critiques of Four Major Novels.* Edited by Carlos Baker. New York: Scribner's, 1962, pp. 156–172. Also reprinted in *Twentieth Century Interpretations of The Old Man and the Sea.* Edited by Katharine T. Jobes. Englewood Cliffs, N.J.: Prentice-Hall, 1968, pp. 27–33.

Baker, Sheridan.   *Ernest Hemingway.* New York: Holt, Rinehart, and Winston, 1967, pp. 126–135.

Barbour, James and Robert Sattelmeyer.   "Baseball and Baseball Talk in *The Old Man and the Sea,*" in *Fitzgerald/Hemingway Annual 1975,* pp. 281–287.

Barnes, Lois L.   "The Helpless Hero of Ernest Hemingway," in *Science and Society.* XVII (Winter, 1953), pp. 1–8.

Burhans, Clinton S., Jr.   "*The Old Man and the Sea*: Hemingway's Tragic Vision of Man," in *American Literature.* XXXI (January, 1960), pp. 446–455. Reprinted in *Hemingway and His Critics: An International Anthology.* Edited by Carlos Baker. New York: Hill and Wang, 1961, pp. 259–268. Also reprinted in *Ernest Hemingway: Critiques of Four Major Novels.* Edited by Carlos Baker. New York: Scribner's, 1962, pp. 150–155.

Cooperman, Stanley.   "Hemingway and Old Age: Santiago as Priest of Time," in *College English.* XXVII (December, 1965), pp. 215–220.

Gurko, Leo.   *Ernest Hemingway and the Pursuit of Heroism.* New York: Crowell, 1968, pp. 159–174.

Handy, William J.   "A New Dimension for a Hero: Santiago of *The Old Man and the Sea,*" in *Six Contemporary Novels: Six Introductory Essays in Modern Fiction.* Edited by William O.S. Sutherland, Jr. Austin: University of Texas Department of English, 1962, pp. 58–75.

Harada, Keiichi.   "The Marlin and the Shark: A Note on *The Old Man and the Sea,*" in *Hemingway and His Critics: An International Anthology.* Edited by Carlos Baker. New York: Hill and Wang, 1961, pp. 269–276.

Kashkeen, Ivan. "Alive in the Midst of Death," in *Hemingway and His Critics: An International Anthology*. Edited by Carlos Baker. New York: Hill and Wang, 1961, pp. 162–179.

Lewis, Robert W., Jr. *Hemingway on Love*. Austin: University of Texas Press, 1965, pp. 199–213.

Moseley, Edwin M. *Pseudonyms of Christ in the Modern Novel*. Pittsburgh: University of Pittsburgh Press, 1962, pp. 205–313.

Rahv, Philip. *Image and Idea: Twenty Essays on Literary Themes*. New York: New Directions, 1957, pp. 192–195.

Rosenfield, Claire. "New World, Old Myths," in *Twentieth Century Interpretations of* The Old Man and the Sea. Edited by Katharine T. Jobes. Englewood Cliffs, N.J.: Prentice-Hall, 1968, pp. 41–55.

Rovit, Earl. *Ernest Hemingway*. New York: Twayne, 1963, pp. 85–94.

Sanderson, Stewart. *Hemingway*. New York: Grove, 1961, pp. 113–118.

Schorer, Mark. "With Grace Under Pressure," in *New Republic*. CXXVII (October 6, 1952), pp. 19–20. Reprinted in *Ernest Hemingway: Critiques of Four Major Novels*. Edited by Carlos Baker. New York: Scribner's, 1962, pp. 132–134.

Waldhorn, Arthur. *A Reader's Guide to Ernest Hemingway*. New York: Noonday, 1972, pp. 189–199.

Weeks, Robert P. "Fakery in *The Old Man and the Sea*," in *College English*, XXIV (December, 1962), pp. 188–192. Reprinted in *Twentieth Century Interpretations of* The Old Man and the Sea. Edited by Katharine T. Jobes. Englewood Cliffs, N.J.: Prentice-Hall, 1968, pp. 34–40.

Wood, Cecil. "On the Tendency of Nature to Imitate Art," in *Minnesota Review*. VI (1966), pp. 140–148.

Wylder, Delbert E. *Hemingway's Heroes*. Albuquerque: University of New Mexico Press, 1969, pp. 199–222.

Young, Philip. *Ernest Hemingway*. New York: Rinehart, 1952, pp. 93–105. Reprinted in *Twentieth Century Interpretations of* The Old Man and the Sea. Edited by Katharine T. Jobes. Englewood Cliffs, N.J.: Prentice-Hall, 1968, pp. 18–26.

Zabel, Morton Dauwen. *Craft and Character in Modern Fiction: Texts, Method, and Vocation*. New York: Viking, 1957, pp. 321–326.

THE SUN ALSO RISES

Type of work: Novel
Author: Ernest Hemingway (1899–1961)
Time of plot: 1920's
Locale: Paris and Pamplona, Spain
First published: 1926

The Sun Also Rises, *a major novel of the 1920's, treats the aimlessness of a group of American and English expatriates who represent the so-called "lost generation" following the disillusionment of World War I. Unlike most of the other characters, who cynically acquiesce in their own moral disintegration, Jake Barnes searches for a personal, proto-existential code of values.*

Principal Characters

Robert Cohn, a Jewish writer living in Paris in the 1920's. He and Jacob Barnes are friends, though Barnes delights in needling him. Cohn seems to mean well, but he has a talent for irritating all his acquaintances. When Cohn meets Lady Brett Ashley, he immediately brushes off Frances Clyne, his mistress, and spends a few days at San Sebastian with Brett. He now feels that she is his property, though she plans to marry Michael Campbell. Cohn has the temerity to join a group from Paris (including Brett and Michael) going to the fiesta in Pamplona, Spain. When Brett is smitten by a young bullfighter and sleeps with him, Cohn, reputedly once a middleweight boxing champion at Princeton, gives the bullfighter a pummeling. Cohn's personality has many contradictions: in general, he is conceited, but is unsure of himself as a writer; he seems both obtuse and sensitive; he evokes pity from his friends, yet they all thoroughly dislike him.

Jacob Barnes (Jake), the narrator, an American expatriate also living in Paris, where he works as a correspondent for a newspaper. In World War I he was wounded in the groin and as a result is sexually impotent. This injury negates the love he has for Brett and her love for him. Seeming to work very little, Barnes spends a great deal of time in cafés, drinking and talking. His greatest problems in life are trying to adjust himself to the nature of his injury and trying to work out some sort of personal philosophy; two of his thoughts almost solve the latter problem: "You can't get away from yourself by moving from one place to another" and "Enjoying living was learning to get your money's worth and knowing when you had it." Barnes is a lover of good food and drink, an expert trout fisherman, and an "aficionado" of the bullfight. Although he drinks as much as the other characters, some of whom are given to passing out, he has the happy faculty of remaining keen and alert.

Lady Brett Ashley, an English woman separated from her husband. Her first lover died of dysentery during the war and she is getting a divorce from Lord Ashley. She plans to marry Michael Campbell, but really she is in love with Barnes, perhaps because she knows he is unattainable, because they can never sexually consummate their love. She is a drunkard and is wildly promiscuous, as is shown by her affairs with Cohn and. the young bullfighter, Pedro Romero; but she seems as lost in life as Barnes and she is an appealing woman, one whose successive affairs remind the reader of a little girl trying game after game to keep herself from being bored. In the end she is determined to settle down with Campbell, even though he is nastily talkative when drunk; but in spite of her resolutions Lady Brett seems destined to work her way through life from bed to bed.

Bill Gorton, a witty American friend of Barnes. With Barnes he fishes for trout in Spain and attends the fiesta in Pamplona.

Michael Campbell, Lady Brett's fiancé. He is pleasant when sober but very frank and blunt when drunk.

Pedro Romero, a young bullfighter of' great promise who has an affair with Brett, but who is jilted when he says he wants to marry her and when she realizes she is not good for him.

Count Mippipopolous, a friend of Brett's who would like always to drink champagne from magnums; he is kind to Brett and Jake in Paris.

Montoya, the proprietor of the hotel in Pamplona where the established, truly good bullfighters stay; the hotel thus becomes the headquarters of Barnes' wild vacationers.

The Story

Jake Barnes knew Robert Cohn in Paris shortly after the first World War. Somehow Jake always thought that Cohn was typical of the place and the time. Cohn, the son of wealthy Jewish parents, had once been the middleweight boxing champion of Princeton. He never wanted anyone to forget that fact. After leaving college, he had married and had lived incompatibly with his wife until she ran off with another man. Then in California he met some writers and decided to start a little, arty review of his own. He also met Frances Clyne, who became his mistress, and when Jake knew Cohn the two were living unhappily in Paris, where Cohn was writing his first novel. Cohn wrote and boxed and played tennis, and he was always careful not to mix his friendships. A man named Braddocks was his literary friend. Jake Barnes was his tennis friend.

Jake Barnes was an American newspaperman who had fought with the Italians during the war. His own private tragedy was a war wound which had emasculated him so that he could never marry Lady Brett Ashley, a young English war-widow with whom he was in love. In order not to think too much about himself, Jake spent a lot of time listening to the troubles of his friends and drinking heavily. When he grew tired of Paris, he went on fishing trips to the Basque country or to Spain for the bullfights. One night, feeling lonely, Jake asked Georgette, a girl of the streets, to join him in a drink at the Café Napolitain. They dined on the Left Bank, where Jake met a party of his friends, including Robert Cohn and Frances Clyne. Later Brett Ashley came in with a group of young men. It was evident that Cohn was attracted to her, and Frances was jealous. Brett refused to dance with Cohn, however, saying that she had a date with Jake in Montmartre. Leaving a fifty-franc note with the café proprietor for Georgette, Jake left in a taxi with Brett for a ride to the Parc Montsouris. They talked for a time about themselves without mentioning what was in both their minds, Jake's injury. At last Brett asked Jake to drive her back to the Café Select.

The next day Cohn cornered Jake and asked him questions about Brett. Later, after drinking with Harvey Stone, another expatriate, on the terrace of the Café Select, Jake met Cohn and Frances, who announced that her lover was dismissing her by sending her off to London. She abused Cohn scornfully and taunted him with his inferiority complex while he sat quietly without replying. Jake was embarrassed. The same day Jake received a telegram from his old friend, Bill Gorton, announcing his arrival on the *France*. Brett went on a trip to San Sebastian with Robert Cohn. She thought the excursion would be good for him.

Jake and Bill Gorton had planned to go to Spain for the trout fishing and the bullfights at Pamplona. Michael Campbell, an Englishman whom Brett was to marry, had also arrived in Paris. He and Brett arranged to join Jake and Bill at Pamplona later. Because Cohn had gone to San Sebastian with Brett and because she was staying now with Mike Campbell, everyone felt that it would be awkward if Cohn accompanied Jake and Bill on their trip. Nevertheless, he decided to join them at Bayonne. The agreement was that Jake and Bill would first go trout fishing at Burguete in the mountains. Later the whole party would meet at the Montoya Hotel in Pamplona for the fiesta.

When Jake and Bill arrived in Bayonne, they found Cohn awaiting them. Hiring a car, they drove on to Pamplona. Montoya, the proprietor of the hotel, was an old friend of Jake's because he recognized Jake as a true *aficionado*—one who is passionate about the bullfight. The next morning Bill and Jake left by bus for Burguete, both riding atop the ancient vehicle with several bottles of wine and an assortment of Basque passengers. At Burguete they enjoyed good fishing in the company of an Englishman named Wilson-Harris.

Once back in Pamplona, the whole party had gathered for the festival of San Fermin. The first night they went to see the bulls come in, to watch the men let the savage bulls out of the cages one at a time. Much wine made Mike Campbell loquacious and freed his tongue so that he harped constantly on the fact that Cohn had joined the group, although he knew he was not wanted. At noon on Sunday the fiesta exploded. The carnival continued for seven days. Dances, parades, religious processions, the bullfights—these and much wine furnished the excitement of that hectic week. Also staying at the Montoya Hotel was Pedro Romero, a bullfighter about twenty years old, who was extremely handsome. At the fights Romero acquitted himself well, and Brett fell in love with him, a fact she admitted with embarrassment to Jake. Brett and the young man met at the hotel; Romero soon became interested in her.

Besides the bullfights, the main diversion of the group was drunken progress from one drinking spot to another. While they were in the Café Suizo, Jake told Cohn that Brett had gone off with the bullfighter to his room. Cohn swung at both Mike and Jake and knocked them down. After the fight Cohn apologized, crying all the while. He could not understand how Brett could go off with him to San Sebastian one week and then treat him like a stranger when they met again. He planned to leave Pamplona the next morning.

The next morning Jake learned that after the fight Cohn had gone to Pedro Romero's room, where he found Brett and the bullfighter together. Cohn had beaten Romero badly. But that day, in spite of his swollen face and battered body, Romero performed beautifully in the ring, dispatching a bull which had recently killed another torero. That night, after the fights, Brett left Pamplona with Romero. Jake got very drunk.

The fiesta over, the party dispersed. Bill Gorton went back to Paris, Mike Campbell to Saint Jean de Luz. Jake was in San Sebastian when he received a wire from Brett asking him to come to the Hotel Montana in Madrid. Taking the express, Jake met her the next day. Brett was alone. She had sent Pedro Romero away, she said, because she thought she was not good for him. Then, without funds, she had sent for Jake. She had decided to go back to Mike, she told Jake, because the Englishman was her own sort.

After dinner Jake and Brett rode around in a taxi, seeing the sights of Madrid. This, Jake reflected wryly, was one of the few ways they could ever be alone together—in bars and cafés and taxis. Both knew the ride was as purposeless as the war-wrecked world in which they lived, as aimless as the drifting generation to which they belonged.

Critical Evaluation

Upon its publication in 1926, *The Sun Also Rises* was instantly accepted as one of the important American novels of the post-World War I period. Part of this recognition was due to the superficial fact that sophisticated readers "identified" current expatriate "celebrities" among the book's characters, but, as most of these personages faded into obscurity, this *roman à clef* aspect of the novel soon lost its appeal. A more important reason for the book's immediate success is that it perfectly captured the mood and style of the American artistic and intellectual "exiles" who drank, loved, and searched for meaning on the Paris Left Bank in the aftermath of that first world struggle.

The overall theme of *The Sun Also Rises* is indicated by Hemingway's two epigraphs. Gertrude Stein's comment that "you are all a lost generation" suggests the ambiguous and pointless lives of Hemingway's exiles as they aimlessly wander about the Continent drinking, making love, and traveling from place to place and party to party. The quote from Ecclesiastes, which gives the novel its title, implies a larger frame of reference, a sense of permanence, order, and value. If the activities of the characters seem to justify the former quotation, their search for new meanings to replace the old ones—

or at least to enable them to deal with that loss—demonstrates their desire to connect with the latter one.

Early in the novel the hero, Jake Barnes, declines to kiss Georgette, a prostitute, on the grounds that he is "sick." "Everybody's sick. I'm sick too," she responds. But this sickness motif is opposed in another early conversation Jake has, this one with Count Mippipopolous, a most vivid minor character, who tells him "that is the secret. You must get to know the values." The search for "values" and the willingness to pay the price, first to acquire them and then to live by them, are what separates Hemingway's exiles, at least some of them, from simple, pointless hedonism.

At the center of this search for values is the "Hemingway hero," Jake Barnes. As in all of Hemingway's important fictions, *The Sun Also Rises* is a novel of "education"—of learning to live with the conditions faced.

Jake's problem is, of course, complicated by his war injury. Having been emasculated in combat, Jake's "affair" with Lady Brett Ashley takes on a comical aspect—as he himself freely admits. But Hemingway has a very serious intention: Jake's wound is a metaphor for the condition of the entire expatriate group. They have all been damaged in some fundamental way by the war—physically, morally, psychologically, economically—and their aimless existence can be traced back to it. But the real symbolic importance of Jake's wound is that it has deprived him of the *capacity* to perform sexually, but it has not rid him of the *desire*. The people in *The Sun Also Rises* fervently want meaning and fulfillment, but they lack the ability and equipment to find it.

The heroes in Hemingway's major works learn the "values" in two ways: through their own actions and by contact with other characters who already know them. These "exemplars" understand the values either from long, hard experience, like Count Mippipopolous, or intuitively, automatically, like the bullfighter, Pedro Romero. But such heroes never articulate these values; they only embody them in action. Indeed, once talked about they become, in the Hemingway lexicon, "spoiled." Jake's education can be most clearly seen in his relationship to three characters: Robert Cohn, Pedro Romero, and Lady Brett Ashley.

Critics have speculated on why Hemingway begins the novel with a long discussion of Robert Cohn, a relatively minor character. The reason is simple: if it is hard to say exactly what the values *are,* it is easy to say what they *are not* and Robert Cohn embodies the old, false, "romantic" values that Hemingway is reacting against.

In the beginning Jake feels that Cohn is "nice and awful," but tolerates and pities him as a case of "arrested development." By the end of the book he thoroughly hates him. Cohn's flaws include a false sense of superiority—reinforced by his pugilistic skills—and a romantic attitude toward himself and his activities that distorts his relationship wth everyone around him. To reinforce this false romanticism, Cohn alters reality to suit his preconceptions. Falling "in love" with Brett, he refuses to see her realistically, but idealizes her. When she spends a weekend with him, because she thinks it would be "good for him," he treats it as a great affair and demands the "rights" of a serious lover, striking out at all the other men who approach her. In short, Cohn's false perception of reality and his self-romanticization underscore his chief fault, the cardinal sin in Hemingway's view: Cohn refuses to "pay his bill."

Cohn's romantic self-image is finally destroyed by the book's "exemplar," the bullfighter Pedro Romero. After being introduced to Brett by Jake, Romero becomes enamoured of her and they go off together. Affronted that Brett has been "taken" from him, Cohn reacts predictably and forces the young man into a prolonged fist fight. But, although totally outmanned as a boxer, Romero refuses to give in to Cohn. After absorbing considerable punishment, Romero, by sheer will, courage, and endurance, rallies to defeat and humiliate his opponent. His romantic bubble deflated, Cohn bursts into tears and fades from the novel.

It is appropriate that Cohn's false values be exposed by Pedro Romero, because his example is also central to the educations of both Jake and Brett. As an instinctively great bullfighter, Romero embodies the values in action and especially in the bullring. In a world bereft of religious certainties, Hemingway saw the bullfighter's performance as an aesthetic ceremony which substituted for obsolete religious ritual. Without transcendental meanings, man's dignity must come from the manner in which he faces his certain destiny; the bullfighter, who repeatedly does so by choice, was, for Hemingway, the supreme modern hero, providing he performs with skill, precision, style, and without "falsity" (that is, making it look harder or more dangerous than it really is). Shortly before the bullfight, Jake's group watches the local citizenry "run with the bulls" down the main street of the town. They see one man gored to death from behind. The following day that same bull is presented to Romero and he kills it perfectly by standing directly in front of it as he drives home his sword. This obvious symbolism states in a single image the most important of all the values, the need to confront reality directly and honestly.

But it is not only Pedro's example that helps to educate Jake, but also Jake's involvement in the Brett-Romero affair. His role as intermediary is the result of his "would-be" romance with her. They have long been in love and deeply frustrated by Jake's "funny-sad" war injury. Yet, despite the impossibility of a meaningful relationship, Jake can neither accept Brett as a "friend" nor cut himself off from her—although he knows that such a procedure would be the wisest course of action. She can, therefore, only be a "temptress" to him; she is quite accurate when she refers to herself as "Circe."

The only time in the book when Jake feels whole and happy is when he and Bill Gorton take a fishing trip at Bayonne. There, in a world without women, they fish with skill and precision, drink wine, naturally chilled in the stream, instead of whiskey, relate to the hearty exuberance of the Basque peasantry, and feel serene in the rhythms of nature. But once they return and Jake meets Brett at San Sebastian, his serenity is destroyed.

Jake puts his group up at a hotel owned by Montoya, an old friend and the most honored bullfighting patron. Montoya is an admirer and accepts Jake as a true *aficionado,* that is, one who truly understands and appreciates bullfighting not merely with his intellect, but with his whole being, his *passion.* Montoya even trusts Jake to the point of asking advice about the handling of this newest, potentially greatest young bullfighter, Pedro Romero. When Jake presents Brett to Pedro, fully understanding the implications of his act, he violates his trust with Montoya. His frustrated love for Brett exposes Pedro to her potentially corrupting influence. Jake's realization of his own weakness in betraying Romero, plus the fact that it has cost him his *aficionado* status, leaves him a sadder, wiser Hemingway hero.

But Pedro is not destroyed because Brett sends him away before she can do any damage. Of course more than simple altruism is involved in her decision. Life with Pedro held the possibility of wholeness for her—as it held the possibility of dissipation for him. So by sending him away she relinquishes her "last chance" for health and happiness rather than risk damaging her lover.

Whether or not Jake's insights and Brett's final "moral act" give meaning to the lives of these exiles is problematical. During their Bayonne fishing trip, Jake's friend Bill Gorton sings a song about "pity and irony" and that seems to be the overall tone of the book, and especially of the ending: pity for the personal anguish and aimless searching of these people, but ironic detachment toward characters whose lives and situations are, at best, at least as comical as they are tragic.

Bibliography

Baker, Carlos. *Hemingway: The Writer as Artist.* Princeton, N.J.: Princeton University Press, 1963, pp. 75–93. Reprinted in *Ernest Hemingway: Critiques of Four Major Novels.* Edited by Carlos Baker. New York: Scribner's, 1962, pp. 11–17. Also reprinted in *The Merrill Studies in* The Sun Also Rises. Edited by William White. Columbus, Oh.: Merrill, 1969, pp. 48–59.

Baker, Sheridan. *Ernest Hemingway.* New York: Holt, Rinehart, and Winston, 1967, pp. 40–55.

Beach, Joseph Warren. *American Fiction, 1920–1940.* New York: Macmillan, 1941, pp. 79–83, 105–108.

Benson, Jackson J. *Hemingway: The Writer's Art of Self-Defense.* Minneapolis: University of Minnesota Press, 1969, pp. 30–43.

Canby, Henry Seidel. "Introduction," in *The Sun Also Rises*. New York: Modern Library, 1930.

Cochran, Robert W. "Circularity in *The Sun Also Rises*," in *Modern Fiction Studies*. XIV (Autumn, 1968), pp. 297–305.

Cowley, Malcolm. "Introduction," in *The Sun Also Rises*. New York: Scribner's, 1962. Reprinted in *The Merrill Studies in* The Sun Also Rises. Edited by William White. Columbus, Oh.: Merrill, 1969, pp. 91–106.

Farrell, James T. *The League of Frightened Philistines*. New York: Vanguard, 1945. Reprinted in *Ernest Hemingway: Critiques of Four Major Novels*. Edited by Carlos Baker. New York: Scribner's, 1962, pp. 4–6. Also reprinted in *Ernest Hemingway: The Man and His Work*. Edited by John K.M. McCaffery. Cleveland, Oh.: World, 1950, pp. 221–225. Also reprinted in *The Merrill Studies in* The Sun Also Rises. Edited by William White. Columbus, Oh.: Merrill, 1969, pp. 53–57.

Frohoch, W.M. *The Novel of Violence in America*. Dallas: Southern Methodist University Press, 1958, pp. 167–176. Reprinted in *Ernest Hemingway: The Man and His Work*. Edited by John K.M. McCaffery. Cleveland, Oh.: World, 1950, pp. 261–271.

Gurko, Leo. *Ernest Hemingway and the Pursuit of Heroism*. New York: Crowell, 1968, pp. 55–80.

Halliday, E.M. "Hemingway's Narrative Perspective," in *Sewanee Review*. LX (Spring, 1952), pp. 203–209. Reprinted in *Ernest Hemingway: Critiques of Four Major Novels*. Edited by Carlos Baker. New York: Scribner's, 1962, pp. 174–182. Also reprinted in *Modern American Fiction*. Edited by Walton Litz. New York: Oxford University Press, 1963, pp. 215–227.

Levy, Alfred J. "Hemingway's *The Sun Also Rises*," in *Explicator*. XVII (February, 1959), item 37.

Lewis, Robert W., Jr. *Hemingway on Love*. Austin: University of Texas Press, 1965, pp. 19–35. Reprinted in *The Modern American Novel: Essays in Criticism*. Edited by Max Westbrook. New York: Random House, 1966, pp. 93–113.

Mizener, Arthur. *Twelve Great American Novels*. New York: New American Library, 1967, pp. 120–141.

Rovit, Earl. *Ernest Hemingway*. New York: Twayne, 1963, pp. 147–162. Reprinted in *The Merrill Studies in* The Sun Also Rises. Edited by William White. Columbus, Oh.: Merrill, 1969, pp. 58–72.

Sanderson, Stewart. *Hemingway*. New York: Grove, 1961, pp. 40–50.

Schroeter, James. "Hemingway's *The Sun Also Rises*," in *Explicator*. XX (November, 1961), item 28.

Scott, Arthur L. "In Defense of Robert Cohn," in *College English*. XVIII (March, 1957), pp. 309–314.

Spilka, Mark. "The Death of Love in *The Sun Also Rises*," in *Twelve Original Essays on Great American Novels*. Edited by Charles Shapiro. Detroit: Wayne State University Press, 1958, pp. 238–256. Reprinted in *Hemingway and His Critics: An International Anthology*. Edited by Carlos Baker. New York: Hill and Wang, 1961, pp. 80–92. Also reprinted in *Ernest Hemingway: Critiques of Four Major Novels*. Edited by Carlos Baker. New York: Scribner's, 1962, pp. 18–25. Also reprinted in *Hemingway: A Collection of Critical Essays*. Edited by Robert P. Weeks. Englewood Cliffs, N.J.: Prentice-Hall, 1962, pp. 127–138. Also reprinted in *The Merrill Studies in* The Sun Also Rises. Edited by William White. Columbus, Oh.: Merrill, 1969, pp. 73–85.

Stallman, R.W. "*The Sun Also Rises*—But No Bells Ring," in *The Houses That James Built and Other Literary Studies*. East Lansing: Michigan State University Press, 1961, pp. 173–191.

Stephens, Robert O. "Ernest Hemingway and the Rhetoric of Escape," in *The Twenties—Poetry and Prose: Twenty Critical Essays*. Deland, Fla.: Everett/Edwards, 1966, pp. 82–86.

Waldhorn, Arthur. *A Reader's Guide to Ernest Hemingway*. New York: Noonday, 1972, pp. 93–112.

Woolf, Virginia. *Granite and Rainbow*. London: Hogarth, 1958, pp. 85–92.

Wylder, Delbert E. *Hemingway's Heroes*. Albuquerque: University of New Mexico Press, 1969, pp. 31–65.

Young, Philip. *Ernest Hemingway*. New York: Rinehart, 1952, pp. 82–88. Reprinted in *Ernest Hemingway: Critiques of Four Major Novels*. Edited by Carlos Baker. New York: Scribner's, 1962, pp. 7–10. Also reprinted in *The Merrill Studies in* The Sun Also Rises. Edited by William White. Columbus, Oh.: Merrill, 1969, pp. 86–90.

JOSEPH HERGESHEIMER

Born: Philadelphia, Pennsylvania (February 15, 1880)
Died: Sea Isle City, New Jersey (April 25, 1954)

Principal Works

NOVELS: *The Lay Anthony*, 1914; *Mountain Blood*, 1915; *The Three Black Pennys*, 1917; *Gold and Iron*, 1918 (*Wild Oranges, Tubal Cain, The Dark Fleece*); *Java Head*, 1919; *Linda Condon*, 1919; *Cytherea*, 1922; *The Bright Shawl*, 1922; *Balisand*, 1924; *Tampico*, 1926; *The Party Dress*, 1929; *The Limestone Tree*, 1931; *The Foolscap Rose*, 1934.

SHORT STORIES: *The Happy End*, 1919; *Quiet Cities*, 1928.

BIOGRAPHY AND HISTORY: *Swords and Roses*, 1929; *Sheridan*, 1931.

AUTOBIOGRAPHY: *The Presbyterian Child*, 1923; *From an Old House*, 1925.

TRAVEL SKETCHES: *San Cristóbal de la Habana*, 1920.

Joseph Hergesheimer was born of Pennsylvania Dutch stock in Philadelphia, Pennsylvania, on February 15, 1880. Shy, and frequently ill as a child, he attended Quaker School and, planning a career as a painter, enrolled at the Philadelphia Academy of Fine Arts in 1897. At twenty-one, he inherited enough money to allow him to live and paint in Italy for a few years, but he suffered a nervous breakdown and returned to the United States, abandoning painting for a career as a writer.

Progress as a writer was slow; there were lean years of trial-and-error apprenticeship. In 1907 he married Miss Dorothy Hemphill, settled in West Chester, Pennsylvania, and made that city his home for the rest of his writing career. His first novel, *The Lay Anthony*, appeared in 1914. His success followed rapidly, and became established with the novel *The Three Black Pennys* in 1917. This is a realistic but exotically styled novel set against the Pennsylvania iron industry and deals with three generations of a single family of iron-masters. His best fiction combines realism and romance, usually against historical settings, and includes such books as *Java Head, Linda Condon, The Bright Shawl, Balisand*, and *The Limestone Tree*. He also wrote short stories; the historical-biographical sketches in *Swords and Roses*; a biography of Sheridan; an account of the restored Pennsylvania farmhouse where he made his home, *From an Old House*; and some critical articles. For nearly twenty years before his death, on April 25, 1954, at Sea Isle City, New Jersey, Hergesheimer wrote very little for publication.

Bibliography

Autobiographical material will be found in *The Presbyterian Child*, 1923, and *From an Old House*, 1925. See also James Branch Cabell, *Joseph Hergesheimer, An Essay in Interpretation*, 1921; *idem, Some of Us*, 1930; Geoffrey West,

"Joseph Hergesheimer," *Virginia Quarterly Review*, VIII (1932), 95–108; and Leon Kelly, "America and Mr. Hergesheimer," *Sewanee Review*, XL (1932), 171–193. A study, which includes a bibliography, is Ronald E. Martin, *The Fiction of Joseph Hergesheimer*, 1965.

THE THREE BLACK PENNYS

Type of work: Novel
Author: Joseph Hergesheimer (1880–1954)
Time of plot: c. 1750–1910
Locale: Pennsylvania
First published: 1917

The Three Black Pennys. *a family chronicle, is also a selective history of American culture, the first of the Pennys representing the beginning of an enterprising culture, the second representing the essential crudeness of the early nineteenth century, and the last representing the effete qualities of a Victorian generation which passed away without ever understanding the modern society supplanting it.*

Principal Characters

Howat Penny, the dark-skinned, somber-eyed, jut-chinned son of the owner of Myrtle Forge. A free-spirited, strong-willed man, he loves the Pennsylvania wilderness rather than his father's iron works. Once he has fallen in love with Ludowika and possessed her, he has no scruples about taking her from her husband; but the theft is unnecessary because Winscombe dies.

Ludowika Winscombe, the young Anglo-Polish wife of an elderly British envoy; in love with Howat Penny and later his wife. After a background of social life in London she finds Pennsylvania life interesting but somewhat crude. She submits to Howat's forcefulness, however, and becomes Mrs. Penny.

Jasper Penny, Howat's great-grandson, a widower; headstrong, rebellious, and independent like his ancestor whom he resembles physically. Guilt leads him to rescue Eunice and provide for her. He is unable to persuade Susan to marry him until both have lost their vigor; and their son, the second Howat's father, is the weakened product of their diminished selves.

Susan Brundon, Jasper's sweetheart, mistress of a girls' school and friend of Jasper's cousins, the Jannans. Pale, blue-eyed, high-cheeked, a very proper Victorian, she rejects Jasper's marriage proposal because she thinks herself an unsuitable mother for Eunice. After Essie's death, however, she does marry him.

Howat Penny, Jasper's and Susan's grandson, the final issue of a declining family. A delicate aesthete and antiquarian who lives a quiet bachelor life, he is shocked by Mariana's interest in Polder. Howat is a symbol of family decay.

Mariana Jannan, Howat's cousin, a modern young woman whom old-fashioned Howat cannot understand. Howat sees in her something of the first Howat and Jasper combined, a person of vigor and independence in contrast to his own negativeness.

James Polder, Mariana's lover, grandson of Eunice; a blunt, self-made man. Deserted by a slatternly wife, he takes Mariana as his mistress until he can get a divorce.

Felix Winscombe, Ludowika's cold, sardonic husband.

Eunice Scofield, Jasper's illegitimate daughter, later legally adopted and named Penny.

Essie Scofield, her repulsive mother whom Jasper finally pays off permanently.

Gilbert Penny, the first Howat's father.

Stephen Jannan, Jasper's cousin, a lawyer.

Daniel Cusler, Essie's leech-like young lover who is killed while visiting her.

The Story

The Penny family was English, except for a Welsh ancestor whose blood cropped out from time to time among his descendants. Those who showed the Welsh strain were called black Pennys by their relatives in an attempt to describe the mental make-up of individuals to whom it was applied. Howat was the first black Penny in over a hundred years; the last one had been burned to death as a heretic by Queen Elizabeth, long before the family had emigrated to the Colonies.

Living at Myrtle Forge, on the edge of the Pennsylvania Wilderness, Howat Penny was far more interested in the deep woods than he was in becoming an ironmaster. Nor did the appearance of Ludowika Winscombe make him any more satisfied or contented with his life.

Ludowika Winscombe, the young Polish wife of an elderly British envoy, had been left at the Penny home while her husband traveled through the Colonies on the king's business. Before long Howat Penny fell in love with her. Ludowika warned him, however, that she was a practical person who felt it was best for her to remain married to her husband rather than to run away with a young frontiersman. Howat stubbornly told her that she would have to marry him, for he would permit nothing to stand in the way of their happiness.

Winscombe returned ill to Myrtle Forge and Howat Penny found himself acting as Winscombe's nurse. It was an ironic situation filled with tension. Howat Penny waited for the old man to die. Ludowika was torn between two desires. She wanted Howat Penny, but she hated to face a life with him in the wilderness. The climax came late one night while Howat and Ludowika sat by the sick man's bed while Winscombe made a gallant effort to remain alive. Howat and Ludowika dared not even look at each other for fear of what they might see behind each other's eyes. Early in the morning the old man died. As they faced each other in the gray dawn Howat and Ludowika realized that she was destined to remain with him in Pennsylvania and never to see London again.

Three generations later the Welsh Penny blood again appeared in the person of Howat's great-grandson, Jasper. By that time the forge, which had been the beginning of the Penny fortune, had been replaced by a great foundry with many furnaces. Jasper Penny was a rich man, steadily growing richer by supplying the tremendous amounts of iron needed for the new railroads in the United States.

Jasper Penny had never married. Like his great-grandfather Howat, he was a man of great passions whose energies were spent in building up his foundry and fortune. He was still painfully reminded, however, of his earlier indiscretions with a woman who had borne him an illegitimate daughter. The woman hounded Jasper for money and he found it easier to give her money than it was to refuse her demands.

He saw very little of Eunice, his daughter, for he assumed that she would be cared for by her mother as long as he paid all expenses. One day in Philadelphia Jasper decided, on impulse, to visit Eunice. He discovered her, ill-clothed and underfed, in the home of a poor family, and, horrified, he took her away with him. Not knowing what to do with her, he finally placed her in a school in New York.

In Philadelphia Jasper had also met Susan Brundon, mistress of a girls' school and friend of a distant branch of Jasper's family. Jasper fell in love with her and in his abrupt fashion proposed marriage. Being honest, he told her that he had an illegitimate child. Susan refused to marry Jasper because she felt that his first duty was to Eunice's mother.

Shortly after his proposal Jasper was involved in a murder. Eunice's mother had killed another lover and suspicion fell on Jasper Penny. He hated to involve Susan Brundon in the sordid affair, but he found that the only way he could clear himself was through her testimony that he had been with her when the crime was committed.

After the trial Susan told Jasper that she could not marry him until Eunice's mother was dead, that she could not have the past intruding itself upon her love for him after they were married. Almost a decade passed before they were finally able to marry.

The last of the black Pennys was also the last of the family name, for the family died out with the second Howat Penny, the grandson of Jasper Penny and Susan Brundon. Howat was a bachelor who lived alone in the country near the site of the original Penny forge. Interested in music and art, he had never married, and the management of the Penny foundries had gone out of his hands. Possessed of a comfortable fortune, he had in the closing years of his life the companionship of Mariana Jannan, a cousin. She was a young woman in her twenties and little understood by old-fashioned Howat.

He did not understand Mariana because he could not understand her generation. Because Jasper's son and grandson had never had anything to do with that branch of the family descended from Jasper's illegitimate daughter, Howat was horrified when Mariana told him that she was in love with James Polder, a distant cousin.

Howat thought Mariana mad to fall in love with James Polder, who had begun working in the Penny foundries as a boy. The fact that he had worked his way up to a position of importance failed to redeem him in old Howat's eyes.

Polder finally ran away with an actress. Three years after his marriage, Mariana and Howat Penny called on him and his wife. Polder, unhappy with his slatternly wife, had begun drinking heavily. Howat, at Marianna's insistence, invited Polder to visit his home in the country. Polder accepted. Shortly afterward he learned that his wife had deserted him and returned to the stage. He no longer cared; in love once more, he and Mariana realized they should never have permitted family differences to come between them.

Mariana's relatives, shocked by the affair, protested to Howat. Howat himself said nothing, for he now felt that he was too old and understood too little of modern life to intrude in the affairs of Mariana and Polder. Although he was as much Mariana's friend as ever, he could not understand how she was able to live with Polder as his mistress while they waited for his wife to divorce him. Howat believed until the end of his life that women should be protected from reality. Even when he knew he was dying, he said nothing to Mariana, who sat reading by his side. The delicacy of his sensibilities prevented him from shocking her with the fact of his approaching death and kept him from saying goodbye to her when he died, the last of the three black Pennys.

Critical Evaluation

Hergesheimer's third novel, *The Three Black Pennys* was published two years after D. H. Lawrence's *The Rainbow*. Lawrence's novel, suppressed in England, was declared obscene by the Bow Street Magistrate, who ordered police to seize copies at the booksellers and at the press. Hergesheimer's novel, on the other hand, was widely popular; together with *Java Head* (1919) it established for the author a major reputation during the early 1920's. Apart from their different publication histories, the novels in many ways are similar. Both treat the theme of mating—successful or unsuccessful—of three generations of a family, the Brangwens for Lawrence and the Pennys for Hergesheimer; both examine, almost as a mystique, a special quality of "blood" that distinguishes members of the family; both begin with a marriage involving a "mixed" blood line from a Polish widow—Lydia Lensky in *The Rainbow* and Ludowika Winscombe in *The Three Black Pennys*—and show its effects upon the indigenous English or Welsh-American stock of the males of the family; both attempt, through symbolism concerning time, place, and character, to record the history of culture for their respective countries; both show, again through symbol and story, the diminishing vitality of the original family stock, from Ursula's failure in love (she marries in *Women in Love*) to the last Howat Penny's feeble bachelorhood that terminates his line; finally, both novels deal with the larger issues of vitality and degeneration, progress and decay.

Yet the novels, despite their remarkable similarities in theme, are markedly different in their effects. Lawrence's symbols, whether used on a conscious or subconscious Freudian-Jungian level, are worked integrally into the structure of his book; Hergesheimer's symbols—particularly those concerning the relationship between the men and the iron—are all quite obvious. They add substance to the narrative, but do not provide additional levels of significance, nor do they turn the story into myth. Furthermore, Lawrence's concept of "blood consciousness," both a psychological and moral argument, is carefully elaborated in the lives of the Brangwens; Hergesheimer's treatment of the "black" strain (that is, the Welsh ancestry) in the Penny family's blood-inheritance is superficial, a mere plot device without a psychological or moral frame of reference. Whether the "black" Welsh blood represents a behavioral atavism or is an odd coincidence of personality, its appearance over several generations is never fully explained. Finally, Lawrence's novel treats the partial or complete failures in sexuality as symbols for the disintegration of modern culture; Hergesheimer, however, treats the failures as isolated examples, without moving from the specific instance to the general malaise of American culture. Thus Lawrence's novel is clearly in the dominant tradition of modern psychological fiction. Hergesheimer's is a period piece, well crafted and entertaining, but not an innovative work of literature.

Nevertheless, critics in 1917 praised *The Three Black Pennys* for the author's accurate research into the history of the nation, for his mastery of prose style, and for his ability to create vigorous characters. As a chronicle, the novel contrasts with the popular sentimental romances of the time. In the reconstruction of three periods in America's past, the late Colonial period (concerning the first Howat Penny), the mid-nineteenth century (Jasper Penny), and the turn of the nineteenth century (the last Howat Penny), Hergesheimer is a realist with a scrupulous eye for details. Dividing the novel into "The Furnace," "The Forge," and "The Metal," the author shows how the lives of the "black" Pennys and their contemporaries relate to the growth of industrial America.

Before the Revolutionary War Gilbert Penny establishes in Pennsylvania the Myrtle Forge, a product of his own energy, persistence, and optimism. He and his rebellious son Howat are men of determination; their vision of America is one of struggle leading to power. Three generations later, Jasper Penny, Howat's great-grandson, inherits a mighty industrial complex built around the family's original forge. Like his ancestors, Jasper is concerned with power. A business magnate, he is accustomed to getting his way. But his own impetuosity nearly destroys his happiness. Entangled romantically with Essie Scofield, a worthless woman whom he had seduced and made pregnant while he was still a young man, he cannot in his mature years convince his true love, the idealistic Susan Brundon, to marry him. She insists that they wait until Essie's death. The child born of their middle age comes to represent the languishing vitality of the Penny family. By the time of the last "black" Penny, the effete second Howat, the family's failure to produce an heir corresponds with its decline from a position of industrial power. The foundry is silent, and Howat, merely the caretaker of the past, has memories of his energetic forebears to remind him of his own impotence.

To re-create a sense of the past, Hergesheimer unobtrusively works his research into the Penny chronicle. Without bogging down in the recital of historical facts, he allows the story to carry the reader forward. As a masterful stylist, he evokes setting with a few selective phrases, rather than a profusion of details. Compared to regional realists like his contemporaries Ellen Glasgow or Willa Cather, rarely is he able to describe a setting so fully that it comes alive in all its parts. Even the description of the Myrtle Forge lacks a sense of immediacy. However, Hergesheimer does create an impressionistic feeling for the scene—not from the close observation of particulars but the careful choice of meaningful details which linger in the memory.

To be sure, Hergesheimer's command of style is more impressive than his characterizations. Although his early critics admired the first two romantic Pennys, they appear, from a modern standpoint, deficient in psychological complexity. The first Howat Penny is described, at the beginning, as reclusive and tactless to the point of surliness—a kind of American Heathcliff mysteriously suffering from ambiguous passions. When he falls in love with Ludowika, he changes at once from a sullen misanthrope to an ardent, almost demonic lover. Jasper, also driven by contradictory passions, is the philandering cad with Essie, the practical-minded and affectionate father with Eunice, and the gentle, diffident lover of Susan. The greatest problem in psychology, however, is the last Howat, the American Victorian. If the strain of "black" Welsh blood is said to distinguish those Pennys "impatient of assuaging relationships and beliefs," how can the feeble aesthete belong to the same strain as the impetuous first Howat or the ruthless tycoon Jasper? Apart from his inability to relate to the younger generation, particularly to Mariana Jannan, Howat appears to lack the element of violent, contradictory passions that sets the other "black" Pennys at odds with their peers. A touching, pathetic figure, he represents a dying breed. Yet the reader does not understand whether the fault for his failure lies in Howat's times or in himself. Nevertheless, the portrait of the last Howat, though psychologically blurred, is interesting enough to arouse the reader's sympathies. More than his cardboard-romantic ancestors, he resembles a Henry James hero, morbidly introspective, sensitive but fastidious, capable of tender emotions but little direct action. With him the line of the "black" Pennys comes to an end.

DUBOSE HEYWARD

Born: Charleston, South Carolina (August 31, 1885)
Died: Tryon, North Carolina (June 16, 1940)

Principal Works

NOVELS: *Porgy*, 1925; *Angel*, 1926; *Mamba's Daughters*, 1929; *Peter Ashley*, 1932; *Lost Morning*, 1936; *Star Spangled Virgin*, 1939.
SHORT STORY: *The Half-Pint Flask*, 1929.
POEMS: *Carolina Chansons: Legends of the Low Country*, 1922 (with Hervey Allen); *Skylines and Horizons*, 1924; *Jasbo Brown and Selected Poems*, 1931.
PLAYS: *Porgy*, 1927 (with Dorothy Heyward); *Brass Ankle*, 1931; *Mamba's Daughters*, 1939 (with Dorothy Heyward).

DuBose Heyward was born in Charleston, South Carolina, on August 31, 1885. His formal schooling ended when he left high school to work. After an attack of poliomyelitis at eighteen, he worked as a cotton checker on the Charleston waterfront. At twenty-one he established with a boyhood friend a fairly prosperous insurance firm in Charleston. About this time Heyward began to write short stories and poetry, and in 1920, with John Bennett and Hervey Allen, he organized the Poetry Society of South Carolina. Heyward edited the *Year Book* (1921–1924) of the society and was elected its president in 1924. Allen and Heyward collaborated in the verse collection, *Carolina Chansons* and the latter published a second volume of poetry, *Skylines and Horizons*, in 1924. Heyward had begun to attend the MacDowell Colony in 1921 and there he met and married Dorothy Hartzell Kuhns, herself a playwright, in 1923. Their only child, Jenifer, was born in 1930.

In 1924 Heyward relinquished his insurance business in Charleston and undertook a series of lecture tours. His first novel, *Porgy*, was based on Negro life in Charleston and published in 1925. The hero is a crippled beggar who defends Bess, his woman, from her former lover, Crown, and eventually kills him, only to lose her to a drunken sport who abducts her to Savannah. A second novel, *Angel*, had a background of the North Carolina mountains. A long short story, "The Half-Pint Flask," was published in the *Bookman* (1927) and reprinted in book form two years later. *Mamba's Daughters* was a more ambitious novel of white and Negro people in Charleston. Next came *Peter Ashley*, a historical novel of South Carolina before the Civil War. In these works Heyward became the first white author to treat Negroes honestly, sincerely, and sympathetically, and to represent the Gullah dialect of the sea islands authentically.

With the assistance of Dorothy Heyward, *Porgy* was considerably tightened, dramatized, and produced in 1927 in New York and later in London. *Mamba's Daughters* was similarly produced in 1939. An original play, *Brass Ankle*, appeared in 1931. He also wrote two less successful novels, *Lost Morning* and *Star Spangled Virgin.*

The story of Porgy first caught the attention of George Gershwin in 1926, but it was not until 1935 that the opera *Porgy and Bess*, based on the play, reached the stage. Gershwin wrote the music, the Heywards the libretto, and the Heywards and Ira Gershwin the lyrics. This was the first and has been the most successful serious American folk opera.

DuBose Heyward died at Tryon, North Carolina, June 16, 1940.

Bibliography

The chief study of Heyward is Frank Durham, *DuBose Heyward*, 1954. See also Emily Clark, *Innocence Abroad*, 1931; and Frank M. Durham, *DuBose Heyward's Use of Folklore in His Negro Fiction*, 1961.

PORGY

Type of work: Novel
Author: DuBose Heyward (1885–1940)
Time of plot: Early twentieth century
Locale: Charleston, South Carolina
First published: 1925

In 1918 DuBose Heyward clipped a story from the newspaper about a crippled goat-cart beggar, but it was not until 1925 that the article came to life as the novel Porgy. *Transcending the traditional stereotypes, Heyward depicts a heroic but doomed protagonist who takes on mythic proportions as he searches for dignity and happiness in a modern world that does not allow for freedom, dignity, or happiness.*

Principal Characters

Porgy, an old, crippled Negro beggar who travels about Charleston in a goat-cart. He is frail in body but his hands are powerful. He says little but observes much. When Bess moves in and becomes his woman after Crown has fled following Robbins' murder, Porgy is transformed from an impassive observer of life to a lover of children as well as of Bess. Fearful of losing Bess to Crown, Porgy kills him; but he loses her anyway. Vividly, realistically, and somewhat poetically portrayed, Porgy is one of the most appealing Negro characters in American fiction, but a very different one from J. C. Harris's Uncle Remus or the Negroes in Roark Bradford's stories.

Crown, a stevedore, slow-witted, powerful, brutal, and dangerous, especially when drunk. He is stabbed by Porgy when he breaks into Porgy's room. Crown's body is later found in the river, but the loyalty of Porgy's friends prevents his being identified as Crown's murderer.

Bess, his woman, who lives with Porgy during Crown's absence but who returns briefly to Crown on the day of the Negro picnic. While living with Porgy she is less immoral than amoral, if judged according to the morality of the white race. Neither she nor her friends see anything improper in such conduct. Made drunk by stevedores during Porgy's absence in jail, she is taken to Savannah. Supposedly she returns to her old life.

Robbins, a weekend gambler but otherwise a good provider. He is murdered by Crown, who falsely suspects him of cheating at dice.

Serena, his wife, who adopts Jake and Clara's baby after Porgy is jailed on a contempt charge.

Peter, an old Negro arrested as a witness to Robbins' murder.

Sportin' Life, a flashy New York octoroon who sells "happy dus'" (dope).

Maria, Porgy's friend, operator of a small cook-shop.

Jake, a fisherman drowned when a hurricane wrecks his boat.

Clara, his wife, also drowned during the
hurricane. Bess and Porgy keep her baby
after her death until the baby is taken by
Serena.

Simon Frasier, a Negro "lawyer" who
grants illegal divorces for a dollar.

Alan Archdale, a white lawyer, Porgy's
friend.

The Story

Porgy, a crippled black beggar, lived in a brick tenement called Catfish Row,
once a fine old Southern mansion in Charleston, South Carolina. Different from
the beggars of his race Porgy sat silently, vaguely acknowledging the coins
dropped in his cup.

Porgy's one vice was gambling, and in a gambling session one evening in April,
Crown, a stevedore who thought he had been cheated, murdered Robbins, a good
provider and family man, as Porgy watched. But when the white law investigated
the murder, Porgy wisely disclaimed knowledge of it. Peter, Porgy's source of
transportation, was not so wise, and found himself imprisoned as a material witness.

Deprived of mobility, the resourceful Porgy contrived his own transportation—
a homemade cart and a goat to pull it. Even though he was met on the city streets
with mocking amusement and chastising looks, the cart gave Porgy new freedom.
He no longer had to stay at one stand all day; he could roam widely.

In June Porgy's sense of freedom was increased when Bess, Crown's woman,
came to live with him. Porgy became a new man, less an impassive observer of
life. He even developed a tender affection for children. But Porgy's happiness was
short-lived.

Ironically, on the day of the grand parade and picnic of "The Sons and Daughters of Repent Ye Saith the Lord," Crown came upon Bess cutting palmetto
leaves for the picnic on Kittiwar Island. Bess succumbed to the snakelike charm
of Crown. At the end of the day when she returned to Porgy, it was only with the
promise that in the fall, when cotton shipments provided stevedoring work in
Savannah, she would again be Crown's woman. Bess admitted to Porgy that his
suspicions over her whereabouts during the picnic were justified and both of them
deplored their dismal fates.

In September, while the "Mosquito Fleet" was at the fishing bank, the hurricane flag was suddenly raised over the custom house, and Clara, a fisherman's
wife, shuddered with fear for her husband, Jake, whom she had warned not to go
out in his boat. After an ominous calm, the hurricane struck the city. The water
of the bay, driven by the shrieking wind, rose above the sea wall, crossed the
street, and invaded the ground floor of Catfish Row. Forty frightened blacks huddled in the great second-story ballroom of the old mansion. During a lull in the
storm Clara saw the wreck of her husband's boat near the wharf and left her
baby with Bess to go out into the flood. A few minutes later she was overwhelmed

during a sudden return of the storm's fury, and Bess and Porgy were left with her baby.

In October, drays loaded with heavy bales of cotton came rumbling down the street. In Catfish Row there was excitement and happiness, for stevedoring jobs and money were plentiful again. But the coming of the cotton portended disaster for Porgy. In an effort to avert disaster and free Bess from her imprisonment to Crown, Porgy murdered the returned Crown. Next day the body was found in the nearby river.

A kind of communal sigh of relief went up from Catfish Row when the police left without having made any arrests. But when one of the buzzards that had fed upon Crown's body lit on the parapet above Porgy's room, the frightened Porgy felt that doom was in store for him. The next day, having been asked to identify Crown's body at the morgue, Porgy fled in terror, hotly pursued by a patrol wagon full of officers. Passersby laughed at the ridiculously one-sided race. Porgy was caught at the edge of town, but by the time he had been brought downtown, he was no longer needed, since another Negro had identified the body. Crown was declared to have come to his death at the hands of a person or persons unknown, but Porgy was jailed for contempt of court.

When he returned from jail, Porgy found his adopted baby with a neighboring woman. From a neighbor he learned that some stevedores had got Bess drunk and taken her off to Savannah. Porgy knew that she would never return. Porgy's family, freedom, and joy had lasted one summer. In the end, Porgy sat alone, an old man left with only the mockery of past freedom and happiness in the figure of his goat.

Critical Evaluation

Born into the white aristocracy of Charleston, South Carolina, DuBose Heyward became a minor figure in the Harlem Renaissance. He saw the transition of the black man in America as a tragedy that transcended race and characterized a general post World War I disillusionment with civilization and a longing for primitive innocence.

In a six-part structure that constitutes a series of vignettes, Heyward presents a microcosm of the black man through Porgy, a hopelessly crippled, enslaved man whose life is controlled by the arbitrary whims of both society and nature. The structure of the novel reflects subtle shifts between Porgy's limited existence in Catfish Row and the external forces that control his life. The narrative moves from the calm of ordinary existence, to internal strife and murder in the Row, to the external forces of "legal" society that parallel the disruptive natural forces of the hurricane. In all of the moves the prevalent mood is pessimism; freedom and joy are fleeting and accidental.

Within the chance happenings of life Porgy's efforts for happiness and freedom are ludicrous and his life no more than a vicarious experience—a "waiting."

Through the extended metaphor of gambling, Heyward characterizes Porgy's existence. It is always chance that dominates Porgy's life. A chance murder at the weekly crap game begins the alterations in Porgy's life—which force him to be independent. Porgy, with his contrived cart and goat, ventures to his begging stations amid jeers and horrified glances after the arbitrary imprisonment of Peter, his driver. The murder also brings him Bess, the murder's girlfriend. From tragedy there emerges in Porgy's life more happiness and independence than he has ever known. The destructive hurricane brings life to Porgy and Bess, as they adopt the child of parents lost in the storm.

But such happiness is transient, for the arbitrary forces of man, society, and nature move without mercy and reassert Porgy's dependence. Porgy murders Crown to free Bess and is imprisoned after he superstitiously flees from the law, which is represented by the buzzard that perches on Porgy's roof after Crown's murder; Bess succumbs to fear, and seeks escape in alcohol; the adopted baby is lost.

In *Porgy*, Heyward portrays the alteration of the essential rhythms of black life from strength of faith and strength of community. In modern society he depicts those strengths in the process of displacement by the suffering brought about by change. Porgy, representative of all black men, is mythological in his journey which leaves him isolated, old, and subject to a world he can neither control nor avoid.

In 1935, George Gershwin's opera *Porgy and Bess* first reached the stage. Gershwin wrote the music, DuBose and Dorothy Heyward the libretto, and the Heywards and Ira Gershwin the lyrics of this successful American folk opera. The success of this adaptation assures *Porgy* and Heyward a place of recognition in not only America, but also the world.

Bibliography

Allen, Hervey. *DuBose Heyward: A Critical and Biographical Sketch.* New York: George H. Doran Company, 1970.

Durham, Frank. *DuBose Heyward: The Man Who Wrote* Porgy. Columbia: University of South Carolina Press, 1954.

Durham, Frank. "Porgy Comes Home—at Last!" in *South Carolina Review.* 2, ii, pp. 5–13.

Slavick, William H. "Going to School to DuBose Heyward," in *Studies in the Literary Imagination.* 7, ii, pp. 105–29.

LANGSTON HUGHES

Born: Joplin, Missouri (February 1, 1902)
Died: New York, N.Y. (May 22, 1967)

Principal Works

POETRY: *The Weary Blues*, 1926; *Fine Clothes to the Jew*, 1927; *The Dream Keeper*, 1932; *The Way of White Folks*, 1934; *A New Song*, 1938; *Shakespeare in Harlem*, 1942; *Freedom's Plow*, 1943; *Jim Crow's Last Stand*, 1943; *Fields of Wonder*, 1947; *One-Way Ticket*, 1949; *Montage of a Dream Deferred*, 1951; *Ask Your Mama: 12 Moods for Jazz*, 1961; *The Panther and the Lash*, 1967.

NOVELS: *Not Without Laughter*, 1930; *Simple Speaks His Mind*, 1950; *Simple Takes a Wife*, 1953; *Simple Stakes a Claim*, 1957; *Tambourines to Glory*, 1958; *Simple's Uncle Sam*, 1965.

SHORT STORIES: *The Ways of White Folks*, 1934; *Laughing to Keep From Crying*, 1952; *Something in Common and Other Stories*, 1963.

PLAYS: *Mulatto*, 1935; *Little Ham*, 1935; *Troubled Island*, 1935; *When the Jack Hollers*, 1936; *Joy to My Soul*, 1937; *Front Porch*, 1938; *The Sun Do Move*, 1942; *Simply Heavenly*, 1957; *Tambourines to Glory*, 1963.

HISTORIES: *A Pictorial History of the Negro in America*, 1956; *Fight for Freedom: The Story of the NAACP*, 1967; *Black Magic: A Pictorial History of the Negro in American Entertainment*, 1967.

AUTOBIOGRAPHIES: *The Big Sea: An Autobiography*, 1940; *I Wonder as I Wander: An Autobiographical Journey*, 1956.

Langston Hughes, who heralded the literary movement known as the "Harlem Renaissance," was one of the most prolific of American writers. He was born in Joplin, Missouri, on February 1, 1902, the son of James Nathaniel Hughes and Carrie Mercer. On his father's side, both great-grandfathers were white, one a Jewish slave trader, the other a Kentuckian of Scottish blood who ran a distillery. On his mother's side, his great-grandfather was a white Virginia planter, Quarles, who claimed to be descended from Francis Quarles, the seventeenth century English poet. In addition, one of his grandmothers had Cherokee blood. She had been the wife of Lewis Sheridan Leary, a victim of John Brown's raid on Harper's Ferry, prior to her marriage to Hughes' grandfather.

This racial background contributed to Hughes's unhappy childhood. His father, who had been refused the bar examination because of his race, abandoned the family and went to Mexico to make a career in a nonwhite world. His mother had attended the University of Kansas but was unable to get decent jobs because of her race and consequently was unable to support Hughes. For several of his weaning years, he was brought up by the grandmother who had been Leary's wife. This was the only period of stability in his early life. The grandmother imbued the young boy with a sense of his black heritage and had a pronounced influence in shaping the later course of his life.

Hughes discovered writing in high school where his initial models were Paul Laurence Dunbar and Carl Sandburg. In 1921 he entered Columbia University, and in June of the same year his poem, "The Negro Speaks of Rivers," was published in the *Crisis*. He left school after a year and began his wanderings by signing on a ship as a kitchen hand. This gave him the opportunity to see most of the African ports and work as a dishwasher at a night club, "Le Grande Duc," in Paris. His rise to fame was an accidental occurence. In 1925, while he was employed as a busboy at the Wardman Park Hotel in Washington, he had the occasion to wait on Vachel Lindsay, then at the height of his fame. Hughes got up the courage to approach Lindsay and gave him three of his poems, "Jazzonia," "Negro Dancers," and "The Weary Blues." Next morning, the newspapers quoted Lindsay as saying that he had discovered a busboy poet, and when Hughes came to work there were reporters waiting to interview him. The publicity which followed placed him among the eminent young poets in America.

Hughes soon proved that he was no fluke, He won literary awards; he received excellent reviews for *The Weary Blues* (1926) and *Fine Clothes to the Jew* (1927); and his poetry readings were very successful. Lindsay had advised him to work diligently and study hard, and he tried to implement this plan by enrolling in Lincoln University on a grant from Amy Spingarm. He also acquired a new sponsor, Mrs. Rufus Osgood Mason, an elderly widow, and was financially secure for the first time in his life. In 1929, he graduated from Lincoln University, and in the same year he finished his first novel, *Not Without Laughter*. The novel, which was published in 1930, focused on the simple humdrum of day-to-day black life and was generally acclaimed. The success of his novel also brought about the break with his patron, Mrs. Mason. Mrs. Mason had provided him with economic and even literary help and now evidently wanted to shape his career. Hughes's independent spirit would not permit it.

This crisis changed the future course of his life. He felt that somehow his relationship with Mrs. Mason had never transcended the traditional white-black bond. He was also poor again (though his books received good reviews, very few copies sold), and he went back to seek his own roots among the poor black people and find a bond with them. He was fiercely independent and worked hard to be an original writer with original views.

From 1931 to 1937 his thirst to see new places got hold of him. He traveled over the southern United States, visited Negro colleges, and made his way to Mexico and Haiti. In 1932 he visited the Soviet Union with a group of blacks who were invited there to make a movie on black life in America, and he went on to travel around the world. He spend most of 1937 in Spain, as correspondent for the Baltimore *Afro-American*, covering the civil war. In 1938 his wanderings ended and he returned to the United States.

Meanwhile, Hughes had managed to establish himself as a major black writer and the progenitor of the "Harlem Renaissance." He became a major dramatist and his play *Mulatto* was the first dramatic success by a black writer. To infuse the sense of black pride and culture into the mainstream of black life, he established the Harlem Suitcase Theater in New York and the New Negro Theater in Los Angeles. He also redirected his talents to produce a volume of short stories, *The Ways of White Folks*, and two volumes of poems.

In the latter part of his life, Langston Hughes went on to further develop his talents. He wrote a screenplay, three books on the history of blacks in the United States; and two autobiographies, *The Big Sea* (1940) and *I Wonder as I Wander* (1956); two volumes of short stories; five novels; seven volumes of poetry; and a host of plays. His prolific career was, however, made all the more memorable by the creation of Jesse B. Simple, a character which has become as much a part of our myth and tradition as Huck Finn or George Babbitt. Simple was first introduced by Hughes in 1943 in the *Chicago Defender*, and he later became the protagonist of the series of "Simple" novels, the last of which was published in 1965.

Simple symbolizes the mistreated, ignorant, shackled black Everyman, who, with all his problems, manages to retain a courageous, generous and spirited "never say die" outlook on life. After one of his unpleasant experiences Simple says: "I have been caught in the rain, caught in jails, caught short in my rent, caught with the wrong woman—but I am still there." Through Simple, Hughes projects his vision of the eventual outcome of the blacks' struggle for viability, for Simple represents the eternal indestructable spirit.

Langston Hughes died in a New York hospital on May 22, 1967. He will be remembered as the first black to make a successful strictly literary career. But he was also an innovater of the highest order. He presented us with a colloquiality drawn from the rich fabric of black life. In his best works, he approximates the great writers of his age; intwined with the pathos, biting wit and sheer drama is a daring vision of life—a vision based on the eternal quality of the human spirit.

Bibliography

There is no standard edition of Hughes' works. Important biographies include Rebecca Barton, *Witnesses for Freedom*, 1948; Donald Dickinson, *A Bio-Bibliography of Langston Hughes*, 1967; James Emanual, *Langston Hughes*, 1967; and Milton Meltzer, *Langston Hughes: A Biography*, 1968. Also see Robert A. Bone, *The Negro Novel in America*, 1968; N. I. Huggins, *Harlem Renaissance*, 1972; and Jean Wagner, *Black Poets of the U.S.A.: Racial and Religious Feelings in Black Poetry from Paul Laurence Dunbar to Langston Hughes*, 1972. More specialized studies are found in the following: James Emanuel, *The Short Stories of Langston Hughes*, 1962; Raymond Quinot, *Langston Hughes, ou L'Étoile Noire*, 1964; Jean Wagner, *Les Poètes Nègres des États-Unis*, 1963; T. J. Spencer and Clarence Rivers, "Langston Hughes: His Style and Optimism," *Drama Critique* VII (Spring, 1964); and James Presley, "The American Dream of Langston

Hughes," *Southwest Review* XLVIII (Autumn, 1963). Also see the Special Langston Hughes number of *College Language Association Journal* XI, No. 4 (June, 1968), and the special supplement on Hughes of *Freedomways* VIII, No. 2 (Spring, 1968).

NOT WITHOUT LAUGHTER

Type of work: Novel
Author: Langston Hughes (1902–1967)
Time of plot: ca. 1910
Locale: a small Kansas town
First published: 1930

Rather than develop an intensely dramatic plot, Langston Hughes chose to construct in Not Without Laughter *the coming-of-age of Sandy Rodgers as one possible metaphor for the black experience.*

Principal Characters

Sandy Rodgers, a ten-year-old black child growing up shortly before World War I in a small Kansas town called Stanton. Unlike many heroes in a novel, Sandy's life is not marred by overwhelming calamity or distinguished by great achievement. Rather he is seen by the reader as representative of a particular type of black experience. Sandy is a good boy and one may assume that the stability of his character is a consequence of the love and protection given him by his grandmother, Aunt Hager Williams. Although Sandy's character is tested by bearable poverty and non-violent racial discrimination, Aunt Hager provides him the security that his likeable but often absent father, Jimboy, does not. Through Sandy's tolerant and sympathetic eyes, the reader learns of the variety and vitality of blacks who are neither Southern nor ghetto-locked. The extremes in Sandy's experience as he journeys to manhood are seen in his two aunts: Harriett, a defiant and hostile blues singer, and Tempy, a cold, respectable woman who denies her blackness. When Sandy leaves Kansas at the age of sixteen to join his mother in a one-room tenement in Chicago, he seems to have learned enough from his childhood experience not only to survive in the city but to prevail as well.

Aunt Hager Williams, Sandy's religious, hardworking grandmother. Her importance is partly revealed through her three daughters, Annjee, Harriett, and Tempy who, collectively, express the range of possibilities in the black experience. Her significance in terms of the plot is considerable—she serves as Sandy's protectoress. Even though each of her daughters deserts her, Aunt Hager continues to wash and iron the clothes of white people in order to keep Sandy fed and in school. She is free of hatred toward whites, a consequence of her close relationship to her white mistress during and after the Civil War. Her death is free of trauma and tragedy. While she has suffered much, she has maintained her dignity.

Annjelica (Annjee) Rodgers, Sandy's mother. She is a loving mother who works as a cook and housekeeper for the demanding Rice family. Stronger than her love for her son, however, is her desire to be with her husband, Jimboy. In spite of illness, she leaves Kansas and follows Jimboy from Detroit to Toledo to Chicago. There she ends up living in a single room next to an elevated railroad. Her desire for Sandy to help support her as an elevator operator is cut short by her sister Harriett who plans to support Sandy's education.

Jimboy Rodgers, the guitar-playing, virile

husband of Anjee and father of Sandy. Although Jimboy loves his son and takes him to carnivals when he is in town, he leaves Anjee and Sandy in a continual state of financial distress, as Aunt Hager constantly points out. His odyssey through the industrial cities of the North ends when he is drafted and sent to Europe.

Harriett Williams, Aunt Hager's bright, fun-loving daughter. Harriett ignores her mother's religion and tolerance of whites in favor of a career as a blues singer. When Harriett's prospects at home seem in jeopardy, she goes off with the circus, returns home, and then falls under the influence of her loose, street-walking friend, Maudel. She eventually goes to Kansas City, and from there she becomes a success on the black vaudeville circuit.

Temperance (Tempy) Siles, wife of Arkin Si-les, a property-owning postal clerk. She is the least sympathetic of Aunt Hager's daughters. Her concern for propriety leads her to ignore her washerwoman mother. Yet she takes Sandy into her home after Aunt Hager dies and concerns herself with his education.

Jimmy Lane, one of Sandy's childhood companions. Used primarily as a foil to Sandy, Jimmy quits school to work as a bellhop and seems headed toward an aimless life characterized by drinking and wenching.

Pansetta Young, one of the black students at Sandy's predominantly white high school. She is Sandy's first romantic interest, but Sandy's innocent inattention leads her to spend afternoons with the likes of Jimmy Lane.

Essay-Review

Readers familiar with the indignation and rage dramatized by black writers such as James Baldwin and Toni Morrison may find *Not Without Laughter* surprisingly free of anger and dramatic tension. Hughes's novel does indeed remind its audience of the inequities blacks have experienced at the hands of whites. Aunt Hager Williams literally works herself to death laundering white people's clothes, and her daughter, Anjee, labors under the unreasonable demands of her white employer, Mrs. Rice. Yet Aunt Hager rejects the unfocused anger of her youngest daughter, Harriett, who hates all whites, even Jesus. Without a trace of irony, Aunt Hager tells the impressionable Sandy that "...I's kept a room in ma heart fo 'em, 'cause white folks needs us, even if they don't know it."

Rather than dramatize the atrocities that whites have committed against blacks, Hughes chooses to employ Aunt Hager, her three daughters, and one grandson as a microcosm of the black experience. Although they live neither in the South nor the ghettoes of a Northern city, their home, a small, tranquil Kansas town, contains the general obstacles that confronted blacks before World War I. Aunt Hager is resigned to her lot and cheerfully cares for her neighbors, black and white. She finds what solace she can in the church and her family. Her daughters are not so sanguine. Anjee, Sandy's mother, invests her hopes in a man, the rambling, virile Jimboy. Against her mother's wishes she leaves Kansas and her son to follow Jimboy from one Northern city to the next. Tempy, Aunt Hager's eldest, stays in Stanton, but abandons her mother as well. She marries a postal clerk, and invests emotionally in the respectability symbolized by the Episcopal Church that she joins. The youngest daughter, Harriett, has no regard for marriage, the church, or respectability. Once she escapes from the world of prostitution, she finds success singing on the black vaudeville circuit.

The three sisters all care for Sandy in their way, and each protects or intervenes on his behalf at some crucial time in his growth to manhood. As flawed as each daughter may be in her own way, Hughes refuses to condemn them. Each has a particular kind of courage and decency. Tempy may be unkind to her mother, but she genuinely cares for Sandy, as does her opposite, the fun-loving profligate, Harriett. The combined examples of his grandmother, mother, and aunts provides the female-dominated hero Sandy with a wealth of insight and tolerance. Such a range in experience, along with formal education, will allow Sandy to navigate the stormy waters of his coming adult years in the urbanized North.

While Hughes expresses concern for the black experience generally, he is most successful at capturing the individual priorities of the Williams women. The depiction of Anjee's sexual love for Jimboy, a love that leads her to leave her only son, is both sympathetic and remarkably candid. Hughes is at his best, however, when he portrays Harriett and her attraction to the world of black sensuality. In the best scene in the novel, the reader follows Harriett to a black dance and the music of Benbow's Famous Kansas City Band. Amidst the odors of fried fish, Sen Sens, and hair oil, "The four black men in Benbow's wandering band were exploring depths to which mere sound had no busines to go. Cruel, desolate, unadorned was their music now, like the body of a ravished woman on the sun-baked earth. . . ." Through Harriett, Hughes reveals his capacity to capture the particular rhythms of black communal life.

If Hughes succeeds in making one see and feel the texture of much of the black experience, he finds less success in other matters. Although the novel's thematic interest in the hero coming of age is obvious, the reader feels that the history of most any other major character would have been more interesting than Sandy's. A related problem is the lack of tension that characterizes the plot generally. Even though his father and mother both leave him with an impoverished old woman who eventually dies, Sandy's life is remarkably free of any dramatically felt conflict. The reader never really worries about him. Similarly, the death of Aunt Hager elicits scarcely any response at all—either from Sandy or the reader. When his mother summons Sandy to Chicago, he apparently feels neither intense relief nor joy. Compared with a Bigger Thomas or Ralph Ellison's Invisible Man, Sandy is dull, and his history is distressingly serene.

The novel's value as a social history of a time and place the reader might not have known otherwise and its successful characterization of supporting characters compensate for the lack of tension in the somewhat episodic plot. If Sandy himself does not engage the reader fully, the world of Aunt Hager and her daughters frequently does. One also experiences the pleasure of a flexible prose that moves with ease from the clear formal language of the narrator to the complex rhythms of black spoken English.

Bibliography

Bone, Robert A.   *The Negro Novel in America.* Rev. ed. New Haven, Conn.: Yale University Press, 1965.

Bontemps, Arna.   "The Harlem Renaissance," in *Saturday Review of Literature*, XXX (March 22, 1947), pp. 12–13, 44.

Brawley, Benjamin.   *The Negro Genius.* New York: Dodd, Mead, 1937.

Davis, Arthur P.   *From the Dark Tower.* Washington, D.C.: Howard University Press, 1974.

Emanuel, James A.   *Langston Hughes.* New York: Twayne, 1967.

Gloster, Hugh M.   *Negro Voices in American Fiction.* Chapel Hill: University of North Carolina Press, 1948.

Jackson, Blyden.   "A Golden Mean for the Negro Novel," in *CLA Journal*, III (December, 1959), pp. 81–87.

Kinnamon, Keneth.   "The Man Who Created Simple," in *Nation*, CCV (December 4, 1967), pp. 599–601.

Littlejohn, David.   *Black on White: A Critical Survey of Writings by American Negroes.* New York: Grossman, 1966.

Margolies, Edward.   *Native Sons: A Critical Study of Twentieth-Century Negro Authors.* Philadelphia: Lippincott, 1968.

Nichols, Lewis.   "Langston Hughes Describes the Genesis of His *Tambourines to Glory*," in *The New York Times*, section 2 (October 27, 1963), p. 3.

O'Daniel, Therman B., ed.   *Langston Hughes, Black Genius.* New York: William Morrow, 1971.

Presley, James.   "The American Dream of Langston Hughes," in *Southwest Review*, XLVIII (Autumn, 1963), pp. 380–386.

OLIVER LaFARGE

Born: New York City (December 19, 1901)
Died: Albuquerque, New Mexico (August 2, 1963)

Principal Works

AUTOBIOGRAPHY: *Raw Material*, 1945.

NOVELS: *Laughing Boy*, 1929; *Long Pennant*, 1933; *Sparks Fly Upward*, 1931. *The Enemy Gods*, 1937; *The Copper Pot*, 1942.

SHORT STORIES: *All the Young Men*, 1935; *Behind the Mountains*, 1956; *Pause in the Desert*, 1957; *The Door in the Wall*, 1965.

SCIENTIFIC WORKS: *Tribes and Temples*, with Frans Blom, 1927: *The Year Bearer's People*, with Douglas S. Byers, 1931; *Santa Eulalia: the Religion of a Cuchumatan Indian Town*, 1947.

MISCELLANEOUS: *Introduction to American Indian Art*, 1931; *As Long as the Grass Shall Grow*, 1940; *A Man's Place*, 1940; *The Changing Indian*, 1942; *War Below Zero*, 1944; *The Eagle in the Egg*, 1949.

POETRY: "Draft Names Drawn," 1941.

Oliver LaFarge was born into a distinguished family which could trace its history to Colonial times. His full name was Oliver Hazard Perry LaFarge II in honor of his notable great-great grandfather Commodore Oliver Hazard Perry and his uncle Oliver H. P. LaFarge. Oliver's father, Grant LaFarge, was a prominent architect and illustrator who maintained homes in New York City and on Narragansett Bay, Rhode Island, where Oliver spent long summers learning to ride and sail. Oliver's grandfather, John LaFrage, was a well known painter and artist in stained glass; and his older brother, Christopher LaFarge, was also a published writer. Oliver was always conscious of this cultural heritage and believed that it sometimes served as a handicap in his writing. His family's genteel traditions and social expectations may well have caused a rebellion in the young man which resulted in his life-long interest in aboriginal cultures.

From an early age LaFarge had longed to become a writer, and he had his first literary experience as editor of the school magazine. In 1920 he entered Harvard, where he wrote for the Harvard student publications. He continued his literary activities as an undergraduate and became president of the board of editors, as well as a member of the student council. In his senior year, he was elected class poet and *Scribner's Magazine* published an essay he had written.

His college major, however, was anthropology, not literature. Harvard's major research in anthropology was in the American Southwest, and the next summer LaFarge participated in a field trip to the Four Corners area of New Mexico, Colorado, Utah, and Arizona. The following summer he returned with another expedition to the Navajo Reservation. In 1924 he received a Bachelor of Arts degree *cum laude* with a major in anthropology from Harvard. At his graduation, LaFarge read an original poem called "Baccalaureate Hymn" in which he expressed his belief that no man's life is without purpose and should not be without commitment. He maintained those convictions throughout his life. After graduation he spent his third summer on the Navajo Reservation then returned to begin graduate studies at Harvard. During that summer of 1924, LaFarge traveled with two companions over a hundred miles on a crosscountry trip on horseback from the Four Corners area to the Grand Canyon. He learned to speak Navajo, and the friendly Navajos christened him Harzi Nex, Tall Cliff Dweller.

In 1922, LaFarge's father had been commissioned to illustrate Elsie Clews Parsons' *American Indian Life* and this had further strengthened his son's interest in the American Indians. In *Raw Material*, LaFarge said of his father that he was a great outdoors man, a wilderness man who had a gift for getting on with Indians and who knew them well. He visited in many of their homes and wrote about their ceremonies and customs. His father was an important influence on his attitudes and values. His mother, Florence Bayard Lockwood, had always been active in civic affairs and was very conscious of social responsibilities. This was no doubt influential in shaping LaFarge's concern for those less fortunate economically then himself. His first impressions of Indian people were lasting ones and they created an enduring empathy and concern that would result in a life time of action on their behalf.

That fall when LaFarge returned to Harvard to begin graduate studies, he stayed only one semester. He was awarded the Hemenway Fellowship in Anthropology 1924–1926, was appointed assistant in ethnology in the Department of Middle American Research at Tulane University, and was invited to become assistant director of the Tulane expedition to Central America. He joined the expedition to Guatemala in early 1925. In 1926 he again spent the summer in Arizona, after which he returned to Tulane where he became a part of the third Tulane expedition to Guatemala. Since he was a part of several expeditions under the auspices of Tulane, New Orleans became his home base for two and a half years.

It was there in the French Quarter that LaFarge wrote *Laughing Boy*. He was on a half-time appointment at Tulane, where he was writing up the results of his research in the field. He was also writing short stories and articles to eke out a living. One story, "North is Black," was printed in a literary magazine, *The Dial*, and included in *Best American Short Stories of 1927*. It was a story based on a Navajo experience. Ferris Greenslet, editor of Houghton Mifflin, saw the story and expressed an interest in LaFarge's writing. That was enough encouragement for LaFarge to begin serious work on *Laughing Boy*.

He returned to Harvard in 1928 and received his Master of Arts degree in anthropology in May, 1929. He had worked on the degree sporadically since 1924 but with many interruptions caused by his absences for expeditions. He returned to New Orleans where *Laughing Boy* was completed and published in 1929. In 1930 it won the Pulitzer Prize.

William Faulkner was living in New Orleans during the two and a half years that LaFarge was working at Tulane and living in the French Quarter. They saw each other on numerous occasions and it has been suggested that LaFarge supplied much of the information about the history, customs and beliefs of his Indians that Faulkner used in his own works. LaFarge's knowledge of and enthusiasm for Indians erupted on every occasion. At parties in the Quarter, he often talked about the Southwest, chanted Navajo songs, performed tribal dances, and even wore beaded Indian headbands.

It is evident that LaFarge's first novel, *Laughing Boy*, was the result of his admiration and respect for Navajo people and what he saw as their vanishing way of life. He loved the desert regions of the Southwest and his nostalgic attitude colored the personal experiences he wove into the novel. The novel's success created the opportunities for LaFarge to begin his life's work on behalf of the American Indians.

LaFarge was married to Wanden E. Mathews Spetember 28, 1929, in New York City. They had two children, a son, Oliver Albee who later assumed the name Peter, and a daughter Povy Anya. An accelerated social life together with the Great Depression forced LaFarge to capitalize on the success of *Laughing Boy* by writing romantic Indian stories for popular magazines. He also tried other modes and themes, but these attempts met with little success.

When John Collier was made Commissioner of Indian Affairs during Franklin D. Roosevelt's first term, he sent Oliver LaFarge on assignment to the Southwest to work with the Navajos, Hopis, and Apaches. During the thirties and forties there, LaFarge produced four novels, numerous short stories and many articles on the Indian situation.

In 1930 the Eastern Association on Indian Affairs elected him to its Board of Directors and in 1933 he was elected president. In In June 1937, there was a merger of the Eastern Association on Indian Affairs with the Indian Defense Association. It became the Association of American Indian Affairs and LaFarge became the president. He served from 1932 to 1941 and from 1947 until his death in 1963. His concern for Indian rights brought him disillusionment and frustrations when later administrations ignored conditions and abandoned Indian programs. During those times he continued his writings, but nothing he wrote ever again achieved the popularity of *Laughing Boy*.

LaFarge and his wife Wanden were divorced in 1937. She received custody of their two children and there was an estrangement between him and his children which lasted many years and was never entirely reconciled. LaFarge was married in 1939 to Consuelo Olille Cabeza de Baca of Santa Fe. They chose Santa Fe as their home and lived there until his death. They had one son, John Pendarica.

LaFarge's scholarly training, his artistic impulse, and his ancestral heritage were often in conflict. He felt the necessity to measure up to societal expectations but at the same time the inclination to live a free and easy individualistic existence. He knew he could write easily and well the scholarly articles expected in his profession, but he longed to express the characters and situations that filled his imagination. He said that the greatest disappointment of his life was that he was never again able to achieve the success of *Laughing Boy*. That was, however, no small feat for the classic novel of Navajo culture not only won the Pulitzer Prize but has been translated into several foreign languages, and the total sales have exceeded a quarter of a million copies.

LaFarge died August 2, 1963. At his funeral representatives of the Meccasukee Seminole tribe, the Cheyenne tribe, and the All Pueblo Council of New Mexico served as honorary pall bearers. His monument has been the slim little volume *Laughing Boy* composed when he was only twenty-eight.

LAUGHING BOY

Type of work: Novel
Author: Oliver La Farge (1901–1963)
Time of plot: 1915
Locale: The American Southwest, Arizona and New Mexico
First published: 1929

Laughing Boy *is a romantic story of the conflict between a consuming love that brings a new, non-Indian way of life to a naïve Indian man and the resulting loss of family, friends, and mores of the familiar, traditional Navajo lifestyle during the early part of the twentieth century.*

Principal Characters

Laughing Boy, a naïve, traditional, young Navajo man. He is also called Went Away, Blind Eyes, Sings Before Spears, and Slayer of Enemy Gods in the traditional Indian way of giving a new name to a person because of an important event or attribute in his life. Laughing Boy is from the Tahtachini clan which lived at T'o Tlakai in the remote northern area of the Navajo Nation. He has had almost no experience with non-Indian people or customs and so is easily deceived by Slim Girl. He is a skilled silversmith and jeweler who likes working with his hands, participating in "sings" and ceremonies, breeding and racing horses, and gambling. Laughing Boy is enchanted by Slim Girl, marries her, then struggles to somehow live in two very different worlds with loyalties and values in each.

Slim Girl, a beautiful young Navajo girl of the Bitahni clan whose parents are dead and who has no living relatives. She is also called Lillian, Came With War, and affectionately, Hasche Lto'i (goddess). Slim Girl has been away from the reservation at "white" school for six years. She is most familiar with the non-Indian world, and has lost many of her Navajo traditions and attitudes. She lives at Chiziai, a border town. Slim Girl wants to behave in a traditional Navajo fashion but does not know how. She had an Apache grandmother, and Slim Girl's impulses are difficult to control. She loves Laughing Boy, but her thirst for revenge for her loss of traditions and her treatment in a non-Indian world is her dominant concern.

Jesting Squaw's Son, Laughing Boy's best friend. He is used as a counterpoint for Laughing Boy and to illustrate the traditional Navajo values and behavior. He is a "long hair," as Laughing Boy was before his marriage.

Red Man, a treacherous, young Navajo man who has adopted many non-Indian ways. He, also, lives in Chiziai, a town on the border of the Navajo reservation. Red Man is a rejected suitor of Slim Girl. Filled with dissatisfaction and the compulsion for revenge, he accidentally shoots Slim Girl while aiming at Laughing Boy, the source of his misery.

Wounded Face, Laughing Boy's uncle and his spiritual "father." He tries to persuade Laughing Boy not to marry Slim Girl.

Yellow Singer, an old, drunken Navajo medicine man who lives in Chiziai. He "sings" over Laughing Boy and Slim Girl to perform a marriage ceremony in exchange for a bottle of whiskey. Laughing Boy does not understand why he seems so strange. Laughing Boy has never drunk whiskey and does not know its effects before he meets Slim Girl.

George Hartshorn, Slim Girl's American lover who cares for her but cannot accept the idea of a "squaw" for a wife.

Mountain Singer, a traditional Navajo medicine man. He is the spiritual leader of the Tahtachini clan. He conducts the ten-day Night Chant which Laughing Boy and Slim Girl attend. He sits in the family council to discuss Laughing Boy's marriage and its consequences and to give guidance.

Two Boys, Laughing Boy's biological father who taught him silversmithing and who is concerned for his welfare.

Spotted Horse, Laughing Boy's younger uncle.

Walked Around, Laughing Boy's mother.

Boy's Son, Laughing Boy's brother.

Bay Horse, Laughing Boy's brother-in-law.

Essay-Review

The romantic love story *Laughing Boy* won the Pulitzer Prize for the best novel in 1930, and it still offers much to the current reader. While many readers simply enjoy the romance, others may profit more from the revelations of Navajo culture at a time when that world was undergoing vast changes. The theme and historical period, the setting, and the colorful characters are fused to create an enduring piece of American literature. While Oliver LaFarge was an anthropologist by training, his interest in the American Indians and his empathy for their plight provided the stimulus necessary for him to create a ficitional account which has become a classic.

LaFarge chose 1915 as an appropriate time for his novel. The early part of the twentieth century was a time for fundamental adjustments in the lives of the Navajo people. LaFarge used the confrontation between the Indian and non-Indian cultures as a central theme for his story. The results of exposure to new ways and different values is shown through the lives of both Laughing Boy and Slim Girl. The novel's characters are representative of many other Navajo at that time and in that place.

At the turn of the century, the Navajo nation was a vast, sparsely populated, semi-arid reservation. The region in northwest New Mexico and northeast Arizona had been the home of the Navajo people for many generations and was set aside for their permanent use as a reservation on June 1, 1868. The Navajos are a semi-nomadic people who are primarily shepherds. They live in permanent family-oriented communities from which they go out to tend their flocks. Like most American Indians, the Navajos value the extended family; it is of primary importance to them. Not only do they live near their families and clan members, but they mutually support each other. Family acceptance and good relationships are essential to their well being. Laughing Boy came from that environment.

Slim Girl, a beautiful young Navajo-Apache girl, had been taken from her traditional environment and sent away to school, where she had been forbidden to speak Navajo and was encouraged to adopt "white" customs. She was introduced to Christianity when she lived with a minister and his family. Slim Girl's experience is representative of many Indians who were emotionally confused by this whole process. It was difficult for Slim Girl to understand this very different concept which places values on things and attitudes which were foreign to Indian philosophy. Slim Girl chose "the Jesus path" however, and sought to conform to the new standards. But, in doing this, she was forced to reject and forget the traditional Navajo ways. When she was betrayed by Christianity and the non-Indian world, Slim Girl was caught between the two cultures and could be a part of neither. She feared and distrusted the "white" world and learned to hate it. In typical Indian fashion she sought revenge.

Laughing Boy, by contrast, was from a very traditional environment. His family lived on the northern part of the reservation, the most remote area. Laughing Boy's only contact with non-Indians was at the trading post where he sometimes went for supplies. He found the behavior of the white men there amusing but difficult to understand. He had never seen a town, did not know what a jail was, and had only heard of whiskey. Oliver LaFarge used Laughing Boy to demonstrate traditional attitudes and behaviors before the change that was inevitable.

In addition to Laughing Boy and Slim Girl, LaFarge used other characters in the novel to demonstrate Navajo types of that time. Yellow Singer is an elderly Navajo who had been a respected medicine man on the reservation but who became a drunken bum in the little town of Chiziai. Yellow Singer did not know how to handle "this new drink" and soon the next drink of whiskey became his primary concern and preoccupation. Although he remembers the old ways, and is able to perform the wedding ceremony for Slim Girl and Laughing Boy, the old ways have lost importance for him as he sinks into an alcoholic existence. La Farge was aware of the devastating effects of alcohol on Indians and the resulting loss of traditions. He simply foresaw what is now a national concern. Yellow Singer is a symbol for that eventuality.

By contrast, Mountain Singer is a traditional medicine man. LaFarge used Mountain Singer's respected place in the Navajo community to point up the degradation of Yellow Singer. LaFarge's choice of names for characters seems somewhat obvious viewed from this distance, but the religious association often made with mountains and the yellow color associated with infection and pus are illustrative of the characters. And, of course, medicine men are known as "singers" because of the various ceremonies which are sung as healing rites.

Jesting Squaw's Son is an appropriate counterpart for Laughing Boy. They are intimate boyhood friends whose lives are very similar until they met the young Indian women with whom they fall in love. Laughing Boy ignores his traditional customs and lack of family approval to marry Slim Girl. His marriage, while passionate and beautiful, becomes less and less fulfilling until the relationship ends in her death. Jesting Squaw's Son, when he discovers that he and his love are from the same clan, accepts the taboo and immediately gives up the relationship. While he is totally miserable for a time, he recovers in a few weeks and returns to the reservation resigned to his loss. LaFarge seems to be saying that an Indian's ignoring of traditions can not produce lasting happiness.

George Hartshorn, Slim Girl's American lover, serves as an additional contrast to Laughing Boy. George also sincerely loves Slim Girl; he provides a house, supplies, and small luxuries for her. But, he is unwilling to make the personal sacrifices that Laughing Boy does. He cannot ignore the criticism of his own culture and accept Slim Girl for what she is. In the end, George suffers humiliation and the loss of Slim Girl while Laughing Boy "had nearly lost her but now he had her forever." This value for romantic love underscores the major theme of the novel.

The characters in *Laughing Boy* are rather flat. Only Laughing Boy is revealed in any depth. The reader is conscious of the function of various characters to make a point, but they are not developed in enough detail to make them more than types. One gradually becomes aware of Slim Girl's confused value system, but the narrator is never omniscient and the reader is made aware that she suffered deep conflicts only through her behavior and the recounting of her youthful experiences. She longs to retain the traditions she has lost; she wants to be Navajo, but she does not remember how. Slim Girl's character is developed sufficiently to support the novel's themes, but not sufficiently to make her a memorable character.

The almost mystical Navajo values for silversmithing and weaving are illustrated very effectively. They are the most important symbols in the novel. Laughing Boy is a silversmith who loves his work and who fashions his dreams into beautifully finished objects. It is much more than a craft for him; it is an art. His favorite silver bow-guard is a piece much admired by others and considered "lucky" by him. It is a symbol of tradition and of the essence of Laughing Boy, who at Slim Girl's death places the bow-guard in the grave with her. He leaves his most valued possession and his personal symbol with her.

The weaving of rugs and blankets is a symbol for Slim Girl. At first Slim Girl does not know how to weave, but she recognizes the traditional value of weaving and struggles to learn the craft. Her first efforts are amateurish but she doggedly continues. As she includes her ambitions and dreams into her designs, her skill grows until her products also become beautiful and admired. The rugs illustrate Slim Girl's developing life and the harmony and balance that she is discovering. After her death, Laughing Boy saves her most beautiful rug to keep as the emblem of her perfection for him.

An interesting bit of Indian philosophy is incorporated into the novel's structure. Indians generally value the circle as a symbol of unity and completeness. They tend to see life as cyclic rather than linear. LaFarge has structured his novel in that pattern. The novel begins with Laughing Boy on his way to a ceremonial sing. It ends the same way. The cycle is complete. The search for harmony and completeness is the single most important concept in Navajo culture and LaFarge uses that perfect balance effectively in the structure of his novel.

Some accurate details about Navajo life are skillfully woven into the plot. Traditional attitudes, practices, beliefs, names, ceremonies, even foods are incorporated into the story. These realistic details provide the authenticity to make the story believable, but the plot is not complex nor are the characters.

Early reviewers praised LaFarge's sympathetic treatment of Navajos in *Laughing Boy*, which was one of the first successful novels about Indians. The novel was immediately popular and was selected as the November 1929 selection of the Literary Guild. The novel's popularity was to some extent, no doubt, a nostalgic support for the "noble savage" concept. But, the novel has an intrinsic value also.

Laughing Boy is a novel which reads easily, and its theme is clearly recognized. The language is not difficult since LaFarge deliberately used monosyllabic words. The situations are apparent, the characters distinguishable, and the plot interesting and charming. Because of its simplicity and romantic interest, it is a novel especially appropriate for adolescent readers. The more sophisticated reader will find the lack of complexity refreshing or empty as his taste dictates. The novel has been criticized as being sentimental, and LaFarge himself acknowledged that he probably lacked the self-discipline to handle the emotions effectively. *Laughing Boy* is useful, however, to illustrate Navajo customs and attitudes of that time and to help the reader become aware of differences between novels written about Indians and novels written by Indians. Although current criticism is lacking, quite probably the modern knowledgeable reader will consider *Laughing Boy* an over simplification of a complex and still to be resolved situation.

Bibliography

Allen, Charles. "The Fiction of Oliver La Farge," in *University of Arizona Quarterly*. I (Winter 1945).

Austin, Mary. "A Navajo Tale," in *The Saturday Review of Literature*. 6 (November 9, 1929), pp. 262–263.

Bird, John. "The Future of Oliver La Farge," in *Bookman*. LXXII (September, 1930), p. 13.

Bunker, Robert. "Oliver La Farge: In Search of Self," in *New Mexico Quarterly* XX (Summer, 1950), pp. 211–224.

Gaston, Edwin, W., Jr. *The Early Novel of the Southwest*. Albuquerque: University of New Mexico Press, 1961.

Krefft, James H. "A Possible Source for Faulkner's Indians: Oliver La Farge's *Laughing Boy*," in *Tulane Studies in English*. XXIII (1978), pp. 187–192.

McNickle, D'Arcy. *Indian Man: A Life of Oliver La Farge*. Bloomington: Indiana University Press, 1971.

Pearce, T. M. "New Worlds in View: Novels," in *Oliver La Farge.* New York: Twayne Publishers Inc., 1972.

Powell, Lawrence Clark. *Books, West and Southwest.* Los Angeles: Ward Ritchie, 1957.

Van Doren, Carl. *The American Novel, 1789–1939.* New York: Macmillan, 1946.

Van Doren, Carl. "Why the Editorial Board Selected *Laughing Boy*," in *Wings.* III, No. 11 (November, 1929), pp. 4–5.

SINCLAIR LEWIS

Born: Sauk Center, Minnesota (February 7, 1885)
Died: Rome, Italy (January 10, 1951)

Principal Works

NOVELS: *Our Mr. Wren*, 1914; *The Trail of the Hawk*, 1915; *The Innocents*, 1917; *The Job*, 1917; *Free Air*, 1919; *Main Street*, 1920; *Babbitt*, 1922; *Arrowsmith*, 1925; *Mantrap*, 1926; *Elmer Gantry*, 1927; *The Man Who Knew Coolidge*, 1928; *Dodsworth*, 1929; *Ann Vickers*, 1933; *Work of Art*, 1934; *It Can't Happen Here*, 1935; *The Prodigal Parents*, 1938; *Bethel Merriday*, 1940; *Gideon Planish*, 1943; *Cass Timberlane*, 1945; *Kingsblood Royal*, 1947; *The God-Seeker*, 1949; *World So Wide*, 1951.

SHORT STORIES: *Selected Short Stories of Sinclair Lewis*, 1935.

PLAY: *Jayhawker*, 1935 (with Lloyd Lewis).

The literary decade of the 1920's was dominated by two figures: H. L. Mencken and (Harry) Sinclair Lewis, who, more than any other writers, gave to that era of "debunking" its special tone. Quite appropriately, Lewis was born in Sauk Center, Minnesota ("Gopher Prairie"), on February 7, 1885, the son of Dr. Emmet J. Lewis, who furnished him with part of the character of Arrowsmith. After graduating from Yale in 1908, Lewis spent many years at all sorts of work, mainly journalism, wandering from California to the East Coast. His first marriage, to Grace Hegger in 1914, ended in divorce in 1925; in 1928 he married the famous newspaper correspondent, Dorothy Thompson, from whom he was divorced in 1942.

Lewis presents the rather unusual phenomenon of a writer who, after a period of purely conventional apprenticeship, suddenly found his true expression and for a decade produced a series of extremely important novels, only to relapse for the rest of his career into work of no lasting significance. Thus, his earlier and later novels can be disregarded. It was in five books written during the 1920's that he said what he had to say, and even during these years he wrote the undoubtedly second-rate *Mantrap*.

Before 1920, Lewis had published five novels, all insignificant; then, according to legend, he announced that he was at last going to write a book to please himself. The result was *Main Street*, which had an immediate and enormous success following its unheralded publication in 1920. Using the knowledge gained as a youth spent in a typical small town, Lewis shattered forever the sentimental tradition clinging around American village life. Though he located Gopher Prairie in the part of the country that he knew best, Lewis made it clear that his story would have been much the same in any small town in the United States: they are all alike, he implied, in their pettiness, dreariness, and dullness, victims of the "village virus" which destroys initiative and makes the complacent inhabitants intolerant of values other than their own. For them, Gopher Prairie is the ultimate triumph of civilization.

In *Babbitt*, his most successfully executed novel, Lewis undertook a more representative theme: the character of the typical businessman, the "go-getter" with his materialistic standards, hypnotized by his own slogans of success, yet gnawingly aware that his life is somehow empty. His tragi-comic revolt is short-lived, but it symbolizes the failure of American middle-class life to bring any real satisfaction to these people who are materially so successful and comfortable.

Arrowsmith did not infuriate so many readers, since its satire of commercialized science did not touch as many individuals and it contained the sympathetic character of Leora, the hero's first wife. It is a competent novel, with some memorable figures, but it is more limited than the other books Lewis wrote during this period. Yet it was probably his most popular novel and the one for which he was offered the Pulitzer Prize in 1926. This prize he refused.

The next novel, *Elmer Gantry*, was Lewis' most slashing attack on any segment of American life and the book that angered the greatest number of people. In it Lewis satirized with intense bitterness the more fundamentalist sects of American Protestantism. The main character, a clergyman, is a monster of hypocrisy equal to any of the villains of Dickens, yet at the end of the novel, after a temporary reversal, he is poised for further triumphs—a biting comment on America. Also included was a caricature of a famous evangelist of that period. The novel is naïve, for Lewis knew very little about religion, but the attack was badly needed at a time when churchmen had put the weight of their churches behind Prohibition and similar hypocrisies. Yet its very timeliness for 1927 makes it more "dated" than the other novels Lewis wrote during this period.

In *Dodsworth* Lewis returned to the scenes of *Babbitt*, dealing now with the very rich members of that world. His aim was to point out that American life, even at this high financial level of ease and security, is an empty thing, that the very success, so much striven for, does not bring happiness, that the typical American, preoccupied with making money, does not know what to do with himself once the money is made. Added to this picture was that of Dodsworth's wife, seeking in a series of affairs, each more hectic than the last, for some romantic thrill that she feels she has missed.

Although Lewis wrote ten more novels and, in 1930, became the first American to be awarded the Nobel Prize for literature, his important work had been completed by the end of the 1920's. He was a typical product of the decade which, with Mencken, he had dominated, and they together accomplished a much-needed task. Their pungent satire, appealing to the younger generation, successfully punctured the great national complacency; never again, as has often been pointed out, could Americans regard themselves with the same placid self-satisfaction. The cult of "boosterism" had received a mortal wound.

Even in his best novels, Lewis was an extremely uneven writer and apparently totally lacked the power of self-criticism. His often naïve view of social problems was probably the result of his early socialist sympathies; he resembled Dickens in his over-simplification of human situations. Yet he had something of Dickens' power of creating caricatures, which he used in place of characters: we have never known a man exactly like Babbitt, but he is a composite of all the business-men of our acquaintance. In addition, Lewis possessed an eye for characteristic detail and an ear for actual American speech which, added to his careful preparation, give to his novels a solid reality. He was the perfect photographer; each scene, each speech is authentic and recognizable.

Lewis died in Rome on January 10, 1951. His last novel, *World So Wide*, appeared after his death.

Bibliography

The definitive biography is Mark Schorer, *Sinclair Lewis, An American Life*, 1961. Grace Hegger Lewis has presented a highly personal portrait in *With Love from Gracie: Sinclair Lewis, 1912–1925*, 1956. Earlier biographical studies include Oliver Harrison, *Sinclair Lewis*, 1925; and Carl Van Doren, *Sinclair Lewis: A Biographical Sketch*, 1933. Biographical details may also be found in *From Main Street to Stockholm: Letters of Sinclair Lewis, 1919–1930*, edited by Harrison Smith, 1952, and *The Man from Main Street: A Sinclair Lewis Reader*, 1953.

For critical commentary see Carl Van Doren, *The American Novel*, 1921 (rev. ed., 1940); Vernon L. Parrington, *Sinclair Lewis: Our Own Diogenes*, 1927; Régis Michaud, *The American Novel To-day*, 1928; Vernon L. Parrington, *Main Currents in American Thought*, Vol. III, 1930; Alfred Kazin, *On Native Grounds*, 1942; C. Carroll Hollis, "Sinclair Lewis: Reviver of Character," in *Fifty Years of the American Novel, 1900–1950*, edited by Harold C. Gardiner, S.J., 1951; Edward Wagenknecht, *Cavalcade of the American Novel*, 1952; Frederick J. Hoffman, *The Twenties: American Writing in the Postwar Decade*, 1955; and Mark Schorer, ed., *Sinclair Lewis: A Collection of Critical Essays*, 1962.

See also Howard Mumford Jones, "Mr. Lewis's America," *Virginia Quarterly Review*, VII (1931), 427–432; Lewis Mumford, "The America of Sinclair Lewis," *Current History*, XXXIII (1931), 529–533; Granville Hicks, "Sinclair Lewis and the Good Life," *English Journal*, XXV (1936), 265–273; Lloyd Morris, "Sinclair Lewis, His Critics and Public," *North American Review*, CCXLV (1938), 381–390; Joseph E. Baker, "Sinclair Lewis, Plato, and the Regional Escape," *English Journal*, XXVIII (1939), 460–468; Leo and Miriam Gurko, "The Two Main Streets of Sinclair Lewis," *College English*, IV (1943), 288–293; and Frederick I. Carpenter, "Sinclair Lewis and the Fortress of Reality," *ibid.*, XVI (1955), 416–423.

BABBITT

Type of work: Novel
Author: Sinclair Lewis (1885–1951)
Time of plot: The 1920's
Locale: Zenith, fictional Midwestern town
First published: 1922

Babbitt *is a pungent satire about a man who typifies complacent mediocrity. Middle-class businessman George F. Babbitt revels in his popularity, his automobile, and his ability to make money. He drinks bootleg whiskey, bullies his wife, and ogles his manicurist. Because he is firmly grounded in realism,* Babbitt *is one of American fiction's most memorable characters; his very name has entered the language as a synonym for the widespread phenomenon he represents.*

Principal Characters

George F. Babbitt, a satirically-portrayed prosperous real estate dealer in Zenith, a typical American city. He is the standardized product of modern American civilization, a member of the Boosters' Club, hypnotized by all the slogans of success, enthralled by material possessions, envious of those who have more, patronizing towards those who have less, yet dimly aware that his life is unsatisfactory. His high moment comes when, after delivering a speech at a real estate convention, he is asked to take part in a political campaign against Seneca Doane, a liberal lawyer who is running for mayor. As a result of his campaign efforts, Babbitt is elected vice-president of the Boosters. His self-satisfaction is shattered when his one real friend, Paul Riesling, shoots his nagging wife and is sent to prison. For the first time Babbitt begins to doubt the values of American middle-class life. He has a love affair with a client, Mrs. Judique, and becomes involved with her somewhat bohemian friends; he publicly questions some of the tenets of Boosterism; he refuses to join the Good Citizens'

League. But the pressure of public opinion becomes too much for him; when his wife is taken ill, his brief revolt collapses, and he returns to the standardized world of the Boosters' Club.

Myra Babbitt, his colorless wife, whom he married because he could not bear to hurt her feelings. She lives only for him and the children.

Verona Babbitt, their dumpy daughter. Just out of college, she is a timid intellectual whose mild unconventionality angers her father. He is relieved when she marries Kenneth Escott.

Theodore (Ted) Babbitt, their son. A typical product of the American school system, he hates study and the thought of college. He elopes with Eunice Littlefield, thus winning his father's secret admiration, for he has at least dared to do what he wanted.

Paul Riesling, Babbitt's most intimate friend since college days. With the soul of a musician, he has been trapped into a lifetime of manufacturing tar-roofing and is burdened with a shrewish wife.

Goaded to desperation, he shoots her and, though she lives, is sent to prison.

Zilla Riesling, Paul's nagging wife. With a vicious disposition that is made worse by having too much time on her hands, she finally drives Paul to the point of shooting her.

Mrs. Daniel (Tanis) Judique, a widow with whom Babbitt has a brief affair as a part of his revolt against conventionality.

Seneca Doane, a liberal lawyer, the anathema of all the solid businessmen of Zenith.

William Washington Eathorne, a rich conservative banker. He represents the real power behind the scene in Zenith.

Charles and
Lucille McKelvey, wealthy members of Zenith's smart set. The Babbitts are hopeful of being accepted socially by the McKelveys but do not succeed.

Ed and
Mrs. Overbrook, a down-at-heels couple.

They are hopeful of being accepted socially by the Babbitts but do not succeed.

The Rev. Dr. John Jennison Drew, the efficient, high-powered pastor of Babbitt's church.

Vergil Gunch, a successful coal dealer. He is prominent in all the civic organizations to which Babbitt belongs.

T. Cholmondeley (Chum) Frink, a member of Babbitt's social group. He is a popular poet whose work is syndicated throughout the country.

Howard Littlefield, Babbitt's next-door neighbor. An economist for the Zenith Street Traction Company, he can prove to everyone's satisfaction that Zenith is the best of all possible worlds.

Eunice Littlefield, his flapper daughter. She elopes with Ted Babbitt to the public surprise and indignation of both families but to Babbitt's secret delight.

Kenneth Escott, a newspaper resporter. After a tepid courtship, he finally marries Verona Babbitt.

The Story

George F. Babbitt was proud of his house in Floral Heights, one of the most respectable residential districts in Zenith. Its architecture was standardized; its interior decorations were standardized; its atmosphere was standardized. Therein lay its appeal for Babbitt.

He bustled about in a tile and chromium bathroom in his morning ritual of getting ready for another day. When he went down to breakfast, he was as grumpy as usual. It was expected of him. He read the dull real estate page of the newspaper to his patient wife, Myra. Then he commented on the weather, grumbled at his son and daughter, gulped his breakfast, and started for his office.

Babbitt was a real estate broker who knew how to handle business with zip and zowie. Having closed a deal whereby he forced a poor businessman to buy a piece of property at twice its value, he pocketed part of the money and paid the rest to the man who had suggested the enterprise. Proud of his acumen, he picked up the telephone and called his best friend, Paul Riesling, to ask him to lunch.

Paul Riesling should have been a violinist, but he had gone into the tar-roofing business in order to support his shrewish wife, Zilla. Lately she had made it her practice to infuriate doormen, theater ushers, or taxicab drivers, and then ask Paul to come to her rescue and fight them like a man. Cringing with embarrassment, Paul would pretend he had not noticed the incident. Later, at home, Zilla would accuse him of being a coward and a weakling.

So sad did Paul's affairs seem to Babbitt that he suggested a vacation to Maine together—away from their wives. Paul was skeptical, but with magnificent assurance Babbitt promised to arrange the trip. Paul was humbly grateful.

Back in his office Babbitt refused a raise for one of his employees. When he got home, he and his wife decided to give a dinner party, with the arrangements taken bodily from the contents of a woman's magazine, and everything edible disguised to look like something else.

The party was a great success. Babbitt's friends were exactly like Babbitt. They all became drunk on prohibition-period gin, were disappointed when the cocktails ran out, stuffed themselves with food, and went home to nurse headaches.

Sometime later Babbitt and Myra paid a call on the Rieslings. Zilla, trying to enlist their sympathy, berated her husband until he was goaded to fury. Babbitt finally told Zilla that she was a nagging, jealous, sour, and unwholesome wife, and he demanded that she allow Paul to go with him to Maine. Weeping in self-pity, Zilla consented. Myra sat calmly during the scene, but later she criticized Babbitt for bullying Paul's wife. Babbitt told her sharply to mind her own business.

On the train, Babbitt and Paul met numerous businessmen who loudly agreed with each other that what this country needed was a sound business administration. They deplored the price of motor cars, textiles, wheat, and oil; they swore that they had not an ounce of race-prejudice; they blamed Communism and socialism for labor unions which got out of hand. Paul soon tired of the discussion and went to bed. Babbitt stayed up late, smoking countless cigars, and telling countless stories.

Maine had a soothing effect upon Babbitt. He and Paul fished and hiked in the quiet of the north woods, and Babbitt began to realize that his life in Zenith was not all it should be. He promised himself a new outlook on life, a more simple, less hurried way of living.

Back in Zenith, Babbitt was asked to make a speech at a convention of real estate men which was to be held in Monarch, a nearby city. He wrote a speech contending that real estate men should be considered professionals and called realtors. At the meeting he declaimed loudly that real estate was a great profession, that Zenith was God's own country—the best little spot on earth—and to prove his statements quoted countless statistics on waterways, textile production, and lumber manufacture. The speech was such a success that Babbitt instantly won recognition as an orator.

Babbitt was made a precinct leader in the coming election. His duty was to speak to small labor groups about the inadvisability of voting for Seneca Doane, a liberal, in favor of a man named Prout, a solid businessman who represented the conservative element. Babbitt's speeches helped to defeat Doane. He was very proud of himself for having Vision and Ideals.

On a business trip to Chicago, Babbitt spied Paul Riesling sitting at dinner with a middle-aged but pretty woman. Later, in his hotel room, Babbitt indignantly demanded an explanation for Paul's lack of morality. Paul told Babbitt that he could no longer stand living with Zilla. Babbitt, feeling sorry for his friend, swore that he would keep her husband's secret from Zilla. Privately, Babbitt envied Paul's independence.

Babbitt was made vice-president of the Booster's Club. He was so proud of himself that he bragged loudly when his wife called him at the office. It was a long time before he understood what she was trying to tell him; Paul had shot his wife.

Babbitt's world collapsed about him. Though Zilla was still alive, Paul was in prison. Babbitt began to question his ideas about the power of the dollar. Paul was perhaps the only person Babbitt had ever loved. Myra had long since become a habit. The children were too full of new ideas to be close to their father. Babbitt felt suddenly alone. He began to criticize the minister's sermons. He no longer visited the Athletic Club, rarely ate lunch with any of his business acquaintances.

One day a pretty widow Mrs. Judique, came to his office and asked him to find her a flat. Babbitt joined her circle of bohemian friends. He drank more than he had ever drunk in his life. He spent money wildly. Two of the most powerful men in town requested that he join the Good Citizen's League—or else. Babbitt refused to be bullied. For the first time in his life he was a human being. He actually made friends with his arch-enemy, Seneca Doane, and discovered that he liked his liberal ideas. He praised Doane publicly. Babbitt's new outlook on life appealed to his children, who at once began to respect him as they never had before. But Babbitt became unpopular among his business-boosting friends. When he again refused to join the Good Citizen's League, he was snubbed in the streets. Gradually Babbitt found that he had no real resources within himself. He was miserable.

When Myra became ill, Babbitt suddenly realized that he loved his colorless wife. He broke with Mrs. Judique. He joined the Good Citizen's League. By the time Myra was well again, there was no more active leader in the town of Zenith than George F. Babbitt. Once more he announced his distrust of Seneca Doane. He became the best Booster the club ever had. His last gesture of revolt was private approval of his son's elopement. Outwardly he conformed.

Critical Evaluation

Zenith, "the Zip City—Zeal, Zest, and Zowie," is Sinclair Lewis' satirical composite picture of the typical progressive American "business city" of the 1920's, and middle-aged, middle-class Midwesterner George F. Babbitt is its average prosperous citizen. Everything about Zenith is modern. A few old buildings, ramshackle witnesses of the city's nineteenth century origins, are embarrassing, discordant notes amid the harmony of newness produced by shining skyscrapers, factories, and railroads. One by one the old buildings are surrounded and bulldozed. The thrust of all energies in the city is toward growth: one of Zenith's most booming businesses is real estate; one of its favorite occupations is the religious tallying and charting of population increase.

As Lewis presents his characters, however, the reader discovers that the prosperity and growth of Zenith has been inversely proportional to the intellectual bankruptcy and spiritual stagnation of its inhabitants. Because they subscribe to the values of Zenith's culture, which are all based on the "Dollar Ethic," Lewis' characters think in terms of production and consumption, judge people on the grounds of their purchasing power, and seek happiness in the earning and spending of money. This creed of prosperity permeates every aspect of society. It is evident not only in political and economic beliefs (discussion between Babbitt and his friends about government affairs is limited to the monotonous refrain, "What this country needs is a good, sound business administration"), but in moral and religious attitudes as well. Thus, Dr. Drew attracts followers to his "Salvation and Five Percent" church with a combined cross-and-dollar-sign approach. Even more sinister is the facility with which the upright Babbitt carries through crooked deals in his real estate business. In one maneuver, he plots with a speculator to force a struggling grocer to buy the store building (which he has been renting for years) at a scalper's price. The money ethic is so elemental to Babbitt's conscience that he honestly feels nothing but delight and pride when the deal is completed; his only regret is that the speculator carries off nine thousand dollars while Babbitt receives a mere four hundred and fifty dollar commission. At the same time, Babbitt—with no inkling of his hypocrisy—discourses on his virtue to his friend Paul Riesling, touting his own integrity while denigrating the morality of his competitors.

The value placed on money also determines Zenith's aesthetic standards. There is no frivolity about the city's architecture; the most important structures are the strictly functional business buildings. Other structures, such as the Athletic Club—where the businessmen go to "relax" and discuss weighty matters of finance—are gaudy, unabashed copies of past styles; the Club's motley conglomeration includes everything from Roman to Gothic to Chinese. The culmination of literary talent in Zenith is the work of Chum Frink, whose daily newspaper lyrics are indistinguishable from his Zeeco car ads. He comes to Babbitt's dinner party fresh from having written a lyric in praise of drinking water instead of poison booze; with bootleg cocktail in hand, he identifies the American genius as the fellow who can run a successful business or the man who writes the Prince Albert Tobacco ads.

But most important of all, the prosperity ethic is at the heart of social norms in Zenith; it is the basis upon which each citizen judges his individual worth. Lewis' novel includes caricatures of men in every major field of endeavor: Howard Littlefield is the scholar; T. Cholmondeley Frink, the poet; Mike Monday, the popular preacher; Jake Offut, the politician; Vergil Gunch, the industrialist. Yet despite their various professions, these men are identical in their values; they are united in their complacent pride at their own success, and in their scorn for those who haven't "made it." A man is measured by his income and his possesions. Thus, Babbitt's car is far more than his means of transportation, and his acquisition of gimmicks like the nickle-plated cigar cutter more than mere whim; both car and cigar cutter are affirmations of competence and virility. But the more Babbitt and his peers strive to distinguish themselves through ownership, the more alike they seem. Thus, the men of Zenith, since they are saturated day after day with the demands of the business life and its values, are even more alike than the women, who are not as immersed in the "rat race" as their husbands.

Mercilessly revealing and minutely detailed as the portrait of Zenith is, however, *Babbitt* would not be the excellent novel it is if Lewis had stopped at that. But in addition to being an exposé of shallowness, the novel is the chronicle of one man's feeble and half-conscious attempt to break out of a meaningless and sterile existence. In the first half of the book, George Babbitt is the Zenithite *par excellence*; but in the realtor's sporadic bursts of discontent, Lewis plants seeds of the rebellion to come. Babbitt's complacency is occasionally punctured by disturbing questions: Might his wife be right that he bullied Zilla only to strut and show off his strength and virtue? Are his friends really interesting people? Does he really love his wife and enjoy his career? These nagging questions and the pressures in his life finally build sufficient tension to push Babbitt to the unprecedented step of taking a week's vacation in Maine without his wife and children. The trip relieves his tension and dissolves the questions, and he returns to another year in Zenith with renewed vigor and enthusiasm for Boosters, baseball, dinner parties, and real estate.

It takes the personal tragedy of his friend Paul Riesling to really shock Babbitt out of his routine way of life; Paul's shooting of his wife and consequent imprisonment, which occur approximately midway in the novel, shake Babbitt to his foundations. The Babbitt of the first half of the story is a parody; the Babbitt of the second half, a weak and struggling human being. After Paul goes to prison, Babbitt, to all appearances, throws over his whole previous life style: he drinks, smokes, and curses; he frequents wild parties, befriends the city's "bohemian set," adopts radical opinions, and has a love affair. All these things are part of his rebellion against stifling circumstances and his attempt to escape into individuality. The attempt fails because he lacks the inner strength to be independent, and his revolt is ultimately little more than a teapot tempest. Whether preaching the philosophy of the Elks or rebelliously praising the radical politics of Seneca Doane, whether giving a dinner party with his wife or sneaking out to see Mrs. Judique, Babbitt never truly acts on his own.

Thus, by the end of the novel, Babbitt has "returned to the fold," joining the Good Citizen's League and redoubling his zeal in behalf of Zenith Booster activities. But even though Babbitt lacks the strength to break out of his mold, Lewis does not imply that he is unchanged by his experience. On the contrary, Babbitt rediscovers his love for his wife, and learns something about himself. The Babbitt at the close of the novel has grown in awareness, even if he has proven himself incapable of essentially changing his life. If he has lost his own individuality, he is still able to hope for better things for his son Ted, of whose elopement he secretly approves.

Bibliography

Blake, Nelson M. *Novelist's America: Fiction as History, 1910–1940.* Syracuse, N.Y.: Syracuse University Press, 1969, pp. 23–33, 36–38.

Cole, E.R. "George Babbitt: Mock-Hero of a Mock-Epic," in *Descant.* X (Winter, 1966), pp. 21–25.

Dooley, D.J. *The Art of Sinclair Lewis.* Lincoln: University of Nebraska Press, 1967, pp. 81–95.

Friedman, Philip Allan. "*Babbitt*: Satiric Realism in Form and Content," in *Satire Newsletter.* IV (1966), pp. 20–29.

Geismar, Maxwell. *The Last of the Provincials: The American Novel, 1915–1925.* Boston: Houghton Mifflin, 1947, pp. 88–96. Reprinted in *The Modern American Novel: Essays in Criticism.* Edited by Max Westbrook. New York: Random House, 1966, pp. 48–56.

Grebstein, Sheldon. *Sinclair Lewis.* New York: Twayne, 1962, pp. 73–85.

Griffin, Robert J. "Sinclair Lewis," in *American Winners of the Nobel Literary Prize.* Edited by Warren G. French and Walter E. Kidd. Norman: University of Oklahoma Press, 1968, pp. 47–50.

Hilfer, Anthony C. "Sinclair Lewis: Caricaturist of the Village Mind," in *The Revolt from the Village, 1915–1930.* Chapel Hill: University of North Carolina Press, 1969, pp. 167–176.

Hoffman, Frederick J. *The Twenties: American Writing in the Postwar Decade.* New York: Viking, 1955, pp. 364–370.

Hollis, C. Carroll. "Sinclair Lewis: Reviver of Character," in *Fifty Years of the American Novel: A Christian Appraisal.* Edited by Harold C. Gardiner. New York: Gordian Press, 1968, pp. 98–99.

Lewis, Robert W. *"Babbitt* and the Dream of Romance," in *North Dakota Quarterly.* XL (1972), pp. 7–14.

Light, Martin. *The Quixotic Vision of Sinclair Lewis.* West Lafayette, Ind.: Purdue University Press, 1975, pp. 73–84.

Lundquist, James. *Sinclair Lewis.* New York: Frederick Ungar, 1973, pp. 40–44, 70–74.

Mencken, H.L. "Portrait of an American Citizen," in *Sinclair Lewis: A Collection of Critical Essays.* Edited by Mark Schorer. Englewood Cliffs, N.J.: Prentice-Hall, 1962, pp. 20–22.

Petrullo, Helen B. *"Babbitt* as Situational Satire," in *Kansas Quarterly.* I (1969), pp. 89–97.

Pugh, D.G. "Baedekers, Babbittry, and Baudelaire," in *The Twenties: Fiction, Poetry, Drama.* Edited by Warren G. French. Deland, Fla.: Everett/ Edwards, 1975, pp. 87–99.

Quincy, James R. "George Babbitt's Quest for Masculinity," in *Ball State University Forum.* X (1969), pp. 4–7.

————. "Release Motif and Its Impact in *Babbitt,"* in *Sinclair Lewis Newsletter.* I (Spring, 1969), pp. 4–5.

Rothwell, Kenneth S. "From Society to Babbittry: Lewis' Debt to Edith Wharton," in *Journal of the Central Mississippi Valley American Studies Association.* I (Spring, 1960), pp. 32–37.

Schorer, Mark. *Sinclair Lewis: An American Life.* New York: McGraw, 1961, pp. 341–360.

Walcutt, Charles C. "Mud Huts of Intellect: Sinclair Lewis's *Babbitt,"* in *Man's Changing Mask: Modes and Methods of Characterization in Fiction.* Minneapolis: University of Minnesota Press, 1966, pp. 240–246.

West, Rebecca. *"Babbitt,"* in *New Statesman.* (October 21, 1922). Reprinted in *Sinclair Lewis: A Collection of Critical Essays.* Edited by Mark Schorer. Englewood Cliffs, N.J.: Prentice-Hall, 1962, pp. 23–26.

ELMER GANTRY

Type of work: Novel
Author: Sinclair Lewis (1885–1951)
Time of plot: 1915–1925
Locale: Midwest America
First published: 1927

Essay-Review

Sinclair Lewis wrote *Elmer Gantry* at the height of his fame, in the middle of the remarkable decade of the 1920's that began for Lewis with *Main Street* and ended with *Dodsworth* and saw not only *Babbitt* and *Arrowsmith* but also their author's refusal of a Pulitzer Prize that had been awarded to him. Yet curiously, *Elmer Gantry* gives us a first hint of the waning of Lewis' powers. Before this novel Lewis had served a long apprenticeship, and had achieved great success. From 1915 to 1920 he wrote fifty short stories and five novels, trying out his themes and characterizations, sketching out his satiric portraits of various types; not the least among these were religious types, though the climax of that kind of portraiture was not to come until *Elmer Gantry* appeared in 1927.

Main Street burst upon the world in 1920, the result of several years of research to establish the realistic foundation upon which his satires were to rest. His book was a sensational best-seller, and apparently it occurred to Lewis that he could repeat his success if he would only, in a programmatic way, turn his satiric eye upon the various aspects of American life in sequence. After his exposure of the village he next chose Zenith, a middle-sized city, and George F. Babbit a middle-class businessman. Then he applied his attention (now in collaboration with Dr. Paul de Kruif) to medicine, public health, and medical experimentation. Other projects flashed through his mind and were rejected, until he at last found a challenging project he could eagerly work upon, the ministry; and he began to consider how he could assemble ideas, plot, character, and especially background for what would later become *Elmer Gantry*. Undertaking an exposure of hypocrisy in religion was a formidable and dangerous task, but Lewis felt confidently ready for it. In *Babbit* he had written of Mike Monday, the evangelist; Mrs. Opal Emerson Mudge, leader of the New Thought League; and the Reverend John Jennison Drew, author of *The Manly Man's Religion*.

Following his usual method of research, he sought expert advice to provide the background for his novel. Acquainted with a minister in Kansas City, he went there to find some of his material. He gathered a weekly "seminar" of local pastors of many faiths and sects; after luncheon, there might be a session on "The Holy Spirit," with Lewis challenging, pressing, arguing, and thus absorbing material. Gradually, characters and plot took shape. Elmer Gantry was to be Lewis' most extravagant faker, a salesman of religion with no real knowledge of theology and no scruples or morals, a stupid man who would exploit his parishioners as he climbed to success from village to town to city, a seducer of women, a man of greed.

Elmer Gantry, captain of the football team at Terwillinger College, was known as "Hell-cat" to his classmates and especially to his roommate, a drinking, and carousing friend, Jim Lefferts. Then something happened to convert Gantry from being the heathen that he was; he was taken up with the moment. He had met Judson Roberts, the ex-football star who had a following among members of the "manly" set. Gantry's mother had been urging him to give his soul to God and so at a prayer meeting Elmer was swept up and converted with a mob of other "saved" people, while his mother, Judson Roberts, and his disbelieving classmates looked on. From that point on, Lewis exposed Gantry's cheap education, revealed his mistaken, temporary, and even fradulent initial religious impulses, surrounded him with religionists of neither character nor morality, carried him through several near-catastrophes, only to allow Gantry to recover and rise further still.

Gantry was ordained a minister at Mizpah Theological Seminary. During his time there he was sent to a spur-line town, Schoenheim, with an assistant, Frank Shallard. Shallard, noting Gantry's questionable motives toward Lulu Bains, a deacon's daughter, reproached Elmer and threatened to take the matter to Dean Trosper. Gantry caught Shallard off guard and reminded him that his faith was shaky and that if Dean Trsoper were to know of this it would end Shallard's career at the seminary. When Shallard realized that someone else was aware of this problem, he left the post at Schoenheim and devoted his time to added study. But in his effort to set against Gantry some men of good will and genuine religiosity, Lewis' imagination and understanding failed him, and no true opponent, no convincing expression of what religion could mean, or be, emerges from the book. Frank Shallard, Elmer's chief antagonist, remains only a shadowy character; finally his doubts get the best of him and he leaves the ministry in order to put his Christian principles into practice—and he is painfully defeated.

But Gantry's troubles with Lulu Bains had just begun; she informed him that they must get married and thus Gantry was forced into announcing his betrothal to her. He finally managed to get Lulu involved with an innocent but willing bystander, and in this way he was able to break the engagement.

Gantry left Schoenheim, supposedly heartbroken, and was sent to a new post in Monarch. On his way to preach the Sunday sermon he met Ad Locust, a traveling salesman for the Pequot Farm Implement Company. When Gantry became too drunk to show up at the church, he was fired from the seminary, even though he remained an ordained Baptist minister. Elmer then took a job with the Pequot Farm Implement Company and worked for them for two years. While in Sautersville, Nebraska, he met Sharon Falconer, a woman evangelist. He followed her and eventually became her assistant and lover. Everything went well for Gantry until the opening of Sharon's Waters of Jordan Tabernacle, which burned, killing a large number of the attending worshipers and Sharon.

Gantry then took up with Mrs. Evans Riddle, but he was kicked out of her group when she discovered that he was stealing from the collection. He then moved to a Methodist pastorate after teaching his own school of thought for a brief time. At this post he married Cleo Benham. After several successful charges in larger churches, Gantry was given a large church in New York. Gantry had not lived a pious life even after his marriage, and he became involved with his secretary, Mrs. Hettie Dowler. Those who opposed him used this opportunity to get back at him for his hellfire and brimstone sermons in which he spared no one. The newspapers got wind of the scandal and printed it, but T. J. Riggs saved Gantry from ruin. Gantry swore he would never again desire another woman, but as he knelt to pray because of his congregation's faith in him, he noticed at the same time the ankles of a new and attractive choir member.

Lewis has shown us a large gallery of ministerial frauds, such as Mrs. Riddle, the New Thought leader who taught classes in Concentration, Prosperity, Love, Metaphysics, Oriental Mysticism, and the Fourth Dimension, as well as how to keep one's husband. Another example is Judson Roberts, the state secretary of the Y.M.C.A., a young giant with curly hair and a booming voice that he used to bring in the big fellows.

Lewis gave much of his attention to his portrait of Sharon Falconer, the beautiful and somewhat mad female evangelist who preaches in a majestic temple, then leads Gantry to her retreat in the hills where she allows herself to be seduced on an altar she has built to such pagan goddesses as Astarte. Sharon says she has visions and confesses that she hates little vices like smoking and swearing but loves big ones like lust and murder. Yet from some confused notions about God Sharon derives sufficient strength to stand at the pulpit in her burning tabernacle and attempt to quell the panic of the mob of her parishioners, while Gantry knocks aside dozens of helpless people and is able to escape. Into such scenes as these, and into the final episode in which Gantry narrowly is saved from entrapment in the old badger game, Lewis poured all his vitality. But what critics have missed, and what seems to suggest the first waning of Lewis' powers, is the lack of any real opposition, referred to before. In Gantry himself there seems to be no decency, and therefore there are no alternatives contending in his soul. In the "good" characters there is insufficient understanding and fortitude, and they neither supply important alternatives nor force Gantry to any choices. In this book Lewis displayed his virtuosity as a satirist, but he also indulged it and failed to find for it any opposition in positive values. Thus, as a satirist of American life, he was by now really beginning to repeat himself, and it turned out to be essentially true (though not without some occasional exceptions) that he was to go on for about twenty-five years looking here and there for aspects of American life to expose, exploiting as best he could his earlier brilliance at recording the clichés of our lives and language but not advancing to any new understanding either for himself or for his readers. Meanwhile, the world moved on. If he was right that there was hypocrisy and corruption in the religious practices of America, his portrait was also incomplete in not showing us some of the glimmer that would begin to be fanned into the light of leadership that religion is trying to provide in the crises of today.

Bibliography

Blake, Nelson M. *Novelist's America: Fiction as History, 1910–1940.* Syracuse, N.Y.: Syracuse University Press, 1969, pp. 39–44.

Canby, Henry Seidel. "Vicious Ignorance," in *Saturday Review of Literature.* III (March 12, 1927), pp. 637, 640.

Davies, Horton. *A Mirror of the Ministry in Modern Novels.* New York: Oxford University Press, 1959, pp. 28–35.

Dooley, D.J. *The Art of Sinclair Lewis.* Lincoln: University of Nebraska Press, 1967, pp. 125–135.

Geismar, Maxwell. *The Last of the Provincials: The American Novel, 1915–1925.* Boston: Houghton Mifflin, 1947, pp. 101–105.

Genthe, Charles V. "*The Damnation of Theron Ware* and *Elmer Gantry*," in *Research Studies.* XXXII (1964), pp. 334–343.

Grebstein, Sheldon N. *Art of Sinclair Lewis.* New York: Twayne, 1962, pp. 99–107.

Griffin, Robert J. "Sinclair Lewis," in *American Winners of the Nobel Literary Prize.* Edited by Warren G. French and Walter E. Kidd. Norman: University of Oklahoma Press, 1968, pp. 42–44.

Hilfer, Anthony C. "*Elmer Gantry* and That Old Time Religion," in *The Revolt from the Village: 1915–1930.* Chapel Hill: University of North Carolina Press, 1969, pp. 177–192.

Hollis, C. Carroll. "Sinclair Lewis: Reviver of Character," in *Fifty Years of the American Novel: A Christian Appraisal.* Edited by Harold C. Gardiner. New York: Gordian Press, 1968, pp. 100–101.

Krutch, Joseph Wood. "Mr. Babbitt's Spiritual Guide: A Review of Sinclair Lewis's *Elmer Gantry*," in *Nation* (March 16, 1927), pp. 291–292. Reprinted in *Sinclair Lewis: A Collection of Critical Essays.* Edited by Mark Schorer. Englewood Cliffs, N.J.: Prentice-Hall, 1962, pp. 36–38.

Light, Martin. *The Quixotic Vision of Sinclair Lewis.* West Lafayette, Ind.: Purdue University Press, 1975, pp. 98–107.

Lundquist, James. *Sinclair Lewis.* New York: Frederick Ungar, 1973, pp. 49–53, 76–80.

Schorer, Mark. *Sinclair Lewis: An American Life.* New York: McGraw, 1961, pp. 475–483.

Shillito, Edward. "*Elmer Gantry* and the Church in America," in *Nineteenth Century.* CI (May, 1927), pp. 739–748.

West, Rebecca.   *The Strange Necessity.* New York: Viking, 1927, pp. 295–308. Reprinted in *Sinclair Lewis: A Collection of Critical Essays.* Edited by Mark Schorer. Englewood Cliffs, N.J.: Prentice-Hall, 1962, pp. 39–45.

MAIN STREET

Type of work: Novel
Author: Sinclair Lewis (1885–1951)
Time of plot: c. 1910–1920
Locale: Small Midwestern town
First published: 1920

In this portrait of a typical small Midwestern town called Gopher Prairie, Lewis satirizes the smug complacency, narrow-mindedness, hypocrisy, and resistance to change of the small-town mentality. Despite its social criticism, however, Main Street reflects Lewis' affection for his home town of Sauk Center, Minnesota, upon which Gopher Prairie was based.

Principal Characters

Carol Kennicott, an idealistic girl eager to reform the world. Interested in sociology and civic improvement, she longs to transform the ugliness of Midwestern America into something more beautiful. Having married Dr. Will Kennicott, she moves to his home in Gopher Prairie, Minnesota, a hideous small town indistinguishable from hundreds of similar communities. There she shocks and angers the townspeople by her criticisms and by her attempts to combat the local smugness. To its citizens Gopher Prairie is perfection; they can see no need for change. To her, it is an ugly, gossipy, narrow-minded village, sunk in dullness and self-satisfaction. Her efforts to change the town fail, and she drifts into a mild flirtation with Erik Valborg, a Swedish tailor with artistic yearnings. Frightened by the village gossip, she and Kennicott take a trip to California; but on her return she realizes that she must get away from both her husband and Gopher Prairie. After some argument, she and her small son leave for Washington, where she stays for more than a year. The flight is a failure, for she finds Washington only an agglomeration of the small towns in America. She returns to Gopher Prairie, realizing that it is her home. Her crusade has failed; she can only hope that her children will accomplish what she has been unable to do.

Dr. Will Kennicott, Carol's husband, a successful physician in Gopher Prairie. Though he loves Carol, he is dull and unimaginative, unable to enter her world or to understand her longings. He is the typical self-satisfied citizen of a small town.

Guy Pollock, a lawyer. Though sensitive and intellectual, he is the victim of the "village virus" that has deprived him of all initiative. At first he appears to Carol as the most hopeful person in town, but he disappoints her with his timidity and conventionalism.

Vida Sherwin, a teacher in the High School. Though better educated, she is as satisfied with the Gopher Prairie standards as are the other citizens. She marries Raymond Wutherspoon.

Raymond Wutherspoon, a sales clerk in the Bon Ton Store. A pallid, silly man, he marries Vida Sherwin. He goes to France during World War I and returns as a major.

Erik Valborg, a tailor in Gopher Prairie, the son of a Swedish farmer. Handsome and esthetically inclined, he attracts Carol, and they have a mild flirtation. But gossip drives him from the town; he goes to Minneapolis and is last seen playing small parts in the movies.

Bea Sorenson, a farm girl who comes to Gopher Prairie to find work. She is as much fascinated by the town as Carol is repelled. She becomes the Kennicotts' hired girl and Carol's only real friend. She marries Miles Bjornstam and has a son. She and the little boy both die of typhoid fever.

Miles Bjornstam, the village handy man and radical, one of the few genuine people in Gopher Prairie and one of the few

who understand Carol. He marries Bea Sorenson; when she and their child die, he leaves the town.

Mrs. Bogart, the Kennicotts' neighbor. She is the epitome of village narrow-mindedness.

Sam Clark, a hardware dealer and solid citizen.

Percy Bresnahan, born in Gopher Prairie but now a successful automobile manufacturer in Boston. He visits his home for occasional fishing trips and stoutly maintains that it is God's country. Heavy-handed, jocular, and thoroughly standardized, he is the forerunner of George F. Babbitt.

James Blauser, known as "Honest Jim." A professional hustler and promoter, he is hired to start a campaign for a Greater Gopher Prairie. Not much is accomplished.

Hugh, Will and Carol's first child, on whom she lavishes her attention.

The Story

When Carol Milford was graduated from Blodgett College in Minnesota, she determined to conquer the world. Interested in sociology, and village improvement in particular, she often longed to set out on a crusade of her own to transform dingy prairie towns to thriving, beautiful communities. When she met Will Kennicott, a doctor from Gopher Prairie, and listened to his praise of his home town, she agreed to marry him. He had convinced her that Gopher Prairie needed her.

Carol was essentially an idealist. On the train, going to her new home, she deplored the run-down condition of the countryside and wondered about the future of the northern Middle West. Will did not listen to her ideas sympathetically. The people were happy, he said. Through town after town they traveled, Carol noting with sinking heart the shapeless mass of hideous buildings, the dirty depots, the flat wastes of prairie surrounding everything, and she knew that Gopher Prairie would be no different from the rest.

Gopher Prairie was exactly like the other towns Carol had seen, except that it was a little larger. The people were as drab as their houses, as flat as their fields. A welcoming committee met the newlyweds at the train. To Carol, all the men were alike in their colorless clothes, over-friendly, over-enthusiastic. The Kennicott house was a Victorian horror. But Will said he liked it.

Introduced to the townsfolk at a party held in her honor, Carol heard the men talk of motor cars, train schedules, "furriners," and praise Gopher Prairie as God's own country. The women were interested in gossip, sewing, and cooking, and most of them belonged to the two women's clubs, the Jolly Seventeen and the Thanatopsis Club. At the first meeting of the Jolly Seventeen, Carol brought wrath upon her head when she stated that the duty of a librarian was to get people to read. The town librarian staunchly asserted that her primary trust was to perserve the books.

Carol did many things which were to cause her great unhappiness. She hired a maid and paid her the over-generous sum of six dollars a week. She gave a party with an Oriental motif. Sometimes she even kicked off a slipper under the table and revealed her arches. The women frowned on her unconventional behavior. Worse, she redecorated the old Kennicott house and got rid of the mildew, the ancient bric-a-brac, the dark wallpaper. Will protested against her desire to change things.

Carol also joined the Thanatopsis Club, for she hoped to use the club as a means of awakening interest in social reform. But the women of Gopher Prairie, while professing charitable intentions, had no idea of improving social conditions. When Carol mentioned that something should be done about the poor people of the town, everyone firmly stated that there was no real poverty in Gopher Prairie. Carol also attempted to raise funds for a new city hall, but no one could see that the ugly old building needed to be replaced. The town voted against appropriating the necessary funds.

Will Kennicott bought a summer cottage on Lake Minniemashie. There Carol enjoyed outdoor life and during the summer months almost lost her desire for reform. But when September came she hated the thought of returning to Gopher Prairie.

Carol resolved to study her husband. He was well thought of in the town, and she romanticized herself as the wife of a hard-working, courageous country doctor. She fell in love with Will again on the night she watched him perform a bloody but successful operation upon a poor farmer. But Carol's praise of her husband had little effect. Will was not the romantic figure she had pictured. He accepted his duties as a necessary chore, and the thought that he had saved the life of a human being did not occur to him. His interest in medicine was identical with his interest in motor cars. Once more Carol turned her attention to Gopher Prairie.

Carol, trying to interest the Thanatopsis Club in literature and art, finally persuaded the members to put on an amateur theatrical. But enthusiasm soon waned. Carol's choice of a play, Shaw's *Androcles*, was vetoed, and *The Girl from Kankakee* put in its place. Carol considered even that choice too subtle for Gopher Prairie, but at least the town's interest in the theater had been revived.

After three years of marriage, Carol discovered that she was pregnant. Almost immediately the neighborhood became interested in her condition. When her son was born, she resolved that some day she would send little Hugh away from Gopher Prairie, to Harvard, Yale, or Oxford.

With a new son and the new status of motherhood, Carol found herself more a part of the town, but she devoted nine-tenths of her attention to Hugh and had little time to criticize the town. She wanted a new house, but she and Will could not agree on the type of building. He was satisfied with a square frame house. Carol had visions of a Georgian mansion, with stately columns and wide lawns, or a white cottage like those at Cape Cod.

Then Carol met a tailor in town, an artistic, twenty-five-year-old aesthete, with whom she imagined herself in love. She often dropped by his shop to see him, and one day Will warned her that the gossip in town was growing. Ashamed, Carol promised she would not see him again. The tailor left for Minneapolis.

Carol and Will decided to take a trip to California. When they returned three months later, Carol realized that her attempt to escape Gopher Prairie had been unsuccessful. For one thing, Will had gone with her. What she needed now was to get away from her husband. After a long argument with Will, Carol took little Hugh and went off to Washington, where she planned to do war work. But hers was an empty kind of freedom. She found the people in Washington an accumulation of the population of thousands of Gopher Prairies all over the nation. Main Street had merely been transplanted to the larger city. Disheartened by her discovery, Carol had too much pride to return home.

After thirteen months, Will went to get her. He missed her terribly, he said, and begged her to come back. Hugh was overjoyed to see his father, and Carol realized that inevitably she would have to return to Gopher Prairie.

Home once more, Carol found that her furious hatred for Gopher Prairie had burned itself out. She made friends with the clubwomen and promised herself not to be snobbish in the future. She would go on asking questions—she could never stop herself from doing that—but her questions now would be asked with sympathy rather than with sarcasm. For the first time she felt at last that she was wanted. Her neighbors had missed her. For the first time Carol felt that Gopher Prairie was her home.

Critical Evaluation

Sinclair Lewis frequently had difficulty in determining in his own mind whether his works were meant as bitterly comic satires of American life and values or whether they were planned as complex novels centering around the lives of the series of characters he made famous. One of the difficulties of reading Lewis is that these two conflicting sorts of writing are both present in many of his works, and frequently at odds with each other. This is demonstrably true of *Main Street* which cannot simply be called a satire of life in small-town America. For all the satire of small-town attitudes and values,

Lewis is not unequivocal in his attack as a satirist might be expected to be. Actually, he finds quite a lot of value in the best *Main Street* has to offer, and he seems to see Carol Kennicott's reconciliation with the town at the end of the novel as a triumph more than a failure on her part. Thus, though *Main Street* is, as it has been frequently called, a revolt against the village, it is a revolt marked by the complexity of Lewis' attitude toward Gopher Prairie and toward its real-life counterpart, Sauk Center, Minnesota, where Lewis spent his early years.

Lewis' characters, particularly Will and Carol Kennicott, are another complicating factor in this novel which prevents its being simply a satire. Unlike the one-dimensional figures typical of satire, the Kennicotts develop into somewhat rounded characters who demand attention and sympathy in their own rights. Carol in particular, as the central figure of the novel, is developed more novelistically than satirically as Lewis traces her development from a very naïve and foolishly idealistic young woman into a more tolerant and understanding human being. Ironically, for the reader to adopt only the critical and satiric portrait of the small town which lies at the surface of *Main Street* would be for him to embrace the same overly-simplistic attitudes which characterized Carol at the beginning of the novel, and which she must escape as evidence of her maturity.

During the early part of the century, Americans tended to accept on faith the premise that all that was best in life was epitomized by the small-town environment. Though by no means the first author to attack this premise, Lewis with *Main Street* achieved the widespread popularity which gave new prominence to this revolt against the small town. Lewis, himself a small-town boy, knew at first hand the discrepancy between the vision of the village as a Utopia and the actuality of its bleak cultural and moral atmosphere. As Lewis makes clear in his prologue, *Main Street* is an analogue for all such towns, and by his treatment of Gopher Prairie, Lewis sought to strike a satiric blow at the very heartland of America. Rather than a Utopia, Lewis discovers in the provincial mentality of the small town a surfiet of hypocrisy, bigotry, ignorance, cruelty, and, perhaps most damning of all, a crippling dullness and conformity which is essentially hostile to any possibility of intellectual or emotional life. Ironically, though, even while ruthlessly exposing these negative qualities of the small town, Lewis finds, particularly in the matter-of-fact courage and determination of Will Kennicott, some of the very qualities which have given the small town its reputation as the strength of America. The fact is, Lewis was himself ambivalent in his attitude toward the village, and this indecisiveness creeps into the novel to mitigate his castigation of middle America.

The action of the novel centers around Carol Kennicott's discovery of the nature of life and society in Gopher Prairie, and culminates with her eventual compromise with the town. For Lewis' purposes, Carol is an excellent device to enable him to expose the bleak heart of the midwestern town by contrasting its qualities and values with her own. Young, educated, intelligent, and idealistic, Carol can bring the vision to Gopher Prairie to see what it lacks, and so far as that is her purpose, she performs well. It is when she performs as a character in her own right that we begin to see Lewis' attitude toward her as being more complicated than simply approving her values in contrast to those of the town. Carol's idealism is accompanied by a naïveté and intolerance which but poorly qualify her to accomplish the reforms she advocates because she can only hope to change Gopher Prairie by becoming part of it. The polarization she brings about by trying too much too soon makes it improbable that she should ever be able to realize her ambitions for the town unless she learns to accommodate to—though not necessarily to approve of —its values. After running away to Washington only to discover that the values of the city are not too different from those of the village, Carol is in a better position to adopt a more tolerant attitude toward the villagers. As we see her at the end of the novel, she has made an effort to come to terms with her environment by working to evolve realistic reforms rather than seeking a radical overthrow of entrenched values and institutions. In losing her naïveté, Carol gains in terms of her ability to confront reality, and even to change it over a period of time.

Actually, most of Carol's reforms are too superficial really to cure what Lewis called the village virus. Her concern is more with manners than values, and she would only substitute the slick sophistication of the city for the provincial dullness she finds so intolerable. The perfect foil to her is Will Kennicott who, while epitomizing all the worst of the town's boorishness, goes about his daily medical practice with quiet efficiency, determination, and even courage that Lewis clearly admires. Will's presence makes it impossible simply to accept Carol's assessment of the vulgarity of the town as Lewis' final word. It is Gopher Prairie that finally triumps as Carol reconciles herself to its full reality.

Bibliography

Aaron, Daniel. "Sinclair Lewis: *Main Street*," in *The American Novel from James Fenimore Cooper to William Faulkner*. Edited by Wallace Stegner. New York: Basic Books, 1965, pp. 166–179.

Blake, Nelson M. *Novelist's America: Fiction as History, 1910–1940*. Syracuse, N.Y.: Syracuse University Press, 1969, pp. 12–23.

Bogardus, E.S. "Social Distance in Fiction: Analyses of *Main Street*," in *Sociology and Social Research*. (November–December, 1929), pp. 174–180.

Coard, Robert L. "College and Schoolhouse in *Main Street*," in *Sinclair Lewis Newsletter*. I (Spring, 1969), pp. 3–4.

Dooley, D.J. *Art of Sinclair Lewis.* Lincoln: University of Nebraska Press, 1967, pp. 57–82.

Douglas, George H. *"Main Street* after Fifty Years," in *Prairie Schooner.* XLIV (Winter, 1970–1971), pp. 338–348.

Downs, Robert B. "Revolt from the Village," in *Famous American Books.* New York: McGraw-Hill, 1971, pp. 257–265.

Gannett, Lewis. "Looking Backwards—Sinclair Lewis: *Main Street,"* in *Saturday Review of Literature.* XXXII (August 6, 1949), pp. 31–32.

Geismar, Maxwell. *The Last of the Provincials: The American Novel, 1915–1925.* Boston: Houghton Mifflin, 1947, pp. 84–88.

Grebstein, Sheldon N. *Sinclair Lewis.* New York: Twayne, 1962, pp. 61–73.

Griffin, Robert J. "Sinclair Lewis," in *American Winners of the Nobel Literary Prize.* Edited by Warren G. French and Walter E. Kidd. Norman: University of Oklahoma Press, 1968, pp. 32–34.

Gurko, Leo and Miriam Gurko. "The Two Main Streets of Sinclair Lewis," in *College English.* IV (February, 1943), pp. 288–292.

Hackett, Francis. *"Main Street,"* in *The Critic as Artist: Essays on Books, 1920–1970.* Edited by Gilbert A. Harrison. New York: Liveright, 1972, pp. 145–149.

Herron, Irma H. *The Small Town in American Literature.* Durham, N.C.: Duke University Press, 1939, pp. 377–390.

Hilfer, Anthony C. *The Revolt from the Village, 1915–1930.* Chapel Hill: University of North Carolina Press, 1969, pp. 158–192.

Hollis, C. Carroll. "Sinclair Lewis: Reviver of Character," in *Fifty Years of the American Novel: A Christian Appraisal.* Edited by Harold C. Gardiner. New York: Gordian Press, 1968, pp. 97–98.

Krutch, Joseph Wood. "Sinclair Lewis," in *Nation.* (February 24, 1951), pp. 179–180. Reprinted in *Sinclair Lewis: A Collection of Critical Essays.* Edited by Mark Schorer. Englewood Cliffs, N.J.: Prentice-Hall, 1962, pp. 147–150.

Light, Martin. *The Quixotic Vision of Sinclair Lewis.* West Lafayette, Ind.: Purdue University Press, 1975, pp. 60–72.

Lundquist, James. *Sinclair Lewis.* New York: Frederick Ungar, 1973, pp. 19–22, 35–40.

McCarthy, John F. "A New Look at an Old Street," in *English Journal.* LVII (October, 1968), pp. 985–987.

Mencken, H.L. "Consolation," in *Sinclair Lewis: A Collection of Critical Essays.* Edited by Mark Schorer. Englewood Cliffs, N.J.: Prentice-Hall, 1962, pp. 17–19.

Petrullo, Helen B. *"Main Street, Cass Timberlane* and Determinism," in *South Dakota Review.* VII (Winter, 1969–1970), pp. 30–42.

Schier, Donald. *"Main Street* by Sinclair Lewis," in *Carleton Miscellany.* IV (Fall, 1963), pp. 95–101.

Schorer, Mark. *Sinclair Lewis: An American Life.* New York: McGraw, 1961, pp. 267–297.

HORACE MCCOY

Born: Pegram Station, Tennessee (April 14, 1897)
Died: Beverly Hills, California (December 15, 1955)

Principal Works

NOVELS: *They Shoot Horses, Don't They?* 1935; *No Pockets in a Shroud*, 1937; *I Should Have Stayed Home*, 1938; *Kiss Tomorrow Goodbye*, 1948; *Scalpel*, 1952.

In 1946, a dispatch from Paris to the New York *Times Book Review* revealed a rather odd aspect of the effect of American fiction on the Continent and in England: Horace McCoy was being "hailed as the peer of Steinbeck and Hemingway" and regarded as the first American existentialist. American writers and readers may well have asked, who is Horace McCoy in the United States that he should have made such an impact, as an American, in Europe? In 1946 he was the forgotten author of one of the best tough-guy novels of the 1930's—*They Shoot Horses, Don't They?*—a short, terse, first person description of a dance marathon that ends in a mercy killing. His second novel, *No Pockets in a Shroud*, the violent story of a newspaperman's attempt to expose crime in Dallas politics, first appeared in England and was published in America only in paperback (1948). While *I Should Have Stayed Home*, an account of the despairing lives of two Hollywood extras, was published in the United States, it commanded little attention, despite its being one of the better "Hollywood" novels. McCoy's fourth novel, *Kiss Tomorrow Goodbye*, (1948), the violent tale of a Phi Beta Kappa scholar turned gangster, offered little to explain McCoy's importance in Europe. His last novel, *Scalpel* (1952), the story of a coal miner's ruthless rise to riches as a surgeon, reveals qualities in McCoy's fiction that may account for his appeal: violence, despair, frustration, and a compressed, vivid, muscular style.

One must go back to *They Shoot Horses, Don't They?* to understand McCoy's impact. In some ways it is a better example than James M. Cain's *The Postman Always Rings Twice* of the "pure" tough-guy novel; it is neither linked to the detective story, as are the hardboiled novels of Dashiell Hammett and Raymond Chandler, nor is it similar to the tough-guy proletarian fiction of B. Traven. McCoy's short novel projects in terms of a natural symbolism—the dance marathon—a universal image of modern man's futile, Sisyphian labor. As an expression of existential outlook, it deserves comparison with Camus' *The Stranger* (1942).

Horace McCoy started work as a newsboy when he was twelve. As a house-to-house salesman, he traveled the South. In New Orleans and Dallas, he drove a taxi. During World War I, he served as a pilot and was wounded in France. From 1922 to 1930, he worked as a reporter and sports editor on the Dallas *Journal*. He was one of the founders of the Dallas Little Theater. On periodic pilgrimages to

Paris, he became acquainted with F. Scott Fitzgerald, was associated with *Transition*, began writing stories that were published in obscure literary magazines, and attracted the attention of anthologists such as Edward J. O'Brien.

After 1930, he wandered the California coast, picking vegetables and fruit in the Imperial and San Joaquin Valleys. He picketed in strikes, was a soda jerk, a bodyguard to a politician, a bouncer in a marathon dance contest, and a movie extra. And he once doubled for a sick wrestler. He began to write for the movies in 1933 when the gangster novels and films were making their strongest impact; several of his own novels have been made into movies with actors such as James Cagney. The most recent film adaptation of one of his novels was *They Shoot Horses, Don't They?* in 1969.

Bibliography

There is little material on McCoy available. See Thomas Sturak, "Horace McCoy's Objective Lyricism," *Tough Guy Writers of the Thirties*, edited by David Madden, 1968; Robert M. Coates, Afterword to *They Shoot Horses, Don't They?*, 1966; and Edmund Wilson's essay *The Boys in the Back Room*, 1940.

THEY SHOOT HORSES, DON'T THEY?

Type of work: Novel
Author: Horace McCoy (1897–1955)
Time of plot: The 1930's
Locale: An amusement pier near Hollywood, California
First published: 1935

Essay-Review

Horace McCoy's *They Shoot Horses, Don't They?* is an excellent example of the tough-guy fiction that flourished during the 1930's. Full of violence, sex, and hard-boiled talk, McCoy's five novels resemble the works of Hammett, Chandler, Cain, and B. Traven.

But Robert, the young narrator who aspires to become a film director like Eisenstein, is no hoodlum. His tough tone simply reflects the effect a brutalizing experience has had upon him. An unemployed movie extra in the middle of the depression, Robert meets Gloria, a not very attractive, unemployed extra who persuades him to enter a marathon dance contest as her partner. Both have come to Hollywood, glamor capital of the world, from small Southern towns, lured by the American dream of sudden success. After an unsuccessful suicide attempt before she left home, Gloria is now being "razzed" by an expert—God; but she lacks the courage to kill herself. Her verbal signature throughout the contest is some variation on the refrain, "I wish I was dead." Opposed to this total despair is Robert's typical American optimism; but he ends a victim of Gloria's nihilistic vision. Robert and Gloria exist only in terms of their situation as contestants; they have almost no past, and their future is violent death.

The contest is held on an amusement pier in an old building that was once a public dance hall. One hundred and forty couples enter: professional marathon dancers and amateurs, like Robert and Gloria. Floor judges, nurses, and a house doctor are in attendance; contestants are allowed to continue only if they are in good physical condition. The dancing area is thirty by one hundred feet; there are loge, circus, or general admission seats, and a bar. Contestants dance one hour and fifty minutes; during the ten-minute rest intervals, they sleep, eat, shave, bathe, excrete, change clothes. The trick is to learn to do several things at once. After the first week, contestants need not dance, they must simply keep moving; all employees of the hall must constantly be in motion. Local sponsors of individual couples provide equipment and costumes, the company name across the chest, the contestant's number on his back. Thus, Robert and Gloria become "Jonathan Beer." Specialty numbers draw a shower of silver; but one couple, who do a lifeless tap-dance, declare that you are better off without a specialty. In the derby, a nightly fifteen-minute heel-and-toe endurance race, Robert soon stops trying to win and strives merely to keep from coming in last, to avoid being disqualified. If a dancer loses his partner, because of menstrual pains or a heart attack, for instance, he may couple with another lone survivor; casualties are scarcely missed. A tub of ice water awaits those who faint; thus is Robert shocked out of a dream of being a film director. The main inducement for staying in the contest is that one knows where his next meal is coming form; food and bed are free as long as the contestant endures. For the winning couple the purse is one thousand dollars, and every one has the same chance, according to Rocky Gravo, the master of ceremonies. There is also the chance of being "discovered" by a movie producer, though after the second day each contestant resembles a zombie. It is a contest of "endurance and skill"; one must have the skill to endure.

Gloria's attitude is overwhelmingly cynical. She and Robert are on a merry-go-round; when the dance is over, they will get off where they got on. Eating and sleeping is merely a postponing of death. Responding to Robert's expression of sympathy for one of the dancers who is arrested as a fugitive murderer, Gloria suggests that they are all condemned fugitives. "Socks," the promoter, appreciates the publicity; anything that draws the crowds is good. He asks Gloria and Robert to get married on the dance floor as a "high class" entertainment feature; they can get a divorce after the contest closes. Gloria refuses; Robert is afraid the angry promoter will disqualify them. Gloria, who wishes she had never been born, encourages one of the dancers who is pregnant to abort the child because it will only end up the same way.

In the 1920's and the 1930's, dance marathons, an import from Europe, were held in every major American city. Hollywood is a particularly apt symbolic setting for McCoy's marathon: it represents the public Eden to which few are admitted; the rejects end up on the dance floor. The roll call of actual celebrities among the spectators is effective, more so today since we can see what fame comes to. In the context of the depression, the spectators are the corrupt rich being amused by the antics of the work horses, but ultimately spectator and dancer reverse roles. Just as the dance, symbol of the new postwar morality, became perverted by the marathon, sexual perversion is part of the experience. Gloria is about to submit to lesbians to get what she wants; Mrs. Layden, a wealthy old woman who comes every night to watch, lusts for Robert. Robert and Gloria are not in love; there is not even a sexual tie. About to do a favor for a nymphomaniac dancer under the bandstand, Robert is interrupted by a voice in the dark; later, he learns that Gloria was nearby with Rocky. Rocky's monotonous exhortation to the orchestra, the dancers (especially the female), and the audience is "Give!"

When a rich spectator finally shows an interest in her, Gloria, ironically, is too devoid of hope to respond. She declares that she is glad she is through with life. In the midst of a fight in the bar, the cause of which is never disclosed, five shots are fired. Mrs. Layden, on her way to the platform to judge the derby, is an accidental target. Ironically, old Mrs. Layden wanted to live to make love to young Robert, while Gloria wishes the bullet had struck herself. Without a winner, the marathon ends on the dictate of chance. Robert and Gloria walk out onto the pier. She persuades him that she is no good to herself nor to anyone else, that she is better off dead. He shoots her to put her out of her misery. Ironically, his lawyer instructs Robert to throw himself on the mercy of the court; but the court gives him, against his will, what he gave Gloria at her own request—oblivion.

While the marathon dance symbolizes man's predicament in the 1930's, it is almost perfect as a symbolic expression of the universal human predicament. While McCoy's central symbolic action is realistically true and stark, and never literary, the dance draws to itself many traditional connotations that enhance the significance of the marathon. In mythic terms, the grinding dance is like Sisyphus' struggle to push his rock to the top of the mountain; the ten-minute rest periods are like his moment of freedom as he returns to his burden on the plain. In the simple event of the dance, we experience a pure existential situation that exemplifies the absurd nature of life.

Among the most effective motifs, all of which McCoy develops quite naturally, is the incessant pounding of the ocean under the floor; like the slow ticking of the clock and the slow movement of its hands in relation to the movements of the dancer's legs, the surf counterpoints the dance. Robert used to love the ocean; now he hates it. Gloria observes that the waves have been moving for a million years; it is between the rising and falling of a wave that Robert honors her plea that he shoot her. Robert used to dislike the sun; now he tries to absorb every moment of sunlight that falls through a crack in the roof of the windowless hall. Gloria observes that he moves like a ballet dancer as he follows the dime-sized ray of sun. McCoy suggests the existential idea that man can expect only rare moments of natural bliss. Ironically, the brief respite, by allowing time to reflect on its context, is sometimes too bitter, and Robert is glad when the siren calls him back to the dance floor.

The form of this novel is strictly congruent with all its elements. Juxtaposition is McCoy's most effective technique for controlling and conceptualizing his raw material. Robert's story is presented as an interior monologue, the thirteen unlucky parts of which are juxtaposed to fragments of the sentence of death which a judge is pronouncing upon him. On the first page a single statement directs the prisoner to stand. The next page begins as he stands up. The ironic immediacy of the sentence lends an immediacy to Robert's memory of the dance. The initial image is Gloria's face the moment after Robert fires the gun; at the end, the firing itself is depicted. Thus, the brevity of the novel gives the impression of a single juxtaposition. The marriage ceremony on the dance floor is juxtaposed to the Lord's prayer, which is juxtaposed to the killings in the bar. Another graphic device is the score box that heads the last four chapters, showing: ELAPSED HOURS. COUPLES REMAINING. As the hours accumulate, the judge's words grow larger and larger on the page. On the last he invokes God's mercy on the prisoner's soul.

As he tells it from the vantage of the prisoner's dock, Robert comments briefly (in italics) on his own story. Before he shoots Gloria, he recalls the shooting of his grandfather's horse when Robert was a child. Thus, the present was given in the past; the sentence he hears now, as he recalls the past, was passed during the dance, before the murder, because it is inherent in the nature of things. McCoy's structure gives us a sense of the simultaneity of the sentence with the conditions that produced the "crime." Robert concludes that while the tune varies, the dance, one's experiences, are the same; nothing is new. The novel is superbly compressed: Robert's meeting Gloria is briefly described and their parting briefly depicted: the 879-hour-long dance is the large center of the action. The brevity of the killing and of the sentence, of the book itself, is an ironic comment on the length, the prolonged agony of the dance. It is singularly appropriate that dance-murder-trial be compressed within the judge's sentence.

JOHN PHILLIPS MARQUAND

Born: Wilmington, Delaware (November 10, 1893)
Died: Newburyport, Massachusetts (July 16, 1960)

Principal Works

NOVELS: *The Unspeakable Gentleman,* 1922; *The Black Cargo,* 1925; *Warning Hill,* 1930; *Haven's End,* 1933; *The Late George Apley,* 1937; *Wickford Point,* 1939; *H. M. Pulham, Esq.,* 1941; *So Little Time,* 1943; *B. F.'s Daughter,* 1946; *Point of No Return,* 1949; *Melville Goodwin, U.S.A.,* 1951; *Sincerely, Willis Wayde,* 1955.

MISCELLANEOUS: *Thirty Years,* 1954.

John P(hillips) Marquand is, in the opinion of many readers, the inheritor of the mantle of Sinclair Lewis as an attentive reporter of social customs, personal ambitions, and class structures in modern American society; but unlike Lewis, whose social satire is laid on with a heavy hand, Marquand presents his pictures of upper-class New England life with a clarity and simplicity that keep the reader from immediately sensing the real bitterness of the novelist's observations. Indeed, Marquand works a vein of good-mannered but tart social comment that can be found also in the novels of William Dean Howells and Ellen Glasgow.

Marquand was admirably equipped for the task to which he set himself in his fiction. He was born in Wilmington, Delaware, on November 10, 1893, into a well-to-do family with New England connections; his great-aunt was the celebrated Margaret Fuller of Transcendentalist fame, and his ancestral town of Newburyport, Massachusetts, is a town whose aura of tradition he reflected in *Wickford Point* and other novels. But Marquand's youth was not a financially secure one; his family lost money in the crash of 1907, and when Marquand went to Harvard (Class of '15), he was forced to depend on scholarships and the help of friends. Marquand had a keen sense of being ostracized and consequently was able to look at his chosen subject-matter from both sides of the tracks; his recognition from the Harvard *Lampoon* did not close the wound which social exclusion from the university clubs had given him.

After college Marquand accumulated war experience on the Mexican border and in France, but he did not find this experience of danger and fear especially suggestive in a literary way. More stimulating were several years spent in an advertising agency in New York; he could not take seriously an office full of Phi Beta Kappas involved in merchandising. After two years with the New York *Tribune* he returned to New England to write his first novel, a cloak-and-dagger narrative titled *The Unspeakable Gentleman.* For almost a decade and a half afterwards, until the appearance of *The Late George Apley* in 1937, Marquand was a productive writer of stories that appeared regularly in the *Saturday Eve-*

ning Post and *Collier's*, work that, in Marquand's own later judgment, naïvely accepts the morality of the success story and the superficial social observation of a fashionable photographer. Toward the end of this period he had great success with a series of detective stories about a Japanese detective, Mr. Moto, who, understandably, had to be withdrawn from circulation about 1941 but who was revived in *Stopover, Tokyo* (1957).

Against the advice of friends, Marquand wrote his first serious novel, *The Late George Apley*, and had the satisfaction of winning the Pulitzer Prize. The novel, an attack on the Brahmin class of Boston, is, like Marquand's later social dissections, doubly chilling because of the simplicity and quietness with which the attack goes forward. The failure of his central character to achieve his own early hopes and to respond to the real chances for life and experience furnishes a pattern for many of the later Marquand novels. The hero of many a subsequent tale is shrewd enough to see what he really is or could be; he is not adventurous enough to realize this vision and instead accepts the "diminished thing" (the phrase is that of Robert Frost, another New Englander) that is life according to the wishes of one's wife and the pressures of one's "social role."

Marquand was married twice, each time, as one of his characters would put it, "very well." Marquand's first wife, from whom he was divorced in 1935, warned him of his projected novel about Apley: "That's a good book to write if you want to leave Boston, that's all."

Marquand's own career since 1937 was one of unwavering success measured by the books he had written: *Wickford Point, H. M. Pulham, Esq., So Little Time, Point of No Return, Sincerely, Willis Wayde*, and others. Meanwhile membership on the board of a book club, involvement in the productions of stage verisons of several of his novels, and continuous writing were activities protracting his early success as a writer for the "slicks" into his second career as a writer whose social comment and criticism were taken with real seriousness. For example, Granville Hicks pointed out that Marquand was a better observer of class structure in Newburyport than were W. Lloyd Warner and his staff of sociologists in their scientific study of the Massachusetts town in *The Social Life of a Modern Community*. But negative criticism points to the continued deftness of Marquand's style; apparently such criticism would be pleased if Marquand had written with less skill. Other critics are not pleased that Marquand in the long run accepted and tolerated a society whose shortcomings he identified brilliantly. As to this latter point, it may be doubted that a person who rejected the social structure that tolerates Willis Wayde and other Marquand characters could write of the perplexed heroes with the understanding which Marquand always summoned.

Bibliography

The writer is the subject of a literary study done in the Marquand manner, Philip Hamburger's *J. P. Marquand, Esq.*, 1952; there is also John J. Gross, *John*

P. Marquand, 1963; and C. Hugh Holman, *John P. Marquand*, 1965. There is also a recent biography, Millicent Bell's *Marquand: An American Life*, 1979. For briefer criticism and commentary see also the essay on Marquand in Joseph Warren Beach, *American Fiction, 1920–1940*, 1941; and Charles A. Brady "John Phillips Marquand: Martini-Age Victorian," in *Fifty Years of the American Novel, 1900–1950*, edited by Harold C. Gardiner, S.J., 1951; Harlan Hatcher, "John Phillips Marquand," *College English*, I (1939), 107–118; Herschel Brickell, "Miss Glasgow and Mr. Marquand," *Virginia Quarterly Review*, XVII (1941), 405–417; Nathan Glick, "Marquand's Vanishing American Aristocracy: Good Manners and the Good Life," *Commentary*, IX (1950), 435–441; and Granville Hicks, "Marquand of Newburyport," *Harper's*, CC (1950), 101–108.

THE LATE GEORGE APLEY

Type of work: Novel
Author: John P. Marquand (1893–1960)
Time of plot: Late nineteenth and early twentieth centuries
Locale: Boston
First published: 1937

In this brilliantly constructed novel, the satire is double-edged, aimed not only at the society portrayed but at the style of the book itself, for Mr. Willing, the supposed biographer of these memoirs of George Apley, is as much a source of satire as Apley himself. The humor is subtle and often gentle, but always accurate and knowing.

Principal Characters

George William Apley, a proper Bostonian carefully trained since childhood to be a respectable member of Boston Brahmin society. Though as a college student he belittled the Brahmin pride of family, he acquired it himself as he matured, and later he attempted to pass it on to his children. Undistinguished academically at Harvard, he had been active in campus affairs and a member of a select club. Unfit for active business, he derived his income from investments and from his father's substantial legacy. Though he admired Emerson's writings he never became an Emersonian nonconformist; in fact, he believed that the individual in society must submit to the common will. Like his father and his Uncle William, he was a generous giver to worthy causes.

John Apley, his son, who stirred George's heart with pride over his war service, including a wound, and who later married a girl of good family. It was John who requested the writing of his father's life story.

Eleanor Apley, his daughter. She greatly disappointed George by marrying a journalist.

Catharine Bosworth Apley, his wife, whose marriage to George was unexciting but successful. According to his sister Amelia, George simply let Catherine and her family dominate him.

Mr. Willing, George Apley's biographer, staid, polished, and politely dull. Like George himself, Mr. Willing is snobbish, for he is also a Brahmin. In accordance with John's request, he includes along with George's commendable characteristics and actions some derogatory and unsavory details in his life; but he attempts to excuse these as minor aberrations in an essentially admirable man.

Mary Monahan, an attractive girl whose love affair with George ended when George's parents removed him from such a lower-class association.

William Apley, George's uncle, a wealthy businessman who spent little on himself and scorned ostentation but who was secretly a generous philanthropist. He controlled the Apley mills and opposed labor unions. When over eighty he shocked the family by marrying his nurse.

Amelia Apley, George's sister. She was more independent and forceful than George.

O'Reilly, a lawyer who tricked George into a scandal.

Horatio Apley, holder of a diplomatic post in Rome.

Thomas and

Elizabeth Hancock Apley, George's parents.

Miss Prentiss, the young nurse whom Uncle William married.

Newcomb Simmings, Amelia Apley's husband.

Louise Hogarth Apley, John's wife. She is a divorcee but when George learns that she is from a fine family, he is satisfied.

William Budd, Eleanor's husband.

The Story

George William Apley was born on Beacon Hill, on January 25, 1866. The Apleys were an old family in Massachusetts. Thomas, known in the old records as Goodman Apley, had emigrated from England to America and settled in Roxbury in 1636. Goodman Apley's son, John, had graduated from Harvard in 1662. From his time there had been an Apley in Harvard in each succeeding generation. John Apley's son, Nathaniel, established himself in Boston. A later Apley, Moses, became a shipping master and laid the foundation of the Apley fortune. Moses Apley was George Apley's grandfather.

George Apley grew up in a quiet atmosphere of wealth and social position. He learned his parents' way of living calmly and with fortitude. In an orderly way he was introduced to the polite world, at first through visits to relatives; later, through study at Harvard.

His Harvard days were probably the high point of his life. He was sent to Harvard to weld those qualities of gentlemanly behavior which private grammar school and parents together had tried to encourage. His parents were anxious that he should make friends with the right people. George was carefully instructed in the ways of high-minded gentlemen. His training was indicated by a theme in which he wrote a description of a Boston brothel in terms expressing his repulsion and shock. In the gymnasium George won distinction as a boxer. Moreover, he became a member of the Board of the Harvard *Lampoon*. He was taken into the Club, an honor his father appreciated greatly. In his junior and senior years he took part in the musical extravaganzas of the Hasty Pudding Club. In spite of these activities he never neglected his studies, and he was known as a respectable student with grades placing him in the middle of his class at graduation.

While in college, he fell in love with an impossible girl, Mary Monahan. The affair was cut short by the Apleys and never referred to publicly. Shortly thereafter his family prescribed a sea voyage for him. When he returned home he took up the study of law and became a member of the board for the Boston Waifs' Society.

George was instructed in the shrewd businesslike manners and knowledge of the Apleys. He was sent to work with his Uncle William for one summer. William sensed that his nephew would never make a good businessman and advised that George should be put into law or made a trustee of other peoples' money, not his own. As a result George, like many of his friends, never went actively into business, but spent his lifetime clipping coupons.

In February, 1890, George followed his parents' wishes and suitably became engaged to Catharine Bosworth. Both his father-in-law and his own father saw to it that the young couple had a summer cottage and a house for the winter. The two mothers were equally solicitous. George discovered that he had married not only Catharine but also her family.

As the years passed, George devoted his time to charitable groups, learned societies, and to writing for his clubs. One of his papers, "Jonas Good and Cow Corner," was said to be among the best papers read before the Browsers in fifty years.

His first child's name was a subject for debate in his own and Catharine's family. The name, John, common to both families, was finally chosen. His second child was a daughter, Eleanor.

Shortly after his sister Amelia's marriage, George's father died of an apoplectic stroke. He left a million dollars to Harvard, other large sums to his charities, and the remainder of his fortune in trust for his family. George had to pay a sum of money to a woman who claimed she had borne a son to his father. Although he did not believe the charge, he paid rather than cause scandal in the family.

George invested in a place known as Pequod Island and there he took his friends when he wanted to get away from Boston. On the island he and his friends condescended to share the campfire with their guides. Planned as a male retreat, the island was soon overrun with literary lights of the times invited by George's wife and sister.

As his son grew up, George noted an increasing desire on the part of the younger generation to be wild and careless with money. Later, George began to realize that he and his generation had let much slip and that Boston was going to the Irish. He gave his name to the "Save Boston Association" as he considered his membership an Apley duty. He also interested himself in bird lore and philosophy and took as much personal concern as possible in the affairs of his children. When his mother died in 1908, George counted her death as one of his most poignant tragedies.

When George's son entered Harvard, George took a new interest in the university and noted many changes he did not like.

Old Uncle William, now over eighty, still controlled the Apley mills and held out successfully against the new labor unions. One day the old man shocked his family by marrying his nurse, a Miss Prentiss.

His daughter Eleanor's marriage was completely unsatisfactory to George because she did not induce her husband to give up his job for a position in the Apley mills and to take up residence near her family. But George was proud of his son John for his service at the front. George himself belonged to the Home Guards. When John married a girl of good connections after the war, George was doubly pleased.

At last George came into opposition with a man named O'Reilly, whom George planned to have brought before criminal court on charges of extortion. However, O'Reilly tricked George into a scandal. George intended to have the whole case cleared in court, but before the trial he received a note from his one-time sweetheart, Mary Monahan. After an interview with her, he settled the case quietly and bought off his opponents.

In 1928 he became a grandfather. As soon as the baby had been born, George telegraphed Groton to include his grandson's name among the entrance applicants.

In his last years George took interest in the new novels, condemning those too blatant in their description of sex and fighting against the inclusion of some of them in the Boston libraries. His own copy of *Lady Chatterly's Lover* he hid in the silver safe to keep his daughter from seeing it. He defied prohibition as an abuse of his rights and kept a private bootlegger on principle because he thought it important to help break the prohibition law.

He thought, too, that the colossal fortunes being gathered by the uneducated should be handed over to the government. In the autumn of 1929 he and his wife made a trip to Rome, where they visited Horatio Apley, recently appointed to a diplomatic post there. George was absent from America when the stock market crash came. His financial affairs did not suffer greatly, but, his health breaking, he began to plan his will and his funeral.

George Apley died in December, 1933.

Critical Evaluation

The Late George Apley, considered by many to be the best of John P. Marquand's novels, was a turning point in its author's career. For fifteen years prior to its publication Marquand had, as a "slick" popular writer, enjoyed considerable commercial success, but no critical recognition. *The Late George Apley,* however, was immediately recognized as an important book and its author was promoted by the critics from "popular" to "serious" writer. This elevation was certified when the novel earned Marquand the Pulitzer Prize in 1938. Throughout the remaining years of his writing career he confirmed and further consolidated this reputation, although never completely abandoning the commercial marketplace.

The Late George Apley is the first of a trilogy of novels in which Marquand minutely describes and analyzes the social patterns, behaviors, mores, and conflicts in upper class Boston society during the rapidly changing 1880-1920 period. This novel pictures that part of old Boston society with Puritanical antecedents and commercial traditions, the second of the books, *Wickford Point* (1939), shows the decline of Bostonians with Transcendentalist ancestors and artistic pretensions, while the last, *H. M. Pulham, Esquire* (1941), examines the present day (1920-1940) Boston businessman as he tries to accommodate his geographical and class inheritances to the pressures of the contemporary world.

In each of these books Marquand explores the ways in which social forms and cultural assumptions left over from the past bind those in the present; how, in short, those environments which evolved to assure familial and social protection, identity, and continuity, become prisons for the individuals who inherit them.

This is most obvious in *The Late George Apley*. Actually, the book chronicles three Apley generations. George's father, Thomas, represents the old nineteenth century individualistic businessman. He is highly intelligent, austere, rigid, hard working, and uncompromising. His relationship with his son is reserved and formal, almost institutionalized, although he shows concern and, on occasion, affection for the boy. The doubts that are to plague his son are foreign to Thomas. He knows who he is and what his roles are as father, as businessman, as member of the community, and as "Apley." When he and George have their only real public disagreement, the older man emphatically quashes George's fuzzy democratic ideas: "You and I do not stand for the common good. We stand for a small class; but you don't see it. . . . Nobody sees it but me and my contemporaries." But Thomas is saved from Robber Baron status by a sincere Puritan "stewardship" ethic; he truly believes that the Apley position and fortune are signs of Godly favor and that the money must be conserved and shared with the community—but only on terms dictated by that "small class" of superior people at the top of the social pyramid.

George Apley envies his father his certainty and strength, but cannot emulate him personally. Early in his life he accepts the verdict of his Uncle William, and subsequently Thomas, that he is "not a businessman," that he is "too easy going" and "erratic" and so accepts permanent placement as an investment counselor (of other people's money), lawyer, and civic leader. George assumes from the beginning that his environment is the only one he "could have survived in," but neither he nor the reader can ever be sure. He is never able to test his well-meaning mediocrity; he is given the opportunity neither to succeed nor to fail, but only to fit into a predetermined groove.

In his youth George makes a few feeble attempts at nonconformity; he chooses some dubious friends, questions a few Apley dogmas, and, most importantly, has a brief, intense love affair with a middle-class Irish Catholic girl. It is squelched, of course; George is sent on a Grand Tour and Mary Monahan becomes a sad memory (until the end of the book). But throughout his life George is plagued by the sense that he is trapped and is living a life filled with activity, but devoid of action or meaning. The most important events of his life are family disputes: what to name the baby, how to prevent cousin John from divorcing his wife, where to bury cousin Hattie, whether or not to move the rose bushes.

George's few attempts to find even momentary respite from his milieu fail before they begin. He travels abroad, but carries Boston with him. "I am a raisin," he says, "in a slice of pie which has been conveyed from one plate to another." He buys an island as a masculine retreat from Bostonian formality and its guardians, the womenfolk, and before he knows it, the ladies arrive and "Boston has come to Pequod Island." Throughout his life he suspects that he cannot escape the "net" (young John's phrase) of an environment that stifles more than it supports, and shortly before his death he acknowledges it. Worst of all he realizes that it has cost him the one important thing that he might have had from his life—happiness.

As his father before him, George tries to pass the Apley ethic down to his own son. John rebels more directly and emphatically than his father did. His social and political views baffle and alarm George. John pushes the rebellion further by refusing to join his father's firm, by going to New York City, and by marrying a divorcée. He is much more attuned to the modern world than his father is, and his World War I experiences at the front have matured and sophisticated him. But, in the end, John proves to be his father's son; he returns to Boston and sets up housekeeping at Hillcrest, the family estate. George dies secure in the knowledge that the Apley niche in Boston remains filled; the cycle continues.

But *The Late George Apley* is more than a sad story of the environment's tyranny over individuals. For all of the bleakness of its conclusions, the novel is most entertaining and amusing. The comedic and satiric center of the novel lies in its narrator, Mr. Willing. Marquand decided to tell the story as "a novel in the form of a memoir" for two reasons: first, to parody the then common sub-literary genre of the "collected papers" and, more importantly, to filter the information about the Apleys through the mind and language of a character even more dogmatically committed to the proper Bostonian vision of life.

Willing understands none of George Apley's incipient rebellions and his son's more blatant social improprieties. Much of the novel's rich humor and gentle satire comes from his fussy, polite, pseudo-literary apologies and rationalizations for the errant Apley behavior. In the end, in spite of Willing's stuffy shortsightedness, the reader gets to know and understand the subject very well, is amused and saddened by his weaknesses and narrowness, but is finally tolerant of, and sympathetic toward, the late George Apley.

Bibliography

Beach, Joseph Warren. *American Fiction, 1920–1940.* New York: Russell and Russell, 1960, pp. 259–270.

Goodwin, George. "The Last Hurrahs: George Apley and Frank Skeffington," in *Massachusetts Review.* I (May, 1960), pp. 461–471.

Gordon, Edward J. "What's Happened to Humor?," in *English Journal.* XLVII (1958), pp. 127–133.

Greene, George. "A Tunnel from Persepolis: The Legacy of John Marquand," in *Queen's Quarterly.* LXXIII (Autumn, 1966), pp. 343–349.

Gross, John J. *John P. Marquand.* New York: Twayne, 1963, pp. 31–50.

Holman, C. Hugh. *John P. Marquand.* Minneapolis: University of Minnesota Press, 1965.

Johnson, Robert O. "Mary Monahan: Marquand's Sentimental Slip?," in *Research Studies.* XXXIII (December, 1965), pp. 208–213.

Macauley, Robie. "Let Me Tell You About the Rich . . . ," in *Kenyon Review.* XXVII (Autumn, 1965), pp. 664–666.

Oppenheimer, Franz. "Lament for Unbought Grace: The Novels of John P. Marquand," in *Antioch Review.* XVIII (Spring, 1958), pp. 41–45.

Stuckey, W.J. *The Pulitzer Prize Novels: A Critical Backward Look.* Norman: University of Oklahoma Press, 1966, pp. 112–116.

Warren, Austin. "The Last Puritan," in his *The New England Conscience.* Ann Arbor: University of Michigan Press, 1966, pp. 195–201.

MARGARET MITCHELL

Born: Atlanta, Georgia (November 8, 1900)
Died: Atlanta (August 16, 1949)

Principal Work

NOVEL: *Gone with the Wind*, 1936.

Margaret (Munnerlyn) Mitchell, born in Atlanta, Georgia, on November 8, 1900, was the daughter of Eugene Muse Mitchell, an attorney and president of the Atlanta Historical Society. Atlanta's history meant Civil War history, and the perceptive young daughter of the Mitchell household developed a keen interest in this event and its lingering impact even as a child. What she later did with this lore caused the biggest splash in American publishing history. To describe her one novel requires superlatives: biggest seller in a single day (50,000 copies) and in a single year (2,000,000 copies); most widely translated (22 languages); longest fiction translated into Braille (30 volumes); greatest motion picture hit (seen by 91,000,000 people in 17,000 theaters, earned a profit of $30,000,000 for producers).

Margaret Mitchell attended Smith College for one year and later received an honorary M.A. degree from that institution. Required to return home when her mother died, she started a career in journalism on the Atlanta *Journal* as "Peggy Mitchell" in 1922. Three years later she married John R. Marsh, a power company executive, to whom she dedicated her book. A year later a slow-healing sprained ankle caused her to resign her position with the newspaper and the ten-year writing job which resulted in *Gone with the Wind* got under way, the last part first.

The title taken from Ernest Dowson's poem "Cynara," *Gone with the Wind* was published on June 30, 1936, and among the many awards which followed were the Pulitzer Prize in 1937 and the American Booksellers' Association award in the same year. The book owes its immense popular appeal to its sustained narrative and the finely drawn characters. Scarlett O'Hara and Rhett Butler become vivid personalities whose all-too-human emotions absorb the reader and keep him racing along through 1,037 pages.

Margaret Mitchell wrote no other book. On a summer evening in 1949 she was struck down by a taxicab on an Atlanta street and died shortly thereafter, on August 16.

Bibliography

Biographical and critical material on Margaret Mitchell is scarce. There is only Finis Farr, *Margaret Mitchell of Atlanta, The Author of Gone with the Wind*, 1965. For brief discussions see Frank Ernest Mott, *Golden Multitudes*, 1941,

255–258; and Ernest E. Leisy, *The American Historical Novel*, 1950, 171–173. See also "Backdrop for Atlanta," *Time*, XXVIII (July 6, 1936), 62; and Editorial, *Saturday Review of Literature*, XVII (January 8, 1938), 8.

GONE WITH THE WIND

Type of work: Novel
Author: Margaret Mitchell (1900–1949)
Time of plot: 1861–1873
Locale: Atlanta and Tara Plantation, Georgia
First published: 1936

Principal Characters

Scarlett O'Hara, a Georgia belle. Gently bred on Tara plantation and the wife of Charles Hamilton, she finds herself, through the fortunes of war, a widow and the mistress of a ruined plantation with a family to feed. With an indomitable will to survive and an unquenchable determination to keep Tara, she improves her fortunes with the aid of her own native abilities and opportunistic marriages to Frank Kennedy and Rhett Butler.

Ashley Wilkes, Scarlett O'Hara's sensitive, sophisticated neighbor, with whom she fancies herself in love until, through adversity, he is shorn of the aura of romance with which she has endowed him and shows himself for the weakling that he is.

Rhett Butler, a cynical, wealthy blockade runner, Scarlett O'Hara's third husband. Knowing Scarlett for the unscrupulous materialist that she is, he nevertheless admires her will to survive and is plagued with a love for her which he finally overcomes just as she discovers that it is he and not Ashley Wilkes that she loves.

Charles Hamilton, Scarlett's first husband, whom she marries for spite.

Frank Kennedy, Scarlett's second husband, whom she marries for money.

Melanie (Hamilton) Wilkes, Ashley Wilkes' reticent, ladylike wife.

Gerald O'Hara and
Ellen O'Hara, Scarlett's parents.

Bonnie Blue Butler, the daughter of Scarlett O'Hara and Rhett Butler.

Suellen O'Hara, Scarlett's sister.

Miss Pittypat, Melanie Wilkes' aunt.

India Wilkes, Ashley Wilkes' sister.

Mammy, Scarlett's nurse.

Essay-Review

Gone with the Wind, one of the best-selling novels of all time, is the story of the subjugation of a proud people by war and the harsh "reconstruction" that followed. Swept along with these events is the beautiful, headstrong daughter of a wealthy plantation owner who, when reduced to poverty and hardship in the wake of Sherman's cruel and vicious destruction of the countryside, used her feminine wiles to regain her lost wealth. Having at last attained this goal, she was unable to hold the one man she really loved.

A historical romance of prodigious proportions, this first novel by an unknown author went through twelve printings within two months of publication. Its 1,037 pages enthralled millions, the sales in a single year exceeding two million copies.

The novel has been translated into more than two dozen languages and after many years, sales continue at a pace brisk enough to please any publisher. The motion picture lived up to Hollywood's most studied superlatives and attained worldwide popularity.

The unprecedented success of Margaret Mitchell's only novel may be attributed to a combination of the author's style—a sustained narrative power combined with remarkable character delineation—and the universality of her subject, the struggle for survival when the accustomed security of civilized life is abruptly swept away and the human spirit suddenly stands alone. In spite of the fast-moving narrative, one is aware of this underlying thread of universality, this familiarity with human tragedy that all men can understand.

Perhaps the most lasting impression one gets from the novel, however, is the skill with which Mitchell handles her characterizations. Scarlett O'Hara is, without question, one of the memorable characters in fiction. So lifelike did she become in the public mind that the producers of the motion picture preferred not to risk an established actress in the role and be accused of miscasting; they sent to England for a relatively unknown young actress to portray the fire and passion flashing from the tempestuous Scarlett.

The story of Scarlett O'Hara alone would be reason enough for a best-seller; many books have achieved such eminence on far less. This daughter of Irish temper and French sensibilities displays stark and bold emotions that grip the reader. He follows her intense, futile love for Ashley Wilkes, her spiteful marriage to Charles Hamilton, her opportunistic stealing of her sister's fiancé Frank Kennedy, her grasping arrangement of convenience with Rhett Butler. He is sometimes appalled at her callous use of her sex to gain her ends; he looks in vain for some sign of lofty ideals in this woman; and yet, in spite of all this, he finds laudable her will to survive and her contempt for her conquerors.

Three other characters stand out, admirably drawn but not quite inspiring the amount of interest created by Scarlett. Rhett Butler, dissolute son of Charleston blue bloods, is a cynical, materialistic blockade runner who consorts openly with the enemy and scoffs at patriotic ideals. Forceful, masculine, he is accustomed to taking what he wants. His one unfulfilled desire is the love of Scarlett and this frustration finally breaks his spirit. When at last, after several years of unhappy marriage, he gains her love as Ashley defaults, Rhett, now a bitter, fleshy toper, has already reached his decision to leave her.

Ashley Wilkes, the weak-willed object of Scarlett's misguided passion, depicts the impractical idealist dependent on a stronger will to solve life's problems for him. When Scarlett observes his unstable reaction to his wife's death she is finally able to see him as he really is. Shorn of his cavalier manners and the aura of courtly romance she had bestowed upon him, he becomes in her eyes an ineffectual weakling and the sterility of her forbidden love is at last apparent.

Melanie, in a way the winner despite her death at the end of the novel, found happiness and tranquility in her devotion to her insecure husband. Reticent, ladylike, saccharine, but intellectually attuned to Ashley, there is never any question that she, not Scarlett, should be Ashley's wife.

High-spirited Scarlett was sixteen when the Civil War began. She fancied herself in love with Ashley Wilkes, the sensitive, sophisticated son at a neighboring plantation, but he did not acknowledge her love. Upon the announcement of his engagement to his soft-spoken cousin Melanie Hamilton, Scarlett impetutously married Melanie's brother Charles, to that surprised young man's pride and delight. Less than a year later Scarlett was a war widow and an unwilling mother.

Here the novel loses the tempo of leisurely plantation life and takes on the urgency of a region at war. Leaving her father's plantation, Tara, Scarlett traveled twenty-five miles to Atlanta to stay with her dead husband's relatives. Later, as Atlanta was besieged by Sherman's troops, Scarlett returned home to Tara through the battle lines at night in a wagon provided by Rhett. With her were Melanie and Ashley's day-old son whom Scarlett had delivered as guns sounded in the distance.

Approaching Tara through the battle-scarred countryside she saw that most of the plantation mansions had been looted and burned by the enemy. Tara had been spared as a headquarters, though the outbuildings and baled cotton had been burned and the hogs, cows, and chickens killed. Scarlett's mother, too ill with fever to be moved as the soldiers approached, died with her beloved Tara filled with Yankee conquerors. Her father's mind, unable to stand these shocks, was gone. Now the sheltered Southern belle was faced with the formidable prospect of feeding, from a plantation stripped bare by the ruthless invaders, her father, her child, two sisters, Melanie, and the few servants who remained faithfully behind when the others ran off.

These are the events that helped to shape the character of Scarlett O'Hara and they explain the hardness, the avarice, that prompted many of her actions. For example, she was determined to hold on to Tara and when the carpetbaggers arbitrarily levied an extra three-hundred-dollar tax with the expectation of taking over the property for unpaid taxes, Scarlett unhesitatingly married storeowner Frank Kennedy, who was engaged to her sister Suellen, and he dutifully paid the three-hundred-dollar tax.

The art of Margaret Mitchell makes such reprehensible acts seem normal under the circumstances, for the author has skillfully brought us along the same harsh road Scarlett has traveled and we, being thus exposed to the same experiences, understand, even condone, her responses.

Once Scarlett had learned the law of the jungle her native abilities came into their own. Borrowing money from Rhett, she bought and operated successfully a sawmill and soon was financially secure. When Frank was killed by occupation troops she married Rhett, who had amassed half a million dollars during the war as a blockade runner. But even the birth of a child, Bonnie Blue, did not bring happiness to this union because of the love for Ashley to which Scarlett absurdly clung. Rhett, always jealous of this will-of-the-wisp emotion, was unable to cope with what he could not understand. Ironically, Rhett overcame his love for Scarlett just as she was discovering that it was he, not Ashley, whom she loved. When she tried to tell him this, Rhett announced brusquely that she was too late, that he was leaving her forever. There was no mistaking the finality of his words but, characteristically, Scarlett, the self-confident schemer, would not accept them as such.

Gone with the Wind is not a happy book. There are flicks of humor, but for the most part a deadly seriousness pervades the novel and in the end the callous, grasping cynicism of the leading characters mocks them and, properly, only an empty loneliness remains.

A natural question concerns the position of *Gone with the Wind* and its author in world literature. On the strength of her one novel Margaret Mitchell certainly cannot be called a great author. Whether her outstanding book will rank as a great novel will not be decided by those who consider the question at this early date. If the work eventually achieves first rank, it will be because Scarlett O'Hara continues to convey to future readers the same essence of human behavior that we ourselves see in her now.

FRANK NORRIS

Born: Chicago, Illinois (March 5, 1870)
Died: San Francisco, California (October 25, 1902)

Principal Works

NOVELS: *Moran of the Lady Letty*, 1898; *Blix*, 1899; *McTeague*, 1899; *A Man's Woman*, 1900; *The Octopus*, 1901; *The Pit*, 1903; *Vandover and the Brute*, 1914. SHORT STORIES: *A Deal in Wheat and Other Stories*, 1903; *The Third Circle*, 1909. ESSAYS: *The Responsibilities of the Novelist*, 1903.

Frank Norris wrote in 1899: "Tell your yarn and let your style go to the devil. We don't want literature, we want life." Yet the life he portrayed in his novels was more naturalistic—emphasizing the brutality in man, the sordid in experience—than realistic; and his works are more the dramatization of his obsession with power and bigness than the "truth" of either the times or the characters of his fiction.

The oldest son of a wealthy jewelry manufacturer and a doting mother, he was born in Chicago on March 5, 1870, and christened Benjamin Franklin Norris, Jr. When he was fourteen, his family moved to San Francisco; the bustling and varied life of that city as well as his wide reading stimulated his boyish imagination and turned him away from all thoughts of a business career. Encouraged by his mother, he began the study of art and spent a year at the Atelier Julien in Paris. In 1890 he entered the University of California, read Darwin and Zola, and began *McTeague*. After four years at the university, without taking a degree, he transferred to Harvard. There, encouraged by Professor Lewis E. Gates, he worked at *McTeague* and completed *Vandover and the Brute*.

During the Boer War he was in South Africa as a correspondent for the San Francisco *Chronicle*. After editorial experience on *The Wave*, a magazine published in San Francisco, he went to New York to work for the S. S. McClure syndicate. In 1898 he went to Cuba to report on the Spanish-American War. Following his return to New York, he married and became a reader for the firm of Doubleday, Page and Company. As a publisher's reader, he was the discoverer of Theodore Dreiser's *Sister Carrie* (1900).

Physically frail as a boy, Norris had greatly admired his powerful, aggressive father, but was rejected by him because of the boy's obedience to his artistic, possessive mother. When his parents were divorced, Norris apparently suffered a form of psychological split; his brief career as a writer has been explained as an attempt at refusion by attempting big things to please his father while traveling along the path of art which his mother has laid out for him. He never completed either of the two great trilogies he planned, yet his books gave promise of what he might have achieved as a writer of the naturalistic school. In his projected Epic of the Wheat, for example, he wished to express his indignation over as well as his admiration for the men who through organization and exploitation had taken over the economic and social control of America. The expansion of the railroads alone had produced vast outer conflicts and inner tensions, the latter principally because there was no frontier left for the less aggressive and the ethical to flee to. Norris wrote of both the aggressors and those in conflict with them, but in his emphasis on the business of social conflict rather than on character, in his preoccupation with the sordid, shocking, and depressing, and in his obsession with size and violence, he was frequently the traditional romantic in reverse. In addition, he mixed his literary styles, sometimes writing realistically and sometimes weaving into his work an almost mystic poetical quality. This fusion of the naturalistic and the poetic makes him a distinctive writer, as well as an artistic failure in all his novels except *McTeague*.

Vandover and the Brute, although published last, was the first written of his novels. (The loss of the manuscript during the San Francisco fire accounts for the long-delayed publication). It is a thinly disguised tale of Norris' own attempt to find release from his unhappy relationship with his incompatible parents, a work in which he relived his own defeats in dilettante debauchery and prophesied his doom as a broken cleaner of closets. Of little interest for the average reader today, it curiously fits a prejudice of the time in its philosophy that anyone born to wealth deserved a miserable and impoverished end.

Superior in every way to the Nietzschean primitivism of *Moran of the Lady Letty* and the semi-autobiographical *Blix*, *McTeague* also presents the theme of indulgence and punishment, but within a milieu quite different from that of Norris himself. More objective in treatment, it is also more a work of the creative imagination in the manner of Zola; melodramatic situations and exaggeration of the degree of brutality and avarice in American life mar but do not destroy the sheer driving power of narrative in this story of a crude, brutal dentist corrupted by his passion for gold.

Norris was not to find another subject suited to his talents until he conceived his Epic of the Wheat. In *The Octopus*, the first novel of his proposed trilogy, he tells of the planting and harvesting of the wheat; the fertile land is presented as a symbol of force in a plot centering on conflict between the farmers of the San Joaquin Valley in California and the Southern Pacific Railroad, an industrial octopus with tentacles of steel. In this novel the human antagonists are doomed to defeat, but the prevailing mood of pessimism is in part redeemed by a conclusion which suggests the tradition of the sentimental novel in its assurance that everything has occurred for the best, that no matter how many lives are destroyed in the production of wheat more lives are sustained by it as food. *The Pit* continues the story of wheat through the speculation and exploitation of the Chicago grain market. This novel is less an artistic melange, but the work suffers from the writer's reversion to memories of his own family for some of his situations and scenes. In it the main protagonists are drawn after his father and mother, with the mother choosing the wrong lover (a businessman rather than an artist) for her husband. As in the case of *The Octopus*, the characters are overdrawn and the naturalistic tone is blurred by the note of personal mysticism at the end.

Norris had sketchily outlined a third novel, *The Wolf*, which would deal with the need for and the consumption of wheat abroad. But this book, like the trilogy he had planned on the Battle of Gettysburg, was never written. He died in San Francisco on October 25, 1902, from the post-operative effects of appendicitis.

Bibliography

The writings of Frank Norris were collected in the limited Argonaut Manuscript Edition and a trade edition, 10 vols., 1928. A later collection of previously unpublished stories and sketches is *Frank Norris of "The Wave,"* edited by Oscar Lewis, 1931. The standard biography is Franklin Walker, *Frank Norris: A Biography*, 1932. The best critical work is Ernest Marchand, *Frank Norris: A Study*, 1942, which contains a bibliography. See also Kenneth S. Lynn, *The Dream of Success*, 1955; Warren French, *Frank Norris*, 1962; William B. Dillingham, *Frank Norris: Instinct and Art*, 1969; and Richard Chase, *The American Novel and Its Tradition*, 1957. A special study is Richard A. Davidson, ed., *Studies in The Octopus*, 1969.

McTEAGUE

Type of work: Novel
Author: Frank Norris (1870–1902)
Time of plot: 1890's
Locale: San Francisco and Death Valley
First published: 1899

Generally considered Norris' best novel, McTeague follows the lives of three people drawn inevitably to catastrophe through their own inherited qualities acted upon by environmental forces. The novel is powerful and terrifying in its evocation of a naturalistic world in which people are victims of forces beyond their control.

Principal Characters

McTeague (Mac), a massive, slow-witted man with a blond mustache and enormously strong hands. An unlicensed dentist, McTeague sometimes pulls teeth with his bare hands. He snoozes away Sunday afternoons in his dentist chair until he meets Trina Sieppe, the cousin and fiancée of his friend, Marcus Schouler. His friend sees that McTeague and Trina are attracted and with fairly good grace accepts the situation. Many of McTeague's violent and even repulsive qualities are highlighted by incidents in the novel. At an outing Marcus and McTeague wrestle; Marcus, envious and angry, bites off McTeague's ear lobe; the dentist, in turn, breaks Marcus' arm. In adversity, McTeague's brutality is intensified by drink. Sadistically, he bites his wife's fingers until they are infected and have to be amputated. Adversity can only intensify his desperation, and one is not surprised when he beats his wife to death and then flees the consequences. In the middle of the desert he is met by his former friend, now a member of the sheriff's posse; again a violent struggle is the only response McTeague can give. He kills his friend, but not before Marcus has handcuffed them together under the boiling sun. McTeague's death, like his life, is brutish. Readers have considered McTeague's career, as related by Norris, a triumph of realistic description.

Marcus Schouler, who lives above McTeague's dental office. The two men are friends. Smaller than McTeague but gifted with more intelligence, Marcus broods over the loss of his fiancée and her prize money and is petty enough to report McTeague to the authorities for practicing without a license. By fate or by sheer perversity he binds his enemy to his own corpse with handcuffs; the two face eternity only hours apart.

Trina Sieppe, McTeague's wife, trained to be a thrifty housewife by her Swiss parents. She overdevelops this trait after she wins five thousand dollars in a lottery. She spends every spare moment carving small wooden Noah's Ark animals for her uncle's "import" business. Although counting coins is her only joy, she does buy a huge gold tooth as a sign for her husband's dental office. Sexually subservient to her husband's physical strength, she cannot protect herself from his drunken fury when he bites her finger tips. Her character shows only vestigial kindness, and her miserliness leads to her death.

Grannis, an aged English bookbinder, comforted each night by the delicate sounds of his neighbor's teatray on the opposite side of a partition. The tray belongs to the seamstress next door.

Miss Parker, a genteel dressmaker. She responds with fluttering heart when she hears Grannis and his supper tray. They marry.

Zerkov, a junk dealer.

Maria Macapa, a maid who collects junk for Zerkov. She raves about "gold dishes" once owned by her family. These ravings lead Zerkov to marry Maria. But a head blow ends her aberration and in frustration Zerkov kills her.

Papa and
Mamma Sieppe, Trina's parents, elderly Swiss immigrants.

The Story

McTeague, born in a small mining town, worked with his unambitious father in the mines. But his mother saw in her son a chance to realize her own dreams. The opportunity to send him away for a better education came a few years after McTeague's father had died. A traveling dentist was prevailed upon to take the boy as an apprentice.

McTeague learned something of dentistry, but he was too stupid to understand much of it. When his mother died and left him a small sum of money, he set up his own pratice in an office-bedroom in San Francisco. McTeague was easily satisfied. He had his concertina for amusement and enough money from his practice to keep him well supplied with beer.

In the flat above McTeague lived his friend, Marcus Schouler. Marcus was in love with his cousin, Trina Sieppe, whom he brought to McTeague for some dental work. While they were waiting for McTeague to finish with a patient, the cleaning women sold Trina a lottery ticket.

McTeague immediately fell in love with Trina. Marcus, realizing his friend's attachment, rather enjoyed playing the martyr, setting aside his own love in order that McTeague might feel free to court Trina. He invited the dentist to go with him to call on the Sieppe family. From that day on McTeague was a steady visitor at the Sieppe home. To celebrate their engagement, McTeague took Trina and her family to the theater. Afterward they returned to McTeague's flat, to find the building in an uproar. Trina's lottery ticket had won five thousand dollars.

In preparation for their wedding, Trina was furnishing a flat across from McTeague's office. When she decided to invest her winnings and collect the monthly interest, the dentist was disappointed, for he had hoped to spend the money on something lavish and exciting. But Trina's wishes prevailed. With that income and McTeague's earnings, as well as the little that Trina earned from her hand-carved animals, the McTeagues could be assured of a comfortable life.

Marcus slowly changed in his attitude toward his friend and his cousin. One day he accused McTeague of stealing Trina's affection for the sake of the five thousand dollars. In his fury he struck at his old friend with a knife. McTeague was not hurt, but his anger was thoroughly aroused.

In the early months after their wedding, McTeague and Trina were extremely happy. Trina was tactful in the changes she began to make in her husband. Gradually she improved his manners and appearance. They both planned for the time when they could afford a home of their own. Because of those plans they had their first real quarrel. McTeague wanted to rent a nearby house, but Trina objected to the high rent. Her thriftiness was slowly turning into miserliness. When McTeague, unknown to her, rented the house, she refused to move or to contribute to the payment of the first month's rent which signing of the lease entailed.

Some days later they went on a picnic to which Marcus was also invited. Outwardly he and McTeague had settled their differences, but jealousy still rankled in Marcus. When some wrestling matches were held, Marcus and the dentist were the winners in their bouts. It now remained for the two winners to compete. No match for the brute strength of McTeague, Marcus was thrown. Furious, he demanded another match. In that match Marcus suddenly leaned forward and bit off the lobe of the dentist's ear. McTeague broke Marcus' arm in his anger.

Marcus soon left San Francisco. Shortly thereafter an order from City Hall disbarred McTeague from his practice because he lacked college training. Marcus had informed the authorities.

Trina and McTeague moved from their flat to a tiny room on the top floor of the building, for the loss of McTeague's practice had made Trina more niggardly than ever. McTeague found a job making dental supplies. Trina devoted almost every waking moment to her animal carvings. She allowed herself and the room to become slovenly, she begrudged every penny they spent, and when McTeague lost his job she insisted that they move to even cheaper lodgings. McTeague began to drink, and drinking made him vicious. When he was drunk, he would pinch or bite Trina until she gave him money for more whiskey.

The new room into which they moved was filthy and cramped. McTeague grew more and more surly. One morning he left to go fishing and failed to return. That night, while Trina was searching the streets for him, he broke into her trunk and stole her hoarded savings. After his disappearance Trina learned that the paint she used on her animals had infected her hand. The fingers of her right hand were amputated.

Trina took a job as a scrub woman, and the money she earned together with the interest from her five thousand dollars was sufficient to support her. Now that the hoard of money that she had saved was gone, she missed the thrill of counting over the coins, and so she withdrew the whole of her five thousand dollars from the bank and hid the coins in her room. One evening there was a tap on her window. McTeague was standing outside, hungry and without a place to sleep. Trina angrily refused to let him in. A few evenings later, drunk and vicious, he broke into a room she was cleaning. When she refused to give him any money, he beat her until she fell unconscious. She died early next morning.

McTeague took her money and went back to the mines, where he fell in with another prospector. But McTeague was haunted by the thought that he was being followed. One night he stole away from his companion and started south across Death Valley. The next day, as he was resting, he was suddenly accosted by a man with a gun. The man was Marcus.

A posse had been searching for McTeague ever since Trina's body had been found, and as soon as Marcus heard about the murder he volunteered for the manhunt. While the two men stood facing each other in the desert, McTeague's mule ran away, carrying on its back a canteen bag of water. Marcus emptied his gun to kill the animal, but its dead body fell on the canteen bag and the water was lost. The five thousand dollars was also lashed to the back of the mule. As McTeague went to unfasten it, Marcus seized him. In the struggle McTeague killed his enemy with his bare hands. But as he slipped to the ground, Marcus managed to snap one handcuff to McTeague's wrist, the other to his own. McTeague looked stupidly around, at the hills about a hundred miles away, and at the dead body to which he was helplessly chained. He was trapped in the parching inferno of the desert that stretched away on every side.

Critical Evaluation

McTeague presents a unique challenge to the critic. It is a gripping story of human emotions and the relentless pressures of heredity and environment that distort the soul; it is also a melodrama with stereotyped characters, lurid action, and a creaking machinery of symbols that includes everything from dental equipment to snarling dogs. Nevertheless, despite its obvious weaknesses, *McTeague* is exactly what Alfred Kazin has said it is: "The first great tragic portrait in America of an acquisitive society." Norris' novel initiates the literary treatment of a theme that eventually informed significant American literary works such as Theodore Dreiser's "An American Tragedy" and Arthur Miller's "Death of a Salesman."

McTeague himself is a crude but well-meaning hulk of a man whose gentle temper suggests "the draft horse, immensely strong, stupid, docile, obedient." His brutishness is under control as long as he can putter with his dentistry and sleep off his steam beer in the dental chair. Once he is eroticized by Trina, however, McTeague is sucked into a world of feelings that undermine the self-control his undisturbed life has made possible. Once he and Trina marry, McTeague becomes vulnerable to her avarice and Marcus' jealousy and envy. These destructive emotions, not characteristic of McTeague himself, release the underlying primitiveness of his character. When Marcus bites McTeague's ear lobe during the wrestling match at the family picnic, the gentle "draft horse" rises with "the hideous yelling of a hurt beast, the squealing of a wounded elephant . . . . It was something no longer human; it was rather an echo from the jungle." For Norris, man is fundamentally an animal, his world ruled by harsh laws of survival.

McTeague's brutalization is tragic because the humanity he had achieved was so touching in its vulnerability. Also he is strikingly innocent of avarice. Although the release of McTeague's brutish animal quality results in two slayings, Norris suggests greater dehumanization in the mad greed of Trina counting her gold coins and Zerkov dreaming of Maria's gold plate. McTeague becomes an animal, but they defy nature itself in the hideousness of their moral and psychological deformity.

It is here that the melodramatic elements of the novel threaten its power. Nevertheless, Norris succeeds in conveying the irony that the nonbrutes in an acquisitive society are more lethal than the brutes, or innocents, who are not conceived in its bowels. McTeague comes from a nonurban world, and it is a testimony to his instincts for self-preservation that he flees back to the mountains after killing Trina. She, Marcus, and Zerkov are all shaped by the city and its acquisitive and artificial environment, and they are all annihilated violently to dramatize the hopelessness of their origins.

Perhaps Norris overdoes the pettiness and petit-bourgeois traits of Trina's Swiss family Sieppe. And his portrait of the psychotic Zerkov hovers close to anti-Semitism. But the shallowness of the characterizations serves a larger symbolic purpose. All these people are what they are because their environment is a kind of hell, a swarming, competitive world. If Norris indulges in harsh stereotypes, it is because society produces them. "I never truckled . . . . I told them the truth. They liked it or they didn't like it. What had that to do with me?" This was Norris' literary creed, and he adhered to it relentlessly in other Naturalist works of social criticism such as *The Octopus* (1901) and *The Pit* (1903). Even in situations that unobservant readers might dismiss as sentimentalism, Norris preserves his sardonic and tough-minded view of the world. The budding love affair between old Mister Grannis and Miss Baker, which reads like a contrast to the deteriorating marriage of McTeague and Trina, is, in reality, a bitter comment on the frustrations of isolation in the congested city. These two old people have conducted their romance through the wall that separates their rooms for so long that their final coming together is a cruelly ironic comment on the life they have never lived.

The central symbol in *McTeague* is gold. Everyone craves it: Maria, the servant girl, is full of stories about the ancestral gold plate of her family. She captivates Zerkov with descriptions of it and steals gold fillings from McTeague's dental parlor. Trina counts her gold coins into the night, deriving a fiercer erotic joy from this than from the bear hugs of her husband. Marcus covets Trina's lottery winnings and finally brings about his own death in struggling over the gold with McTeague in the middle of Death Valley. Only McTeague is indifferent to the glitter of gold. For him it is merely a tool of his trade. When he runs off with Trina's money, he is motivated not by greed, as all critics of the novel agree, but by revenge.

Erich von Stroheim made a famous film of *McTeague* and called it *Greed*. He is said to have followed *McTeague* page by page, "never missing a paragraph." Any reader of *McTeague* will agree that Norris moves through his story with what Kenneth Rexroth has called "a relentless photographic veracity." Scene after scene unfolds with a visual precision and crispness that leaves an indelible impression on the mind and does much to dispel the reservations that the melodramatic action arouses. There is a relentless and powerful movement in these pictures. From the opening scenes describing McTeague on a Sunday in his cozy dental office slumbering or lazily playing his concertina, to the violent closing scene of the novel in which McTeague and Marcus are locked in a violent death struggle in the middle of the greatest wasteland in America, the reader is swept steadily along to increasingly arresting visual involvements. The eye wins over the mind. The environment is rendered with a concreteness that reveals its central power in the novel.

Bibliography

Brooks, Van Wyck. "Introduction," in *McTeague, A Story of San Francisco*. Greenwich, Conn.: Fawcett, 1960.

Chase, Richard. *The American Novel and Its Tradition*. Garden City, New York: Doubleday, 1957, pp. 188–192. Reprinted in *McTeague, A Story of San Francisco*. Edited by Donald Pizer. New York: Norton, 1977, pp. 341–344.

Collins, Carvel. "Introduction," in *McTeague, A Story of San Francisco*. New York: Rinehart, 1955. Reprinted in *The American Novel from James Fenimore Cooper to William Faulkner*. Edited by Wallace Stegner. New York: Basic Books, 1965, pp. 97–105.

Cooperman, Stanley. "Frank Norris and the Werewolf of Guilt," in *Modern Language Quarterly*. XX (September, 1959), pp. 252–258.

Dillingham, William B. *Frank Norris: Instinct and Art*. Lincoln: University of Nebraska Press, 1969, pp. 104–109, 115–119. Reprinted in *McTeague, A Story of San Francisco*. Edited by Donald Pizer. New York: Norton, 1977, pp. 354–361.

————. "The Old Folks of *McTeague*," in *Nineteenth-Century Fiction*. XVI (September, 1961), pp. 169–173. Reprinted in *McTeague, A Story of San Francisco*. Edited by Donald Pizer. New York: Norton, 1977, pp. 344–348.

Dreiser, Theodore. "Introduction," in *The Argonaut Manuscript Limited*

Edition of Frank Norris' Works, Volume VIII. Garden City, N.Y.: Doubleday, 1928, pp. vii–xi.

French, Warren. *Frank Norris.* New York: Twayne, 1962, pp. 62–75.

Frohock, W.M. *Frank Norris.* Minneapolis: University of Minnesota Press, 1968, pp. 9–16.

Geismar, Maxwell. *Rebels and Ancestors: The American Novel, 1890–1915.* Boston: Houghton Mifflin, 1953, pp. 14–21. Reprinted in *McTeague, A Story of San Francisco.* Edited by Donald Pizer. New York: Norton, 1977, pp. 332–337.

Goldman, Suzy B. "*McTeague* and the Imagistic Network," in *Western American Literature.* VII (Summer, 1972), pp. 83–99.

Hill, John S. "Trina Sieppe: First Lady of American Literary Naturalism," in *University of Kansas City Review.* XXIX (Autumn, 1962), pp. 77–80.

Howells, William Dean. "A Case in Point," in *Literature.* I (March 24, 1899), pp. 241–242. Reprinted in *McTeague, A Story of San Francisco.* Edited by Donald Pizer. New York: Norton, 1977, pp. 325–327.

Johnson, George W. "Frank Norris and Romance," in *American Literature.* XXXIII (March, 1961), pp. 57–60.

Kazin, Alfred. "American Naturalism: Reflections from Another Era," in *The American Writer and the European Tradition.* Edited by Margaret Denny and William H. Gilman. Minneapolis: University of Minnesota Press, 1950, pp. 121–131.

Marchand, Ernest. *Frank Norris: A Study.* New York: Octagon Books, 1964, pp. 56–67.

Martin, Jay. *Harvests of Change: American Literature, 1865–1914.* Englewood Cliffs, N.J.: Prentice-Hall, 1967, pp. 249–252.

Morgan, H. Wayne. *American Writers in Rebellion from Twain to Dreiser.* New York: Hill and Wang, 1965, pp. 114–120.

Pizer, Donald. "Evolutionary Ethical Dualism in Frank Norris's *Vandover and the Brute* and *McTeague,*" in *PMLA.* LXXVI (December, 1961), pp. 552–560.

———. *The Novels of Frank Norris.* Bloomington: Indiana University Press, 1966, pp. 23–31, 63–85.

Powell, Lawrence Clark. *California Classics: The Creative Literature of the Golden State.* Los Angeles: Ward Ritchie, 1971, pp. 175–184.

Rexroth, Kenneth. "Afterword," in *McTeague, A Story of San Francisco.* New York: New American Library, 1964, pp. 341–348.

Walcutt, Charles C. *American Literary Naturalism, A Divided Stream.*
Minneapolis: University of Minnesota Press, 1956, pp. 125, 128–132. Re-
printed in *McTeague, A Story of San Francisco.* Edited by Donald Pizer.
New York: Norton, 1977, pp. 337–341.

JULIA PETERKIN

Born: Laurens County, South Carolina (October 31, 1880)
Died: Fort Motte, South Carolina (August 10, 1961)

Principal Works

NOVELS: *Black April*, 1927; *Scarlet Sister Mary*, 1928; *Bright Skin*, 1932.

SHORT STORIES: *Green Thursday*, 1924.

SKETCHES: *Roll, Jordan, Roll*, 1933; *A Plantation Christmas*, 1934.

Julia Mood Peterkin, best known for her novel *Scarlet Sister Mary*, was one of the earliest authors to write sympathetically and realistically about the black people in the South. Her writing career was brief, but during the period between 1924 and 1932 she wrote three novels, many short stories, and various sketches of plantation life.

She was born in Laurens County, daughter of Julius Andrew and Alma Archer Mood. She attended Converse College and in 1896 received her B.A. degree. A year later she was granted her M.A. She spent the next ten years at Fort Motte teaching in a small school. In 1903 she married William George Peterkin, the owner of Lang Syne Plantation at Fort Motte. They had one child, a son, William George. It was at Lang Syne Plantation that she became acquainted with a group of Gullah blacks, descendants of the first Africans brought to the plantation as slaves and who had chosen to stay on the land to farm after emancipation. Living in the same slave-quarter houses that had been built by their ancestors, the people had retained many of the old customs and beliefs. Their language and speech patterns, highly musical and colorful, were to the untrained ear not altogether comprehensible. In an autobiographical sketch, Peterkin wrote that her early attempts to communicate with the Gullahs were difficult and embarrassing. But "little by little I learned their words. . . .I soon found that their quaint dialect was not only musical and expressive but filled with wit and wisdom." She came to learn not only their language but also how they approached life with courage and grace. Their vivid customs, their earthy wisdom and ways, became the materials of her fiction.

Peterkin's first writing efforts were encouraged by another South Carolinian, Henry Bellamann, who was later to publish the highly successful novel *Kings Row*. In 1921, Bellamann, impressed by Peterkin's abilities, brought Carl Sandburg to Lang Syne Plantation. Sandburg was full of praise and encouragement; however, noting the possibility that his reaction might be prompted by courtesy and kindness, Peterkin sought the advice of the "toughest critic" in the country, H. L. Mencken. Mencken was not only impressed, but he also wrote Emily Clark, in Virginia, who was then editor of *The Review*. Clark, in turn, requested material from Peterkin. In October of 1921 *The Review* printed a sketch, "From Lang

Syne Plantation," and Mencken's *Smart Set* printed Peterkin's first short story, "The Merry-Go-Round."

Published steadily after that, her stories represented a break in the literary traditions of the time. Like those of DuBose Heyward, her characters were strong and compelling people, not the stereotypes of blacks that the public and critics expected. Graphic in detail and realistic in its presentation of the life of the black people she knew, "Missy Twins" was found by Mencken to be "too terrible" and by Emily Clark, although she printed it, to be "grim and terrible." After publication of the story, the journal heard from its outraged and shocked Southern readers.

Green Thursday, a collection of twelve short stories all concerning the lives of Gullahs of South Carolina, was published in 1924; and although it received favorable reviews throughout the country, it was reviewed by only one paper in South Carolina. Ignored by the local press, Peterkin was, moreover, denounced by many women's clubs; and letters attacking her poured in to the newspapers. In spite of these racist outpourings, Peterkin continued to write, and in 1926 the story "Maum Lou" was chosen for publication in the O. Henry Memorial volume. The following year Peterkin's first novel, *Black April*, was published. Although it lacks clear focus, the novel remains interesting in its further exploration of the same region and characters of the short stories and sketches.

In 1928, *Scarlet Sister Mary* appeared, and that spring it was awarded the Pulitzer Prize. Using the same locale and many of the characters from her earlier stories, Peterkin created in this novel her strongest and most memorable character, Sister Mary. Widely and extensively praised, the novel was also made into a Broadway play which unfortunately starred Ethel Barrymore playing Mary in black face. Although the play met with success, it had a short run because Barrymore became ill.

Negative reactions to Peterkin's works continued in South Carolina, however, to the extent that *Scarlet Sister Mary* was banned by the public libraries. But in the face of national acclaim, acceptance was growing; and when the library in Gaffney, South Carolina, banned the book, it was printed serially by the local newspaper.

Bright Skin, published in 1932, brings Peterkin's characters into closer contact with the outside world and the twentieth century. Like *Scarlet Sister Mary*, the major theme of *Bright Skin* concerns the relationships and conflicts between the needs of the individual and the role society expects him or her to fulfill. Unlike *Scarlet Sister Mary*, *Bright Skin* is a sad book, lamenting a passing time and a loss of innocence. *Roll, Jordan, Roll* published in 1933, is a collection of factual sketches of life and people on Lang Syne Plantation and a text for photographs by Dora Ulman. Peterkin's last publication, published in 1934, was a small and sentimental sketch called *A Plantation Christmas*.

From the first, Peterkin had assisted her husband in the management of Lang Syne Plantation, and as his health declined, she assumed greater responsibilities,

In the 1940 Census, she listed her occupation as "farmer."

Spanning less than a decade Peterkin's writing was notable, winning critical acclaim and national and international acceptance. Eventually, even in her own state she came to be recognized. Converse College awarded her an Honorary D.D.L. in 1927; and after winning the Pulitzer Prize, she became a sought after public speaker. Most important, however, is that she broke the traditions of the genteel Southern lady writer and the vogue of the plantation romance based on a mythical Southern aristocracy living in a Camelot surrounded by happy and loyal blacks. Her break with this tradition aroused local hostility, but Peterkin persisted in writing what she knew from her own experience to be "true." For this, she won praise from the black press. W. E. B. Du Bois, for example, called *Green Thursday* a beautiful book. More recently, Margaret Just Butcher in *The Negro in American Culture* praised Peterkin for her intuitive understanding of black folkways, for her creation of vivid characters who are not rigidly defined types, and for what she did to establish the folk tale in legitimate perspective.

In spite of the praise by blacks, however, Peterkin's work has in the recent decades received almost no critical attention from the scholarly community.

Bibliography

The most extensive work on Peterkin appears in *Contemporary American Authors* by Fred B. Millett (New York, 1940); "The Life and Works of Julia Peterkin," an unpublished M.A. thesis (University of Georgia, 1956); and in the introductory essay that Frank Durham provides in his *Collected Short Stories of Julia Peterkin* (South Carolina, 1970).

SCARLET SISTER MARY

Type of work: Novel
Author: Julia Peterkin (1880–1961)
Time of plot: Early twentieth century
Locale: Southern coastal lowlands, U.S.A.
First published: 1928

Winner of the Pulitzer Prize in 1928 for Scarlet Sister Mary, *Peterkin wrote several other novels, but none as good. Previous to the publication of* Scarlet Sister Mary, *portraits of black people in plantation literature conformed to derogatory stereotypes of a race, but Peterkin brought new insights and authentic characterization to a people and a land.*

Principal Characters

Mary, left without parents, her father disappearing before she is born and her mother dying shortly after childbirth, is brought up by her "Auntie," Maum Hannah, in the small community that formerly had been the slave quarters of a large plantation. After baptism into her church, she is called Sister Mary. *Scarlet* refers to the ten "scarlet" sins she commits.

Maum Hannah, a member of Heaven's Gate Church, a midwife and nurse, who rears Mary after the death of Mary's mother.

Budda Ben, Maum Hannah's son. Crippled by an accident, he earns his living cutting kindling wood. Because of his quick temper he finds it impossible to stay a member of the Church for very long at a time, but he is both father and brother to Mary.

July, Mary's husband. He is a gambler, a crap shooter and poker player, who dances, and sings and plays reels on his guitar. He deserts Mary shortly after the birth of their son and goes off to live in town with Cinder.

June, July's brother. Hardworking and dependable, he is also in love with Mary. After July has left the Quarter, June fathers Mary's second child.

Cinder, Mary's cousin, who has always wanted July and finally succeeds, with the help of Daddy Cudjoe, in getting July to leave Mary.

Doll, sister of June and July, married to Andrew, one of the sternest deacons of the Church. She loses no occasion to reproach Mary for all of her "sin" children.

Unex, short for Unexpected, son of July and Mary. Unex leaves the Quarter at an early age to go north to find work. He returns to Mary with his newly born daughter after the death of his young wife. Suffering from the same illness, he, too, dies, in spite of all that Maum Hannah and Mary do to save him.

Seraphine, daughter of Mary and June. She goes off to school to earn a diploma and returns unwed, bringing to her mother a newly born child on the same night that Mary gives birth to twin boys.

Daddy Cudjoe, an old man who knows all the old conjures and magic. He makes a charm for Cinder which helps her lure July into town. Too late Mary goes to him for a charm to win July back from Cinder. But the charm that Daddy Cudjoe makes for Mary proves to be the best charm he has ever made. It brings Mary every man she desires. In the end, it works on the deacons of the Church, causing them to allow her to return to the Church.

Essay-Review

Peterkin's characters are descendants of Gullah Africans who stayed on the land to live and work long after the plantation owners had disappeared. Their speech and customs are virtually unchanged by the twentieth century, and it is Peterkin's use of the people's folkways and wisdom that gives *Scarlet Sister Mary* its special quality and effects.

Mary gains the name Sister upon entering the church. Later, she marries July, but she loses him to Cinder. With the help of a charm she obtains from Daddy Cudjoe, Mary attracts any man she desires, bearing a child by one of them every other year. Mary remains proud, however, that she can support her family and that she never has to rely on the fathers' of her children. Even though her "scarlet" sins have barred her from the church, Mary thinks that one day she will be accepted again. After her eldest son dies, Mary spends the night weeping and praying. She has a vision, in which her son tells her to pray for forgiveness for each of her "scarlet" sins. She does so and feels herself forgiven. When she relates the story of her vision to the deacons in the church, who must decide if the vision is from God or Satan, Mary wears her charm. The deacons, after all, are men. They decide in her favor and accept Mary into the church again. Upon leaving the church, Daddy Cudjoe asks for the charm, as he assumes Mary will have no further need of it. Mary refuses to return it, however, saying, "E's all I got now to keep me young."

Peterkin writes in a modified dialect in an attempt to capture the particularly musical speech of the Gullahs; and to a large extent she succeeds in her effort, as in the translation of Sister Mary to "Si May-e," when the lilting pattern that is characteristic of their speech emerges. There are, however, occasional translations, as in "box" for guitar, and some instances when meaning remains obscure.

In her attempts to present the patterns of life of the Gullahs, Peterkin shows the subtle blending of customs and rituals, as in the description of Mary's wedding. The brightly dressed "waiters" and the twelve little flower girls dressed in white with flowers and ribbons flying, march in a circle (dancing is forbidden). As the bride and groom appear, there is much laughter and shouting. The occasion is solemn only when the marriage service is read by Reverend Duncan; but when the minister gives Mary a sudden smacking kiss, the festivities begin. "Brer Dee took his place beside a long table under the hackberry tree at the side of the house and began bawling in a high-keyed voice, 'Come on up, brudders an' sisters! Put you presents on de table, so you can get you cake an' wine. Don' stand back.' "

Christmas is another big event in the life of the Quarter. Here, too, Peterkin describes the blend of tribal and western customs and rituals. The scene of the celebration is set against a huge bon fire at the end of the street. Crowds of men and women of all ages move around the fire chanting a ritualistic game. Firecrackers are popping, and sky rockets and Roman candles momentarily light up the sky. At midnight, at the sound of cowbells being rung, Christians and "sinners" alike gather at the meeting place to watch and pray through the night, the members seated in the front and the "sinners" standing in the back or outside. It is a night, the people believe, when even the animals fall on their knees and pray.

The numbers of people attending the parties at Foolishness where the "sinners" hold their festivities suggest that the "sinners" outnumber the church members; but here, too, Gullah traditions are apparent. Flooded by the blood red light of a great fire, the people dance to the beat of the drum and the music of a fiddle. Great pots of food bubble and cook over the fire. People drink corn liquor and sing and dance through the night, "pleasuring" themselves.

Throughout the novel the people are shown to be intimately related to nature. Aware of the tides, the phases of the moon, the seasons of the year, they predict events and relate their lives to these natural occurrences. Special, also, is their relationship to their animals. Mary's rooster, for example, crows three times to announce the impending arrival of a visitor, and Mary is able to sit so still by a shining pool that both shy birds and a gray fox come out to drink.

Details like these create a special authenticity, but the real significance of the novel lies in its themes and the carefully drawn character of Mary, who is caught within the structure of conflicts affecting the lives of the group as well as the ones which arise from her own heart and mind. The central and overriding theme is expressed through the juxtaposition of Heaven's Gate Church and Foolishness— the demands of the religion and the people's natural drives and desires, the role which a woman is expected to play as opposed to her individual needs, the double standard by which men and women are judged.

Mary is exceptional. She possesses the strength to defy the church which does not allow the same sexual freedom for women as it does for men. Her child, conceived before marriage is not only a sin but a "scarlet" sin. She accepts the condemnation of the church but resolves to repent later. She believes in Heaven and fears Hell, but she also believes in the forgiving nature of Jesus. She is unable, however, to accept a way of life which would require her to be ruled by a man. Even when July returns after fifteen years and she experiences the same powerful feelings that she had known as a young girl, she finds the strength to send him away. Nor will she acknowledge the fathers of her other children. She is proud that she is capable of taking care of her large family, that she can do a man's work in the fields, and that her children are happy and healthy. She is satisfied that her life is uncomplicated by the unfair demands that a man would make upon her; and she is content with Daddy Cudjoe's charm which draws to her the men who will add pleasure to her life.

Torn between grief over losing July and anger at being deserted when he first leaves with Cinder, Mary becomes withdrawn, feeling herself unable to cope with life. But because she is essentially strong, she is able to find within herself the confidence to take control of her life. She regains her vibrant nature and pleasure in life that is to remain with her throughout her adult years. She gives credit for these attributes to the charm made for her by Daddy Cudjoe, and she refuses to relinquish it even though she knows it is a "sinful" thing.

Throughout the novel Mary is contrasted with other women characters, particularly with her two cousins, Doll and Cinder. Doll is a good church member. She is married to Andrew, one of the main deacons of the church who is a hardworking man, a good provider, a good Christian, and by community standards, a perfect husband. But Doll lives a life so circumscribed and restricted by convention that she feels cheated and helpless to do anything about it. She grows mean and nagging in spirit, dislikes and is disliked in return by everyone. Anger and bitterness drive her finally into a violent outburst when she destroys everything in her home which can be destroyed. Cinder is not a "good" woman. She openly pursues the man she wants and runs off to live with him. but she, too, is trapped in a role that is defined by a relationship with a man without whom her life loses meaning or significance; and when July deserts her she becomes "a poor pitiful soul, living in a broken-down shack, filled with wharf-rats and water bugs. Her black skin was ashy and dried up on her bones, not a decent tooth was in her head, yet she still grieved for July."

At the end of the novel, from a wisdom born of self-knowledge, Mary is triumphant. She has had it all: her charm, her pleasures, her children, and now even, when she is ready, her church.

Although *Scarlet Sister Mary* won for Peterkin the Pulitzer Prize in 1928 and established her position in American letters, and although the novel was made into a play starring Ethel Barrymore (who performed in black face), the book has received almost no critical attention.

Bibliography

Butcher, Margaret Just. *The Negro in American Culture.* New York: New American Library, 1957.

Clark, Emily. *Innocence Abroad.* New York: Alfred A. Knopf, Inc., 1931.

Davidson, Donald. "Julia Peterkin," in *The Spyglass: Views and Reviews, 1924–1930,* ed. John Tyree Fain. Nashville: Vanderbilt University Press, 1931.

DuBois, W. E. B. "The Browsing Reader," in *The Crisis.* XIX (December, 1924), p. 81.

Durham, Frank. *Collected Short Stories of Julia Peterkin.* Columbia: University of South Carolina Press, 1970.

Maddox, Marilyn Price. "The Life and Works of Julia Mood Peterkin." Unpublished M.A. Thesis. Athens: University of Georgia, 1956.

Millett, Fred B. *Contemporary American Authors.* New York, 1940.

Richardson, Eudora Ramsay. "The South Grows Up," in *Bookman* LXX (January, 1930), p. 548.

CONRAD RICHTER

Born: Pine Grove, Pennsylvania (October 13, 1890)
Died: Pottsville, Pennsylvania (October 30, 1968)

Principal Works

NOVELS: *The Sea of Grass,* 1937; *The Trees,* 1940; *Tacey Cromwell,* 1942; *The Free Man,* 1943; *The Fields,* 1946; *Always Young and Fair,* 1947; *The Town,* 1950; *The Light in the Forest,* 1953; *The Lady,* 1957; *The Waters of Kronos,* 1960; *A Simple Honorable Man,* 1962; *The Grandfathers,* 1964; *The Trees, The Fields, The Town,* published in one volume as *The Awakening Land,* 1966; *A Country of Strangers,* 1966; *The Aristocrat,* 1968.

SHORT STORIES: *Early Americana,* 1936.

PHILOSOPHICAL STUDY: *The Mountain on the Desert: A Philosophical Journey,* 1955.

JUVENILE: *Over the Blue Mountain,* 1967.

Our leading specialist in early Americana, Conrad (Michael) Richter was born on October 13, 1890, in Pine Grove, Pennsylvania, a town which his great-grandfather, a major in the War of 1812 and a local store and tavern keeper, helped to name. His father was a minister, as were his grandfather, a great-uncle, and an uncle; he felt that his interest in the American past went back beyond them to earlier ancestors who were soldiers, country squires, traders, farmers. During his boyhood, as his father moved from charge to charge, he became familiar with sections of the state where old habits of living and speech still survived, and these early impressions are reflected in his books. In those days it was expected that he would study for the ministry, but at fifteen he finished high school and went to work driving a wagon over the mountains of central Pennsylvania.

A variety of jobs followed—work in a machine shop, in a coal breaker, on a farm, reporting for Johnstown and Pittsburgh papers. At nineteen he was editor of a country weekly. For two years he worked as a private secretary in Cleveland, Ohio. After a brief mining venture in the Coeur d'Alenes he returned to Pennsylvania to set up a small publishing business of his own. During the next decade his writing was divided between magazine fiction and several nonfiction books of scientific-philosophical theorizing such as *Human Vibration* (1925) and *Principles of Bio-physics* (1927). *Brothers of No Kin,* a collection of short stories, was published in 1924. He married Harvena M. Achenbach in 1915. The Richters had one daughter, Harvena, a poet and short story writer.

In 1928 Conrad Richter sold his business and moved his family to New Mexico. Interested from childhood in stories of pioneer days, he found in the American Southwest a region not long removed from the everyday realities of the frontier experience. Out of the files of old newspapers, diaries, letters, land deeds, account books, and from tales heard at first hand from older settlers in the Southwest, he filled his notebooks with material which eventually became the short stories collected in *Early Americana*. Chronologically and technically, these stories make a good introduction to the whole body of his fiction because they reveal the working of a specialized point of view. Projected by memory or time into a middle distance where his people act freely, away from the distractions and confusion of the present, the rigors and dangers of the frontier do not enlarge upon life for pictorial or dramatic effect, they are its actual substance. If the present intrudes briefly on the past, as it does in several of these stories, it is only because the lives of his people extend into our own time. In these stories the reader may trace the development of a narrative method. It is not the simple pastness of the past that is important but the effect gained by a useful frame of reference.

In *The Sea of Grass*, his first novel, the story of the passing of the great ranges is told long after the events have taken place by an observer who has reflected on the meaning of deeds of betrayal and violence viewed years before. On a domestic level the account of Colonel Jim Brewton and his cattle empire, of the wife who deserted him for a self-seeking politician, and of their outlaw son parallels a picture of the spacious land ravaged by conflict and greed. The same mold of reminiscence shapes *Tacey Cromwell*, in which the vividly realized atmosphere of an Arizona mining town in its boom days is the background for the story of a dance-hall fancy woman, her gambler lover and his small half-brother, and the miner's orphan whom she adopts. Her attempts at respectability fail when the children are taken from her by the town's prim housewives and her lover deserts her to make a proper marriage. Tacey's story is moving but never sentimentalized, realistically presented by a boy innocent of the social implications but candidly observant of the results. *Always Young and Fair*, also told by an observer, presents a small-town heiress who after the death of her lover in the Spanish-American War renounces the world as represented by the Pennsylvania community in which she lives. In his other, more objective, novels Richter limited his story to the point of view and the idiom of his period. *The Free Man* tells of Henry Dellicker, a Palatine redemptioner who ran away from his Philadelphia master and as Henry Free made a new life for himself among the freedom-loving Pennsylvania German settlers resisting British authority on the farming frontier beyond the Blue Mountains. *The Light in the Forest* deals with a white boy reclaimed from his Indian captors. His efforts to return to the wild forest life and his friendship with a young Indian uncover deeper meanings, the Emersonian idea that for everything given in human society something fundamental is taken away. *The Lady* marks a return to Richter's earlier method; this story of some events surrounding an unsolved disappearance in the New Mexico Territory is told by a youthful observer and participant.

Conrad Richter's major work is the trilogy made up of *The Trees*, *The Fields*, and *The Town*, novels tracing the history of a pioneer family in the Ohio Valley from the wilderness years of the eighteenth century to the period of the Civil War.

The story, following the life of Sayward Luckett from girlhood in the woods to matriarchal old age in the town of Americus, Ohio, begins with a picture of the hardship and waste which frontier life imposed on those who subdued the savage land and ends with its characters involved in the political, social, and moral problems of modern society. These books are wholly in the American grain; on a deeper level than that of action and character they touch upon matters complex and still obscure in the national consciousness: the restlessness, the violence, the communal guilt and shame, the inner loneliness, the secret fears. That Richter saw in his writing undertones of symbolism and myth is indicated by *The Mountain on the Desert*, a book written to extend the themes of his novels and to define his vitalistic philosophy. This deeper texture makes the past a necessary condition of his work, not to create a painted backdrop for appropriate action, but to effect a dimension which gives spatial depth to his perspective of meaning.

The Waters of Kronos, which received The National Book Award for fiction in 1961, and *A Simple Honorable Man* are the first two volumes of another trilogy which the author did not live to complete. In these novels he returned to the Pennsylvania of his ancestors and wrote two quietly beautiful stories of the Donner family and the past recaptured. Both books received the highest critical praise. His last two novels, *The Grandfathers* and *The Aristocrat*, were generally held to be good but not as impressive as his earlier work.

Bibliography

Conrad Richter's article, "The Early American Quality," *Atlantic Monthly*, CLXXXVI (September, 1950), 26–30, provides insight into his literary point of view and historical interests. For criticism see Edwin W. Gaston, *Conrad Richter*, 1965; Robert J. Barnes, *Conrad Richter*, 1968; Bruce Sutherland, "Conrad Richter's Americana," *New Mexico Quarterly*, XV (1945), 413–422; Dayton Kohler, "Conrad Richter: Early Americana," *College English*, VIII (1947), 221–227; Frederic I. Carpenter, "Conrad Richter's Pioneers: Reality and Myth," *College English*, XII (1950), 77–82; and John T. Flanagan, "Folklore in the Novels of Conrad Richter," *Midwest Folklore*, II (1952), 5–14.

THE SEA OF GRASS

Type of work: Novel
Author: Conrad Richter (1890–1968)
Time of plot: 1885–1910
Locale: The Southwest
First published: 1936

The Sea of Grass, *a sweeping drama of the cattle-grazing country in America at the end of the nineteenth century, conveys vividly the atmosphere of the space and freedom of the West. The novel is unusual in its championing of the large landholders over the homesteaders. Indeed, Colonel Jim Brewton stands as a kind of epic hero in the book, the last of a dying breed in the face of the petty encroachments of civilization.*

Principal Characters

Colonel Jim Brewton, a pioneer rancher. He stages a bitter but losing fight against the encroachment of homesteaders who come West to fence and farm the free range. A proud man, the Colonel claims his range as his empire, and he has only contempt for the "nesters" who would destroy it with wheat crops. He marries a vivacious young woman from St. Louis who brightens his home and his life for a time. But after bearing three children, one not his, she tires of her rough, monotonous existence on the ranch and deserts her husband for a period of fifteen years. Although aware that one of her children is not his, the Colonel rears the boy as his own and buries him as a full-fledged member of the family.

Hal Brewton, the Colonel's nephew, who deplores the inevitable changes he sees taking place all around him. He detests the homesteaders who spoil the range, and he resents Lutie's "Eastern ways," which mean new furniture, flowers growing in the yard, frequent guests and visitors. Returning home from medical school to establish his practice, he finds that the sea of grass of his youth is gone forever.

Lutie Cameron, a charming young woman who comes to Salt Fork from St. Louis to marry Colonel Brewton. She soon turns the ranch house into a center for gay parties and distinguished guests, and for a while she seems to adjust satisfactorily to her new way of life. She bears three children, one by her favorite dancing partner, a young lawyer named Brice Chamberlain. Eventually tiring of the harsh ranch life she leaves the Colonel, expecting Brice to go away with her. Nothing is heard from her for fifteen years. Then one day she unexpectedly returns, without explanations, and the Colonel takes her back as though she had never been away. Meanwhile he has reared her illegitimate son and with the force of his personality has kept local gossip to a minimum.

Brice Chamberlain, who as a young lawyer takes the homesteaders' side in a trial. Though he loses the trial, he continues to fight the free-range policy of

Colonel Brewton and eventually sees the "nesters" win out. He becomes Lutie's lover and fathers a son by her, but, being a cowardly man, he lacks the courage to leave town with her as planned when the Colonel appears at the station wearing a gun.

Brock Brewton, Lutie's son by Brice Chamberlain. Realizing as a youth that he is illegitimate, he grows up bitter and resentful; to avenge himself he turns to drinking, gambling, cheating at cards, and, eventually, to outlawry. When he is trapped by a posse and shot, the Colonel defiantly claims the body as that of his own son and buries it on the Brewton ranch.

Jimmy and **Sarah Beth Brewton,** the children of Lutie and the Colonel.

The Story

Hal Brewton never forgot the day he stood on the railroad platform at Salt Fork, where he waited to meet Lutie Cameron, who was arriving from St. Louis to marry his uncle, Colonel Jim Brewton, owner of the vast Cross B Ranch. At present Colonel Brewton was involved in a range war with nesters coming to rip the sod off the grazing lands in order to raise wheat.

On the day of Lutie's arrival two of the colonel's cowhands were being tried for shooting at a homesteader on the Brewton range. Although the colonel's lawyer, Henry McCurtin, won the case, the opposition lawyer, young Brice Chamberlain, protested indignantly that the victory would not be permanent. Colonel Brewton was contemptuous of the lawyer's warnings.

Lutie Cameron was a lovely woman, too lovely for that still-wild territory. When men saw her, she won them completely. Only Hal refused to be moved by her charm. All that winter in an academy at Lexington, Missouri, he thought of her as part of the destruction coming from the East to destroy the sea of grass he loved.

The following summer he returned to a changed ranch house. Lutie had filled it with furniture and flowers and had planted a row of cottonwoods and tamarisks about it. Guests from the whole territory came and went. Officers from the Army posts, officials of the railroad companies, neighboring ranch men—all found ample welcome at the home of Colonel and Mrs. Brewton.

The old-timers who had known the colonel before he had married Lutie hoped she would settle down after her babies came. The babies were born, two boys and a girl; however, Lutie did not settle down. The third baby was scarcely in its cradle before she was dancing with Brice Chamberlain as her favored partner. Colonel Brewton ignored the gossip which was whispered about Lutie.

Local politics shifted with the administration in Washington, for the territory depended upon appointments to its judicial staffs. For a while Brice Chamberlain had influential support from Washington. Then, during another administration, the forces which backed Colonel Brewton were in power, and the incoming tide of settlers seemed to be checked. Hal read of the change with great pleasure, but when he returned to Salt Fork he discovered that Chamberlain was still in his law office on the Salt Fork plaza. He learned that hundreds of settlers were waiting nearby for a change in government which would permit them to stake claims upon the miles of land held by men like Colonel Brewton.

Then Lutie calmly announced that she was leaving her husband and children. She explained that she had had enough of the flat grass country and the fighting between ranchers and homesteaders. She claimed she would be able to get possession of her three children, Jimmy, Brock, and Sarah Beth later, by court action.

The town was informed that Mrs. Brewton was leaving for a visit in St. Louis. Most of the people knew better. Their feelings were confirmed when they saw Brice Chamberlain with a bag packed, ready to head east on the same train. But the colonel paced the station platform, a gun belt buckled under his broadcloth coat. Chamberlain did not board the train.

A few days later the colonel sent Hal to Denver, to give Lutie a thousand dollars. He knew that his wife's cowardly lover had no intention of following her. But Hal could find no trace of Lutie in Denver. At the same time a new administration appointed Chamberlain a judge of the district court. Back in Salt Fork, Hal saw the white-covered wagons of the emigrant trains moving westward into the range country.

When Colonel Brewton planned to run the homesteaders off his land, a troop of cavlary from Fort Ewing was sent to guard him until all chances of his stopping the land-grabbers were gone.

Studying for his medical degree, Hal spent three more years away from Salt Fork. When he returned, he discovered that his sea of grass had been hopelessly despoiled. His uncle seemed much older. The Brewton children were growing up wild, for their mother had never sent for them.

One day Hal saw Jimmy and Brock fighting in the dusty Salt Fork street. Then a nester among the onlookers called out that he was betting on the Chamberlain brat. So Hal heard for the first time the rumor that Brock was not his uncle's son. Hal fired at the nester but missed. When Colonel Brewton appeared, the crowd, even the jeering nesters, grew quiet.

As young Brock grew older, he became the image of Brice Chamberlain. It was obvious that he realized the truth and resented it. He took to gambling, drinking, and barroom brawling. At last he was caught cheating in a card game. For that disgrace Colonel Brewton could not forgive him, but he continued to indulge the boy and pay his debts.

By that time Hal was practicing medicine in Salt Fork. He was glad when Sarah Beth, who had been away at school, returned and began to look after her father.

One day Brock shot and killed Dutch Charley, who had accused Brock of using a woman to help him cheat at cards. Brock was locked up, but Brice Chamberlain soon got him out of jail. When Brock returned home, he defied Colonel Brewton and said he was leaving the Brewton ranch to go to work for Brice Chamberlain's interests. This last blow to the colonel's pride permanently wrecked his health.

Brock now took the name of Chamberlain, an act which cut the old colonel still more. Brock began to ride wild, shooting up towns and staging reckless holdups. He became the talk of the Southwest for his daring lawlessness. At last he was trapped by a posse of homesteaders and held at bay in a cabin by twenty or thirty vigilantes.

That same day Lutie Brewton unexpectedly returned. She was fifteen years older, but she still carried herself with quiet self-possession. Lutie immediately assumed her place in her household as though she had been away fifteen days, not fifteen years.

Meanwhile the colonel rode out to the cabin where Brock was holding off the sheriff and the armed and angry nesters. With Hal, who had been summoned to attend a wounded deputy, he broke through to Brock, who lay dying from a bullet wound in his lung. They brought his body back across desolate country scorching in raw sunlight with nesters' families huddled about sagging shacks and plows rusting in fields where wheat would not grow in hot, rainless summers. Sand was beginning to drift among dugouts and rotting fence posts.

Brock was buried on the Brewton ranch. The stone inscribed with the name "Brock Brewton" was the old colonel's challenge to all gossip and speculation around Salt Fork. He and Lutie took up their life where she had broken it off years before, and no one every dared ask either the colonel or his wife where she had been. It seemed to Hal that the colonel had found peace at last.

Critical Evaluation

The Sea of Grass is a very good "Western," as well as a significant contribution to the naturalistic tradition in American literature. Employing an almost Homeric mode of narration and description, Richter develops a view of the relationship between land and human personality which is quite reminiscent of Norris and Steinbeck.

In addition to the three main characters, there is the New Mexico prairie itself, which assumes an almost personal presence in the novel. The moral quality of the Colonel, Lutie, and Brock is revealed as they each establish their own particular relation to "the sea of grass." In the Colonel, long grappling with and empathy for the land have produced immense courage, endurance, and directness. Lutie's own vitality and courage are, when tested by the range, found to spring from shallower sources. She must impose her own designs on frontier reality in order to survive psychologically. Ultimately she cannot endure and escapes to "civilization," the essential qualities of which are embodied in Brice Chamberlain. Brock, who in effect has two fathers, is destroyed by his inability to resolve the conflict between nature (Colonel Brewton) and civilization (Judge Chamberlain).

This conflict is also played out in the struggle between the Cross B and the nesters. Chamberlain, with his cultivated abstractions, pictures the Colonel as merely greedy. In fact, the old pioneer wishes to protect the land from despoliation by the rootless, opportunistic farmers. He refuses to sympathize with their very real plight simply because he knows that the land bears them no such sympathy. The drought which drives them away proves the absurdity of Chamberlain's political machinations and vindicates the Brewton ethic of Stoic patience.

Richter envisions nature as a beautiful yet terrifying Presence which radically determines human destiny. In the novel, he communicates this view by giving the tale overtones of Greek epic poetry. The narrator, Hal Brewton, sings of a forgotten age of heroes. Like Homer, he repeats certain key poetic formulae again and again. Colonel Brewton, though a plain citizen, is really a New Mexico king, and Lutie his venerated queen. Like classical myth, the plot of *The Sea of Grass* moves in great temporal circles, with new sons emerging to assume the old roles in the same fate-controlled drama.

Bibliography

Barnes, Robert J. *Conrad Richter.* Austin, Tex.: Steck-Vaughn, 1968, _ pp. 16–25.

Carpenter, Frederic I. "Conrad Richter's Pioneers: Reality and Myth," in *College English.* XII (November, 1950), pp. 77–84.

Edwards, Clifford D. *"The Sea of Grass* and Richter's Tragic Vision," in *Conrad Richter's Ohio Trilogy: Its Ideas, Themes, and Relationship to Literary Tradition.* The Hague: Mouton, 1970, pp. 81–94.

Flanagan, John T. "Conrad Richter, Romancer of the Southwest," in *Southwest Review.* XLIII (Summer, 1958), pp. 189–196.

Folsom, James K. *The American Western Novel.* New Haven, Conn.: Yale University Press, 1966, pp. 94–98.

Gaston, Edwin W., Jr. *Conrad Richter.* New York: Twayne, 1965, pp. 74–84.

Harris, Jim R. "New Mexico History: A Transient Period in Conrad Richter's *The Sea of Grass,*" in *Southwestern American Literature.* V (1975), pp. 62–67.

Kohler, Dayton. "Conrad Richter: Early Americana," in *College English.* VIII (February, 1947), pp. 223–224.

Sutherland, Bruce. "Conrad Richter's Americana," in *New Mexico Quarterly Review.* XV (Winter, 1945), pp. 418–419.

Wagenknecht, Edward. *Cavalcade of the American Novel.* New York: Holt, 1952, pp. 436–437.

ELIZABETH MADOX ROBERTS

Born: Perryville, Kentucky (October 30, 1881)
Died: Orlando, Florida (March 13, 1941)

Principal Works

NOVELS: *The Time of Man*, 1926; *My Heart and My Flesh*, 1927; *Jingling in the Wind*, 1928; *The Great Meadow*, 1930; *A Buried Treasure*, 1931; *He Sent Forth a Raven*, 1935; *Black Is My Truelove's Hair*, 1938.
SHORT STORIES: *The Haunted Mirror*, 1932; *Not by Strange Gods*, 1941.
POEMS: *Under the Tree*, 1922; *Song in the Meadow*, 1940.

Among the writers who have given new perspectives to Southern life and character in fiction, Elizabeth Madox Roberts is notable for her sympathetic portrayal of humanity and the poetic qualities of her style. To the folk materials of her region she added the techniques of the modern novel of sensibility. As a result the final effect of her writing is quite different from anything found in the older local colorists whose stories demonstrate an art based on pictures of the quaint and strange enclosing sentimental or melodramatic plots. Local in her choice of setting but never provincial in outlook, she transformed her Kentucky background into a landscape of the imagination and the spirit, filled it with living figures realistically and regionally true to its manners and its climate but recognizable as part of the greater human world as well.

Elizabeth Madox Roberts was born in Perryville, October 30, 1881, in the Pigeon River country where her family had settled generations before. Among her earliest recollections were a grandmother's stories of ancestors who came over Boone's Trace in the 1770's; thus the history of Kentucky became for her a personal account of family tradition. Ill during much of her early life, she lived for several years in the Colorado Rockies after her graduation from high school. *In the Great Steep's Garden*, an uneven but promising first book of poems, appeared in 1915. Two years later she entered the University of Chicago, from which she was graduated in 1921. During her undergraduate days, a member of a literary group that included Glenway Wescott and Yvor Winters, she wrote poetry and prose, winning the McLaughlin Prize for essay writing and the Fisk Prize for a group of poems which, expanded, became *Under the Tree*, published in 1922.

Roberts came to the writing of fiction after several false starts during the years of her literary apprenticeship in New York. One novel had been started but abandoned in despair and another was left unfinished when she began *The Time of Man*, which brought her critical recognition and public fame in 1926. Working on her second novel during a stay in California, she wrote day after day in her Santa Monica apartment, watched from her windows the rolling surf of the Pacific, and grew eager to return to Kentucky. Perhaps that is why the limits of the state expand to become a satirical symbol of American civilization in her third novel, *Jingling in the Wind*, rewritten from an unfinished version preceding *The Time of Man*. When these books appeared, however, Roberts had already returned to Kentucky to make her permanent home in Springfield. Having found in the tradition and life of her own region those roots and ties which the writer must possess if his work is to draw any meaning from man's relation to his time and place, in her life as in her books she made a segment of the Kentucky landscape her measure of the larger world.

This was a child's world in *Under the Tree*, a poetic anthology of childhood impressions. But the same world has grown vast and strangely cruel to Ellen Chesser in *The Time of Man* as she scrawls her name with a fingertip upon empty air and ponders the mystery of her identity. Among her people pioneering impulses have dwindled to the restlessness of the tenant farmer; her life is a series of removals through a tragic cycle of love, desertion, marriage, and the beginning of another pilgrimage when her children have begun to repeat in legend fashion the story of her earlier migrations. A work of poetic realism, the novel is as timeless as a pastoral or a folk ballad and seemingly as effortless in design. Darkness of the spirit hangs over *My Heart and My Flesh*, in which the aristocratic, futile world of Theodosia Bell dissolves in hunger, madness, and the emotional shock of murder. *Jingling in the Wind*, a less successful effort, brings *Candide* and *Alice in Wonderland* into Kentucky, and attempts a travesty on the Babbitts, professional optimists, and brisk salesmen of our industrial civilization. *The Great Meadow*, a re-creation of the historic past, is a prose monument to the pioneer: in the story of Diony Hall, her heroine, Roberts tried to catch the spirit and even the accents of her grandmother's tales of the settlement of Kentucky.

A Buried Treasure is an old morality story retold, presenting the situation which arises when a pot of hidden gold brings unexpected wealth to those who do not know what to do with it. The short stories of *The Haunted Mirror* represent further crystallization of experience, a compression of inarticulate lives into moments of significance and perception: an awakening to life in "The Sacrifice of the Maidens," the terror of love in "The Scarecrow," the candid spectacle of death in "Death at Bearwallow," the tragedy of violence in "Record at Oak Hill." *He Sent Forth a Raven*, set against the first two decades of the present century, dramatizes in mystic and poetic fashion the conflict between the outer realities of man's world and darker passions of the human spirit.

The cloudy mysticism which critics and readers found puzzling in *He Sent Forth a Raven* does not appear in her last novel, *Black Is My Truelove's Hair*. As simple in outline as the folk song from which its title was taken, it is saved from thematic bareness by Roberts' richly colored landscapes and her sensitive perceptions of her people. The novel is a prose ballad of love betrayed, a ballad with a happy ending, however, and it is written in prose that sings.

Elizabeth Madox Roberts never forgot that she was a poet before she became a novelist. From time to time, in the intervals between books, her poems appeared in various magazines. In 1940 the best of these were printed in *Song in the Meadow*, a collection of lyrics in which she spoke in her own person as a poet. *Not by Strange Gods*, a second book of short stories, was her last published work. She died of anemia in Orlando, Florida, on March 13, 1941.

Bibliography

There is no authorized biography. The first expanded critical study is Harry M. Campbell and Ruel E. Foster, *Elizabeth Madox Roberts: American Novelist*, 1956. For criticism in books and periodicals see also Harlan Hatcher, *Creating the Modern American Novel*, 1935; Edward Wagenknecht, *Cavalcade of the American Novel*, 1952; Earl H. Rovit, *Herald to Chaos: The Novels of Elizabeth Madox Roberts*, 1960; Frederick P. W. McDowell, *Elizabeth Madox Roberts*, 1963; Glenway Wescott, "Elizabeth Madox Roberts: A Personal Note," *Bookman*, LXXI (1930), 12–15; Mark Van Doren, "Elizabeth Madox Roberts: Her Mind and Style," *English Journal*, XXI (1932) 521–528; J. Donald Adams, "Elizabeth Madox Roberts," *Virginia Quarterly Review*, XII (1936), 80–90; Francis L. Janey, "Elizabeth Madox Roberts," *Sewanee Review*, XLV (1937), 388–410; Alex M. Buchan, "Elizabeth Madox Roberts," *Southwest Review*, XXV (1940), 463–481; Dayton Kohler, "Elizabeth Madox Roberts: A Regional Example," *Mountain Life and Work*, XXII (Fall, 1946), 5–8; Earl H. Rovit, "Recurrent Symbols in the Novels of Elizabeth Madox Roberts," *Boston University Studies in English*, II (Spring, 1956), 35–54; and Robert Penn Warren, "Elizabeth Madox Roberts: Life Is from Within," *Saturday Review*, XLVI (9 March 1963), 20–21, 38.

THE TIME OF MAN

Type of work: Novel
Author: Elizabeth Madox Roberts (1886–1941)
Time of plot: Early twentieth century
Locale: Kentucky
First published: 1926

Although The Time of Man *is not, from the strictly Marxian sense of social class struggle, a protest novel, Roberts examines in powerful detail the grueling and often unrewarded toil of Kentucky migrant farmers. Yet she shows, in balance, their inner strength, love of the soil, and fierce independence.*

Principal Characters

Ellen Chesser Kent, a farm girl and woman with an introspective mind and a poetic imagination. Though uneducated, she resembles the well-read Diony Hall Jarvis ("The Great Meadow") in her consciousness of herself as a separate identity. Hate fills her when Jonas deserts her for Sallie Lou, and she hates Hester for the lustful effect she has on Jasper.

Henry Chesser, her father, a restless tenant farmer who works for various farmers; usually meek and timid but occasionally roused to anger. He loves to talk.

Nellie, her mother, a simple farm woman.

Jasper Kent, her husband, a hard worker and a fighter when angered, as when Albert steals his pigs. Accused of barn burning, he is acquitted. Unjustly accused of another burning, he is savagely beaten by masked raiders. He packs up his family to take them far away.

Jonas Prather, her fiancé who marries Sallie Lou Brown instead of Ellen.

Hep Bodine,

Mrs. Bodine, and
Emphira Bodine, a family on one farm where the Chessers are tenants.

Tessie, Ellen's friend, a fortuneteller with whom Ellen wants to travel instead of living on the Bodine farm.

Joe Trent, a college boy and energetic farm worker who likes Ellen but seems to look down on her.

Mr. Al and
Miss Tod Wakefield, owners of the Wakefield farm, on which they raise turkeys.

Scott MacMurtrie, a farmer.

Miss Cassie, his wife, a strong and independent woman who nevertheless hangs herself when Scott and Amanda run away together.

Amanda Cain, a cousin of Miss Cassie.

Dorine Wheatley, a merry, gay friend of Ellen.

Sebe Townley, a kind and gentle friend of Ellen, who cannot forget his big ears.

Mrs. Wingate, an old, half-mad woman for whom Jasper sharecrops.

THE TIME OF MAN by Elizabeth Madox Roberts. By permission of the publishers, The Viking Press, Inc. Copyright, 1926, by The Viking Press, Inc.

Albert, her son, a heavy-drinking trouble-maker who steals Jasper's pigs and sells them. Jasper thrashes him.

Joe Phillips, a farmer who offers Jasper work and a house on his farm and who

later becomes interested in Ellen.

Jule Nestor, a prostitute, the memory of whom troubles Jonas' conscience.

Hester Shuck, a wench whom Jasper visits.

The Story

Henry and Nellie Chesser had been on the road a long time. People sometimes called the Chessers and their friends gipsies, and they did tell fortunes and swap horses and mules. But Henry liked the earth, and he worked as a tenant for different farmers from time to time. Only his restless spirit kept him from settling somewhere permanently.

One day Henry's wagon broke down. The others could not wait for the Chessers, and Henry haunted the smithy, hoping to speed repairs. But when Hep Bodine offered him twenty dollars a month, a tenant house, and a garden spot, he accepted. The house had only one room and a loft, but it was better than sleeping outside.

Henry's daughter, Ellen, was greatly disappointed. She hated to leave Tessie, her great friend, the fortune-teller. Ellen knew no one on the Bodine farm, nor did she make friends easily. Mrs. Bodine even ordered her out of the berry patch. Only Joe Trent, home from college, noticed her.

Joe was elegant, always wearing shoes and clothes of different kinds of cloth. He would joke with Ellen as she got in the firewood. She was growing up, and Joe awakened some spark of longing in her thin body. Then one day Joe drove past her with Emphira Bodine. He pretended not to see Ellen in her skimpy skirt above her bare feet and legs. After that, Joe would stand behind a big bush where the men from the house could not see him and call to Ellen. Ellen was ashamed. She was glad when her father decided to move over to the Wakefield farm.

Their new house was better; even the loft had once been papered. Miss Tod Wakefield let Ellen look after the turkeys for money wages. So with setting out tobacco plants, getting in the firewood, and going regularly to the big barnyard, she settled into a pleasant routine. By fall Nellie was able to get Ellen a store dress and new shoes.

In an old abandoned barn where she went to look for turkey eggs she often noticed Amanda Cain waiting in the hay loft for Scott MacMurtrie, who was married to Miss Cassie. All the field workers knew of the affair, and they discussed eagerly how Miss Cassie would lay into Scott when she learned he was carrying on with her cousin Amanda, for Miss Cassie was strong and independent. One day Scott and Amanda disappeared. That night Ellen was awakened by the tolling bell on the MacMurtrie place. She hurried over, outdistancing her father, who thought the barn must be on fire. Ellen found the old Negress pulling the bell rope in a frenzy. Miss Cassie had hanged herself.

Dorine moved into one of the tenant houses. She was merry and gay and attracted others to her. She and Ellen became friends. At her house Ellen went to her first party. Shy, she hoped desperately that no one would notice her. But in her agony of timidity she sang a ballad her father had taught her, and she was accepted as one of the group. At their dances and games and on their Sunday walks she went sometimes with Jonas Prather but more often with Sebe Townley. Sebe was kind and gentle, but she liked Jonas better.

Jonas took little part in their gay dances. He would call the figures and then retire with the old folks. He seemed to withdraw from contact with girls; some even said he had got religion.

One night Jonas told Ellen he wanted her to marry him. When he went away to work for wages, he promised to come back during the summer to get married. Ellen had a letter from him and she wrote him a letter in return. But the summer wore on and Jonas did not come. At last she heard that Jonas had married Sallie Lou.

When Henry rented a patch of twenty-five acres called the Orkeys place, Ellen felt a sense of escaping from her troubles. Their new home had once been a toll house. It contained three rooms on one floor, and Ellen's bedroom was weathertight.

The nearest neighbors were on the Wingate place. Old Mrs. Wingate, half mad, sat suspiciously in her house all day long and Jasper Kent worked her farm on half shares. Albert Wingate, the son, seldom came to the farm, and when he did appear he would often be roaring drunk. He would beg or steal money from his mother and sometimes he would turn the house upside down looking for more. When he began driving off cattle in which Jasper had a half interest, Jasper felt his anger mount.

Although Jasper prudently kept his own pigs in a corral far from the house, Albert discovered them. One morning Jasper found the corral empty; Albert had sold the pigs to a passing trader. That night Albert and Jasper fought in the barn. Jasper was stronger than his opponent. Then Albert drew a gun. Jasper wrested it away and threw it in the brush. But in the fighting Jasper forgot his lantern on the barn floor. When the building went up in flames, Jasper fled. He had been in jail before, and he was afraid.

He found work on the Phillips farm. Joe Phillips offered a house to Jasper. So Jasper and Ellen were married and set up housekeeping in their own place. Their house was tight, and Joe promised to add a room. Ellen was carrying her first child and was very content with her marriage.

The letter they had been dreading came, an indictment for arson drawn up against Jasper for the burning of the Wingate barn. Henry was Jasper's witness and Jasper was freed. At last Ellen and Jasper seemed to be free of all care; they had only to work the land and raise their family. Each year they had another child.

Following the custom of the migrant people, they left the Phillips farm. It became a matter of indifference to Ellen where she lived; a year on the Goodrich place, a year on the McKnight farm—it was all the same. Then they moved back to the Phillips farm. Joe Phillips, greatly attracted to Ellen, spoke sweet words to her. When Jasper began to go off for all-night carouses, Ellen accepted Joe's attentions. She did not tell Jasper right away about the new baby she was carrying. When she did, Jasper was bitter and swore it was Joe's. But when the sickly child was born, Jasper was very fond of it. The baby died in its third year.

When a nearby barn burned, suspicion unjustly fell on Jasper. One night masked raiders came to their home, seized Jasper while he slept, and bound him with ropes. They beat him savagely. Ellen brought him in and washed his bleeding welts. Jasper was greatly shamed.

The family loaded all their goods on the wagon and set out. They scarcely knew where they were going, but it would be far away. As they went they dreamed of a homeplace of land they could call their own. Perhaps they could even set out trees for an orchard, somewhere, someday.

Critical Evaluation

In *The Time of Man,* Elizabeth Madox Roberts draws on her own first-hand knowledge of poor rural whites in Kentucky—where she was born and reared—to present a stark portrait of impoverishment balancing between hope and despair. The tenant farmer's lot, of course, has never been an easy one, but the field workers and tenant farmers in Roberts' novel appear in especially dire straits. For them, it seems that each small advance is followed by a setback twice as large. In those days before government welfare programs, sheer endurance was their only defense against misfortune.

However, the wellsprings of their endurance derive from complex sources. For the easy assumption is that the poor work only because of need. Although necessity is indeed a compelling motivation, the characters in *The Time of Man* work for other reasons as well. The Chessers, Ellen and Henry, and the others, for example, are psychologically and spiritually compelled to work: they get satisfaction from farming the land, and they believe unquestioningly in the virtues of work. Despite occasional straying, they are nevertheless devoted to their families and have a strong sense of responsibility toward them. It may thus be said that they embody some of the most powerful tenets of the Protestant work ethic—a startling testimony, under the circumstances, to the ubiquity and the force of middle-class values even among the poor.

And the Chessers, the Kents, and their friends and neighbors are certainly poor, with a poverty that often extends to intellectual and emotional deprivation as well. For they are so preoccupied with the struggle for survival that they rarely, if ever, question or challenge the assumptions upon which the social system, or even their own lives, is based. Essentially unsophisticated people, they have no anxieties in the modern clinical sense, for their view of the present and their vision of the future are geared to the basic necessities for survival. Hence, they have worries and they have fears—of the most primitive sort. But identity crises and abstract intellectualizing do not concern them. In this sense, therefore, the novel's title, *The Time of Man*, must be construed as ironic, for the novel itself deals with people who have been denied access to the dignity of being "Man," part of mankind, and part of the human race.

O. E. RÖLVAAG

Born: Dønna, Helgeland, Norway (April 22, 1876)
Died: Northfield, Minnesota (November 5, 1931)

Principal Works

NOVELS: *Amerika-breve*, 1912 (*Letters from America*; as Paul Mørck); *Paa glemte veie*, 1914 (*On Forgotten Paths*; as Paul Mørck); *To tullinger*, 1920 (*Two Simpletons*); *Laengselens baat*, 1921; *I de dage*, 1924 (*In Those Days*); *Riket grundlaegges*, 1925 (*The Kingdom Is Founded*); *Giants in the Earth*, 1927 (translated from *I de dage* and *Riket grundlaegges*); *Peder Seier*, 1928 (*Peder Victorious*); *Pure Gold*, 1930 (translation of *To tullinger*); *Their Father's God*, 1931 (translation of *Den signede dag*, 1931); *The Boat of Longing*, 1933 (translation of *Laengselens baat*).

ESSAYS: *Omkring faedrearven*, 1925 (*Concerning Our Heritage*).

O(le) E(dvart) Rölvaag was born on April 22, 1876, on the Island of Dønna off the coast of Norway. Although his father was a veterinarian, the family was one of peasant fishermen stock, and for a time young Rölvaag also secured his livelihood from the sea. His formal education was slight, for he had only a few weeks' schooling a year. In 1896, determined to come to America, he refused the command of a fishing boat and emigrated to South Dakota. There he worked for a year on an uncle's farm to earn enough money to attend college.

At home Rölvaag had been regarded as a poor student but an avid reader, particularly the novels of Cooper, Dickens, Haggard, Marryat, Dumas, and Verne, as well as those of such Scandinavian writers as Topelius, Lie, and Bjørnson. In this country he added to his love of reading a strong incentive to learn and during the next six years achieved a brilliant record in scholarship. He first attended Augustana College, a small preparatory school in Canton, South Dakota, and from there went to St. Olaf College at Northfield, Minnesota, graduating with honors in 1905. He then returned to Norway for a year of graduate study at the University of Oslo prior to accepting a position in the Department of Norwegian at St. Olaf.

His relations with St. Olaf continued until a few months before his death a quarter of a century later. He settled in Northfield, married Marie Bergdahl in 1908, and became a citizen of the United States in 1908. In 1910 he received a Master of Arts degree from St. Olaf and eventually was honored with a full professorship. His career as a writer began somewhat obscurely during these years of scholastic activity. Upon his return to St. Olaf he had written his first novel, *Nils og Astri, eller Brudstykker av Norsk-Amerikansk Folkeliv . . .Fragments of Norwegian-American Popular Life*), but this work had gone unpublished. He continued his literary efforts now with *Letters from America* which was printed in

Norwegian under a pseudonym in 1912. It was Rölvaag's belief that close relationships between the American immigrants and their fellows in the homeland should be maintained, and his early novels were an attempt to secure this relationship. Written in Norwegian, they depicted the trials and the triumphs of pioneers in the New World.

Rölvaag's interest in the preservation of his homeland culture caused him some difficulty with the rise of strong national feeling during World War I, but criticism and abuse only increased his determination. He continued to write in Norwegian and to advocate the maintenance of Scandinavian folkways in the face of all opinion to the contrary. This was his belief and practice throughout his life, but eventually he was to exchange his native Norwegian for his adopted English in his creative work. This change was brought about through the help of the journalist Lincoln Colcord. Rölvaag had published two novels in Norwegian, *I de dage* and *Riket grundlaegges*, both of which dealt with the struggles of the early Norwegian settlers in the Dakotas. Colcord, appreciating the power of these two works, persuaded Rölvaag to turn them into English, working with him to help the novelist capture American idiom in its clearest form. The result was *Giants in the Earth*, Rölvaag's great "Saga of the Prairie," published in 1927.

Three more novels in English, *Peder Victorious*, *Pure Gold*, and *The Boat of Longing*, followed his first work in his adopted language, but no other could match the strength or scope of his masterpiece, and it is on *Giants in the Earth* that his reputation as a novelist still rests. The book, praised by such critics as Vernon Parrington and such fellow Midwestern writers as Carl Sandburg, has been lauded as "the finest and most powerful novel that has been written about pioneer life in America."

The success of Rölvaag's writings in English failed to diminish his interest in his native language or old-world traditions. He was made a Knight of St. Olaf by King Haakon in 1926 and was a guest of the Norwegian government at the Ibsen centennial celebration in 1927–1928. Although there were many such demands on his time, he continued his teaching in spite of the fact that he suffered from angina pectoris, a disease to which he finally succumbed at Northfield on November 5, 1931, three months after his retirement from St. Olaf.

Bibliography

There is no collected edition of Rölvaag's work. The authorized biography is Theodore Jorgensen and Nora O. Solum, *Ole Edvart Rölvaag: A Biography*, 1939. The best brief account of his career is the essay by Elinar Haugen in the *Dictionary of National Biography*. Perhaps the best introduction to the novels is Vernon L. Parrington, *Main Currents of American Thought*, III, 1930.

For criticism see also Julius E. Olson, "Rölvaag's Novels of Norwegian Pioneer Life in the Dakotas," *Scandinavian Studies and Notes*, IX (1926); George L. White, Jr., "Ole Edvart Rölvaag: Prophet of a People," *Scandinavian Themes in American Fiction*, 1937; Percy H. Boynton, *America in Contemporary Fiction*,

1940; Joseph E. Baker, "Western Man Against Nature: *Giants in the Earth*," *College English*, IV (1942), 19–26; Richard Beck, "Rölvaag, Interpreter of Immigrant Life," *North Dakota Quarterly*, XXIV (1956), 26–30; Robert Steensma, "Rölvaag and Turner's Frontier Thesis," *North Dakota Quarterly*, XXVII (1959), 100–104; and Carroll D. Laverty, "Rölvaag's Creation of the Sense of Doom in *Giants in the Earth*," *South Central Bulletin* 27, iv (1967), 45–50.

GIANTS IN THE EARTH

Type of work: Novel
Author: O. E. Rölvaag (1876–1931)
Time of plot: Late nineteenth century
Locale: The Dakotas
First published: 1924–1925

A significant saga of American pioneer life, the novel's theme is man's struggle to wrench an existence from the land and establish a culture despite the antagonism of the stubborn earth. It is the story of Per Hansa, a Norwegian who becomes the founder of a settlement in the bleak Dakota territory. Remorselessly fighting Indians, his wife, the weather, claim jumpers, and the despondency of his fellow settlers, Hansa is a study in human fortitude.

Principal Characters

Per Hansa, as his friends call him, born **Peder Hansen** and later renamed **Peder Holm** to fit his new life in the Dakota Territory. A strong, self-reliant man who came to America to be near his best friend and great hero, Per Hansa saves his small Norwegian pioneer community by his ingenuity and perseverance in the face of great odds. Though beset by family problems, the powerful man turns his wilderness tract into the finest farmland, superior to all the other farms in the region. He is loving, cheerful, and even-tempered, except for a few black and angry moods caused mostly by his wife's piety on the one hand and her lack of wifely respect on the other. He goes to his certain death in a blizzard for the spiritual comfort of his best friend.

Beret, his beautiful, pious, superstitious wife, who sees the giants or trolls of destruction come out of the untamed prairie. She often confounds her enterprising husband with sharp criticism of his seemingly dishonest acts, such as removing claim jumpers' stakes from their land. She suffers from a mental disorder brought on by childbirth and depression

over their hard life, but after a traveling preacher sets her mind at ease she becomes the loving wife of former years, with only her dark piety causing discord. It is she who persuades the dying friend that he needs the ministrations of the preacher; thus she sends her husband out into the blizzard that claims his life.

Ole Haldor,
Hans Kristian,
Anna Marie, and
Peder Seier, their four children, the latter born on Christmas day of their first year in the wilderness. Ole and Hans are useful to their father and mother, while the younger sister And-Ongen (Happy Duckling) keeps them all cheered by her sunny looks and disposition. The new arrival, christened Per Victorious in a touching frontier ceremony, is born with a caul or helmet, a sign of future greatness which the mother hopes will mean he will become a minister.

Hans Olsa, born **Hans Olsen,** who later changes his name to **Hans Vaag,** after his wife's birthplace. Hans Olsa, the leader of the community and the great friend of Per Hansa, is as steady as he is strong. Only once is he roused to anger when an Irish claimjumper curses him; and then one sledge-hammer blow with his great fist fells the man and a great swoop of the Norwegian's arms throws the poor fellow into his own wagon. Hans performs christening ceremonies, fills out the legal papers, opens up new lands, and generally manages the pioneering community's business. His wife Sörine cares for the Hansa child while Beret is ill, looks after the bachelor Solum brothers when they are teaching the neighborhood youngsters, and ministers gently to the needy immigrants. Their daughter is a favorite among Per Hansa's boys. Hans Olsa loses his life as the result of exposure and frostbite, and he dies waiting for the preacher he knows his friend Per will bring safely through the blizzard.

Sorine, Hans Olsa's devoted wife.

Sofie, their daughter.

Syvert Tönseten, the foolish, garrulous justice of the peace of the community. Although his wife Kjersti is a favorite of the group, Tönseten is embittered because he has no children and because he is never consulted on matters of importance. While Kjersti is beloved for her secret generosity, Syvert is laughed at for his pompous ways. He keeps the Solum brothers from leaving the community, but he offsets the value of keeping them on as schoolteachers by displaying his own authority in the classroom.

Henry and
Sam Solum, the Norwegian-American brothers who come with the wagon train from Minnesota. Both good boys, Henry shows goods sense and courage at all times, though Sam develops these pioneer qualifications as he grows to manhood. Since they speak English, they interpret for the group.

The Story

Per Hansa moved all his family and his possessions from Minnesota into the Dakota territory. His family consisted of his wife, Beret, and three children, Ole, Anna Marie, and Hans Kristian. Beret was fearful and sad, for she had been uprooted too often and the prarie country through which they traveled seemed bleak, lonely, savage.

Per Hansa staked out his claim near the family of Hans Olsa at Spring Creek. Then Beret announced that she was carrying another child. Money was scarce. Per Hansa faced overwhelming odds and thoughts of the great risks he was taking kept him awake long after Beret and the children slept. Being something of a poet, Per Hansa thought at times that the land spoke to him, and often he watched and listened and forgot to keep to his work as he cleared his land and built his house. He labored from before dawn until after dark during those long, northern summer days.

When Indians came and drove away the settlers' cows, only Per Hansa had the courage to follow after them. Only he had the sense to doctor a sick Indian. Beret mistrusted his wisdom for foolishness and there were harsh words between them. The grateful Indian gave Per Hansa a pony. Then Per Hansa went on a buying expedition and returned with many needed supplies and, what was more, news of coming settlers.

The next summer Per Hansa discovered claim stakes which bore Irish names. The stakes were on his neighbor's land; the homesteaders had settled where others had already filed claim. Secretly he removed the stakes and burned them but not before Beret realized what he was doing. She began to worry over her husband's deed. Per Hansa sold some potatoes to people traveling through and awoke the slumbering jealousy of his neighbors.

In midsummer more people arrived, the settlers who had set out the stakes that Per Hansa had burned. They called the Norwegians claim jumpers, but after a fight they took up other land nearby. Per Hansa managed to sell some of his goods to them. That fall more Norwegians came. The little community was thriving. But Beret, depressed by the open spaces and her fear that her husband had done a bad thing, brewed a dark remorse within herself. Day by day she brooded over her lonely life, and she covered her window at night because of her nameless fears. At least Per Hansa on his infrequent trips around to different settlements met other people.

When winter came Per Hansa rested. He could sleep long hours while the winds blew outside, but his wife worried and fretted. He began to quarrel with her. Soon, however, he noticed that his neighbors were suffering hardship and privation. The unmarried young men who had settled near the Hansas were planning to desert the settlement. It required all his ability to convince them to stay and to face the desolate, bitter winter to its end.

The settlers began to talk of a school which would move from house to house so that the parents might learn English along with the children.

During the winter Per Hansa became lost in a blizzard and only his tremendous strength and courage saw him and his oxen safely through the storm to the Trönders' settlement. The following day, forgetting how Beret must be worrying about him, he stayed on and cut a load of wood to take back home with him.

His next expedition was to bargain with the Indians for furs. He suffered greatly from exposure and lost two toes through frostbite.

When spring came, Per Hansa could not wait to get into his fields to plant his wheat. His friends thought he was planting too early. And so it seemed, for snow fell the next day and freezing weather set in. Determined not to lose heart, Per Hansa decided to plant potatoes in place of the wheat. Beret took to her Bible, convinced that evil was working its way into their lives. Then, unexpectedly, their wheat came up.

Another couple arrived. They were exhausted with travel, the wife saddened by the death of her son on the prairie. Per Hansa and Beret took them in. When they moved on, greater despondency seized Beret. She felt some doom was working its way closer and closer to her life.

That summer grasshoppers destroyed much of the grain. Most of Per Hansa's crop was saved, but Beret took his good fortune only as a sign that the underground trolls, or evil spirits, were planning greater ruin for her and her husband.

In the following years the scourge of the grasshoppers returned. Many of the settlers were ruined. Some starved. Some went mad. One summer a traveling Norwegian minister took up residence with them to plan a religious service for the whole community. His coming worked a change in Per Hansa's household. Per Hansa took courage from it and consolation, but deeper and stranger grew the reveries in Beret's mind. Because it was the largest house in the district the minister held a communion service in Per Hansa's cabin. Disconnected parts of the service floated all that week in Beret's head. Her mind was filled with strange fancies. She began to think of Peder Victorious, her youngest child, who was born on the prairie, as a saviour who would work their salvation.

As the autumn came on, the great plains seemed hungry for the blood and strength of those who had come to conquer it.

That winter Hans Olsa froze his legs and one hand. In spite of all that Per Hansa and the others did for their neighbor, Hans Olsa grew weaker. Beret stood beside him, predicting that he had not long to live. She put into the sick man's mind the idea to send for the minister. Per Hansa thought that Hans Olsa was weak in calling for a minister and that the way to throw off illness was to get out of bed and go to work. He had never spared himself, nor had he spared his sons. He was the man to go for the minister, but this time he was unwilling to set out on a long winter journey. Hans Olsa was a good man; he did not need a minister to help him die. The weather itself was threatening. However, Per Hansa reconsidered. His sons were digging a tunnel through snow to the pigsty. Inside, his wife was preparing a meal for him. They watched as he took down his skis and prepared to make the journey for the sake of his dying friend. He did not look back at his house or speak farewell to Beret as he started out.

So Per Hansa, on his errand of mercy, walked into the snowstorm. There death overtook him.

Critical Evaluation

Ole Rölvaag was born in the Helgoland district of Norway and lived there until he was twenty years of age. He attended school irregularly; his ambition to become a poet, once broached in the family circle, brought a discouraging barrage of ridicule. At fourteen he left school entirely and went out with the Lofoten fishing fleet. He seemed destined to pursue this hard vocation all his life, and the prospect brought him little contentment. Though considered by his family as too stupid to learn, he read voraciously, both Norwegian and foreign authors. His reading gave him a view of the possibilities of life that made the existence to which he was bound seem intolerably circumscribed. When he had been a fisherman for five years, something occurred which forced him to a decision. The master of his boat, whom he greatly admired, offered to stake him to a boat of his own. Ole realized that if he accepted the offer, he would never be anything but a fisherman, so he declined it and emigrated to America.

For three years he farmed for an uncle in South Dakota; then at the age of twenty-three, with great trepidation, he entered a preparatory school in Canton, South Dakota. Six years later he was graduated *cum laude* from St. Olaf College. After a year of postgraduate study in Oslo, he took the chair of Norwegian literature at St. Olaf, which he held until his death.

By the time Rölvaag began work on *Giants in the Earth* at age forty-seven, he had already written five novels, of which four had been published. All were written in Norwegian, published in Minneapolis, and read exclusively by the Norwegian-speaking population of the Midwest. All the works deal with aspects of the Norwegian settlement, and so appealed strongly to an audience of immigrants. *Giants in the Earth* and its sequel *Peder Victorious* are his only works either to be translated into English or to be published in Scandinavia. Springing from a European artistic tradition, but treating matters utterly American, they are perhaps unique in both American and foreign literatures.

The European and specifically Norwegian elements that distinguish *Giants in the Earth* are its orientation toward the psychology rather than the adventures of its characters, and its strain of Nordic pessimism. The characters of Beret and Per Hansa illustrate two complementary facets in the psychology of the Norwegian settlers. In Per Hansa the desire to own and work his own land, to "found a new kingdom," seems to feed on the hazards he encounters. The brute resistance of the soil, the violence of the weather, the plagues of grasshoppers, the danger from Indians, the dispute over the claim-stakes only spur him on to greater feats of daring, endurance, and ingenuity. Every victory over misfortune makes him feel more lucky, and fuels his dream of a prosperous freehold for himself and his children. Freed from the cramped spaces and conventions of an old culture, he embraces the necessities of the new life joyfully, trusting in his instinct for the fitness of things to help him establish a new order. Beret, on the other hand, takes no joy in pioneer life and is instead deeply disturbed at having to leave an established way of life to confront the vast, unpeopled plains: uprooted, she feels morally cast adrift, as if her ethical sense, indeed her very identity, were attached to some physical place. Beret sees Per Hansa's exultant adaptability to pioneer life as evidence of the family's reversion to savagery. For a man to shelter with his livestock, to change his name or give his child a strange name, to parley with Indians, to christen in the absence of a minister—all these things indicate to her a failure of conscience, a giving up of the hallmarks of civilization.

Yet she, like Per, has brought her worst troubles with her from home. Her growing despondency about Per's and her neighbor's spiritual condition springs from her own sense of sin in having borne Ole out of wedlock. She sees herself as the deserving object of divine retribution; in her deranged state she takes every escape from disaster as a sign that God has marked her for some still more awful punishment. The very openness that thrills Per Hansa with its endless potentialities fills her with dread: "Here, far off in the great stillness, where there was nothing to hide behind—here the punishment would fall!" And Per, bearing her in his heart, is drawn down in the vortex of her despair.

Ironically, it is only after Beret regains her courage and her faith through religious ministration and ceases to expect calamity from minute to minute, that Per Hansa dies. It even seems as if she sends him out to die. But from an aesthetic point of view, his death is necessary to the work itself. For all its realism and modernity of tone, *Giants in the Earth* is a saga, and as sagas must, it ends with the death of heroes. Per Hansa and Hans Olsa are heroes of epic stature and like the heroes of old legend they complement each other's virtues. They have loved each other from their youth, and in their prime their strength and wit combine to carve a new home out of the wilderness. And like Beowulf braving the dragon, they sacrifice themselves in a last great struggle with the prairie before it succumbs to the plow and the fence. Thus "the great plain drinks the blood of Christian men and is satisfied." The deaths of Hans Olsa and Per Hansa signal the passing of the time of legend, when giants walked the earth, and one man could do the work of ten; they signal as well the beginning of a more comfortable time of clapboard houses and coffee hot and plentiful, and of heroes of a wholly different kind.

UPTON SINCLAIR

Born: Baltimore, Maryland (September 20, 1878)
Died: Bound Brook, New Jersey (November 25, 1968)

Principal Works

NOVELS: *The Journal of Arthur Stirling*, 1903; *The Jungle*, 1906; *The Metropolis*, 1908; *King Coal*, 1917; *100%*, 1920; *They Call Me Carpenter*, 1922; *Oil! A Novel*, 1927; *Boston*, 1928; *Mountain City*, 1930; *Roman Holiday*, 1931; *Co-op*, 1936; *Little Steel*, 1938; *World's End*, 1940; *Between Two Worlds*, 1941; *Dragon's Teeth*, 1942; *Wide Is the Gate*, 1943; *Presidential Agent*, 1944; *Dragon Harvest*, 1945; *A World to Win*, 1946; *Presidential Mission*, 1947; *One Clear Call*, 1948; *O Shepherd, Speak!*, 1949; *Another Pamela; or, Virtue Still Rewarded*, 1950; *The Return of Lanny Budd*, 1953; *What Didymus Did*, 1954; *It Happened to Didymus*, 1958; *Affectionately Eve*, 1961.

PLAYS: *Plays of Protest*, 1912; *Singing Jailbirds*, 1924; *Bill Porter*, 1925; *Oil!*, 1925; *Depression Island*, 1935; *Marie Antoinette*, 1939; *The Enemy Had It Too*, 1950.

ESSAYS AND STUDIES: *Our Bourgeois Literature*, 1905; *The Profits of Religion*, 1918; *The Brass Check: A Study in American Journalism*, 1919; *The Goose-Step: A Study of American Education*, 1923; *The Goslings: A Study of the American Schools*, 1924; *Mammonmart*, 1925; *The Cup of Fury*, 1956.

AUTOBIOGRAPHY: *My Lifetime in Letters*, 1960; *The Autobiography of Upton Sinclair*, 1962.

Upton (Beall) Sinclair was one of the most prolific, widely read, and least recognized writers of his time. The trouble lies probably in the tractarian nature of his writings, for from the beginning of his career Sinclair was a reformer. His book, *The Cup of Fury*, published in 1956, is an analysis of the effect of alcohol, with the conclusion that other writers, had they abstained from liquor like Upton Sinclair, would have been greater writers and would have written much more. The book is, in effect, an old-fashioned temperance tract, an attempt to reform.

Born in Baltimore, Maryland, on September 20, 1878, Sinclair began his career as a prodigy. He finished secondary school when he was twelve and became a student at the City College of New York at the age of fourteen. From the age of fifteen he supported himself in part by writing stories for the pulp magazines. After finishing college, he married in 1900 and, while threatened with poverty, began to write serious novels. His first five books, published between 1901 and 1906, gave him little encouragement, for they produced together less than a thousand dollars. Before leaving college Sinclair had become a Socialist, and his political views influenced his writing. His first fame came with the publication of *The Jungle*, an exposé of the Chicago stockyards which, in its final chapters, becomes a mere Socialist tract. With the proceeds of this book, which was a best seller that still finds readers, Sinclair founded Helicon Hall, a cooperative community at which Sinclair Lewis was temporarily a furnace man. Upton Sinclair continued to write at a furious pace, also becoming a publisher during 1918–1919 with *Upton Sinclair's Magazine*. Beginning with *The Profits of Religion*, in 1918, he wrote a series of non-fictional works on the effects of capitalism in America, from the viewpoint of a Socialist. The series, which has the collective title of *The Dead Hand*, reviewed such phases of American culture as the schools, the colleges, newspapers and publishing, art, and literature.

In private life, as well as in public life, Upton Sinclair had difficulties. He was divorced in 1911 and remarried in 1913. In 1915 he and his second wife, Mary Craig Kimbrough, a poetess, moved to California. In 1923 Sinclair founded the California chapter of the American Civil Liberties Union. Several times he ran for political office, seeking seats in the U.S. House of Representatives and the Senate. He also ran for the governorship of California, twice as a Socialist and once, in 1934, as a Democratic nominee.

In his novels of the period 1917–1940, Upton Sinclair exploited many areas of contemporary life. *King Coal* described conditions in the Colorado coal fields. *Oil!* described life in the oil fields of California, with looks also at the young motion picture industry. *Little Steel* described conditions and strikes in the steel mills during the 1930's.

During the thirteen years between 1940 and 1953, Upton Sinclair labored at a series of novels relating the events of the whole world from 1913 to 1950, including World War I, the peace negotiations after that war, the rise to power of Hitler and Mussolini, the Spanish Civil War, the Munich debacle, Roosevelt's election and re-elections, World War II, and the aftermath of World War II. The whole series is tied together picaresquely and romantically by the character of Lanny Budd, son of a wealthy munitions manufacturer. Lanny Budd, a young man with Socialist leanings, travels far and wide, meets many people, happens usually to be at the right spot at the right time, and even serves as a special agent for Franklin D. Roosevelt.

More recent works by Sinclair include *Another Pamela* (1950), a twentieth-century version of Richardson's novel about virtue rewarded; *The Enemy Had It Too*, a play about the atomic age; and *A Personal Jesus* (1952), Sinclair's own interpretation of the Christ.

Probably no contemporary American writer of fiction has been read by so many people in this country and abroad or been translated into so many languages. Upton Sinclair has been a best seller in other countries when he was not one at home, but that popularity probably rests on social and political bases, rather than on any artistic values. At times Sinclair employed pseudonyms, among them Clarke Fitch, Frederick Garrison, and Arthur Stirling.

Bibliography

There are two convenient compilations of Sinclair's work, *An Upton Sinclair Anthology*, edited by I. O. Evans, 1934; and *Upton Sinclair Anthology*, edited by Irving Stone and Lewis Browne, 1947. Of primary interest is Sinclair's auto-biography, *American Outpost: A Book of Reminiscences*, 1932 (published in England as *Candid Reminiscences: My First Thirty Years*). A significant early evaluation is Floyd Dell, *Upton Sinclair: A Study in Social Protest*, 1927. A range of critical estimates may be found in Van Wyck Brooks, *Emerson and Others*, 1927; Harry Hartwick, *The Foreground of American Fiction*, 1934; Harlan Hatcher, *Creating the Modern American Novel*, 1935; and A. H. Quinn, *American Fiction*, 1936. See also Walter Lippmann, "Upton Sinclair," *Saturday Review of Literature*, IV (1928), 641–643; and George J. Becker, "Upton Sinclair: Quixote in a Flivver," *College English*, XXI (1959), 133–140.

THE JUNGLE

Type of work: Novel
Author: Upton Sinclair (1878–1968)
Time of plot: Early twentieth century
Locale: Chicago
First published: 1906

The power of this novel derives from the anger the author felt at the sociaι injustices of the meat-packing industry. An honestly told and gripping story, The Jungle at the time of its publication aroused public sentiment and eventually led to reforms in the practices of the meat industry.

Principal Characters

Jurgis Rudkus, a Lithuanian peasant immigrant who works in the Chicago stockyards. Victimized, hurt at the plant, and jailed for attacking a man who takes his wife to a house of prostitution, he finally hears a Socialist speaker and joins the party because of the rebirth of hope and faith it offers.

Ona, Jurgis' wife, who sells herself to her boss for money for the family. She dies in childbirth.

Connor, a stockyards boss attracted by Ona.

Antanas, Jurgis' baby, who drowns when left unattended.

Elzbieta, Ona's stepmother, and the mother of six.

Stanislovas, the oldest son of Elzbieta, who lies about his age to get a job.

Antanas Rudkus, Jurgis' aged father, who kicks back part of his wages in order to keep his job. He dies of tuberculosis.

Jonas, Elzbieta's brother, who works at the stockyards.

Jack Duane, a Chicago safe-cracker who shows Jurgis how to get quick money.

Marija, Ona's orphan cousin, who loses her job at the stockyards and becomes a prostitute.

The Story

While he was still a peasant boy in Lithuania, Jurgis Rudkus had fallen in love with a gentle girl named Ona. When Ona's father died, Jurgis, planning to marry her as soon as he had enough money, came to America with her family. Besides the young lovers, the emigrant party was composed of Antanas, Jurgis' father; Elzbieta, Ona's stepmother; Jonas, Elzbieta's brother; Marija, Ona's orphan cousin, and Elzbieta's six children.

By the time the family arrived in Chicago they had very little money. Jonas,

THE JUNGLE by Upton Sinclair. By permission of the author and the publishers, The Viking Press, Inc. Copyright, 1905, 1906, 1933, 1946, by Upton Sinclair.

Marija, and Jurgis at once got work in the stockyards. Antanas tried to find work, but he was too old. They all decided that it would be cheaper to buy a house on installments than to rent. A crooked agent sold them a ramshackle house which had a fresh coat of paint and told his ignorant customers that it was new.

Jurgis found his job exhausting, but he thought himself lucky to be making forty-five dollars a month. At last Antanas also found work at the plant, but he had to give part of his wages to the foreman in order to keep his job. Jurgis and Ona saved enough money for their wedding feast and were married. Then the family found that they needed more money. Elzbieta lied about the age of her oldest son, Stanislovas, and he too got a job at the plant. Ona had already begun to work in order to help pay for the wedding.

Antanas worked in a moist, cold room where he developed consumption. When he died, the family had scarcely enough money to bury him. Winter came, and everyone suffered in the flimsy house. When Marija lost her job the family income diminished. Jurgis joined a union and became an active member. He went to night school to learn to read and speak English.

At last summer came with its hordes of flies and oppressive heat. Marija found work as a beef trimmer, but at that job the danger of blood poisoning was very great. Ona had her baby, a fine boy, whom they called Antanas after his grandfather. Winter came again, and Jurgis sprained his ankle at the plant. Compelled to stay at home for months, he became moody. Two more of Elzbieta's children left school to sell papers.

When Jurgis was well enough to look for work again, he could find none, because he was no longer the strong man he had been. Finally he got a job in a fertilizer plant, a last resource, for men lasted only a few years at that work. One of Elzbieta's daughters was now old enough to care for the rest of the children, and Elzbieta also went to work.

Jurgis began to drink. Ona, pregnant again, developed a consumptive cough and was often seized with spells of hysteria. Hoping to save the family with the money she made, she went to a house of prostitution with her boss, Connor. When Jurgis learned what she had done, he attacked Connor and was sentenced to thirty days in jail. Now that he had time to think, Jurgis saw how unjustly he had been treated by society. No longer would he try to be kind, except to his own family. From now on he would recognize society as an enemy rather than a friend.

After he had served his sentence, Jurgis went to look for his family. He found that they had lost the house because they could not meet the payments and had moved. He found them at last in a rooming-house. Ona was in labor with her second child, and Jurgis frantically searched for a midwife. By the time he found one, Ona and the child had died. Now he had only little Antanas to live for. He tried to find work. Blacklisted in the stockyards for his attack on Connor, he finally found a job in a harvesting machine factory. Shortly afterward he was discharged when his department closed down for a lack of orders.

Next he went to work in the steel mills. In order to save money he moved near the mills and came home only on weekends. One weekend he came home to find that little Antanas had drowned in the street in front of the house. Now that he had no dependents, he hopped a freight train and rode away from Chicago. He became one of the thousands of migratory farm workers; his old strength came back in healthful surroundings.

In the fall Jurgis returned to Chicago. He got a job digging tunnels under the streets. Then a shoulder injury made him spend weeks in a hospital. Discharged with his arm still in a sling, he became a beggar. By luck he obtained a hundred-dollar bill from a lavish drunk. When he went to a saloon to get it changed, however, the barkeeper tried to cheat him out of his money. In a rage Jurgis attacked the man. He was arrested and sent to jail again. There he met a dapper safe-cracker, Jack Duane. After their release, Jurgis joined Duane in several hold-ups and became acquainted with Chicago's underworld. At last he was making money.

Jurgis became a political worker. About that time the packing plant workers began to demand more rights through their unions. When packing house operators would not listen to union demands, there was a general strike. Jurgis went to work in the plant as a scab. One day he met Connor and attacked him again. Jurgis fled from the district to avoid a penitentiary sentence. On the verge of starvation, he found Marija working as a prostitute. Jurgis was ashamed to think how low he and Marija had fallen since they came to Chicago. She gave him some money so that he might look for a job.

Jurgis was despondent until one night he heard a Socialist speak. Jurgis believed that he had found a remedy for the ills of the world. At last he knew how the workers could find self-respect. He found a job in a hotel where the manager was a Socialist. It was the beginning of a new life for Jurgis, the rebirth of hope and faith.

Critical Evaluation

"Here it is at last! The *Uncle Tom's Cabin* of wage slavery! And what *Uncle Tom's Cabin* did for black slaves, *The Jungle* has a large chance to do for the white slaves of today." So wrote Jack London in 1905. His hopes were exaggerated, for labor's Magna Carta, the Wagner Act, was not enacted until 1935. Nevertheless, Sinclair's muckraking classic was a singularly important factor leading to the Pure Food and Drug Act.

In *The Jungle*, superb investigative journalism and the art of a master melodramatist combine. Sinclair spent two months gathering his material; he ate in settlement houses, visited workers at home, interviewed strike leaders, and spoke to professional and political leaders who knew "the Yards." On a Sunday stroll he happened into a Lithuanian wedding and so obtained his characters. At first, publishers balked, so horrifying were Sinclair's revelations. Finally, after verifying key facts, Doubleday sent the book to press.

Sinclair was invited to the White House to advise an outraged Roosevelt on the conduct of a secret Presidential investigation. Only the charge that men who had fallen into lard vats went out to the world as "Armour's pure leaf lard" could not be substantiated.

The effectiveness of Sinclair's story lies in the gradual and relentless way in which the picture of a terrifyingly oppressive system is revealed. He allows us to believe, with Jurgis, that some hope exists in "the American way." Then, even the few positive factors are shown to be related to corruption. The democratic institutions which might have provided a means of change have all been bought off by the "Machine." The opportunity to "rise" causes men to betray their fellow workers and countrymen.

The Jungle is a naturalistic work: Jurgis' environment forces him into violence and crime; fault lies with "the system," not with him. But Sinclair's pessimism is not like that of Zola. The Socialism he preached implied a human ability (collectively expressed) to master that system.

Bibliography

Becker, George J. "Upton Sinclair: Quixote in a Flivver." in *College English*. XXI (December, 1959), pp. 133, 139–140.

Bloodworth, William A., Jr. *Upton Sinclair*. Boston: Twayne, 1977, pp. 44–64.

Brooks, Van Wyk. *Confident Years: 1885–1915*. New York: Dutton, 1952, pp. 373–376.

Chalmers, David M. *The Social and Political Ideas of the Muckrakers*. New York: Citadel, 1964, pp. 93–95.

Dekle, Bernard. *Profiles of Modern American Authors*. Rutland, Vt.: Charles E. Tuttle, 1969, pp. 70–74.

Downs, Robert Bingham. *Books That Changed America*. New York: Macmillan, 1970, pp. 144–151.

Filler, Louis. *Crusaders for American Liberalism*. New York: Harcourt, 1939, pp. 157–170.

Harris, Leon. *Upton Sinclair: American Rebel*. New York: Thomas Y. Crowell, 1975, pp. 70–77, 367–369.

Hatcher, Harlan. *Creating the Modern American Novel*. New York: Farrar and Rinehart, 1935, pp. 127–129.

Knight, Grant C. *The Strenuous Age in American Literature*. Chapel Hill: University of North Carolina Press, 1954, pp. 177–178.

Loggins, Vernon. *I Hear America*. New York: Thomas Y. Crowell, 1937, pp. 267–269.

Marcosson, Isaac Frederick. *Adventures in Interviewing*. New York: John Lane, 1919, pp. 280–289.

Marsh, Edward Clark. *"The Jungle,"* in *The Bookman.* XXIII (April, 1906), pp. 195–197.

Rideout, Walter B. *Radical Novel in the United States, 1900–1955; Some Interrelations of Literature and Society.* Cambridge, Mass.: Harvard University Press, 1956, pp. 30–37.

Straumann, Heinrich. *American Literature in the Twentieth Century.* New York: Harper & Row, 1965, pp. 11–14.

Swados, Harvey. *A Radical's America.* Boston: Little, Brown, 1962, pp. 3–11.

Weinberg, Arthur Myron and Lila Weinbert. *The Muckrakers: The Era in Journalism That Moved America to Reform—The Most Significant Magazine Articles of 1902–1912.* New York: Simon and Schuster, 1961, pp. 205–206.

Yoder, Jon A. *Upton Sinclair.* New York: Frederick Ungar, 1975, pp. 31–49.

JOHN STEINBECK

Born: Salinas, California (February 27, 1902)
Died: New York, N.Y. (December 20, 1968)

Principal Works

NOVELS: *Cup of Gold*, 1929; *To a God Unknown*, 1933; *Tortilla Flat*, 1935; *In Dubious Battle*, 1936; *Of Mice and Men*, 1937; *The Grapes of Wrath*, 1939; *The Moon Is Down*, 1942; *Cannery Row*, 1945; *The Wayward Bus*, 1947; *Burning Bright*, 1950; *East of Eden*, 1952; *Sweet Thursday*, 1954; *The Short Reign of Pippin IV: A Fabrication*, 1957; *The Winter of Our Discontent*, 1961.

SHORT STORIES: *The Pastures of Heaven*, 1932; *Saint Katy the Virgin*, 1936; *The Red Pony*, 1937; *The Long Valley*, 1938; *The Pearl*, 1947.

MISCELLANEOUS: *The Forgotten Village*, 1941; *Sea of Cortez*, 1941; *Bombs Away*, 1942; *A Russian Journal*, 1948; *Once There Was a War*, 1958; *Travels with Charley; In Search of America*, 1962; *Letters to Alicia*, 1965; *Journal of a Novel: The East of Eden Letters*, 1969.

PLAY: *Burning Bright; A Play in Three Acts*, 1951.

John (Ernst) Steinbeck's career as a novelist allows us to view a man who has enjoyed great popularity and, for long periods of time, serious literary acclaim. This double success is in part due to the fact that his books gave expression to the social and economic tensions that were at work during the period of his greatest success. *The Grapes of Wrath*, in particular, appeared at an opportune moment when the fate of the "Okies" in his novel seemed also to reflect the fate of the nation.

Steinbeck once wrote inquirers for biographical data: "Please feel free to make up your own facts about me as you need them. I can't remember how much of me really happened and how much I invented. . . . Biography by its very nature must be half-fiction." Nevertheless, the records show that he was born in Salinas, California, on February 27, 1902. His father was active in local politics, and his mother was a schoolteacher in the Big Sur country. At nineteen Steinbeck went to Stanford University, where intermittent enrollment and part-time jobs for six years did not lead to a degree. From California he went to New York via the Panama Canal by freighter and continued to live by casual jobs as newspaperman, hod carrier on the construction of New York buildings, chemist, and day laborer. In retrospect, this drifting career seems admirably designed to fit him to be the novelist of the submerged classes and to speak for those who were not able to speak for themselves.

Steinbeck's first three books sold fewer than three thousand copies, but after the popular attention given *Tortilla Flat* in 1935 he moved rapidly into the literary spotlight. *In Dubious Battle* is a study of the confused currents of self-interest and generous emotion involved in a strike of California fruit pickers. In it one sees, as one has seen ever since, Steinbeck's generous social sympathies qualified by his personal skepticism about the possibility of reform and social progress. This same sympathy played over two itinerant farm hands in *Of Mice and Men*. In these novels phases of life that more conventionally trained writers would be powerless to handle took on vivid reality.

Steinbeck's full critical acclaim came in 1939 with *The Grapes of Wrath*, awarded the Pulitzer Prize in 1940 and hailed as the twentieth century *Uncle Tom's Cabin*. Social dislocation, the private well-being, the havoc wrought by uninformed prejudice—all these important themes find expression in this work. The chief family in the novel, the Joads, became as famous as Sinclair Lewis' Babbitt of twenty years before; both are almost common nouns in our language. Critics were able to point out that the Joads are the "noble savages" of the twentieth century, endowed with much the same dignity and purity of intent that Rousseau and his followers once imagined existed in the American Indian. Critics also pointed to literary sophistication in the novel; interchapters of general comment have a Whitmanesque note, and the conclusion that some readers found shocking is a carefully contrived passage of symbolism.

No subsequent book of Steinbeck's has made a similar impact on the national consciousness, but in novels like *Cannery Row* Steinbeck underlined his claims to a class and a region as his proper subject matter. Certain veins of inverse sentimentality are easy to distinguish in both *Cannery Row* and *The Wayward Bus*; it is a self-evident truth that in Steinbeck's world the virtues of generosity and kindness are found only on the lower rungs of the social ladder, among those very persons whom more fortunate persons call "sinners." It is also apparent that Steinbeck resented the increasing mechanization of our culture and, in romanticizing the dignity of the poor and the outcast, he defended the proper dignity of all men.

East of Eden is a story which, in a sense, is about Steinbeck's own people, one that comes into a focus in a study of the reaction two brothers give to past scandal in their family; the ner'er-do-well brother survives the shock of discovering his mother's profession, but the brother who has lived for conscious purity and uprightness disintegrates when confronted by the truth. In this novel Steinbeck appeared once more as the advocate of unconscious, spontaneous patterns of behavior. The posthumously published *Journal of a Novel* gives an account of writing of this book.

Steinbeck's career, subsequent to his initial success, was one which mingled travel, journalism, and public utterance on questions of the day. At his best he touched the conscience of his generation and, incidentally, showed us how that conscience works.

Bibliography

Four critical studies important for general reference on the man and his books are Harry T. Moore, *The Novels of John Steinbeck: A First Critical Study*, 1939; Peter Lisca, *The Wide World of John Steinbeck*, 1957; F. W. Watt, *John Steinbeck*, 1962; and Joseph Fontenrose, *John Steinbeck: An Introduction and Interpretation*, 1963. See also Lewis Gannett, *John Steinbeck, Personal and Bibliographical Notes: A Pamphlet*, 1939. A useful introduction to the work is *The Portable Steinbeck*, edited by Pascal Covici, with an introduction by Lewis Gannett, 1943 (enlarged, 1946).

For briefer studies see Percy H. Boynton, *America in Contemporary Fiction*, 1940; Edmund Wilson, *The Boys in the Back Room*, 1941; Maxwell Geismar, *Writers in Crisis*, 1942; W. M. Frohock, *The Novel of Violence in America*, 1950; John S. Kennedy, "John Steinbeck: Life Affirmed and Dissolved," in *Fifty Years of the American Novel*, edited by Harold C. Gardiner, S.J., 1952; Charles Child Walcutt, *American Literary Naturalism, A Divided Stream*, 1957; Claude E. Jones, "Proletarian Writing and John Steinbeck," *Sewanee Review*, XLVIII (1940), 445–456; Frederic I. Carpenter, "The Philosophical Joads," *College English*, II (1941), 315–325; Lincoln R. Gibbs, "John Steinbeck, Moralist," *Antioch Review*, II (1942), 172–184; Woodburn Ross, "John Steinbeck: Earth and Stars," *Missouri Studies in Honor of A. H. R. Fairchild*, 1946; and Frederick Bracher, "Steinbeck and the Biological View of Man," *Pacific Spectator*, III (1949), 302–310. The most ambitious treatment of Steinbeck criticism to date is *Steinbeck and His Critics: A Record of Twenty-five Years*, a collection of comprehensive and significant essays edited by E. W. Tedlock, Jr., and C. V. Wicker, 1957.

THE GRAPES OF WRATH

Type of work: Novel
Author: John Steinbeck (1902–1968)
Time of plot: 1930's
Locale: Southwest United States and California
First published: 1939

A bitter chronicle of the exodus of farm families from the Dust Bowl during the 1930's, this work is a harsh indictment of our capitalistic economy. Searching for work in California, the Joads begin their long journey. Treated like enemies by the businessmen along their path, the older members of the family die, and those remaining are herded into migrant camps where the poor help one another to survive.

Principal Characters

Tom Joad, Jr., an ex-convict. Returning to his home in Oklahoma after serving time in the penitentiary for killing a man in self-defense, he finds the house deserted, the family having been pushed off the land because of dust bowl conditions and in order to make way for more productive mechanization. With Casy, the preacher, he finds his family and makes the trek to California in search of work. During labor difficulties Tom kills another man when his friend Casy, who is trying to help the migrant workers in their labor problems, is brutally killed by deputies representing the law and the owners. He leaves his family because, as a "wanted" man, he is a danger to them, but he leaves with a new understanding which he has learned from Casy: it is no longer the individual that counts but the group. Tom promises to carry on Casy's work of helping the downtrodden.

Tom Joad, Sr., called **Pa,** an Oklahoma farmer who finds it difficult to adjust to new conditions while moving his family to California.

Ma Joad, a large, heavy woman, full of determination and hope, who fights to hold her family together. On the journey to California she gradually becomes the staying power of the family.

Rose of Sharon Rivers, called **Rosasharn,** the married, teen-age daughter of the Joads. Her husband leaves her, and she bears a stillborn baby because of the hardships she endures. As the story ends she gives her own milk to save the life of a starving man.

Noah, the slow-witted second son of the Joads. He finally wanders off down a river when the pressures of the journey and his hunger become too much.

Al, the third son of the Joads. In his teens, he is interested in girls and automobiles. He idolizes his brother Tom.

Ruthie, the pre-teen-age daughter of the Joads.

Winfield, the youngest of the Joads.

Uncle John, the brother of Tom Joad, Sr.

He is a lost soul who periodically is flooded with guilt because he let his young wife die by ignoring her illness.

Grampa Joad, who does not want to leave Oklahoma and dies on the way to California. He is buried with little ceremony by the roadside.

Granma Joad, also old and childish. She dies while crossing the desert and receives a pauper burial.

Jim Casy, the country preacher who has given up the ministry because he no longer believes. He makes the trek to California with the Joads. He assumes the blame and goes to jail for the "crime" of a migrant worker who has a family to support. He is killed as a "red" while trying to help the migrant workers organize and strike for a living wage.

Connie Rivers, Rosasharn's young husband, who deserts her after arriving in California.

Floyd Knowles, a young migrant worker with a family, called a "red" because he asks a contractor to guarantee a job and the wages to be paid. He escapes from a deputy sheriff who is attempting to intimidate the workers. Tom Joad trips the deputy and Jim Casy kicks him in the back of the head.

Muley Graves, a farmer who refuses to leave the land, although his family has gone. He remains, abstracted and lonely, forced to hide, hunted and haunted.

Jim Rawley, the kind, patient manager of a government camp for the migrant workers.

Willy Feeley, a former small farmer like the Joads; he takes a job driving a tractor over the land the Joads farmed.

Ivy Wilson, a migrant who has car trouble on the way to California with his sick wife Sairy. The Joads help them and the two families stay together until Sairy becomes too ill to travel.

Sairy Wilson, Ivy's wife. When the Wilsons are forced to stay behind because of her illness, she asks Casy to pray for her.

Timothy Wallace, a migrant who helps Tom Joad find work in California.

Wilkie Wallace, his son.

Aggie Wainwright, the daughter of a family living in a box car with the Joads while they work in a cotton field. Al Joad plans to marry her.

Jessie Bullitt,
Ella Summers, and
Annie Littlefield, the ladies' committee for Sanitary Unit Number Four of the government camp for migrant workers.

The Story

Tom Joad was released from the Oklahoma state penitentiary where he had served a sentence for killing a man in self-defense. He traveled homeward through a region made barren by drought and dust storms. On the way he met Jim Casy, an ex-preacher; the pair went together to the home of Tom's people. They found the Joad place deserted. While Tom and Casy were wondering what had happened, Muley Graves, a die-hard tenant farmer, came by and disclosed that all of the families in the neighborhood had gone to California or were going. Tom's folks, Muley said, had gone to a relative's place preparatory to going west. Muley was the only sharecropper to stay behind.

All over the southern Midwest states, farmers, no longer able to make a living because of land banks, weather, and machine farming, had sold or were forced out of the farms they had tenanted. Junk dealers and used-car salesmen prof-iteered on them. Thousands of families took to the roads leading to the promised land, California.

Tom and Casy found the Joads at Uncle John's place, all busy with prepara-tions to leave for California. Assembled for the trip were Pa and Ma Joad; Noah, their mentally backward son; Al, the adolescent younger brother of Tom and Noah; Rose of Sharon, Tom's sister, and her husband, Connie; the Joad children, Ruthie and Winfield; and Granma and Grampa Joad. Al had bought an ancient truck to take them west. The family asked Jim Casy to go with them. The night before they started, they killed the pigs they had left and salted down the meat so that they would have food on the way.

Spurred by handbills which stated that agricultural workers were badly needed in California, the Joads, along with thousands of others, made their torturous way, in a worn-out vehicle, across the plains toward the mountains. Grampa died of a stroke during their first overnight stop. Later there was a long delay when the truck broke down. Small business people along the way treated the migrants as enemies. And, to add to the general misery, returning migrants told the Joads that there was no work to be had in California, that conditions were even worse than they were in Oklahoma. But the dream of a bountiful West Coast urged the Joads onward.

Close to the California line, where the group stopped to bathe in a river, Noah, feeling he was a hindrance to the others, wandered away. It was there that the Joads first heard themselves addressed as *Okies*, another word for tramps.

Granma died during the night trip across the desert. After burying her, the group went into a Hooverville, as the migrants' camps were called. There they learned that work was all but impossible to find. A contractor came to the camp to sign up men to pick fruit in another county. When the Okies asked to see his license, the contractor turned the leaders over to a police deputy who had accom-panied him to camp. Tom was involved in the fight which followed. He escaped, and Casy gave himself up in Tom's place. Connie, husband of the pregnant Rose of Sharon, suddenly disappeared from the group. The family was breaking up in the face of its hardships. Ma Joad did everything in her power to keep the group together.

Fearing recrimination after the fight, the Joads left Hooverville and went to a government camp maintained for transient agricultural workers. The camp had sanitary facilities, a local government made up of the transients themselves, and simple organized entertainment. During the Joads' stay at the camp the Okies successfully defeated an attempt of the local citizens to give the camp a bad name and thus to have it closed to the migrants. For the first time since they had arrived in California, the Joads found themselves treated as human beings.

Circumstances eventually forced them to leave the camp, however, for there was no work in the district. They drove to a large farm where work was being offered. There they found agitators attempting to keep the migrants from taking the work because of unfair wages offered. But the Joads, thinking only of food, were escorted by motorcycle police in to the farm. The entire family picked peaches for five cents a box and earned in a day just enough money to buy food for one meal. Tom, remembering the pickets outside the camp, went out at night to investigate. He found Casy, who was the leader of the agitators. While Tom and Casy were talking, deputies, who had been searching for Casy, closed in on them. The pair fled, but were caught. Casy was killed. Tom received a cut on his head, but not before he had felled a deputy with an ax handle. The family concealed Tom in their shack. The rate for a box of peaches dropped, meanwhile, to two-and-a-half cents. Tom's danger and the futility of picking peaches drove the Joads on their way. They hid the injured Tom under the mattresses in the back of the truck and told the suspicious guard at the entrance to the farm that the extra man they had had with them when they came was a hitchhiker who had stayed on to pick.

The family found at last a migrant crowd encamped in abandoned boxcars along a stream. They joined the camp and soon found temporary jobs picking cotton. Tom, meanwhile, hid in a culvert near the camp. Ruthie innocently disclosed Tom's presence to another little girl. Ma, realizing that Tom was no longer safe, sent him away. Tom promised to carry on Casy's work in trying to improve the lot of the downtrodden everywhere.

The autumn rains began. Soon the stream which ran beside the camp overflowed and water entered the boxcars. Under these all but impossible conditions, Rose of Sharon gave birth to a dead baby. When the rising water made their position no longer bearable, the family moved from the camp on foot. The rains had made their old car useless. They came to a barn, which they shared with a boy and his starving father. Rose of Sharon, bereft of her baby, nourished the famished man with the milk from her breasts. So the poor kept each other alive in the depression years.

Critical Evaluation

The publication of John Steinbeck's *The Grapes of Wrath* caused a nationwide stir in 1939. This account of the predicament of migrant workers was taken more as social document than as fiction. Some saw it as an exposé of capitalist excesses; others, as a distorted call to revolution. Frequently compared to *Uncle Tom's Cabin,* it was awarded the Pulitzer Prize for 1940.

Recent literary critics, taking a second look at the novel, have often lumped it with a number of other dated books of the 1930's as "proletarian fiction." A careful reader, however, recognizes that beneath this outraged account of an outrageous social situation lies a dynamic, carefully structured story which applies not just to one era or society, but to the universal human predicament.

As a social document, the novel presents such a vivid picture of oppression and misery that one tends to doubt its authenticity. Steinbeck, however, had done more than academic research. He had journeyed from Oklahoma to California, lived in a migrant camp, and worked alongside the migrants. (Peter Lisca reports that after the novel appeared, the workers sent Steinbeck a patchwork dog sewn from scraps of their clothing and wearing a tag labeled "Migrant John.") Before making the motion picture, which still stands as one of the great films of the era, Darryl F. Zanuck hired private detectives to verify Steinbeck's story; they reported that conditions were even worse than those depicted in the book. The political situation was a powder keg; Freeman Champney has remarked that "it looked as if nothing could avert an all-out battle between revolution and fascism in California's great valleys."

Social injustice was depicted so sharply that Steinbeck himself was accused of being a revolutionary. Certainly he painted the oppressive economic system in bleak colors. Warren French argues convincingly, however, that Steinbeck was basically reformer, not revolutionary; that he wanted to change the attitudes and behavior of people—both migrants and economic barons—not overturn the private enterprise system. Indeed, Steinbeck observes that ownership of land is morally edifying to a man.

Steinbeck once declared that the writer must "set down his time as nearly as he can understand it," and that he should "serve as the watchdog of society . . . to satirize its silliness, to attack its injustices, to stigmatize its faults." In *The Grapes of Wrath,* he does all these things, then goes further to interpret events from a distinctly American point of view. Like Whitman, he expresses love for all men and respect for manual labor. Like Jefferson, he asserts a preference for agrarian society in which men retain a close, nourishing tie to the soil: his farmers dwindle psychologically as they are separated from their land, and the California owners become oppressors as they substitute ledgers for direct contact with the soil. Like Emerson, Steinbeck demonstrates faith in the common man and in the ideal of self-reliance. He also develops the Emersonian religious concept of an oversoul. The preacher, Jim Casy, muses " . . . maybe that's the Holy Sperit—the human sperit—the whole shebang. Maybe all men got one big soul ever'body's a part of it." Later Tom Joad reassures Ma that even if he isn't physically with her, "Wherever they's a fight so hungry people can eat, I'll be there. Wherever they's a cop beatin' up a guy, I'll be there. . . . I'll be in the way kids laugh when they're hungry an' they know supper's ready. . . . "

This theme, that all men essentially belong together, are a part of one another and of a greater whole that transcends momentary reality, is what removes *The Grapes of Wrath* from the genre of timely proletarian fiction and makes it an allegory for all men in all circumstances. Warren French notes that the real story of this novel is not the Joads' search for economic security, but their education, which transforms them from self-concern to a recognition of their bond with the whole human race. At first, Tom Joad is intensely individualistic, interested mainly in making his own way; Pa's primary concern is keeping bread on his table; Rosasharn dreams only of traditional middle-class success; and Ma, an Earth-Mother with a spine of steel, concentrates fiercely upon keeping the "fambly" together. At the end, Tom follows Casy's example in fighting for human rights; Pa, in building the dike, sees the necessity for all men to work together; Rosasharn forgets her grief over her stillborn child and unhesitatingly lifts a starving man to her milk-filled breast; and Ma can say, "Use' ta be the fambly was fust. It ain't so now. It's anybody. Worse off we get, the more we got to do." Thus the Joads have overcome that separation which Paul Tillich equates with sin, that alienation from others which existentialists are so fond of describing as the inescapable human condition.

It is interesting to note how much *The Grapes of Wrath,* which sometimes satirizes, sometimes attacks organized Christian religion, reflects the Bible. In structure, as critics have been quick to notice, it parallels the story of the Exodus to a "promised land." Symbolically, as Peter Lisca observes, the initials of Jim Casy are those of Jesus Christ, another itinerant preacher who rebelled against traditional religion, went into the wilderness, discovered his own gospel, and eventually gave his life in service to others.

. Language, too, is frequently Biblical, especially in the interchapters which, like a Greek chorus, restate, reinforce, and generalize from the specific happenings of the narrative. The cadences, repetitions, and parallel lines all echo the patterns of the Psalms—Ma Joad's favorite book.

Even the title of the novel is Biblical; the exact phrase is Julia Ward Howe's, but the reference is to Jeremiah and Revelation. The grapes have been a central symbol throughout the book: first of promise, representing the fertile California valleys, but finally of bitter rage as the Midwesterners realize they have been lured West with false bait, that they will not partake of this fertility. The wrath grows, a fearsome, terrible wrath; but, as several interchapters make clear, better wrath than despair, because wrath moves to action. And Steinbeck would have his people act, in concert and in concern for one another—and finally prevail over all forms of injustice.

Bibliography

Beach, Joseph Warren. *American Fiction, 1920–1940.* New York: Macmillan, 1942, pp. 325–347. Reprinted in *Steinbeck and His Critics: A Record of Twenty-five Years.* Edited by E.W. Tedlock, Jr. and C.V. Wicker. Albuquerque: University of New Mexico Press, 1957, pp. 250–265.

Blake, Nelson Manfred. *Novelist's America: Fiction as History, 1910–1940.* Syracuse, N.Y.: Syracuse University Press, 1969, pp. 139–162.

Bowden, Edwin T. *The Dungeon of the Heart: Human Isolation and the American Novel.* New York: Macmillan, 1961, pp. 138–148. Reprinted in *A Casebook on* The Grapes of Wrath. Edited by Agnes McNeill Donohue. New York: Crowell, 1968, pp. 195–203.

Bowron, Bernard. *"The Grapes of Wrath*: A 'Wagons West' Romance," in *Colorado Quarterly*. III (Summer, 1954), pp. 84–91. Reprinted in *A Companion to* The Grapes of Wrath. Edited by Warren French. New York: Viking, 1963, pp. 208–216.

Carpenter, Frederic I. "The Philosophical Joads," in *College English*. II (January, 1941), pp. 315–325. Reprinted in *A Casebook on* The Grapes of Wrath. Edited by Agnes McNeill Donohue. New York: Crowell, 1968, pp. 80–89.

Chametsky, Jules. "The Ambivalent Endings of *The Grapes of Wrath*," in *Modern Fiction Studies*. XI (Spring, 1965), pp. 33–44. Reprinted in *A Casebook on* The Grapes of Wrath. Edited by Agnes McNeill Donohue. New York: Crowell, 1968, pp. 232–244.

Crockett, H. Kelly. "The Bible and *The Grapes of Wrath*," in *College English*. XXIV (December, 1962), pp. 193–199. Reprinted in *A Casebook on* The Grapes of Wrath. Edited by Agnes McNeill Donohue. New York: Crowell, 1968, pp. 105–114.

Donohue, Agnes McNeill. " 'The Endless Journey to No End': Journey and Eden Symbolism in Hawthorne and Steinbeck," in *A Casebook on* The Grapes of Wrath. Edited by Agnes McNeill Donohue. New York: Crowell, 1968, pp. 257–266.

Eisinger, Charles E. "Jeffersonian Agrarianism in *The Grapes of Wrath*," in *University of Kansas City Review*. XIV (1947), pp. 149–154. Reprinted in *A Casebook on* The Grapes of Wrath. Edited by Agnes McNeill Donohue. New York: Crowell, 1968, pp. 143–150.

Fontenrose, John. *John Steinbeck: An Introduction and Interpretation*. New York: Barnes & Noble, 1963, pp. 67–83.

French, Warren. *"The Grapes of Wrath*," in *A Study Guide to Steinbeck: A Handbook to His Major Works*. Edited by Tetsumaro Hayashi. Metuchen, N.J.: Scarecrow, 1974, pp. 29–46.

————. *John Steinbeck*. New York: Twayne, 1975, pp. 92–102.

Frohock, Wilbur M. *The Novel of Violence in America*. Boston: Beacon Press, 1964, pp. 129–134.

Geismar, Maxwell. *Writers in Crisis: The American Novel, 1925–1940*. Boston: Houghton Mifflin, 1961, pp. 239–241, 263–266. Reprinted in *A Casebook on* The Grapes of Wrath. Edited by Agnes McNeill Donohue. New York: Crowell, 1968, pp. 134–142.

Griffin, Robert J. and William A. Freedman. "Machines and Animals: Pervasive Motifs in *The Grapes of Wrath*," in *Journal of English and Germanic Philology*. LXII (July, 1963), pp. 569–580. Reprinted in *A Casebook on* The Grapes of Wrath. Edited by Agnes McNeill Donohue. New York: Crowell, 1968, pp. 219–231.

Levant, Howard. *The Novels of John Steinbeck: A Critical Study.* Columbia: University of Missouri Press, 1974, pp. 93–129.

Lisca, Peter. *The Wide World of John Steinbeck.* New Brunswick, N.J.: Rutgers University Press, 1958, pp. 144–177.

Lutwack, Leonard. *Heroic Fiction: The Epic Tradition and American Novels of the Twentieth Century.* Carbondale: Southern Illinois University Press, 1971, pp. 47–63.

McElderry, Bruce R., Jr. *"The Grapes of Wrath:* In the Light of Modern Critical Theory," in *College English.* V (March, 1944), pp. 308–313. Reprinted in *A Companion to* The Grapes of Wrath. Edited by Warren French. New York: Viking, 1963, pp. 199–208.

Marks, Lester J. *Thematic Design in the Novels of John Steinbeck.* New York: Humanities Press, 1969, pp. 66–82.

Moore, Harry Thornton. *The Novels of John Steinbeck: A First Study.* Chicago: Normandie House, 1939, pp. 53–72.

Mosley, Edwin M. *Pseudonyms of Christ in the Modern Novel: Motifs and Methods.* Pittsburgh: University of Pittsburgh Press, 1962, pp. 163–174. Reprinted in *A Casebook on* The Grapes of Wrath. Edited by Agnes McNeill Donohue. New York: Crowell, 1968, pp. 209–217.

Poore, Charles. "Introduction," in *The Grapes of Wrath.* New York: Harper's Modern Classics, 1951, pp. vii–xv.

Taylor, Walter F. *"The Grapes of Wrath* Reconsidered," in *Mississippi Quarterly.* XII (Summer, 1959), pp. 136–144. Reprinted in *A Casebook on* The Grapes of Wrath. Edited by Agnes McNeill Donohue. New York: Crowell, 1968, pp. 185–194.

Watt, F.W. *Steinbeck.* New York: Grove, 1962, pp. 63–75.

IN DUBIOUS BATTLE

Type of work: Novel
Author: John Steinbeck (1902–1968)
Time of plot: The 1930's
Locale: California
First published: 1936

One of the most successful proletarian novels written in the United States, In Dubious Battle *is a forceful book, with vivid characterizations and a sharp, angry focus. A story of the clash of social and economic forces during the early part of the Depression of the 1930's, this intensely vital narrative stands among the best of Steinbeck's novels.*

Principal Characters

Mac, a Communist labor organizer who organizes a fruit pickers' strike. After many hardships, in the face of starvation and imminent eviction, the strike seems doomed. Then Mac rallies the strikers with a stirring speech over the body of his friend and co-organizer, Jim Nolan, who is shot when he and Mac are enticed into a trap.

Jim Nolan, the friend and co-organizer who is finally killed. The son of a workingman whose death was caused by policemen's blows, he has come to communism by way of starvation and early ill-treatment.

London, the leader of the fruit pickers.

Doc Burton, a philosopher and skeptic. He does much to maintain the sanitation of the camp and the strikers' health during the strike. Things worsen after his disappearance. It is in response to

a report that he is lying wounded in a field that Jim and Mac rush out into the trap in which Jim is killed.

Al Townsend, the owner of a lunch cart. He gives handouts to the strikers, for whom he feels sympathy. His father permits the strikers to camp on his farm.

Lisa London, the daughter of the camp leader. Mac's influence around the camp greatly increases after he, giving the impression he is a doctor, delivers Lisa of a baby.

Joy, an old and crippled comrade who is killed in an early conflict. Mac's speech on this occasion does much to unify the workers.

Dick, a handsome comrade who uses his charms on women in order to get food for the strikers.

The Story

Jim Nolan's father was a workingman driven to his death by the blows of police clubs and pistol butts. As a youngster Jim witnessed both his father's courage and his despair; he saw his mother lose even her religious faith as poverty and starvation overwhelmed the family.

Older, but still keenly remembering his youth, with the scars of brutality and starvation deeply embedded in his heart, Jim Nolan became a member of the Communist Party. He was assigned to work with Mac, an able, experienced organizer. Together they became fruit pickers, at a time when the fruit growers had cut wages even lower than the workers had thought possible. A strike was brewing and Mac and Jim determined to hurry it along and to direct its course.

Luck was with them. Shortly after their arrival at the camp of the workers, Mac, by giving the impression that he was a doctor, delivered Lisa, daughter of the camp leader, of a baby. Word of his accomplishment spread throughout the area. After Mac and Jim became friendly with London, leader of the camp, and the other workers, they persuaded the fruit pickers to organize and to strike for higher wages and better living conditions. This was not easy to do. As usual, the orchard owners had made effective use of Communism as a bogey. Furthermore, the vigilantes were a constant menace, not to mention deputies, troops,and strikebreakers, all hirelings of the fruit growers. In addition, the authorities could always close down the camp by maintaining that it violated the sanitation laws and was a menace to public health. There was also the problem of money and food; the poor migrant workers desperately needed work to supply their daily necessities.

But at last a strike was called. On the night that the strikers were to sneak out to meet the strikebreakers called in by the owners, Mac and Jim were ambushed by vigilantes. They succeeded in escaping, but Jim was shot in the arm. Word of their plan for the next morning had leaked out, and they suspected that a stool pigeon was in their midst. Nevertheless, the next day they marched out to meet the strikebreakers at the railroad station, and to implore them not to fight against their fellow workers.

Although the police had assembled in force, they seemed afraid of the strikers. During the encounter, Joy, an old and crippled comrade, was shot and killed. The strikers carried the body back to the camp, and over the body of their comrade Mac delivered a fiery and eloquent speech, exhorting the strikers to carry on and to fight to the finish. This action proved to be the best of all possible spurs to bring the workers together, and the strikers were aroused to carry on the struggle even more fiercely.

Luck was with them in other ways. They had persuaded the father of Al Townsend, who owned a lunch cart and gave handouts to Party members, to allow them to camp on his farm, after they promised him that his crop would be picked and that his property would be protected. Doc Burton, a philosopher and skeptic, took charge of the sanitation, thus protecting the camp against the health inspectors. Dick, a handsome comrade, used his charms on women in order to get money and food for the strikers.

Meanwhile the owners tried everything to break up the strike. They attempted to intimidate the workers, to divide them, to bribe London, but all their efforts failed. Then another problem arose. The owners had an article published in which it was stated that the county was feeding the strikers. The report was not true, but those who sympathized with the strikers believed it and stopped helping them altogether. Dick was getting far fewer results from his endeavors, and the situation became desperate.

Mac was often on the point of losing his head, of letting his anger get the best of him, so that the strategy of the strike was sometimes imperiled. By contrast, Jim grew more able, more hardened. He ignored the women of the camp who sought to lure him into their tent, and did not allow his feeling for Lisa to become anything more than a casual, friendly relationship. Thus he provided a sort of balance for his emotional comrades.

Conditions grew worse. The strikers had practically no money, no food. Dick finally managed to get a cow and some beans, but the food sufficed for only a few days. Meanwhile, Doc Burton had vanished. Without his help, the sick and the wounded could not be attended to, and the sanitation of the camp grew progressively worse. One night someone managed to outwit the guards and set a barn afire. The barn and an adjacent kennel housing some favorite pointers were totally destroyed. The next day the owner called in the sheriff to evict the strikers.

The strike seemed lost. The spirits of the men were at a very low ebb, and they gave signs of yielding. On the following night a boy came and told Jim and Mac that Doc Burton was lying wounded in a field. They rushed out, only to realize, when they were fired upon, that they had fallen into a trap. Mac called out a word of warning and fell to the ground. When he got up, after the firing had stopped, he called out to Jim. He got no answer. Jim was dead. By that time the shots had aroused the others and they came forward. Over the body of his comrade and friend, Mac made a strong and rousing speech, urging the workers to stick together, to fight on, and to win the strike.

Critical Evaluation

In Dubious Battle, Steinbeck's fifth book—the first after *Tortilla Flat* (1935), which had brought him immediate fame—solidified his literary reputation. As an embodiment of the author's reforming vision, derived from the explosive social and economic problems of California in the 1930's, this novel is his most obviously "proletarian" comment on class struggle. It has been looked upon by critics as the source for his Pulitzer Prize-winning masterpiece, *The Grapes of Wrath* (1939). Although its dialogue captures the rough idiom of the migrant workers and strike organizers, the novel is too "pat" in the inevitability of plot and abrupt character development to be considered among Steinbeck's best work.

Yet it is notable for Doc Burton's expression of the concept of "groupman," an organic, animal-like entity which Jim, the hero, learns to recognize as something quite apart from the individual men who compose it. Jim realizes that "the Holy Land, Democracy, Communism," are only words invented by group-man to "reassure the brains of individual men" and that the group has a will of its own that no individual can discern accurately. The novel's major theme is the organizers' recognition that anger must be sublimated into wrath; only then can it be dispassionate and indifferent enough to become mechanistically effective. Steinbeck presents his story with the stark realism of the muckrakers. The idyllic pastoral vision of Frost's "After Apple Picking" is trampled by the actual brutality of the applepickers' lives; only at the end does Mac even taste an apple—and that is a withered one. Jim, a person of feeling and dreams contrasted to Mac who is "too busy to feel" because he is always planning, moves from frustrated bystander to charismatic leader to symbolic martyr. And Mac, the pragmatist, finally realizes that Jim is more useful dead than alive.

Bibliography

Fontenrose, Joseph. *John Steinbeck: An Introduction and Interpretation.* New York: Holt, Rinehart, 1963, pp. 42–53.

French, Warren. *John Steinbeck.* New York: Twayne, 1975, pp. 76–81.

Frohock, W.M. *The Novel of Violence in America.* Boston: Beacon Press, 1964, pp. 124–143.

Geismar, Maxwell. *Writers in Crisis: The American Novel Between Two Wars.* Boston: Houghton Mifflin, 1942, pp. 260–263.

Hartt, Julian N. *The Lost Image of Man.* Baton Rouge: Louisiana State University Press, 1964, pp. 74–76.

Levant, Howard. *The Novels of John Steinbeck: A Critical Study.* Columbia: University of Missouri Press, 1974, pp. 74–92.

Lisca, Peter. *The Wide World of John Steinbeck.* New Brunswick, N.J.: Rutgers University Press, 1958, pp. 108–129.

Marks, Lester J. *Thematic Design in The Novels of John Steinbeck.* New York: Humanities Press, 1969, pp. 58–63.

Moore, Harry Thornton. *The Novels of John Steinbeck: A First Study.* Chicago: Normandie House, 1939, pp. 40–47.

Morsberger, Robert E. "Steinbeck's Zapata: Rebel versus Revolutionary," in *Steinbeck: The Man and His Work.* Edited by Richard Astro and Tetsumaro Hayashi. Corvallis: Oregon State University Press, 1971, pp. 51–54.

Perez, Betty L. "*In Dubious Battle,*" in *A Study Guide to Steinbeck: A Handbook to His Major Works.* Edited by Tetsumaro Hayashi. Metuchen, N.J.: Scarecrow, 1974, pp. 47–68.

Walcutt, Charles C.　*American Literary Naturalism: A Divided Stream.* Minneapolis: University of Minnesota Press, 1956, pp. 260–262.

Watt, F.W.　*Steinbeck.* New York: Grove, 1962, pp. 51–58.

Whipple, Thomas K.　*Study Out the Land.* Berkeley: University of California Press, 1943, pp. 109–110.

OF MICE AND MEN

Type of work: Novel
Author: John Steinbeck (1902–1968)
Time of plot: Twentieth century
Locale: Salinas Valley, California
First published: 1937

John Steinbeck compresses the tragic story of Of Mice and Men *into three days with dramatic intensity (it was later turned into a successful play), stark realism, and deep sympathy. In that brief time Curley has his hand smashed, his wife is murdered, the old swamper's dog is killed, Lennie loses his life, and George shoots his best friend.*

Principal Characters

Lennie Small, a simple-minded man of great size and strength. His dream is to have a chicken and rabbit farm with his friend George Milton, and to be allowed to feed the rabbits. George tells him about the farm over and over and keeps Lennie in line by threatening not to let him feed the rabbits. The two men are hired to buck barley on a ranch. Lennie crushes the hand of the owner's son, kills a puppy while stroking it, and breaks a woman's neck, all unintentionally.

George Milton, Lennie's friend, a small and wiry man. He assumes responsibility for his simple friend and in the new job does the talking for both. At last, after the unintentional killing by Lennie, George knows that he can no longer save his friend and, after telling him once again of their plan for the farm, he shoots him.

Candy, a swamper on the barley ranch. He makes George's and Lennie's dream seem possible, for he has three hundred and fifty dollars and wants to join them.

Curley, the son of the ranch owner. Vain of his ability as a prizefighter and jealous of his slatternly bride, he provokes Lennie into squeezing his hand. Pleased that Curley's hand has been broken, his wife comes to make advances to Lennie, who accidentally kills her.

Slim, the jerkline skinner on the ranch. He gives Lennie the puppy and persuades Curley to say his hand was caught in a machine.

Crooks, the colored stable hand. Cool to Lennie at first, he is disarmed by Lennie's innocence.

The Story

Late one hot afternoon two men carrying blanket rolls trudged down the path that led to the bank of the Salinas River. One man—his companion called him George—was small and wiry. The other was a large, lumbering fellow whose arms hung loosely at his sides. After they had drunk at the sluggish water and washed their faces, George sat back with his legs drawn up. His friend Lennie imitated him.

The two men were on their way to a ranch where they had been hired to buck barley. Lennie had cost them their jobs at their last stop in Weed, where he had been attracted by a girl's red dress. Grabbing at her clothes, he had been so frightened by her screaming that George had been forced to hit him over the head to make him let go. They had run away to avoid a lynching.

After George had lectured his companion about letting him talk to their new employer when they were interviewed, Lennie begged for a story he had already heard many times. It was the story of the farm they would own one day. It would have chickens, rabbits, and a vegetable garden, and Lennie would be allowed to feed the rabbits.

The threat that Lennie would not be allowed to care for the rabbits if he did not obey caused him to keep still when they arrived at the ranch the next day. In spite of George's precautions, their new boss was not easy to deal with. He was puzzled because George gave Lennie no chance to talk.

While the men were waiting for the lunch gong, the owner's son Curley came in, ostensibly looking for his father, but actually to examine the new men. After he had gone, Candy, the swamper who swept out the bunkhouse, warned them that Curley was a prizefighter who delighted in picking on the men and that he was extremely jealous of his slatternly bride.

Lennie had a foreboding of evil and wanted to leave, but the two men had no money with which to continue their wanderings. But by evening Lennie was happy again. The dog belonging to Slim, the jerkline skinner, had had pups the night before, and Slim had given one to simple-minded Lennie.

Slim was easy to talk to. While George played solitaire that evening, he told his new friend of the incident in Weed. He had just finished his confidence when Lennie came in, hiding his puppy inside his coat. George told Lennie to take the pup back to the barn. He said that Lennie would probably spend the night there with the animal.

The bunkhouse had been deserted by all except old Candy when Lennie asked once more to hear the story of the land they would some day buy. At its conclusion the swamper spoke up. He had three hundred and fifty dollars saved, he said, and he knew he would not be able to work many more years. He wanted to join George and Lennie in their plan. George finally agreed, for with Candy's money they would soon be able to buy the farm they had in mind.

Lennie was still grinning with delighted anticipation when Curley came to the bunkhouse in search of his wife. The men had been taunting him about her wantonness when he spied Lennie's grin. Infuriated with the thought that he was being laughed at, Curley attacked the larger man. Lennie, remembering George's warnings, did nothing to defend himself at first. Finally he grabbed Curley's hand and squeezed. When he let go, every bone had been crushed.

Curley was driven off to town for treatment, with instructions from Slim to say that he had caught his hand in a machine. Slim warned him that the truth would soon be known if he failed to tell a convincing story.

After the others had started to town with Curley, Lennie went to talk to Crooks, the colored stable buck, who had his quarters in the harness room instead of the bunkhouse. Crooks' coolness quickly melted before Lennie's innocence. While Lennie told the colored man about the dream of the farm, Candy joined them. They were deep in discussion of the plan when Curley's wife appeared, looking for her husband. The story about her husband and the machine did not deceive her, and she hinted that she was pleased with Lennie for what he had done. Having put an end to the men's talk, she slipped out noiselessly when she heard the others come back from town.

Lennie was in the barn petting his puppy. The other workmen pitched horseshoes outside. Lennie did not realize that the dog was already dead from the mauling he had innocently given it. As he sat in the straw, Curley's wife came around the corner of the stalls. He would not speak to her at first, afraid that he would not get to feed the rabbits if he did anything wrong, but the girl gradually managed to draw his attention to her and persuaded him to stroke her hair.

When she tried to pull her head away, Lennie held on, growing angry as she tried to yell. Finally he shook her violently and broke her neck.

Curley's wife was lying half-buried in the hay when Candy came into the barn in search of Lennie. Finding Lennie gone, he called George, and while the latter went off to get a gun the swamper spread the alarm. The opportunity to catch the murderer was what Curley had been looking for. Carrying a loaded shotgun, he started off with the men, George among them.

It was George who found Lennie hiding in the bushes at the edge of a stream. Hurriedly, for the last time, he told his companion the story of the rabbit farm, and when he had finished Lennie begged that they go at once to look for the farm. Knowing that Lennie could not escape from Curley and the other men who were searching for him, George put the muzzle of his gun to the back of his friend's head and pulled the trigger. Lennie was dead when the others arrived.

Critical Evaluation

Five years before *Of Mice and Men* appeared Steinbeck showed his interest in what he called "unfinished children of nature," in a collection of short stories entitled *Pastures of Heaven*. Lennie Small is perhaps the finest expression of the writer's lifelong sympathy for the abused common man. Like *Tortilla Flat,* which brought Steinbeck immediate fame in 1935, and *In Dubious Battle* (1936), *Of Mice and Men* is set in the Salinas Valley of California where the writer himself spent many years as a migrant worker like the characters he depicts. Although he would go on to win the Pulitzer Prize for *The Grapes of Wrath* in 1939, and the Nobel Prize in 1962, Steinbeck's artistic temperament remained wedded to his concern with working-class problems that developed from his experience in this valley.

Yet *Of Mice and Men* is in no way a political statement. Its simplicity and grace make it a universal metaphor for the inhumanity of the human condition. Lennie—with his "shapeless face," his bear-like movements, his brute gentleness, and his selective forgetfulness—is one of the most sympathetic melodramatic figures of modern fiction (akin to Faulkner's Benjy, but more immediately accessible). He is not only convincingly childlike but is also consciously so—because he knows what will reinforce his relationship with George, the one thing he values besides all small, soft creatures. But just as Lennie's uncontrollable strength destroys those creatures inevitably, Lennie himself must be destroyed. George destroys him, out of love, because George recognizes that, like Candy's dog, Lennie does not belong in a world that does not protect the innocent from the inhumanity of selfish men. George's tragic action is the last gesture in their extraordinary relationship—a relationship the others fail to understand because it is based on tenderness rather than greed.

Bibliography

Allen, Walter. *The Modern Novel in Britain and the United States.* New York: Dutton, 1964, pp. 163–164.

Beach, Joseph Warren. *American Fiction: 1920–1940.* New York: Russell and Russell, 1960, pp. 322–324.

Burgum, Edwin Berry. "The Sensibility of John Steinbeck," in *Steinbeck and His Critics: A Record of Twenty-five Years.* Edited by E.W. Tedlock, Jr. and C.V. Wicker. Albuquerque: University of New Mexico Press, 1957, pp. 109–112.

Dusenbury, Winifred L. *The Themes of Loneliness in Modern American Drama.* Gainesville: University of Florida Press, 1960, pp. 45–50.

Fontenrose, Joseph. *John Steinbeck: An Introduction and Interpretation.* New York: Holt, Rinehart, 1963, pp. 53–59.

French, Warren. *John Steinbeck.* New York: Twayne, 1975, pp. 87–91.

Geismar, Maxwell. *Writers in Crisis.* Boston: Houghton Mifflin, 1942, pp. 237–270.

Gurko, Leo. *Angry Decade.* New York: Harper & Row, 1968, pp. 217–219.

Levant, Howard. *The Novels of John Steinbeck: A Critical Study.* Columbia: University of Missouri Press, 1974, pp. 130–144.

Lisca, Peter. "Motif and Pattern in *Of Mice and Men*," in *Modern Fiction Studies.* II (Winter, 1956–1957), pp. 228–234. Reprinted in his *The Wide*

World of John Steinbeck. New Brunswick, N.J.: Rutgers University Press, 1958, pp. 130–143.

Marks, Lester.   *Thematic Structure in the Novels of John Steinbeck.* New York: Humanities Press, 1969, pp. 58–65.

Moore, Harry T.   *The Novels of John Steinbeck: A First Critical Study.* Port Washington, N.Y.: Kennikat, 1968, pp. 47–52.

Slater, John F.   *"Of Mice and Men,"* in *A Study Guide to Steinbeck: A Handbook to His Major Works.* Edited by Tetsumaro Hayashi. Metuchen, N.J.: Scarecrow, 1974, pp. 129–154.

Spilka, Mark.   "Of George and Lennie and Curley's Wife: Sweet Violence in Steinbeck's Eden," in *Modern Fiction Studies.* XX (1974), pp. 169–179.

Watt, F.W.   *Steinbeck.* New York: Grove, 1962, pp. 58–62.

Wilson, Edmund.   "The Californians: Storm and Steinbeck," in *New Republic.* CIII (December 9, 1940), pp. 784–787.

BOOTH TARKINGTON

Born: Indianapolis, Indiana (July 29, 1869)
Died: Indianapolis (May 19, 1946)

Principal Works

NOVELS: *The Gentleman from Indiana*, 1899; *Monsieur Beaucaire*, 1900; *The Conquest of Canaan*, 1905; *His Own People*, 1907; *The Flirt*, 1913; *Penrod*, 1914; *The Turmoil*, 1915; *Penrod and Sam*, 1916; *Seventeen*, 1916; *The Magnificent Ambersons*, 1918; *Ramsey Milholland*, 1919; *Alice Adams*, 1921; *Gentle Julia*, 1922; *The Midlander*, 1923; *Growth*, 1927 (*The Turmoil, The Magnificent Ambersons*, and *The Midlander*); *Penrod Jashber*, 1929; *Young Mrs. Greeley*, 1929; *Presenting Lily Mars*, 1933; *Little Orvie*, 1934; *The Heritage of Hatcher Ide*, 1941; *The Fighting Littles*, 1941; *Kate Fennigate*, 1943; *Image of Josephine*, 1945.

SHORT STORIES: *In the Arena*, 1905; *The Fascinating Stranger and Other Stories*, 1923.

PLAYS: *The Guardian*, 1907 (with Harry Leon Wilson); *Mister Antonio*, 1916; *The Gibson Upright*, 1919 (with Harry Leon Wilson): *Clarence*, 1919.

REMINISCENCES: *The World Does Move*, 1928.

(Newton) Booth Tarkington was born in Indianapolis, Indiana, on July 29, 1869. He attended Phillips Exeter Academy and Purdue University and was graduated from Princeton. Primarily interested in art, he preferred to make drawing his career, until financial necessity turned him to writing. After an inauspicious beginning he gradually achieved loyal popularity from readers and considerable acclaim from critics. His first popular success in fiction was *Monsieur Beaucaire*, a romantic novelette that helped call attention to his first novel, *The Gentleman from Indiana*, which had appeared in 1899. Today, Tarkington is perhaps most widely known for his stories of youth and teen-agers: *Penrod, Penrod and Sam, Penrod Jashber*, and *Seventeen*. These are "American Boy" stories, comic but very human and appealing. Perhaps his best novel, *Alice Adams* appeared in 1921 and won the Pulitzer Prize for fiction in 1922. *The Magnificent Ambersons* had earlier won the same prize. In 1933 Tarkington was awarded the Gold Medal of the National Institute of Arts and Letters. Tarkington was twice married, to Miss Laurel Louisa Fletcher, of Indianapolis, in 1902, and to Miss Susannah Robinson, of Dayton, Ohio, in 1912. He was a prolific writer, with successful ventures in the short story and the drama, but it is chiefly as a novelist that he is remembered. Among his other representative novels are *The Conquest of Canaan, His Own People, The Flirt, The Turmoil, Ramsey Milholland, Gentle Julia, The Midlander*, and *Young Mrs. Greeley*. A trilogy dealing with the industrial development of the Middle West came out in 1927 under the title of *Growth*;

it included *The Turmoil, The Magnificent Ambersons*, and *The Midlander*. Tarkington, who suffered difficulties with his eyesight for years, became totally blind in 1930, but his sight was partially restored by a series of operations. For the last thirty-five years of his life he divided his time between his home in Indianapolis and his house in Kennebunkport, Maine. He died May 19, 1946, in Indianapolis.

Bibliography

The only full-length biography is James Woodress, *Booth Tarkington: Gentleman from Indiana*, 1955, a work based extensively on the Tarkington papers at Princeton University. Two other works indispensible to Tarkington studies are the unfinished autobiography, *As It Seems to Me, Saturday Evening Post*, CCXIV (July 5–August 23, 1941); and Dorothy R. Russo and Thelma L. Sullivan, *A Bibliography of Booth Tarkington, 1869–1946*, 1949. See also Robert C. Holliday, *Booth Tarkington*, 1918; Asa D. Dickinson, *Booth Tarkington: A Sketch*, 1926, (pamphlet); and Kenneth Roberts, *I Wanted to Write*, 1949. Two articles are W. T. Scott, "Tarkington and the 1920's," *American Scholar*, XXVI (1957), 181–194; and John D. Seelye, "That Magnificent Boy-Penrod Once Again," *Virginia Quarterly Review*, XXXVII (1960), 591–604.

ALICE ADAMS

Type of work: Novel
Author: Booth Tarkington (1869–1946)
Time of plot: Early twentieth century
Locale: A small Midwestern town
First published: 1921

Tarkington's modest style creates a quiet atmosphere and tolerant, sympathetic stance from which the author can make observations that are often sharply critical of small-town manners and morals.

Principal Characters

Alice Adams, a dreamer whose family is not rich enough to send her to college. She tries to attract attenion by affected mannerisms. Disappointed in every ambition, she finally stops daydreaming and, reluctantly, enrolls in Frincke's Business College.

Virgil Adams, her father, an employee of the Lamb Wholesale Drug Company and part discoverer of the formula for a special glue. The co-discoverer has died. The failure of Virgil's project to manufacture the glue is responsible for his having a stroke.

Mrs. Adams, Alice's socially ambitious mother, who nags her husband to make more money but ends up taking in boarders.

Walter Adams, their son, who has stolen three hundred dollars from his employer. He is more interested in gambling with waiters than in dancing with his sister at Mildred's party.

Mildred Palmer, Alice's best friend.

Frank Dowling, a fat, unpopular boy who is the only one attentive to Alice at the dance.

Arthur Russell, a distant relative of the Palmers who is momentarily interested in Alice, then finds her posing repulsive.

Mr. Lamb, who builds his own glue factory and destroys Virgil Adams' prospects.

Charley Lohr, who brings the Adamses news that the absconding Walter has left town.

The Story

Alice Adams had been reared in a town in which each person's business was everybody's business, sooner or later. Her father, Virgil Adams, worked for Lamb and Company, a wholesale drug factory in the town, where he also obtained a job for his son Walter. Alice had been one of the town's young smart set while she was in high school, but when the others of the group had gone to college Alice had remained behind because of economic reasons. As time passed she felt increasingly out of things. To compensate for a lack of attention, Alice often attracted notice to herself by affected mannerisms.

Alice had been invited to a dance given by Mildred Palmer, who, according to Alice, was her best friend. Walter had also been invited so as to provide her with an escort. Getting Walter to go out with Alice, however, was a process which took all the coaxing and cajoling that Mrs. Adams could muster. On the night of the dance Alice departed in a made-over formal, carrying a homemade bouquet of wild violets, and with an unwilling escort who was driving a borrowed flivver. The party itself turned out no better than its inauspicious beginning. Alice was very much a wallflower except for the attentions of Frank Dowling, a fat, unpopular boy. Toward the end of the evening Mildred Palmer introduced Alice to a new young man, Arthur Russell, a distant relative of the Palmers. It was rumored that Mildred and Arthur would become engaged in the near future. Alice asked Arthur to find her brother, whom she had not seen since the second dance. When Arthur found Walter shooting dice with the Negro waiters in the cloakroom Alice was mortified.

A week later Alice accidently met Arthur Russell and he walked home with her. During their walk Alice learned that Arthur had asked for an introduction to her at the dance. Flattered, Alice built up for herself a background which did not exist. Arthur asked for permission to call on her.

But Arthur failed to appear the next evening. Several nights later, after Alice had helped with the dishes, she was sitting on the front porch when Arthur finally came to call. To hold his interest, Alice asked him to promise not to listen to any gossip about her. As time went on, she repeated her fear that someone would talk about her. Her protestations were something Arthur could not understand.

For many years Mrs. Adams had been trying to convince her husband to leave his job at Lamb and Company and go into business for himself. Her idea was that he could start a factory to manufacture glue from a formula he and another young man at Lamb and Company had discovered years before. Meanwhile the other man had died and the only people who knew the formula were Mr. Lamb and Mr. Adams. Mr. Lamb had lost interest in the formula. Mr. Adams felt that his wife's scheme was dishonest, and in spite of her nagging he refused to do as she wished. But after Mr. Lamb's granddaughter failed to invite Alice to a dinner party she was giving, Mrs. Adams convinced her husband that the true reason was their own poor economic status. In that way she finally won his grudging agreement to her plan.

Without delay, Mr. Adams began to organize his new business. Walter refused to join him because Mr. Adams would not give him three hundred dollars immediately. But Mr. Adams needed all his money for his new project. He sent Mr. Lamb a letter of resignation, telling of his intention to start a glue factory. He expected some sort of action or at least an outburst on Mr. Lamb's part when he read the letter, but nothing was forthcoming. He went ahead with his arrangements and began to manufacture his glue.

Alice's mother decided the time had come to invite Arthur to dinner, and Alice agreed with great reluctance. An elaborate meal was prepared; a maid was hired to serve, and Mr. Adams was forced into his dress suit. But the dinner was a dismal failure, and everyone, including Arthur, was extremely uncomfortable. Arthur had more reason than the rest for being so, for he had heard Mr. Adam's venture discussed in the most unfavorable light. He had also heard some uncomplimentary remarks about Alice. Before dinner was over, a friend named Charley Lohr came to speak to Mr. Adams. When both her mother and father failed to return to the table, Alice and Arthur went out to the porch. She soon dismissed him, knowing that something had come between them. When she went into the house, Charley Lohr informed her that her brother had been caught short in his accounts and had skipped town.

Mr. Adams decided to get a loan from the bank the first thing in the morning in order to pay back what Walter had taken. However, when he went to his factory in the morning, he discovered that the building which had been erected across the street from his was in reality another glue factory, one started by Mr. Lamb. His hopes of obtaining money on his factory were shattered. Then Mr. Lamb rode up to gloat over his retaliation. Mr. Adams angrily accused Mr. Lamb of waiting until Walter got into trouble before announcing his new factory and thereby making Mr. Adams' property practically worthless. He worked himself into such a state that he had a stroke.

Mr. Lamb, feeling sorry for Mr. Adams, offered to buy him out, and Mr. Adams was forced to agree. Now there was no income in the family. Mrs. Adams decided to take in boarders, and Alice finally made up her mind to enroll in Frincke's Business College. She had lost more than Arthur Russell; she had lost her daydreams as well.

Critical Evaluation

Alice Adams and Booth Tarkington's other masterpiece of Americana, *The Magnificent Ambersons,* together present a surprisingly broad and perceptive picture of small town life in the first decades of the twentieth century. Because he was writing of people and places he knew intimately, the author brought an unusual understanding and insight to his portrayals. Tarkington's style, deceptively simple, actually is the perfect vehicle for his stories; his prose is clean and supple and does not distract from the vivid characterizations or well-thought-out plots. He was a superior craftsman, and *Alice Adams* is an excellent example of his sensitivity and skill.

The novel hinges on the personality of Alice. Tarkington sees into this young girl with amazing insight; her little dreams, her self-delusions, her battles with reality, all are portrayed with a touching honesty and affection.

The scene in which Alice, dressed in simple but good taste attends a party full of pushy, overdressed small town "society belles" is a pointed commentary on American taste and social standards.

The reader cares deeply about Alice's little humiliations and attempts to rise beyond the limitations of her station. Her efforts to make her modest home nice and to provide a fine dinner when the young man comes to visit are painfully futile, however well-intentioned. Her little tragedies are the tragedies of everyday life for millions of people, and are captured with a deft hand. Many readers will pause and think, "Yes, that's true, that's the way it is." For many of the efforts and emotions described in the novel are so true to human nature that they do not date any more than those of the Bennett sisters in Jane Austen's *Pride and Prejudice*.

Alice Adams won the Pulitzer Prize for fiction in 1921, but Tarkington's novels have suffered a temporary eclipse. There is no doubt, however, that *Alice Adams* will endure as an honest and touching picture of real people in genuine struggles with their world.

Bibliography

Baldwin, Charles C. *The Men Who Make Our Novels*. New York: Dodd, Mead, 1924, pp. 477–478.

Collins, Joseph. "The New Mr. Tarkington," in *Bookman*. LXV (March, 1927), pp. 12–21.

Crowley, Richard. "Booth Tarkington: Time for Revival," in *America*. XC (February 13, 1954), pp. 508–510.

Fennimore, Keith J. *Booth Tarkington*. New York: Twayne, 1974, pp. 85–89.

Herron, Ima Honaker. *The Small Town in American Literature*. Durham, N.C.: Duke University Press, 1939, pp. 341–344.

Loggins, Vernon. "Booth Tarkington," in *I Hear America . . . Literature in the United States Since 1900*. New York: Biblo and Tanner, 1967, pp. 342–343.

Lovett, Robert Morss. "Alice of the Adamses," in *New Republic*. XXXII (June 29, 1921), pp. 147–148.

Meyer, Gerard P. "Afterword," in *Alice Adams*. New York: New American Library, 1961.

Oriens, G. Harrison. *A Short History of American Literature*. New York: Crofts, 1940, p. 285.

Scott, Winfield Townley. "Tarkington and the 1920's," in *American Scholar*. XXVI (Spring, 1957), pp. 181–194. Reprinted in his *Exiles and Fabrications*. Garden City, N.Y.: Doubleday, 1961, pp. 95–113.

Sorkin, Adam J. " 'She Doesn't Last, Apparently': A Reconsideration of Booth Tarkington's *Alice Adams*," in *American Literature*. XLVI (1974), pp. 182–199.

Stuckey, W.J. *The Pulitzer Prize Novels: A Critical Backward Look.* Norman: University of Oklahoma Press, 1966, pp. 35–39.

Van Doren, Carl. *The American Novel, 1789–1939.* New York: Macmillan, 1947, pp. 263–264.

Wagenknecht, Edward. *Cavalcade of the American Novel.* New York: Holt, 1952, pp. 247–248.

Woodress, James *Booth Tarkington, Gentleman from Indiana.* Philadelphia: Lippincott, 1954, pp. 245–250.

Wyatt, Edith Franklin. "Booth Tarkington: The Seven Ages of Man," in *North American Review*. CCXVI (October, 1922), pp. 499–512.

B. TRAVEN
Traven Torsvan

Born: Chicago, Illinois (?) (1900 ?)
Died: Mexico City, Mexico (March 27, 1969)

Principal Works:

NOVELS: *Das Totenschiff,* 1926 (*The Death Ship*); *Der Wobbly,* 1926; *Der Schatz der Sierra Madre,* 1927 (*The Treasure of the Sierra Madre*); *Die Brücke im Dschungel,* 1929 (*The Bridge in the Jungle*); *Die weisse Rose,* 1929 (*The White-Rose*); *Der Karren,* 1931 (*The Carreta*); *Sonnenschöpfung,* 1936 (*Sun-Creation*); *Der Marsch ins Reich der Caoba,* 1933 (*March to Caobaland,* 1961); *Die Rebellion der Gehenkten,* 1936 (*The Rebellion of the Hanged*); *Die Troza,* 1936; *Ein General kommt aus dem Dschungel,* 1940 (*The General from the Jungle*); *Macario,* 1949.

SHORT STORIES: *Der Busch,* 1930 (*The Bush*); *The Night Visitor and Other Stories,* 1966.

NONFICTION: *Die Regierung,* 1931 (*Government*).

TRAVEL: *Das Land des Frühlings,* 1928.

Almost every statement about B. Traven, the most famous international literary mystery of the twentieth century, must end with a question mark. In a comment on his life and work, Traven said, "of an artist or writer, one should never ask an autobiography, because he is bound to lie. . . . If a writer, who he is and what he is, cannot be recognized by his work, either his books are worthless, or he himself is." His readers should look for him, he said, along and between the lines of his works.

When a New York publisher rejected his first two novels on the grounds that they lacked commercial possibilities and a finished style, Traven took them to Germany; they were published, and he became famous. From the beginning, he refused to allow his fascinating life and personality to be exploited for publicity, In 1963, he refused a literary prize from Germany. His agents in Mexico City protected him from most of the numerous letters addressed to him, many from editors all over the world.

Until Hitler banned his books for their radical point of view on the exploitation of the worker, Traven would not allow his work to appear in the United States. Finally, Alfred A. Knopf persuaded him to release the American rights, and five novels appeared in this country; a classic motion picture was made from *The Treasure of the Sierra Madre.* In his native country (he stated that he was an American), his novels are less appreciated than elsewhere; they have sold millions of copies in thirty languages. In Europe he is considered a major figure in contemporary fiction, and in the judgment of twenty or more nations, *The Death*

Ship is one of America's greatest novels.

Sorting among the scattered bits of information about Tavern, one can be fairly certain of these "facts": he was born about 1900 in Chicago; his parents were poor Norwegian-Swedish immigrant workers. A life of hard work began when he was seven. Though he was truant much of the time, he read a great many borrowed books. At ten he sailed on a tramp freighter as a cabin boy. The port of Mazatlán was one of this first exposures to Mexico, to which he returned again and again before settling in that tropical region where he spent most of his mature life. But for a decade, he sailed the world under several flags and worked at a great variety of laborer's jobs in Mexico. At some time he probably belonged to the IWW Wobblies. Traven wrote and spoke German, French, Spanish, and English fluently; he also spoke two of the unwritten Indian languages of southeast Mexico.

Traven's sixteen novels are concerned with the common man, laboring on ships and in the jungles of Mexico. His characters speak the slang of the early twentieth century with an immigrant accent. There is much description of landscapes and seascapes, and he has a special interest in depicting strong, courageous women, children, and the personalities of certain animals. The hard-core center of most of his realistic fiction is work. Among his books are sociological studies, documentaries, Mexican travel books illustrated with his own photographs, and Mexican folk tales. His outlook was that of the self-educated worker—sardonic and ironic, expressed, even in crawling misery, with wit and ribald humor. His novels depict men with a great appetite for life struggling to survive, always within the immediate vicinity of death.

One third of Traven's novels are in the first person; all have a strong autobiographical basis. But whether told in the third person or in the first, his novels aggressively state his radical revolutionary sentiments. He is alienated not only from Western civilization in general but from any formal creed or ideology in particular. In *The Death Ship*, Gerard Gales, who reappears in several of the novels, speaks of national and international bureaucracy as the irreconcilable enemy of individual freedom. Though one may be tempted, because of Traven's radical thinking and adventurous life, to associate him with Jack London, he is more a philosophical revolutionary in the tradition of Thoreau, whose love of privacy he shared. Much of his work resembles American proletarian fiction, although most of it was written several years before novels in that genre began to appear. And because of the attitude toward life that he and his characters demonstrate in action and speech, Traven may be regarded as one of the finest of the tough-guy novelists.

Bibliography

There are a number of articles dealing with questions about Traven's life. See Hubert Jannach, "The B. Traven Mystery," *Books Abroad*, XXXV (Winter, 1961), 28–29; *ibid.*, "B. Traven—An American or German Author," *German*

Quarterly, XXXVI (November, 1963); R. Recknagel, "B. Traven: Beiträge zur Biographie," 1966; "The Great Traven Mystery," *New Yorker*, XLIII (July 22, 1967), 82+; and Judy Stone, "The Mystery of B. Traven," *Ramparts*, VI (1967), 31–49+.

The B. Traven feature in the Winter, 1963, issue of *The Texas Quarterly*, edited by C. H. Miller and R. E. Pujan, contains the first biographical notes and tell-tale excerpts from his novels to be authorized by Traven himself for publication in the United States. See also John Fraser, "Splendour in the Darkness: B. Traven's *The Death Ship*," *Dalhousie Review*, XLIV (1964), 35–43; and C. H. Miller, "B. Traven, Pure Proletarian Writer," *Proletarian Writers of the Thirties*, edited by David Madden, 1968. Miller's introduction to *The Night Visitor and Other Stories* and the bibliography of Traven's work concluding it are also helpful.

For additional material see E. R. Hagemann, "A Checklist of the Work of B. Traven and the Critical Estimates and Bibliographical Essays on Him, Together with a Brief Biography," *Papers of the Bibliographical Society of America*, LIII, 1 (1959), 36–67.

THE DEATH SHIP

Type of work: Novel
Author: B. Traven (1900–1969)
Time of plot: The 1920's
Locale: Belgium, Holland, France, Spain, the Mediterranean Sea
First published: 1926

Essay-Review

Based on the author's own experiences, written when he was about twenty-four, *The Death Ship* is unique, apparently free of direct influences, just as B. Traven is in some ways unlike any other writer. The book may be classified as a proletarian novel, written in the style of tough-guy fiction. But its thesis is not as doctrinaire, as deliberately worked out as that of a proletarian novel, nor is its style as conscious as that of a tough-guy novel.

For Gerard Gales, the young American narrator, stranded in Antwerp when his ship returns to New Orleans without him, the passport has displaced the sun as the center of the universe. Unable to prove his citizenship, he is a man without a country, and his physical presence is no official proof of his birth. Like Kafka's K. in *The Trial*, he moves through a labyrinth of bureaucracy; officials empowered to dispense passports, certificates, sailors-books, receipts, affidavits, seals, and licenses conduct the inquisition of the modern age. The war for liberty and democracy has produced a Europe in which to be hungry is human, to lack a passport is inhuman—unless you are rich.

A victim of nationalism, moving among fading echoes of speeches on international brotherhood, Gerard is an individualist. Immigration officials conspire to smuggle him from Belgium into Holland, then back into Belgium, then into France, where he is jailed for riding a train without a ticket and later sentenced to be shot as a suspected spy. Ironically, when he senses the universal animosity toward Americans and pretends to be a German, he is treated royally. In Spain he is left entirely alone. A people politically oppressed, the Spanish seem freer than other men and Gerard loves them. But the peasants are so good to him that he feels useless and hates himself; he senses the error in a Communist state where the individual is denied the privilege of taking his own risks. Because he is a sailor without a ship, and because he wants to return to his girl, Gerard signs aboard *The Yorikke.*

If he once thought that the world consisted of deckhands and men who made paint, he descends now into a sailor's hell as drag man in a stokehold. Its name obscured on the bow, *The Yorikke*, too, appears to lack a proper birth certificate; but though she seems ashamed of her name, Gerard exhibits a kind of nationalism himself when he withholds his true name and country and signs on as an Egyptian; no American would sail on such a ship, and he realizes that, despite its many faults, he loves his country and is wretchedly homesick. *The Yorikke* resembles no ship he has ever seen; she appears to be insane. A model death ship, she has no life jackets. A death ship is so called because her owners have decided to scuttle her for the insurance. The crew, desperate men called "deads," at the end of their tether when they come aboard, do not know when the ship will go down. The sea, Gerard imagines, will probably eructate the diseased ship for fear of infection. No supplies—spoons, coffee cups, blankets—are provided; the men repeatedly steal a single bar of soap from one another until it has been through every filthy hand; conditions are worse than in a concentration camp. The only thing in ample supply is work, and if a man tries to collect overtime on a ship pathologically committed to profits he may find himself in a black hold with rats that would terrify a cat. Traven conveys a vivid sense of what "she" means as pronoun for a ship; Gerard constantly describes *The Yorikke* in very intimate and telling female terms.

Gerard admires his mysterious captain whose intelligence sets him apart from the old style pirate. He takes care of his men, and they would rather sink with the ship than inform the authorities that she is carrying contraband for the Riffs. *The Yorikke* crew is the filthiest Gerard has ever seen; the men wear bizarre rigs and rags. Some appear to have been shanghaied off the gallows. In the towns, other sailors shun them; men, women, and children fear them; and the police, afraid they may leave the town in ashes, follow them.

The filthiest member of the black gang is the drag man, who must perform extra and loathsome chores. Work is at the center of this novel—the struggle to get it, and, under extreme conditions, the horror and ultimate beauty of it. Delight in conveying an inside view is a characteristic of tough-guy literature. Gerard gives all the details of various work routines. One of the most horrific passages in literature is Traven's description of putting back fallen grate bars while the boiler is white hot. After his first bout at what becomes a daily task, Gerard declares that he is free, unbound, above the gods; he can do what he wishes and curse the gods, because no hell could be greater torture.

Gerard resurrects the freshness of the cliché that men become like machines. He feels like a gladiator for Caesar's fight-to-the-death spectacles. Bravery on the battlefield is nothing when compared to the bravery of men who do certain work to keep civilization afloat. No flag drapes the bodies of casualties; they go like garbage over the fantail. On a death ship no laws keep a man in line; each worker is crucially necessary and work is a common bond. With no sense of heroics, Gerard helps save two men and is himself saved. His true countrymen, he discovers, are those workers who are scalded and scorched at the same furnace with him; he does not desert because his friend Stanislav would then have to work alone. Though Traven appears to show how men grow accustomed to misery and filth, he insists that nobody really gets used to them; one simply loses the capacity to feel and becomes hard-boiled. Few fictive descriptions of the life, the hopes, the illusions and attitudes of the doomed sailor, his qualities of ingenuity, improvisation, and audacity are as complete as Traven's.

Ironically, just as Gerard, despite his misery, learns to live and laugh on the ship, he senses *The Yorikke*'s imminent doom. A further irony comes when Gerard and Stanislav are shanghaied from *The Yorikke* to serve on the new but disastrously slow *Empress of Madagascar*, which is to be scuttled in a few days. But the *Empress* kills her plotting captain and stands like a tower between the rocks before she sinks. Stanislav eats like a shipowner before he drowns. He and Gerard are safely tied to a piece of wreckage, but Stanislav has a hallucination in which he sees *The Yorikke* leaving the dock. Wanting to go with her, he detaches himself and slips into the sea. Not yet rescued, Gerard pays his respects to his comrade in the last lines of the novel.

The style of the story—rough, garrulous, full of completely justified profanity—sounds translated, but it is consistent with Gerard's semi-literate immigrant background. Though these qualities become wearisome in three hundred pages, the sheer energy of the telling achieves a special eloquence. Traven is overly fascinated by the way words come about; Gerard indulges in figurative rhetoric; many of his wisecracks seem lame, probably because his slang is dated. Humor, wit, and comedy are interwoven quite naturally among the darks of Traven's narrative. The style provides an amplification of theme through the play of language. Although Traven does not set up satirical situations, his diction and metaphorical pretenses create a satrirical distortion in the telling of such episodes as those involving bureaucracy.

No plot, no story line as such holds the novel together; narratively, it seems split in half, but the handling of theme, the picaresque looseness, and the personality of the narrator create an appropriate effect to the material. The static quality is relieved by sudden transitions and by the frequent use of tales and anecdotes, as in *The Treasure of the Sierra Madre*. Gerard is a storyteller who never tires of retelling a tale. The consulate scenes are repetitious; we get variations on the same routine, though speeded up and foreshortened sometimes; and toward the end, Stanislav tells Gerard a story about himself that closely resembles Gerard's earlier experiences. Gerard is especially fond of ridiculing popular fiction and movie versions of the seafaring life; the difference between living and listening to an experience is discussed in the beginning and at the end. Gerard tells his general story the way a sailor would, commenting with joking metaphors and reflecting constantly on the meaning of events. The reader is visualized as a captive audience for a man who has at last found a way to speak without interruption on various social, political, and economic conditions. The novel has some poignant moments, too, but, as is typical of the tough-guy novel, sentimentality occasionally intrudes.

Gerard and Stanislav are not to be associated with the victims of recent literature. They are more victims of the nature of things than of conditions that can be reformed. Gerard may gripe with every breath he takes, but he does not whine. He proudly insists that he can do work any man can do, anywhere. He contemptuously refuses to bow to circumstance. He refuses to blame the shipowners; having failed to take his fate in his own hands by jumping ship, he has no right to refuse to be a slave. But he can hope that he will be resurrected from the "deads" by his own will and fortitude. He knows that for the courageous man who survives the ordeal of *The Yorikke* anything is possible. By going to the bottom of agony in his daily task of replacing grate bars, Gerard comes out with a kind of peace, aware of his place in a universe that now has meaning in he slightest thing. This earned romanticism enables him to see beauty in the conventionally ugly.

Although Gerard covers, directly to the reader and in dialogue, almost every grievance of the laborer of the first twenty-five years of this century, he is not interested in easy working conditions and fringe benefits. Repeatedly, he preaches the gospel of hard work, not because work is good for the soul, which seems less involved than muscle, but because it is good for man the animal. Unlike proletarian writers, Traven achieves a kind of mystique about work. One thinks of Albert Camus' Sisyphus: for his disobedience of the officials, Sisyphus was condemned to the futile task of rolling a huge rock to the top of a mountain, after which it rolled back down to the plain. Camus likened this labor to that of the proletariat. Unintentionally, perhaps, Traven has translated Sisyphus' mythic task into existential reality. The intentions of the novel are uncertain; but at moments it appears to be an allegory about the laboring class. Working unseen at sea, deep in the black hole of an ash pit, these men, who were never born, in a sense, who are without a country, go to their deaths on a ship that does not exist officially. Gerard constantly speaks of the ship metaphorically as being over five thousand years old. The flag is so dirty it could represent any country, and thus represents all. Many nationalities are represented among the crew; each nameless person is called, ironically, by the name of the country he claims, but which has denied his existence.

NATHANAEL WEST

Born: New York, N.Y. (October 17, 1903 ?)
Died: El Centro, California (December 22, 1940)

Principal Works

NOVELS: *The Dream Life of Balso Snell*, 1931; *Miss Lonelyhearts*, 1933; *A Cool Million*, 1934; *The Day of the Locust*, 1939.

Nathanael West's literary life has an irony which almost parodies his own novels. Completely original and a deadly serious craftsman, he achieved in his short life little fame, except among a discerning few, and no popular success. Now, some years after his death, paperback editions have sold in the hundred thousands, and his *Complete Works* (1957) won critical acclaim and a place on bestseller lists.

Born Nathan Weinstein, in New York City, October 17, 1903 (?), he used the name Nathaniel von Wallenstein-Weinstein in Brown University (Ph.B., 1924), where he was labeled eccentric and a genius, and nicknamed "Pep" for the opposite characteristics the word suggests. Literary friends included I. J. Kapstein, Quentin Reynolds, and S. J. Perelman, who later married his sister Laura; but he wrote few pieces for undergraduate publications. In Paris during 1925–1926 he came under surrealist influences and wrote his first novel, *The Dream Life of Balso Snell*, a fantasy on his hero's wanderings inside the Trojan Horse, where he meets a naked man in a derby writing about Saint Pucc (a flea who lived in Christ's armpit), and a twelve-year-old boy wooing his schoolmistress with Russian journals. This work was ignored following its publication in 1931.

Back in New York, West worked as a hotel manager, as associate editor of *Contact* with William Carlos Williams in 1932, and also as associate on *Americana* with George Grosz in 1933. *Contact* and a third little magazine, *Contempo*, contained early drafts of *Miss Lonelyhearts*, the story of an agony columnist who is destroyed when he takes too seriously the problems and miseries of his correspondents. This minor classic was issued in 1933 by a publisher who shortly afterward went bankrupt. By the time copies and plates were rescued from the unpaid printer by another publishing house, demand for the book had ceased.

West's third and weakest novel, *A Cool Million*, is a broad satire on the Horatio Alger myth, in which Lemuel Pitkin loses his teeth, eye, scalp, money, and eventually his life after being victimized by capitalists, communists, and neofascists. It was quickly remaindered.

Unsuccessful as a short story writer and playwright, West made a living in Hollywood writing B-grade movies. Here he took five years to finish his most mature work, *The Day of the Locust*, and in 1940 he married Eileen McKenney, of *My Sister Eileen* fame. Seven months later, on December 22, they were killed together in an auto crash at El Centro, California.

Although *The Day of the Locust* has Hollywood as its locale and minor actors and hangers-on from the periphery of the studios as its characters, the novel is no more about motion pictures than *Miss Lonelyhearts* is about newspapers. Fantastic and exaggerated in theme and treatment, West's two chief novels convey, more clearly than most twentieth century fiction, a sense of horror and revulsion from the universe man lives in and the world he makes for his fellows and himself.

Bibliography

There are two book-length studies: James F. Light, *Nathanael West: An Interpretive Study*, 1961; and Randall Reid, *The Fiction of Nathanael West: No Redeemer, No Promised Land*, 1967.

Useful critical material is found in Robert M. Coates, Introduction to the New Directions edition of *Miss Lonelyhearts* (1946); Edmund Wilson, "Postscript," *The Boys in the Back Room*, 1941, reprinted in *Classics and Commercials*, 1950; Daniel Aaron, "The Truly Monstrous: A Note on Nathanael West," *Partisan Review*, XIV (1947), 98–106; Alan Ross, "The Dead Centre: An Introduction to Nathanael West," *Horizon*, XVIII (1948), 284–296, reprinted, with changes, in the Grey Walls Press edition of *Miss Lonelyhearts*, 1949, and the *Complete Works*, 1957; Richard B. Gehman, "Nathanael West: A Novelist Apart," *Atlantic*, CLXXXVI (1950), 69–72, reprinted in the New Directions edition of *The Day of the Locust*, 1950; Cyril M. Schneider, "The Individuality of Nathanael West," *Western Review*, XX (1955),7–28, 254–256; Arthur Cohen, "Nathanael West's Holy Fool," *Commonweal*, LXIV (June 15, 1956), 276–278; and James F. Light, "*Miss Lonelyhearts*: The Imagery of Nightmare," *American Quarterly*, VIII (1956), 316–327. See also William White, "Nathanael West: A Bibliography," *Studies in Bibliography*, XI (1958), 207–224.

MISS LONELYHEARTS

Type of work: Novel
Author: Nathanael West (Nathan Weinstein, 1903–1940)
Time of plot: Late 1920's
Locale: New York City
First published: 1933

Miss Lonelyhearts *was one of the first, and remains one of the best, examples of black humor in contemporary American fiction. This highly charged, bitterly ironical vision of a man destroyed by his hypersensitivity to the contradictions and pains of the modern world remains, along with* The Day of the Locust *(1939), one of the two minor masterpieces that West completed in his tragically short life.*

Principal Characters

Miss Lonelyhearts, the male writer of advice to the lovelorn on the New York "Post-Dispatch." The lovelorn column, considered a necessity for the increase in the paper's circulation and regarded by its staff as a joke, becomes an agony to its writer as he sees that the letters he receives are genuine cries for help from the very depths of suffering. In an attempt to escape the pain of the realization that he is the victim of the joke rather than its perpetrator, he turns in vain to drink, to love-making, and to a vacation in the country with a girl who loves him. Finally, in the delirium of illness, he imagines himself identified with the Christ whose image has long haunted him. As the crippled Peter Doyle approaches his room, Miss Lonelyhearts runs toward him with arms outstretched to receive him in his healing embrace. His gesture is mistaken for an intended attack and he is shot.

Willie Shrike, the feature editor, who is Miss Lonelyhearts' boss. He turns the knife in Miss Lonelyhearts' agony by his unending mockery of the desperate cries for help in the lovelorn letters and of the attempts at escape with which men delude themselves.

Mary Shrike, Willie Shrike's wife, whom Miss Lonelyhearts tries in vain to seduce.

Betty, a girl who is in love with Miss Lonelyhearts. Hoping to cure his despair, she takes him to the country. The attempt fails, since the letters are not forgotten.

Peter Doyle, a cripple who consults Miss Lonelyhearts about the meaning of the painful and unremunerative round of his existence. Later, he accuses the columnist of the attempted rape of his wife and shoots him in a struggle following a gesture which the cripple mistakes for an intended attack.

Fay Doyle, Peter Doyle's wife. Dissatisfied with her life with her crippled husband, she seeks out Miss Lonelyhearts and tries to seduce him.

MISS LONELYHEARTS by Nathanael West. By permission of the publishers, Farrar, Strauss & Cudahy, Inc. Copyright, 1933, by Nathanael West.

The Story

Miss Lonelyhearts found it hard to write his lovelorn column in the New York *Post-Dispatch*: the letters were not funny, there was no humor as desperate people begged for help. Sick-of-it-all, for example, with seven children in twelve years, was pregnant again and ill, but being a Catholic she could not consider an abortion and her husband would not let her alone; Desperate, a sixteen-year-old girl, a good dancer with a good shape and pretty clothes, would like boy friends, but cried all day at the big hole in the middle of her face (should she commit suicide?); Harold S., fifteen, wrote that his sister Gracie, thirteen, deaf, dumb, and not very smart, had something dirty done to her by a man, but Harold could not tell their mother Gracie was going to have a baby because her mother would beat her up. Shrike, the feature editor and Miss Lonelyhearts' tormentor, was no help at all: instead of the same old stuff, he said, Miss Lonelyhearts ought to give his readers something new and hopeful.

At Delehanty's speak-easy, where Miss Lonelyhearts went to escape his problems, his boss still belabored him about brooding and told him to forget the Crucifixion and remember the Renaissance. Meanwhile, he was trying to seduce Miss Farkis, a long-legged woman with a childish face. He also taunted the columnist by talking of a Western sect which prayed for a condemned slayer with an adding machine, numbers being their idea of the universal language.

Miss Lonelyhearts' bedroom walls were bare except for an ivory Christ nailed with large spikes, and the religious figure combined in a dream with a snake whose scales were tiny mirrors in which the dead world took on a semblance of life. First he was a magician who could not move his audience by tricks or prayer; then he was on a drunken college spree with two friends. Their attempt to sacrifice a lamb before barbecuing it, with Miss Lonelyhearts chanting the name of Christ, miscarried when the blade broke on the altar and the lamb slipped out of their bloodied hands. When the others refused to go back to put the lamb out of its misery, Miss Lonelyhearts returned and crushed its head with a stone.

One day, as he tried to put things in order, everything went against him: pencils broke, buttons rolled under the bed, shades refused to stay down, and instead of order on the skyline he found chaos. Miss Lonelyhearts remembered Betty, who could bring order into his world, and he went to her apartment. But he realized that her world was not the world and could never include the readers of his column; his confusion was significant and her order was not. Irritated and fidgety, he could neither talk to her nor caress her, although two months before she had agreed to marry him. When she asked if he were sick, he could only shout at her; when she said she loved him, he could only reply that he loved her and her smiling through tears. Sobbing that she felt swell before he came and now felt lousy, she asked him to go away.

At Delehanty's he listened to talk of raping a woman writer, and as he got drunker he heard friends mock Shrike's kidding him; but whiskey made him feel good and dreams of childhood made the world dance. Stepping back from the bar, he collided with a man holding a beer. The man punched him in the mouth. With a lump on his head, a loose tooth and a cut lip, Miss Lonelyhearts walked in the fresh air with Ned Gates. In a comfort station they met an old man with a terrible cough and no overcoat, who carried a cane and wore gloves because he detested red hands. They forced him to go to an Italian wine cellar. There they told him they were Havelock Ellis and Krafft-Ebing and insultingly mocked him with taunts of his homosexuality. When Miss Lonelyhearts twisted his arm— imagining it was the arm of Desperate, Broken-hearted, or Sick-of-it-all—the old man screamed, and someone hit the columnist with a chair.

Instead of going to the office after Shrike phoned him, Miss Lonelyhearts went to the speak-easy; he knew Shrike found him too perfect a butt for his jokes to fire him. Needing a woman, he phoned Mary, Shrike's wife, whom he had never seduced, although she hated her husband and used Miss Lonelyhearts to arouse Shrike. At a night club, in a cab, and at her apartment door, Miss Lonelyhearts tried to talk Mary into sleeping with him; but Shrike opened the door, ending that scheme.

The next day Miss Lonelyhearts received a letter from Fay Doyle, unhappily married to a cripple, asking for an appointment. Although he first threw the letter away, he retrieved it, phoned her to meet him in the park, and took her to his apartment. In the intervals of making love, she told of her married life and her child Lucy, whose father was not Doyle.

Physically sick and exhausted in his room for three days, he was comforted by Betty, who tried to get him to quit his Lonelyhearts job. He said he had taken the job as a joke, but after several months the joke had escaped him. Pleas for help made him examine his values and he became the victim of the joke. While Betty suggested he go to the country with her, Shrike broke into the room, taunted him to escape to the South Seas, hedonism, art, suicide, or drugs, and ended by dictating an imaginary letter from the columnist to Christ.

After he had been ill for a week, Betty finally persuaded Miss Lonelyhearts to go with her to her aunt's Connecticut farm. They camped in the kitchen, sat near a pond to watch frogs, deer, and a fawn, and slept on a mattress on the floor. They walked in the woods, swam in the nude, and made love in the grass.

After several days they returned to the city. Miss Lonelyhearts knew that Betty had failed to cure him; he could not forget the letters. He vowed to attempt to be humble. In the office he found a lengthy letter from Broad Shoulders, telling of her troubles with a crazy husband.

About a week later, while Shrike was pulling the same familiar jokes in Delehanty's, the bartender introduced Miss Lonelyhearts to Peter Doyle, a cripple whose wife wanted the columnist to have dinner at their house. After labored conversation, Doyle gave him a letter about his problems: he must pull his leg up and down stairs for $22.50 a week; his wife talked money, money, money; a doctor prescribed a six months' rest. When their hands touched under the table, they were at first embarrassed, but then they held hands in silence.

As they left the speak-easy, very drunk, to go to Doyle's, the cripple cursed his wife and his foot. Miss Lonelyhearts was happy in his humility. When Mrs. Doyle tried to seduce the columnist, he failed to respond. Meanwhile, her husband called himself a pimp and at his wife's request went out to get gin. Failing to find a message to show Mrs. Doyle her husband loved her, and disgusted by her obscene attempts to get him to sleep with her, Miss Lonelyhearts struck her again and again before he ran out of the house.

Following a three days' illness, Miss Lonelyhearts was awakened by five people, including Shrike and his wife, all drunk, who wanted to take him to a party at the editor's home. Betty was one of the party. Shrike wanted to play a game in which he distributed letters from Miss Lonelyhearts' office file and made taunting comments. When the columnist could stand it no longer, he followed Betty out, dropping unread the letter given him, which Shrike read to the crowd. It was from Doyle, accusing Miss Lonelyhearts of trying to rape the cripple's wife.

Miss Lonelyhearts told Betty he had quit the Lonelyhearts job and was going to look for work in an advertising agency. She told him she was going to have a baby. Although he persuaded her to marry him and have the baby instead of an abortion, by the time he left her he did not feel guilty; he did not feel, in fact, for his feeling, conscience, sense of reality, and self-knowledge were like a rock.

The next morning he was in a fever. The Christ on his wall was shining, but everything else in the room seemed dead. When the bell rang and he saw Doyle coming up the stairs, he imagined the cripple had come to have Miss Lonelyhearts perform a miracle and make him whole. Misunderstanding the outspread arms, Doyle put his hand in a newspaper-wrapped package as Betty came in the door. In the struggle the gun Doyle carried went off and Miss Lonelyhearts fell, dragging the cripple with him.

Critical Evaluation

Nathanael West, born Nathan Weinstein, graduated from Tufts in 1924 with a major in Philosophy. Immediately upon graduation he left for Paris where he remained for two years. On his return from abroad he took a job as a hotel night clerk, a job for which he was not particularly suited but which enabled him to write. In 1931 his first short novel *The Dream Life of Balso Snell* was privately printed; it was remarkably unsuccessful. His next work, *Miss Lonelyhearts,* appeared in 1933; if anything, its lack of success surpassed his first novel—the publisher was forced to declare bankruptcy. In the same year he went to Hollywood where he lived until his death. While there he was acquainted with such prominent authors as William Faulkner and F. Scott Fitzgerald, and there in 1940 he married Eileen McKenny, famous as *My Sister Eileen* (written by Ruth McKenny). He and his wife were killed on December 22, 1940, in an automobile accident.

West was obsessed with the daydreams people live. Though Jewish, he considered Christ and the Christ figure the ultimate dream, a concept more comprehensible when one considers that, for West as for many other authors (Cervantes is a notable example), the word dream is synonymous with ideal. In *Miss Lonelyhearts* West explores the modern answers to man's dilemma. Miss Lonelyhearts himself is the central figure of the novel, the observer through whose eyes the reader sees a modern wasteland. The wasteland motif is represented by the letters which Miss Lonelyhearts receives. In each of these letters sex and the failure of sex are the central conflicts: a woman destroyed by repeated pregnancy; a noseless girl for whom sex is impossible; a retarded child who has been raped.

Obsessed with the pain of others, Miss Lonelyhearts confuses compassion with identification. He becomes a Christ figure who embraces his suppliant children with erotic abandon. He renders unto Eros what is Christ's in a confused and tormented ministry. Shrike's taunting remarks all originate in his contempt for Miss Lonelyheart's original assumption that pure good is a true, human motivation. Determined to make Miss Lonelyhearts confront his own corruption, Shrike taunts him with gibes ridiculing his spiritual vanity. In the end Miss Lonelyhearts becomes an integral part of the very wasteland he thought he could redeem. The gospel of Shrike, the Mephistophelian naysayer, is confirmed by the totally ridiculous sacrifice of Miss Lonelyhearts in the arms of Peter Doyle. Miss Lonelyhearts' dream of Christ like self-sacrifice is parodied in the farcical embrace of seducer and cuckold rolling down the stairs.

Bibliography

Abrahams, Roger D. "Androgynes Bound: Nathanael West's *Miss Lonelyhearts*," in *Seven Contemporary Authors: Essays on Cozzens, Miller, West, Golding, Heller, Albee, and Powers.* Edited by Thomas B. Whitbread. Austin: University of Texas Press, 1966, pp. 49–72.

Andreach, Robert J. "Nathanael West's *Miss Lonelyhearts*: Between and Dead Pan and the Unborn Christ," in *Modern Fiction Studies.* XII (Summer, 1966), pp. 251–260.

Distasi, Lawrence W. "Aggression in *Miss Lonelyhearts*: Nowhere to Throw the Stone," in *Nathanael West: The Cheaters and the Cheated, A Collection of Critical Essays.* Edited by David Madden. Deland, Fla.: Everett/ Edwards, 1973, pp. 83–101.

Frank, Mike. "The Passion of Miss Lonelyhearts According to Nathanael West," in *Studies in Short Fiction.* X (Winter, 1973), pp. 67–73.

Geha, Richard, Jr. "*Miss Lonelyhearts*: A Dual Mission of Mercy," in *Hartford Studies in Literature.* III (1971), pp. 116–131.

Hand, Nancy Walker. "A Novel in the Form of a Comic Strip: Nathanael West's *Miss Lonelyhearts*," in *The Serif*. V (June, 1968), pp. 14–21.

Hickey, James W. "Freudian Criticism and *Miss Lonelyhearts*," in *Nathanael West: The Cheaters and the Cheated, A Collection of Critical Essays*. Edited by David Madden. Deland, Fla.: Everett/Edwards, 1973, pp. 111–150.

Jackson, Thomas H., Editor. *Twentieth Century Interpretations of* Miss Lonelyhearts: *A Collection of Critical Essays*. Englewood Cliffs, N.J.: Prentice-Hall, 1971.

Kunkel, Francis L. "Wrestlers with Christ and Cupid," in *Passion and the Passion: Sex and Religion in Modern Literature*. Philadelphia: Westminister Press, 1975, pp. 129–156.

Light, James F. "*Miss Lonelyhearts*: The Imagery of Nightmare," in *American Quarterly*. VIII (Winter, 1956), pp. 316–327.

Lorch, Thomas M. "Religion and Art in *Miss Lonelyhearts*," in *Renascence*. XX (Autumn, 1967), pp. 11–17.

_____. "West's *Miss Lonelyhearts*: Skepticism Mitigated?," in *Renascence*. XVIII (Winter, 1966), pp. 99–109.

Madden, David. "A Confluence of Voices: *Miss Lonelyhearts*," in his *Nathanael West: The Cheaters and the Cheated, A Collection of Critical Essays*. Deland, Fla.: Everett/Edwards, 1973, pp. 77–82.

Nelson, Gerald B. "Lonelyhearts," in *Ten Versions of America*. New York: Knopf, 1972, pp. 77–90.

Orvell, Miles D. "The Messianic Sexuality of *Miss Lonelyhearts*," in *Studies in Short Fiction*. X (Spring, 1973), pp. 159–167.

Pritchett, V.S. "*Miss Lonelyhearts*," in his *The Living Novel and Later Appreciations*. New York: Random House, 1964, pp. 76–82.

Richardson, Robert D., Jr. "*Miss Lonelyhearts*," in *University of Kansas City Review*. XXXIII (Winter, 1966), pp. 151–157.

Smith, Marcus. "The Crucial Departure: Irony and Point of View in *Miss Lonelyhearts*," in *Nathanael West: The Cheaters and the Cheated, A Collection of Critical Essays*. Edited by David Madden. Deland, Fla.: Everett/Edwards, 1973, pp. 103–110.

_____. "Religious Experience in *Miss Lonelyhearts*," in *Nathanael West: A Collection of Critical Essays*. Edited by Joy Martin. Englewood Cliffs, N.J.: Prentice-Hall, 1971, pp. 74–90.

EDITH WHARTON

Born: New York, N.Y. (January 24, 1862)
Died: St. Brice sous Foret, France (August 11, 1937)

Principal Works

NOVELS: *The Touchstone,* 1900; *The Valley of Decision,* 1902 (2 vols.); *Sanctuary,* 1903; *The House of Mirth,* 1905; *The Fruit of the Tree,* 1907; *Madame de Treymes,* 1907; *Ethan Frome,* 1911; *The Reef,* 1912; *The Custom of the Country,* 1913; *Summer,* 1917; *The Marne,* 1918; *The Age of Innocence,* 1920; *The Glimpses of the Moon,* 1922; *A Son at the Front,* 1923; *Old New York,* 1924 (*False Dawn: The Forties, The Old Maid: The Fifties, The Spark: The Sixties, and New Year's Day: The Seventies*); *The Mother's Recompense,* 1925; *Twilight Sleep,* 1927; *The Children,* 1928; *Hudson River Bracketed,* 1929; *The Gods Arrive,* 1932; *The Buccaneers,* 1938.

SHORT STORIES: *The Greater Inclination,* 1899; *Crucial Instances,* 1901; *The Descent of Man,* 1904; *The Hermit and the Wild Woman,* 1908; *Tales of Men and Ghosts,* 1910; *Xingu,* 1916; *Here and Beyond,* 1926; *Certain People,* 1930; *Human Nature,* 1933; *The World Over,* 1936; *Ghosts,* 1937.

POEMS: *Artemis to Actaeon,* 1909; *Twelve Poems,* 1926.

CRITICISM: *The Writing of Fiction,* 1925.

AUTOBIOGRAPHY: *A Backward Glance,* 1934.

Edith Newbold Jones was born in New York City on January 24, 1862, into a wealthy, upper middle-class family of distinguished ancestry. She learned as a girl, according to her own account, to love good literature, good English, and good manners. Traveling extensively with her socially active parents, and reading under the encouragement of tutors, she acquired a perspective of people and an enjoyment of literature which led her into writing stories on her own. With the publication of poetry and stories in magazines her literary career began. But her own social circle disapproved of her work, and she in turn discovered that their good manners were motivated by status rather than love. In 1885 she married Edward Wharton, a Boston banker, but their marriage was clouded by the husband's mental breakdown. In 1907, following the example of her literary mentor and personal friend, Henry James, Mrs. Wharton went abroad to live and settled permanently in France. However, she did not forget her society; she contemplated it from a distance and re-created it in art with irony and nostalgia.

Though Edith Wharton must be considered a major writer because of her artistry, her themes are somewhat less important today than they were during the first quarter of the twentieth century. One theme she treated was that the very conventions of conduct in America tend to stifle creative activity; the second, that the rising *nouveaux riches* were adulterating the purity of upper-class standards.

Essentially a writer of manners, she never attained the dispassionate view of her material that Jane Austen did, and her works are tragedies rather than comedies. Most of her novels tell the same story: the plight of an innocent victimized by the stultifying conventions of the group or the difficulties of the noble in heart in an ignoble society, a society whose lip service to the conventions makes its successful members hypocrites and its few honest ones victims. The antagonists are essentially evil, and their inevitable triumph is the real tragedy. However, the very defeat of the protagonists gives them a spiritual victory, for their defeat, as in *The House of Mirth*, is the result of their moral integrity.

All of her works are colored by the business of maneuvering for position, usually social. The first work to achieve critical recognition was the novel *The House of Mirth*, published in 1905. The protagonist, Lily Bart, a sensitive, ethical girl, is punished by society for following the direction of her sympathies rather than the demands of the "respectable"; she makes attractive friendships rather than socially acceptable ones, is snubbed by family and old acquaintances, and commits suicide in an agony of bewildered despair. In line with the literature of revolt of the period, this novel was unique in the restraint of its style, and perhaps all the more effective for its keyed-down qualities.

Edith Wharton rejected the "middle" class with prejudiced scorn. *The Custom of the Country* is cutting in its delineation of the character of the barbarian climber, Undine Spragg. However, she felt for the lower class, especially the rural, the same sympathy and identification with its victims of convention. *Ethan Frome* is a classic story of tragic frustration. Ethan, a farmer, marries out of loneliness. When his wife's cousin comes to live with them in poverty, and they fall in love—the first love in both their lives—they cannot see any way out to consummate their love; so they attempt suicide. Mrs. Wharton, as she does in many of her short stories, adds an ironic denouement to this plot: the suicide attempt fails, both are crippled, and the wife-in-name who refused to allow them their freedom is chained to them forever as their nurse. The novel *Summer* is similar in subject, milieu, and theme.

The Age of Innocence presents a starkly classic quality in its picture of the inevitablity of spiritual destruction suffered by two noble people because of their moral flaw, which allows their social status to take precedence over love. The protagonists, Newland Archer and Ellen Olenska, are defeated by a code of their group, a group that willingly breaks the codes only when there is an assurance of not getting caught. "It was a dull association of material and social interests held together by ignorance on the one side and hypocrisy on the other." This novel comes closest to the polished perfection of the manners genre in that there is a comic tone that restrains the pathos of the dilemma of Newland and married Ellen who, afraid to face ostracism, must either destroy their love for each other or destroy themselves. The very restraint allows the perceptive reader to live the tragedy of their thwarted emotional lives, and the impression is deep and lasting.

After 1920 only the short stories continued as art; the novels were mechanical repetitions of the earlier works or quickly contrived propaganda pieces, like *A Son at the Front*. The world that Edith Wharton had known was gone and there was little more to say.

The success of Wharton's work was achieved by "disengaging crucial moments from the welter of existence," keeping the plot true to the characters' motivations, and using a language that was dispassionate yet moving in its clarity and restraint. Before she died, at St. Brice sous Foret, France, on August 11, 1937, she had received more honors for her work than any other woman writer in American history.

Bibliography

There is no definitive biography of Edith Wharton. Her autobiography, *A Backward Glance*, was published in 1934 and reprinted in 1964. A biographical study is Percy Lubbock, *Portrait of Edith Wharton*, 1947; a critical study, Nevius Blake, *Edith Wharton: A Study of Her Fiction*, 1953. For earlier biographical and critical works see Katherine F. Gerould, *Edith Wharton: A Critical Study*, 1922; Robert M. Lovett, *Edith Wharton*, 1925; and E. K. Brown, *Edith Wharton: Étude Critique*, 1935. The best criticism is to be found in Irving Howe, ed., *Edith Wharton: A Collection of Critical Essays*, 1962.

See also Percy H. Boynton, *Some Contemporary Americans*, 1924; Régis Michaud, *The American Novel To-day*, 1928; N. Elizabeth Monroe, *The Novel and Society*, 1941; Alfred Kazin, *On Native Grounds*, 1942; also Percy Lubbock, "The Novels of Edith Wharton," *Quarterly Review*, CCXXIII (1915), 182–201; Charles K. Trueblood, "Edith Whartoon," *Dial*, LXVIII (1920), 80–91; Frances T. Russell, "Melodramatic Mrs. Wharton," *Sewanee Review*, XL (1932), 425–437; E. K. Brown, "Edith Wharton," *Études Anglaises*, II (1938), 12–26; Edmund Wilson, "Justice to Edith Wharton," *New Republic*, XCV (1938), 209–213; and Larry Rubin, "Aspects of Naturalism in Four Novels by Edith Wharton," *Twentieth Century Literature*, II (1957), 182–192.

THE AGE OF INNOCENCE

Type of work: Novel
Author: Edith Wharton (1862–1937)
Time of plot: Late nineteenth century
Locale: New York City
First published: 1920

The Age of Innocence *is a subtle yet unmistakable indictment of stratified New York high society in 1920. Wharton is reminiscent of Henry James both in her psychological probing of characters' emotions and motivations and in her degree of craftsmanship. However, she maintains a style less obscure and less involved than that of James.*

Principal Characters

Newland Archer, a young lawyer who is a member of New York's high society. Married to May Welland, a girl from his own class, he falls in love with Ellen Olenska and for a time considers running away with her. He never does so because he is bound by his ties of marriage and convention.

Countess Ellen Olenska, A New York girl of good family who has married a Polish nobleman but now wishes a divorce from him. Intelligent and beautiful, she comes back to New York, where she tries to fit into the life she had known before her marriage. She falls in love with Newland Archer. When the young attorney, persuaded by her family, urges her not to seek a divorce, she leaves for Europe without him. Years later Archer's son visits Ellen in Paris.

May Welland Archer, Newland's wife, a typical New York socialite with all the restrictions and forms adopted by that class. She triumphs over Ellen Olenska and saves her marriage with the announcement that she is to become a mother.

Mr. Welland and

Mrs. Welland, May's parents. Rich, conservative, puritanical, they are somewhat shocked by the discovery that their relative, Ellen, plans to divorce her husband. Clannishly, however, they give in her honor a party at which they announce the engagement of their daughter to Newland Archer.

Mrs. Catherine Mingott, May's grandmother, the mother of Mrs. Welland and a proud old aristocrat who dominates the clan.

Medora Mingott, May's aunt and Ellen's former chaperone. Flighty but goodnatured, she brings Ellen back to the family home in New York after Ellen and her husband have separated.

Mr. van der Luyden and
Mrs. van der Luyden, members of the old, conservative aristocracy. They generously offer to receive Ellen after she has been snubbed by others of her class.

Julius Beaufort, a successful New York businessman. Married, he carries on affairs on the side. Eventually he goes bankrupt.

Mrs. Beaufort, his wife, a fat, pleasant

woman tolerant of her husband's philanderings.

Fanny Beaufort, the daughter of Julius by one of his mistresses. She marries Dallas Archer.

Dallas Archer, the son of May and Newland Archer. He manages to cut the ties of formal society which have held his father captive for so long, marries Fanny Beaufort, and leads a more relaxed and happier life than his father's.

Ned Winsett, one of Newland Archer's friends, a journalist who tries to win Archer over to a less restrictive life.

Reggie and
Mrs. Chivers, Newland Archer's fashionable but understanding friends. They entertain him when he is trying to have a rendezvous with Ellen.

Jane Archer, Newland's wise and clever little sister. She has an ear for gossip and spends much time talking over tidbits of information with her mother.

Mrs. Archer, Newland's widowed mother. She intercedes for Ellen with the van der Luydens and manages to persuade them to give a dinner party for her after she has been snubbed by the rest of New York society.

Mrs. Lemuel Struthers, a lively, fat woman much interested in musicians and artists. She is considered quite vulgar by the "better" families.

Mr. Letterblau, the senior partner of the law firm for which Newland Archer works. He directs the young attorney to handle the Olenska divorce case.

Lawrence Lefferts, a society friend of the Archers and the Wellands.

The Story

Newland Archer, a handsome and eligible young attorney engaged to lovely May Welland, learned that the engagement would be announced at a party to welcome his fiancée's cousin, Countess Ellen Olenska. This reception for Ellen constituted a heroic sacrifice on the part of the many Welland connections, for her marriage to a ne'er-do-well Polish count had not improved her position so far as rigorous and straight-laced New York society was concerned. The fact that she contemplated a divorce action also made her suspect, and, to cap it all, her rather bohemian way of living did not conform to what her family expected of a woman who had made an unsuccessful marriage.

Newland Archer's engagement to May was announced. At the same party Archer was greatly attracted to Ellen. Before long, with the excuse that he was making the cousin of his betrothed feel at home, he began to send her flowers and call on her. To him she seemed a woman who offered sensitivity, beauty, the promise of a life quite different from that he could expect after his marriage to May.

He found himself defending Ellen when the rest of society was attacking her contemplated divorce action. He did not, however, consider breaking his engagement to May, but constantly sought reasons for justifying what was to the rest of his group an excellent union. With Ellen often in this thoughts, May Welland's cool beauty and correct but unexciting personality began to suffer in Archer's estimation.

Although the clan defended her against all outsiders, Ellen was often treated as a pariah. Her family kept check on her, trying to prevent her from indulging in too many bohemianisms, such as her strange desire to rent a house in a socially unacceptable part of town. The women of the clan also recognized her as a dangerous rival, and ruthless Julius Beaufort, whose secret dissipations were known by all, including his wife, paid her marked attention. Archer found himself hating Julius Beaufort very much.

Convincing himself that he was seeing too much of Ellen, Archer went to St. Augustine to visit May, who was vacationing there with her mother and her hypochondriac father. In spite of her cool and conventional welcome and her gentle rebuffs to his wooing, her beauty reawakened in him a kind of affection, and he pleaded with her to 'advance the date of their wedding. May and her parents refused because their elaborate preparations could not be completed in time.

Archer returned to New York. There, with the aid of the family matriarch, Mrs. Manson Mingott, he achieved his purpose, and the wedding date was advanced. This news came to him in a telegram sent by May to Ellen, which Ellen read to him just as he was attempting to advance the intimacy of their relationship. Archer left Ellen's house and found a similar telegram from May to himself. Telling his sister Janey that the wedding would take place within a month, he suddenly realized that he was now protected against Ellen and himself.

The ornate wedding, the conventional European honeymoon which followed, and May's assumption of the role of the proper wife, soon disillusioned Archer. He realized that he was trapped, that the mores of his society, helped by his own lack of courage, had prepared him, like a smooth ritual, for a rigid and codified life. There was enough intelligence and insight in Archer, however, to make him resent the trap.

On his return to New York, he continued to see Ellen. The uselessness of his work as junior attorney in an ancient law firm, the stale regimen of his social life, and the passive sweetness of May did not satisfy that part of Archer which set him apart from the rest of his clan.

He proposed to Ellen that they go away together, but Ellen, wise and kind, showed him that such an escape would not be a pleasant one, and she indicated that they could love each other only as long as he did not press for a consummation. Archer agreed. He further capitulated when, urged by her family, he advised Ellen, as her attorney and as a relative, not to get a divorce from Count Olenski. She agreed, and Archer again blamed his own cowardice for his action.

The family faced another crisis when Julis Beaufort's firm, built upon a framework of shady financial transactions, failed, ruining him and his duped customers. The blow caused elderly Mrs. Mingott to have a stroke, and the family rallied around her. She summoned Ellen, a favorite of hers, to her side, and Ellen, who had been living in Washington, D. C., returned to the Mingott house to stay. Archer, who had not met Ellen since he advised her against a divorce, began seeing her again, and certain remarks by Archer's male acquaintances along with a strained and martyrlike attitude which May had adopted, indicated to him that his intimacy with Ellen was known among his family and friends. The affair came to an end, however, when Ellen left for Paris, after learning that May was to have a baby. It was obvious to all that May had triumphed, and Archer was treated by his family as a prodigal returned. The rebel was conquered. Archer made his peace with society.

Years passed. Archer dabbled in liberal politics, interested himself in civic reforms. His children, Mary and Dallas, were properly reared. May died when Archer was in his fifties. He lamented her passing with genuine grief. He watched society changing, and saw the old conservative order give way, accepting and rationalizing innovations of a younger, more liberal generation.

One day his son Dallas, about to be married, phoned him and proposed a European tour, their last trip together. In Paris, Dallas revealed to his father that he knew all about Ellen Olenska and had arranged a visit to her apartment. But when they arrived, Archer sent his son ahead, to pay his respects, while he remained on a park bench outside. A romantic to the end, incapable of acting in any situation which made demands on his emotional resources, he sat and watched the lights in Ellen's apartment until a servant appeared on the balcony and closed the shutters. Then he walked slowly back to his hotel. The past was the past; the present was secure.

Critical Evaluation

Edith Wharton's *The Age of Innocence* is probably one of her most successful books because it offers an inside look at a subject the author knew very well, that is, New York society during the 1870's. That was her milieu, and her pen captures the atmosphere of aristocratic New York as its inhabitants move about in their world of subtleties, innuendoes, and strict adherence to the dictates of fashionable society. Edith Wharton describes those years for herself as "safe, guarded, and monotonous." Her only deviation as a young adult consisted in frequent journeys abroad and summers in Newport. Her marriage to Edward Wharton, a prominent Bostonian, assumed the same character as her own early life until it became apparent that he suffered from mental illness and would have to be hospitalized. During World War I, Edith Wharton worked for the allies and received the French Cross of the Legion of Honor for her work with the Red Cross in Paris. Most critics agree that her best years as a novelist were from 1911 to 1921, during which time she produced *Ethan Frome,* a grim New England study, and *The Age of Innocence,* for which she was awarded the Pulitzer Prize.

Edith Wharton's most successful theme (like that of her friend Henry James) was the plight of the young and innocent in a world which was more complicated than they were prepared for. Newland Archer and Ellen Olenska found the society of New York intricate and demanding and, as such, an impediment to their personal searches for happiness and some degree of freedom. *The Age of Innocence* is a careful blending of a nostalgia for the 1870's with a subtle, but nonetheless inescapable, criticism of its genteel timidities and clever evasions.

With respect to Wharton's style it can be generalized that she was not a particularly daring writer, nor an experimenter in form. Rather, she wrote in a comfortable, fixed, formal style which was closely designed. In some instances, her narrative becomes heavy and the intricate play and counterplay of the characters' motives can lose all but the most diligent reader. The author's presence is never forgotten and the reader feels her control throughout the story, as the narrative view is quickly established from the beginning. Wharton's characters are portrayed through their actions, and the clear lines of the plot are visible. Since *The Age of Innocence* so carefully fits a historical niche, its scope is limited and its direction narrow. That is not to say that drama is limited or lacking. On the contrary, in detailing such a small world, the drama is intense even if it is found beneath a sophisticated, polished surface.

Three figures are projected against the historical background of New York society. First, May Welland, the beautiful betrothed of Newland Archer. May was born and bred in traditions and she is completely a product of the system she seeks to perpetuate. Newland observes, after their marriage, that May and her mother are so much alike that he sees himself being treated and placated just as Mr. Welland is by his wife and daughter. There is no doubt that May will never surprise Newland "by a new idea, a weakness, a cruelty or an emotion."

Ellen Olenska, on the other hand, has freed herself from the restraints of society by her experiences abroad and through her subsequent separation from her husband, the Polish Count. Madame Olenska is not only more cosmopolitan; she is also a character of more depth and perception than the other women in the novel. She suggests by her presence as well as by her past experiences a tragic and emotionally involved element in the story. Ellen definitely does not conform to the rules of accepted behavior, yet she moves in a cloud of mystery which makes her an intriguing personality to those who observe her, if even only to criticize. As soon as she and Archer are aware of their feelings for each other, Archer tries to convince Ellen, in a halfhearted way, that one cannot purchase freedom at the expense of another. He has given her an idea by which to live and, in so doing, has unknowingly destroyed his one opportunity to find a new freedom for himself.

Newland Archer is, in many ways, a typical Wharton masculine figure. He is a man set apart from the people he knows by education, intellect, and feeling, but lacking the initiative and courage to separate himself physically from the securities of the known. The movement of the plot in *The Age of Innocence* is established by the transition from one position to another taken by Archer in his relations with either May or Ellen. Archer's failure to break the barriers of clan convention lead him to an ironic abnegation, for in the last pages of the novel we see Newland retreating from the opportunity to meet with Ellen—an opportunity his eager son Dallas is quick to arrange. Dallas is anxious to meet Ellen, for he heard from his mother shortly before she died that Archer had given up the thing he had most wanted (namely, Ellen) for her. It is sad to see that Archer, the object of two loves, has never been able to satisfy or be satisfied by either. The tragedy in the novel rests with May, for it is she who appeared to be the most innocent and naïve; yet in the end, she is, perhaps, the most aware of them all. She has suffered quietly through the years, knowing that her husband's true desires and passions were elsewhere. Dallas' generation observes the whole situation out of context as "prehistoric." He dismisses the affair rather casually, for his contemporaries have lost that blind adherence to social custom that the Archers, Wellands, and the rest knew so well.

The Age of Innocence is a novel of manners which delineates a very small world, yet under the surface we see a world of suffering, denial, and patient resignation—a situation which deserves more attention and reflection than one might give at first reading.

Bibliography

Auchincloss, Louis. *Edith Wharton*. Minneapolis: University of Minnesota Press, 1961, pp. 29–31.

Beach, Joseph Warren. *The Twentieth-Century Novel: Studies in Technique*. New York: Appleton-Century-Crofts, 1932, pp. 294–298.

Canby, Henry Seidel. *Definitions: Essays in Contemporary Criticism*. New York: Harcourt, Brace, 1931, pp. 212–216.

Coolidge, Olivia. *Edith Wharton, 1862–1937*. New York: Scribner's, 1964, pp. 181–184.

Coxe, Louis O. "What Edith Wharton Saw in Innocence," in *New Republic*. CXXXII (June 27, 1955), pp. 16–18. Reprinted in *Edith Wharton: A Collection of Critical Essays*. Edited by Irving Howe. Englewood Cliffs, N.J.: Prentice-Hall, 1962, pp. 155–161.

Doyle, Charles C. "Emblems of Innocence: Imagery Patterns in Wharton's *The Age of Innocence*," in *Xavier University Studies*. X (1971), pp. 19–25.

Gargano, James W. "*The Age of Innocence*: Art or Artifice?," in *Research Studies*. XXXVIII (March, 1970), pp. 22–28.

Gelfant, Blanche Housman. *The American City Novel*. Norman: University of Oklahoma Press, 1954, pp. 107–119.

Hopkins, Viola. "The Ordering Style of *The Age of Innocence*," in *American Literature*. XXX (November, 1958), pp. 345–357.

Jacobson, Irving F. "Perception, Communication, and Growth as Correlative Themes in Edith Wharton's *The Age of Innocence*," in *Agora.* II (1973), pp. 68–82.

Kellogg, Grace. *The Two Lives of Edith Wharton: The Woman and Her Work.* New York: Appleton-Century, 1965, pp. 224–232.

Kronenberger, Louis. "Edith Wharton's New York: Two Period Pieces," in *Michigan Quarterly Review.* IV (Winter, 1965), pp. 3–13. Reprinted in *The Polished Surface: Essays in the Literature of Worldliness.* New York: Knopf, 1969, pp. 256–270.

Lawson, Richard H. *Edith Wharton.* New York: Frederick Ungar, 1977, pp. 15–27.

Lewis, R.W.B. "Introduction," in *The Age of Innocence.* New York: Scribner's, 1968.

Lindberg, Gary H. *Edith Wharton and the Novel of Manners.* Charlottesville: University Press of Virginia, 1975, pp. 76–86, 100–108, 128–137, 151–157.

Lyde, Marilyn Jones. *Edith Wharton: Convention and Morality in the Works of a Novelist.* Norman: University of Oklahoma Press, 1959, pp. 4–7, 95–98.

McDowell, Margaret B. *Edith Wharton.* New York: Twayne, 1976, pp. 92–104.

Mizener, Arthur. "Edith Wharton: *The Age of Innocence*," in *Twelve Great American Novels.* New York: New American Library, 1967, pp. 68–86.

Moseley, Edwin M. "*The Age of Innocence*: Edith Wharton's Weak Faust," in *College English.* XXI (December, 1959), pp. 156–160.

Nevius, Blake. *Edith Wharton.* Berkeley: University of California Press, 1953, pp. 177–189. Reprinted in *Edith Wharton: A Collection of Critical Essays.* Edited by Irving Howe. Englewood Cliffs, N.J.: Prentice-Hall, 1962, pp. 162–171.

Niall, Brenda. "Prufrock in Brownstone: Edith Wharton's *The Age of Innocence*," in *Southern Review.* IV (November, 1971), pp. 203–214.

Robinson, James A. "Psychological Determinism in *The Age of Innocence*," in *Markham Review.* V (1975), pp. 1–5.

Rubin, Larry. "Aspects of Naturalism in Four Novels by Edith Wharton," in *Twentieth Century Literature.* II (January, 1957), pp. 186–188.

Walton, Geoffrey. *Edith Wharton: A Critical Interpretation.* Rutherford, N.J.: Fairleigh Dickinson University Press, 1970, pp. 130–138.

Wolff, Cynthia Griffin. *A Feast of Words: The Triumph of Edith Wharton.* New York: Oxford University Press, 1977, pp. 310–334.

ETHAN FROME

Type of work: Novel
Author: Edith Wharton (1862–1937)
Time of plot: Late nineteenth century
Locale: Starkfield, Massachusetts
First published: 1911

Unrepresentative though it is of Wharton's works, Ethan Frome *is the most critically acclaimed and most popular. Wharton's terse depiction of Ethan's wasted talents and passions becomes a cynical fable describing the triumph of a trivial, conventional society over the ambitious, creative individual.*

Principal Characters

Ethan Frome, a farmer frustrated in his ambition to become an engineer or a chemist, and in his marriage to a nagging, sour, sickly wife. He falls in love with his wife's good and lovely cousin, Mattie Silver, who comes to live with them. When his wife finally drives the girl away, Ethan insists on taking her to the station. Ethan and Mattie decide to take a sleigh ride they have promised themselves and, in mutual despair over the impending separation, they resolve to kill themselves by running the sled against a tree. But they are not killed, only permanently injured, and Ethan's wife is to look after them for the rest of their lives.

Zenobia Pierce Frome (Zeena), Ethan's wife, a distant cousin who nursed his mother during a long illness. The marriage is loveless, and Zeena is sickly and nagging.

Mattie Silver, Zeena's cousin, who comes to live with the Fromes. She returns Ethan's love, and once when Zeena spends a night away from home, she and Ethan spend a happy evening together, not making love but sitting quietly before the fire, as Ethan imagines happily married couples do. Mattie feels that she would rather die than leave Ethan, but in the crash she suffers not death, but a permanent spine injury, and must submit thereafter to being nursed by Zeena.

Ruth Varnum and Ned Hale, a young engaged couple whom Ethan observes stealing a kiss. On his night alone with Mattie he tells her wistfully about it; it is as close as he comes to making advances.

The Story

Ethan Frome was twenty-one years old when he married Zenobia Pierce, a distant cousin who nursed his sick mother during her last illness. It was a wedding without love. Zenobia, called Zeena, had no home of her own, and Ethan was lonely. So they were married. But Zeena's talkativeness, which had been pleasing to Ethan during his mother's illness, quickly subsided, and within a year of their marriage Zeena developed the sickliness which was to plague her husband all her life. Ethan became increasingly dissatisfied with his life. He was an intelligent and ambitious young man who had hoped to become an engineer or a chemist. But he soon found himself chained to a wife he detested and a farm he could not sell.

The arrival of Mattie Silver brightened the gloomy house considerably. Mattie, Zeena's cousin, had come to Starkfield partly because she had no other place to go and partly because Zeena felt in need of a companion around the house. Ethan saw in Mattie's goodness and beauty every fine quality that Zeena lacked.

When Zeena suggested that Ethan help Mattie find a husband, he began to realize how much he himself was attracted to the girl. When he went to a church social to bring Mattie home and saw her dancing with the son of a rich Irish grocer, he realized that he was jealous of his rival and in love with Mattie. On his way home with her, Ethan felt his love for Mattie more than ever, for on that occasion as on others, she flattered him by asking him questions on astronomy. His dreams of happiness were short-lived however, for when he reached home Zeena was her nagging, sour self. The contrast between Zeena and Mattie impressed him more and more.

One day Ethan returned from his morning's work to find Zeena dressed in her traveling clothes. She was going to visit a new doctor in nearby Bettsbridge. Ordinarily Ethan would have objected to the journey because of the expensive remedies which Zeena was in the habit of buying on her trips to town. But on that occasion he was overjoyed at the news of Zeena's proposed departure, for he realized that he and Mattie would have the house to themselves overnight.

With Zeena out of the way, Ethan again became a changed man. Later in the evening, before supper, Ethan and Mattie sat quietly before the fire, just as Ethan imagined happily married couples would do. During supper the cat broke Zeena's favorite pickle dish, which Mattie had used to brighten up the table. In spite of the accident, they spent the rest of the evening happily. They talked about going sledding together, and Ethan told shyly—and perhaps wistfully—that he had seen Ruth Varnum and Ned Hale, a young engaged couple, stealing a kiss earlier in the evening.

In the morning Ethan was happy, but not because of anything out of the ordinary the night before. In fact, when he went to bed, he remembered sadly that he had not so much as touched Mattie's fingertips or looked into her eyes. He was happy because he could imagine what a wonderful life he could have if he were married to Mattie. He got glue to mend the pickle dish, but Zeena's unexpected return prevented him from repairing it. His spirits were further dampened when Zeena told him that the Bettsbridge doctor considered her quite sick. He had advised her to get a girl to relieve her of all household duties, a stronger girl than Mattie. She had already engaged the new girl. Ethan was dumbfounded by this development. In her insistence that Mattie be sent away Zeena gave the first real hint that she may have been aware of gossip about her husband and Mattie. When Ethan told Mattie of Zeena's decision, the girl was as crestfallen as Ethan. Zeena interrupted their lamentations, however, by coming downstairs for something to eat. After supper she required stomach powders to relieve a case of heartburn. In getting the powders, which she had hidden in a spot supposedly unknown to Mattie, Zeena discovered the broken pickle dish, which had been carefully reassembled in order to give the appearance of being unbroken. Having detected the deception and learned that Mattie was responsible for the broken dish, Zeena called Mattie insulting names and showed plainly that the girl would be sent away at the earliest possible moment.

Faced with the certainty of Mattie's departure, Ethan thought of running away with her. But his poverty, as well as his sense of responsibility to Zeena, offered no solution to his problem, only greater despair. On the morning Mattie was to leave Starkfield, Ethan, against the wishes of his wife, insisted on driving Mattie to the station. The thought of parting was unbearable to both. They decided to take the sleigh ride that Ethan had promised Mattie the night before. Down the hill they went, narrowly missing a large elm tree at the bottom. Mattie, who had told Ethan that she would rather die than leave him, begged until Ethan agreed to take her down the hill a second time and run the sled into the elm at the bottom of the slope. But they failed to hit the tree with force sufficient to kill them. The death they sought became a living death, for in the accident Mattie suffered a permanent spine injury and Ethan an incurable lameness. The person who received Mattie into her home, who waited on her, and who cooked for Ethan was—Zeena.

Critical Evaluation

Ethan Frome is a compact novelette which etches with acid the existential tragedy of misspent lives and talent gone awry. In it, Edith Wharton depicts Ethan Frome and Mattie Silver as intelligent and fundamentally decent human beings whose souls—and finally, whose bodies—are crushed by meaningless but inexorable social conventions, represented by Zeena Frome.

Ethan in particular reflects Wharton's view that twentieth century America has repudiated the fine nineteenth century values which Wharton cherishes so deeply, for Ethan stands for all those bygone qualities which she admires. He has a good mind, commendable ambition, and strong integrity. A twentieth century Ethan might, for example, think of killing Zeena—and possibly even attempt it—but Wharton's nineteenth century man, living in an inhospitable twentieth century, is instead slowly destroyed by a society which has no use for him or his anachronistic values. In the end, he is tended by Zeena, who takes care of him much as a museum curator takes care of ancient artifacts entrusted to him.

Although *Ethan Frome* is unusual in the large corpus of Wharton's work for its revelations about the author's bitterness toward what she views as the shallowness of modern industrial society, it is by no means unique. Wharton earlie⁻ treated a similar theme in *The House of Mirth* (1905), a novel frequently paired with *Ethan Frome* for purposes of comparison. And indeed the likenesses are there. Like Ethan, for instance, Lily Bart in *The House of Mirth* is meant for a better life than she has. But in her pursuit of what she clearly deserves, she is subjected to calumny, deceit, and fraud which finally drive her to a fatal overdose of sedatives. These two simple tragedies stand out from Wharton's other work, which concerned itself largely with complex socio-moral conflicts, but they are certainly not inferior, despite their apparently anomalous position. In fact, *Ethan Frome* is considered by many to be Wharton's finest work.

Bibliography

Auchincloss, Louis. *Edith Wharton.* Minneapolis: University of Minnesota Press, 1961, pp. 21–22. Reprinted in *Seven Modern American Novelists.* Edited by William V. O'Connor. Minneapolis: University of Minnesota Press, 1964, pp. 25–26.

Bernard, Kenneth. "Imagery and Symbolism in *Ethan Frome*," in *College English.* XXIII (December, 1961), pp. 178–184.

Bewley, Marius. "Mrs. Wharton's Mask," in *New York Review of Books.* (September 24, 1964), pp. 7–9. Reprinted in *Masks and Mirrors: Essays in Criticism.* New York: Atheneum, 1970, pp. 145–153.

Brennan, Joseph X. "*Ethan Frome*: Structure and Metaphor," in *Modern Fiction Studies.* XII (Winter, 1961), pp. 347–356.

Bruce, Charles. "Circularity: Theme and Structure in *Ethan Frome*," in *Studies and Critiques.* I (1966), pp. 78–81.

Coolidge, Olivia. *Edith Wharton, 1862–1937.* New York: Scribner's, 1964, pp. 112–114.

Deegan, Dorothy Yost. *The Stereotype of the Single Woman in American Novels.* New York: Octagon Books, 1969, pp. 56–66.

DeVoto, Bernard. "Introduction," in *Ethan Frome.* New York: Scribner's, 1938, pp. v-xviii.

Freemantle, Anne. "Edith Wharton: Values and Vulgarity," in *Fifty Years of the American Novel: A Christian Appraisal.* Edited by Harold C. Gardiner. New York: Scribner's, 1951, p. 24.

Hafley, James. "The Case Against *Ethan Frome*," in *Fresco.* I (1961), pp. 194–201.

Herron, Ima H. *The Small Town in American Literature.* Durham, N.C.: Duke University Press, 1939, pp. 138–140.

Iyengar, K.R. Srinivasa. "A Note on *Ethan Frome*," in *Literary Criticism.* V (Winter, 1962), pp. 168–178.

Kazin, Alfred. "Edith Wharton and Theodore Dreiser," in *On Native Grounds.* New York: Reynal and Hitchcock, 1942, p. 81. Reprinted in *Edith Wharton: A Collection of Critical Essays.* Edited by Irving Howe. Englewood Cliffs, N.J.: Prentice-Hall, 1962, pp. 92–93.

Kellogg, Grace. *The Two Lives of Edith Wharton: The Woman and Her Work.* New York: Appleton-Century, 1965, pp. 159–174.

Lawson, Richard H. *Edith Wharton.* New York: Frederick Ungar, 1977, pp. 67–75.

Lewis, R.W.B. *Edith Wharton, A Biography.* New York: Harper & Row, 1975, pp. 308–311.

Lubbock, Percy. "The Novels of Edith Wharton," in *Quarterly Review.* CCXXIV (January, 1915), pp. 182–201. Reprinted in *Edith Wharton: A Collection of Critical Essays.* Edited by Irving Howe. Englewood Cliffs, N.J.: Prentice-Hall, 1962, pp. 43–61.

McDowell, Margaret B. *Edith Wharton.* New York: Twayne, 1976, pp. 64–71.

Nevius, Blake. "*Ethan Frome* and the Themes of Edith Wharton's Fiction," in *New England Quarterly.* XXIV (June, 1951), pp. 197–207. Reprinted in *Edith Wharton: A Study of Her Fiction.* Berkeley: University of California Press, 1953, pp. 117–124, 127–130. Also reprinted in *Edith Wharton: A Collection of Critical Essays.* Edited by Irving Howe. Englewood Cliffs, N.J.: Prentice-Hall, 1962, pp. 130–136.

Ransom, John Crowe. "Characters and Character: A Note on Fiction," in *American Review.* VI (January, 1936), pp. 271–275.

Thomas, J.D. "Marginalia on *Ethan Frome*," in *American Literature.* XXVII (November, 1955), pp. 405–409.

Trilling, Lionel. "The Morality of Inertia," in *Great Moral Dilemmas in Literature, Past and Present.* Edited by Robert M. MacIver. New York: Harper, 1956, pp. 37–46. Reprinted in *Edith Wharton: A Collection of Critical Essays.* Edited by Irving Howe. Englewood Cliffs, N.J.: Prentice-Hall, 1962, pp. 137–146.

Walton, Geoffrey. *Edith Wharton: A Critical Interpretation.* Rutherford, N.J.: Fairleigh Dickinson University Press, 1970, pp. 72–74, 78–83.

Wolff, Cynthia Griffin. *A Feast of Words: The Triumph of Edith Wharton.* New York: Oxford University Press, 1977, pp. 163–184.

THE HOUSE OF MIRTH

Type of work: Novel
Author: Edith Wharton (1862–1937)
Time of plot: Early twentieth century
Locale: New York
First published: 1905

One of Wharton's finest novels, this is the story of a girl alone trying to survive in a hypocritical and shallow society, in which a young woman's only assets are her beauty and her ability to amuse the rich who might be her protectors. The book is a devastating criticism of the emptiness and cruelty of people who calculate individual worth only in terms of dollars.

Principal Characters

Lily Bart, a fascinating, beautiful young woman sacrificed to the false ideals of New York social life, the belief that a "good" marriage is preferable to a happy one and that appearances must be maintained, regardless of the expense. Through the machinations of a jealous wife whose husband has fallen in love with Lily, the hapless girl is eventually brought to social disgrace, poverty, and death.

Lawrence Selden, an intellectual young bachelor lawyer in love with Lily. Although he prefers to remain on the outskirts of New York high society, he is popular and invited into many fashionable homes. Always in the background, he tries to steer Lily's life for her, but he is too weak to marry her.

Gertrude Farish, called Gerty, Selden's cousin, who lives alone in a modest apartment and is much taken up with philanthropy. In desperation, Lily goes to her for help, but Gertrude can offer her little solace.

Mr. Rosedale, a young Jewish financier who is trying to enter the upper brackets of New York society. At the beginning of the story, when Lily retains her position in society, he wants to marry her. Later, after her conduct has been questioned and she is willing to marry him, he is no longer interested.

Percy Gryce, a shy young man protected from designing women by his strong-minded, possessive mother. He is much taken with Lily Bart because she shows great interest in his collection of Americana. Eventually he is frightened off because of Lily's popularity with other men, and he ends up marrying Gwen Van Osburgh.

Mrs. Gryce, Percy's mother, a monumental woman with the voice of a public orator and a mind divided between concern for her son and the iniquities of her servants.

George Dorset, a mournful dyspeptic, unhappily married. He falls in love with Lily and thus arouses his wife's jealousy and resentment, bringing about the scandal which contributes to Lily's downfall.

Bertha Dorset, George Dorset's garrulous, pretty wife, who is vicious in her treatment of Lily Bart after she has learned that her husband has grown fond of the girl. Mrs. Dorset behaves indiscreetly with Ned Silverton, carries on a clandestine correspondence with Lawrence Selden, and has several other affairs, but she cannot tolerate her husband's affection for Lily.

Ned Silverton, a handsome, weak young "poet of passion." Spoiled by wealthy patronesses, he develops too expensive a taste for bridge and incurs many gambling debts.

Mrs. Carrie Fisher, a striking divorcee. She takes pity on Lily in the midst of that young woman's poverty and tries to establish for her connections that will help her out of her predicament.

Mrs. Peniston, Lily's aunt, the widowed sister of Hudson Bart, who takes charge of her niece after the death of Lily's parents. Mrs. Peniston gives Lily little affection; however, she leaves her ten thousand dollars when she dies, with instructions that Lily is to use the money in payment of her debts.

Charles Augustus Trenor, called **Gus,** an investment broker, and
Judy Trenor, prominent New York society people. Lily is invited to many parties and cruises on their yacht. Mrs.

Trenor seems to exist solely as a hostess, while Mr. Trenor is in Wall Street and deeply interested in his business affairs. He invests for Lily some money she has won at bridge and gets large returns from the small sum. Later Lily finds out that the returns have been from Trenor's pocket and that she owes him ten thousand dollars. This debt and its implications horrify Lily and her attempt to repay it precipitates the cause of her breakdown and subsequent death from an overdose of chloral.

Jack Stepney and
Grace Stepney, Lily Bart's cousins. Typical in their conforming attitudes, they obey all the social forms and are shocked by Lily's behavior.

Gwen Van Osburgh, the girl, "reliable as roast mutton," whom Percy Gryce marries. She has a deep affinity with Gryce; they share the same prejudices and ideals and have the same ability to make other standards nonexistent by ignoring them.

Mr. Wetherall and
Mrs. Wetherall, guests at Bellemont, the Dorset estate. They belong to the vast group of people who go through life without neglecting to perform a single one of the gestures executed by the social puppets that surround them.

The Story

Selden enjoyed watching Lily Bart put a new plan into operation. She was a very beautiful and clever young lady, and no matter how impromptu any action of hers appeared, Selden knew that she never moved without a definitely worked out plan.

Lily had almost no money of her own; her beauty and her good family background were her only assets. Her father had died soon after a reversal of his financial affairs, and her mother had drilled into her the idea that a wealthy marriage was her only salvation. After her mother's death, Lily was taken in by her aunt, Mrs. Peniston. Mrs. Peniston supplied her with fashionable clothes and a good home, but Lily needed jewels, gowns, and cash to play bridge if she were to move in a social circle filled by wealthy and eligible men.

Mr. Rosedale, a Jewish financier, would gladly have married Lily and provided her with a huge fortune, for he wanted to be accepted into the society in which Lily moved. But Lily thought that she still had other prospects less repulsive to her, the most likely one being Percy Gryce, who lived protected from scheming women by his watchful widowed mother.

Lily used her knowledge of his quiet life to her advantage. Selden, Lily, and Gryce were all house guests at the home of Gus and Judy Trenor, and the opportunity was a perfect one for Lily, who assumed the part of a shy, demure young girl. But when Gryce was ready to propose, she let the chance slip away from her, for Lily really hated the kind of person she had become. In addition, although Selden was poor and offered her no escape from her own poverty, she was attracted to him because only he really understood her.

Gus Trenor offered to invest some of Lily's small income, and over a period of time he returned to her more than eight thousand dollars, which he assured her was profit on the transaction. With that amount she was able to pay most of her creditors and reopen her charge accounts. Gus seemed to think, however, that his wise investment on her account should make them better friends than Lily felt was desirable.

In the meantime, Lily unexpectedly got possession of some letters which Bertha Dorset had written to Selden. Bertha had once loved Selden, but George Dorset's fortune was great and she had left Selden for George. She continued to write to Selden after her marriage.

When Gus Trenor began to get more insistent in his demands for Lily's companionship, she became really worried. She knew that people were talking about her a great deal and that her position in society was precarious. She turned to Selden for advice. He told her that he loved her for what she could be, but that he could give her nothing now. He had no money, and he would not even offer her his love because he could not love her as she was, a scheming, ruthless fortune-hunter.

One night Lily received a message that Judy Trenor wanted her to call. When she arrived at the Trenor home, Lily found Gus there alone. He had sent the message. Gus told her then that the money had not been profit on her investment, but a gift from him. When he intimated that she had always known the money was from him personally, Lily was terrified, but at last she managed to get out of the house. She knew then that there was only one thing for her to do. She must accept Rosedale's offer of marriage. But before she wrote to Rosedale accepting his offer, the Dorsets invited her to take a Mediterranean cruise on their yacht. The moment of decision was postponed for a time.

Selden also left New York. Unknown to her, he had seen Lily leave the Trenor house on the night Gus had tricked her into thinking Judy wanted her to call. Selden had always refused to believe the unsavory stories circulating about Lily, but the evidence of his own eyes, he thought, was too plain to be ignored. When he met Lily abroad, he treated her with courteous disinterest.

Lily returned to New York. Her aunt, Mrs. Peniston, had died, leaving Lily ten thousand dollars. Lily planned to repay Gus Trenor with her inheritance, and she found intolerable the delay in settling her aunt's estate. Meanwhile Bertha Dorset's insinuations about Lily's conduct abroad, coupled with the talk about Lily and Gus Trenor, finished Lily's reputation. She took various positions, until at last she was reduced to working in the factory of a milliner. She had first offered to accept Rosedale's former proposal of marriage, but she was no longer useful to Rosedale since her fall from favor, and he refused to marry her. He knew that Lily had the letters Bertha had written Selden, and he also knew that George Dorset no longer loved his wife and would gladly marry Lily. It seemed to Rosedale that Lily had only two alternatives, either to take George Dorset away from Bertha or to go to Bertha with the letters and force her to receive Lily once more.

At first Lily's feeling for Selden made her shrink from doing anything that would harm him. Then she lost her position. Without money to buy food or to pay for her room in a dingy boarding-house, she reluctantly took the letters and started to the Dorset home. On the way she stopped to see Selden. When he again told her that he loved her, or rather that he would love her if she would only give up her greed for wealth and position, she gave up her plan and, unseen by him, dropped the letters into the fireplace. Then she thanked him for the kindness he, and he alone, had given her, and walked out into the night.

When she returned to her room, she found the check for the ten thousand dollars of her inheritance. She sat down at once and wrote a check to Gus Trenor for the amount she owed him and put it in an envelope. In another envelope she placed the ten thousand dollar check and addressed the envelope to her bank. She put the two envelopes side by side on her desk before she lay down to sleep.

But sleep would not come. At last she took from her bureau a bottle of chloral, which she had bought for those nights when she could not sleep. She poured the contents of the bottle into a glass and drank the whole. Then she lay down again upon her bed.

The next morning, feeling a sudden need to see Lily at once, Selden went early to her rooming-house. There he found a doctor already in attendance and Lily dead from an overdose of chloral. On her desk he saw the two envelopes. The stub of the open checkbook beside them told the whole story of Lily's last effort to get her accounts straight before she died. He knew then that his love for her had been justified, but the words he spoke as he knelt by her bed came too late.

Critical Evaluation

"Life is the saddest thing," Edith Wharton once wrote, "next to death." *The House of Mirth* perhaps comes as close to tragedy as any novel written in America. Neglected by a generation bored with stories of high society, *The House of Mirth* is now recognized as one of Wharton's outstanding works. One reason for this recognition is that the novel deals with more than high society. It contains the very arresting sequence in which Lily Bart works in the millinery factory. Here Wharton examines the oppression of laborers, a recurring theme in her work, although she is not so sentimental as to overlook the cruelty of those same laborers toward one another. She also explores the character of Mr. Selden, who is not a member of the upper class. But Selden and the millinery factory do not alone explain the novel's newfound appeal.

The House of Mirth is primarily about the degradation of the members of the upper class, and it is one of the most powerful novels of its kind. It illustrates, in bold and clear detail, what the members of the upper class—the "right people"—undergo to keep their places in that class: the meaningless rituals, their loveless marriages, their face-saving loans to friends. Also illustrated is the pervasive influence of the "right people" on those who do not belong, and who should be, but are not, able to see the emptiness of class values. Rosedale, an outsider because of his birth and religion, is overpowered by a need to belong. To satisfy this need, he has worked hard to acquire a fortune; to satisfy this need, he is willing to marry Lily Bart, even if he has to assume her debts.

Lily Bart is a victim of her birth into the upper class. Her artistic sensitivity might have developed into a superior talent, but has been allowed to atrophy because of her acceptance of the teaching that ladies of her class have only one destiny—to make a "good marriage." Thus educated, Lily pursues this "good marriage" in the way a businessman would pursue a good investment, passing up Rosedale in the hope that Percy Gryce might be available. Yet her good qualities get the better of her just as she has almost won Percy Gryce. To maintain her contacts and her place in society, she is obliged to play bridge and to gamble away money she does not have. She misses a second chance to marry Rosedale when the Dorsets invite her on a trip to Europe, thinking that they are thus helping out a fellow member of high society by taking her away from her troubles. The trip, however, ends in disaster, causing Lily to feud with Mrs. Dorset and ruin herself as a respectable members of the upper class. No longer eligible for protection by her social peers, or for marriage to the social-climbing Rosedale, Lily must seek a job. She goes to work in the millinery factory, and there discovers that birth and breeding do not provide one with usable skills.

Lily's ruin is partly treated as a naturalistic drama in which the victim of environment and chance is inexorably crushed. A sense of fatality hangs over the book. But throughout, most especially toward the end, the possibility of escape presents itself, in the person of Selden. At the beginning, he is willing to rescue Lily from the emptiness of being one of the "right people." At the end, he tenders an offer, subject to entirely reasonable conditions, to rescue her from poverty and uselessness. But she is essentially unable to communicate with him, despite her concern that he not be victimized by her corrupt entanglements. Such lack of communication is as much a theme of *The House of Mirth* as is criticism of high society.

Like many communicative failures in real life, that of *The House of Mirth* takes many forms. At first, it is Lily who cannot express her love for Selden because he is not one of the "right people." She offends him by offering to be his friend while continuing her mercenary search for a "good marriage." Later, it is Selden who becomes harsh toward Lily because of unfounded suspicion, although he cannot set aside his genuine feeling for her. In the end, and most pathetically, it is Lily who cannot reach out, because she feels unworthy of Selden.

Most of the action is told from Lily's viewpoint. But, at the beginning, the middle, and the end, it is the story of Selden. A sympathetic character because of the genuineness of his love and because of his freedom from the false values of high society, Selden nevertheless suffers from an inability to see things in context, and, no less than Lily, from a failure to make his true feelings known. For this, he assumes a disproportionate share of the blame for Lily's death.

The House of Mirth can be seen as either the story of Lily or the story of Selden. Lily's story is an indictment of a class, and is somewhat limited in its appeal by the subsequent changes which have occurred in our society. The American upper class is no longer as powerful or prestigious as it was in Edith Wharton's time, and its values have changed. Its members betray a certain amount of guilt because of their privileges and the interests of the quest for proper marriages has been mitigated. Even so, Lily's story is relevant so long as meaningless social rituals, class envy, and the belief that women can have only limited destinies continue.

Bibliography

Auchincloss, Louis. *Edith Wharton.* Minneapolis: University of Minnesota Press, 1961, pp. 11–17. Revised and reprinted in *Pioneers and Caretakers: A Study of Nine Women Novelists.* Minneapolis: University of Minnesota Press, 1961, pp. 25–29.

Bristol, Marie. "Life Among the Ungentle Genteel: Edith Wharton's *The House of Mirth*," in *Western Humanities Review.* XVI (Autumn, 1962), pp. 371–374.

Coolidge, Olivia. *Edith Wharton, 1862–1937.* New York: Scribner's, 1964, pp. 81–83.

Dahl, Curtis. "Edith Wharton's *The House of Mirth*: Sermon on a Text," in *Modern Fiction Studies.* XXI (1975), pp. 572–576.

Gargano, James W. "*The House of Mirth*: Social Futility and Faith," in *American Literature.* XLIV (March, 1972), pp. 137–143.

Gelfant, Blanche Housman. *The American City Novel.* Norman: University of Oklahoma Press, 1954, pp. 107–119.

Grumbach, Doris. "Reconsideration," in *New Republic.* CLXVIII (April 21, 1973), pp. 29–30.

Howe, Irving. "A Reading of *The House of Mirth,*" in *Edith Wharton: A Collection of Critical Essays.* Edited by Irving Howe. Englewood Cliffs, N.J.: Prentice-Hall, 1962, pp. 119–129.

Kellogg, Grace. *The Two Lives of Edith Wharton: The Woman and Her Work.* New York: Appleton-Century, 1965, pp. 106–114, 121–123.

Kronenberger, Louis. "Edith Wharton's New York: Two Period Pieces," in *Michigan Quarterly Review.* IV (Winter, 1965), pp. 3–13. Reprinted in *The Polished Surface: Essays in the Literature of Worldliness.* New York: Knopf, 1969, pp. 256–270.

Lawson, Richard H. *Edith Wharton.* New York: Frederick Ungar, 1977, pp. 29–39.

Lewis, R.W.B. *Trials of the Word.* New Haven, Conn.: Yale University Press, 1965, pp. 129–147.

Lindberg, Gary H. *Edith Wharton and the Novel of Manners.* Charlottesville: University Press of Virginia, 1975, pp. 61–67, 87–93, 122–128.

Lubbock, Percy. "The Novels of Edith Wharton," in *Quarterly Review.* CCXXIV (January, 1915), pp. 182–201. Reprinted in *Edith Wharton: A Collection of Critical Essays.* Edited by Irving Howe. Englewood Cliffs, N.J.: Prentice-Hall, 1962, pp. 43–61.

Lyde, Marilyn Jones. *Edith Wharton: Convention and Morality in the Work of a Novelist.* Norman: University of Oklahoma Press, 1959, pp. 115–118, 171–173.

McDowell, Margaret B. *Edith Wharton.* New York: Twayne, 1976, pp. 43–52.

McIlvaine, Robert. "Edith Wharton's American Beauty Rose," in *Journal of American Studies.* VII (August, 1973), pp. 183–185.

Nevius, Blake. *Edith Wharton: A Study of Her Fiction.* Berkeley: University of California Press, 1953, pp. 53–62.

Poirier, Richard. "Edith Wharton: *The House of Mirth,*" in *The American Novel from James Fenimore Cooper to William Faulkner.* Edited by Wallace Stegner. New York: Basic Books, 1965, pp. 117–132. Expanded and reprinted in *A World Elsewhere: The Place of Style in American Literature.* New York: Oxford University Press, 1966, pp. 215–235.

Rideout, Walter B. "Edith Wharton's *The House of Mirth,*" in *Twelve Original Essays on Great American Novels.* Edited by Charles Shapiro. Detroit: Wayne State University Press, 1958, pp. 148–176.

Rubin, Larry. "Aspects of Naturalism in Four Novels by Edith Wharton," in *Twentieth Century Literature*. II (January, 1957), pp. 182–186.

Trilling, Diana. *"The House of Mirth* Revisited," in *Harper's Bazaar.* LXXXI (1947), pp. 126–127, 181–186. Reprinted in *Edith Wharton: A Collection of Critical Essays*. Edited by Irving Howe. Englewood Cliffs, N.J.: Prentice-Hall, 1962, pp. 103–118.

Vella, Michael W. "Technique and Theme in *The House of Mirth*," in *Markham Review*. II (May, 1970), pp. 17–20.

Walton, Geoffrey. *Edith Wharton: A Critical Interpretation*. Rutherford, N.J.: Fairleigh Dickinson University Press, 1970, pp. 44–63.

Wolff, Cynthia Griffin. *A Feast of Words: The Triumph of Edith Wharton*. New York: Oxford University Press, 1977, pp. 109–133.

THORNTON WILDER

Born: Madison, Wisconsin (April 17, 1897)
Died: Hamden, Connecticut (December 7, 1975)

Principal Works

NOVELS: *The Cabala*, 1926; *The Bridge of San Luis Rey*, 1927; *The Woman of Andros*, 1930; *Heaven's My Destination*, 1934; *The Ides of March*, 1948; *The Eighth Day*, 1967.

PLAYS: *The Angel That Troubled the Waters and Other Plays*, 1928; *The Long Christmas Dinner and Other Plays*, 1931; *Our Town*, 1938; *The Merchant of Yonkers*, 1939; *The Skin of Our Teeth*, 1942; *The Matchmaker*, 1955 (revised from *The Merchant of Yonkers*).

Thornton (Niven) Wilder's work displays individual qualities of wit, imagination, and careful workmanship, all combined with beauty and precision of style. As a novelist and playwright he always followed his own course, even in decades when the literary current was flowing in quite different channels, such as naturalism, reportage, social documentation. Among the veering trends by which his contemporaries reacted to the special concerns of our time, his work took root in the humaneness and restraint of a classical tradition. A literary figure of some distinction in his own right, he was also a teacher of students on both sides of the Atlantic, and in this role he helped to create a cultural link between the Old World and the New.

Wilder was born in Madison, Wisconsin, on April 17, 1897, the son of Amos P. Wilder, who was at that time editor of the *Wisconsin State Journal*. When he was nine, he accompanied his family to China, where his father was consul general at Hong Kong and Shanghai. This was the first of a series of wanderings and international contacts which in part shaped the outward pattern of his life and the inward habit of detached observation characteristic of his novels and plays. He finished high school in California and in 1915 entered Oberlin College, only to leave that school two years later for service in the Coast Artillery Corps during World War I. After the war he transferred to Yale, received his B.A. degree in 1920, studied for a year at the American Academy in Rome, and in 1921 became an instructor in a preparatory school at Lawrenceville, New Jersey. In 1926 he received his M.A. degree from Princeton.

In the same year he published his first novel, *The Cabala*, the gracefully written story of a young American in postwar Rome and his contacts with a group of talented and wealthy aristocrats who exert a mysterious influence on affairs of state and Church. Drawn into their secret confidences and councils, he sees them at last for what they are: the pagan gods of Europe grown old and unable, in spite of their ancient wisdom, to save themselves from the sufferings and follies of ordinary humanity. With a great leap in time and space, Wilder's imagination moved to Colonial Peru for his second novel, *The Bridge of San Luis Rey*, a brief but evocative retelling of events in five lives snuffed out in the collapse of a bridge on the road between Lima and Cuzco. The stories are beautifully told; not without irony, Wilder seeks to discover the working of a providential plan in the disaster, and only at the end does the reader perceive that his characters represent in their different persons the bitterness, innocence, sorrow, and humility of love. Some critics, noting his use of the celebrated French letter writer Madame de Sévigné as the model for one of his characters, suggested that there was a strong element of pastiche in Wilder's writing. It is, in fact, an open secret that Wilder's mind often found imaginative stimulus in a forgotten nineteenth century play, in Roman histories, in work as modern as James Joyce's *Finnegans Wake*. What his critics minimize, however, is Wilder's own note, his detached but not unkind gaze to which he subjects the materials toward which his mind and imagination turned. Thus his third novel, *The Woman of Andros*, is more than a story based on the *Andria* of Terence; it is another probing into hidden meanings in human experience, presented through man's blundering impulses toward truth in a twilight age that waited for the birth of a great faith.

Although Wilder's sources are usually "literary," his manipulation of them is not pedantic; he displays in whatever he touched the same sure craftsmanship and the working of a mind enlivened by considerable imagination and wit. In *Heaven's My Destination* he took the pattern of the picaresque novel and imposed on it a new subject matter, evangelistic activity in the Middle West, so that the story of George Brush becomes the amusing yet touching saga of a cornfed Faithful and his travels through a modern Vanity Fair. *The Ides of March*, epistolary in form, takes for its subject events in the closing years of Julius Caesar's life; unlike the usual popular historical novel, however, this book represents full knowledge of a past period and full imaginative and artistic domination over it. *The Eighth Day*, the story of a fictitious murder, seemed to one critic to recall *The Bridge of San Luis Rey* in that it dealt with the effect of "a central and violent event on a widening circle of characters."

The same note of controlled experimentation sounds in Wilder's plays. His two most noteworthy, *Our Town* and *The Skin of Our Teeth*, are at once experimental and derivative in form; we can trace his progress toward these efforts in the one-act plays and dramatic character sketches written during his Lawrenceville years and collected in *The Angel That Troubled the Waters* and *The Long Christmas Dinner*. *Our Town* is the account of life in a New England village, but it is acted out on a bare stage, much in the manner of Oriental drama, and the lack of furnishings such as those which clutter the modern stage becomes an effective device in centering attention upon events which make this play a morality drama revealing the religious feeling that underlies Wilder's best work. *The Skin of Our Teeth* takes elements from Joyce and European expressionism and tells, in terms of the trials and temptations of one household, of the full course of human history on the planet. But beneath this surface diversity Wilder's own note persists, the point of view of the wise observer who is not involved in what he sees but who does not, for that reason, despise what he is observing in the failures and triumphs of mankind. The play became a subject of literary controversy when critics pointed out his debt to Joyce, but much of this curious critical flurry was negated by the fact that Joyce had in turn borrowed from the theories of Giovanni Battista Vico, eighteenth century Italian philosopher, in the writing of *Finnegans Wake*.

Wilder's intellectual history lies open to view in his novels and plays. During World War II he served as a combat-intelligence officer with the Air Force in Italy. He taught at the University of Chicago and at Harvard and gave special courses of lectures before various universities and learned societies throughout Europe. His last work was *The Matchmaker*, a revised version of *The Merchant of Yonkers*, first presented in 1939. Wilder died in 1975.

Bibliography

For biographical and critical studies see Linda Simon, *Thornton Wilder: His World*, 1979; Rex Burbank, *Thornton Wilder*, 1961; Bernard Grebanier, *Thornton Wilder*, 1964; Malcolm Goldstein, *The Art of Thornton Wilder*, 1965; and Donald Haberman, *The Plays of Thornton Wilder*, 1967. Three of his novels were reprinted in the *Thornton Wilder Trio*, 1956, for which Malcolm Cowley wrote a discerning and helpful preface. For criticism see Edmund Wilson, *Classics and Commercials*, 1950, and *Shores of Light*, 1952; Pierre Loving, "The Bridge of Casuistry," *This Quarter*, II (1929), 150–161; E. G. Twitchett, "Thornton Wilder," *London Mercury*, XXII (1930), 32–39; Robert McNamara, "Phases of American Religion in Thornton Wilder and Willa Cather," *Catholic World*, CXXXV (1932), 641–649; E. K. Brown, "A Christian Humanist, Thornton Wilder," *University of Toronto Quarterly*, IV (1935), 356–370; Dayton Kohler, "Thornton Wilder," *English Journal*, XXVII, (1939), 1–11; Martin Gardner, "Thornton Wilder and the Problem of Providence," *University of Kansas City Review*, VII (1940), 83–91; J. J. Firebaugh, "The Humanism of Thornton Wilder," *Pacific Spectator*, IV (1950), 426–438; and Arthur H. Ballet, " 'In Our Living and in Our Dying,' " *English Journal*, XLV (1956), 243–249. For a Marxian view of Wilder see also Michael Gold, "Wilder: Prophet of the Genteel Christ," *New Republic*, LXIV (1930), 266, and "The Economic Interpretation of Wilder," *ibid.*, LXV (1930), 31–32.

THE BRIDGE OF SAN LUIS REY

Type of work: Novel
Author: Thornton Wilder (1897–1975)
Time of plot: Early eighteenth century
Locale: Peru
First published: 1927

Set in Peru during its golden days as a Spanish colony, the plot of this novel is built around an investigation into the lives of five people who are killed when a bridge collapses. The investigation is made by a friar who witnesses the tragedy, and asks himself the philosophical question, "Was the event a random accident, or part of God's plan?" Always popular and widely read for its excellent character sketches, The Bridge of San Luis Rey won the Pulitzer Prize in 1927.

Principal Characters

Brother Juniper, a Spanish friar who tries to prove that the collapse of the bridge of San Luis Rey in Peru is an act showing the wisdom of God, who properly sent five persons to their deaths in the accident. For his book, which is condemned by the Church, the friar is burned at the stake.

The Narrator, who finds a copy of Brother Juniper's eighteenth century book and reconstructs for the reader the lives of the five persons who died when the bridge collapsed.

The Marquesa de Montemayor, an ugly woman with a beautiful daughter. She is highly possessive and selfish, first to her daughter and then to Pepita, her maid. By reading a letter from Pepita to an abbess the Marquesa learns her own nature, becomes contrite, and resolves to be a better woman, only to die the next day when the bridge collapses.

Pepita, maid for the Marquesa de Montemayor, who dies also when the bridge collapses. She is unhappy when she is sent from her convent by the Abbess

Madre María del Pilar, whom she loves, to serve the noblewoman. Her letter confessing her unhappiness reveals to the Marquesa the noblewoman's thoughtless and self-centered life.

Uncle Pio, an actor who discovers La Périchole singing in a tavern. He makes a great actress and singer of her, and comes to love her. He is disappointed by the girl, who becomes the mistress of the viceroy and soon is too proud for her own good. Uncle Pio takes her illegitimate child to rear, but the next day he and the child are victims of the collapse of the bridge.

Jaime, illegitimate son of La Périchole and the viceroy. He dies when the bridge collapses.

Esteban, a young man whose twin brother gives up his love for La Périchole because of the affection between the two brothers, foundlings reared by the Abbess Madre María del Pilar. Manuel dies, and his brother, who becomes a victim of the bridge's collapse, is inconsolable.

La Périchole, an actress who is overly

---

proud, especially after becoming the viceroy's mistress. Her pride diminishes when smallpox destroys her beauty. She puts her son in the care of Uncle Pio the day before both of them die.

Manuel, twin brother of Esteban. He hides his love for La Périchole so he will not hurt his brother's feelings, but in a delirium, close to death, he reveals his secret passion.

The Abbess Madre María del Pilar, who befriends the twin brothers, Esteban and Manuel, as well as Pepita, the girl who becomes the Marquesa de Montemayor's maid. The Abbess is a wise and kindly woman.

Doña Clara, cynical daughter of the Marquesa de Montemayor. She learns too late of her mother's change of heart and inner goodness.

The Story

On Friday, July the twentieth, 1714, the bridge of San Luis Rey, the most famous bridge in Peru, collapsed, hurling five travelers into the deep gorge below. Present at the time of the tragedy was Brother Juniper, who saw in the event a chance to prove, scientifically and accurately, the wisdom of that act of God. He spent all his time investigating the lives of the five who had died, and he published a book showing that God had had a reason to send each one of them to his death at exactly that moment. The book was condemned by the Church authorities, and Brother Juniper was burned at the stake. He had gone too far in explaining God's ways to man. Through a strange quirk of fate, one copy of the book was left undestroyed, and it fell into the hands of the author. From it, and from his own knowledge, he reconstructed the lives of the five persons.

The Marquesa de Montemayor had been an ugly child, and was still homely when she grew up. Because of the wealth of her family, she was fortunately able to marry a noble husband, by whom she had a lovely daughter, Doña Clara. As she grew into a beautiful young woman, the marquesa's daughter became more and more disgusted with her crude and unattractive mother, whose possessive and over-expressive love left Doña Clara cold and uncomfortable. The daughter finally married a man who took her to Spain. Separated from her one joy in life, the marquesa became more eccentric than before and spent her time writing long letters to her daughter in Spain.

In order to free herself of some of her household cares, the marquesa went to the Abbess Madre María del Pilar and asked for a girl from the abbess' school to come and live with her. So Pepita, unhappy that her beloved teacher was sending her away from the school, went to live with the marquesa.

When the marquesa learned by letter that Doña Clara was to have a child, she was filled with concern. She wore charms, bought candles for the saints, said prayers, and wrote all the advice she could discover to her daughter. As a last gesture, she took Pepita with her to pay a visit to a famous shrine from which she hoped her prayers would surely be heard. On the way the marquesa happened to read one of Pepita's letters to her old mistress, the abbess. From the letter the marquesa learned just how heartless she had been in her treatment of the girl, how thoughtless and egotistic. She realized that she had been guilty of the worst kind of love toward her daughter, love that was sterile, self-seeking, and false. Aglow with her new understanding, she wrote a final letter to her daughter, telling her of the change in her heart, asking forgiveness, and showing in wonderful language the change that had come over her. She resolved to change her life, to be kind to Pepita, to her household, to everyone. The next day she and Pepita, while crossing the bridge of San Luis Rey, fell to their deaths.

Esteban and Manuel were twin brothers who had been left as children on the doorstep of the abbess' school. She had brought them up as well as she could, but the strange relation between them was such that she could never make them talk much. When the boys were old enough, they left the school and took many kinds of jobs. At last they settled down as scribes, writing letters for the uncultured people of Lima. One day Manuel, called in to write some letters for La Périchole, fell in love with the charming actress. Never before had anything come between the brothers, for they had always been sufficient in themselves. For his brother's sake Manuel pretended that he cared little for the actress. Shortly afterward he cut his leg on a piece of metal and became very sick. In his delirium he let Esteban know that he really was in love with La Périchole. The infection grew worse and Manuel died.

Esteban was unable to do anything for weeks after his brother's death. He could not face life without him. The abbess finally arranged for him to go on a trip with a sea captain who was about to sail around the world. The captain had lost his only daughter and the abbess felt he would understand Esteban's problem and try to help him. Estaban left to go aboard ship, but on the way he fell with the others when the bridge broke.

Uncle Pio had lived a strange life before he came to Peru. There he had found a young girl singing in a tavern. After years of his coaching and training, she became the most popular actress of the Spanish world. She was called La Périchole, and Uncle Pio's greatest pleasure was to tease her and anger her into giving consistently better performances. All went well until the viceroy took an interest in the vivacious and beautiful young actress. When she became his mistress, she began to feel that the stage was too low for her. After living as a lady and becoming prouder and prouder as time went on, she contracted smallpox. Her beauty was ruined, and she retired to a small farm out of town, there to live a life of misery over her lost loveliness.

Uncle Pio had a true affection for his former protégée and tried time and again to see her. One night, by a ruse, he got her to talk to him. She refused to let him help her, but she allowed him to take Jamie, her illegitimate son, so that he could be educated as a gentleman. The old man and the young boy set off for Lima. On the way they came to the bridge, and died in the fall when it collapsed.

At the cathedral in Lima a great service was held for the victims. Everyone considered the incident an example of a true act of God, and many reasons were offered for the various deaths. Some months after the funeral, the abbess was visited by Doña Clara, the marquesa's daughter. Doña Clara had finally learned what a wonderful woman her mother had really been. The last letter had taught the cynical daughter all that her mother had so painfully learned. The daughter, too, had learned to see life in a new way. La Périchole also came to see the abbess. She had given up bemoaning her own lost beauty, and she began a lasting friendship with the abbess. Nothing could positively be said about the reason for the deaths of those five people on the bridge. Too many events were changed by them; one could not number them all. But the old abbess believed that the true meaning of the disaster was the lesson of love for those who survived.

Critical Evaluation

The Bridge of San Luis Rey marked the beginning of a key stage in Wilder's development and also revealed the essential dimensions of the artistic program he would follow. His first novel, *The Cabala* (1926), had viewed the decadent aristocracy of contemporary Rome through the eyes of a young American student. In the tradition of Henry James and Edith Wharton, the highly autobiographical work suffered by comparison and was not praised by the critics. But *The Bridge of San Luis Rey,* which vividly evoked a forgotten era and a type of society utterly foreign to Wilder's experience, sold three hundred thousand copies in its first year and made its author a celebrity. The descripition of early eighteenth century Peru was, in Edmund Wilson's estimation, "solid, incandescent, distinct." This success confirmed Wilder's intention to make abundant use of historical materials, and he set his next novel, *The Woman of Andros* (1930), in post-classical Greece. *The Bridge of San Luis Rey* also served notice that a major philosophical and theological writer had entered the literary scene. The engaging simplicity of the book drew its readers towards problems no less recondite than those of the justice of God, the possibility of disinterested love, and the role of memory in human relationships. That Wilder's subsequent works consistently returned to these themes was a surprise to no one, so powerfully had this novel stated them.

The Christianity which inspires and informs *The Bridge of San Luis Rey* is existential and pessimistic. "Only one reader in a thousand notices that I have asserted a denial of the survival of identity after death," Wilder once remarked of the book. He also denies the value of the apologetic task which Brother Juniper undertakes. For even if human reason could "scientifically demonstrate" God's providence—a proposition Wilder rejects —man would inevitably employ this knowledge in a self-aggrandizing manner. The inherent mystery of the divine intention is a check to human pride. And pride is Wilder's overriding concern, especially that pride which cloaks itself in the guise of "unselfish love." If there is providence, Wilder suggests, it most clearly operates as something which exposes the egoistic taint in all love and reveals to the lover his need to be forgiven both by the one he loves and the social community.

Despite the ostensible importance of Brother Juniper, Uncle Pio, and Esteban, only Wilder's female characters develop sufficiently to gain awareness of the meaning of the novel's action. The marquesa undergoes the clearest transformation. The maternal love which she cultivates so assiduously is neither spontaneous nor generous. Rather, the marquesa craves her daughter's affection as an antidote to her own insecurity. Her imagination first magnifies the daughter's virtues and prestige; then, to assuage a deep self-loathing, she demands from this "great lady" a meticulous and servile devotion. Aware of her manipulative impulses, the marquesa is nevertheless powerless to conquer them. And she is not aware of how her distorted passion causes misery to those around her. The revelation of Pepita's agonized loneliness shames and humiliates her. But she thereby gains the strength to eliminate the element of tyranny in the love she bears for her daughter.

Because La Périchole (Camila) appears in each of the three tales, she is the novel's most real character. Her satirical attack on the marquesa becomes ironic when, later on, her own ugliness and avarice also make her the object of gossip and scorn. And like the marquesa, she does not believe herself to be intrinsically valuable. But Uncle Pio, who first treated Camila as something to dominate and take aesthetic delight in, now loves her unconditionally. Her willingness to accept this fact and express her love causes him to suffer and isolates her unnaturally from society. Such a painful yet liberating acceptance is made possible both by Pio's persistence and her love for Jaime. Her grief, and the possibility of disinterested love which it implies, moves her at last to present her disfigured self to society.

Even though her moral insight makes the abbess the standard against which all in the novel is measured, she too must suffer and grow. Unlike the abstract and detached Brother Juniper, she makes herself vulnerable to the pains which love and service involve. Unlike the marquesa, she does not demand instant expressions of servile devotion from those who love her. But she does yearn to have her work remembered, to gain that (in Wilder's view illusory) immortality which comes to those who labor for great causes. Consequently, she manipulates Pepita much as Uncle Pio manipulates Camila. That Pepita died lonely and forsaken reveals to the abbess the results of her misguided passion. Her faith undergoes a purification when she confronts the fact that "Even memory is not necessary for love."

The episode of Esteban and Manuel does not fit neatly into the pattern Wilder generally establishes. Some critics have suggested that Wilder here meant to deal with homosexual love. This view is partially refuted by the heterosexual activity of both youths and by Esteban's evident unwillingness to stand between Manuel and Camila. But does Esteban unconsciously attempt to retain possession of his brother, communicating his feelings through the uncanny channels of sympathy which bind these twins? Even if this were so, there remains the fact that Manuel also is unable to conceive of a separation. The tale thus seems to constitute a digression, one which serves to underscore the enormous mystery and intensity of all relationships of love. It is linked to the central thematic pattern by Esteban's deep feelings for the abbess, which enables him to reach out to another human being despite his tragic sorrow.

For Wilder, it is almost impossible for human beings to live serenely and faithfully knowing that their personalities will neither be remembered by society nor allowed to survive death in a hereafter. This prospect creates an anxiety which pervades all their efforts to love. They persistently use the beloved to prove themselves worthy and immortal. Then to love are added additional, degrading elements. Men never realize, in the abbess' words, that "the love will have been enough." Wilder's views could have led him to enormous sentimentality but in truth, *The Bridge of San Luis Rey* is extraordinarily stark. It is sustained only by the single hope that "all those impulses of love return to the love that made them."

Bibliography

Burbank, Rex. *Thornton Wilder.* New York: Twayne, 1961, pp. 44–57.

Goldstein, Malcolm. *The Art of Thornton Wilder.* Lincoln: University of Nebraska Press, 1965, pp. 49–62.

Grebanier, Bernard. *Thornton Wilder.* Minneapolis: University of Minnesota Press, 1964, pp. 15–20.

Haberman, Donald. *The Plays of Thornton Wilder, a Critical Study.* Middletown, Conn.: Wesleyan University Press, 1967, pp. 31–34.

Kuner, M.C. *Thornton Wilder: The Bright and the Dark.* New York: Crowell, 1972, pp. 62–79.

Papajewski, Helmut. *Thornton Wilder.* Translated by John Conway. New York: Frederick Ungar, 1968, pp. 91–108.

Stuckey, W.J. *The Pulitzer Prize Novels; a Critical Backward Look.* Norman: University of Oklahoma Press, 1966, pp. 74–81.

THOMAS WOLFE

Born: Asheville, North Carolina (October 3, 1900)
Died: Baltimore, Maryland (September 15, 1938)

Principal Works

NOVELS: *Look Homeward, Angel,* 1929; *Of Time and the River,* 1935; *The Web and the Rock,* 1939; *You Can't Go Home Again,* 1940.

SHORT STORIES: *From Death to Morning,* 1935; *The Hills Beyond,* 1941.

PLAYS: *The Return of Buck Gavin,* 1924 (in *Carolina Folk-Plays: Second Series,* edited by Frederick H. Koch); *Mannerhouse,* 1948.

BELLES-LETTRES: *The Story of a Novel,* 1936.

LETTERS: *Thomas Wolfe's Letters to His Mother,* edited by J. S. Terry, 1943; *The Letters of Thomas Wolfe,* edited by Elizabeth Nowell, 1956.

MISCELLANEOUS: *A Note on Experts,* 1939; *Gentlemen of the Press,* 1942; *A Western Journal,* 1951; *Notebooks,* edited by Richard S. Kennedy and Paschal Reeves, 1970.

Thomas (Clayton) Wolfe was born October 3, 1900, in Asheville, North Carolina. He was the youngest child in the family, with older brothers and sisters. His father, W. O. Wolfe, was a stonecutter who had been born in central Pennsylvania and who went south to live soon after the Civil War. His mother was Julia Westall, of Asheville. Wolfe was educated in public schools until he was twelve, when he was entered at the North State School under the direction of Mr. and Mrs. J. M. Roberts. Attending school here until graduation (1912–1916), he entered the University of North Carolina (1916–1920). His stay at Chapel Hill was maturing and exciting; he stood well in his classes, became interested in the Carolina Playmakers and wrote plays of his own in which he acted, and became one of the most popular and outstanding figures on the campus of his time. Encouraged by Professor Frederick H. Koch of the Playmakers, Wolfe decided to do graduate work at Harvard in George Pierce Baker's 47 Dramatic Workshop, and to make playwriting his career.

He remained three years at Harvard, two of them as student, taking his A.M. degree in 1922, and hoping to place at least one of his plays for Broadway production. During his years at Harvard, his father died, and Wolfe accepted a teaching appointment as instructor in English at New York University. He began teaching in February, 1924.

Soon afterward he was diverted from playwriting to fiction. *Look Homeward, Angel* was started in England in 1924, when Wolfe made his first visit abroad; it was finished in 1928, placed by Madeleine Boyd with Maxwell Perkins, managing editor of Scribner's, and published in October, 1929. The book was generally well received; only at home in North Carolina were the reactions antagonistic. The turmoil occasioned by *Look Homeward, Angel* in his home town hurt Wolfe; he was naïvely surprised that his novel should be so patently recognized for what it was, a very thinly disguised autobiography, and he avoided a return to Asheville until the year before his death.

Recognition came slowly for Wolfe, but surely. In 1930, in his address of acceptance of the Nobel Prize for literature, Sinclair Lewis paid Wolfe tribute on the basis of his only book, *Look Homeward, Angel*, and prophesied a great future for the younger novelist. In the meantime Wolfe was working on a second novel, a continuation of the story of Eugene Gant, which was published in 1935 as *Of Time and the River*. Although equally autobiographical, *Of Time and the River* stirred no local animosities in Asheville, perhaps because the scenes of the book were removed to Boston, New York, and Europe. In the summer of 1935 Wolfe was invited to speak at a writers' conference at Boulder, Colorado, where he delivered a series of lectures which became an account of the writer's craft and which was published the following year as *The Story of a Novel*. Also published in 1935 were the sketches and short stories called *From Death to Morning*.

By 1937 Wolfe had come to a momentous decision with himself: he had smarted from criticism and gossip which suggested too much dependence upon the guiding editorship of Maxwell Perkins, and so Wolfe decided to change publishers and become "far more objective in his approach to fiction." He signed a new contract with Harper and Brothers, and delivered to his new editor the continuing development of "the book," a work in progress incorporating some changes which Wolfe mistakenly believed to be much greater than they actually were. "The book"—Wolfe's name for the constantly accumulating manuscript of his writings—was still the story of Eugene Gant-Thomas Wolfe. Now, however, the chief protagonist was renamed George Webber, and he varied somewhat in physical appearance and family background from Eugene Gant, but the other circumstances were much the same. In 1937 Wolfe returned to Asheville to find himself recognized as famous and forgiven for the shock of *Look Homeward, Angel*; but other things had also changed, and Wolfe, the man, like Gant-Webber, the character, discovered that "You can't go home again."

In the Spring of 1938 Wolfe was invited to lecture at Purdue University. From there he started on a trip to the Far West, stopping at Denver and making a great sweep through the National Park country. In Seattle he was ill with a cold, locally diagnosed as pneumonia; he was removed to a hospital and his brother Fred was called West to attend him. When his condition grew worse, Fred Wolfe was joined by his sister, Mrs. Mabel Wheaton. Consulting physicians suspected a brain tumor; certainly an operation was indicated. The family conference determined that any operation should be done at Johns Hopkins, in Baltimore, and there Wolfe was brought in August. The operation revealed multiple tuberculosis of the brain. Wolfe never came out of the coma which followed the operation, and he died in Baltimore on September 15, 1938, less than a month before his thirty-eighth birthday. His body was taken to Asheville for burial; only in death could the wanderer "go home again."

Wolfe's third and fourth novels, *The Web and the Rock* and *You Can't Go Home Again*, were readied for posthumous publication by Edward C. Aswell, Wolfe's editor and personal friend at Harper. The novels added stature to Wolfe's increasing position as a major writer, and brought his fictional work to a reasonable conclusion. In 1941 appeared *The Hills Beyond*, another series of short stories and sketches, and "The Hills Beyond," a fragmentary and incomplete novel introducing some of the Gant-Webber family members of an earlier time in the Carolina mountains. *Mannerhouse*, a play first written by Wolfe during his stay at Harvard, appeared in published form in 1948. His *Letters to His Mother* came out in 1943. *The Letters of Thomas Wolfe*, collected and edited by his literary agent, Elizabeth Nowell, appeared in 1956; these letters constitute what amounts to an autobiography.

Before his death Thomas Wolfe was already becoming a legend. Everything about him was greater than lifesize. He was six feet five inches tall; his capacities for vividly rendering sense impressions and physical appetites and energies were widely known and praised; his books confirmed the statement of the American Dream better than it had been expressed since Walt Whitman, and characters of his fiction had already entered general allusive consciousness. He is still a controversial figure, but his popularity seems to continue growing and to encourage new studies and new converts.

Bibliography

The definitive biography is Elizabeth Nowell, *Thomas Wolfe*, 1960. Herbert J. Muller, *Thomas Wolfe*, 1947, is the pioneer critical study. Other biographical and critical studies include Pamela Hansford Johnson, *Thomas Wolfe: A Critical Study*, 1947 [*Hungry Gulliver: An English Critical Appraisal*]; Agatha B. Adams, *Thomas Wolfe: Carolina Student*, 1950; Daniel L. Delakas, *Thomas Wolfe: La France et les romanciers français*, 1950; T. C. Pollock and Oscar Cargill, *Thomas Wolfe at Washington Square*, 1954; Louis D. Rubin, Jr., *Thomas Wolfe: The Weather of His Youth*, 1955; C. Hugh Holman, *Thomas Wolfe*, 1960; Richard S. Kennedy, *The Window of Memory: The Literary Career of Thomas Wolfe*, 1962; and Bruce R. McElderry, *Thomas Wolfe*, 1964. Related materials are found in Hayden Norwood, *The Marble Man's Wife*, 1947; and Maxwell Perkins, *Editor to Author: The Letters of Maxwell E. Perkins*, edited by John Hall Wheelock, 1950; and T. C. Pollock and Oscar Cargill, eds., *The Correspondence of Thomas Wolfe and Homer Andrew Watts*, 1954.

For articles on Wolfe in books see Herbert J. Muller, *Modern Fiction: A Study of Values*, 1937; Joseph Warren Beach, *American Fiction, 1920–1940*, 1941; Maxwell Geismar, *Writers in Crisis*, 1942; Alfred Kazin, *On Native Grounds*, 1942; George Snell, *Shapers of American Fiction, 1798–1947*, 1947; E. B. Burgum, *The Novel and the World's Dilemma*, 1947; F. J. Hoffman, *The Modern*

Novel in America, 1900–1950, 1951; Gerald S. Sloyan, "Thomas Wolfe: A Legend of a Man's Youth in His Hunger," in *Fifty Years of the American Novel*, edited by Harold C. Gardiner, 1952; and Louis D. Rubin, Jr., "Thomas Wolfe in Time and Place," in *Southern Renascence*, edited by Rubin and Robert D. Jacobs, 1953.

See also Hamilton Basso, "Thomas Wolfe: A Portrait," *New Republic*, LXXXVII (1936), 199–202; Dayton Kohler, "Thomas Wolfe: Prodigal and Lost," *College English*, I (1939), 1–10; William Braswell, "Thomas Wolfe Lectures and Takes a Holiday," *ibid.*, 11–22; John Peale Bishop, "The Sorrows of Thomas Wolfe," *Kenyon Review*, I (1939), 7–17; Henry T. Volkening, "Thomas Wolfe: Penance No More," *Virginia Quarterly Review*, XV (1939), 196–215; E. K. Brown, "Thomas Wolfe: Realist and Symbolist," *University of Toronto Quarterly*, X (1941), 153–166; John M. Maclachan, "Folk Concepts in the Novels of Thomas Wolfe," *Southern Folklore Quarterly*, IX (1945), 28–36; Margaret Church, "Thomas Wolfe: Dark Time," *Publications of the Modern Language Association*, LXIV (1949), 629–638; and Betty Thompson, "Thomas Wolfe: Two Decades of Criticism," *South Atlantic Quarterly*, LXIX (1950), 378–392.

The Portable Thomas Wolfe, 1946, contains an excellent introduction by Maxwell Geismar.

LOOK HOMEWARD, ANGEL

Type of work: Novel
Author: Thomas Wolfe (1900–1938)
Time of plot: 1900–early 1920's
Locale: North Carolina
First published: 1919

An attempt to re-create the whole American experience in Wolfe's own terms, this sprawling novel combines a large cast of brilliant and vital characters and a chaotic, romantic representation of the United States in the early days of this century. In the center of this swirling mass stands the young hero Eugene Gant— Wolfe himself—trying to cope with the world and with his own emotions and genius.

Principal Characters

Eugene Gant, a shy, imaginative, awkward boy. The youngest child in a tumultuous family, with a wastrel father and a penny-pinching mother, he passes through childhood alone and misunderstood, for there is no family affection. He is precocious, with an insatiable appetite for books. He hates his mother's penuriousness, the family jealousies, and the waste of all their lives, yet is fascinated by the drunken magniloquence of his father. His salvation is the private school he is allowed to attend, for the Leonards, who operate it, develop and shape his mania for reading. At fifteen he enters the state university, where he is considered a freak although he does brilliantly in his studies. He has his first bitter love affair with Laura James during that summer. In his sophomore year he becomes something of a campus personality. The great tragedy of these years is the death of his brother Ben, who had loved him in his own strange abrupt fashion. Just before he leaves for Harvard for graduate study, his brother Luke asks him to sign a release of his future inheritance on the excuse that he has had his share of their parents' estate in extra schooling. Knowing that he is being tricked by his grasping and jealous family, he signs so that he can break away from them forever.

Oliver Gant, his father, a stonecutter from Pennsylvania who has wandered to North Carolina and married there. Hating his wife and her miserly attitude, he is drunken and promiscuous, yet fascinating to his children because of his wild generosities and his alcoholic rhetoric. He is the exact opposite of his wife: she has an overpowering urge to acquire property and he wants none of it. He will not go with her when she moves to another house so that she can take in boarders. Their entire marriage has been an unending war, but she wins at last, for his failing health forces him to live with her.

Eliza Gant, Oliver's wife and Eugene's mother, the daughter of a family named Pentland from the mountains. They have all grown prosperous through financial acumen and native thrift. Eliza has an instinctive feeling for the future value of

real estate and an almost insane penuriousness; she acquires land until she is
a wealthy woman. She alienates Eugene
by the stinginess which will never allow
her to enjoy the money that she has accumulated. She is rock-like in her im-
mobility, absorbed in her passion for
money and her endless, involved reminiscences.

Ben Gant, their son, silent and withdrawn, yet capable of deep affection for
Eugene. He dies of pneumonia because
his mother will not call a reliable doctor
in time. His is a wasted life, for he was
endowed with potentialities that were
never realized.

Steve Gant, another son. He is a braggart
and wastrel, with all of his father's worst
qualities but none of his charm.

Luke Gant, another son. He is a comic
figure, stuttering, generous, and ineffectual.

Helen Gant, a daughter. She has her
father's expansive nature and takes his
side against her mother. She is the only
member of the family who can handle
Gant when he is drunk.

Daisy Gant, another daughter. She is
a pretty but colorless girl who plays little
part in the family drama.

Margaret Leonard, wife of the principal
of the private school that Eugene attends.
She directs his haphazard reading so as
to develop the best in his mind; she
really takes the place of the mother who
has had no time for him.

Laura James, a young girl five years
older than Eugene, who is spending the
summer at Eliza's boarding house. Eugene falls in love with her and she with
him. But when she returns home, she
writes that she is to marry a man to
whom she has been engaged for a year.

The Story

Eugene, the youngest child in the Gant family, came into the world when Eliza
Gant was forty-two years old. His father went on periodic drinking sprees to forget his unfulfilled ambitions and the unsatisfied wanderlust which had brought
him to Altamont in the hills of old Catawba. When Eugene was born, his father
was asleep in a drunken stupor.

Eliza disapproved of her husband's debauches, but she lacked the imagination
to understand their cause. Oliver, who had been raised amidst the plenty of a
Pennsylvania farm, had no comprehension of the privation and suffering which
had existed in the South after the Civil War, the cause of the hoarding and ac-
quisitiveness of his wife and her Pentland relations in the Catawba hill country.

Eliza bore the burden of Oliver's drinking and promiscuousness until Eugene
was four years old. Then she departed for St. Louis, taking all the children but
the oldest daughter, Daisy, with her. It was 1904, the year of the great St. Louis
Fair, and Eliza had gone to open a boarding-house for her visiting fellow towns-
men. The idea was abhorrent to Oliver. He stayed in Altamont.

Eliza's sojourn in St. Louis ended abruptly when twelve-year-old Grover fell ill
of typhoid and died. Stunned, she gathered her remaining children to her and
went home.

Young Eugene was a shy, awkward boy with dark, brooding eyes. He was, like
his ranting, brawling father, a dreamer. He was not popular with his schoolmates,

who sensed instinctively that he was different, and made him pay the price; and at home he was the victim of his sisters' and brothers' taunts and torments. His one champion was his brother Ben, though even he had been conditioned by the Gants' unemotional family life to give his caresses as cuffs. But there was little time for Eugene's childish daydreaming. Eliza believed early jobs taught her boys manliness and self-reliance. Ben got up at three o'clock every morning to deliver papers. Luke had been a *Saturday Evening Post* agent since he was twelve. Eugene was put under his wing. Although the boy loathed the work, he was forced every Thursday to corner customers and keep up a continuous line of chatter until he broke down their sales resistance.

Eugene was not yet eight when his parents separated. Eliza had bought the Dixieland boarding-house as a good investment. Helen remained at the old house with her father. Daisy married and left town. Mrs. Gant took Eugene with her. Ben and Luke were left to shift for themselves, to shuttle back and forth between the two houses. Eugene grew to detest his new home. When the Dixieland was crowded, there was no privacy, and Eliza advertised the Dixieland on printed cards which Eugene had to distribute to customers on his magazine route and to travelers arriving at the Altamont station.

But although life at the boarding-house was drabness itself, the next four years were the golden days of Eugene's youth, for he was allowed to go to the Leonards' private school. Margaret Leonard, the tubercular wife of the schoolmaster, recognized Eugene's hunger for beauty and love and was able to find in literature the words that she herself had not the power to utter. By the time he was fifteen Eugene knew the best and the greatest lyrics almost line for line.

Oliver Gant, who had been fifty when his youngest son was born, was beginning to feel his years. Although he was never told, he was slowly dying of cancer.

Eugene was fourteen when the World War broke out. Ben, who wanted to join the Canadian Army, was warned by his doctor that he would be refused because he had weak lungs.

At fifteen, Eugene was sent to the university at Pulpit Hill. It was his father's plan that Eugene should be well on his way toward being a great statesman before the time came for old Oliver to die. Eugene's youth and tremendous height made him a natural target for dormitory horseplay, and his shy, awkward manners were intensified by his ignorance of the school's traditions and rituals. He roomed alone. His only friends were four wastrels, one of whom contributed to his social education by introducing him to a brothel.

That summer, back at the Dixieland, Eugene met Laura James. Sitting with her on the front porch at night, he was trapped by her quiet smile and clear, candid eyes. He became her lover on a summer afternoon of sunlit green and gold. But Laura went home to visit her parents and wrote Eugene that she was about to marry a boy to whom she had been engaged for nearly a year.

Eugene went back to Pulpit Hill that fall, still determined to go his way alone. Although he had no intimates, he gradually became a campus leader. The commonplace good fellows of his world tolerantly made room for the one who was not like them.

In October of the following year Eugene received an urgent summons to come home. Ben was finally paying the price of his parents' neglect and the drudgery of his life. He was dying of pneumonia. Eliza had neglected to call a competent doctor until it was too late, and Oliver, as he sat at the foot of the dying boy's bed, could think only of the expense the burial would be. As the family kept their vigil through Ben's last night, they were touched with the realization of the greatness of the boy's generous soul. Ben was given, a final irony, the best funeral money could buy.

With Ben went the family's last pretenses. When Eugene came back to the Dixieland after graduation, Eliza was in control of Oliver's property and selling it as quickly as she could in order to use the money for further land speculations. She had disposed of their old home. Oliver lived in a back room at the boarding-house. His children watched each other suspiciously as he wasted away, each concerned for his own inheritance. Eugene managed to remain unembroiled in their growing hatred of each other, but he could not avoid being a target for that hatred. Helen, Luke, and Steve had always resented his schooling. In September, before he left for Harvard to begin graduate work, Luke asked Eugene to sign a release saying that he had received his inheritance as tuition and school expenses. Though his father had promised him an education when he was still a child and Eliza was to pay for his first year in the North, Eugene was glad to sign. He was free, and he was never coming back to Altamont.

On his last night at home he had a vision of his dead brother Ben in the moonlit square at midnight; Ben, the unloved of the Gants, and the most lovable. It was for Eugene as well a vision of old, unhappy, unforgotten years, and in his restless imagination he dreamed of the hidden door through which he would escape forever the mountain-rimmed world of his boyhood.

Critical Evaluation

Essentially plotless, *Look Homeward, Angel* covers roughly the first twenty years of the life of both Thomas Wolfe and his autobiographic hero, Eugene Gant. The three sections of the novel portray the first three stages in Eugene's life: his first twelve years, his four years at the Leonards' school, and his four years at the university. Wolfe's subtitle, "A Story of the Buried Life," partly suggests the way in which the story is developed. Though there is much external action, talk, and description, the reader is frequently taken into the consciousness of Eugene as well as into that of Ben, of Eliza, and of Gant. Eugene's double inheritance from his rhetoric-spouting, self-pitying, histrionic father and his more practical and dominating mother, brings him into a series of conflicts with family, school, society, and all that is outside himself. He is the young artist seeking isolation from a world that constantly impinges upon him. Like most highly imaginative and passionately intense young persons, he reacts through both mind and senses to this external world, and his responses are often phrased in a lyrical prose that sweeps the reader emotionally along with Eugene. Young Gant is inclined to take himself very seriously, as when he becomes a hero in his many fantasies. Yet he is capable of self-mockery, particularly as he is growing out of adolescence during his university years. Stylistically, the novel shows an amazing variety: sensuous, evocative description; symbolism with shifting meanings; realistic, pungent dialogue; bawdy humor; parody and burlesque; satire; fantasy; and dithyrambic passages in which the author becomes intoxicated with the flow of his own words. The shifts of style are often so abrupt that the reader needs a keen awareness to appreciate what Wolfe is doing. *Look Homeward, Angel* is a novel of youth slowly developing into maturity, and perhaps it is best appreciated by readers who can more or less identify with young Eugene. Yet older readers can also lose themselves in it, remembering the turmoil, the joys, and the sorrows of their own maturation.

Bibliography

Albrecht, W.P. "The Titles of *Look Homeward, Angel*: A Story of the Buried Life," in *Modern Language Quarterly.* XI (March, 1950), pp. 50–57. Reprinted in *The Merrill Studies in* Look Homeward, Angel. Edited by Paschal Reeves. Columbus, Oh.: Merrill, 1970, pp. 97–106.

Aswell, Edward C. "An Introduction to Thomas Wolfe," in *The Enigma of Thomas Wolfe: Biographical and Critical Selections.* Edited by Richard Walser. Cambridge, Mass.: Harvard University Press, 1953, pp. 103–108.

Budd, Louis J. "The Grotesques of Anderson and Wolfe," in *Modern Fiction Studies.* V (Winter, 1959–1960), pp. 304–310. Reprinted in *The Merrill Studies in* Look Homeward, Angel. Edited by Paschal Reeves. Columbus, Oh.: Merrill, 1970, pp. 126–133.

Carlile, Robert Emerson. "Musical Analogues in Thomas Wolfe's *Look Homeward, Angel*," in *Modern Fiction Studies.* XIV (Summer, 1968), pp. 215–223.

Chamberlain, John. "*Look Homeward, Angel*," in *Bookman.* LXX (December, 1929), pp. 449–450. Reprinted in *The Idea of an American Novel.* Edited by Louis D. Rubin, Jr. and John Rees Moore. New York: Crowell, 1961, pp. 344–346.

Cowley, Malcolm. *A Second Flowering: Works and Days of the Lost Generation.* New York: Viking, 1973, pp. 156–190.

DeVoto, Bernard. "Genius Is Not Enough," in *Saturday Review.* XIII (April 25, 1936), pp. 3–4, 14–15. Reprinted in *Thomas Wolfe: Three Decades of*

Criticism. Edited by Leslie A. Field. New York: New York University Press, 1968, pp. 131–138. Also reprinted in *Thomas Wolfe: A Collection of Critical Essays.* Edited by Louis D. Rubin, Jr. Englewood Cliffs, N.J.: Prentice-Hall, 1973, pp. 72–79.

Evans, Elizabeth. "Music in *Look Homeward, Angel*," in *Southern Literary Journal.* VIII (Spring, 1976), pp. 62–73.

Geismar, Maxwell. *Writers in Crisis.* New York: Houghton Mifflin, 1942, pp. 187–235. Reprinted in *The Enigma of Thomas Wolfe: Biographical and Critical Selections.* Edited by Richard Walser. Cambridge, Mass.: Harvard University Press, 1953, pp. 109–119. Also reprinted in *The Merrill Studies in* Look Homeward, Angel. Edited by Paschal Reeves. Columbus, Oh.: Merrill, 1970, pp. 56–65.

Gurko, Leo. *Thomas Wolfe: Beyond the Romantic Ego.* New York: Crowell, 1975, pp. 49–78.

Hill, John S. "Eugene Gant and the Ghost of Ben," in *Modern Fiction Studies.* XI (Autumn, 1965), pp. 245–249. Reprinted in *The Merrill Studies in* Look Homeward, Angel. Edited by Paschal Reeves. Columbus, Oh.: Merrill, 1970, pp. 134–139.

Holman, C. Hugh. *Thomas Wolfe.* Minneapolis: University of Minnesota Press, 1960.

Johnson, Pamela Hansford. *Thomas Wolfe: A Critical Study.* Toronto: William Heinemann, 1947, pp. 34–45. Reprinted in *The Merrill Studies in* Look Homeward, Angel. Edited by Paschal Reeves. Columbus, Oh.: Merrill, 1970, pp. 147–154.

Kennedy, Richard S. *The Window of Memory: The Literary Career of Thomas Wolfe.* Chapel Hill: University of North Carolina Press, 1962, pp. 124–161.

————. "Wolfe's *Look Homeward, Angel* as a Novel of Development," in *South Atlantic Quarterly.* LXIII (Spring, 1964), pp. 218–226. Reprinted in *Thomas Wolfe: Three Decades of Criticism.* Edited by Leslie A. Field. New York: New York University Press, 1968, pp. 195–204. Also reprinted in *The Merrill Studies in* Look Homeward, Angel. Edited by Paschal Reeves. Columbus, Oh.: Merrill, 1970, pp. 82–90.

McElderry, Bruce R., Jr. "The Durable Humor of *Look Homeward, Angel*," in *Arizona Quarterly.* XI (Summer, 1955), pp. 123–128. Reprinted in *Thomas Wolfe: Three Decades of Criticism.* Edited by Leslie A. Field. New York: New York University Press, 1968, pp. 189–194. Also reprinted in *The Merrill Studies in* Look Homeward, Angel. Edited by Paschal Reeves. Columbus, Oh.: Merrill, 1970, pp. 91–96.

————. *Thomas Wolfe.* New York: Twayne, 1964, pp. 45–66.

Moser, Thomas C. "Thomas Wolfe: *Look Homeward, Angel,*" in *The American Novel from James Fenimore Cooper to William Faulkner.* Edited by Wallace Stegner. New York: Basic Books, 1965, pp. 206–218. Reprinted in *Thomas Wolfe: A Collection of Critical Essays.* Edited by Louis D. Rubin, Jr. Englewood Cliffs, N.J.: Prentice-Hall, 1973, pp. 116–127.

Muller, Herbert J. *Thomas Wolfe.* Norfolk, Conn.: New Directions, 1947, pp. 44–54.

Reaver, J. Russell and Robert I. Strozier. "Thomas Wolfe and Death," in *The Modern American Novel: Essays in Criticism.* Edited by Max Westbrook. New York: Random House, 1966, pp. 79–89. Reprinted in *The Merrill Studies in* Look Homeward, Angel. Edited by Paschal Reeves. Columbus, Oh.: Merrill, 1970, pp. 117–125.

Rubin, Larry. "Thomas Wolfe and the Lost Paradise," in *Modern Fiction Studies.* XI (Autumn, 1965), pp. 250–258. Reprinted in *The Merrill Studies in* Look Homeward, Angel. Edited by Paschal Reeves. Columbus, Oh.: Merrill, 1970, pp. 107–116.

Rubin, Louis D., Jr. *The Faraway Country: Writers of the Modern South.* Seattle: University of Washington Press, 1963, pp. 72–104. Reprinted in *Thomas Wolfe: Three Decades of Criticism.* Edited by Leslie A. Field. New York: New York University Press, 1968, pp. 59–84. Also reprinted in *The Merrill Studies in* Look Homeward, Angel. Edited by Paschal Reeves. Columbus, Oh.: Merrill, 1970, pp. 140–146.

Walser, Richard. *Thomas Wolfe: An Introduction and Interpretation.* New York: Barnes & Noble, 1961, pp. 4–15, 39–47, 53–94, 125–138. Reprinted in *The Merrill Studies in* Look Homeward, Angel. Edited by Paschal Reeves. Columbus, Oh.: Merrill, 1970, pp. 66–79.

Watkins, Floyd C. *Thomas Wolfe's Characters: Portraits from Life.* Norman: University of Oklahoma Press, 1957, pp. 4–37.

OF TIME AND THE RIVER

Type of work: Novel
Author: Thomas Wolfe (1900–1938)
Time of plot: 1920's
Locale: Harvard, New York, France
First published: 1935

Subtitled A Legend of Man's Hunger in His Youth, *this long novel is a sequel to* Look Homeward, Angel: *it enjoys the youthful freshness and enthusiasm of the earlier work, yet benefits from Wolfe's growing experience as a stylist. Modeled after the author, Eugene Gant has an insatiable appetite for experience; a lonely and frightened man of seemingly inexhaustible energy, he attends Harvard, teaches at New York University, and tours France in his search to find meaning through action.*

Principal Characters

Eugene Gant, a young Southerner, just graduated from the State University and on his way to Harvard for advanced study. He is eager to leave the drab world of his childhood: his jealous family, the dreary boarding house run by his mother. But he finds Harvard disappointing, the famous drama class of Professor Hatcher disillusioning, for the students are intellectual frauds. In Boston he meets his eccentric uncle, Bascom Pentland, and has a brief love affair with a commonplace girl. He finds one good friend, however, in Francis Starwick, Hatcher's assistant. Starwick's sophistication fascinates Eugene, yet it somehow seems unreal. After a winter at Harvard and a summer of hoping that his play will be produced, Eugene goes to New York as instructor in a city university. There he renews his friendship with Robert Weaver from his home town and with Joel Pierce from Harvard. Weaver, with his drunkenness, causes only trouble; Pierce, with his vast wealth, is fascinating but disillusioning. During his vacation Eugene goes first to England, which he detests, and then to Paris, where he meets Starwick, who is with two young Boston women, Elinor, a divorcée, and Ann, an unmarried girl. After a drunken summer in Paris Eugene realizes the tragic situation: that he loves Ann but that she loves Starwick, and that Starwick has become a homosexual. Breaking away from the doomed trio, Eugene goes to Orléans. After a fantastic experience with two French noblewomen, he returns to America. On the ship he sees a woman named Esther and knows that she is to be his fate.

Oliver Gant, Eugene's father, who dies of cancer. Although his drunken profligacy has made the family life a nightmare, his death makes his children realize what a remarkable man he was.

Eliza Gant, Eugene's mother. Tenacious

in her acquisition of property, infinitely stubborn, lost in her web of recollection, she has become a powerful woman.

Francis Starwick, assistant to Professor Hatcher of Harvard. Mannered and pretentious yet intelligent, he seems to Eugene the acme of sophistication. He is loved by Ann, but her love is wasted, for he is homosexual.

Bascom Pentland, Eugene's eccentric uncle, living in Boston.

Joel Pierce, a member of an immensely rich family. He introduces Eugene to the world of great wealth, which fascinates yet repels him.

Robert Weaver, a young man from Eugene's home town. Joining Eugene in New York, he becomes a nuisance because of his drunkenness.

Abe Jones, a Jewish student in Eugene's class in New York. He shows Eugene the hard, bitter world of the lower-class New York Jews.

The Countess de Caux, a slightly mad Frenchwoman whom Eugene meets in Orléans. She is interested in using him for her own financial advantage.

The Marquise de Mornay, to whom the Countess de Caux introduces Eugene on the pretext that he is a well-known journalist. Although the Marquise is a great lady, it develops that she has permitted the introduction for the purpose of getting Eugene to raise money in America for a hospital in France.

Elinor, a slightly older woman from Boston, where she has left her husband and child. Knowing that she has ruined herself forever at home, she joins Eugene and Starwick during their drunken vacation in Paris. She is the leader of the group, domineering and essentially cruel.

Ann, an unmarried Boston girl accompanying Elinor. Eugene falls in love with her, to find that she loves Starwick, whose homosexuality makes that love impossible.

Esther [Jack], a lovely Jewess with "dove's eyes" whom Eugene sees as he is boarding the ship to return to America. He knows that she is to become the "target of his life."

The Story

Eugene Gant was leaving Altamont for study at Harvard. His mother and his sister Helen stood on the station platform and waited with him for the train that would take him north. Eugene felt that he was escaping from his strange, unhappy childhood, that the train would take him away from sickness and worry over money, away from his mother's boarding-house, the Dixieland, away from memories of his gruff, kind brother Ben, away from all ghosts of the past. While they waited, they met Robert Weaver, who was also on his way to Harvard. Mrs. Gant said that Robert was a fine boy, but that there was insanity in his family. She told Eugene family scandals of the town before the train came puffing in.

Eugene broke his trip in Baltimore to visit his father, who was slowly dying of cancer. Old Gant spent much of his time on the sunlit hospital porch, dreaming of time and of his youth.

At Harvard, Eugene enrolled in Professor Hatcher's drama class. Hungry for knowledge, he browsed in the library, pulling books from the library shelves and reading them as he stood by the open stacks. He wrote plays for the drama workshop. Prowling the streets of Cambridge and Boston, he wondered about the lives of people he met, whose names he would never know.

One day he received a note from Francis Starwick, Professor Hatcher's assistant, asking Eugene to have dinner with him that night. As Eugene had made no friends at the university, he was surprised by Starwick's invitation. Starwick turned out to be a pleasant young man who welcomed Eugene's confidences but returned none.

In Boston Eugene met his uncle, Bascom Pentland, and his wife. Uncle Bascom had once been a preacher, but he had left the ministry and was now working as a conveyancer in a law office.

One day Eugene received a telegram telling him that his father was dying. He had no money for a ticket home, and so he went to see Wang, a strange, secretive Chinese student who roomed in the same house. Wang gave him money and Eugene went back to Altamont, but he arrived too late to see his father alive. Old Gant died painfully and horribly. Only with his death did his wife and children realize how much this ranting, roaring old man had meant in their lives.

Back at Harvard, Eugene and Starwick became close friends. Starwick always confused Eugene when they were together; Eugene had the feeling that everything Starwick did or said was like the surface of a shield, protecting his real thoughts or feelings underneath.

One night Robert Weaver came to Eugene's rooms. He was drunk and shouting at the top of his voice. He wanted Eugene to go out with him, but Eugene finally managed to get him to bed on a cot in Wang's room.

Eugene dreamed of becoming a great playwright. After he had completed his course at Harvard, he went back to Altamont and waited to have one of his plays accepted for production on Broadway. That was a summer of unhappiness and suspense. His plays were rejected. While visiting a married sister in South Carolina, he ran into Robert Weaver again. The two got drunk and landed in jail.

In the fall Eugene went to New York to become an English instructor at a city university. After a time Robert Weaver appeared. He had been living at a club, but now he insisted that Eugene get him a room at the apartment hotel where Eugene lived. Eugene hesitated, knowing what would happen if Weaver went on one of his sprees. The worst did happen. Weaver smashed furniture and set fire to his room. He also had a mistress, a woman who had married her husband because she knew he was dying and would leave her his money. One night the husband found his wife and Weaver together. There was a scuffle. The husband pulled a gun and attempted to shoot Weaver before he collapsed. It looked very much as if Eliza Gant's statement about insanity in the Weaver family were true.

Eugene also renewed a college friendship with Joel Pierce, the son of a wealthy family. At Joel's invitation he went to visit at the magnificent Pierce estate along the Hudson River. Seeing the fabulously rich close at hand for the first time, Eugene was both fascinated and disappointed.

At vacation time Eugene went abroad, first to England, where he lived with the strange Coulson family, and then to France. In Paris he met Starwick again, standing enraptured upon the steps of the Louvre. Starwick was doing Europe with two women from Boston, Elinor and Ann. Elinor, who had left her husband, was mistakenly believed by her friends to be Starwick's mistress. Eugene went to see the sights of Paris with them. Ann and Elinor paid all of Starwick's bills. One night, in a cabaret, Starwick got into an argument with a Frenchman and accepted a challenge to duel. Ann, wanting to end the ridiculous affair, paid the Frenchman money to satisfy him for damages to his honor.

Eugene attempted to make love to Ann, but when she resisted him he realized that she was in love with Starwick. What made the affair even more tragic was Eugene's discovery that Ann's love was wasted because Starwick was a homosexual.

Disgusted with the three, Eugene went to Chartres by himself. From Chartres he went to Orleans. There he met an eccentric old countess who believed that Eugene was a correspondent for the New York *Times*, a journalist planning to write a book of travel impressions. She secured for him an invitation to visit the Marquise de Mornaye, who was under the mistaken impression that Eugene had known her son in America.

Eugene went to Tours. There in that old town of white buildings and narrow, cobble-stoned streets, memories of America suddenly came flooding back to him. He remembered the square of Altamont on a summer afternoon, the smell of woodsmoke in the early morning, the whistle of a train in the mountain passes. He remembered the names of American rivers, the parade of the states that stretched from the rocky New England coastline across the flat plains and high mountains to the thunder of the Pacific slope, the names of battles fought on American soil. He remembered his family and his own childhood. He felt that he had recaptured the lost dream of time itself.

Homesick, he started back to America. One day he caught sight of Starwick and his two women companions in a Marseilles café, but he went away before they saw him.

He sailed from Cherbourg. On the tender taking passengers out to the great ocean liner he suddenly heard an American voice above the babble of the passengers grouped about him. He looked. A woman pointed eagerly toward the ship, her face glowing with an excitement as great as that Eugene himself felt. A woman companion called her Esther. Watching Esther, Eugene knew that she was to be his fate.

Critical Evaluation

Thomas Wolfe was six feet five inches tall and enormously heavy. Born in 1900, and endowed with a Niagara of uncontrollable energy, he thirsted wildly for life. He felt that he must visit all lands, pace all streets, follow all rural trails, meet all people, scan all faces, eat all food, drink all liquors, read all literature, love all women, capture all beauty, and "write, write, write." Time was his most lethal foe, and he predicted that only death, disease, or madness could stop him. Unable to curb his own intensity, he lamented a compulsion to do "too much of everything." Even in writing, he was devoid of the ability to select. He had great writing skills and was considered a literary phenomenon after 1929, when he published his first novel *Look Homeward, Angel,* which was followed in 1935 by *Of Time and the River.* At one time, William Faulkner considered him the best American novelist.

A slow-moving but intense novel of more than nine hundred pages that has the theme of a silent river flowing through time and darkness, *Of Time and the River* has passage after passage of splendid prose. The river always flows, always changes, but is always the same as it drinks dark and silent tides that "flow strangely from inland America." At twilight the river joins the harbor, which flows into the sea, but always the river runs like life itself through the secret night, groping like the novel for life's meaning. At times the purpose of the fine but endless descriptions of kitchens, foods, fields, woods, people, and trees is as mysterious as life's purpose is to Eugene Gant. Seasons are likened to the passing of life. October and November are painted so beautifully that they are reminiscent of Catholic concepts of November, the month of the souls in purgatory, when leaves and plants are dying, awaiting winter.

Besides its haunting vision of nocturnal America, the novel gives an unflattering view of "the mongrel and anonymous compost" of America's population. Bitter loathing is aimed at mediocre people, but also at Eugene Gant-Thomas Wolfe himself. There are also fine street scenes of America and Europe. America's culture is scrutinized, and its fierce energy recognized, but the horror of mediocrity, of the common man, and of human flesh with its pasty complexion and "sagging folds" is stressed. We see jaded and weary people with lackluster eyes traveling through tunnels, the same faces that Eugene has seen everywhere in a thousand places and on a thousand occasions. The novel's ponderous pace does not change, and satiric irony is ladled out at Jews, middle-class Americans, rural police, laborers, uneducated people, and blacks. Most Jews are described in less than effusive terms, although there finally appears one good Jew, Fried. Some critics feel that Wolfe hurled his ironic darts at Jews because even though they were beyond the pale of "high" society in the 1920's, as was Wolfe himself, they were, unlike Wolfe, able to laugh and not be hurt. Blacks in the novel seem to have microscopic intellects, but an even more ghastly picture is drawn of two ultra-libidinous priests gorging themselves hoggishly at a sidewalk cafe in Marseilles, France. The lechery of these two fictional libertines is supreme, but several unkind critics have seen Thomas Wolfe autobiographically reincarnated in the enormous, bulky ringleader of the astounding pair. Such characterizations induced Leslie A. Fiedler to allege that the novel should be placed "not in a children's library, but in a high school library, on the shelf of masturbatory dreams."

Intellectual snobbery is endemic throughout the book, along with repetition and pessimism. But war's folly is lampooned, as well as the apparent hypocrisy of the conflict between age and youth. The problems confronting college youth, in an age when moral values are starting to be held in abeyance, are well drawn. So are the scenes of freshmen life in a large university, when youths sometimes deny God at seventeen and then stumble on without fixed goals.

Eugene Gant, like Thomas Wolfe, is lonely and has groundless fears. He feels that he can never be happy, and his wanderlust leads him over two continents, experiencing, tasting, always seeing. But he is looking for a secret portal to real life, as he gazes hungrily at the street scenes of America and Europe, asking himself: "Where shall I go? What shall I do?" He seeks reality through satiation, or possibly the reverse, and is obsessed by the passing of time's river. When Eugene arrives in England he feels the same loneliness that Wolfe calls "time-far," but he finds English street crowds more mellow, warm, and open than crowds in New England. Eugene is still choking in his own spiritual darkness, so the mark of dark time is visible in England, and, while breathing the gray European air, he realizes that it lacks the sparkle of America's. He journeys from England to France; naked desolation smothers his life, and he eventually realizes that he is an exile in Europe. He yearns for the remembered beauty of American landscapes, the vast fields, and distant blue hills and decides to return. In some ways, however, he has grown only in blubbery flesh, not in nobility. And even though he meets Esther, as he is about to sail back, he is still lonely.

Thomas Wolfe died in 1938, leaving vast stacks of written pages that were published posthumously as *The Web and the Rock* (1939) and *You Can't Go Home Again* (1940). His terminal illness struck suddenly just after he had finished the two gigantic manuscripts. Like Eugene Gant, Wolfe's main problem in life was loneliness; it could never have been solved in any other way.

Bibliography

DeVoto, Bernard. "Genius is Not Enough," in *Saturday Review.* XIII (April 25, 1936), pp. 3–4, 14–15. Reprinted in *Thomas Wolfe: Three Decades of Criticism.* Edited by Leslie A. Field. New York: New York University Press, 1968, pp. 131–138. Reprinted in *The Enigma of Thomas Wolfe: Biographical and Critical Selections.* Edited by Richard Walser. Cambridge, Mass.: Harvard University Press, 1953, pp. 140–148. Also reprinted in *Thomas Wolfe: A Collection of Critical Essays.* Edited by Louis D. Rubin, Jr. Englewood Cliffs, N.J.: Prentice-Hall, 1973, pp. 72–79.

Gurko, Leo.   *Thomas Wolfe: Beyond the Romantic Ego.* New York: Crowell, 1975, pp. 79–108.

Halperin, Irving. "Wolfe's *Of Time and the River*," in *Explicator.* XVIII (November, 1949), item 9. Reprinted in *Thomas Wolfe: Three Decades of Criticism.* Edited by Leslie A. Field. New York: New York University Press, 1968, pp. 217–220.

Holman, C. Hugh.   *Thomas Wolfe.* Minneapolis: University of Minnesota Press, 1960.

Johnson, Pamela Hansford.   *Thomas Wolfe: A Critical Study.* Toronto: William Heinemann, 1947, pp. 45–54.

Kennedy, Richard S.   *The Window of Memory: The Literary Career of Thomas Wolfe.* Chapel Hill: University of North Carolina Press, 1962, pp. 199–209, 259–273.

Lyons, John O.   *The College Novel in America.* Carbondale: Southern Illinois University Press, 1962, pp. 77–85, 141–144.

McElderry, Bruce R., Jr.   *Thomas Wolfe.* New York: Twayne, 1964, pp. 67–87.

Muller, Herbert J.   *Thomas Wolfe.* Norfolk, Conn.: New Directions, 1947, pp. 55–76.

Reeves, Paschal. "Wolfe's *Of Time and the River*," in *Explicator.* XXVI (October, 1967), item 18.

Walser, Richard.   *Thomas Wolfe: An Introduction and Interpretation.* New York: Barnes & Noble, 1961, pp. 25–45, 72–103, 121–129.

Warren, Robert Penn.   "A Note on the Hamlet of Thomas Wolfe," in *American Review.* V (May, 1935), pp. 191–208. Reprinted in *Selected Essays.* New York: Random House, 1958, pp. 170–183. Also reprinted in *The Enigma of Thomas Wolfe: Biographical and Critical Selections.* Edited by Richard Walser. Cambridge, Mass.: Harvard University Press, 1953, pp. 120–132. Also reprinted in *Thomas Wolfe: Three Decades of Criticism.* Edited by Leslie A. Field. New York: New York University Press, 1968, pp. 205–216.

Watkins, Floyd C.   *Thomas Wolfe's Characters: Portraits from Life.* Norman: University of Oklahoma Press, 1957, pp. 49–65.

THE WEB AND THE ROCK

Type of work: Novel
Author: Thomas Wolfe (1900–1938)
Time of plot: 1900–1928
Locale: North Carolina, New York, Europe
First published: 1939

This partly autobiographical "education" novel, structurally uneven but with scenes of great emotional intensity, is marked by contrasts of innocence with sophistication, the mountain folk of North Carolina with the cosmopolitan smart set of Manhattan, the freedoms of America with the insidious beginnings of National Socialism in Germany. Wolfe's story is continued in You Can't Go Home Again.

Principal Characters

George Webber, a lonely child reared by a family-proud aunt and uncle in the small city of Libya Hill, North Carolina. His childhood is the bleak existence of a youngster taken up by charity. As a youth he is an omnivorous, voracious reader who yearns to acquire the power of writing great novels, hoping someday to write about the two-sided world he knows—the side of the rich and the side of the poor. After attending college George moves to New York, only to find that he is as lonely among the big city's millions of people as he was in a small town. Even a trip to Europe gives him no satisfaction, for he is a silent, brooding, distrustful man. His salvation, ultimately, is a love affair lasting several years, an experience that brings him out of himself. His mistress helps him lose his childish illusions about fame and greatness. His self-knowledge is complete when, during a trip to Europe, he awakens in a hospital after a sordid brawl to recognize that life is knowing one's self completely.

Mrs. Esther Jack, a successful, well-known designer of stage sets in New York. She meets George Webber aboard ship, falls in love with him, and becomes his mistress and counselor for several years, although she is fifteen or twenty years older than her lover. She brings George to meet many well-known people and to realize that life is more than mere fame. She encourages George to write, and with her help his long-sought novel begins to take shape. But she dominates George so much that he is forced to leave her, lest her very goodness and love become his undoing as a writer.

Mr. and Mrs. Joyner, George's uncle and aunt, who rear him after his mother's death. They are proud of their family and try to turn the boy against his father.

Mr. Webber, George's father, who deserts his wife and child to run off with another woman. Despite his father's behavior, George loves and admires the man. Mr. Webber's death brings George a small inheritance that enables him to attend college and to travel to Europe.

The Story

George Webber's childhood was one of bleakness and misery. He was really a charity ward, even though he lived with his aunt and uncle. For George's father had deserted him and his mother and had gone off to live with another woman. After the death of George's mother, her Joyner relatives took George into their home, where the boy was never allowed to forget that he had some of the blood of the Webbers mixed with his Joyner blood. Strangely, all his good and beautiful dreams were dreams of his father, and often he hotly and passionately defended his father to the Joyners. His love for his father made his childhood a divided one. George hated the people his aunt and uncle called good; and those they called bad, he loved. A lonely child, George kept his thoughts and dreams to himself rather than expose them to the ridicule of the Joyners. But the picture of that happy, joyful world of his father, and others like him, stayed with him during those bleak years of his childhood. When George was sixteen, his father died, leaving the boy a small inheritance. With that money, George left the little southern town of Libya Hill and went to college. There he found knowledge, freedom, life. Like many other young men, George wasted some of that freedom in sprees of riotous and loose living. But he also used his freedom to read everything he could get his hands on, and he was deeply impressed with the power of great writers. George was beginning to feel the need of getting down some of his thoughts and memories on paper. He wanted to write of the two sides of the world—the bright, gay world of the people who had everything and the horrible, dreary world of the derelicts and the poor.

His college years ended, George fulfilled the dream of every country boy in the nation; he went to the city, to the beautiful, wonderful enfabled rock, as he called New York.

The city was as great and as marvelous as George had known it would be. He shared an apartment with four other boys; it was a dingy, cheap place, but it was their own apartment, where they could do as they pleased. But George found the city a lonely place in spite of its millions of people and its bright lights. There was no one to whom he was responsible nor to whom he belonged. He thought he would burst with what he knew about people and about life, and, since there was no one he could talk to about those things, he tried to write them down. He began his first novel.

The next year was the loneliest one George had ever known. He drove himself mercilessly. He was wretched, for the words torturing his mind would not go on the paper as he wanted them to. At the end of a year he took the last of his ineritance and went to Europe. He hoped to find there the peace of mind he needed to finish his book.

The cities of Europe did not hold his salvation. He was still lonely and bitter because he could not find the answer to the riddle of life. He went back to New York. But the city was no longer an unfriendly enemy, for George had found Esther.

They had met on the ship bound for New York. Esther was Mrs. Esther Jack, a well-known and successful stage set designer. She was fifteen or twenty years older than George, but she was also younger in many ways, for Esther loved people and believed in them. Where George was silent and distrustful, Esther was open and trusting. George sometimes felt that theirs was the greatest love of all times, at once brutal and tender, passionate and friendly, so deep that it could not last. But for the next three years he was the king of the world. To Esther, George told all his dreams, all his memories, all his formerly wordless thoughts about life and people.

George failed to realize at first that Esther meant more than a lover to him. Gradually he came to know that through her he was becoming a new person, a man who loved everyone. For the first time in his life George Webber belonged to someone. Since he was no longer lonely, the torture and the torment left him. At last his book began to take shape, to become a reality. George Webber was happy.

Slowly the magic of his affair with Esther began to disappear. He still loved her more than he believed possible, knew that he would always love her; but they began to quarrel, to have horrible, name-calling scenes that left them both exhausted and empty, even the quarrels that ended with passionate lovemaking. At first George did not know the reason for those scenes, although he always knew that it was he who started them. Slowly he began to realize that he quarreled with Esther because she possessed him so completely. He had given her his pride, his individuality, his dreams, his manhood. Esther had also unknowingly been a factor in his disillusionment, for through her he had met and known the great people of the world—the artists, the writers, the actors—and he had found those people disgusting and cheap. They had destroyed his childhood illusions of fame and greatness, and he hated them for it.

When his novel was finished, Esther sent the manuscript to several publishers she knew. After months had passed without his hearing that it had been accepted, George turned on Esther in one final burst of savage abuse and told her to leave him and never return. Then he went to Europe again.

Although he had gone to Europe to forget Esther, he did nothing without thinking of her and longing for her. Esther wrote to him regularly, and he paced the floor if the expected letter did not arrive. But he was still determined to be himself, and to accomplish his purpose he must not see Esther again.

One night, in a German beer hall, George got into a drunken brawl and was badly beaten up. While he was in the hospital, a feeling of peace came over him for the first time in ten years. He looked into a mirror and saw his body as a thing apart from the rest of him. And he knew that his body had been true to him, that it had taken the abuse he had heaped upon it for almost thirty years. Often he had been almost mad, and he had driven that body beyond endurance in his insane quest—for what he did not know. Now he was ready to go home again. If his first novel should not be published, he would write another. He still had a lot to say. The next time he would put it down right, and then he would be at peace with himself. George Webber was beginning to find himself at last.

Critical Evaluation

In *The Story of a Novel* (1936), Wolfe responded to critics' complaints that he could write only about his own life and that his Scribners editor, Maxwell Perkins, was responsible for organizing the material of his first two novels, *Look Homeward, Angel* (1929) and *Of Time and the River* (1935). He promised to write in a more "objective," disciplined style; and to prove that he could, without assistance, structure his sprawling fiction, he severed his professional association with Perkins. In July 1938, two months before he died following a brain operation, Wolfe submitted to his new editor, Edward C. Aswell, the manuscript from which his last two novels, *The Web and the Rock* and *You Can't Go Home Again,* were assembled. Although somewhat more objective, more finely controlled, than his earlier fiction, the novels continue the supreme subject of all his work: the story of his own life reshaped into myth.

George Webber, described as monkeylike with long arms and an awkward, ambling gait, scarcely resembles the tall, hawklike Eugene Gant of *Look Homeward, Angel.* Yet he is surely another psychological portrait of Wolfe, the tormented artist among Philistines. In the first part of *The Web and the Rock,* the author attempts to provide for his hero a new family and social background. But the Joyners, despite their vitality, are mere copies of the Pentlands; Lybia Hill resembles Altamont; and the moody, romantic Webber recalls the young Eugene. Some of the minor characters, notably the baseball hero Nebraska Crane and Aunt Maw, are brilliantly drawn. And the chapter "The Child by Tiger," originally published as a short story, reveals Wolfe's great power to create tragic myth. Above all, the strength of the first part of the book rests upon the author's heroic vision of the townspeople and the mountain folk of North Carolina—a stock of enterprising, stubborn, passionately independent souls. They represent the mysterious "web" of the earth. Like Webber, a child of the mountain folk, they are tied by threads of destiny not only to the land but also to the seasons, the workings of time. As an artist, Webber understands intuitively the heart of things, the patterns of life and dreams.

In roughly the second half of the novel, Wolfe contrasts the "web" of the earth with the "rock" of the city of New York. At this point in his writing, he abandons, for the most part, his scheme of objectivity and deals with the experiences of his own life. Webber meets and falls in love with Esther Jack (the same Esther who first appears to Eugene Gant in the "Faust and Helen" chapter of *Of Time and the River*)—in real life the stage designer and artist Aline Bernstein. With remarkable frankness Wolfe describes the tragic course of the affair between these markedly different personalities: the egotistic, brilliant, despotic provincial genius and his mistress, a sophisticated, sensitive, upper-middle class Jewish wife and mother. As a realist Wolfe is at his best detailing scenes of lovemaking and eating, of tempestuous quarrels and passionate reconciliations. Throughout the extended part of the book dealing with the love affair—for all its excesses and absurdities—Wolfe is able to touch the reader: George and Esther truly care about each other. They try desperately to make their fragile relationship endure.

Yet the theme of the novel is the fragility of all dreams. The "rock" of New York, which George once loved as well as feared, begins to crumble in this novel; it will betray its fullest stresses in *You Can't Go Home Again*. The city, founded upon greed and selfish power, has no soul. To escape from his own sense of ruin, George visits pre-Nazi Germany, already ripe for the advent of a Hitler. George hopes to recapture, among the drunken revelers at a Munich Oktoberfest, the sense of joy of his own manhood. But he becomes violent, a savage fighting the beer hall swaggerers, and is terribly beaten. By the end of the novel, he wishes to return to America so that he might establish his dreams once again upon a foundation that will endure: upon the "web" of his failing sense of the earth, and upon the "rock" of an already insecure civilization. In the last chapter, "The Looking Glass," Webber comes to understand the futility of these dreams.

Bibliography

Braswell, William. "Introduction," in *The Web and the Rock*. New York: Harper's Modern Classics, 1958, pp. ix–xix.

Chase, Richard. "Introduction," in *The Web and the Rock*. New York: Dell, 1960, pp. 7–19.

Earnest, Ernest. "The American Ariel," in *South Atlantic Quarterly*. LXV (Spring, 1966), pp. 192–200.

Fadiman, Clifton. "*The Web and the Rock*," in *New Yorker*. XV (June 24, 1939), pp. 82–84. Reprinted in *The Enigma of Thomas Wolfe: Biographical and Critical Selections*. Edited by Richard Walser. Cambridge, Mass.: Harvard University Press, 1953, pp. 149–153.

Gurko, Leo. *Thomas Wolfe: Beyond the Romantic Ego*. New York: Crowell, 1975, pp. 108–136.

Holman, C. Hugh. *Thomas Wolfe*. Minneapolis: University of Minnesota Press, 1960.

Johnson, Pamela Hansford. *Thomas Wolfe: A Critical Study*. Toronto: William Heinemann, 1947, pp. 55–69.

Kennedy, Richard S. "Thomas Wolfe's Don Quixote," in *College English*. XXIII (1961), pp. 185–191.

————. *The Window of Memory: The Literary Career of Thomas Wolfe*. Chapel Hill: University of North Carolina Press, 1962, pp. 388–402.

McElderry, Bruce R., Jr. *Thomas Wolfe.* New York: Twayne, 1964, pp. 90–98.

Muller, Herbert J. *Thomas Wolfe.* Norfolk, Conn.: New Directions, 1947, pp. 112–121.

Priestley, J.B. "Introduction," in *The Web and the Rock.* London: William Heinemann, 1947, pp. ix–xii.

Reeves, Paschal. "Esther Jack as Muse," in *Modern Fiction Studies.* XI (Autumn, 1965), pp. 275–285. Reprinted in *Thomas Wolfe: Three Decades of Criticism.* Edited by Leslie A. Field. New York: New York University Press, 1968, pp. 221–228.

Rubin, Louis D., Jr. *Thomas Wolfe: The Weather of His Youth.* Baton Rouge: Louisiana State University Press, 1955, pp. 69–104.

Walser, Richard. *Thomas Wolfe: An Introduction and Interpretation.* New York: Barnes & Noble, 1961, pp. 91–104.

Watkins, Floyd C. *Thomas Wolfe's Characters: Portraits from Life.* Norman: University of Oklahoma Press, 1957, pp. 84–110.

YOU CAN'T GO HOME AGAIN

Type of work: Novel
Author: Thomas Wolfe (1900–1938)
Time of plot: 1929–1936
Locale: New York, England, Germany
First published: 1940

Wolfe's final novel continues the story of George Webber from The Web *and the* Rock. *A sprawling yet powerful and often lyrical book,* You Can't Go Home Again *examines with realistic detachment the failed promises of America during the Depression, but shows how the dream of freedom, though difficult to establish, is vastly superior to the poisonous promises of Nazi Germany.*

Principal Characters

George Webber, a young writer in the first flush of success as a novelist. He learns that success brings enemies and that success is sometimes empty of meaning. His great aim in life, idealist that he is, is to write the truth, to portray people as they are, the great and small, the rich and poor. He faces disillusionment at every turn. He finds that his fellow men are greedy after the world's goods; he finds, too, that they do not relish his truthful portrayal of them. George again visits Germany, a place he loves, only to find that country filled with fear and persecution in the 1930's, during the Nazi regime. He returns home to the United States to preach in new novels against selfishness and greed, hoping he can awaken the people of his own land to arise and defeat the forces which are threatening the freedom of mankind.

Foxhall Edwards, an editor for a publishing house who becomes George Webber's friend and trusted adviser for a time. He is a genius at encouraging young writers to find themselves and to win the confidence they need to produce literary art. He is also a skeptical person who believes that if man is not destined for freedom, he must accept this fact. Edwards' fatalism is at odds with George's idealistic desire to better the lot of mankind by working to change conditions. These divergent attitudes cause a break in the friendship between the two men.

Lloyd McHarg, a successful American novelist who has won world-wide fame based upon a number of excellent novels. He has found fame to be empty and searches for something, he knows not what. McHarg's disillusionment is a bitter lesson for young, idealistic George Webber, for whom McHarg has been a symbol of greatness as a man of letters.

Esther Jack, an older woman who has been George's mistress in the past and becomes so again for a time after he has achieved success. He leaves her a second time when he decides that in order to find himself, he must leave Esther's sophisticated set and get to know the common people of the world.

Else von Kohler, a beautiful, intelli-

gent young German woman with whom   visiting Germany during the 1930's.
George has a tender romance while re-

The Story

As George Webber looked out of his New York apartment window that spring day in 1929, he was filled with happiness. The bitter despair of the previous year had been lost somewhere in the riotous time he had spent in Europe, and now it was good to be back in New York with the feeling that he knew where he was going. His book had been accepted by a great publishing firm, and Foxhall Edwards, the best editor of the house, had been assigned to help him with the corrections and revisions. George had also resumed his old love affair with Esther Jack, who, married and the mother of a grown daughter, nevertheless returned his love with tenderness and passion. This love, however, was a flaw in George's otherwise great content, for he and Esther seemed to be pulling different ways. She was a famous stage designer who mingled with a sophisticated artistic set. George thought that he could find himself completely only if he lived among and understood the little people of the world.

Before George's book was published, he tried for the first time to go home again. Home was Libya Hill, a small city in the mountains of Old Catawba. When the aunt who had reared George died, he went back to Libya Hill for her funeral. There he learned that he could never really go home again, for home was no longer the quiet town of his boyhood but a growing city of money-crazy speculators who were concerned only with making huge paper fortunes out of real estate.

George found some satisfaction in the small excitement he created because he had written a book which was soon to be published. But even that pleasure was not to last long. For when he returned to New York and the book was published, almost every citizen in Libya Hill wrote him letters filled with threats and curses. George had written of Libya Hill and the people he knew there. His only motive had been to tell the truth as he saw it, but his old friends and relatives in Libya Hill seemed to think that he had spied on them through his boyhood in order to gossip about them in later years. Even the small fame he received in New York, where his book was favorably reviewed by the critics, could not atone for the abusive letters from Libya Hill. He felt he could redeem himself only by working feverishly on his new book.

George moved to Brooklyn, first telling Esther goodbye. This severance from Esther was difficult, but George could not live a lie himself and attempt to write the truth. And in Brooklyn he did learn to know and love the little people—the derelicts, the prostitutes, the petty criminals—and he learned that they, like the so-called good men and women, were all representative of America. His only real friend was Foxhall Edwards, who had become like a father to George. Edwards was a great man, a genius among editors and a genius at understanding and encouraging those who, like George, found it difficult to believe in anything during the depression years. Edwards, too, knew that only through truth could America and the world be saved from destruction; but, unlike George, he believed that the truth cannot be thrust suddenly upon people. He calmly accepted conditions as they existed. George raged at his friend's skepticism.

After four years in Brooklyn, George finished the first draft of his new book. Tired of New York, he thought that he might find in Europe the atmosphere he needed to complete his manuscript. In London he met Lloyd McHarg, the embodiment of all that George wanted to be. George yearned for fame in that period of his life. Because his book had brought him temporary fame, quickly extinguished, he envied McHarg his world reputation as a novelist. George was disillusioned when he learned that McHarg thought fame an empty thing. He had held the world in his hand for a time, but nothing had happened. Now he was living feverishly, looking for something he could not name.

When his manuscript was ready for publication, George returned to New York, made the corrections Edwards suggested, and then sailed again for Europe. He went to Germany, a country he had not visited since 1928. In 1936, he was more saddened by the change in the German people than he had been by anything else in his life. He had always felt a kinship with the Germans, but they were no longer the people he had known before. Persecution and fear tinged every life in that once proud country, and George, sickened, wondered if there were any place in the world where truth and freedom still lived.

There were, however, two bright horizons in his visit to Germany. The first was the fame which greeted him on his arrival there. His first book had been well received, and his second, now published, was a great success. For a time he basked in that glory, but soon he, like McHarg, found fame an elusive thing that brought no real reward. His other great experience was his love for Else von Kohler. That was also an elusive joy, for her roots were deep in Germany, and George knew he must return to America to cry out to his own people that they must live the truth and so save America from the world's ruin.

Before he left Germany, he saw more examples of the horror and tyranny under which the people existed, and he left with a heavy heart. He realized once more that one can never go home again.

Back in New York, he knew that he must break at last his ties with Foxhall Edwards. He wrote to Edwards, telling him why they could no longer travel the same path. First he reviewed the story of his own life, through which he wove the story of his desire to make the American people awake to the great need for truth so that they might keep their freedom. He told Edwards, too, that in his youth he had wanted fame and love above all else. Having had both, he had learned that they were not enough. Slowly he had learned humility, and he knew that he wanted to speak the truth to the downtrodden, to all humanity. Because George knew he had to try to awaken the slumbering conscience of America, he was saying farewell to his friend. For Edwards believed that if the end of freedom was to be the lot of man, fighting against that end was useless. Sometimes George feared that the battle was lost, but he would never stop fighting as long as there was hope that America would find herself. He knew at last the real enemy in America. It was selfishness and greed, disguised as a friend of mankind. He felt that if he could only get help from the little people, he could defeat the enemy. Through George, America might go home again.

Critical Evaluation

In May, 1938, having broken with his first editor and "mentor" Maxwell Perkins ("Foxhall Edwards" in the novel), Thomas Wolfe deposited an unfinished manuscript of perhaps a million words on the desk of his new editor, Edward C. Aswell of Harper and Brothers, and left for a tour of the West. In Vancouver he contracted pneumonia, in Seattle it worsened, and finally, after he had been moved to Johns Hopkins in Baltimore, it was found that the illness had triggered the release of previously latent tuberculosis bacteria in his lungs which had gone to the brain; he died on September 15, 1938.

Thus, it was left to Aswell to assemble, organize, and edit Wolfe's admittedly unfinished material into publishable fictions. The major results of Aswell's efforts were the two massive novels that chronicle the life and artistic development of George Webber, *The Web and the Rock* (1939) and *You Can't Go Home Again*. Consequently, the episodic, fragmentary, sometimes even arbitrary structure of these books and the unevenness and occasional excessiveness of the writing must in part be the result of the compositional problems—though these flaws also exist in his two prior works. There is no way of knowing what the final form of the novels would have been had Wolfe lived to complete them to his own satisfaction.

It has been said that Thomas Wolfe wrote only one book during his career, a thinly disguised autobiography. In a sense this is true, but, like Walt Whitman, the American author who seems most like him in artistic intention and attitude, Wolfe saw his own experience as the focal point for the experience of a nation in the process of becoming. Thus, as the major character in Wolfe's novels strives for experience, personal meaning, and a means of artistic expression, he is also trying to seize and formalize the nature and direction of nothing less than American society itself.

You Can't Go Home Again is the most external and social of his four major novels. The title sets the theme and action line of the novel. George cannot go "home" to any of the old places, experiences, or ideas that have formed him, because every time he attempts to do so he either finds a corruption that has destroyed the thing he would return to, or he finds that he has gone beyond that particular experience and has neither the need nor the desire to repeat it. Metaphorically, "home" is the naïve, idealized vision of

America and of his potential place in it that he had held as a young man, but now learns no longer exists and perhaps never did.

When George returns to his home town of Libya Hill to attend his aunt's funeral, he finds the old rural values gone and a new corrupt speculative fever running rampant. Then he sees the collapse of this greedy dream in the beginnings of the Depression. He cannot go back to his physical home because it no longer exists and he is repelled by what has replaced it. But Libya Hill is only a microcosm, a foreshadowing of what he is to encounter. As America enters into the Depression, George comes into painful contact with both the results of the American economic and social systems as he intimately observes both its victims and its victimizers—and he seeks to disassociate himself from both.

It is Europe and especially Germany, however, that brings George to his final understanding. The notion that artistic success and fame will bring him satisfaction is destroyed by his meeting with the famous novelist Lloyd Mc-Harg (a fictionalized Sinclair Lewis), who finds only bitterness, loneliness, and alcohol in his success. George then completes his education in Germany when he is exposed to the horror of the newly powerful Nazi regime. The Nazi horror, thus, is the logical extension and end result of the greed and corruption George has observed in America, perhaps even the America of the not too distant future.

And yet *You Can't Go Home Again* is not a despairing book. It ends with an exhortation. For all the evil and pessimism he has encountered in his education, George continues to feel that mankind in general and America in particular still have the potential to assert their positive capacities and realize the ideals they once possessed. That is where, as an artist in Whitman's "Bardic" tradition, George sees his place in America to be—as a spokesman for that vision.

Bibliography

Beach, Joseph Warren. *American Fiction: 1920–1940.* New York: Macmillan, 1941, pp. 197–215.

Benet, Stephen Vincent. "A Torrent of Recollection," in *Saturday Review of Literature.* XXI (September 21, 1940), p. 5. Reprinted in *The Enigma of Thomas Wolfe: Biographical and Critical Selections.* Edited by Richard Walser. Cambridge, Mass.: Harvard University Press, 1953, pp. 154–157.

Chase, Richard. "Introduction," in *You Can't Go Home Again.* New York: Dell, 1960, pp. 9–21.

Clements, Clyde C. "Symbolic Patterns in *You Can't Go Home Again,*" in *Modern Fiction Studies.* XI (1965), pp. 286–296. Reprinted in *Thomas Wolfe: Three Decades of Criticism.* Edited by Leslie A. Field. New York:

New York University Press, 1968, pp. 229–240.

Cracroft, Richard H. "A Pebble in the Pool: Organic Theme and Structure in Thomas Wolfe's *You Can't Go Home Again*," in *Modern Fiction Studies.* XVII (Winter, 1971), pp. 533–553.

Dessner, Lawrence Jay. "Thomas Wolfe's Mr. Katamoto," in *Modern Fiction Studies.* XVII (Winter, 1971), pp. 561–565.

Gossett, Louise Y. *Violence in Recent Southern Fiction.* Durham, N.C.: Duke University Press, 1965, pp. 5–16.

Gurko, Leo. *Thomas Wolfe: Beyond the Romantic Ego.* New York: Crowell, 1975, pp. 137–158.

Holman, C. Hugh. "Focus on Thomas Wolfe's *You Can't Go Home Again*: Agrarian Dream and Industrial Nightmare," in *American Dreams, American Nightmares.* Edited by David Madden. Carbondale: Southern Illinois University Press, 1970, pp. 149–157.

————. *Thomas Wolfe.* Minneapolis: University of Minnesota Press, 1960.

————. "Thomas Wolfe: Rhetorical Hope and Dramatic Despair," in *Thomas Wolfe and the Glass of Time.* Edited by Paschal Reeves. Athens: University of Georgia Press, 1971, pp. 78–96.

Johnson, Pamela Hansford. *Thomas Wolfe: A Critical Study.* Toronto: William Heinemann, 1948, pp. 69–77.

Kennedy, Richard S. *The Window of Memory: The Literary Career of Thomas Wolfe.* Chapel Hill: University of North Carolina Press, 1962, pp. 299–391, 403–411.

McElderry, Bruce R., Jr. *Thomas Wolfe.* New York: Twayne, 1964, pp. 98–103.

Muller, Herbert J. *Thomas Wolfe.* Norfolk, Conn.: New Directions, 1947, pp. 123–154.

Walser, Richard. *Thomas Wolfe: An Introduction and Interpretation.* New York: Barnes & Noble, 1961, pp. 40–54, 106–118.

Watkins, Floyd C. *Thomas Wolfe's Characters: Portraits from Life.* Norman: University of Oklahoma Press, 1957, pp. 111–132.

RICHARD WRIGHT

Born: Near Natchez, Mississippi (September 4, 1908)
Died: Paris, France (November 28, 1960)

Principal Works

NOVELS: *Native Son*, 1940; *Black Boy*, 1945; *The Outsider*, 1953.
SOCIAL STUDIES: *Twelve Million Black Voices*, 1941; *Black Power*, 1954.

Richard Wright's childhood was an unpleasant one. Born near Natchez, Mississippi, on September 4, 1908, he grew up, according to his own account, as an unruly and unwanted Negro child in the American South. His father, a laborer, deserted the family when Wright was five years old, and Wright's mother became totally paralyzed when the boy was ten. Leaving the home of relatives at the age of fifteen, Wright went to Memphis, Tennessee, where he worked at various unskilled jobs. During the depression years of the 1930's he traveled north, arriving in Chicago in 1934. There, becoming interested in the labor movement and communism, he joined the Communist Party in 1936. He worked on WPA Writers' Projects in Chicago and New York, later became a contributing editor of the *New Masses*.

Wright's "Uncle Tom's Children" won the prize offered by *Story* in 1938. Awarded a Guggenheim Fellowship the following year, he wrote *Native Son*, a ficitional study of a Negro murderer. In 1940 he received the Spingarn Medal for achievement in the field of Negro interests. *Twelve Million Black Voices* is a history of the American Negro and his problems. In 1944 Wright broke with the Communists; an essay describing his career as a Party member was published in *The God That Failed* (1950). *Black Boy* is an autobiographical novel based on Wright's childhood. *The Outsider* is a novel about a Negro's experience as a Communist. *Black Power* is a nonfictional personal study of conditions in Africa, on the Gold Coast, as Wright saw them on a visit to the region in 1953. *Native Son* has been Wright's most popular novel. As a stage play produced in the United States and as a motion picture filmed in Argentina, *Native Son* was fairly successful. The author played the lead role in the motion picture version.

After World War II Wright and his family moved to France because he found life there less difficult. In Paris he associated himself with the existentialist group. He died in a Paris clinic in 1960.

Bibliography

For biographical and critical discussion see H. M. Gloster, *Negro Voices in American Fiction*, 1948; William A. Owens, Introduction to *Native Son*, Harper Modern Classics edition, 1957; James Baldwin, "Many Thousands Gone," *Partisan Review*, XVIII (1951), 665–680; and Nathan A. Scott, "Search for Beliefs: Fiction of Richard Wright," *University of Kansas City Review*, XXIII (1956), 19–24.

NATIVE SON

Type of work: Novel
Author: Richard Wright (1908–1960)
Time of plot: 1930's
Locale: An American city
First published: 1940

Richard Wright was the first black novelist of stature to break into the mainstream of American fiction, and Native Son *is his most representative and powerful book. Wright presents in Bigger Thomas a young man who is driven by anger, frustration, and hatred—directed both at the white world and at himself— that can only explode violently in both directions.*

Principal Characters

Bigger Thomas, a young Negro, frustrated by poverty and race prejudice, who has a pathological hatred of white people. He is reluctantly drawn into alliance with his employer's daughter Mary and her sweetheart, who are crusading with the Communists to help the Negroes. After an evening of drinking, Bigger carries the drunken Mary to her room. To prevent her from making a sound which will alarm her blind mother, he puts a pillow over her face and accidentally smothers her. This act releases all his pent-up emotions. He hides the body in the furnace, tries to get ransom money from his employer, and tries to frame the dead girl's sweetheart. He confesses to his mistress, and after the discovery of the body he hides out with her. But he fears that she will be found and questioned, and so he kills her. The police catch him, and under steady questioning by the prosecuting attorney, he admits his crime. Despite an eloquent plea by his attorney, outlining the social structure that made him what he is, Bigger is sentenced to die. While awaiting death he gets, from talking to his attorney, an understanding that his

persecutors are themselves filled with fear and are not responsible for their social crimes.

Mr. Dalton, a wealthy white man for whom Bigger works as a chauffeur.

Mrs. Dalton, his blind wife.

Mary Dalton, their daughter, crusading with the Communists against racial discrimination. Bigger accidentally smothers her.

Jan Erlone, Mary's sweetheart and fellow crusader. Bigger succeeds so well in throwing suspicion on him for Mary's disappearance that Jan is arrested. After Bigger is arrested, Jan comes to see him and promises help. Jan introduces to Bigger a lawyer from the Communist-front organization for which Jan works.

Boris A. Max, Bigger's lawyer, provided by a Communist-front organization. He argues that society is to blame for Bigger's crime, but he does not succeed in saving Bigger from death. He is able to show Bigger that his enemies are also

NATIVE SON by Richard Wright. By permission of the publishers, Harper & Brothers. Copyright, 1940, by Richard Wright.

driven by fear and must be forgiven.

Bessie Mears, Bigger's mistress, to whom he confides his guilt and whom he kills.

Britten, a detective hired by Dalton to investigate Mary's disappearance.

Buckley, the prosecuting attorney, under whose questioning Bigger breaks down and signs a confession. He makes full use of anti-Communism feeling and race prejudice in prosecuting Bigger.

The Story

In a one-room apartment Bigger Thomas lived with his brother, sister, and mother. Always penniless, haunted by a pathological hatred of white people, driven by an indescribable urge to make others cringe before him, Bigger had retreated into an imaginary world of fantasy.

Through the aid of a relief agency he obtained employment as a chauffeur for a wealthy family. His first assignment was to drive Mary Dalton, his employer's daughter, to the university. Mary, however, was on her way to meet Jan Erlone, her sweetheart. The three of them, Mary and Jan, white people who were crusading with the Communist Party to help the black people, and Bigger, a reluctant ally, spent the evening driving and drinking. When Bigger brought Mary home, she was too drunk to take herself to bed. With a confused medley of hatred, fear, disgust, and revenge playing within his mind, Bigger helped her to her bedroom. When Mary's blind mother entered the room, Bigger covered the girl's face with a pillow to keep her from making any sound that might arouse Mrs. Dalton's suspicions. The reek of whiskey convinced Mrs. Dalton that Mary was drunk, and she left the room. Then Bigger discovered that he had smothered Mary to death. To delay discovery of his crime, he took the body to the basement and stuffed it into the furnace.

Bigger began a weird kind of rationalization. The next morning in his mother's home he began thinking that he was separated from his family because he had killed a white girl. His plan was to involve Jan in connection with Mary's death.

When Bigger returned to the Dalton home, the family was worrying over Mary's absence. Bigger felt secure from incrimination because he had covered his activities by lying. He decided to send ransom notes to her parents, allowing them to think Mary had been kidnaped. But there were too many facts to remember, too many lies to tell. Britten, the detective whom Mr. Dalton had hired, tried to intimidate Bigger, but his methods only made Bigger more determined to frame Jan, who in his desire to protect Mary lied just enough to help Bigger's cause. When Britten brought Bigger face to face with Jan for questioning, Bigger's fear mounted. He went to Bessie, his mistress, who wrung from him a confession of murder. Bigger forced her to go with him to hide in an empty building in the slum section of the city. There he instructed her to pick up the ransom money he hoped to receive from Mr. Dalton.

Bigger was eating in the Dalton kitchen when the ransom note arrived. Jan had already been arrested. Bigger clung tenaciously to his lies. It was a cold day.

Attempting to build up the fire, Bigger accidentally drew attention to the furnace. When reporters discovered Mary's bones, Bigger fled. Hiding with Bessie in the deserted building, he realized that he could not take her away with him. Afraid to leave her behind to be found and questioned by the police, he killed her and threw her body down an air shaft.

When Bigger ventured from his hideout to steal a newspaper, he learned that the city was being combed to find him. He fled from one empty building to another, constantly buying or stealing newspapers so that he could know his chances for escape. Finally he was trapped on the roof of a penthouse by a searching policeman. Bigger knocked him out with the butt of the gun he had been carrying with him. The police finally captured Bigger after a chase across the rooftops.

In jail Bigger refused to eat or speak. His mind turned inward, hating the world, but he was satisfied with himself for what he had done. Three days later Jan Erlone came to see Bigger and promised to help him. Jan introduced Boris A. Max, a lawyer from the Communist front organization for which Jan worked.

Buckley, the prosecuting attorney, tried to persuade Bigger not to become involved with the Communists. Bigger said nothing even after the lawyer told him that Bessie's body had been found. But when Buckley began listing crimes of rape, murder, and burglary which had been charged against him, Bigger protested, vigorously denying rape and Jan's part in Mary's death. Under a steady fire of questions from Buckley, Bigger broke down and signed a confession.

The opening session of the grand jury began. First Mrs. Dalton appeared as a witness to identify one of her daughter's earrings, which had been found in the furnace. Next Jan testified, and under the slanderous anti-Communist questioning, Max rose in protest against the racial bigotry of the coroner. Max questioned Mr. Dalton about his ownership of the high-rent, rat-infested tenements where Bigger's family lived. Generally, the grand jury session became a trial of the race relations which had led to Bigger's crime rather than a trial of the crime itself. As a climax to the session the coroner brought Bessie's body into the courtroom in order to produce evidence that Bigger had raped and murdered his Negro sweetheart. Bigger was returned to jail after Max had promised to visit him. Under the quiet questioning of Max, Bigger at last was able to talk about his crime, his feelings, his reasons. He had been thwarted by white people all his life, he said, until he had killed Mary Dalton; that act had released him.

At the opening session of the trial Buckley presented witnesses who attested Bigger's sanity and his ruthless character. The murder was dramatized even to the courtroom reconstruction of the furnace in which Mary's body had been burned. Max refused to call any of his own witnesses or to cross-examine, promising to act in Bigger's behalf as sole witness for the defense. The next day in a long speech Max outlined an entire social structure, its effect on an individual such as Bigger, and Bigger's particular inner compulsions when he killed Mary Dalton. Pleading for mitigation on the grounds that Bigger was not totally responsible for his crime, he argued that society was also to blame.

· After another race-prejudiced attack by Buckley, the court adjourned for one hour. It reopened to sentence Bigger to death. Max's attempts to delay death by appealing to the governor were unsuccessful.

In the last hours before death Bigger realized his one hope was to communicate his feelings to Max, to try to have Max explain to him the meaning of his life and his death. Max helped him see that the men who persecuted Negroes, poor people, or others, are themselves filled with fear. Bigger could forgive them because they were suffering the same urge that he had suffered. He could forgive his enemies because they did not know the guilt of their own social crimes.

Critical Evaluation

Native Son, when it appeared in 1940, was without precedent in American literature. Previous black writing, including Wright's *Uncle Tom's Children,* had treated blacks as passive and innocent victims of racism suffering their lot in dignified silence. As Wright said of his own earlier work, the reading audience could escape into the self-indulgence of pity on reading such work rather than truly face the hard facts of racism. In Bigger Thomas, Wright created a character who was neither passive sufferer nor innocent victim. Instead, Wright reminded Americans of the full cost of bigotry in social and human terms by dramatizing the deep anger and hate and fear many blacks felt. Years after *Native Son's* appearance, James Baldwin would assert that every black person carries some degree of Bigger Thomas within himself. Perhaps so, but it is to Richard Wright's credit that he was the first American writer to bring those feelings into the open. We are reminded throughout the work that Bigger is a "native son," and his experience is quintessentially a part of the American experience. On the psychological, the sociological, and the philosophical levels, Wright explores the most disturbing implications of what it means to be black in America.

The basic tone of Wright's psychological treatment of Bigger is set in the opening scene in which Bigger and Buddy battle the rat. Here is a symbolic paradigm for the entire novel in which Bigger, like the rat, will be hunted down and destroyed. The rat, it must be understood, operates entirely at the instinctual level, and its viciousness is in response to fear. Recalling that "Fear" is the title of the first section of the novel as "Flight" is of the second suggests that Bigger too is a creature motivated by fear and acting instinctively. This is demonstrably true of his killing Mary Dalton while avoiding detection, and it shows up even earlier in the fight with Gus. Fearful of outside forces, particularly whites, Bigger is equally fearful of the repressed anger within himself as his several comments referring to his concern that he is destined to commit some terrible act indicates. Thus, throughout at least the first two sections of the novel, Bigger, before and after the murder, is operating at the animal level of pure instinct, and it is against this background that his development takes place.

Bigger's psychological state is an obvious result of the sociological conditions prevailing in the novel. As Bigger dramatizes the anger and pain of his race, the Daltons effectively represent the ruling white power structure. It is to Wright's credit that he does not give way to the temptation to create villains, but makes these whites generous, liberal, and humanitarian. It is ironic, of course, that even while giving a "chance" to Bigger and helping in ghetto programs, the Daltons are reaping the proceeds of ghetto housing. Appropriately, Wright uses the metaphor of blindness to characterize the attitude of the Daltons here as he will later to account for Max's failure to comprehend Bigger. But Bigger too is described as blind, because, in this world of Native Son, there is no real possibility of people seeing one another in clear human perspective. All the characters respond to one another as symbols rather than as people.

But Wright's use of the polarities of black and white symbolism are not limited to the literal and racial levels of the novel. The entire world of Native Son, as the story unfolds, is increasingly polarized into a symbolic black-white dichotomy. Especially during Part II, the snow which buries the city under a cold and hostile blanket of white becomes a more complicated manifestation of the white symbolism than that limited to the sociological level. At the same time, Bigger escapes not only into the black ghetto in search of safety and security, he seeks out the black interiors of abandoned buildings to hide both from the freezing snow and the death-dealing white mob. Finally, Bigger's flight ends with his being spread out against the white snow as though crucified.

It is not probable that Wright had heard of European existentialism when he wrote Native Son, so it is all the more remarkable that this novel should so clearly demonstrate concepts which anticipate Wright's embracing of the existentialist philosophy when he went to Europe in the late 1940's. Though Bigger very obviously commits the murder without premeditation, he quickly comes to the realization that somehow that act is the sum of his entire life. Rather than repudiating responsibility for his crime, or seeing himself as a victim of circumstances, either of which would be understandable, Bigger consciously and deliberately affirms the killing as the most creative act of his life. Whereas before he was in the position of constantly reacting—like the rat— he now sees himself as having responsibility for his own fate. Further, the world which before had seemed frighteningly ambiguous is now clearly revealed to him. For the first time in his life, Bigger has a positive sense of his own identity, and a concrete knowledge of how he relates to the world around him. Ironically, Max's case that Bigger is a victim of society threatens to deprive Bigger of the identity he has purchased at such terrible cost to himself, but, facing death at the end of the novel, he reaffirms his belief that he killed for something, and he faces death with the courage born of his one creative moment. Wright's novel is not without faults, particularly the tedious final section in which Max argues a doctrinaire Marxist interpretation of Bigger's crime. Apparently, however, Wright himself could not fully accept this view, since Bigger's reaffirmation of responsibility contradicts Max's determinstic justification. In the final analysis, Bigger's insistence upon responsibility for his act demonstrates the human potential for freedom of act and will, and asserts human possibility in contrast to the Marxist vision of man as an animal trapped in a world he cannot control.

Bibliography

Allen, Walter. *The Modern Novel in Britain and the United States.* New York: Dutton, 1964, pp. 155–158.

Baker, Houston A., Editor. *Twentieth Century Interpretations of* Native Son. Englewood Cliffs, N.J.: Prentice-Hall, 1973.

Baldwin, James. *Notes of a* Native Son. Boston: Beacon Press, 1955, pp. 24–45.

Blake, Nelson. *Novelists' America: Fiction as History 1910–1940.* Syracuse, N.Y.: Syracuse University Press, 1969, pp. 234–253.

Bolton, H. Philip. "The Role of Paranoia in Richard Wright's *Native Son*," in *Kansas Quarterly.* VII (Summer, 1975), pp. 111–124.

Bone, Robert A. *The Negro Novel in America.* New Haven, Conn.: Yale University Press, 1965, pp. 140–152.

Britt, David. "*Native Son*: Watershed of Negro Protest Literature," in *Negro American Literature Forum.* I (Fall, 1967), pp. 4–5.

Cowley, Malcolm. *Think Back on Us.* Carbondale: Southern Illinois University Press, 1967, pp. 355–357.

Emanuel, James A. "Fever and Feeling: Notes on the Imagery in *Native Son*," in *Negro Digest.* XVIII (December, 1968), pp. 16–24.

Ford, Nick A. "The Ordeal of Richard Wright," in *College English.* XV (November, 1953), pp. 87–94.

French, Warren. *The Social Novel at the End of an Era.* Carbondale: Southern Illinois University Press, 1966, pp. 173–179.

Glickesberg, Charles I. "Negro Fiction in America," in *South Atlantic Quarterly.* XLV (October, 1946), pp. 481–488.

Gloster, Hugh M. *Negro Voices in America Literature.* Chapel Hill: University of North Carolina Press, 1948, pp. 228–234.

Hughes, Carl. *The Negro Novelist.* New York: Citadel, 1953, pp. 41–68, 198–206.

Jackson, Blyden. "The Negro's Image of the Universe as Reflected in His Fiction," in *College Language Association Journal.* IV (September, 1960), pp. 22–31.

Jackson, Esther M. "The American Negro and the Image of the Absurd," in *Phylon.* XXII (Winter, 1962), pp. 22–31.

Kennedy, J.G. "The Content and Form of *Native Son*," in *College English.* XXXIV (November, 1972), pp. 269–286.

Kinnamon, Keneth. "*Native Son*: The Personal, Social and Political Background," in *Phylon.* XXX (Spring, 1969), pp. 66–72.

Klotman, Phyllis R. "Moral Distancing as Rhetorical Technique in *Native Son*: A Note of Fate," in *College Language Association Journal.* XVIII (December, 1974), pp. 284–291.

Larsen, R.B.V. "The Four Voices in Richard Wright's *Native Son*," in *Negro American Literature Forum.* VI (Winter, 1972), pp. 105–109.

Merkle, Donald R. "The Furnace and the Tower: A New Look at the Symbols of *Native Son*," in *English Journal.* VI (September, 1971), pp. 735–739.

Nagel, James. "Images of Vision in *Native Son*," in *University Review.* XXXVI (Winter, 1969), pp. 109–115.

Singh, Raman K. "Some Basic Ideas in Richard Wright's Fiction," in *College Language Association Journal.* XIII (September, 1969), pp. 78–84.

Wertham, Frederic. "An Unconscious Determinant in *Native Son*," in *Journal of Clinical Psychology.* VI (1944–1945), pp. 111–115. Reprinted in *Psychoanalysis and Literature.* Edited by Hendrik M. Ruitbeck. New York: Dutton, 1964, pp. 321–325.

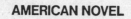

AMERICAN NOVEL

ALPHABETICAL LIST OF TITLES